Accounting Provisions of the Companies Act 1985

Barry Johnson FCA
Matthew Patient FCA
of Deloitte Haskins & Sells

Legal Consultant Editor
Mary Arden MA LLM (Cantab) LLM (Harvard)
of Gray's Inn and Lincoln's Inn, Barrister

ISBN 0 86349 066 2
© Deloitte Haskins & Sells, UK. 1985
Photoset and printed in England by Ebenezer Baylis & Son Ltd.,
The Trinity Press, Worcester and London

Foreword
by Sir John Hoskyns

The consolidation of the Companies Acts has been long overdue. With the increasing complexity of company law any simplification in wording and layout of a consolidating Act is a major step forward and must be welcomed. The Companies Act 1985 provides this step forward by bringing together the five previous Companies Acts. However, even where wording and layout are improved, interpretation of the Act's provisions is always difficult.

In the area of accounts and accounting records the duties for companies and directors alike are highly technical and particularly onerous. Barry Johnson and Matthew Patient are therefore to be congratulated in preparing this detailed explanatory reference work on the accounting provisions of the Companies Act 1985.

Companies and directors have to be aware of an ever increasing number of other regulations that apply to company accounts. One of the useful features of this book is that, in addition to covering the accounting provisions of the Act, it incorporates all the other major regulations concerning company accounts disclosure, therefore doing away with the necessity to consult numerous tomes on a particular subject. Inevitably, at times these other regulations conflict with the law. The authors have considered many of these conflicts and by their illustration and informed comment have explained their implications admirably.

I am therefore very pleased to commend to its users this major new reference work as both relevant and timely and wish it a long and useful existence.

John Hoskyns
July 1985

(Sir John Hoskyns is the Director General of the Institute of Directors.)

Preface

The Companies Act 1985 is the first consolidation of company legislation for 37 years. On 1 July 1985 it repealed five major Companies Acts and much other subordinate legislation. It represents a substantial re-organisation of the existing law, a large part of which relates to company financial reporting.

This book gives detailed explanations of the accounting provisions of the 1985 Act. It also refers throughout to the additional reporting requirements that limited companies have to comply with and that are set out in Statements of Standard Accounting Practice (including exposure drafts), The Stock Exchange's Continuing Obligations for listed companies, and The Stock Exchange's General Undertaking for USM companies. The text includes worked examples and extracts from published financial statements. The financial reporting provisions and schedules of the Act are reproduced. The appendices include a detailed aide-memoire of those disclosure requirements that apply to company financial statements and a model set of financial statements.

The book also includes practical advice and comment we have gained through our work for the National Auditing and Accounting Technical Department of Deloitte Haskins and Sells in advising the Firm's clients, partners and staff.

We hope that finance directors, accountants, legal practitioners, company administrators, financial advisers and auditors will find this book useful.

Our thanks are due to Mary Arden (our legal consultant) and Gabrielle Lumsden (our Firm's legal adviser until her sad death in June 1985), for their advice on the legal content. Also to Charles Silcock for his enormous contribution in drafting and checking the text, Matt Matthews for his editorial style, Rosa Reynolds for her excellent processing of the words, and all the other members of the department for their helpful comments and advice.

Barry Johnson & Matthew Patient

Deloitte Haskins & Sells
London
July 1985

Contents

Contents

Contents

Contents

Contents

Appendices

Companies Act 1985 (extract of the accounting provisions)

Index and Tables

Abbreviations and terms used

accounts	=	financial statements.
the Act/the 1985 Act	=	the Companies Act 1985.
ACT	=	advance corporation tax.
AER	=	All England Law Reports.
APC	=	Auditing Practices Committee.
ASC	=	Accounting Standards Committee.
CACA	=	Chartered Association of Certified Accountants.
CCAB	=	Consultative Committee of Accountancy Bodies (that is, of the ICAEW, ICAS, ICAI, ICMA, CACA and CIPFA).
CC(CP)	=	Companies Consolidation (Consequential Provisions) Act 1985.
Ch	=	Law Reports, Chancery Division.
CIPFA	=	Chartered Institute of Public Finance and Accountancy.
Cmnd	=	Command Paper.
CO	=	Continuing Obligations, Section 5 of The Stock Exchange's 'Admission of Securities to Listing'.
DTI	=	Department of Trade and Industry
EC	=	European Community.
ECU	=	European currency unit.
ED	=	exposure draft.
financial statements	=	accounts.
Fourth Directive	=	EC Fourth Directive on Company Law.
GAAP	=	Generally accepted accounting practice.
GU	=	The Stock Exchange's General Undertaking of the Unlisted Securities Market.
IAS	=	International Accounting Standard.
IASC	=	International Accounting Standards Committee
ICAEW	=	Institute of Chartered Accountants in England and Wales.
ICAI	=	Institute of Chartered Accountants in Ireland.
ICAS	=	Institute of Chartered Accountants of Scotland.
ICMA	=	Institute of Cost and Management Accountants.
ICR	=	Industrial Cases Reports.
MR	=	Master of the Rolls.
NASDAQ system	=	National Association of Securities Dealers Automated Quotation System.
QC	=	Queen's Counsel.
RDG	=	Regional Development Grant.
SC	=	Session Cases.
Sch	=	Schedule to the Companies Act 1985 (4 Sch 85 = 4th Schedule, paragraph 85).
Sec	=	Section(s) of the 1985 Act.
s	=	section of another Act.
SI	=	statutory instrument.
SOI	=	Statement of Intent.
SORP	=	Statement of Recommended Practice.

SSAP	=	Statement of Standard Accounting Practice.
TR	=	Technical release issued by the CCAB.
UK	=	United Kingdom.
US	=	United States of America.
USM	=	Unlisted Securities Market.
VAT	=	Value Added Tax.
WLR	=	Weekly Law Reports.
Yellow book	=	The Stock Exchange's 'Admission of Securities to Listing'.

CHAPTER 1

INTRODUCTION

Chapter 1

Introduction

1.01 The Companies Act 1985 received Royal Assent on 11 March 1985, and it came into force on 1 July 1985. It is the first major consolidation of company law for 37 years, the last being the Companies Act 1948. It repealed the Companies Acts 1948, 1967, 1976, 1980 and 1981.

1.02 Some provisions of these earlier Acts have been consolidated into three other Acts: the Business Names Act 1985, the Company Securities (Insider Dealing) Act 1985 and the Companies Consolidation (Consequential Provisions) Act 1985. The four Acts now represent the state of company law applicable in the UK.

1.03 The consolidated Acts have not amended the law, but instead they have re-stated it in a more convenient form. The consolidation has brought together, in a logical order, subjects that were previously dealt with in a variety of statutes. In addition, the new Acts have been drafted using a more modern style of English. They are, consequently, more readable and easier to understand.

The reason for consolidation

1.04 The consolidation of the Companies Acts 1948 to 1981 mainly became necessary because of the substantial amount of legislation contained in both the Companies Act 1980 and the Companies Act 1981.

1.05 The 1980 Act was passed on 1 May 1980, and it enacted provisions based on the Second EC Directive on company law. This Act represented the first real impact that the EC company law harmonisation programme had on United Kingdom company legislation.

1.06 The Second Directive dealt with the formation of public companies, the allotment of their share capital and the maintenance of their share capital. The Government, in implementing this Directive, extended some of its provisions to apply to private companies also. In addition, the 1980 Act contained provisions relating to directors, and also provisions prohibiting insider dealing.

1.07 The 1981 Act had its origin in the EC Fourth Directive on company law, and so its prime purpose was to implement that Directive. The

Government also took the opportunity to introduce into the 1981 Act provisions that covered other areas. These additional provisions dealt with company names and business names, the setting-up of a share premium account in the event of a merger or a group reconstruction, dealings by a company in its own shares and disclosure of interests in shares.

1.08   The EC company law harmonisation programme is not yet completed. The draft Fifth Directive (directors' responsibilities) is still under discussion in the Council of Ministers, and the Seventh Directive (preparation, content and publication of group accounts) and the Eighth Directive (qualifications and responsibilities of auditors), though approved by the Council, are not due to take effect in the Member States until 1990. Consequently, the Companies Act 1985 is likely to be amended and supplemented when further EC Directives are implemented in the UK. A summary of all the EC company law Directives is given in Appendix III. Moreover, statutory measures of purely domestic origin will also affect the 1985 Act. The new insolvency legislation (for example), which is expected to be enacted later in 1985, will repeal many of those provisions of the 1985 Act that deal with the winding-up of companies.

Commencement of the Act

1.09   All the provisions of the four 1985 Acts came into force on 1 July 1985. During 1984, Parliament approved also two Orders containing various technical amendments to the Companies Acts 1948 to 1981. These Orders are the Companies Acts (Pre-Consolidation Amendents) Order 1984 (SI 1984/134) and the Companies Acts (Pre-Consolidation Amendments) (No. 2) Order 1984 (SI 1984/1169). The amendments that they contain have been included in the new legislation, and the amendments therefore come into force simultaneously with the new Acts. In addition, a revised Table A, modernised to take account of legislation and company practice since 1948, was approved by Parliament on 3 June 1985 and is incorporated in a statutory instrument, The Companies (Tables A to F) Regulations 1985 (SI 1985/805). It also came into effect on 1 July 1985.

Main provisions of the Act

1.10   The Companies Act 1985 is split into 27 parts. A summary of these, together with the arrangement of sections found in the Act, is given on pages 655 to 682.

The aim of this book

1.11   This book explains the accounting provisions of the Companies Act 1985. It deals in particular with the following parts of the Act:

(a) Part V — Share capital, its increase, maintenance and reduction (in particular, Chapter III—Share premiums).

(b) Part VII — Accounts and audit (including provisions that apply to the financial statements of companies generally and provisions that apply to the financial statements of banking, shipping and insurance companies).

(c) Part VIII — Distribution of profits and assets.

(d) Part X — Enforcement of fair dealing by directors.

(e) Part XXIII — Overseas companies.

(f) Schedule 4 — Form and content of company accounts.

(g) Schedule 5 — Miscellaneous matters to be disclosed in notes to company accounts.

(h) Schedule 6 — Particulars in company accounts of loan and other transactions favouring directors and officers.

(i) Schedule 7 — Matters to be dealt with in directors' report.

(j) Schedule 8 — Modified accounts of companies qualifying as small or medium-sized.

(k) Schedule 9 — Form and content of special category accounts.

(l) Schedule 10 — Additional matters to be dealt with in directors' report attached to special category accounts.

(m) Schedule 11 — Modifications of Part VIII where company's relevant accounts are special category.

(n) Schedule 24 — Punishment of offences under the Act. (Those sections that relate to the accounting provisions of the Act are reproduced in Appendix IV.)

All of the Parts and Schedules of the Act that are referred to in *(a)* to *(m)* above are reproduced in full on pages 684 to 883.

1.12 The book follows, in general, the order of the accounting provisions in the Act. The Schedules to the Act are not discussed separately in the book but they are introduced (where necessary) into the text when they apply to the main provisions of the Act that are being considered at that place in the book.

1.13 In addition to explaining the accounting provisions of the Companies Act 1985, this book summarises also, where appropriate, those provisions of generally accepted accounting practice in the United Kingdom that are contained in Accounting Standards, exposure drafts, The Stock Exchange's Continuing Obligations (which apply to listed companies) and The Stock Exchange's General Undertaking (which applies to companies traded on the USM). Consequently, this book serves as a practical guide to the application of the accounting provisions of all the major regulations that companies have to consider when they prepare their annual financial statements. It includes practical comment based on advice given by the National Auditing and Accounting Technical Department of Deloitte Haskins and Sells to the Firm's partners, staff and clients. In order to illustrate matters relating to presentation and disclosure in company financial statements, it includes also extracts from published financial statements of various companies.

The scope of this book

1.14   Unless otherwise stated, the provisions examined in this book apply to those companies that are defined in Section 735 of the Act. The definition in Section 735 embraces companies registered under either the Act or a former Companies Act, and it embraces also companies registered under the Joint Stock Companies Acts. The term 'Joint Stock Companies Acts' means the Joint Stock Companies Acts 1856 and 1857, the Joint Stock Banking Companies Act 1857 and the Act to enable Joint Stock Banking Companies to be formed on the principle of limited liability. [*Sec 735(3)*].

1.15   Companies may be either limited or unlimited. A 'limited' company is a company in which the members' liability is limited by shares or by guarantee. [*Sec 1(2)(a)(b)*]. An 'unlimited' company is a company that does not limit its members' liability. [*Sec 1(2)(c)*]. Limited companies may be either public or private.

1.16   A 'public' company (plc) is a company limited by shares (or, if incorporated before 22 December 1980, by guarantee) where its memorandum states that it is a public company. Such a company must also be registered as a public company, and, before it can do business or exercise any borrowing power, it must satisfy the statutory requirements as to its authorised minimum share capital. [*Sec 1 (3)(4), 117, 118*]. The current 'authorised minimum' share capital that such a company is required to allot before it can do business or exercise any borrowing power is £50,000. [*Sec 118*].

1.17   A private company is any company which is not a public company. [*Sec 1(3)*]. The text of this book draws attention to those requirements of the Act that differ for public companies and private companies respectively.

CHAPTER 2

ACCOUNTING RECORDS AND ACCOUNTING REFERENCE PERIODS

Chapter 2

Accounting Records and Accounting Reference Periods

Introduction

2.01 A company must ensure that it keeps proper accounting records. [*Sec 221(1)*]. A company's directors are under an obligation to present to the company's members, once a year, the company's annual financial statements. [*Sec 227(1)*]. Those financial statements include a profit and loss account for the financial year (or, if it is a company not trading for profit, an income and expenditure account), together with a balance sheet prepared as at the last day of the financial year. [*Sec 227(1)(3)*]. Schedule 4 to the Act lays down detailed rules that companies must follow in preparing their financial statements. Companies will have to consider also other rules that are contained in SSAPs and in other authoritative accounting statements (for example, SORPs and EDs). In addition, if a company is listed on The Stock Exchange, it will have to consider the rules outlined in the Continuing Obligations. Similarly, if the company's shares are traded on The Stock Exchange's USM, it will have to comply with that market's General Undertaking. The accounting records must be sufficient to enable the directors to prepare financial statements that comply with all these rules.

2.02 Furthermore, there may be other legislation that specifies the way in which particular companies should keep their accounting records. For example:

(a) The Housing Act 1980 gives the Secretary of State power to prescribe accounting requirements for registered housing associations. The Secretary of State took advantage of this provision and imposed certain accounting requirements in the Registered Housing Associations (Accounting Requirements) Order 1982 (SI 1982/828). Housing associations have to comply with these requirements in order to ensure that their financial statements give a true and fair view of the financial state of their housing activities.

(b) The Insurance Brokers (Registration) Act 1977 requires all insurance brokers to maintain accounting records that comply with the Insurance Brokers Registration Council (Accounts and Business Requirements) Rules Approval Order 1979 (SI 1979/489) (as amended by the Insurance Brokers Registration Council (Accounts and Business Requirements) (Amendment) Rules Approval Order 1981 (SI 1981/1630)).

9

2.03   This chapter considers the Act's requirements that relate to keeping proper accounting records, the place where those records should be kept, and the period for which they should be retained. It considers also the responsibilities both of a company's directors and of its auditors, and finally it discusses the accounting period that a company's financial statements must cover.

Accounting records

The requirement to keep proper accounting records

2.04   The requirement that every company shall keep proper accounting records is contained in Section 221(1) of the Act. Counsel's interpretation of the meaning of certain words and phrases included in Section 221, and shown in italics below, is explained in paragraph 2.05. This section of the Act says that the accounting records must be sufficient to show and explain the company's transactions and, consequently, to:

(a) *Disclose* with reasonable accuracy the company's *financial position at any time.*

(b) Enable the directors to ensure that any financial statements prepared from the *accounting records* comply with the requirements of the Act.
[*Sec 221(2)*].

A company's accounting records should detail the following:

(a) The sums of money the company received and expended on a *day-to-day* basis, together with explanations of the amounts it received and expended.

(b) *A record of the assets and liabilities* of the company.
[*Sec 221(3)*].

(c) If the company deals in goods:

   (i) *Statements of stocks* the company held at the year end, together with supporting statements of stocktakes.
   (ii) *Statements of all goods sold and purchased* by the company, in sufficient detail to enable the goods and the buyers and sellers to be identified. (This requirement, however, does not apply to companies carrying on retail trades.)
[*Sec 221(4)*].

Counsel's opinion on proper accounting records

2.05   Section 221 of the Act derives from section 12 of the Companies Act 1976. The APC took Counsel's opinion on the interpretation of parts of section 12 and published it in 'True and Fair' (Issue No. 6, Winter 1977/8). The interpretation below is based on that opinion which applies equally to Section 221 of the 1985 Act.

(a) 'Disclose'. The records a company maintains must disclose the basic information from which the financial position can be ascertained. This does not mean that the financial position needs to be displayed in the accounting records after each transaction has been recorded. It does mean, however, that the information from which a statement of the financial position can be prepared is available.

(b) 'Financial position at any time'. The Act clearly recognises that it would be impracticable for the information contained in the accounting records to present a 'true and fair' view of the state of affairs and of the results required to be disclosed in annual financial statements. It recognises also that it is not practicable to draw up financial statements giving a 'true and fair' view at any time during the year. However, the Act does require that directors should have available to them an adequate statement at any time of the company's financial position.

Section 221 seems to indicate that directors should be in a position to prepare, with reasonable accuracy, a statement showing tangible assets, liabilities and pre-tax results at any selected date. Although a company would need to estimate its stocks figure to establish a pre-tax figure, the Act does not necessarily require that the company undertakes a physical stocktake or maintains continuous stock records. (This is a matter for the directors to decide on, and their decision would depend on the company's particular circumstances.) It appears that a company may estimate the results in any of the following three ways:

  (i) By applying gross profit margins to sales to arrive at the cost of sales.
  (ii) By maintaining detailed records of the cost of sales.
  (iii) By maintaining detailed stock records to enable a stock valuation to be performed at any time.

(c) 'Accounting records'. These records need not be in the form of a book. They could, for example, be in a loose leaf binder, or on computer disks or, for prime entry items, in a secure clip of invoices with an add-list attached. The information recorded should be organised and labelled. (A carrier-bag full of invoices is not sufficient.)

(d) 'Day-to-day'. Clearly, transactions cannot be recorded instantaneously. What is necessary is that when the entries are made, each transaction should be shown separately and be identified by its date and an explanation of the matter to which it relates. With retail shops, a record of the day's total cash takings will probably suffice.

(e) 'A record of the assets and liabilities'. The records must include details of all the company's assets and liabilities (such as debtors, creditors and plant and machinery). There is no specific requirement that these records should be updated on a day-to-day basis, but the accounting records should show separately the assets and the liabilities of the company at any particular time. The records must be updated at frequent intervals. Annually is certainly not sufficient. They must also contain details of the dates on which assets are acquired and disposed of, and of the dates on which liabilities are incurred and discharged. (Stocks are, however, excluded from these requirements.)

(f) 'Statements of stocks'. This term is taken to mean a summary supporting the amount included in the financial statements in respect of the stocks held at each financial year end. Also, stocktaking records that support the year-end stocks summary must be retained. The Act imposes an obligation for companies to retain documentation supporting year-end stock valuations, but it allows them considerable flexibility in meeting the requirement to disclose the financial position 'at any time' (see (b) above).

(g) 'Statements of all goods sold and purchased'. The intention of the Act appears to be to ensure that the substance of transactions is properly recorded. With products where the identity of each individual item of the product is irrelevant to the seller and the purchaser, only the product type of each item is relevant, and it is not necessary for each particular item to be identified. In practical terms, the identity of the seller and the purchaser will normally be available from the purchase and sales ledgers.

Directors' duty to account properly

2.06   The CCAB issued a technical release (TR 573) in March 1985 that provides guidance on the main duties and responsibilities, particularly of a financial or accounting nature, that directors owe to their company and its shareholders. This statement sets out what is considered to be best practice rather than what may be acceptable as the legal minimum. It has a section that deals with books of account and other accounting records. The statement gives the following guidance:

"In addition to the statutory requirement to keep proper books of account which show an up-to-date picture of the company's financial position, the directors have an overriding responsibility to ensure that they have adequate information to enable them to discharge their duty to manage the company's business."

2.07   A statement that the ICAEW issued in April 1970 (V17 — now section 1.401 in the ICAEW Members Handbook) gave similar advice to that quoted above, but also contained the following further guidance:

"The directors should therefore ensure that the books and accounting records are:

(a) adequate to meet the statutory requirements;
(b) kept up to date;

12

(c) designed so as to facilitate:

(i) safeguarding the company's assets, and
(ii) the prompt preparation of accounting and management information, adequate for the proper control of the particular business.

The accounting and management information should be in sufficient detail to enable the directors adequately to control, *inter alia*:

(a) cash;
(b) debtors and creditors;
(c) capital expenditure;
(d) stock and work in progress.

In addition, a plan should be prepared against which the subsequent performance of the business can be measured. Periodic management accounts will be necessary to enable actual operating results and cash position to be compared with plan. The extent and frequency of the preparation of such accounts and the level of management to which they are presented will depend on the size, scope, and nature of the business.''

2.08   A company's normal books of account would include:

(a) Cash books.
(b) Sales day book.
(c) Sales returns book.
(d) Purchase day book.
(e) Purchase returns book.
(f) Creditors ledger.
(g) Debtors ledger.
(h) Transfer journal.
(i) General ledger.

These books may be retained in book form, or on computer or in any other suitable readable form. Other books of account may be used to assist directors in the preparation of management accounts. These may include stock books to record continuous stock records used in a company's costing systems.

Auditors' duties

2.09   In addition to the requirement that a company must keep proper accounting records, the company has a duty to appoint auditors, and those auditors must examine any financial statements of the company laid before it in general meeting. They must also report to the members on those financial statements. [*Sec 236(1)*].

13

2.10   The auditors have a right of access at all times to the company's accounting records. They also have a right to require such information and
explanations from the company's officers as they believe they need in
order to form an opinion on those financial statements. [*Sec 237(3)*].
In addition, the auditors have a duty to carry out investigations that
will enable them to form an opinion both on whether the company has
kept proper accounting records, and on whether they have received
proper returns adequate for their audit from those branches they did
not visit. [*Sec 237(1)(a)*]. They should also ensure that the company's
financial statements are in agreement with the accounting records. [*Sec
237(1)(b)*]. If the company has not kept proper accounting records
(including returns from branches), or if the financial statements are
not in agreement with those records, then the auditors must state this
fact in their report. [*Sec 237(4)*]. The Auditing Guideline on audit reports
gives examples of audit reports qualified where proper accounting
records are not kept.

The place where records are to be kept

2.11   A company must keep its accounting records either at its registered
office or at such other place as the directors think fit. The records have
to be available for inspection by the company's officers at all times.
[*Sec 222(1)*]. For this purpose, an officer includes a director, or a
manager, or the company secretary. [*Sec 744*].

2.12   If the accounting records are kept outside Great Britain, then accounts
and returns must be sent to an appropriate place in Great Britain (for
example, the registered office), where they should be available for
inspection at all times. [*Sec 222(2)*].

2.13   These accounts and returns should disclose the company's financial
position at intervals not exceeding six months. They should also enable the directors to ensure that the company's financial statements comply with the form and the content of company financial statements set
out in the Act. [*Sec 222(3)*].

2.14   Where a company operates an overseas branch, the accounting records
themselves may be kept overseas. (Overseas, for this purpose, means
anywhere outside Great Britain, and so it includes Northern Ireland,
the Channel Islands and the Isle of Man.) However, the accounts or
returns that must be returned to Great Britain at least once every six
months should reflect the transactions recorded in those accounting
records. This requirement poses no problem for most of the companies
that have branches overseas, because their overseas entities will usually
return management accounts to Great Britain at regular intervals (normally, monthly). These management accounts will generally satisfy the
requirements of Section 222(3).

The period of retention of records

2.15   The Act requires that a private company should keep its accounting records for three years from the date when they are prepared and a public company should keep its accounting records for six years. However, where a company is being wound up, this requirement is subject to any direction with respect to the disposal of records that may be given under the winding-up rules made pursuant to Section 663. [*Sec 222(4)*].

2.16   The period for which companies should keep their accounting records is governed also by various other statutes. These include the VAT regulations, the Limitation Act 1980 and the Taxes Management Act 1970. These may affect the retention of accounting records in the following ways:

(a) VAT regulations. Those companies that are registered for VAT must keep their records and accounts and other related documents for a period of three years. These documents must be open to inspection by H.M. Customs and Excise at all times.

(b) Limitation Act 1980. The Limitation Act 1980 limits the time period during which an action can be brought as follows:

(i) An action on a contract under seal — 12 years from the date when the cause of action arose.

(ii) An action on a simple contract — 6 years from the date when the cause of action arose.

(iii) A judgment debt — barred after 6 years.

(iv) Interest on a judgment debt — not recoverable more than 6 years after the judgment was made.

(c) Taxes Management Act 1970. The Inland Revenue may generally assess within six years of the chargeable period. But where they suspect fraud or wilful default, the period is unlimited. The Taxes Management Act contains two further rules that may be relevant:

(i) Production of accounts, books and other information. The Inland Revenue may serve notice and require a company to deliver copies of its financial statements (including copies of the auditors' report on those financial statements) to the inspector. It may also require all the company's books, accounts and documents to be made available for inspection by any officers of the Board of Inland Revenue.

(ii) Time limit for recovery of penalties. Recovery of penalties may be commenced at any time within six years after the date on which the penalty was incurred.

2.17   Consequently, the period of time for which a company should keep its accounting records depends primarily on the type of document involved. As a general rule, most accounting records should be kept for a period of at least six years.

2.18   To overcome the problems of storing accounting records, many companies now microfilm them. For VAT purposes, the Customs and Excise accepts records stored on microfilm. However, where a company stores accounting records in this way, the Customs and Excise does require the company to provide it with adequate viewing facilities.

2.19   In court proceedings, a court will normally require the production of the original document. However, where the original document is not available, a court will accept any other evidence of the document. But, in this situation, it will be necessary to prove that the microfilm is a true reproduction of the original document.

2.20   Consequently, before a company destroys any documents that it has microfilmed, it should consider very carefully whether it should retain the original document. It should remember that certain transactions (for example, a property lease) must be evidenced in writing and, therefore, it should not destroy the original document. Also, before a company destroys any accounting records, it should consult its auditors as to whether the microfilmed records will provide them with sufficient audit evidence. The auditors will also want to satisfy themselves that the company imposes adequate controls over the microfilming process.

Penalties for not keeping proper accounting records

2.21   If a company does not keep proper accounting records as required by Sections 221 and 222(1), or does not keep accounts or returns as required by Section 222(2), every director, or manager, or the company secretary will be guilty of an offence and liable to imprisonment or a fine, or both. However, if the officer can show that he acted honestly, and that the default was excusable in the circumstances in which the company's business was carried on, he will not be guilty of the offence. [*Sec 223(1)(3) — see Appendix IV*].

2.22   Similarly, where an officer fails to take all reasonable steps to ensure that the company keeps these accounting records for the required period, or deliberately causes any default by the company in observing this obligation, he will be guilty of an offence and liable to imprisonment or a fine, or both. [*Sec 223(2)(3) — see Appendix IV*].

2.23   Failure to keep proper accounting records may be attributable to negligence, or incompetence or poor administration. In very serious cases, there may be fraudulent intent.

2.24   In addition, sections 15 to 17 of the Theft Act 1968 impose penalties for fraud and false accounting. Section 18 provides that where a company has committed an offence under section 15, 16 or 17 with the consent or connivance of any director or other officer, he, as well as the company, will be criminally liable.

2.25 Also, section 19 makes it a criminal offence for any officer of a company to publish, with intent to deceive the company's members or creditors, any written statement or account that he knows is, or maybe, false on a material point.

2.26 In this connection, any document has to be regarded as a whole. Moreover, even though each part of a statement is strictly true, that statement may be false on material points if, by reason of what is omitted from it, it conveys a false impression of the company's position.

2.27 If a director or any other person is convicted on indictment or summarily of an indictable offence connected with a company's management (which includes failing to keep proper accounting records), he may be disqualified from acting for a specific period in any of the following ways:

(a) As a director of a company.
(b) As a liquidator of a company.
(c) As a receiver or a manager of a company's property.
(d) As a person concerned directly or indirectly in a company's promotion, formation or management.
[*Sec 295, 296*].

Accounting reference periods

The requirement to notify the Registrar of Companies

2.28 Within six months of being incorporated, a company must notify the Registrar of Companies (using Form 2) of the date that it wishes to treat as the date when its accounting reference period comes to an end each year. [*Sec 224(2)*]. If a company does not give notice of this accounting reference date to the Registrar within six months of being incorporated, then, by default, its accounting reference date will be 31 March. [*Sec 224(3)*].

2.29 A company's first accounting reference period starts on the date of incorporation and ends on the accounting reference date. But the period must not be less than 6 months and must not exceed 18 months. Each subsequent accounting reference period will be for 12 months. It will start on the day after the end of the previous accounting reference period and will end with the next accounting reference date. [*Sec 224(4)*].

2.30 A company's financial statements will cover the period that begins with the first accounting day of the reference period and ends on either one of the following two dates:

(a) The date on which the accounting reference period ends.

(b) Another date determined by the directors that is not more than seven days before or after the end of that period.

[*Sec 227(2)*].

Many companies, especially those in the retail trade, find it convenient to prepare their financial statements as at a particular day of the week. This provision of the Act allows them to do so. Where the latter date is chosen, the next accounting reference period will start on the day after that date.

2.31   The date a company chooses for its accounting reference date in the first year after incorporation can alter the accounting requirements considerably. The following two examples illustrate this:

(a) Company A is incorporated on 1 January 1985 and the company does not inform the Registrar of an accounting reference date by 30 June 1985.

The company's accounting reference period, therefore, starts on the date of incorporation (that is, 1 January 1985), and it is deemed to end 15 months later on 31 March 1986. It could not end on 31 March 1985 because the accounting reference period would have been less than six months. The next accounting reference period is for 12 months, and it ends on 31 March 1987.

(b) Company B is incorporated on 1 January 1985 and the company did inform the Registrar by 30 June 1985 that its accounting reference date is 30 September.

Its first accounting reference period starts on the date of incorporation (that is, 1 January 1985), and it ends nine months later on 30 September 1985. The next accounting reference period is for 12 months, and it ends on 30 September 1986.

2.32   As soon as possible after it is incorporated, a company should decide on a date that it wishes to treat as its accounting year end, and it should inform the Registrar within the six-month period allowed. The company should choose the date that is most convenient for it. For example, it should consider carefully the tax implications and also the peak workloads that the business may create (especially in a seasonal business), because it may be inconvenient to have to draw up financial statements at such a time. Unless a company wishes to change its accounting reference date, it is not required to make any further notifications to the Registrar.

Alteration of accounting reference periods

2.33   A company may, at any time, give notice (using Form 3 or 3A) to the Registrar that it wishes to alter its accounting reference date. [*Sec 225(1) (2)*]. The notice may have the effect of either extending or shortening the current reference period, but a company cannot extend its reference period so as to exceed 18 months. [*Sec 225(5)*].

2.34   Consequently, the notice must explicitly specify whether the accounting reference period is to be shortened or lengthened. [*Sec 225(4)*]. It should be noted, however, that where a company informs the Registrar of its intention to change an accounting reference date *after* the end of a period, the notice of change of the accounting reference date will have effect only where both the following apply:

(a) The company is a subsidiary or a holding company of another company, and the new accounting reference date coincides with the accounting reference date of that other company. [*Sec 225(3)(a)*].

(b) The period allowed by Section 242 of the Act for laying and delivering financial statements (that is, ten months for a private company and seven months for a public company, from the end of the accounting reference period) by reference to the *existing* accounting reference date has *not* already expired at the time the company gives notice. [*Sec 225(3)(b)*].

2.35 In addition, where the effect of the notice is to extend the accounting reference period, this will be allowed only where one of the following applies:

(a) No previous accounting reference period has been extended in this way.

(b) A previous period has been extended, but the notice is given not less than five years after the date on which that previous accounting reference period ended.

(c) The company is a subsidiary or a holding company of another company, and the new accounting reference date coincides with that of the other company.
[*Sec 225(6)*].

2.36 The Secretary of State may waive these conditions. [*Sec 225(7)*]. The timing of the notice a company gives to the Registrar of a change in its accounting reference date is crucial to the acceptance of that new date. Consider the following example:

A private company's accounting reference date is 31 December. The company last completed and filed financial statements for the 12-month period ended 31 December 1983. On 31 October 1985, the company informs the Registrar that it wishes to change its accounting reference date to 30 June. (It can do this only if it is a holding company or a subsidiary of another company, and it is changing its accounting reference date to coincide with the accounting reference date of that other company. This is because the notice is given after 31 December 1984, when its last accounting reference period ended.) The company may appear to have two choices: it may either lengthen its accounting reference period and prepare financial statements for the 18-month period to 30 June 1985, or it may shorten its accounting reference period and prepare financial statements for the 6-month period to 30 June 1984. However, if it does the latter, the company will be overdue in filing its financial statements by six months, because, by 31 October 1985, it will be 16 months after the end of its new accounting reference period. This would be an offence under Section 243(1) of the Act and so this option should not be used.

2.37 If the facts in the example given above remained the same, except that the company gave notice of the change of accounting reference date to the Registrar on 1 November 1985, then this notice would not take effect. The reason for this is that the period for filing on the basis of the existing accounting reference date (that is, 31 December 1984) would have already expired (see para 2.34 above).

2.38   An example of the disclosure that should be made when a company changes its accounting reference period is given in Table 1.

Table 1: Illustration of how a change in subsidiaries' accounting reference periods has been accounted for.

Extract from Lloyds Bank Plc Report and Accounts 31 December 1984.

---

1 Change of accounting dates

Lloyds and Scottish Plc and The National Bank of New Zealand Limited have changed their accounting dates from 30 September and 31 October respectively to 31 December and have therefore prepared accounts for the 15 months and 14 months ended 31 December 1984. The consolidated profit and loss account includes their results for the 12 months ended 31 December 1984, whilst the results for the 3 months and 2 months ended 31 December 1983 have been taken direct to reserves. The amount of £8 million credited to reserves reflects a profit before taxation of £17 million, less taxation of £7 million and minority interests of £2 million.

---

20 Reserves

	The Group Lloyds Bank Plc and Subsidiaries	The Group Associated Companies	Lloyds Bank Plc
	£m	£m	£m
Balance at 1 January 1984	1,950	49	1,446
Adjustment for change of accounting dates	8	—	—
Transfer to profit and loss account	(430)	(4)	(419)
Premium arising on issue of shares	4	—	4
Capitalisation issue	(39)	—	(39)
Surplus on revaluation of premises	112	—	72
Premiums on acquisitions during the year	(34)	—	—
Transfer on disposal of associated companies	2	(2)	—
Exchange adjustments	31	2	—
Retained profit for the year	154	14	96
Balance at 31 December 1984	1,758	59	1,160

1,817

Total reserves include the share premium account of Lloyds Bank Plc amounting to £67 million *(1983: £102 million).*

CHAPTER 3

ACCOUNTING AND AUDITING PRINCIPLES AND RULES

Chapter 3

Accounting and Auditing Principles and Rules

Introduction

3.01 When companies prepare their annual financial statements, they must comply with a substantial number of rules and regulations. All registered companies must comply with the accounting provisions of the Companies Act 1985. [*Sec 228*]. This applies whatever a company's status (public or private, limited or unlimited) may be.

3.02 Companies must comply also with *generally accepted accounting practice* in the UK (UK GAAP) that is set out in SSAPs and in SORPs. SSAPs and SORPs are developed by the ASC of the CCAB and are issued by the six governing bodies (ICAEW, ICAS, ICAI, ICMA, CACA and CIPFA). SSAPs and SORPs are authoritative statements on best accounting practice that aim to narrow the areas of difference and variety in the accounting treatment of the matters they deal with.

3.03 A SORP (that is, a Statement of Recommended Practice) is a new category of pronouncement. A SORP will be developed when there is a need for a pronouncement on a specific topic, but when that topic does not require an Accounting Standard. Unlike SSAPs, SORPs will not be mandatory, but companies will be encouraged to comply with the recommendations that they make. No SORPs exist at the date of publication of this book. However, ED 34 will form the first SORP, once it has been debated publicly.

3.04 In addition to SSAPs and SORPs, each professional body issues, from time to time, other statements on accounting matters that form part of UK GAAP. Consequently, as well as being properly prepared in accordance with the Act, financial statements should have regard to UK GAAP.

3.05 The auditors must state in their audit report whether, in their opinion, the financial statements have been properly prepared in accordance with the Act. [*Sec 236(2)(a)*]. In addition, they have a duty, imposed by the Auditing Standards, to draw attention in their report to material departures from the requirements of SSAPs that they do not concur with. Also, The Stock Exchange's Continuing Obligations require a listed company's directors to give, in the company's financial statements, the reasons for any departure from an applicable SSAP. [*CO 21(a)*]. This

23

requirement is also found in The Stock Exchange's General Undertaking for USM companies. [*GU 10(a)*].

3.06   A list of current SSAPs and EDs is given in Appendix V. These statements generally apply to the financial statements of all limited companies (see further paragraph 3.12).

3.07   Those public limited companies that are listed on The Stock Exchange have to comply also with the accounting disclosure requirements that are set out mainly in the Continuing Obligations, Chapter 2, paragraphs 20 to 22. Similarly, companies that are traded on the USM have to comply with the disclosure requirements that are set out in the General Undertaking, paragraph 10.

3.08   The first part of this chapter considers the Act's basic requirement that a company's financial statements must show a true and fair view. It also considers the way in which this requirement interacts with the requirement that the financial statements should comply with SSAPs. The chapter goes on to consider some of the more general accounting principles that apply equally to both the historical cost accounting rules and the alternative accounting rules (discussed further in Chapters 4 and 5 respectively). Finally, it considers the auditors' duties when reporting on a company's financial statements.

True and fair view

3.09   All financial statements drawn up under the Act must present a true and fair view. [*Sec 228(2)*]. This requirement is fundamental. It overrides the requirements of Schedule 4 (which contains detailed *rules* on the format and content of company financial statements) and all other requirements of the Act as to the matters to be included in a company's financial statements. [*Sec 228(3)*].

3.10   The Act illustrates the circumstances in which the true and fair override will come into play. Section 228(4) of the Act states that, where information additional to that which the Act requires is needed for the financial statements to give a true and fair view, those financial statements must include that additional information. Section 228(5) then goes on to provide that a company must depart from that requirement if its circumstances are such that, if it complied with a particular requirement of the Act, and even if it gave additional information, this would not result in a true and fair view.

3.11   It should be stressed, however, that Section 228 envisages that such a departure will be necessary only in 'special circumstances'. When there is a departure, the notes to the financial statements must disclose particulars of the departure, the reasons for it, and its effect. [*Sec 228(6)*].

Table 2 illustrates such a departure in respect of investment properties.

Table 2: Illustration of a company that has departed from the statutory accounting rules in order to show a true and fair view.

Extract from Rosehaugh PLC Report & Accounts 30 June 1984.

Accounting policy

3. Investment properties

Investment properties are subject to annual valuations and are stated at their open market value based on such valuations. Changes in the value of investment properties are disclosed as movements on revaluation reserve. Where investment properties are appropriated within the Group from trading stocks, they are transferred at open market value based on independent professional valuations, with any surplus arising being reported as a movement on revaluation reserve in the Group balance sheet. In accordance with SSAP 19, investment properties, other than leasehold interests with an unexpired term of less than 20 years, are not depreciated; the directors consider that this accounting policy, which represents a departure from the statutory accounting principles, is necessary to provide a true and fair view.

Table 26 in Chapter 7 shows how the effect of the departure is disclosed.

Application of Accounting Standards

3.12 The question then arises as to what is meant by a 'true and fair view'. In particular, there is the question of whether the requirement to show a true and fair view can be extended to include the requirement by the CCAB member councils that all financial statements should comply with the relevant SSAPs. Where a company has not complied with a SSAP, and the company's auditors do not concur with the departure, the auditors have a duty to draw attention to this non-compliance in their audit report. However, this duty is imposed on auditors by the requirements of Auditing Standard No. 2, 'The audit report'; (see para 3.05 above) it is not necessarily imposed by the Act's overriding legal requirement that financial statements must show a true and fair view.

Counsel's opinions on Accounting Standards and 'true and fair'

3.13 In connection with the development of ED 35, 'Accounting for the effects of changing prices' (withdrawn in March 1985), the ASC sought Counsel's opinion on the meaning of 'true and fair', with particular reference to the role of Accounting Standards. Although Counsel gave their opinions on the interpretation of section 149 of the Companies Act 1948, their opinions apply equally to the interpretation of the equivalent Section 228 of the 1985 Act.

3.14 The joint opinion the ASC obtained from Leonard Hoffman QC and Mary Arden is reproduced in full in Appendix VI, together with a similar opinion on 'true and fair' that the ICAS obtained from J.A.D. Hope of the Scottish bar.

3.15   To obtain a full understanding of Counsel's arguments, the opinions should be read in their entirety. However, the opinions make the following important points:

(a) The application of the 'true and fair view' involves judgment in questions of degree. There may sometimes be room for differences of opinion over the method to adopt to give a true and fair view. Because questions of degree are involved when a company is deciding on how much information is sufficient to make its financial statements true and fair, it may take account of (*inter alia*) cost effectiveness.

(b) It is for the court to decide whether financial statements give a true and fair view in compliance with the Act. But the courts will look for guidance to the ordinary practice of accountants. This is principally because the financial statements will not be true and fair unless the quality and quantity of the information they contain is sufficient to satisfy their readers' reasonable expectations. Those expectations will have been moulded by accountants' practices.

(c) SSAPs have a two-fold value to the court. First, they constitute an important statement of professional opinion. Secondly, because accountants are professionally obliged to comply with SSAPs, the readers of financial statements expect those statements to conform with the prescribed standards. Departure from a SSAP without adequate explanation may therefore result in the financial statements not showing a true and fair view.

(d) Consequently, the courts will treat compliance with accepted accounting principles as *prima facie* evidence that the financial statements are true and fair, and deviations from accepted principles will be *prima facie* evidence that they are not true and fair. These presumptions will be either strengthened or weakened by the extent to which the SSAP is accepted and applied in practice. A SSAP has no direct legal effect, but it will have an indirect effect on the content the courts give to the 'true and fair' concept.

(e) The fact that Accounting Standards can change over time does not alter the effect they have on the true and fair view. The concept of 'true and fair view' is dynamic: its content changes but its meaning remains the same.

Accounting principles and rules included in company law

3.16   Many of the accounting principles and rules that are included in SSAPs appear also in Part II of Schedule 4 to the Act. Part II is divided into three sections:

(a) Accounting principles. This section covers the fundamental accounting concepts, and they are discussed below in paragraphs 3.17 to 3.34.

(b) Historical cost accounting rules. This section covers accounting

bases, specific accounting rules, depreciation and amounts necessary to write down cost to a lower net realisable value. These are discussed in Chapter 4.

(c) Alternative accounting rules. This section deals with the accounting treatment of items where the accounting rules applied are designed to take account, in some way, of either inflation or other fluctuations in value (such as the change in a property's value). These are discussed in Chapter 5.

Accounting concepts

3.17   SSAP 2 sets out the four fundamental accounting concepts that underlie the preparation of financial statements. These are: the going concern concept, the consistency concept, the prudence concept and the accruals concept. These, together with a fifth concept that requires assets and liabilities to be valued separately, are reproduced in the Act as the 'accounting principles'.

3.18   A company's directors are permitted to depart from any of the accounting principles where there are special reasons to do so. If they do so, however, the notes to the financial statements must give particulars of the departure, the directors' reasons for it, and its effect. [*4 Sch 15*].

Table 3 illustrates a company that has departed from these accounting concepts for gains arising on translation.

Table 3: *Example of a company that has departed from the accounting principles of Schedule 4.*

Extract from Christies International plc Report & Accounts 31 December 1983.

Note

27 Profit and loss account

In order to comply with Statement of Standard Accounting Practice No. 20 there has been a departure from the accounting principles of Schedule 8 of the Companies Act 1948 [*now Schedule 4 of the Companies Act 1985*] by the inclusion in the profit and loss account balance of unrealised translation gains arising on the translation of the share capital and distributable reserves of the Group's overseas subsidiary Companies. The gains arising during 1983 amounted to £666,000 (1982 £930,000).

The going concern concept

3.19   When a company prepares its financial statements, it uses the presumption that it is carrying on business as a going concern. [*4 Sch 10*]. Of course, this is merely a presumption, and as such it can be rebutted. It would have to be rebutted, for example, if the company was on the brink of being wound up.

3.20   The importance of the going concern concept relates to the bases a company uses to arrive at the amounts at which it states items in the balance sheet. For example, fixed assets are (in effect) valued on the basis of how useful they are to the business as a going concern. If, however, the business is not a going concern, the fixed assets should be valued at their 'break-up' values.

The following example illustrates this:

A company that manufactures a particular children's toy has the following fixed assets:

	Cost £000	Depreciation £000	Net book value £000	Break-up value £000
Factory buildings	500	25	475	350
Plant and machinery	150	75	75	10
	650	100	550	360

The net book value of the fixed assets is £550,000, whereas their break-up value is £360,000. This difference results from two facts. First, in order to adapt the factory from its present use to a different use, it would need to be altered considerably. Secondly, the plant and machinery would have only a scrap value if the company ceased to manufacture the toy.

So long as the company is a going concern, the financial statements will properly reflect the fixed assets at their net book value of £550,000. If, however, the company ran into severe financial difficulty (so that it could no longer be regarded as a going concern), the fixed assets would have to be written down to their break-up value of £360,000. Thus, in order to reflect the fact that the company could no longer be regarded as a going concern, there would need to be a provision of £190,000 to reduce the amount at which the fixed assets were stated in the balance sheet.

3.21   With most companies, if the company changed the presumption that it is a going concern, it would have a considerable effect. In addition to having to make possible provisions against the book value of fixed and current assets, the company would need to make provision for other costs such as redundancy payments, dilapidations, guarantees, etc.

3.22   In a few cases, the effect of ceasing to regard the business as a going concern may be negligible. The question then arises as to whether the financial statements need to disclose that the company is no longer carrying on business as a going concern. Unless there is a statement to the contrary, the Act allows a reader to *presume* that the company is carrying on business as a going concern. Consequently, where necessary, the company should state that it has prepared its financial statements on a break-up basis, even if the effect of doing so has not been significant.

The consistency concept

3.23   In preparing its financial statements, a company must apply accounting policies consistently from one financial year to the next. [*4 Sch 11*].

Without this rule, it would be difficult to ensure comparability from year to year, or to prevent companies manipulating their results. This is because it would be possible for a company to increase or decrease its profit merely by changing its accounting policies.

3.24   There are, of course, circumstances where a change of accounting policy is justified. For example, consider a company that has formerly had insignificant development expenditure, which it has always written off at the time the expenditure was incurred. If the company, as a matter of policy, determined to embark on a large-scale programme of research and development, and if the amounts involved were material, it might then decide to defer as much of the development expenditure as it is permitted to defer. Provided that the company satisfies the separate rules that relate to the capitalisation of development expenditure set out in Chapter 7, paragraphs 7.15 to 7.22, the Act permits the company to change its accounting policy accordingly.

The prudence concept

3.25   A company must use a prudent basis in determining the amount of any item that it includes in its financial statements. [*4 Sch 12*].

3.26   The Act specifies two particular rules in relation to this. The first is that the profit and loss account may include only those profits that have been realised at the balance sheet date. [*4 Sch 12(a)*]. This means that profits may not be anticipated, and so they should be included only when they are earned and ascertained. For this purpose, realised profits are defined as "such profits of the company as fall to be treated as realised profits for the purposes of those accounts in accordance with principles generally accepted with respect to the determination for accounting purposes of realised profits at the time when those accounts are prepared". [*4 Sch 91*].

3.27   This definition may at first sight appear to be rather too general to be useful. However, its purpose is to ensure that the term 'realised profits', for the purposes of the accounting provisions contained in Schedule 4 to the Act, is not construed as having the rather restricted meaning that it has for tax purposes. A company must determine whether a profit or a loss is realised or unrealised in the light of best accounting practice at the time. In accordance with SSAP 2, 'realised' effectively means realised in the form either of cash or of other assets, whose ultimate cash realisation can be assessed with reasonable certainty. An example of an accounting principle contained in an Accounting Standard (and, therefore, 'generally accepted') is the taking of profits on long-term contracts (which is required by SSAP 9). Without this definition of realised profits, such amounts could not be included in the profit and loss account. The concepts of 'realised' and 'distributable' profits are considered further in Chapter 19.

3.28   The second rule that the Act specifies in connection with the prudence
       concept relates to liabilities and losses. A company must take account
       of all liabilities and losses that either have already arisen, or are likely
       to arise, in respect of either the financial year in question or a previous
       financial year. Moreover, they must be included even when they become
       apparent only in the period between the balance sheet date and the date
       on which the directors sign the financial statements. [4 Sch 12(b)]. This
       means, for example, that if a major debtor becomes insolvent after the
       balance sheet date, and if the directors have not already signed the finan-
       cial statements in accordance with Section 238 of the Act, the resulting
       loss must be reflected in the financial statements. SSAP 17 specifically
       requires the disclosure of the date on which the financial statements
       are approved and signed by the directors (see further Chapter 21 para
       21.7).

The accruals concept

3.29   The financial statements must reflect all income and expenditure that
       relate to the financial year in question. This applies irrespective of the
       dates on which amounts fall due to be received or paid. [4 Sch 13].
       The effect of this is that if income and expenditure relate to the cur-
       rent year, they must be accrued in the financial statements. The result-
       ing difference must be shown as either an accrual or a prepayment.

3.30   The Act is silent as to what happens where the accruals concept is incon-
       sistent with the prudence concept. SSAP 2, however, makes it quite
       clear that, in that circumstance, the prudence concept prevails.

The separate valuation of assets and liabilities

3.31   When a company is determining the aggregate amount of any item,
       it must determine separately the amount of each individual asset or
       liability that makes up that item. [4 Sch 14]. Although this rule is not
       described in SSAP 2 as a fundamental accounting concept, it has always
       been inherent in good accounting practice.

3.32   The treatment of investments is a good example of the separate valua-
       tion principle, although the general principle applies equally to other
       items such as stocks. Those investments that are treated as fixed assets
       will normally be accounted for at cost, less write-downs for any per-
       manent decrease in value. Before the implementation of the separate
       valuation rules in the Companies Act 1981, investments (and particu-
       larly those in subsidiaries) were often considered as a whole. If one
       investment had a market value that was less than book value, and all
       the other investments had an excess of market value over book value
       that more than compensated, then investments as a whole were not over-
       stated at book value. Usually, a company made no provision against
       the one overstated investment.

3.33   However, under the 1985 Act, investments have to be considered individually. By law, a provision *must* be made against an investment if there is a permanent decrease in value below cost. This applies irrespective of the value and the quality of the other investments.

3.34   There is a statutory exception to the separate valuation rule, namely that tangible assets and raw materials and consumables may, in certain circumstances, be included in the financial statements at a fixed quantity and value (see Chapter 4 paras 4.35 and 4.36). [*4 Sch 25(1)*]. In addition, there is a further exception, in that, where there is a legal right of set-off, assets and liabilities may be netted (see Chapter 8 paras 8.76 to 8.82).

Auditors' duties under the Act

3.35   Every company (except a dormant company that has passed a resolution not to do so) is under an obligation to appoint auditors at each general meeting at which the company's financial statements are presented. The auditors then hold office from the end of that meeting until the end of the next general meeting at which the company's financial statements are presented. [*Sec 384(1)*].

3.36   The company's auditors are required to report on any financial statements presented at a general meeting. Their report has to state whether, in their opinion:

(a) The balance sheet and the profit and loss account and (if the company has presented group accounts) the group accounts of the company have been *properly prepared in accordance with the Act.*

(b) A *true and fair view* is given in the balance sheet of the state of the company's affairs at the end of the financial year, and is also given in the profit and loss account of the company's profit or loss for that year.

(c) If group accounts are presented, a *true and fair view* is given of the state of affairs and the profit or loss of the company and those of its subsidiaries that the group accounts deal with, so far as concerns the members of the company.

[*Sec 236(1)(2)*].

3.37   The auditors' duties are contained in Section 237 of the Act. The auditors have a duty, *inter alia*, to consider whether:

(a) The company has kept proper accounting records.

(b) They have received proper returns adequate for their audit from those branches they did not visit.

(c) The financial statements they are auditing are in agreement with the accounting records.

The auditors must report if they are not satisfied that these requirements have been complied with. [*Sec 237(1)(2)*]. These duties are discussed further in Chapter 2, paragraphs 2.09 and 2.10.

3.38 In addition, the Act requires the auditors to disclose in their report (so far as they are reasonably able to do so) certain information where that information has not been disclosed elsewhere in the financial statements. This information is as follows:

(a) The chairman's and the directors' emoluments, pensions and compensation for loss of office (as required by Schedule 5, Part V — see Chapter 10 paras 10.44 to 10.75).

(b) The number of employees paid at higher rates (as required by Schedule 5, Part VI — see Chapter 10 paras 10.76 to 10.79).

(c) Loans and other transactions favouring directors and officers (as required by Schedule 6, Parts I to III — see Chapter 11 para 11.82). [*Sec 237(5)*].

Auditors' duties in relation to Accounting Standards

3.39 The explanatory foreword to the SSAPs says that Accounting Standards are authoritative statements on best accounting practice, and are approved by the CCAB member councils. The CCAB councils expect their members, who assume responsibilities in respect of financial statements, to observe Accounting Standards. Accordingly, the councils consider that where members prepare company financial statements, and they find it necessary to depart from applicable Accounting Standards, they should ensure that they disclose the departure and adequately explain it in those financial statements. Unless it would be impracticable or misleading in the context of giving a *true and fair view*, the member should ensure that the company estimates and discloses the financial effect of such a departure.

3.40 In addition, where the members act as auditors or reporting accountants, the onus is on them not only to ensure that any significant departure is disclosed, but also (to the extent that their own concurrence with that departure is either stated or implied) to justify such a departure from any applicable SSAP.

Auditors' duties imposed by Auditing Standards

3.41 Other duties and obligations that auditors must follow are contained in the Auditing Standards and Guidelines. Auditing Standards and Guidelines are developed by the APC, a committee of the CCAB, and are then issued by the councils of five of the governing bodies (that is, the six CCAB bodies excluding the ICMA). Members of these bodies that carry out audits must have regard to these Standards in their work. The explanatory foreword to the Auditing Standards and Guidelines explains their scope and authority.

3.42   The foreword says that "an audit is the independent examination of, and expression of opinion on, the financial statements of an enterprise by an appointed auditor in pursuance of that appointment and in compliance with any relevant statutory obligation. The responsibility for the preparation of financial statements and the presentation of the information included therein rests with the management of the enterprise (in the case of a company, the directors). The auditor's responsibility is to report on the financial statements as presented by management".

3.43   Auditing Standards prescribe the basic principles and practices that members of the bodies of the CCAB are expected to follow when conducting an audit. In observing those Standards, the auditor must exercise his judgment both in determining the audit procedures he needs to perform in the circumstances to afford a reasonable basis for his opinion and in determining the wording of his report.

3.44   The second Auditing Standard, 'The audit report', has the following to say about the expression 'true and fair view':

"The majority of audit reports are issued under the Companies Acts which normally require the use of the words 'true and fair view'. For the purpose of this Standard, therefore, the phrase 'true and fair view' has been retained. When expressing an opinion that financial statements give a true and fair view the auditor should be satisfied, *inter alia*, that:

(a) all relevant Statements of Standard Accounting Practice have been complied with, except in situations in which for justifiable reasons they are not strictly applicable because they are impracticable, or exceptionally, having regard to the circumstances, would be inappropriate or give a misleading view; and

(b) any significant accounting policies which are not the subject of Statements of Standard Accounting Practice are appropriate to the circumstances of the business."

3.45   Consequently, the auditors not only have to report that a company's financial statements comply with the Act, but also have to report where those statements do not comply with a relevant SSAP.

CHAPTER 4

HISTORICAL COST ACCOUNTING RULES

Chapter 4

Historical Cost Accounting Rules

Introduction

4.01 Companies should normally determine the amounts they include in their financial statements in accordance with the historical cost accounting rules. [*4 Sch 16*]. But the Act permits companies to use also certain alternative accounting rules, and these are discussed in Chapter 5.

4.02 Paragraphs 16 to 28 of Schedule 4 set out the rules companies must apply in arriving at the amounts at which they must disclose items in their financial statements. These rules cover:

(a) Fixed assets.
(b) Current assets.
(c) Purchase price and production cost of assets.
(d) Other items.

Each of these is discussed in detail below.

Fixed assets

4.03 The basic rule is that fixed assets are to be shown at either their purchase price or their production cost (see paras 4.20 to 4.34 below), less any provision for depreciation or diminution in value. [*4 Sch 17*]. For this purpose, a fixed asset is defined as any asset that is "intended for use on a continuing basis in the company's activities". [*4 Sch 77*]. Fixed assets include intangible assets, tangible assets and fixed asset investments.

Depreciation and diminution in value

4.04 Where a fixed asset has a limited useful economic life, a company must write off its purchase price or its production cost systematically over the period of that life. [*4 Sch 18*]. Although depreciation is not defined in the Act, it is defined in SSAP 12 as "a measure of the wearing out, consumption or other loss of value of a fixed asset whether arising from use, effluxion of time or obsolescence through technology and market changes". Depreciation is not necessarily intended to result in a company setting aside profits or funds to replace an asset at the end of its

37

useful economic life, but, coincidentally, that result may be the outcome.

4.05   In determining the amount to be written off each asset each year, the Act (and also SSAP 12) specifically requires companies to take account of the asset's estimated residual value at the end of its useful economic life. [*4 Sch 18(b)*]. 'Useful economic life' is not defined in the Act or SSAP 12. However, ED 37, which the ASC published in March 1985, defines an asset's useful economic life as "the period over which *the present owner* will derive economic benefits from its use". Before ED 37 was issued, many people interpreted an asset's useful economic life mentioned in SSAP 12 as meaning the life of the asset itself, and not the period of time over which the present owner would use it. The calculation of depreciation and amortisation is discussed further in Chapter 7.

4.06   A company *must* make provision if *any* fixed asset (including a fixed asset investment) has diminished in value, and this reduction is expected to be *permanent*. In such a case, the company must reduce the amount at which it discloses the asset in its financial statements by the amount of this diminution in value. This requirement applies whether or not the asset has a limited useful economic life. [*4 Sch 19(2)*]. This accords with the treatment required by paragraph 19 of SSAP 12, which says that if, at any time, the directors consider an asset's unamortised cost not to be recoverable in full, the company should write the asset down immediately to its estimated recoverable amount.

4.07   In addition, where a fixed asset *investment* has suffered a diminution in value that the directors consider to be only *temporary*, the Act *permits* the company to make provision in respect of that diminution in value. Accordingly, it permits it to reduce the amount at which the investment is disclosed in its financial statements. [*4 Sch 19(1)*]. It should be stressed that this provision is permissive, not mandatory, in character; the Act imposes no obligation on a company to make such provision, but it may do so if the directors think it prudent. There is no equivalent provision for a temporary diminution in value of a fixed asset other than an investment (see further Chapter 5 paras 5.10 to 5.29).

4.08   It may be difficult for a company to determine whether an asset has suffered either a permanent or a temporary fall in value or, indeed, whether it has suffered *any* fall in value. For example, as regards its investments, a company will have to consider such matters as the net asset value, liquidity, changes in the nature of the business, future trading difficulties, and other such factors. It may also take advice from stockbrokers and other advisers. However, it may be easier for a company to determine whether a tangible fixed asset has suffered a fall in value, and, if so, whether that fall is likely to be temporary or permanent. For example, if a machine will not again generate income, the company should write it down to its net realisable value, because any decrease in value to the business will be permanent.

4.09   Where a company has made provision for a diminution in value, but the factors that gave rise to it no longer apply to any extent, then the company *must* write back the provision to that extent. [4 Sch 19(3)].

4.10   To illustrate these provisions, consider the following example:

The history of a company's fixed assets is as follows:

	Fixed asset investment £000	Tangible fixed asset £000
Cost at 1 January 1983	10	6
Value at 31 December 1985	8	5
Value at 31 December 1986	5*	3*
Value at 31 December 1987	9	4

*This reduction in value is expected at the time to be permanent.

Ignoring the normal depreciation rules for the purposes of this example, the Act applies as follows:

(a) At 31 December 1985, the directors *could* (if they wish) write down the amount of the fixed asset investment to £8,000. (However, they could not write down the value of the tangible fixed asset to £5,000. This is because the reduction in value is not regarded as *permanent*, and only fixed asset investments can be written down in such circumstances.)

(b) At 31 December 1986, the directors *must* write down the amount of the fixed asset investment to £5,000 (whether or not they wrote it down to £8,000 at 31 December 1985). In addition, they *must* write down the value of the tangible fixed asset to £3,000. This is because the fall in value of each of them is expected to be *permanent*.

(c) At 31 December 1987, the directors *must* write back £4,000 in respect of the fixed asset investment and £1,000 in respect of the tangible fixed asset. This is because the reasons that gave rise to the provision for diminution in value of each of them have ceased to apply to that extent.

4.11   Where a company has made any provision for diminution in value, or has written back any provision for diminution in value, it must disclose the amounts involved (either in the profit and loss account or in the notes to the financial statements). [*4 Sch 19*]. The amounts to be disclosed are:

(a) Provisions made in respect of the permanent diminution in value of fixed assets (see para 4.06). [*4 Sch 19(2)*].

(b) Provisions made in respect of the temporary diminution in value of fixed asset investments (see para 4.07). [*4 Sch 19(1)*].

(c) Amounts written back to the extent that the circumstances that gave rise to the provisions no longer apply (see para 4.09). [*4 Sch 19(3)*].

The amounts disclosed must be split between these three headings, but amounts that fall within the same heading may be aggregated. [*4 Sch 19*]. To illustrate this, consider the following example:

In the financial year in question, the following events occurred:

(a) The company wrote down a building by £15,000 and a machine by £7,000, because they had both fallen in value and the fall was expected to be permanent.

(b) The company wrote down an investment in a subsidiary company and a long-term investment by £20,000 and £5,000 respectively, because they had temporarily fallen in value.

(c) The company wrote back to cost an overseas investment that it had previously written down by £3,000, because the circumstances that gave rise to the previous write-down had ceased to apply.

In such circumstances, the aggregate amounts the company must disclose are:

(a) Provisions made in respect of a *permanent* fall in value of
fixed assets   £22,000

(b) Provisions made in respect of a *temporary* fall in value of fixed
asset investments   £25,000

(c) Write-back of provisions no longer required   £3,000

The amounts in *(a)* and *(b)* may not be aggregated together or reduced by the amount in *(c)*.

Other depreciation rules

4.12   SSAP 12 contains two further rules that relate to depreciation.

4.13   First, where an asset's estimated useful life has been revised, the Standard requires that the asset's unamortised cost should be charged over the revised remaining useful life. [*SSAP 12 para 18*]. For example, a company purchased an asset on 1 January 1980 for £100,000, and the asset had an estimated useful life of ten years and a residual value of nil. The company has charged depreciation using the straight-line method at £10,000 per annum. On 1 January 1984, when the asset's net book value is £60,000, the directors review the estimated life and decide that the asset will probably be useful for a further ten years. The company should then amend the annual depreciation charge to charge the unamortised cost (namely, £60,000) over the revised remaining life of ten years. Consequently, it should charge depreciation for the next ten years at £6,000 per annum.

4.14   This revision is not a change in accounting policy, but merely a refinement of that policy. Therefore, it would not be appropriate to make a prior-year adjustment in accordance with SSAP 6.

4.15   Secondly, if there is a change from one method of providing depreciation to another, the unamortised cost of the asset should be written off over the remaining useful life on the new basis. [*SSAP 12 para 20*].

4.16   Consequently, in the example given above, the company may decide that, from 1 January 1984, the sum-of-the-digits method of calculation would be more applicable than the straight-line method. If so, the depreciation charge for 1984 would be £17,143 (namely, £60,000 x $6/(6+5+4+3+2+1)$), because the asset still has a remaining useful life of six years. SSAP 12 says that where the effect of the change is material, it should be disclosed in the year of change. However, it does not require a prior-year adjustment to be made.

4.17 Both of the above rules in SSAP 12 appear also in ED 37. Table 4 shows a group that has changed its accounting policy in respect of fixed assets.

Table 4: Change in the group's fixed assets accounting policy for replacements of fittings and equipment.

Extract from Stakis Public Limited Company Report and Accounts 30 September 1984.

Fixed Assets and Depreciation

Freehold and leasehold properties are stated at valuation at 2nd October 1983 or subsequent cost. All other fixed assets are stated at cost.

In the year to 30th September 1984 the group changed its accounting policy in regard to replacements of fittings and equipment. These were formerly written off against profits as incurred, the original asset remaining, undepreciated, in fixed assets. Replacement fittings and equipment are now capitalised and, together with all existing fittings and equipment, depreciated over their estimated economic lives.

No depreciation is provided on freehold properties other than industrial buildings on the basis that it is the Company's policy to ensure that freehold premises are continually maintained in a sound state of repair and accordingly the directors consider that the lives of such premises are so long and residual values so high that depreciation is unnecessary.

Depreciation is provided on other fixed assets on the following bases:

 (i) Freehold industrial buildings are amortised over their estimated economic lives.

 (ii) Leasehold property is amortised over the last fifty years of the lease, or the unexpired period of the lease, if less.

(iii) Plant, fittings and equipment are depreciated evenly over ten years.

(iv) Motor vehicles are depreciated evenly over four years.

Current assets

4.18 In general, current assets are to be shown at the lower of purchase price or production cost (see paras 4.20 to 4.34) and net realisable value. [*4 Sch 22, 23(1)*]. For example, debtors should be stated after any provision for bad and doubtful debts. For this purpose, current assets are defined as any assets that are not intended for use on a continuing basis in a company's activities. [*4 Sch 77*].

4.19 Where a company has written down the value of a current asset to its net realisable value, but the circumstances that gave rise to the write-down cease to apply to any extent (that is, the net realisable value becomes greater than the amount that the asset was written down to), the company *must* write back the amount of the write-down to that extent. [*4 Sch 23(2)*]. This means that even where an asset regains only part of its value, the company must write it back to that extent.

Purchase price and production cost of assets

General rule

4.20   The Act sets out detailed definitions of an asset's purchase price and production cost.

4.21   Purchase price is defined as the actual price the company paid for the asset (whether the consideration was in cash or otherwise), plus any expenses that were incidental to its acquisition. [*4 Sch 26(1), 90*]. These incidental expenses include, for example, the expenses that the company had to incur in order to get the asset to its present location and into its present condition.

4.22   Production cost is defined as the total of the following amounts:

(a) The purchase price of the raw materials and consumables the company used in producing the asset.

(b) The direct costs of production the company incurred (excluding distribution costs in the case of current assets).

(c) The following other costs that *may* be included:

   (i) A reasonable proportion of indirect overheads, to the extent that they relate to the period of production.
   (ii) Interest on any capital the company borrowed in order to finance the production of that asset, to the extent that it relates to the period of production. Where such interest has been included in the production cost, the fact that it has been included and its amount must be stated in the notes to the financial statements.

[*4 Sch 26(2)-(4)*].

4.23   These provisions of the Act are largely consistent with the provisions of SSAP 9 on stocks and work in progress. However, with stocks and work in progress, SSAP 9 *requires* the valuation to include a reasonable proportion of indirect overheads, whereas the Act merely *permits* it. Therefore, to comply with SSAP 9, companies should take up the option in the Act.

4.24   The Act states that "In the case of current assets distribution costs may not be included in production costs". [*4 Sch 26(4)*]. However, with stocks, a proportion of the costs that a company incurs in distributing goods from its factory to its sales depot may be included in the valuation. SSAP 9 requires that the costs the company incurs in bringing the goods to their present location should be included in the stocks valuation. A company should not include external distribution costs such as those relating to the transfer of goods from a sales depot to an external customer.

4.25 When determining the purchase price or the production cost of their stocks and other fungible items, companies may apply special rules. These rules are considered in Chapter 8, paragraphs 8.52 and 8.53.

Inclusion of interest in purchase price or production cost

4.26 The rise in interest rates and the increased use of borrowed funds in recent years, together with the rules for determining the purchase price or the production cost, have caused companies to reconsider the way in which they treat their borrowing costs. Views differ on what the appropriate accounting treatment should be. Some regard such costs as forming part of the cost of the particular asset with which they can be either directly or indirectly identified.

4.27 Others regard them as essentially period costs that should be charged to income regardless of how the borrowing is applied. As mentioned in paragraph 4.22 above, the Act permits both views.

4.28 In March 1984, the IASC published IAS 23, 'Capitalisation of borrowing costs'. UK companies are not subject to the requirements of IAS 23 until these requirements are incorporated into a UK Accounting Standard. However, the contents of IAS 23 may still be regarded as an indication of best accounting practice.

4.29 IAS 23 does not include a firm recommendation on whether borrowing costs should or should not be included in an asset's value. The Standard states only how the directors should determine borrowing costs if they wish to capitalise them. It says, *inter alia*, that the directors should calculate a 'capitalisation rate' for the period (by relating, for example, the borrowing costs the company incurred for the period to the borrowings outstanding during that period). They should then apply this capitalisation rate to the expenditure on the acquisition, construction or production of the relevant asset.

4.30 IAS 23 does not address the question of whether the amount to be capitalised should be gross or net of tax relief. There is still no clear consensus of opinion in the UK on this important issue. Accordingly, a company may use either basis, provided that it uses that basis consistently and clearly discloses its policy.

4.31 The Stock Exchange requires that the financial statements of a listed company or of a company traded on the USM should indicate both the amount of interest capitalised during the year, and the amount and the treatment of any related tax relief. [*CO 21(g); GU 10(g)*].

Table 5 illustrates how a company complies with the disclosure requirements for capitalised interest. A further example is given in Table 44 in Chapter 10.

> **Table 5: Disclosure of capitalised interest.**
>
> *Extract from The Peninsular and Oriental Steam Navigation Company Annual Report and Accounts 31 December 1984.*
>
> **28** Capitalised interest
> Interest amounting to £3,897,000 has been capitalised during the year (1983—£1,858,000). Relief for this interest will be allowable in full for taxation purposes.
>
> Aggregate capitalised interest included in assets
>
> | | Group | | Company | |
> |---|---|---|---|---|
> | | **1984** | *1983* | **1984** | *1983* |
> | | **£000** | *£000* | **£000** | *£000* |
> | Building land and development properties | **2,135** | *2,518* | — | — |
> | Work in progress | — | *673* | — | — |
> | Tangible assets | **6,297** | *2,121* | **5,973** | *2,121* |
> | | **8,432** | *5,312* | **5,973** | *2,121* |

Unknown purchase price or production cost

4.32   In certain circumstances, an asset's purchase price or production cost is to be taken as the value the company ascribed to the asset in the earliest available record of its value that the company made on or after it either acquired or produced the asset. These circumstances are where there is no record of either of the following:

(a) The actual purchase price or the actual production cost.

(b) Any price, any expenses or any costs that are relevant for determining the purchase price or the production cost.

4.33   This exemption applies also where the relevant record is available, but it could be obtained only with unreasonable expense or delay. [*4 Sch 28*].

4.34   Where a company has determined, for the first time, an asset's purchase price or production cost according to its earliest known value, the company must disclose this fact in the notes to its financial statements. [*4 Sch 51(1)*].

Other items

Assets shown at a fixed amount

4.35   Where certain conditions are satisfied, tangible fixed assets and raw materials and consumables can be shown at a fixed quantity and at a fixed value. These conditions (all of which must be satisfied) are as follows:

(a) The assets must be assets of a kind that are constantly being replaced.

(b) Their overall value must not be material to the assessment of the company's state of affairs.

(c) Their quantity, value and composition must not be subject to material variation.
[*4 Sch 25*].

4.36   Where this provision applies, all subsequent purchases of the assets in question will be charged direct against profit. This provision will enable companies to continue including (for example) loose tools in either tangible fixed assets or stocks, at a fixed quantity and at a fixed value. However, SSAP 9 says that when valuing stocks, a company must choose a method that produces the fairest practicable approximation to actual cost. It says that base stock would not usually bear such a relationship. [*SSAP 9 Appendix 1 para 12*]. Consequently, although permitted by law, the base stock method of valuing stocks is not allowed by SSAP 9.

Excess of money owed over value received

4.37   Where the amount that a company owes a creditor exceeds the value of the consideration it received in the transaction that gave rise to the liability, the company *may* treat the amount of the difference as an asset. [*4 Sch 24(1)*]. If it does so, however, it must write off the amount it shows as an asset by reasonable amounts each year, and it must write off the asset fully before the date on which the debt becomes due for payment. [*4 Sch 24(2)(a)*].

4.38   Any amount the company includes under assets under this provision must be disclosed separately either on the face of the balance sheet or in the notes to the financial statements. [*4 Sch 24(2)(b)*].

4.39   An example of the application of this provision is the accounting treatment of 'deep discounted stock'. This is considered in Chapter 9, paragraphs 9.30 to 9.40.

CHAPTER 5

ALTERNATIVE ACCOUNTING RULES

Chapter 5

Alternative Accounting Rules

Introduction

5.01 Paragraphs 29 to 34 of Schedule 4 to the Act set out the rules companies may apply in arriving at the amounts (other than cost) at which they may disclose items in their financial statements. These amounts may reflect changes in the value of assets (for example, the increase in the value of property) that may arise as a result of general or specific price increases.

5.02 These provisions of Schedule 4 are purely permissive in character. That is to say, provided that companies comply with certain conditions, they may (but are not obliged to) adopt any of the alternative accounting rules set out in the Act.

5.03 Legally, companies may adopt all or any of these rules. So, for example, a company could include stocks in its balance sheet at current cost, and include every other item on an historical cost basis. However, although it might be reasonable for a company to include certain assets at a valuation, if it mixed the historical cost rules and the alternative accounting rules indiscriminately, it might produce meaningless financial statements. Therefore, the overriding requirement for 'truth and fairness' precludes this approach.

5.04 The combined effect of the historical cost and alternative accounting rules is to allow companies to draw up their financial statements under either the pure historical cost convention, or the historical cost convention modified to include certain assets at a valuation, or the current cost convention.

5.05 There is an important difference between SSAP 16 and the alternative accounting rules. SSAP 16 outlines a method whereby a company may disclose information on a current cost basis. It may do this either in a supplementary statement or in its main financial statements. The alternative accounting rules relate to the main financial statements only, and they apply to all cases where those financial statements are adjusted to take account of inflation or other changes in the value of assets.

The alternative accounting rules

5.06 The alternative accounting rules that the Act permits companies to follow when preparing their financial statements are as follows:

(a) Intangible fixed assets may be stated at their current cost. [*4 Sch 31(1)*]. This does not apply to goodwill, which can be shown only at the value of the consideration for which it was acquired (less any amounts by which it has been amortised). This exception is supported also by SSAP 22, paragraph 34(a) (see further Chapter 7 para 7.66).

(b) Tangible fixed assets may be stated either at their market value on the date when they were last valued or at their current cost. [*4 Sch 31(2)*]. This means, for example, that properties may be valued periodically, although ED37 says that if a company follows a policy of revaluing assets, then it should keep the valuations up to date. Consequently, assuming ED 37 becomes a Standard, if a company adopts this alternative accounting rule, it should revalue its assets on a regular basis.

(c) Fixed asset investments may be shown either at their market value on the date on which they were last valued or at a value determined on a basis that the directors think appropriate in the light of the company's circumstances. However, if a company adopts the latter approach, it must state, in the notes to its financial statements, particulars of the method it has adopted, and the reasons for adopting it. [*4 Sch 31 (3)*]. A value determined on a basis that the directors thought appropriate could, for example, include the valuation of unlisted investments on either a net asset basis or an earnings basis. However, it would not be sufficient for the notes merely to state that unlisted investments are included 'at the directors' valuation'.

(d) Current asset investments may be stated at their current cost. [*4 Sch 31(4)*].

(e) Stocks may be stated at their current cost. [*4 Sch 31(5)*].

5.07 The Act does not define 'current cost'. Therefore, where a company chooses to value some assets at their current cost under the alternative accounting rules, that value would normally be determined in accordance with the principles set out in SSAP 16. However, there may be good reasons for choosing some other method of valuation.

The revaluation reserve

General rules

5.08 The Act specifies the following rules that relate to the creation and use of the revaluation reserve:

50

(a) Any difference between the amount of any item that a company has determined according to one of the alternative accounting rules, and the amount that the company would have disclosed if it had adhered to the historical cost convention, must be credited or debited (as applicable) to a 'revaluation reserve'. [*4 Sch 34*].

In determining the amount of this difference, a company should take account, where appropriate, of any provisions for depreciation or diminution in value that it made otherwise than by reference to the value it determined under the alternative accounting rules. It should also take account of any adjustments of any such provisions that it made in the light of that determination. [*4 Sch 34(1)*].

(b) Where the directors consider that any amount standing to the credit of the revaluation reserve is no longer necessary for the purpose of the accounting policies that the company has adopted, then the reserve must be reduced accordingly. [*4 Sch 34(3)*].

The Act restricts the circumstances in which a company can transfer an amount from the revaluation reserve to the profit and loss account. It can do this only where one of the following circumstances exists:

  (i) The amount in question has been previously charged to the profit and loss account.
  (ii) The amount in question represents a realised profit.
  [*4 Sch 34(3)*].

(c) The revaluation reserve must be shown on the face of the balance sheet as a separate amount, although it need not be shown under that name. [*4 Sch 34(2)*].

(d) Where any amount has been either credited or debited to the revaluation reserve, its treatment for taxation purposes must be disclosed in a note to the financial statements. [*4 Sch 34(4)*].

5.09 The implications of these rules in practice are considered in more detail below. The question of whether a revaluation surplus or deficit is realised or unrealised is considered in Chapter 19.

Treatment of revaluation surpluses and deficits

5.10 As mentioned in paragraph 5.08*(a)* above, where a company has valued an item in accordance with one of the alternative accounting rules, the Act says that the revaluation surplus or deficit *must* be credited or debited to a revaluation reserve.

5.11 This means that when a company values its assets in accordance with the alternative accounting rules, it must:

(a) Value each asset separately. (It must do this in order to comply with

51

the separate valuation principle contained in paragraph 14 of Schedule 4.)

(b) Transfer the surplus or deficit that arises on the revaluation of each asset to the revaluation reserve.

5.12 However, where a revaluation deficit arises because of a *permanent* diminution in value of an asset, the alternative accounting rules do not apply. This is because, in such a situation, the historical cost accounting rules require a *provision* to be made for this *permanent* diminution in value. [*4 Sch 19(2)*].

5.13 Paragraph 19(2) of Schedule 4 requires provisions for *permanent* diminutions in value that are not shown in the profit and loss account to be disclosed in a note to the financial statements. The requirement of this paragraph is probably to ensure that the provision is separately disclosed, either in the profit and loss account itself, or in the notes to the financial statements.

5.14 However, an alternative interpretation of paragraph 19(2) could mean that where the provision is not *charged* in the profit and loss account (but it is charged to another reserve), it must be disclosed in a note to the financial statements. If this latter interpretation is correct, it would be acceptable for a company to charge a provision direct to its revaluation reserve, provided that it disclosed that provision in a note to the financial statements.

5.15 The prudence concept, contained both in the Act and in SSAP 2, requires a company to make provision for all known liabilities and losses. SSAP 2 implies very strongly that a company should charge such provisions to the profit and loss account. Therefore, it appears that when a company makes a provision for a *permanent* diminution in an asset's value (in accordance with paragraph 19(2) of Schedule 4), it should charge it to the profit and loss account and not to another reserve. Consequently, the alternative interpretation of paragraph 19(2) of Schedule 4 outlined above would not appear to be acceptable.

5.16 However, when a company applies the alternative accounting rules, it *must* debit to the *revaluation reserve* those deficits that arise from a *temporary* diminution in value of a fixed asset (other than a fixed asset investment). This is because it would seem that the Act does not permit such revaluation deficits to be charged to the profit and loss account, (see Para 5.10 above).

5.17 In January 1985, the ASC issued ED 36 which, if accepted, will revise SSAP 6. ED 36 specifically addresses the question of how a company should treat those deficits that arise from the diminution in value of fixed assets. In paragraph 41, it says that deficits on the revaluation of fixed assets should be debited to the profit and loss account for the year to the extent that they exceed any surplus that is held in the revaluation reserve and is identified as relating to previous revaluations of the same assets.

5.18   In the past, companies have treated revaluation deficits in various ways. The acceptability of these alternative approaches is considered in more detail below. The three alternative approaches that companies have used are as follows:

(a) Take all deficits that arise on the revaluation of individual assets to the profit and loss account.

(b) Take the *net* amount of revaluation surpluses and revaluation deficits to the revaluation reserve.

(c) Take those deficits that arise on the revaluation of individual assets to the revaluation reserve to the extent that the revaluation reserve contains surpluses that arose on previous revaluations of the same assets. Any balance of deficits is then taken to the profit and loss account.

5.19   In method *(a)*, revaluation deficits that arise from both *permanent* and *temporary* diminutions in value would be taken to the profit and loss account. This is not in accordance with paragraph 19 of Schedule 4 (which says that, under the historical cost accounting rules, a company may provide for *temporary* diminutions in value only of fixed asset *investments* and not all fixed assets) nor in accordance with paragraph 34(1) (which says that, under the alternative accounting rules, revaluation deficits should be debited to the revaluation reserve). However, before the Companies Act 1981 became effective, this method was used because it is prudent, and in certain circumstances it may have been justified.

5.20   In method *(b)*, the net amount of revaluation surpluses and revaluation deficits is taken to the revaluation reserve. By contrast, this method does not seem to comply strictly with paragraph 19(2) of Schedule 4 (unless the alternative interpretation of paragraph 19(2) outlined in paragraph 5.14 above is correct). This is because, in this method, provisions for *permanent* diminutions in value are not charged in the profit and loss account. Also, it does not comply either with the proposals made in ED 36 or with the prudence concept stated in SSAP 2.

5.21   Two further problems arise with method *(b)*. First, how should an overall *deficit* (net of revaluation surpluses) be treated? Secondly, if aggregate revaluation deficits are taken to the revaluation reserve, is it possible to have a debit revaluation reserve balance? As mentioned in paragraph 5.10, the Act says that any revaluation deficits that arise when a company adopts the alternative accounting rules must be debited to the revaluation reserve. This implies that it is acceptable in law to have a debit balance on the revaluation reserve. The only reference in the Accounting Standards to the way in which companies must treat an overall deficit on the revaluation reserve is in SSAP 19, 'Accounting for investment properties'. Paragraph 13 of that Standard says:

"Changes in the value of investment properties should not be taken to the profit and loss account but should be disclosed as a movement on an investment revaluation reserve, unless the total of the investment revaluation reserve is insufficient to cover a deficit, in which case the amount by which the deficit exceeds the amount in the investment revaluation reserve should be charged in the profit and loss account."

5.22   Accordingly, when similar circumstances to those outlined in paragraph 13 of SSAP 19 exist, it remains prudent and good accounting practice to charge an overall debit balance on the revaluation reserve to the profit and loss account.

5.23   Method *(c)* takes deficits to the revaluation reserve to the extent that the revaluation reserve contains surpluses that arose on previous revaluations of the same asset. Any balance of deficits is then taken to the profit and loss account. This method is the method outlined in ED 36, and it relates to all revaluation deficits that arise from both *permanent* and *temporary* diminutions in value. This method accords with the separate valuation principle outlined in paragraph 14 of Schedule 4. There is a distinction to be drawn, however, between permanent and temporary diminutions and this is described below.

5.24   In this method, deficits that arise from a *permanent* diminution in an asset's value should only be charged to the revaluation reserve to the extent that that reserve contains a surplus that has arisen on previous revaluations of the same asset. The balance, if a deficit, must be taken to the profit and loss account.

5.25   Where an asset has previously been revalued, a deficit on a subsequent revaluation of the same asset will only be *permanent* to the extent that that deficit exceeds any previous surplus. For example, if an asset costing £100,000 was revalued in 1980 to £120,000 a surplus would have been taken to the revaluation reserve of £20,000. If in 1985 the same asset is revalued at £90,000, it shows a deficit over its previous valuation of £30,000. If this deficit is expected to be permanent, then a provision for the *permanent* diminution in value of the asset (namely, £10,000) should be charged to the profit and loss account. The provision for *permanent* diminution, therefore, represents the deficit that arises on the latest valuation after deducting any surplus that may have arisen on a previous revaluation of the same asset that is still standing to the credit of the revaluation reserve (namely, £30,000 — £20,000) and not the total deficit of £30,000.

5.26   On a revaluation that gives rise to deficits which are *temporary* (for example, the situation when a diminution arises as part of an annual revaluation exercise), it appears that the proposals in ED 36 allow these deficits to be set, to a certain extent, against surpluses on other assets in the revaluation reserve. If the net of surpluses and deficits results in a deficit, the extract from SSAP 19 quoted in paragraph 5.21 above suggests that the company should make a provision of this net amount in the profit and loss account.

5.27   Also, where a deficit that arises from a *temporary* revaluation of assets has been set off against surpluses on other assets, a problem may arise if those other assets are subsequently sold. The sale of those assets would remove the 'cover' for the deficit. This would leave an overall deficit on the revaluation reserve, and this deficit would have to be transferred to the profit and loss account.

5.28   Method *(c)* does not conflict with the Act, except in the one situation where an overall deficit on the revaluation reserve is taken to the profit and loss account. Also, this method complies with the proposals in ED 36, and, if these proposals are accepted, they will become standard accounting practice. Where there is an overall deficit on the revaluation reserve, and this is taken to the profit and loss account (which is the exception mentioned above), this treatment will conflict with both paragraph 19(2) and paragraph 34 of Schedule 4. However, it can be justified on the grounds that it is necessary in order for the financial statements to show a true and fair view. Where this is done, the particulars of the departure from the Act, the reasons for it and its effect will need to be disclosed in the financial statements in accordance with Section 228(6).

5.29   Consequently, of the three methods described above, method *(c)* (that is outlined in paragraphs 5.23 to 5.28 above) is now considered to be best accounting practice, because methods *(a)* and *(b)* conflict both with the Act and with ED 36.

An accounting policy that follows method *(c)* is illustrated in Table 6.

Table 6: *Accounting policy explaining the treatment of revaluation surpluses and deficits.*

Extract from Lonrho Plc Annual Report 30 September 1983.

Revaluation of fixed assets
Investment properties are revalued annually; the net surplus arising therefrom is credited to revaluation reserve.

    For other fixed assets it is Group policy to review regularly their value and, if it is considered appropriate, to obtain professional valuations, which are incorporated into the Group accounts. When that new valuation exceeds the net book value of the relevant asset, the overprovision for accumulated depreciation, which was charged in previous years and is no longer required, is written back to profit and loss account as a reserve movement. Depreciation is charged to profit before tax on the revised book value from the date of valuation. If the valuation is in excess of the original cost of the relevant asset, the surplus over cost is credited to revaluation reserve. A deficit on valuation of a particular asset is charged to profit before tax to the extent that it is not covered by surpluses arising on prior valuations of that asset which have been previously credited to revaluation reserve.

Determination of revaluation surpluses and deficits

5.30   Companies have adopted two different ways of treating their existing accumulated depreciation when they revalue fixed assets.

5.31   The most widespread method is the simple one of comparing the revalued amount with the net book value and taking the difference to the revaluation reserve. This method is illustrated by the following example:

Details of a fixed asset before revaluation are as follows:

	£
Fixed asset at cost	1,000
Accumulated depreciation	400
Net book value	600
The asset is revalued to	1,500

Details of the fixed asset after revaluation are as follows:

	£
Valuation	1,500
Accumulated depreciation	—
Net book value	1,500

The amount transferred to the revaluation reserve is £900 (namely, £1,500 — £600). This includes £400 of accumulated depreciation.

5.32   The alternative approach is to write back the accumulated depreciation of £400 to the profit and loss account and to transfer the difference between the revalued amount of the asset and its historical cost or previous valuation to the revaluation reserve. Using the same example as above, the details of the fixed asset after the revaluation would be identical to those above. However, in this situation, the amount transferred to the revaluation reserve is only £500 (namely, £1,500 — £1,000). The accumulated depreciation of £400 is written back to the profit and loss account. This write-back to the profit and loss account should be made 'above the line'. If it is material, it should be treated as an exceptional item. If assets are revalued and included in the balance sheet under the alternative accounting rules, the valuations should be kept up to date (that is, the assets should be revalued regularly), and because this write-back of accumulated depreciation will arise each time an asset is revalued, the write-back would not normally be considered extraordinary. Consequently, the write-back would not normally be made 'below the line'.

5.33   The legality of this latter approach relies on the wording of paragraph 34(1) of Schedule 4. It says:

"With respect to any determination of the value of an asset of a company [*under the alternative accounting rules*], the amount of any profit or loss arising from that determination (after allowing, where appropriate, for any provisions for depreciation or diminution in value made otherwise than by reference to the value so determined *and any adjustments of any such provisions made in the light of that determination*) shall be credited or (as the case may be) debited to a separate reserve ('the revaluation reserve')."

5.34   The proponents of this approach argue that the write-back to the profit and loss account of the accumulated depreciation is an adjustment to the provision for depreciation made in the light of the revaluation. However, there is a strong body of opinion that is against this approach.

5.35   In March 1985, the ASC issued ED 37, which sets out proposals to revise SSAP 12. Paragraph 22 of ED 37 says that "Depreciation charged prior to the revaluation should not be written back to the profit and loss account ... The difference between the net book amount prior to the revaluation and the revalued amount should be transferred to the revaluation reserve".

5.36   If this section of ED 37 receives sufficient support and is eventually included in a revised Standard, then it will not be acceptable for a company to write back accumulated depreciation to the profit and loss account when it revalues an asset. However, until ED 37 is accepted, this practice *does* remain possible. The question of whether the write-back of accumulated depreciation is realised or unrealised is considered in Chapter 19, paragraph 19.40.

Sale of revalued assets

5.37   As noted in paragraph 5.08*(b)* above, the directors must reduce the revaluation reserve where, in their opinion, it is no longer necessary for the purpose of the accounting policies the company has adopted. The most likely situation where this will happen is where the company sells an asset that it has previously revalued.

5.38   Paragraph 34(3) of Schedule 4 allows a company to make a transfer from the revaluation reserve to the profit and loss account where the amount transferred represents a realised profit.

5.39   Consequently, when a company sells a revalued asset, the Act permits it to credit the profit on the sale (including the amount of the realised revaluation surplus) to the profit and loss account.

5.40   SSAP 6 does not specifically mention how realised revaluation surpluses should be treated. However, in paragraph 13, it does say that the profit and loss account should reflect all profits and losses recognised in the accounts of the year, other than unrealised surpluses on the revaluation of fixed assets. Those surpluses should be credited direct to reserves. This implies that realised surpluses *may* be credited to the profit and loss account.

5.41   ED 16, 'Supplement to extraordinary items and prior year adjustments', was issued in 1975, but it never became a Standard. Paragraph 14 of this exposure draft stated quite clearly how it proposed that realised revaluation surpluses should be treated. It proposed that:

> "When fixed assets are realised, the surpluses or deficits compared with the *book value* should be recognised in the profit and loss account for the year and classified as extraordinary items or otherwise according to their nature. Any reserve identified as being in respect of previously unrealised surpluses on the revaluation of those assets thereby becomes a realised surplus, but *should not* be reported as part of the profit for the year."

Although ED 16 never became standard accounting practice, many companies treat their realised revaluation surpluses on sales of assets in accordance with the proposals made in the exposure draft.

5.42   As mentioned in paragraph 5.17, the ASC recently issued ED 36. This exposure draft reverts to supporting the treatment that was implied in SSAP 6. Paragraph 42 of this exposure draft says:

> "When fixed assets are disposed of, the surpluses or deficits recognised in the profit and loss account for the year should be based on the difference between sale proceeds and *depreciated original cost*. Any reserve identified as being in respect of previously unrealised surpluses on the revaluation of those assets thereby becomes a realised surplus and *will be included* as part of the profit for the year, but should be disclosed separately where material."

At present, this method is only proposed. If the proposal in paragraph 42 of this exposure draft receives sufficient support and is incorporated into a revision of SSAP 6, it will become standard accounting practice. However, until SSAP 6 is revised in this way, both methods are acceptable, and both comply with the Act.

An accounting policy that accords with ED36 is given in Table 7.

Table 7: *Extract of an accounting policy where the profit or loss that arises on the disposal of properties is shown as part of the normal trading of the company.*

Extract from Trusthouse Forte PLC Report & Accounts 31 October 1984.

Properties: Freehold and long leasehold properties are revalued at intervals of not more than seven years and the resultant valuation is included in the balance sheet unless the surplus or deficit is immaterial. Short leaseholds are included in the balance sheet at cost or revaluation prior to 31st October, 1978 plus subsequent additions at cost or valuation at the date of acquisition.

Where the Group disposes of properties in the normal course of trading, the profit or loss arising is included in trading profit. The profit or loss represents the difference between the net proceeds of sale and historical cost.

5.43   The implications of these alternatives can be explained by an example:

Three companies A, B and C buy identical assets on 1 January 1984 for £1,000. Companies B and C revalue their assets at 31 December 1986 to £1,400. Company C again revalues its assets at 31 December 1988 to £1,500. All three companies sell their assets on 31 December 1989 for £2,000. The estimated useful life of the assets at the date of purchase is ten years, and their residual values are nil.

Each company will record the value of the assets in its accounting records as follows:

Fixed asset values

	Company A	Company B	Company C
	£	£	£
Cost 1.1.1984	1,000	1,000	1,000
Three years' depreciation to 31.12.1986	(300)	(300)	(300)
	700	700	700
Revaluation 31.12.1986	—	700	700
Net book value 31.12.1986	700	1,400	1,400
Two years' depreciation to 31.12.1988	(200)	(400)*	(400)*
	500	1,000	1,000
Revaluation 31.12.1988	—	—	500
Net book value 31.12.1988	500	1,000	1,500
One year's depreciation to 31.12.1989	(100)	(200)*	(300)†
Net book value 31.12.1989	400	800	1,200

*The depreciation charges after the first revaluation are calculated as follows:

$$\frac{\text{Net book value}}{\text{Remaining useful life}} = \frac{£1,400}{7 \text{ years}} = £200 \text{ per annum}$$

†The depreciation charge after the second revaluation is calculated as follows:

$$\frac{\text{Net book value}}{\text{Remaining useful life}} = \frac{£1,500}{5 \text{ years}} = £300 \text{ per annum}$$

If the sale proceeds are compared to the net book values at 31 December 1989, the following surpluses arise. They would be credited to the profit and loss account in 1989:

	Company A	Company B	Company C
	£	£	£
Net book value 31.12.1989	400	800	1,200
Sale proceeds	2,000	2,000	2,000
Surplus on disposal	1,600	1,200	800

If no further adjustments are made to the profit and loss account, the effect on each company's profit and loss account over the life of the assets can be summarised as follows:

	Company A	Company B	Company C
	£	£	£
Depreciation charged (six years)	(600)	(900)	(1,000)
Surplus on disposal	1,600	1,200	800
Net effect over life of asset	1,000	300	(200)

5.44   The net effect on the profit and loss account of each company over the life of the assets, therefore, varies considerably. If the surpluses were reported 'above the line' (see para 5.50 below) as part of the company's normal trading, the earnings per share figure would also vary significantly from company to company.

5.45 This apparent inequity has led many companies, when they sell revalued assets, to transfer their realised revaluation surpluses to the profit and loss account. This method accords with the method proposed in ED 36. It would have the following effect on each company's profit and loss account over the life of the assets:

	Company A £	Company B £	Company C £
Depreciation charged (six years)	(600)	(900)	(1,000)
Surplus of sale proceeds over net book value	1,600	1,200	800
Realised revaluation surplus	—	700	1,200
Net effect over life of asset	1,000	1,000	1,000

5.46 Consequently, the net effect on the profit and loss account over the life of the assets is the same for each company. However, the companies have charged different amounts of depreciation each year to the profit and loss account as a result of the revaluations. Accordingly, this in turn affects the profit that each company reports when it disposes of the assets in 1989, as follows:

	Company A £	Company B £	Company C £
Surplus of sale proceeds over net book value	1,600	1,200	800
Realised revaluation surplus	—	700	1,200
Reported profit on disposal	1,600	1,900	2,000

5.47 Again, this will mean that each company's earnings per share figure will differ if the profit on disposal is reported 'above the line' (see para 5.50 below). ED 36, however, also proposes that earnings per share should be calculated before and after extraordinary items. Consequently, even where the profit on disposal is shown as an extraordinary item and it is credited 'below the line', the earnings per share figure calculated after crediting extraordinary items will differ. This anomaly can be overcome, however, by splitting the depreciation charged in the profit and loss account (see further paras 5.64 to 5.83 below).

5.48 Where a company has reduced its revaluation reserve by capitalising a bonus issue (see Chapter 19 para 19.71), a further problem may arise when it sells a revalued asset. ED 36 proposes that SSAP 6 (revised) should require that when a previously revalued asset is disposed of, any previously unrealised surplus on the revaluation of the asset should be included in the profit and loss account for the year. Clearly, this treatment will not be possible where a company has utilised the revaluation surplus to capitalise a bonus issue. Consequently, ED 36 proposes that where the revaluation reserve is insufficient for the company to make this transfer to the profit and loss account for the year, the company will need to transfer an amount from other reserves to the revaluation reserve in order to make up the shortfall.

5.49   One question that remains to be answered is how the realised revaluation surplus should be treated if it is credited to the profit and loss account.

5.50   Where the disposal of fixed assets gives rise to a material surplus or deficit, this should be shown separately as either an exceptional item or an extraordinary item, as appropriate. [*ED 36 para 16*]. The surplus or deficit should be shown as an extraordinary item only if the sale of the asset can be said to derive from events outside the company's ordinary activities. This may be so, for example, where a significant part of a company's business is being discontinued, and a profit arises when that part of the business is disposed of. This profit on the sale would be treated as an extraordinary item (that is, 'below the line'). However, if, for example, a company carries on a retail trade from a number of retail outlets, and it has a policy of selling a number of old outlets and buying a similar number of new outlets each year, any surpluses on sales of properties could be said to derive from the company's ordinary activities. Consequently, these profits are not extraordinary, and they should be disclosed in the profit and loss account as part of the company's ordinary trading results (that is, 'above the line').

An illustration of a company that shows surpluses on disposal of investment properties as an extraordinary item is given in Table 8. Table 7, however, shows a company that treats the profit or loss on disposal of properties as part of its trading profit.

Other uses of the revaluation reserve

5.51   The Act specifies situations where a surplus or a deficit arising from the revaluation of an asset must be either credited or debited, respectively, to the revaluation reserve. However, the Act does not state specifically that this is the *only* situation in which an amount can be debited or credited to the revaluation reserve. Consequently, this raises the question of whether the revaluation reserve can be used for other purposes. For example, can goodwill be written off to the revaluation reserve?

5.52   The DTI's view is that, apart from accounting for deficits that arise on the revaluation of assets, the revaluation reserve may be reduced in *only* the following two further situations:

(a) When a company writes back an amount that is standing to the credit of the reserve, because the directors consider that the amount is no longer necessary for the purpose of the accounting policies the company has adopted.

(b) A company capitalises the reserve in order to issue bonus shares (see further Chapter 19 para 19.71).

5.53   The DTI's view is based on the wording of the EC Fourth Directive, which forms the basis of Schedule 4 to the Act, and on the DTI's papers concerning the drafting of that Schedule. Consequently, the DTI considers, in particular, that goodwill cannot be written off against the revaluation reserve. However, others argue that the Directive's restriction applies only to companies and not to groups and, therefore, *consolidation* goodwill may be written off to the revaluation reserve (see Chapter 7 Para 7.88).

Table 8: Illustration of profits or losses on disposal of investment properties shown as extraordinary items. Revaluation surpluses that relate to the properties that have been sold are transferred from the investment revaluation reserve to extraordinary items.

Extract from The Rank Organisation Plc Report and Accounts 31 October 1984.

Accounting policy

(vii) Depreciation of fixed assets
  Properties held for investment
  (a) Completed investment properties are revalued regularly and the effect is reflected in the investment property revaluation reserve. Profits or losses on disposal are dealt with in extraordinary items and are arrived at by comparing sale proceeds with the revalued book amount at the beginning of the year and making an appropriate transfer from revaluation reserve of the previously unrealised surplus or deficit relating thereto which has become realised as a result of the disposal, to arrive at the realised profit or loss against historical cost.

Note

7 Extraordinary items	1984 £ million	1983 £ million
Profits less (losses) on disposal of investment properties		
Against opening valuation	(27·6)	—
Transfer from investment property revaluation reserve relating thereto	46·5	0·6
Realised on investment properties against historical cost	18·9	0·6
Cost and provision for cost of terminating activities	(21·0)	(28·0)
Exchange differences on repayment of overseas currency loans	—	(0·8)
	(2·1)	(28·2)
Taxation (including relief relating to previous years)	(7·7)	2·7
	(9·8)	(25·5)
Share of extraordinary items of associated companies	9·9	(0·3)
	0·1	(25·8)
Attributable to minorities	(0·1)	0·4
	—	(25·4)

Disclosure of the revaluation reserve

5.54 As noted in paragraph 5.08*(c)* above, the Act requires that the revaluation reserve must be shown on the face of the balance sheet. However, it may be shown under another name. [*4 Sch 34(2)*]. This concession is necessary for several reasons, as discussed below.

5.55 Where a company prepares full current cost financial statements in accordance with SSAP 16, the current cost balance sheet includes a reserve that is referred to in SSAP 16 as the 'Current cost reserve'.

5.56 The current cost reserve will include:

(a) Unrealised revaluation surpluses on fixed assets, stocks and investments.

(b) Realised amounts equal to the cumulative net total of the current cost adjustments made in accordance with the Standard, namely:

(i) The depreciation adjustment (and any adjustments on the disposal of fixed assets).
(ii) The cost of sales adjustment.
(iii) The monetary working capital adjustment.
(iv) The gearing adjustment.

5.57 In effect, this current cost reserve is very similar to the revaluation reserve outlined in the Act. Consequently, the Act allows the term 'Current cost reserve' to be used instead of the term 'Revaluation reserve'. The main difference between the current cost reserve and the revaluation reserve the Act envisages is that the current cost reserve comprises two parts: an unrealised part that includes surpluses on revaluations, and a realised element that includes items (such as the cost of sales adjustment) that have been either debited or credited to the profit and loss account. The unrealised part of the current cost reserve corresponds to the revaluation reserve under the terms of the Act. To avoid confusion, therefore, it is desirable to present the item in the balance sheet, or in the notes to the balance sheet, as follows:

$$
\begin{array}{lc}
\text{Current cost reserve—unrealised} & X \\
\text{—realised} & \underline{X} \\
& \underline{\underline{X}}
\end{array}
$$

5.58 Often, a company's articles of association will govern the way in which the company operates its revaluation reserve, and these articles may stipulate also the name of the reserve. Consequently, the company should use that name in its financial statements. Articles of this nature are commonly found in investment companies and pension funds.

Taxation implications

5.59 The Act requires the taxation implications of a revaluation to be noted in the financial statements. [*4 Sch 34(4)*].

5.60 This does not mean that there must be a statement of whether the amount is taxable or allowable under tax legislation. It means that there must be an explanation of the tax effect of the revaluation.

5.61 The tax effect will often be deferred until a later period. SSAP 15 says that the revaluation of an asset will give rise to a deferred tax timing difference, insofar as the profit or loss that would result from the asset's realisation at the revalued amount is taxable. But this will not apply if the disposal of the revalued asset and of any subsequent replacement assets would not result in a tax liability after taking account of any expected rollover relief. [*SSAP 15 para 20*].

5.62   The Standard requires that tax deferred or accelerated by the effect of timing differences (including any deferred tax on a capital gain) should be accounted for to the extent that it is probable that an asset or liability will crystallise. [*SSAP 15 para 25*]. In addition to making this provision, a company should disclose, in a note to its financial statements, the total amount of deferred tax (including that on capital gains) that it has not provided for. [*SSAP 15 para 40*]. Where capital allowances have been claimed on an asset that is subsequently revalued, then the deferred taxation implications of any balancing charges or allowances will also have to be considered in addition to the deferred tax on any capital gain. The Standard goes on to say that where the potential amount of deferred tax on a revalued asset is not shown because the revaluation does not constitute a timing difference for the reason explained in paragraph 5.61 above, this fact should be stated. [*SSAP 15 para 41*].

5.63   Compliance with the disclosure requirements of SSAP 15 will ensure compliance with paragraph 34(4) of Schedule 4.

The depreciation rules

5.64   Where a company has determined an asset's value in accordance with one of the alternative accounting rules, that value (rather than the purchase price or the production cost) is to be (or else is to be the starting point for determining) the amount at which it discloses that asset in its financial statements. Where the asset in question has been subject to a previous valuation, its value according to the latest revaluation supersedes its previous value as the basis the company should use when including it in its financial statements. Accordingly, any references in the depreciation rules to purchase price or production cost must be substituted by a reference to the value determined by the alternative accounting rules the company applied. [*4 Sch 32(1)*]. This means that, in determining the amount to be written off systematically over a fixed asset's useful economic life, a company must have regard to the asset's value determined according to the latest application of the alternative accounting rules, rather than to its purchase price or its production cost. Even where a company revalues its assets at the end of the year, it is not exempt from providing depreciation against the profits of the year based on the opening cost or valuation and the cost of subsequent additions.

5.65   The Act also says that where the value of any fixed asset has been determined according to the alternative accounting rules, the amount of any provision for depreciation to be charged in the profit and loss account may be either the amount based on the valuation of the asset, or the amount based on its historical cost. However, where the amount so charged is based on historical cost, the difference between that charge and the charge based on the asset's valuation must be disclosed separately. It must be so disclosed either on the face of the profit and loss account or in the notes. [*4 Sch 32(2)(3)*]. This would appear to allow a company to either debit or credit the difference (as appropriate) direct to the revaluation reserve.

5.66   SSAP 12 echoes the Act's rules. The Standard requires that where a company revalues assets, and gives effect to the revaluation in its financial statements, it should base the charge for depreciation on the revalued amount. If this results in a material increase in depreciation compared to previous years' depreciation charges, then the financial statements should disclose in the notes the depreciation charge split between that applicable to original cost and that applicable to the change in value on revaluation. [*SSAP 12 paras 9, 12*].

5.67   The Standard says also that an increase in the value of an asset does not remove the necessity for a company to charge depreciation even where the market value of an asset is greater than its net book value. [*SSAP 12 para 10*].

5.68   Consequently, it is clear that SSAP 12 requires a company to charge depreciation on the revalued amount of the asset. However, although SSAP 12 makes reference to the depreciation charge, it does not specifically state that this charge has to be made in the profit and loss account. Until the provisions of paragraphs 32(2) and (3) of Schedule 4 were enacted in the 1981 Companies Act, it was normal practice for companies to charge all depreciation to the profit and loss account. However, the wording of paragraph 32 seems to indicate that companies may have a choice.

5.69   It appears that the Act allows a company to either debit all of the depreciation charge to the profit and loss account, or split that charge so that it charges the amount based on the historical cost to the profit and loss account, and charges the difference direct to the revaluation reserve.

5.70   The latter possibility (known as 'split depreciation') can best be explained by an example.

In this example, the facts are the same as those outlined in paragraph 5.43 above. The fixed asset values remain the same as before, but, using split depreciation, the amount of depreciation the companies charge to the profit and loss account differs after they revalue the assets. The depreciation charge is split and charged as follows:

Profit and loss account

	Company A	Company B	Company C
	£	£	£
Three years' depreciation to 31.12.1986	300	300	300
Two years' depreciation to 31.12.1988	200	200	200
One year's depreciation to 31.12.1989	100	100	100
	600	600	600

Revaluation reserve

Two years' excess depreciation to 31.12.1988	—	200*	200*
One year's excess depreciation to 31.12.1989	—	100*	200†
	—	300	400
Total depreciation charge	600	900	1,000

*The excess depreciation charge is calculated as follows:

$$\frac{\text{Revalued amount} - \text{historical cost net book value}}{\text{remaining useful life}} = \frac{£1,400 - £700}{7 \text{ years}}$$

$$= £100 \text{ per annum}$$

†The excess depreciation charge is calculated as follows:

$$\frac{\text{Revalued amount} - \text{historical cost net book value}}{\text{remaining useful life}} = \frac{£1,500 - £500}{5 \text{ years}}$$

$$= £200 \text{ per annum}$$

5.71   Using the split depreciation approach the profit and loss account of each company in the example is drawn up on the same basis and suffers identical depreciation charges each year. The reported profit for the year is not affected by *ad hoc* revaluations.

5.72   Consequently, the reported earnings per share figures for these companies will be comparable.

5.73   When the asset is sold, the effect will be as follows:

Revaluation reserve

	Company A	Company B	Company C
	£	£	£
Surplus at 31.12.1986	—	700	700
Two years' excess depreciation to 31.12.1988	—	(200)	(200)
	—	500	500
Surplus at 31.12.1988	—	—	500
	—	500	1,000
One year's excess depreciation to 31.12.1989	—	(100)	(200)
Revaluation reserve at 31.12.1989	—	400	800

5.74   The revaluation reserve balance will be taken to the profit and loss account together with the difference between the sale proceeds and the net book value.

Profit on disposal

	Company A	Company B	Company C
	£	£	£
Net book value 31.12.1989	400	800	1,200
Sale proceeds	2,000	2,000	2,000
Surplus on disposal	1,600	1,200	800
Realised revaluation reserve	—	400	800
Profit on disposal	1,600	1,600	1,600

5.75   Again, the profit each company reports is identical in 1989, and each company's reported earnings per share figures are also identical.

5.76   The Act appears to permit the split depreciation approach and SSAP 12 does not specifically prohibit it. However, there is a contrary opinion that this approach is not acceptable. This opinion is that such a method produces a balance sheet and a profit and loss account that do not 'articulate'. They mean by this that the balance sheet is drawn up on one basis (historical cost modified to include the revaluation of certain assets), whereas the profit and loss account is drawn up on another (historical cost only).

5.77   In this connection, paragraph 16 of ED 37 says that:

"The accounting treatment in the profit and loss account should be consistent with that used in the balance sheet. Hence, the depreciation charge in the profit and loss account for the period should be based on the carrying amount of the asset in the balance sheet, whether historical cost or revalued amount. The whole of the depreciation charge should be reflected in the profit and loss account. No part of the depreciation charge should be set directly against reserves."

5.78   The ASC, therefore, considers that the accounting treatment of balance sheet and profit and loss account items should be consistent (that is, articulated).

5.79   If this proposal is eventually accepted, SSAP 12 will be amended accordingly. Consequently, although the split depreciation method appears to be acceptable at present, it may be prohibited in the future. An example of a company that has adopted the split depreciation method is given in Table 9.

5.80   There is, however, one situation in which the split depreciation approach cannot be used. That situation is where a company prepares full current cost financial statements in accordance with SSAP 16. That Standard requires that the excess depreciation charged on revalued assets (known as the depreciation adjustment) should be charged to the current cost profit and loss account. [*SSAP 16 para 49*].

5.81   Chapter 19 considers realised reserves and distributable profits in detail. However, Section 275(2) of the Act has a bearing on the way in which companies should treat depreciation on revalued assets. This section says that if the revaluation of an asset produces an unrealised profit, then an amount equal to any excess depreciation charged as a result of the revaluation may be treated as a realised profit. This section is concerned only with the determination of distributable profits (and not with the accounting treatment of excess depreciation). Despite this, it suggests that where a company charges the whole of the depreciation based on the revalued assets to the profit and loss account, it may also

---

Table 9: *Illustration of a company that has adopted the 'split depreciation' basis of depreciation.*

Extract from Norcros P.L.C. Report and Accounts 31 March 1984.

Accounting Policy

Depreciation

Depreciation is calculated by the straight line method having regard to the class and life of asset concerned. Depreciation on cost to the Group is charged in arriving at Profit on ordinary activities before taxation. Depreciation on revaluation surpluses is charged against Revaluation Reserve. Principal depreciation rates for plant and vehicles are 10% and 25% respectively. Depreciation on freehold buildings in the United Kingdom, calculated on the basis of individual properties' estimated remaining useful lives, has been provided for the first time. The effect of this change is not considered sufficient to warrant a restatement of previous years' results.

Note

21 Share Premium Account and Other Reserves	Share Premium	Revaluation Reserve	Other Reserves
	£'000	£'000	£'000
Group			
At 31st March, 1983	25,622	8,237	277
Surplus arising on revaluation of property	—	355	—
Surplus on acquisition of minority interests and investment in Associate Company	—	—	341
Currency translation adjustments	—	(262)	—
Additional depreciation on revalued buildings	—	(77)	—
	£25,622	£8,253	£618
Norcros p.l.c.			
At 31st March, 1983	25,622	3,466	—
Currency translation adjustments	—	(143)	—
Revaluation of investments in subsidiaries to underlying net asset value	—	6,056	—
	£25,622	£9,379	—

Included in the Group revaluation reserves is £4,297,000 (1983 – £3,964,000) in respect of surpluses on the revaluation of land and buildings and in the revaluation reserve of Norcros p.l.c. £10,685,000 (1983 – £4,629,000) in respect of surpluses on the revaluation of investments in subsidiaries.

The amount of reserves of Norcros p.l.c. that may not legally be distributed under section 40 of the Companies Act 1980 [*now Section 264 of the Companies Act 1985*] is £36,307,000 (1983 – £30,252,000).

transfer an amount equal to the excess depreciation from the revaluation reserve to the profit and loss account.

5.82 Because the amount transferred from the revaluation reserve to the profit and loss account represents a realised profit, this treatment would not contravene paragraph 34(3) of Schedule 4 (see para 5.08*(b)* above).

5.83 If this transfer was made to the profit and loss account itself, it would be 'below the line' as a transfer from reserves. Therefore, it would not reduce *all* of the anomalies that exist in reported profits when a company revalues depreciable assets (as discussed in paras 5.43 to 5.50 above). However, one anomaly is removed: because the revaluation reserve is systematically reduced over the asset's life, the net profit on the sale of an asset that is credited to the profit and loss account will be the same whether the asset has been revalued or not.

Additional disclosure required

5.84 Where a company has applied any of the alternative accounting rules, the Act requires it to disclose certain information in the notes to its financial statements. [*4 Sch 33(1)*].

5.85 *First*, the notes must state the items affected and the basis of valuation the company has adopted in respect of each such item. [*4 Sch 33(2)*].

5.86 *Second*, either the balance sheet or the notes must disclose, in respect of every item affected (except stocks), *one or other* of the following amounts:

   (a) The comparable amounts determined according to the historical cost convention.

   (b) The differences between those comparable amounts and the actual amounts shown in the balance sheet.
   [*4 Sch 33(3)*].

5.87 For this purpose, 'comparable amounts' means the aggregate amount the company would have shown if it had applied the historical cost convention, and the aggregate amount of the cumulative provisions for depreciation or diminution in value that would have been permitted or required in determining those amounts according to that convention. [*4 Sch 33(4)*].

5.88 To illustrate this requirement, consider the following example:

Details of a company's fixed assets are as follows:

	Cost £	Valuation £
Fixed assets	10,000	15,000
Accumulated depreciation	6,000	4,000
Net book value	4,000	11,000

If the company states the fixed assets in the balance sheet at valuation, the effect of the Act's provisions is to require the balance sheet or the notes to the financial statements to state either the comparable amounts (namely, cost £10,000 and depreciation £6,000) or the difference between the comparable amounts and the amounts at which they are actually stated (namely, £5,000 and £2,000 respectively).

The historical cost net book amount (namely, £4,000) or the difference between the comparable net book amounts (namely, £7,000) is another interpretation of the amounts that are required to be disclosed. This latter disclosure is arguable because the Act refers to the amounts stated in the balance sheet and the amounts so stated will be the net book value of the assets.

5.89   As a result of this requirement, a company that has revalued its fixed assets will have to maintain records of both the historical cost and the valuation of those fixed assets. In addition, the company will have to calculate depreciation on the historical cost as well as on the valuation.

Table 10 shows how a company complies with these disclosure requirements.

Table 10: Disclosure of the historical cost amounts of fixed assets where the assets have been included in the balance sheet at a valuation.

Extract from Arthur Guinness and Sons PLC Report and Accounts 30 September 1984.

Note extract
(a) Land and buildings—the amount shown at cost or valuation includes the following:

	1984 £m	1983 £m
At cost	34·6	18·8
At valuation in 1981 or prior	4·2	17·8
At valuation in 1983	97·0	94·3
At valuation in 1984	17·8	—
	153·6	130·9
Land and buildings included at valuation would have been included on an historical cost basis at:		
Cost	82·4	61·0
Depreciation	9·8	6·9
Net book value	72·6	54·1

5.90   When a company prepares full current cost financial statements as its main financial statements, the above requirement in the Act for the company to disclose additional historical cost information for those assets it has revalued satisfies also the requirements of paragraph 48(c) of SSAP 16.

CHAPTER 6

FORMAT OF FINANCIAL STATEMENTS

Chapter 6

Format of Financial Statements

Introduction

6.01 The general provisions that relate to the format and content of company financial statements are detailed in Schedule 4 to the 1985 Act.

6.02 Schedule 4 sets out two alternative formats for the balance sheet and four alternative formats for the profit and loss account. It also lays down certain general guidelines to be followed. These formats and guidelines are discussed below. In addition, the Schedule requires companies to disclose considerable detail both in the notes to the balance sheet and in the notes to the profit and loss account.

General rules

Choice of formats

6.03 Schedule 4 leaves the choice of particular formats to the company's directors. Once the directors have selected the particular formats that they are going to adopt for the balance sheet and the profit and loss account, they should not subsequently change them without good reason. [4 Sch 2(1)]. An example of such a reason might occur if a company changes both its operations and its accounting methods significantly, and considers that, following the changes, its financial statements fit more naturally into a different format.

6.04 In most situations, however, few companies will have good reason to change their formats, and so they must select carefully the formats that they wish to adopt when they prepare their first set of financial statements after incorporation. If a company does eventually change its formats, it may incur a considerable amount of extra work, because it will have to restate the corresponding amounts for the previous year in accordance with the new formats. In addition, the notes to the financial statements must disclose:

(a) The fact that the company has adopted a different format.

(b) The directors' reasons for the change.
[4 Sch 2(2)].

Headings and sub-headings

6.05   The formats give a list of items either as main headings or as sub-headings. In the balance sheet, main headings are designated either by letters or by Roman numerals, and sub-headings are designated by Arabic numerals. The object of this notation is for identification purposes only, so that the Act can refer to items by their prefix. There is no requirement for financial statements, when they are prepared, actually to show these letters or numbers. [*4 Sch 1(2)*]. In the profit and loss account, most items are designated by Arabic numerals.

6.06   Whichever of the balance sheet formats and profit and loss account formats a company chooses, the company must show the items in the fixed order and under the headings and the sub-headings set out in the formats it has adopted. [*4 Sch 1(1)*]. There are, however, certain exceptions to this rule:

(a) An item may be shown in greater detail than the prescribed formats require. [*4 Sch 3(1)*].

For example, most companies will include motor vehicles under the sub-heading 'Fixtures, fittings, tools and equipment'. Where such motor vehicles are significant in value, additional details may be disclosed as follows:

Fixtures, fittings, tools and equipment:
Motor vehicles   X
Other   X   X

(b) An item representing an asset or a liability, or an item of income or expenditure that is not covered in any of the prescribed formats may be shown separately. [*4 Sch 3(2)*].

An example is where a company holds stocks that do not fall easily within the sub-headings of raw materials and consumables, work in progress, finished goods and goods for resale, and payments on account. Table 11 shows the disclosure adopted by British Sugar plc whose principal activities include sugar refining. Because of the special nature of the company's business, the directors considered that the standard analysis of stocks did not strictly apply, and so they included a more suitable presentation. In addition, new crop expenditure did not fit readily into the formats as either stocks or debtors, and so the directors included it as a separate line.

(c) Items that are preceded by Arabic numerals in the Act may be combined in the company's financial statements where either of the following circumstances apply:

(i) Their individual amounts are not material in assessing the company's state of affairs or profit or loss. [*4 Sch 3(4)(a)*].
(ii) The combination facilitates the assessment of the company's state of affairs or profit or loss (that is, it results in greater clarity). Where this applies, however, the detailed breakdown

of the combined items must be given in the notes to the financial statements. [*4 Sch 3(4)(b)*].

(d) A heading or a sub-heading need not be shown where there is no amount to be included for both the financial year in question and the immediately preceding financial year. [*4 Sch 3(5), 4(3)*].

(e) The arrangement, the headings and the sub-headings of items set out in the formats and preceded by Arabic numerals *must* be adapted if the special nature of the company's business requires this. [*4 Sch 3(3)*].

Table 11: Use of other headings in the balance sheet.

Extract from British Sugar plc Annual report 25 September 1983.

Balance sheet extract

Notes		1983 £000	1982 £000
	Current assets		
	Stocks		
	Consumable stores	34,702	29,724
	Sugar and other products	82,474	30,444
		117,176	60,168
	New crop expenditure	235	12,296
15	Debtors	46,541	33,095
	Cash at bank and in hand	301	1,946
		164,253	107,505

6.07 The Act requires that companies should follow the exact wording of the headings and sub-headings used in the formats [*4 Sch 1(1)*], and this was certainly the intention of the EC Fourth Directive. Nevertheless, many companies are, in practice, departing from this requirement. For example, many companies have described 'land and buildings' as 'property'. It seems that this practice is allowable, provided that the revised wording is not likely to mislead readers of the financial statements. For example, the use of the word 'profit' in the profit and loss account where the result is, in fact, a loss would be misleading and should not be allowed. But it would be acceptable to use the term 'associated companies' instead of the term 'related companies' prescribed in the Act.

6.08 However, the Act does not specifically give companies the freedom to change the wording of headings, and so it is unclear whether it is allowable for companies to do so. In its financial statements for the year ended 31 December 1983, BTR plc changed the wording of certain headings. For example, it used the term 'inventories' instead of 'stocks' and the term 'sales' instead of 'turnover'. This was because the company had substantial shareholders in the USA and elsewhere, and the directors considered that it was desirable to use terms that were familiar to them. The company's auditors followed the strict wording of the law, and they qualified their audit report on the grounds that the financial statements did not comply with the Companies Acts to the extent that certain headings the company had used in its financial statements were not those prescribed in the Companies Act 1981 formats (see Table 12).

Table 12: Example of a departure from the words used in the formats detailed in the Act and the auditors' report thereon.

Extract from BTR plc Annual Report 31 December 1983.

Accounting policy

Companies Act 1981

BTR plc is an international company with substantial interests, inter alia, in the USA. The directors consider it is more meaningful and consistent with established reporting procedures to continue to incorporate descriptions more familiar to shareholders for items in the Profit and Loss Account and Balance Sheet. To accord with the requirements of the Companies Act 1981 for the expression 'Sales' read 'Turnover', for 'Inventories' read 'Stocks', for 'Accounts Receivable' read 'Debtors' and for 'Accounts Payable' read 'Creditors'.

Report of the auditors

to the members of BTR plc

We have examined the accounts of BTR plc set out on pages 27 to 43. These have been prepared under the historical cost convention including the valuation of certain fixed assets. Our audit has been carried out in accordance with approved auditing standards.

In our opinion the accounts give a true and fair view of the state of affairs of the company and of the group, so far as concerns members of the company, at 31 December 1983 and of the profit, changes in retained profit and source and application of funds of the group for the 52 weeks then ended and comply with the Companies Acts 1948 to 1981 except that certain of the headings used in the accounts are not those prescribed.

The accounts do not contain the current cost accounts required by Statement of Standard Accounting Practice No.16.

London	Ernst & Whinney
14 March 1984	Chartered Accountants

6.09   A company should consider the presentation of its financial statements in three stages. First, it should consider which of the formats are most suitable for its purposes. Secondly, if the special nature of its business requires it, it must adapt the arrangement and headings and sub-headings of any items designated by Arabic numerals in the selected formats as set out in Schedule 4. Thirdly, it should consider whether it needs to show any item listed in the formats in greater detail, and, if so, it may do so. (Unlike the adaptation of the formats, which is compulsory if the special nature of a company's business requires it, the reporting company has the option to include greater detail under any heading if it wishes to do so.)

6.10   After having considered the presentation of the financial statements, the company must next consider whether compliance with the requirements of Schedule 4 as regards the format of the financial statements, and compliance with other statutory requirements as to the information to be included in the notes to the financial statements, enable the financial statements to give a true and fair view of the company's affairs as at the end of the financial year. If the company decides that compliance with Schedule 4 would not give a true and fair view (see Chapter 3 para 3.09), it should examine whether the solution to this problem might be to provide additional information in the financial statements. Only if this would still not enable a true and fair view to be given (because of the company's special circumstances) may the company depart from the Schedule 4 requirements to the extent necessary to show such a view. In such a situation, particulars of the departure, the reasons for it, and its effect must be given in the notes to the financial statements (see Chapter 3 para 3.11).

Corresponding amounts

6.11   Corresponding amounts for the year immediately preceding the year in question must be shown. [*4 Sch 4(1)*]. This applies even when no such item exists to be disclosed in respect of the current financial year. [*4 Sch 4(3)*].

6.12   Also, in general, the corresponding amounts for the previous financial year must be given in respect of each item shown in the notes to the financial statements. [*4 Sch 58(2)*]. The only exceptions to this relate to:

(a) The information that must be given about subsidiaries and significant shareholdings under Section 231 of, and Parts I and II of Schedule 5 to, the Act (see Chapter 8).

(b) The information that must be disclosed in respect of loans and other transactions with directors and officers under Sections 232 to 234 and Schedule 6 (see Chapter 11).

(c) Opening and closing balances and movements during the year on both the cost (or valuation) and the accumulated provisions for depreciation or diminution in value of fixed assets (see Chapter 7).

(d) Movements on reserves and provisions for liabilities and charges (see Chapter 9).
[*4 Sch 58(3)*].

6.13   Where the amount for the previous year is not comparable with the amount to be shown in respect of the current year, the previous year's amount must be adjusted. Where this applies, particulars of the adjustment and the reasons for it must be disclosed in the notes to the financial statements. [*4 Sch 4(2)*]. This provision accords with the treatment that SSAP 6 recommends. Under SSAP 6, a prior-year adjustment (that has arisen, for example, because there has been a change of accounting policy during the year) is accounted for by restating the previous year's amount, and, where it is affected, by adjusting the opening balance of retained profits accordingly. Where practicable, the effect of the change should be disclosed by showing the amount involved separately in the restatement of the previous year.

Off-setting

6.14 Asset and liability items may not be set off against each other. Similarly, income and expenditure items may not be set off against each other. [*4 Sch 5*]. Consequently, companies cannot, for example, show hire-purchase liabilities as a deduction from the related asset. (They may, however, deduct from stocks the payments they have received on account of orders. [*Note 8 on the balance sheet formats*].) This rule, which relates primarily to the presentation of items in the financial statements, is discussed more fully in Chapter 8, paragraphs 8.70 to 8.73 on debtors, and in paragraphs 8.76 to 8.82 on bank balances.

The balance sheet

Formats

6.15 The Act sets out two alternative balance sheet formats.

Format 1

6.16 In format 1, net assets can be equated with the aggregate of share capital and reserves. This method of presentation probably represents UK companies' most common practice. The Act does not, however, prescribe the place where the totals should be struck. Consequently, in this format a company can equate total assets less current liabilities, on the one hand, with the aggregate of creditors falling due after more than one year, provisions for liabilities and charges, and capital and reserves, on the other hand. Format 1 is set out on the next two pages and is also illustrated in Table 13.

Format 2

6.17 In format 2, assets are equated with liabilities (which include capital and reserves). Because the information disclosed in format 2 is identical in all respects (apart from one) to the information disclosed in format 1, format 2 has not been reproduced here. The only difference between format 1 and format 2 is that format 2 aggregates, on the face of the balance sheet, creditors due within one year and those due after more than one year. However, in respect of each item included in creditors the split between the amount due within one year and the amount due after more than one year, together with the aggregate, must still be disclosed either on the face of the balance sheet or in the notes. [*Note 13 on the balance sheet formats*]. This method of presentation is more common in some other EC countries (for example, France and Germany) than in the UK. An example of a format 2 balance sheet is given in Table 14.

Balance sheet — Format 1

A   Called-up share capital not paid

B   Fixed assets
   I   *Intangible assets*
      1 Development costs
      2 Concessions, patents, licences, trade marks and similar rights and assets
      3 Goodwill
      4 Payments on account

   II *Tangible assets*
      1 Land and buildings
      2 Plant and machinery
      3 Fixtures, fittings, tools and equipment
      4 Payments on account and assets in course of construction

   III *Investments*
      1 Shares in group companies
      2 Loans to group companies
      3 Shares in related companies
      4 Loans to related companies
      5 Other investments other than loans
      6 Other loans
      7 Own shares

C   Current assets

   I   *Stocks*
      1 Raw materials and consumables
      2 Work in progress
      3 Finished goods and goods for resale
      4 Payments on account

   II *Debtors*
      1 Trade debtors
      2 Amounts owed by group companies
      3 Amounts owed by related companies
      4 Other debtors
      5 Called-up share capital not paid
      6 Prepayments and accrued income

   III *Investments*
      1 Shares in group companies
      2 Own shares
      3 Other investments

   IV *Cash at bank and in hand*

D   Prepayments and accrued income

E   Creditors: amounts falling due within one year
      1 Debenture loans
      2 Bank loans and overdrafts
      3 Payments received on account
      4 Trade creditors
      5 Bills of exchange payable
      6 Amounts owed to group companies
      7 Amounts owed to related companies
      8 Other creditors including taxation and social security
      9 Accruals and deferred income

F   **Net current assets (liabilities)**

G   **Total assets less current liabilities**

H   **Creditors: amounts falling due after more than one year**
      1 Debenture loans
      2 Bank loans and overdrafts
      3 Payments received on account
      4 Trade creditors
      5 Bills of exchange payable
      6 Amounts owed to group companies
      7 Amounts owed to related companies
      8 Other creditors including taxation and social security
      9 Accruals and deferred income

I   **Provisions for liabilities and charges**
      1 Pensions and similar obligations
      2 Taxation, including deferred taxation
      3 Other provisions

J   **Accruals and deferred income**

K   **Capital and reserves**
    I   *Called-up share capital*
    II   *Share premium account*
    III *Revaluation reserve*
    IV *Other reserves*
        1 Capital redemption reserve
        2 Reserve for own shares
        3 Reserves provided for by the articles of association
        4 Other reserves

    V   *Profit and loss account*

Commentary on specific items

6.18   In determining the amount to be shown under 'Net current assets (liabilities)' in format 1, a company must take into account any amount
that is shown separately under the heading 'Prepayments and accrued
income'. [*Note 11 on the balance sheet formats*]. This applies whether
the amount in question is shown as a sub-heading of debtors or as a
main heading. But in view of the layout of format 1, it seems to be
a self-evident requirement. The Fourth Directive stated that, in determining the amount to be shown under 'Net current assets (liabilities)'
in format 1, a company should take into account also any amount that
is shown separately under the main heading 'Accruals and deferred
income'. Presumably this omission from note 11 on the balance sheet
formats was an oversight on the part of the UK legislators when they
were originally drafting the 1981 Companies Act.

Table 13: Illustration of a Format 1 balance sheet.

Extract from Dalgety PLC Annual Report and Accounts 30 June 1984.

Balance sheets as at 30 June 1984

NOTE		Group 1984 £m	Group 1983 £m	Parent company 1984 £m	Parent company 1983 £m
	Fixed assets				
9	Intangible assets	10.5	10.1	—	—
10	Tangible assets	309.1	280.8	0.1	0.1
11	Investments	55.7	31.8	230.2	213.1
		375.3	322.7	230.3	213.2
	Current assets				
12	Stocks	204.1	229.0	—	—
13	Debtors	338.8	278.2	51.0	47.1
14	Investments including deposits	15.3	11.3	1.1	0.8
	Cash at bank and in hand	16.1	8.9	0.2	0.4
		574.3	527.4	52.3	48.3
15	Creditors due within one year	(426.9)	(356.2)	(34.8)	(28.4)
	Net Current Assets	147.4	171.2	17.5	19.9
	Total assets less current liabilities	522.7	493.9	247.8	233.1
16	Creditors due after more than one year	(163.9)	(150.4)	(27.8)	(31.0)
17	Provisions for liabilities and charges	(23.6)	(9.6)	—	—
		335.2	333.9	220.0	202.1
	Capital and reserves				
18	Called up share capital	84.9	84.7	84.9	84.7
19	Share premium account	99.4	98.8	99.4	98.8
	Revaluation reserve	17.8	20.6	—	—
19	Other reserves	19.9	13.0	(4.8)	(3.7)
19	Profit and loss account	99.7	95.3	40.5	22.3
	Dalgety shareholders funds	321.7	312.4	220.0	202.1
	Minority shareholders interests	13.5	21.5	—	—
	Total shareholders interests	335.2	333.9	220.0	202.1

Approved by the Board on 8 October 1984

D L Donne
J G T Hart } Directors

6.19　Where a company discloses holdings in its own shares under the heading 'Investments', it must show separately the nominal value of the shares it holds. [*Note 4 on the balance sheet formats*]. A company will generally hold its own shares only where it has acquired them by forfeiture, or by surrender in lieu of forfeiture, or by way of a gift. [*Sec 143*]. Where a company either purchases or redeems its own shares, those shares are treated as cancelled on purchase or redemption (see Chapter 8 para 8.45). [*Sec 160(4), 162(2)*].

Table 14: Illustration of a Format 2 balance sheet.

Extract from B.A.T. Industries p.l.c. Annual report and accounts 31 December 1984.

Balance sheets
31 December

	Group 1984 £ millions	1983	Company 1984	1983
Assets				
Fixed assets				
Tangible fixed assets (note 13)	2,820	2,041		
Investment in financial services (page 56)	941			
Investments in Group companies (note 15)			2,198	1,276
Investments in associated companies (note 16)	722	544		
Other investments and long term loans (note 17)	312	73	171	
	4,795	2,658	2,369	1,276
Current assets				
Stocks (note 18)	2,640	2,144		
Debtors (note 19)	1,866	1,451	123	151
Current investments (note 20)	286	200	104	
Short term deposits	255	348		
Cash at bank and in hand	222	175		
	5,269	4,318	227	151
Total assets	10,064	6,976	2,596	1,427
Liabilities				
Capital and reserves				
Share capital	367	365	367	365
Share premium account	18	13	18	13
Revaluation reserves	114		20	
Other reserves	495	357	5	
Profit and loss account	2,847	2,109	877	799
Associated companies	435	317		
Interest of ordinary shareholders (note 21)	4,276	3,161	1,287	1,177
Interest of minority shareholders in subsidiaries	422	250		
	4,698	3,411	1,287	1,177
Provisions for liabilities and charges (note 22)	518	348		
Creditors				
Borrowings (note 26)	2,541	1,262	579	16
Creditors (note 27)	2,307	1,955	730	234
Total funds employed	10,064	6,976	2,596	1,427

On behalf of the board
P Sheehy, B P Garraway *Directors*
26 March 1985

6.20   A company must show the amount for creditors in respect of taxation and social security separately from the amount of the other creditors. [*Note 9 on the balance sheet formats*]. This applies in respect both of creditors payable within one year and of those payable in more than one year (see further Chapter 9 paras 9.11 to 9.13).

6.21   In determining the split between creditors due within one year and those due after more than one year, a company should normally treat a creditor as being payable on the earliest date on which payment falls due (that is, the date on which the creditor can require payment) rather than on the earliest date on which it expects to make payment. Although the Act does not specify this treatment, it is prudent and it follows the treatment the Act requires for loans (see Chapter 9 para 9.06).

6.22   Unless a company shows the payments it has received on account of orders as a deduction from stocks, it must show them under creditors. [*Note 8 on the balance sheet formats*].

6.23   The following items may be shown in alternative positions in the balance sheet:

   (a) Called-up share capital not paid. [*Note 1 on the balance sheet formats*].

   (b) Prepayments and accrued income. [*Note 6 on the balance sheet formats*].

   (c) Accruals and deferred income. [*Note 10 on the balance sheet formats*].

6.24   In addition, two other balance sheet items require further comment:

   (a) 'Payments on account' relate, as appropriate, to payments that a company makes in respect of the acquisition of intangible assets, tangible assets or stocks (see Chapter 7 para 7.100 and Chapter 8 para 8.50).

   (b) A 'related company' is any body corporate (other than another group company) in which the investing company holds, on a long-term basis, a qualifying capital interest for the purpose of securing a contribution to the investing company's own activities by exercising any control or influence that arises from that interest (see Chapter 8 paras 8.22 and 8.23).

The profit and loss account

Formats

6.25   As already mentioned, the Act permits companies to use any one of the four alternative formats of the profit and loss account, and it leaves the choice between these formats to the company's directors.

6.26   Unlike the choice between the balance sheet formats, the choice between the profit and loss account formats is significant. A company can choose not only between a vertical presentation (formats 1 and 2) and a presentation in which it shows charges separately from income (formats 3 and 4), but also between classifying expenses by function or by type. Thus, depending on which format a company chooses, its financial statements will contain certain different information.

Classification of expenses by function

6.27   In formats 1 and 3, expenses are classified by function (for example, cost of sales, distribution costs, administrative expenses). These formats, both of which require identical information, have much in common with the management accounts that many UK companies prepare on a regular basis. Format 1, which is the vertical presentation, is set out below and illustrated in Table 15.

Profit and loss account — Format 1

1 *Turnover*
2 *Cost of sales*
3 *Gross profit or loss*
4 *Distribution costs*
5 *Administrative expenses*
6 *Other operating income*
7 *Income from shares in group companies*
8 *Income from shares in related companies*
9 *Income from other fixed asset investments*
10 *Other interest receivable and similar income*
11 *Amounts written off investments*
12 *Interest payable and similar charges*
13 *Tax on profit or loss on ordinary activities*
14 *Profit or loss on ordinary activities after taxation*
15 *Extraordinary income*
16 *Extraordinary charges*
17 *Extraordinary profit or loss*
18 *Tax on extraordinary profit or loss*
19 *Other taxes not shown under the above items*
20 *Profit or loss for the financial year*

Table 15: Illustration of a Format 1 profit and loss account.

Extract from Habitat Mothercare PLC Report and Accounts 25 March 1984.

CONSOLIDATED STATEMENT OF PROFIT AND LOSS

For the fifty-two weeks ended 25th March, 1984
(1983—thirty-nine weeks ended 27th March, 1983)

	1984	1983
	£000	£000
TURNOVER, excluding sales taxes	375,410	243,974
Cost of sales	(312,698)	(205,017)
GROSS PROFIT	62,712	38,957
Distribution costs	(8,726)	(5,368)
Administrative expenses	(18,813)	(10,718)
TRADING PROFIT (Note 2)	35,173	22,871
Share of results of related companies	209	—
Profit on sale of properties	1,455	20
Net interest charges (Note 3)	(1,925)	(544)
OPERATING PROFIT	34,912	22,347
Interest on convertible unsecured loan stock (Note 12)	(3,695)	(2,664)
Provision for employee profit-linked share plan (Note 13)	(600)	(350)
PROFIT ON ORDINARY ACTIVITIES BEFORE TAXATION	30,617	19,333
Tax on profit on ordinary activities (Note 4)	(11,393)	(7,327)
PROFIT ON ORDINARY ACTIVITIES AFTER TAXATION	19,224	12,006
Extraordinary item (Note 5)	(4,500)	—
PROFIT FOR THE FINANCIAL PERIOD	14,724	12,006
Translation adjustments	(858)	2,968
Dividends paid and proposed	(6,877)	(4,232)
PROFIT RETAINED (Note 15)	6,989	10,742
EARNINGS PER SHARE (Note 6)		
Basic	18·2p	11·3p
Fully diluted	15·7p	10·1p

The accounting policies on page 10 and the notes on pages 15 to 21 form an integral part of this Consolidated Statement of Profit and Loss.

Classification of expenses by type

6.28   In formats 2 and 4, expenses are classified by type (for example, raw materials and consumables, staff costs, and depreciation). These formats, both of which require identical information, are in many ways similar to value added statements. Format 2, which is the vertical presentation, is set out below and also illustrated in Table 16.

Profit and loss account — Format 2

1 Turnover
2 Change in stocks of finished goods and in work in progress
3 Own work capitalised
4 Other operating income
5 (a) Raw materials and consumables
*   (b) Other external charges*
6 Staff costs:
*   (a) Wages and salaries*
*   (b) Social security costs*
*   (c) Other pension costs*
7 (a) Depreciation and other amounts written off tangible and intangible
*   fixed assets*
*   (b) Exceptional amounts written off current assets*
8 Other operating charges
9 Income from shares in group companies
10 Income from shares in related companies
11 Income from other fixed asset investments
12 Other interest receivable and similar income
13 Amounts written off investments
14 Interest payable and similar charges
15 Tax on profit or loss on ordinary activities
16 Profit or loss on ordinary activities after taxation
17 Extraordinary income
18 Extraordinary charges
19 Extraordinary profit or loss
20 Tax on extraordinary profit or loss
21 Other taxes not shown under the above items
22 Profit or loss for the financial year

Commentary on specific items

6.29   The Act attaches to the formats certain notes and comments on specific profit and loss account items.

6.30   Where expenses are classified by function, the amounts to be shown under cost of sales, distribution costs and administrative expenses are to be stated after taking into account any necessary provisions for depreciation and for diminution in the value of assets. [*Note 14 on the profit and loss account formats*]. The amounts of the provisions for depreciation, or for the diminution in the value of tangible and intangible fixed assets, must be disclosed separately in the notes to the financial statements. [*Note 17 on the profit and loss account formats*].

6.31   Income or interest derived from group companies must be shown separately from income and interest derived from other sources. [*Note 15 on the profit and loss account formats*]. Similarly, any interest or similar charges payable to group companies must be shown separately. [*Note 16 on the profit and loss account formats*].

Table 16: Illustration of a Format 2 profit and loss account.

Extract from Associated Dairies Group PLC Annual Report and Accounts 28th April 1984.

CONSOLIDATED PROFIT AND LOSS ACCOUNT
for the fifty-two weeks ended 28 April 1984

	Note	£000	1984 £000	52 weeks ended 30 April 1983 £000
Turnover	2		1,755,220	1,519,144
Change in stocks			8,985	9,088
Other operating income			12,523	10,138
			1,776,728	1,538,370
Raw materials and consumables		1,407,838		1,231,531
Staff costs	4	139,735		121,404
Depreciation of tangible fixed assets		19,690		16,635
Other operating charges		114,424		100,693
			1,681,687	1,470,263
Operating profit	4		95,041	68,107
Share of profits in associated company			78	98
Other income	6		9,669	9,367
Interest payable and similar charges	7		(180)	(186)
Profit before taxation			104,608	77,386
Taxation on profit on ordinary activities	8		45,894	32,219
Profit on ordinary activities after taxation			58,714	45,167
Minority interests			(26)	(27)
Profit after taxation and minorities			58,688	45,140
Extraordinary items	9		24,969	2,968
Profit available for appropriation			33,719	42,172
Dividends	10		19,864	14,892
Retained profit for the period	24		13,855	27,280
Earnings per ordinary share	11		8·92p	6·88p

6.32 One other profit and loss account item requires further comment. In the light of present practice in the UK, it is unlikely that any amount would fall to be disclosed under the heading 'Other taxes not shown under the above items'.

Additional disclosure

6.33 All items in the profit and loss account are preceded by an Arabic numeral and so they may be relegated to the notes to the financial statements. Whichever format of profit and loss account a company adopts, the account must, however, show separately on its face the amount of the company's profit or loss on ordinary activities before taxation. [4 Sch 3(6)].

6.34 In addition, whichever format of profit and loss account a company adopts, the account must show separately the allocation of profit or the treatment of loss (as applicable). In particular, it must show:

(a) Any amount that has been set aside, or that it is proposed to set aside, to reserves.

(b) Any amount that has been withdrawn, or that it is proposed to withdraw, from reserves.

(c) The aggregate amount of any dividends that have been paid and that are proposed.
[*4 Sch 3(7)*].

The notes to the balance sheet and the profit and loss account

6.35 Schedule 4 to the Act requires companies to disclose considerable detail in the notes to their financial statements. The objects of the requirements are:

(a) To supplement the information given in the financial statements in respect of any particular items that are shown in either the balance sheet or the profit and loss account.

(b) To give details of anything else that is relevant, in the light of the information so given, to the assessment of the state of the company's affairs.

(c) To explain any particular circumstances that affect items shown in the profit and loss account.
[*4 Sch 37, 52*].

6.36 Any information that the Act requires to be shown by way of a note to the financial statements may, alternatively, be shown in the company's profit or loss account or balance sheet. [*4 Sch 35*]. However, the Act does not permit a company to use the directors' report as an alternative method of disclosure.

Accounting policies

6.37 The notes to the financial statements must set out the accounting policies the company has adopted in determining the amounts to be included in the financial statements. [*4 Sch 36*]. In particular, they must include:

(a) The method of determining the provisions both for depreciation and for diminution in the value of assets. [*4 Sch 36*].

(b) The method of translating foreign currency amounts into sterling. [*4 Sch 58(1)*].

6.38   Accounting policies are defined in SSAP 2 as "the specific accounting bases selected and consistently followed by a business enterprise as being, in the opinion of the management, appropriate to its circumstances and best suited to present fairly its results and financial position".

6.39   The Standard requires companies to disclose by way of a note to their financial statements the accounting policies they judge to be either material or critical in determining the profit or loss for the year and also in stating the financial position at the end of the year. The explanations should be clear, fair, and as brief as possible. [*SSAP 2 para 18*].

6.40   The Standard gives some examples of matters for which different accounting bases are recognised, and that may have a material effect both on reported results and on the financial position. These matters include:

(a) Depreciation of fixed assets.
(b) Treatment and amortisation of intangibles such as research and development expenditure, patents and trademarks.
(c) Stocks and work in progress.
(d) Long-term contracts.
(e) Deferred taxation.
(f) Hire purchase or instalment transactions.
(g) Leasing and rental transactions.
(h) Conversion of foreign currencies.
(i) Repairs and renewals.
(j) Consolidation policies.
(k) Property development transactions.
(l) Warranties for products or services.

This list is not exhaustive, and it will vary according to the nature of the company's operations.

6.41   Many companies disclose their accounting policies as a separate statement that they locate away from the remainder of the notes. This is generally accepted accounting practice and it has the advantage that the accounting policies are given more prominence and are not lost within the individual notes to the financial statements.

6.42   However, there appears to be a slight conflict with SSAP 2 in adopting this presentation, because paragraph 18 of the Standard specifically says: "The accounting policies ... followed for dealing with items which are judged material or critical in determining profit or loss for the year and in stating the financial position should be disclosed by way of note to the accounts". In addition, paragraph 36 of Schedule 4 requires that the accounting policies should be given *in the notes* to the financial statements.

Consequently, to overcome this anomaly, the page numbers that identify the financial statements for the purpose of the directors' adoption
of the financial statements, and for the purpose of the auditors' opinion, should include the statement of accounting policies.

6.43 Where a company's financial statements have been drawn up under
the alternative accounting rules, the accounting convention used should
be stated in those financial statements (see Chapter 5 para 5.85).
However, the company does need to refer to the specific policy for each
item that it has accounted for under the alternative rules and this disclosure would normally be made as part of the company's accounting
policies.

Statements of source and application of funds

6.44 The Act does not specify formats for, or require companies to include
in their financial statements, a statement of source and application of
funds. But SSAP 10 requires all company financial statements that are
intended to show a true and fair view to include a statement of source
and application of funds. The one exception to this requirement is that,
the statement is not required if a company's turnover or gross income
is less than £25,000 per annum. [*SSAP 10 para 9*]. However, if this statement is excluded from the financial statements, the company's auditors need only mention in their report that the funds statement has not
been given and this will not affect their report on the truth and fairness of those financial statements.

6.45 The Standard does not specify a format a company must use in preparing the statement. It only outlines the object of the statement, which
is to show the manner in which the company has financed its operations and used its financial resources. Consequently, the format should
be designed to achieve this objective.

6.46 The only stipulations that the Standard makes about the format of the
statement are that it should show the profit or loss for the year and
the adjustments the company has made to it for those items that do
not involve the movement of funds. Also, the following sources and
applications of funds should be disclosed where they are material:

(a) Dividends paid.

(b) Acquisitions and disposals of fixed assets.

(c) Funds raised by increasing, or funds expended in repaying or
redeeming, either medium-term or long-term loans or the company's
issued capital.

(d) Increases or decreases in working capital (sub-divided into its components), and movements in 'net liquid funds'.
[*SSAP 10 para 11*].

6.47　'Net liquid funds' is defined as cash at bank and in hand and cash equivalents (for example, investments held as current assets), less bank overdrafts and other borrowings repayable within one year of the accounting date. [*SSAP 10 para 8*].

6.48　The statement is required to be audited, and it should show corresponding amounts for the previous period.

6.49　Although there are no set formats for statements of source and applications of funds, the Appendix to SSAP 10 gives various examples of layouts companies may use. Certain of the headings in these examples are, however, inappropriate, because SSAP 10 was issued before the 1981 Companies Act which introduced the formats. An example of the format of a statement of source and application of funds is given below.

Statement of source and application of funds

	£	£	£	£
Source of funds				
Profit on ordinary activities				
before taxation		X		X
Extraordinary items		X		X
		X		X
Adjustments for items not involving				
the movement of funds:				
Depreciation	X		X	
Amounts written off investments	X	X	X	X
Total generated from operations		X		X
Funds from other sources				
Issue of share capital		X		X
Debenture loans		X		X
		X		X
Application of funds				
Dividends paid	(X)		(X)	
Tax paid	(X)		(X)	
Purchase of tangible fixed assets	(X)	(X)	(X)	(X)
		X		X
Increase or (decrease) in working capital				
Stocks		(X)		X
Debtors		X		X
Creditors		(X)		(X)
		X		X
Movement in net liquid funds:				
Cash at bank and in hand	X		X	
Current asset investments	X		(X)	
		X		X
		X		X

6.50   The Standard requires also that the statement of source and application of funds in a group's financial statements should be so framed
as to reflect the group's operations. [*SSAP 10 para 12*]. An illustration
of a company's source and application of funds statement is given in
Table 17.

6.51   Where the holding company either acquires or disposes of subsidiary
companies, these transactions should be reflected in the statement. The
Standard indicates two ways in which these transactions may be disclosed in the statement:

(a) The first method indicates the funds used or the funds generated
from the purchase or sale respectively of subsidiary companies.

(b) The second method shows the increase or decrease in the individual
assets and liabilities the group has acquired or disposed of.

6.52   Whichever method a company uses, it will generally also need to summarise the effect of the acquisition or disposal by way of a footnote
to the statement. Where the company has acquired a subsidiary company, this footnote should indicate how much of the purchase price
has been discharged in cash and how much by the issue of shares. An
example of the type of disclosure that should be made in the footnote
is shown below:

Summary of the effects of the acquisition of Company A

	£000
Net assets acquired:	
Tangible fixed assets	200
Goodwill	20
Stocks	50
Debtors	40
Creditors	(45)
	265
Discharged by:	
Issue of shares	150
Cash paid	115
	265

Table 17: Example of a source and application of funds statement

Extract from Debenhams PLC Annual Report 28 January 1984.

Statement of Source and Application of Funds

	1984 £000	1983 £000
Source of funds:		
Profit on ordinary activities before taxation	**32,657**	19,575
Adjustment for items not involving the movement of funds:		
Depreciation	**12,188**	11,403
Loss on disposal of fixed assets	**1,802**	4,359
Revaluation surplus now realised		
on properties sold	**(3,746)**	(10,610)
Profit retained by related companies	**(9,448)**	—
Other non-cash movements	**(108)**	1,109
	688	6,261
Funds generated from operations	**33,345**	25,836
Funds from other sources		
Proceeds from sale of tangible fixed assets	**9,113**	18,750
Disposal of fixed investments	**3,025**	—
Proceeds from issue of shares	**2,173**	248
Proceeds from issue of shares to minorities	—	14,731
Increase in creditors falling due		
after more than one year	**1,898**	2,821
	16,209	36,550
	49,554	62,386
Application of funds:		
Purchase of tangible fixed assets	**29,464**	26,349
Payment of dividends	**9,465**	8,605
Payment of taxation	**1,662**	3,950
Payment to minorities	**2,140**	—
Purchase of investments held as fixed assets	**3,405**	14,275
Payment for redemption of debentures	**1,515**	240
	47,651	53,419
Increase in working capital:	**1,903**	8,967
Components of increase in working capital:		
Increase in stock	**7,798**	494
(Decrease)/increase in debtors	**(3,983)**	15,970
Increase in current investments	**11,618**	—
Increase in creditors	**(1,579)**	(7,063)
	13,854	9,401
Movement in net liquid funds:		
Increase in overdrafts	**(13,743)**	(2,801)
Increase in cash	**1,792**	2,367
	(11,951)	(434)
	1,903	8,967

Listed companies' historical summaries

6.53   Although the Act does not require a company to include a historical summary of information in its financial statements, many companies do so. This practice arose because the chairman of The Stock Exchange wrote to all listed companies in 1964 recommending that they should include a ten-year historical summary in their annual financial statements.

6.54   In practice, because the historical summary is additional voluntary information, many listed companies now give only a five-year historical summary.

6.55   There is no set format for historical summaries, but the type of information that listed companies normally give in them is illustrated in Table 18 and summarised below:

Balance sheet

(a) Tangible assets.
(b) Other assets.
(c) Net borrowings.
(d) Capital and reserves.
(e) Minority interests.

Profit and loss account

(a) Turnover.
(b) Trading profit.
(c) Interest.
(d) Profit on ordinary activities before taxation.
(e) Taxation.
(f) Profit after taxation.
(g) Extraordinary items.
(h) Minority interests and preference dividends.
(i) Retained earnings.

Statistical information

(a) Earnings per share.
(b) Ordinary dividends per share.
(c) Dividend cover.

6.56   The historical summary will normally show the actual figures that were reported for each year. However, in certain situations, the reported figures may need to be adjusted. The circumstances where adjustments may be necessary are as follows:

(a) Where there is a change in accounting policy, ED 36 says that amounts relating to past years should be restated if this is necessary to ensure that the reported figures for each year are stated on

Table 18: Example of a five-year historical summary.

Extract from Beechams Group p.l.c. Report and Accounts 31 March 1984.

Five Year Summary 1980 – 1984

Years ended 31st March	1984	1983	1982	1981	1980
	£m	£m	£m	£m	£m
Turnover	1,944·0	1,702·4	1,407·0	1,194·7	1,028·4
Profit before interest and taxation	279·6	250·4	210·3	161·0	138·7
Interest	(11·7)	(13·3)	(8·4)	(10·4)	(1·9)
Profit on ordinary activities before					
taxation	267·9	237·1	201·9	150·6	136·8
Tax on profit on ordinary activities	(105·2)	(84·7)	(80·4)	(60·9)	(54·9)
Minority interests	(0·9)	(0·5)	(0·5)	(0·5)	(0·7)
Dividends	(73·5)	(59·6)	(52·3)	(43·5)	(40·7)
Profit retained	88·3	92·3	68·7	45·7	40·5
Employment of Group capital					
Fixed assets	680·2	628·1	467·2	418·0	353·1
Net current assets	634·9	457·8	387·9	320·8	316·7
	1,315·1	1,085·9	855·1	738·8	669·8
Group capital employed					
Loans – falling due after more than					
one year	268·0	312·9	196·9	169·1	144·7
Provisions and other creditors	65·8	62·2	47·2	40·4	34·9
Capital and reserves	975·8	706·9	609·3	527·5	488·6
Minority interests	5·5	3·9	1·7	1·8	1·6
	1,315·1	1,085·9	855·1	738·8	669·8
Net liquid funds					
Investments	36·9	21·7	21·8	19·8	29·2
Cash at bank and in hand	262·3	174·3	119·1	108·8	75·3
Debenture loans—falling due within					
one year	(9·0)	(36·9)	(3·0)	(1·1)	(0·2)
Bank loans and overdrafts—falling					
due within one year	(39·5)	(51·1)	(24·7)	(31·3)	(16·0)
	250·7	108·0	113·2	96·2	88·3
Statistics					
Profit before interest and taxation					
to turnover	14·4%	14·7%	14·9%	13·5%	13·5%
Profit on ordinary activities before					
taxation to turnover	13·8%	13·9%	14·3%	12·6%	13·3%
Profit on ordinary activities before					
taxation to average historical					
capital employed	22·3%	24·4%	25·3%	21·4%	21·1%
Debenture loans, bank loans and					
overdrafts to capital and reserves					
and minority interests	32·3%	56·4%	36·8%	38·1%	32·8%
Earnings per ordinary share of 25p	22·8p	22·9p	18·3p	13·5p	12·3p
Dividends per ordinary share of 25p	10·2p	9·0p	7·9p	6·6p	6·0p
Employees – average number					
employed	35,900	34,300	33,900	34,200	32,900

The above figures have been restated to reflect the changes made in the Group's accounting policies for advance corporation tax and book goodwill.
Earnings and dividends per ordinary share for each year have been adjusted to take account of the bonus element in the rights issue made in June 1983.

a consistent basis. If the figures have not been restated, then this fact should be disclosed. If figures have been restated, then it should also be made clear which years' figures have been restated.

(b) Where fundamental errors have been corrected by a prior-year adjustment, then the historical summary should be changed, and the same rules as in *(a)* above would apply.

(c) Earnings per share figures that are reported should be amended to reflect any:

   (i) New equity shares that have been issued by capitalising reserves.

   (ii) Equity shares that have been split into shares of a lower nominal value.

   (iii) New equity shares that have been issued by way of rights issues.

The earnings per share figures should be adjusted in the ways explained in Chapter 10, paragraphs 10.142 to 10.144. Appendix 2 to SSAP 3 says that the resultant figures should be described as the 'adjusted earnings per share'. They should be set out separately from the other financial information that is not adjusted (for example, in a separate box – see Table 18).

(d) Dividends per share should also be adjusted where there have been changes in the number of equity shares in issue (in the circumstances set out in *(c)*(i),(ii) and (iii) above). Disclosure of the revised dividend in the form of pence per share should be given in a similar way to the adjusted earnings per share (see Table 18).

6.57   The ASC stated in SSAP 16 that it intended to develop an exposure draft indicating how companies should adjust historical summary figures onto a common price basis, but the guidance that was developed remains in the form of a discussion paper entitled, 'Corresponding amounts and ten year summaries in current cost accounts', that the ASC issued in May 1982. Where a company does adjust its historical summary to eliminate the effects of price changes, it should give the basis of the adjustments that it has made, so as to make the summaries meaningful.

6.58   Because an historical summary is not a requirement of law or of Accounting Standards, and it is not required in order for the financial statements to show a true and fair view, the auditors do not need to report on it. They do, however, have to satisfy themselves that the information shown in the summary is consistent with the audited financial statements and that it is not misleading. [*Auditing Guideline, 'Financial information issued with audited financial statements'*].

Application of the rules on formats to half-yearly reports and preliminary profits statements

6.59   The formats set out in the Act apply both to the financial statements of those companies that are limited by either shares or guarantee and to the financial statements of unlimited companies. However, they do *not* apply to half-yearly reports and preliminary profits statements made by listed companies or by companies traded on the USM. These reports and statements can be presented in any reasonable form that includes the items that are disclosable under The Stock Exchange's Continuing Obligations or the USM's General Undertaking. The reason for this is that the formats apply to any financial statements drawn up under Section 227 of the Act, and Section 227 does not apply to half-yearly reports and preliminary profits statements. [*Sec 228 (1)*].

6.60   The information that The Stock Exchange requires listed companies to include in their half-yearly reports and preliminary profits statements is as follows:

(a) An explanatory statement relating to the group's activities and profit or loss during the period. (This is required in half-yearly reports only.)

(b) A statement showing:

    (i) Net turnover.
    (ii) Profit or loss before taxation and extraordinary items.
    (iii) Taxation.
    (iv) Minority interests.
    (v) Profit or loss attributable to shareholders, before extraordinary items.
    (vi) Extraordinary items (net of taxation).
    (vii) Profit or loss attributable to shareholders.
    (viii) Rates and amounts of dividends paid and proposed.
    (ix) Earnings per share.
    (x) Comparative figures.

(c) An explanation of any significant information required to enable investors to make an informed assessment of the trend of the group's activities. (This is required in half-yearly reports only.)

(d) A statement as to whether the information reported has been audited. (This is required in half-yearly reports only.)
[*CO 25*].

6.61   The General Undertaking requires USM companies to keep the Quotations Department of The Stock Exchange informed of any information necessary to enable the shareholders and the public to appraise the position of the company. In particular, USM companies are required to notify the Quotations Department of their preliminary profit announcements for any year, half year or other period and to prepare a half-yearly report.

6.62   However, the USM's General Undertaking does not specify what information half-yearly reports and preliminary profits statements that companies traded on the USM prepare should contain, but as a guide they should normally include similar information to that outlined above for listed companies.

6.63   Abridged accounts (as defined in Section 255 of the Act) are considered further in Chapter 21, paragraphs 21.38 to 21.48.

CHAPTER 7

BALANCE SHEET — FIXED ASSETS

Chapter 7

Balance Sheet — Fixed Assets

Introduction

7.01 This chapter considers the disclosure of fixed assets in a company's financial statements. It also considers some of the problems that arise in determining the value of specific fixed assets.

7.02 The task of determining the purchase price or the production cost of an asset is discussed earlier in Chapter 4, paragraphs 4.20 to 4.34.

Definitions

7.03 Schedule 4 defines all assets as either fixed or current. Assets are fixed assets if the company intends to use them on a continuing basis in its activities. Any assets the company does not intend to use in that way are current assets. [*4 Sch 77*].

7.04 The Act specifically states, however, that the following three items cannot be treated as assets in any company's balance sheet:

(a) Preliminary expenses.

(b) Expenses of, and commission on, any issue of shares or debentures.

(c) Costs of research.
[*4 Sch 3(2)*].

Consequently, these items should not be capitalised, and they must be written off to the profit and loss account.

7.05 There is very little room for flexibility in relation to the general definition of fixed and current assets. A company must include all its assets under one or other of the two main headings of fixed assets and current assets, unless this would mean that its financial statements would not give a true and fair view. So, for example, assets such as investments or a vehicle hire fleet must be categorised as either fixed or current assets, or else be split between the two categories.

7.06 Where a company intends to dispose of a fixed asset, the asset is not 'intended for use on a continuing basis in the company's activities'. If the asset needs to be reclassified as a current asset, then it is not

101

appropriate that it should be included in the balance sheet at an amount that exceeds cost, unless it is either disclosed as stocks or a current asset investment. This is because the alternative accounting rules can only be adopted for stocks and current asset investments and not other current asset items. When a company intends to dispose of a fixed asset, it may be more appropriate for the company to adopt the true and fair override and to retain the asset under fixed assets in a new sub-heading 'Assets held for resale'. A company that has adopted this type of disclosure is shown in Table 19.

Table 19: Example of a fixed asset note where assets that are held for future sale have been disclosed separately.

Extract from Johnson Group Cleaners PLC Annual Report 31 December 1983.

14 Tangible fixed assets

	Freehold	Trading properties Long leasehold	Short leasehold	Non-Trading properties held for future sale (see below)	Plant fixtures and transport	Total
	£000	£000	£000	£000	£000	£000
Cost						
Cost or valuation at 26th December 1982	7,164	694	783	2,472	26,343	37,456
Additions	1,228	111	180	—	6,215	7,734
Assets of new subsidiary	—	—	231	—	483	714
Disposals	(8)	—	(14)	(190)	(1,582)	(1,794)
Transfers	(39)	(95)	93	43	(2)	—
Exchange rate adjustment	48	—	25	—	76	149
At 31st December 1983	8,393	710	1,298	2,325	31,533	44,259
Depreciation						
At 26th December 1982	—	—	401	—	11,860	12,261
Charge for year	—	—	72	—	2,582	2,654
On disposals	—	—	(11)	—	(1,188)	(1,199)
Exchange rate adjustment	—	—	1	—	11	12
At 31st December 1983	—	—	463	—	13,265	13,728
Net book value 1983	8,393	710	835	2,325	18,268	30,531
Net book value 1982	7,164	694	382	2,472	14,483	25,195

Non-trading properties held for future sale	Freehold	Long leasehold	Total
At 26th December 1982	2,090	382	2,472
Disposals	(181)	(9)	(190)
Transfers	40	3	43
At 31st December 1983	1,949	376	2,325

The proceeds of sale of these properties will be used for investment in trading operations. The timing of disposals is uncertain. Since they are held for future sale they are not investment properties as defined in Statement of Standard Accounting Practice No. 19.

Disclosure

7.07 In respect of either the cost or the valuation (before any provisions for depreciation or diminution in value) of each item in the format that is included under the general heading 'Fixed assets' (whether the item is shown on the face of the balance sheet or in the notes), the notes to the financial statements must disclose:

(a) The aggregate amount of that item at both the beginning and the end of the financial year in question.

(b) The effect of any application of the alternative accounting rules during that financial year (see Chapter 5).

(c) The amount of any acquisitions, and the amount of any disposals, during that financial year.

(d) The amount of any transfers of assets to or from that item during that financial year.
[*4 Sch 42(1)(2)*].

7.08 It should be noted that these requirements apply to all categories of fixed assets (whether intangible assets, tangible assets or investments). Moreover, they require the information to be given in respect of each of the sub-headings that are preceded in the formats in the Act by Arabic numerals.

7.09 In addition, the Act requires details to be disclosed about any provisions made in respect of each fixed asset category. The need for, and the calculation of, provisions both for depreciation and for the diminution in value of assets are discussed earlier in Chapter 4, paragraphs 4.04 to 4.17. In particular, the notes must disclose:

(a) The cumulative amount of provisions for either depreciation or the diminution in value of assets at both the beginning and the end of the financial year in question.

(b) The amount of any such provisions that have been made during that financial year.

(c) The amount of any such provisions that have been eliminated during that financial year on the disposal of the fixed assets to which they related.

(d) The amount of any other adjustments made in respect of any such provisions during that financial year.
[*4 Sch 42(3)*].

7.10 Where a company has applied one of the alternative accounting rules to any fixed asset other than listed investments, the notes must disclose the years in which the assets were separately valued (so far as the directors know these) and also the separate values. If any assets were valued during the financial year in question, the notes must also disclose:

(a) The valuers' names or the qualifications of the persons who acted as valuers.

(b) The bases of valuation that the valuers applied.
[*4 Sch 43*].

Intangible assets

7.11   Intangible assets may be capitalised subject to the rules set out in the following paragraphs.

7.12   The balance sheet may include amounts for concessions, patents, licences, trade marks and other similar rights and assets only where either of the following conditions is satisfied:

(a) They were acquired for valuable consideration in circumstances that do not qualify them to be shown as goodwill.

(b) They were created by the company itself.
[*Note 2 on the balance sheet formats*].

7.13   Where intangible assets are capitalised, they must always be amortised over their estimated useful economic lives. [*4 Sch 18*]. Besides applying to those intangibles that are specifically defined in the Act (development costs, concessions, patents, licences, trade marks and goodwill), this requirement applies also to other intangibles such as know-how. Although know-how is not often found in UK financial statements, the bases and the methods of accounting for it should follow generally the accounting principles for development costs.

7.14   The amortisation rules that have to be followed for intangible assets are the same rules that apply to tangible fixed assets which are discussed in Chapter 4, paragraphs 4.04 to 4.17.

Research and development

7.15   The Act permits only *development costs* (but not research costs) to be capitalised, and then only in *special circumstances*. [*4 Sch 20(1)*]. Research costs (whether pure or applied) must be written off through the profit and loss account as they are incurred. [*4 Sch 3(2)(c)*].

7.16   The Act does not define *'development'*. However, SSAP 13 defines development as a company's use of knowledge it has acquired through research, in order to produce new or substantially improved materials, devices, products, processes, systems or services before commercial production begins. Therefore, development is the work a company performs after it has planned or designed a new product or service until the time that this is ready either to be manufactured, or to be put into operation, commercially. For example, a cable television company may capitalise expenditure on the development of its cable service from the time that it receives a franchise until the time that it relays its first programme.

Development costs

7.17   The type of development *costs* that may be capitalised are not defined either in the Act or in SSAP 13. The reason for this is that expenditure that relates to the development of a product or service will vary considerably according to the type of product or service that is being developed.

7.18   However, IAS 9, 'Accounting for research and development', gives some guidance on the type of costs that may be capitalised. IAS 9 says that development costs may include:

(a) Salaries, wages and related costs of personnel.

(b) The costs of materials and services consumed.

(c) The depreciation of equipment and facilities.

(d) A reasonable allocation of overhead costs.

(e) Other related costs, such as the amortisation of patents and licences.

7.19   As an example, a cable television company may wish to capitalise, as development costs, the expenditure it has incurred in:

(a) Raising capital (excluding preliminary or formation expenses, which it must charge to the profit and loss account).

(b) Depreciating capital equipment.

(c) Recruiting personnel and paying their subsequent salary costs.

(d) Applying successfully for a franchise.

(e) Laying cables.

Special circumstances

7.20   Also, the Act does not define the term *'special circumstances'*. Therefore, it is necessary again to look to SSAP 13 for guidance. It seems reasonable to assume that, if all the conditions set out in paragraph 21 of SSAP 13 are met, special circumstances exist, and so development costs may be capitalised. If any one of the conditions is not met, then developments costs must be written off as they are incurred.

7.21   Paragraph 21 of SSAP 13 lays down the following conditions that must all be satisfied if development expenditure is to be capitalised:

(a) There is a clearly defined project.

(b) The expenditure on the project is separately identifiable.

(c) The outcome of the project has been assessed with reasonable certainty as to both its technical feasibility and its ultimate commercial viability.

(d) All costs of the project (including future costs to be incurred) are reasonably expected to be more than covered by related future revenues.

(e) Adequate resources exist, or are reasonably expected to be available, to enable the project to be completed, and to provide any consequential increases in working capital.

7.22   Where these conditions are satisfied, a company can defer development expenditure, but only until commercial production begins. SSAP 13 requires a company to amortise the expenditure it has capitalised from the time that commercial production of the product or service begins. Where a company is developing a product, commercial production begins when the company is manufacturing the product with a view to selling it commercially.

Amortisation

7.23   Amortisation of development expenditure must be allocated to each accounting period on a systematic basis. This can be done by reference to the sales or the use of the product or the service, or by reference to the period over which the product or service is expected to be sold or used. However, the period of amortisation may be difficult to determine. In determining this period, the directors must establish a realistic and prudent number of years over which they expect the development expenditure to produce a benefit. They must decide also whether they expect the benefit to accrue evenly over these years.

7.24   To continue the example of a cable television company, it would normally write its development expenditure off over a period that begins with the date when it first relays programmes and ends on the date that the franchise period ends. However, if, for example, only part of the system is operational during the initial operation period, the company may calculate the amount of amortisation that it charges during that period differently from the amount it charges once the company becomes fully operational. The company may, for instance, calculate the amount of amortisation it charges in this initial operation period by reference to the actual number of subscribers to the service, as compared to the estimate of the final number of subscribers.

Disclosure

7.25   Where development costs are deferred and are shown as an asset in the balance sheet, the notes to the financial statements must disclose:

(a) The period over which the amount of those costs that were originally capitalised is being, or is to be, written off.

(b) The reasons for capitalising the development costs.
[*4 Sch 20(2)*].

7.26　In addition, SSAP 13 requires that the accounting policy followed
should be clearly explained. An illustration of such a policy is given
in Table 20.

> **Table 20: Illustration of an accounting policy for development
> expenditure.**
>
> *Extract from Hestair plc Annual Review 31 January 1984.*
>
> **Development expenditure**
> Development expenditure attributable to major projects whose technical feasibility and
> commercial viability are reasonably assured is capitalised and amortized over a maximum
> of the first three years' sales. Expenditure on pure research is written off in the year
> during which it is incurred.

Provisions for diminution in value

7.27　A company should review at the end of each accounting period the
development expenditure it has capitalised. Where the circumstances
that justified the original deferral of the expenditure no longer apply,
or are considered doubtful, the company should write off immediately
the expenditure to the extent that the company considers it to be
irrecoverable. [*SSAP 13 para 25*]. Consequently, a company will have
to consider the conditions outlined in paragraph 7.21 above at each
year end in order to establish whether it should write off all or some
of the previously capitalised development expenditure.

7.28　This requirement of SSAP 13 may conflict with the Act's requirements.
There is no conflict if the directors expect the diminution in value of
the development expenditure to be permanent, because, in this circumstance, the Act *requires* that provision should be made for the diminution in value of the asset. [*4 Sch 19(2)*]. However, the directors may
consider that a diminution in value of development expenditure is only
temporary. For example, when the financial statements are prepared,
the directors may no longer be able to show that the development project
is technically feasible, but they may believe that the company will find
a solution to the feasibility problem in the future. In the meantime,
however, they propose to provide for the diminution in value of the
development expenditure (which they consider to be *temporary*) in accordance with SSAP 13. However, the Act does not allow a company to
provide against a fixed asset for a *temporary* diminution in value (unless
it is a fixed asset investment). [*4 Sch 19(1)*]. In this situation, the directors should comply with the requirement of SSAP 13, and they should
provide for the temporary diminution in value on the grounds that this

is necessary in order for the financial statements to show a true and fair view. If they do this, they will have to state in the financial statements the details of the departure from the Act, their reasons for the departure, and its effect. [*Sec 228(6)*].

7.29   SSAP 13 states also that, once development costs have been written off, they should not be reinstated, even though the uncertainties that led to the write-off no longer apply. [*SSAP 13 para 26*].

7.30   This requirement contrasts with the Act's requirement, which says that where a company has provided for the diminution in value of an asset, but the factors that gave rise to the provision no longer apply to any extent, then the company *must* write back the provision to that extent. [*4 Sch 19(3)*].

7.31   An ASC working party is currently reviewing SSAP 13, and it will take into account the implications of the Companies Act. However, pending the amendment of SSAP 13, there could be a conflict between the Act's requirement to write back a provision for a diminution in value of an asset that is no longer required, and SSAP 13's requirement not to reinstate capitalised development costs that have been written off. Again, in this situation, it seems that the company should normally comply with the restriction in SSAP 13.

7.32   An alternative approach, in this situation, is to adopt the alternative accounting rules. The alternative accounting rules in the Act allow intangible and tangible fixed assets to be stated at their market value or current cost (see further Chapter 5, para 5.06). Therefore, the development expenditure may be revalued even though it has previously been written off to the profit and loss account. In this circumstance, the value placed on the development expenditure cannot be credited back to the profit and loss account, but there seems to be no reason why these development costs should not in effect be reinstated by crediting an equivalent amount to the revaluation reserve.

7.33   Once capitalised, the development expenditure will be subject to amortisation in the normal way. The amortisation will usually be charged to the profit and loss account. Consequently, if no further entry is made, the development expenditure would in effect be charged to the profit and loss account twice: once when it is originally written off, and again as it is amortised after revaluation. To overcome this anomaly, transfers should be made from the revaluation reserve to the profit and loss account as the amortisation is charged. This is allowable under paragraph 34 of Schedule 4, to the extent that the amount that is being transferred to the profit and loss account has previously been charged to that account. This treatment will not entirely remove the effect of the double charge to the profit and loss account, because the transfer from the revaluation reserve to the profit and loss account must be shown 'below the line'. Consequently, profit before tax and reported earnings will still suffer the development expenditure twice. Alternatively, if the 'split depreciation' approach (discussed in Chapter 5 para 5.64) is accepted, the amortisation can be charged direct to the revaluation reserve. The problem of a double charge to the profit and loss account will not then arise.

Effect on realised reserves

7.34 Where development expenditure is deferred by capitalising it, and the unamortised development expenditure is not treated as a realised loss (see Chapter 19 para 19.76), the note to the financial statements that Schedule 4, paragraph 20(2) requires must also state:

(a) The fact that the amount of unamortised development expenditure is not to be treated as a realised loss for the purposes of calculating distributable profits.

(b) The circumstances that the directors relied upon to justify their decision not to treat the unamortised development expenditure as a realised loss.
[*Sec 269(2)(b)*].

Computer software

Treatment of computer software costs

7.35 Many companies write off the cost of their computer software immediately to the profit and loss account. However, an increasing number of companies capitalise their computer software costs as either tangible fixed assets or intangible fixed assets (for example, see Table 21). These costs may arise in several ways. Consider the following four situations:

(a) A company purchases computer software externally (including, for example, packages for applications such as payroll, or general ledger or other similar packages to be used on the company's own computer). The company should capitalise the cost of such software as a tangible fixed asset. This is because the software complies with the Act's definition of a fixed asset, because the company will generally purchase it to use it on a continuing basis in the company's activities. The SSAP 13 criteria do not apply in this situation, because this expenditure is not development expenditure.

The company should depreciate this software, in common with its other fixed assets, over its estimated useful life. Where a company purchases a software package specifically to run on a particular computer, the software's estimated useful life should generally not exceed the computer's remaining useful life.

Where a company incurs subsequent expenditure to improve the software, it could either write this expenditure off immediately or capitalise it. If this expenditure is capitalised, it should be written off over the remaining useful life of the software package. However, where the improvement costs lead to an extension of the software's useful life, the company will need to revise the depreciation charge, because the asset's life has been extended (see further Chapter 4 para 4.13).

Table 21: Example of an accounting policy for computer software costs.

Extract from Bestobell plc Report and Accounts 31 December 1983.

c Tangible fixed assets

Interests in freehold and long leasehold land and buildings are stated at cost or the latest revalued amounts. Other fixed assets are shown at their purchase cost together with any incidental expenses of acquisition. Government grants received or receivable on qualifying expenditure are applied in reduction of the cost of acquisition of the fixed assets to which the grants relate.

Computer software costs are capitalised only to the extent that they relate to new and proven projects the costs of which exceed £10,000.

Depreciation is calculated so as to write off the cost or revalued amounts of tangible fixed assets on a straight line basis over the expected useful economic lives of the assets concerned. The principal annual rates used for this purpose are:

Freehold and long-term leasehold buildings	2.5%
Plant and machinery	10-20%
Motor vehicles	25%
Furniture, fixtures and fittings	10-20%
Computer software	25%

Certain intangible assets recognised in the accounts in previous years have been written off. This represents a change in policy, the effect of which is referred to in Note 13.

(b) A company employs programmers to develop software for the company's own use. In this situation, two problems exist:

   (i) The company will need to analyse the programmers' time and other expenses in order to identify the costs of developing the software.

   (ii) If the software is not operational at the time the financial statements are prepared, the company will have to provide evidence to demonstrate that the software will be completed successfully.

Provided that it can overcome both of these problems, a company may capitalise this type of computer software cost as a tangible fixed asset. If the software is not fully developed it should be included under the balance sheet heading of 'Payments on account and assets in the course of construction'.

Again, the SSAP 13 criteria are not relevant in assessing whether this expenditure should be capitalised, because the expenditure is not part of a commercial project. The company is merely producing its own fixed assets.

(c) A company buys computer software to incorporate into a product that it is developing. This could include software that an external

software house writes, and that the company will include in computer-controlled equipment it will produce and sell.

This expenditure is a form of development expenditure, and so the question of whether this can be capitalised is covered by the criteria included in SSAP 13. Provided that these criteria are satisfied, the company may capitalise the expenditure, and amortise it over the product's estimated useful life (see paras 7.21 to 7.23 above).

(d) A company's own programmers write software that the company will include in its products. The question of capitalisation will again depend on whether the criteria set out in SSAP 13 are satisfied.

Revaluation of computer software

7.36 Where a company has developed software and it has written it off to the profit and loss account, it may wish to reinstate this asset, at a future date, by revaluing it. The possibility of subsequently reinstating an asset by revaluation is discussed earlier in relation to development expenditure in paragraphs 7.29 to 7.33. This discussion applies equally to computer software costs.

Difficulties in valuing computer software

7.37 In practice it may be very difficult to value both computer software and computer hardware. This is because substantial advances are being made in technology, and also the cost of high technology products and equipment is continually falling. Where an industry is affected by specific inflation, usually there are Government indices that measure the effect that inflation has had in that industry. However, because the market in high technology products such as computer software and hardware is changing so rapidly, the Government is, apparently, unable to publish a meaningful index for this type of equipment.

7.38 The Guidance Notes to SSAP 16 discussed the concept of the modern equivalent asset. They outlined some of the problems involved in valuing assets where technology has changed significantly since the asset was purchased. They also outlined the following four areas that could change markedly with technological advancement:

(a) An asset's initial capital cost.
(b) An asset's operating costs.
(c) An asset's life.
(d) An asset's output.

Companies should consider all these areas if they decide to value computer software or hardware. Further comment on this subject appears in a research study, entitled 'The reliability of special current cost measurements', published in 1984, that Professor Bryan Carsberg undertook on behalf of the ICAEW.

Goodwill

7.39   Goodwill may be shown as an asset only if it was acquired for valuable consideration. [*Note 3 on the balance sheet formats*].

7.40   This means that companies cannot capitalise goodwill if, for example, it is internally generated. This accords with the requirement in SSAP 22 that companies or groups may recognise goodwill in their financial statements only if it has arisen from a purchase transaction.

7.41   The Act does not define goodwill. However, SSAP 22 defines it as the difference between the value of a business as a whole and the aggregate of the fair values of its separable net assets. [*SSAP 22 para 21*].

7.42   SSAP 22 is broadly consistent with the Act, but in some respects it takes a stronger line. For example, whereas the Act does not apply to goodwill that arises on consolidation, SSAP 22 deals with all purchased goodwill, including goodwill arising on consolidation. This particular example may change in the future, because it is likely that when the EC Seventh Directive is enacted in the UK (see Chapter 17 para 17.03), the treatment of consolidation goodwill that the Act requires will follow the treatment set out in SSAP 22.

7.43   SSAP 22 requires a company or a group to adopt one of the following two definite policies with regard to purchased goodwill:

(a) Purchased goodwill should be eliminated from the financial statements by immediate write-off against reserves (not as a charge in the profit and loss account).

(b) It should be carried as an intangible fixed asset in the balance sheet, and amortised to the profit and loss account over its useful economic life.

SSAP 22 prefers the approach in *(a)* above and this method is illustrated in Table 22.

7.44   The amount to be attributed to purchased goodwill should be the difference between the *fair value of the consideration given* for the business and the aggregate of the *fair values of the scparable net assets acquired*. [*SSAP 22 para 29*].

7.45   Where a company acquires an unincorporated business, it will account for the cost of the business it has acquired by attributing fair values to the separable net assets it has acquired. If the fair value of the consideration the company gave differs from the aggregate of the fair values of the separable net assets it acquired, the difference will be purchased goodwill. The company will identify separately this purchased goodwill in its accounting records. This purchased goodwill may be either positive or negative.

> **Table 22:** *Illustration of the treatment of goodwill. This example shows goodwill written off immediately against reserves which is the method preferred by SSAP 22.*

Extract from Reuters Holdings PLC Report and Accounts 31 December 1984.

Accounting policy

Goodwill   Purchased goodwill is written off against reserves in the year of acquisition.

Note

20 Capital and reserves

Group

	Called up share capital £000	Share premium account £000	Profit and loss account £000	Minority interest £000	Total £000
31 December 1983 (see note 1)	36,096	—	27,335	1,717	65,148
Shares issued during the year	3,331	57,387	—	—	60,718
Flotation costs	—	(9,588)	—	—	(9,588)
Retained for the year	—	—	32,757	897	33,654
Purchased goodwill written off	—	—	(2,464)	(52)	(2,516)
Increase in shareholders' equity arising on minority conversions (see note 22)	—	—	1,102	(562)	540
31 December 1984	39,427	47,799	58,730	2,000	147,956

Fair value of the consideration given

7.46   Where one company acquires another company, and it does not use merger accounting, it will include in its own balance sheet the shares in the acquired company at cost based on the fair value of the consideration it gave. [*SSAP 22 para 18*]. SSAP 22 defines the term 'fair value' as the amount for which an asset or a liability could be exchanged in an arm's length transaction. [*SSAP 22 para 25*]. However, SSAP 22 gives no guidance on how to ascertain the fair value of the consideration given. The ASC is currently developing guidance on this problem.

7.47   Where a company acquires another company for cash, the fair value of the consideration will be the cost to the acquiring company of the investment. However, the fair value of the consideration is more difficult to determine when the consideration includes an issue of shares.

7.48   Where the acquiring company is listed, and the acquisition is either a Class 1 or a Class 2 transaction, then the announcement given to The Stock Exchange's Company Announcement Office will include details of the aggregate value of the consideration, and it will explain how this is to be satisfied. The figure of consideration that is announced will normally be based on The Stock Exchange price of the shares on the day before the announcement. The figure of consideration that is announced would normally be taken to be the fair value of the consideration given for the acquisition.

7.49   If the acquisition is not a Class 1 or a Class 2 transaction, or if the acquiring company is unlisted, it may be difficult to ascertain the fair value of the consideration. In these circumstances, the fair value of the consideration would have to be based on a fair value of the shares acquired.

7.50   Where a company issues its own shares as part of the consideration for an acquisition, the listed price before the acquisition will invariably exceed the nominal value of the shares issued. Where Section 131 of the Act does not entitle the company to merger relief (see Chapter 18), Section 130 requires the premium on the shares issued to be transferred to a share premium account. Consequently, the value of the consideration has a direct bearing on the amount of the share premium account.

Fair value of separable net assets acquired

7.51   Where one company acquires another company, the separable net assets from the point of view of the acquiring company will be the *shares* in the acquired company, not the individual assets and liabilities of the acquired company. The fair value of the consideration given will normally equal the fair value of the shares acquired. Consequently, when one company acquires another company, purchased goodwill will normally not arise in the *holding company's* balance sheet.

7.52   Where the fair value of the shares acquired is not the same as the fair value of the acquired company's individual assets and liabilities, goodwill will arise on consolidation.

For example, Company H acquires a listed company, Company S, for £10 million, even though The Stock Exchange capitalisation of Company S is only £9 million and the value of its separable net assets is £8 million. The total of The Stock Exchange capitalisation is based on the number of shares multiplied by The Stock Exchange price. However, The Stock Exchange price is the price for only small parcels of shares. The market may put a different value on a controlling interest in the company. Consequently, the £10 million consideration is more likely to represent the fair value of the shares that the holding company has acquired. Therefore, purchased goodwill will not arise in the holding company's financial statements but, in this example, £2 million of goodwill will arise on consolidation.

Treatment in the holding company's financial statements

7.53   The investment in the acquired company should be recorded in the acquiring company's books at cost. In the example above, the investment would be recorded in the acquiring company's books of account at £10 million.

7.54   SSAP 22 does not require an adjustment to be made in the holding company's financial statements to the carrying value of the shares in the acquired company in respect of any consolidation goodwill written off either in the group accounts or in the subsidiary's or associate's financial statements. However, the holding company should write down the investment's carrying value to reflect any permanent diminution in value.

7.55   This accords with the legal requirements both for the purchased goodwill that companies carry, and for the purchased goodwill (other than consolidation goodwill) that groups carry. In particular, Schedule 4, paragraph 19(2) requires a company or a group to make provision for any permanent diminution in value of any fixed asset.

7.56   If, however, in the example in paragraph 7.52 above, the value of the investment in Company S (including the goodwill element) subsequently diminished permanently in value to (say) £9,200,000, then Company H should write down its investment in Company S to that figure in its holding company balance sheet.

7.57   Paragraph 66 of Schedule 4 exempts consolidation goodwill from the requirement in paragraph 19(2). Consequently, under the Act, provision does not have to be made for any permanent diminution in value of consolidation goodwill. In addition, a special category company (see Chapter 13) does not, under the Act, have to make provision for any permanent diminution in value of consolidation goodwill, because such a company is not subject to Schedule 4. However, because SSAP 22 applies to all companies, the Standard introduces a requirement similar to paragraph 19(2) in respect of consolidation goodwill and for special category companies.

7.58   Section 275 of the Act says that, unless a provision is one in respect of the diminution in value of a fixed asset that appears on a revaluation of, or consideration by the directors of the value of, all the company's fixed assets (other than goodwill), it must be treated as a realised loss. Consequently, unless a provision for a permanent diminution in value of purchased goodwill results from a revaluation of, or consideration by the directors of the value of, all the company's fixed assets (other than goodwill), it must be treated as a realised loss (see further Chapter 19 para 19.41). However, the immediate write-off of goodwill to reserves as recommended by SSAP 22 is not a provision, and so it need not be regarded as a realised loss. This is considered further in paragraphs 7.85 to 7.90 below.

Treatment in the group accounts

7.59   On consolidation, a group should attribute the cost of the investment to the acquired company's separable net assets. It should do this by stating them at their fair values. [*SSAP 22 para 19*]. Any difference between the total of these fair values and the investment's carrying value (that is, the fair value of the purchase consideration) represents purchased goodwill arising on consolidation. The group should then eliminate this goodwill from its accounts by either immediate write-off or amortisation. The amortisation method is illustrated in Table 23.

Table 23: *Example of an accounting policy where goodwill is amortised over its useful economic life.*

Extract from The British Petroleum Company p.l.c. Annual report & accounts 31 December 1984.

GOODWILL
Goodwill is the excess of purchase consideration over the fair value of net assets acquired. It is capitalised and amortised over its estimated useful economic life, limited to a maximum period of five years.

Reorganisation costs anticipated at the time of acquisition

7.60   When one company purchases another company, the acquiring company may foresee various reorganisation costs arising from the business combination. These reorganisation costs may be needed to combine the business of the acquired company into the existing group's management objectives. For example, reorganisation costs could include redundancy and closure costs arising from the acquiring company's decision to streamline the business of the acquired company.

7.61   When ascribing fair values to the separable net assets of the acquired company, the acquiring company should determine a fair value for the provisions needed for reorganisation costs. The acquiring company should also determine a fair value for provisions for other similar items that were taken into account when arriving at the purchase price of the acquired company.

7.62   These provisions will reduce the net fair value of the separable assets acquired, and so will increase the amount of goodwill, if the goodwill figure is positive.

7.63   Where provisions for anticipated losses and reorganisation costs are needed, they should be included in the consolidated balance sheet heading of 'Provisions'. The provisions may be incorporated into the books of the acquired company, or alternatively they may be dealt with as a consolidation adjustment.

Difference between goodwill and other intangible assets

7.64   SSAP 22 defines goodwill as the difference between the value of a business as a whole and the aggregate of the fair values of its separable net assets. Separable net assets include intangible assets. Companies will probably now try to identify intangible assets when they acquire a business so that the figure of goodwill that arises on consolidation is kept to a minimum. Intangible assets are concessions, patents, licences, trade marks and similar rights and assets. [*4 Sch formats; SSAP 22 para 18*]. Other examples include publishing titles, franchise rights and customer lists.

7.65   Where a company identifies intangible assets (excluding purchased goodwill—see para 7.66 below) on the acquisition of a business, it should incorporate them in its balance sheet at their fair value (see para 7.11). In subsequent years, companies may revalue these intangible assets to their current cost (see paras 7.29 to 7.33). Some companies may wish to have the option of revaluing as many of their intangible assets as possible (for example, in order to strengthen their balance sheets). Consequently, these companies should ensure that they identify all intangible assets when they acquire a business.

Revaluation of purchased goodwill

7.66   SSAP 22 says that a company or group should not revalue purchased goodwill. [*SSAP 22 para 34(a)*]. This accords with the legal requirements for companies and groups, because Schedule 4, paragraph 31(1) does not permit the revaluation of goodwill. The Standard effectively introduces a similar prohibition also for special category companies and special category groups, which Schedule 4 does not cover.

Acceptability of using both elimination methods

7.67   An individual company's circumstances may require it to adopt different policies in relation to the goodwill that arises on different acquisitions. For example, a company may generally follow the preferred policy of immediate write-off, but it may need to adopt the policy of amortising goodwill on an unusually large acquisition because of the effect that an immediate write-off would have on its reserves. This treatment is acceptable under SSAP 22, but the use of several different elimination methods will need to be clearly explained to avoid the financial statements not showing a true and fair view.

Existing goodwill

7.68   SSAP 22 became standard accounting practice in respect of financial statements relating to accounting periods beginning on or after 1 January 1985.

7.69   On the introduction of the Standard, a company or group should normally write off any existing positive goodwill it carries in its balance sheet direct against reserves. [*SSAP 22 para 36*]. Alternatively, if a company or group has previously carried goodwill in its balance sheet at unamortised cost, but now chooses to adopt the amortisation policy, then it should calculate what the result would have been had the amortisation policy been in effect when it purchased the goodwill. The company or group should then write off as a prior-year adjustment to reserves (to realised reserves, with a company) any amount that it would already have written off by the time the Standard came into effect. The company or group should amortise any remaining balance over the remaining useful economic life of the goodwill.

7.70   However, the Standard does include certain transitional provisions that apply principally to companies and groups that have accumulated a large balance of purchased goodwill.

7.71   Difficulties could arise for such companies and groups if they had to write all or part of this goodwill off to reserves immediately by way of a prior-year adjustment. Consequently, paragraph 37 of the Standard outlines transitional provisions that companies and groups can adopt as an alternative to the normal treatment of existing goodwill as described above.

7.72   Paragraph 37 states that a company or group may eliminate any positive goodwill it is carrying in its balance sheet at the time the Standard came into effect by amortising it prospectively over not more than its remaining useful economic life. 'Amortising it prospectively' means that the amortisation period begins when the Standard was introduced. Consequently, there is no need for a prior-year adjustment to reserves.

7.73   The transitional provisions also apply to a company or group that has adopted an amortisation policy as from a date later than the date on which it purchased the goodwill. Such a company or group may continue to amortise the balance of goodwill over not more than its remaining useful economic life. Where companies or groups adopt the transitional provisions, they need not adjust the last period's corresponding figures.

Treatment of negative goodwill

7.74   Companies and groups should credit negative goodwill direct to reserves. 'Negative goodwill' is the term used for any excess of the aggregate of the fair values of the separable net assets acquired over the fair value of the consideration given. Negative goodwill is the mirror image of positive goodwill. SSAP 22 does not require a company or group to set up a separate reserve for negative goodwill. Where a company or group does set up a separate reserve, an appropriate description in the financial statements would be 'Negative goodwill' or 'Capital reserve on consolidation'. This item should be included under 'Other reserves' in the balance sheet format.

Disclosure

7.75   The notes to the financial statements should explain the accounting policy the company or group follows in respect of goodwill. [*SSAP 22 para 39*].

7.76   An example of an accounting policy note that a company may disclose if it writes goodwill off immediately to reserves, and subsequently makes a transfer between unrealised and realised reserves (see para 7.86), is as follows:

> "Purchased goodwill arising on the acquisition (as opposed to merger) of a new subsidiary represents the excess of the fair value of the consideration given over the aggregate of the fair values of the separable net assets acquired. *(Negative goodwill represents the excess of the aggregate of the fair values of the separable net assets acquired over the fair value of the consideration given.)* The group eliminates purchased goodwill *(other than negative goodwill)* from the financial statements by immediate write-off against unrealised reserves other than the revaluation reserve. The group then transfers the amount written off from unrealised reserves to realised reserves by equal annual instalments over the purchased goodwill's estimated useful economic life. *(Negative goodwill is credited direct to unrealised reserves and an amount is then transferred from unrealised reserves to realised reserves in line with the depreciation or realisation of the original assets acquired in the business combination that gave rise to the negative goodwill.)*"

7.77   If a company adopts the amortisation method, the accounting policy note may retain the first two sentences from the example above and add the following:

> "The group eliminates purchased goodwill *(other than negative goodwill)* from the financial statements by amortisation through the profit and loss account. The group amortises such purchased goodwill by equal annual instalments over the purchased goodwill's estimated useful economic life."

7.78   Where a company or group has made any acquisitions during the year, it should show the amount of purchased goodwill, where this is material, separately for each acquisition. [*SSAP 22 para 40*].

7.79   Where a company or group selects the amortisation method, it should show purchased goodwill as a separate item under intangible fixed assets in the balance sheet until the time it is fully written off. [*SSAP 22 para 41*]. The disclosure requirement in paragraph 41 of SSAP 22 accords with the Schedule 4 formats, which require that a company or group should show purchased goodwill (to the extent that it has not been written off) separately under the heading of intangible fixed assets. For a group, purchased goodwill may include goodwill arising on consolidation. It may also include any goodwill that exists in a subsidiary's financial statements which arose when that subsidiary acquired another business.

7.80   Paragraph 41 of SSAP 22 requires a company or group also to show the movement on the goodwill account during the year. Paragraph 42 of Schedule 4 contains a similar requirement. A company or group should show the cost, the accumulated amortisation and the net book value of goodwill both at the beginning and at the end of the year.

7.81   In addition, a company or group must show in respect of goodwill:

(a) The effect that any acquisitions, any disposals and any transfers have had on cost during the year.

(b) The amount of goodwill amortised during the year.

(c) The amount of any adjustments to accumulated amortisation that have arisen from any disposals.

(d) The amount of any other adjustments to accumulated amortisation. [*4 Sch 42*].

7.82   Furthermore, paragraph 21(4) of Schedule 4 and paragraph 41 of SSAP 22 both require a company to disclose the period it has selected for amortising the goodwill relating to each of its major acquisitions. Paragraph 21(4) of Schedule 4 to the Act requires the company also to disclose its reasons for choosing that period. The requirement in SSAP 22 applies in respect of consolidation goodwill, and to special category companies. However, because paragraph 21(4) of Schedule 4 does not apply to special category companies, and is specifically excluded in respect of consolidation goodwill by paragraph 66, the *reason* for choosing a particular amortisation period does not have to be stated for consolidation goodwill, or by a special category company.

7.83   As noted in paragraph 7.94, the Standard permits a company or group to select different useful economic lives for the goodwill that arises on different acquisitions. Consequently, a company or group may need to disclose several amortisation periods, with each one relating to different elements of the goodwill total.

7.84   The following example shows how a group might comply with the disclosure requirements of both the Act and SSAP 22.

Balance sheet (extract)

	Note	1985 £000	1984 £000
Fixed assets			
Intangible assets			
Concessions and patents		5	5
Goodwill	10	93	81
		98	86

Note 10 — Goodwill

	£000
Cost at 1 January 1985	115
Elimination of fully amortised goodwill	(15)
Goodwill arising from acquisition during year	20
Cost at 31 December 1985	120

Accumulated amortisation at 1 January 1985	34
Charge to profit and loss account	8
Elimination of accumulated amortisation on fully amortised goodwill	(15)
Accumulated amortisation at 31 December 1985	27

Net book value at 31 December 1985	93

Net book value at 31 December 1984	81

(a) Goodwill of £100,000 arose from the acquisition of XYZ Ltd in 1981. The economic life of this goodwill has been estimated at 20 years, and the goodwill is being amortised over that period, commencing in 1981.

(b) Goodwill of £20,000 arose from the acquisition of three subsidiaries in 1985. This goodwill is being amortised over its estimated useful economic life of ten years, commencing in 1985.

(c) Goodwill of £15,000 arose from the acquisition of ABC Ltd in 1971. That goodwill was amortised over 15 years, and so has now reached the end of its useful economic life. Consequently, the cost and the accumulated amortisation have been eliminated from the financial statements.

Note: In this example, the figures in Note 10 have been arrived at by combining the three separate elements of the goodwill account as follows:

	(a) £000	(b) £000	(c) £000	Total £000
Cost at 1 January 1985	100	—	15	115
Elimination	—	—	(15)	(15)
Addition	—	20	—	20
Cost at 31 December 1985	100	20	—	120
Accumulated amortisation at 1 January 1985	20	—	14	34
Charge	5	2	1	8
Elimination	—	—	(15)	(15)
Accumulated amortisation at 31 December 1985	25	2	—	27
Net book value at 31 December 1985	75	18	—	93
Net book value at 31 December 1984	80	—	1	81

7.85   As mentioned in paragraph 7.43, paragraph 32 of SSAP 22 says that companies should normally eliminate purchased goodwill (other than negative goodwill) immediately on acquisition against reserves. Paragraph 2 of Appendix 2 to SSAP 22 discusses whether this policy when it is adopted by an individual company reduces *realised* reserves. That paragraph concludes that an immediate write-off of goodwill (excluding, therefore, consolidation goodwill) does *not* constitute an immediate reduction of realised reserves (unless the goodwill is considered to have suffered a permanent diminution in value). However, even where goodwill is not immediately written off against realised reserves, the elimination of purchased goodwill by an individual company must ultimately result in a realised loss. This eventual realised loss arises because purchased goodwill has a limited useful life.

7.86   The effect of this paragraph is to give a choice of two options to an individual company that writes goodwill off immediately to reserves. The first option is that the company may write the goodwill off immediately to realised reserves. The second option is that the company may write the goodwill off immediately to a suitable unrealised reserve, and then transfer the amount written off from unrealised reserves to realised reserves on a systematic basis over the useful economic life of the goodwill. The second option will have the same effect ultimately on distributable reserves as the amortisation method that paragraph 34 of SSAP 22 permits.

7.87   A company may wish to use the second option above where it has insufficient realised reserves to cover the immediate write-off of the purchase cost of the goodwill.

7.88   In practice, the most common unrealised reserve is the revaluation reserve that arises when a company revalues some or all of its fixed assets. However, paragraph 34(3) of Schedule 4 limits the uses that a company may make of the revaluation reserve. This paragraph states:

   "The revaluation reserve shall be reduced to the extent that the amounts standing to the credit of the reserve are in the opinion of the directors of the company no longer necessary for the purpose of the accounting policies adopted by the company; but an amount may only be transferred from the reserve to the profit and loss account if either:

   (a) the amount in question was previously charged to that account; or

   (b) it represents realised profit."

7.89   Consequently, it may be inappropriate for a company to charge the write-off of goodwill against the revaluation reserve, because it appears that the revaluation reserve can be reduced only in one of the ways outlined above. Also, if the write-off was made to this reserve, the company would not be able to transfer the goodwill subsequently to realised reserves in line with Appendix 2 of SSAP 22. This is because the amount in question was not previously charged to the profit and loss account, and it does not represent a realised profit. However, there is still some uncertainty as to whether this restriction applies also to groups and, consequently, to goodwill arising on consolidation. The possibility of writing goodwill off against the revaluation reserve is discussed further in Chapter 5, paragraphs 5.51 to 5.53.

7.90   Where negative goodwill arises in the financial statements of an individual company, it should credit it initially to an unrealised reserve. [*SSAP 22, Appendix 2 para 3*]. The company may then transfer the negative goodwill from that unrealised reserve to realised reserves. This transfer should be in line with the depreciation or the realisation of the assets acquired in the business combination that gave rise to the goodwill in question. However, the distinction between realised and unrealised reserves is not relevant for negative consolidation goodwill. The reason for this is that it is individual companies, not groups, that make distributions, and so the crediting of negative consolidation goodwill to reserves has no effect on the distributable profits of an individual company.

Useful economic life

7.91 The Act makes no attempt to define the 'useful economic life' of goodwill. However, guidance on how to determine the useful economic life of purchased goodwill is given in Appendix 1 of SSAP 22.

7.92 Although SSAP 22 does not specify either a minimum or a maximum amortisation period, Appendix 1 says that the useful economic life of purchased goodwill is the period over which benefits may reasonably be expected to accrue from that goodwill. In the period following the acquisition, the value of the purchased goodwill is considered to diminish, although it may be replaced by non-purchased goodwill. The total goodwill (both purchased and non-purchased) may either remain constant or increase or decrease. However, when a company or group is determining the useful economic life of purchased goodwill, it should not take into account any actions or expenditure or other circumstances after the date of the acquisition, because these subsequent events create non-purchased goodwill. The purchased goodwill whose useful life is being determined is only that which existed and was recognised at the time of the acquisition.

7.93 Several factors may be relevant in determining the useful economic life of purchased goodwill, and a company or group should assess these factors at the time it makes the acquisition. They include the following:

(a) Expected changes in products, markets or technology.
(b) The expected period of future service of certain employees.
(c) Expected future demand, competition or other economic factors that may affect current advantages.

7.94 It is not possible to specify general rules regarding the useful economic life over which purchased goodwill should be written off. The ASC considers that it is inappropriate to indicate a maximum number of years for the amortisation period. Furthermore, a company or group may select different useful economic lives for the goodwill that arises on its different acquisitions.

Tangible assets

7.95 The Act sets out in the formats the following four categories of tangible assets:

(a) Land and buildings.
(b) Plant and machinery.
(c) Fixtures, fittings, tools and equipment.
(d) Payments on account and assets in course of construction.

7.96   The Act also requires that land and buildings be split between freehold, long leasehold and short leasehold. [*4 Sch 44*]. For this purpose, a lease includes an agreement for a lease. It will be a long lease if it still has 50 years or more to run at the end of the financial year in question. Otherwise, it will be a short lease. [*4 Sch 83*].

7.97   Many companies face practical problems when categorising their tangible assets into these four fairly restrictive headings. In particular, some companies find it difficult to decide whether certain assets should be described as 'Plant and machinery' or 'Fixtures, fittings, tools and equipment'. Some companies also have difficulty in deciding the category in which to include motor vehicles.

7.98   In practice, companies categorise their assets according to the nature of their particular business. As a general rule, companies treat major manufacturing assets (including motor vehicles involved in the manufacturing process—for example, fork-lift trucks and cranes) as 'Plant and machinery'. They include other assets not involved in the manufacturing process in 'Fixtures, fittings, tools and equipment'. Companies that prepare manufacturing accounts for management accounts purposes will probably already have a ready analysis of tangible fixed assets between 'Plant and machinery' and 'Fixtures, fittings, tools and equipment'. The assets on which a company charges depreciation in the manufacturing account will normally be 'Plant and machinery'.

7.99   Because the Act allows a company to show any item in greater detail than the format it adopts requires, a company may, for example, disclose the amount for motor vehicles as a subdivision of either 'Plant and machinery' or 'Fixtures, fittings, tools and equipment'. [*4 Sch 3(1)*]. Also, where an asset does not fall under any of the headings given in the formats, paragraph 3(2) of Schedule 4 allows a company to include the amount of it under a separate heading (for example, see Table 24). Consequently, motor vehicles could be included in the balance sheet as a separate item.

Payments on account and assets in course of construction

7.100 'Payments on account' represent payments a company makes in respect of tangible assets that it has not yet taken delivery of. 'Assets in course of construction' will represent the cost of purchasing and installing fixed assets ahead of their productive use. The timing of the transfer of an asset from this category to the appropriate heading will vary. A company will not normally charge depreciation on an asset that is in the course of construction until it is completed and it is transferred to an asset heading that is appropriate (see table 24).

Table 24: Example of a company that has used additional headings to categorise its fixed assets.

Extract from Fleet Holdings P.L.C. Report & Accounts 30 June 1984.

13. Tangible fixed assets	The Group						
	Land and Buildings		Plant and equip-	Motor		Finance	
	Freehold £000	Short leases £000	ment £000	vehicles £000	Films £000	leases £000	Total £000
Balance at 1 July 1983:							
At Valuation	9,178	—	—	—	—	—	9,178
At Cost	8,041	1,987	36,757	2,276	4,114	938	54,113
Foreign exchange translation differences	—	3	30	1	—	—	34
Reallocation	35	—	(35)	—	—	—	—
Additions	221	237	2,409	291	3,900	—	7,058
Disposals	(360)	—	(785)	(1,295)	—	—	(2,440)
At 30 June 1984	17,115	2,227	38,376	1,273	8,014	938	67,943
Accumulated depreciation:							
Balance brought forward at 1 July 1983	—	381	12,792	1,415	10	94	14,692
Foreign exchange translation differences	—	3	18	1	—	—	22
Provision for the year	—	87	1,880	409	502	94	2,972
Disposals	—	—	(664)	(1,131)	—	—	(1,795)
At 30 June 1984	—	471	14,026	694	512	188	15,891
Net book value at 30 June 1984	17,115	1,756	24,350	579	7,502	750	52,052
Net book value at 30 June 1983	*17,219*	*1,606*	*23,965*	*861*	*4,104*	*844*	*48,599*

Included in the cost of plant and equipment is £9,251,000 *(1983—£9,743,000)* (of which £356,000 *(1983—£557,000)* was incurred in the year) representing assets which have not yet been brought into use and which have not been depreciated. In the opinion of the directors there has been no diminution in the value of these assets since acquisition. The directors anticipate that whilst these assets will be brought into use in due course some further delay is expected to take place before this occurs in respect of assets with a cost of £9,070,000 *(1983—£9,080,000)*. Assets with a cost of £848,000 *(1983—£3,946,000)* previously unused have been brought on line in the year.

Assets costing £5,249,000 *(1983—£4,923,000)* have been fully depreciated and are still in use.

Depreciation of tangible assets

7.101   A company will normally include those tangible fixed assets that have a limited useful economic life in its balance sheet at their purchase price or production cost less a provision for depreciation. [*4 Sch 17,18*]. If a company adopts the alternative accounting rules, these assets may be shown in the balance sheet at market value or current cost. [*4 Sch 31(2)*].

7.102   The calculation of depreciation and the rules that relate to depreciation that are contained both within the Act and in SSAP 12 are discussed in more detail in Chapter 4, paragraphs 4.04 to 4.17 and Chapter 5, paragraphs 5.64 to 5.83.

7.103 The provision for depreciation will be based on the difference between cost (or valuation) and residual value. In an extreme situation, if the residual value is high, it is possible that very little depreciation will be required. If a company fails to provide a small amount of depreciation because it is not material, the company can nevertheless regard itself as complying in principle with both the Act and SSAP 12 on accounting for depreciation.

7.104 This treatment is echoed in ED 37, which the ASC issued in March 1985, which deals with the proposed revision of SSAP 12. ED 37 includes a provision that it may not be appropriate for a company to charge depreciation in respect of what would normally be a depreciable asset. But this would apply only where an asset is maintained to such a standard that either of the following applies:

(a) The estimated residual value is either equal to or greater than its net book amount.

(b) Its estimated useful economic life is either infinite or of such length that any depreciation charge would be insignificant.

7.105 In assessing whether any depreciation should be charged, the ASC believes that regard should be had not only to the physical condition of the asset, but also to the risk of obsolescence. Also, the asset should be maintained on a regular basis, and this cost should be charged in the profit and loss account. An example of a company that has adopted this type of policy is given in Table 25 below and another example is given in Table 4 on page 41.

Table 25: *Example of a company whose directors do not depreciate properties because the resultant depreciation charge would be immaterial.*

Extract from Bass PLC Annual Review 30 September 1984.

Accounting policy extract

d) Freehold properties comprising hotels and United Kingdom public houses are maintained, as a matter of company policy, by a programme of repair and refurbishment such that the residual values of these properties taken as a whole are at least equal to their book values. Having regard to this, it is the opinion of the directors that depreciation of any such property as required by the Companies Act 1981 and standard accounting practice would not be material.

7.106 The exposure draft also says that the depreciation methods used should be those that are the most appropriate having regard to the types of assets and their uses in the business. Consequently, there is a range of acceptable depreciation methods. Although the straight-line method is the simplest one to apply, it may not always be the most suitable.

7.107 In addition, the exposure draft defines an asset's useful economic life as the period over which the *present* owner will derive economic benefits from using it. Any useful economic life remaining at the end of the present owner's period of ownership should be taken into account in determining the residual value. The reason for this is that the residual value to be used in calculating depreciation should be the asset's estimated value at the end of this period. However, the estimated residual value should exclude the effects of inflation.

7.108 Neither the Act nor SSAP 12 specifically covers those matters dealt with in the exposure draft that are outlined above. At present, therefore, companies do not have to follow these proposals, but they may choose to do so.

7.109 Where a company does not wish to depreciate its assets because it considers the charge for depreciation would not be material, it should first consider the following two matters:

(a) Although a depreciation charge may not be material in any one year, the cumulative depreciation can, within a few years, have a material effect on the financial statements. Consequently, materiality will need to be judged in connection with other key items (for example, retained profits and the book values of the relevant assets).

(b) Although a depreciation charge may not be significant in a particular year, a similar charge may have a significant effect on the financial statements of a following year. This can occur, for example, where a company's profit decreases because its business has contracted.

Government grants

7.110 SSAP 4 says that grants relating to fixed assets should be credited to revenue over the asset's expected useful life. This may be achieved by either of the following two means:

(a) Reducing the fixed asset's cost of acquisition by the amount of the grant (for example, see Table 21).

(b) Treating the amount of the grant as a deferred credit, and transferring a proportion of this to revenue annually.

7.111 Counsel has advised that accounting for Government grants by deduction from the cost of the assets to which the grants relate (method *(a)* above) involves a departure from paragraph 17 of Schedule 4 (which requires fixed assets to be shown at their purchase price or production cost). The purchase price can only mean the sum paid to the supplier. However, unless the grant is in effect returnable, method *(a)* would not involve the offset of a liability against an asset contrary to paragraph 5 of Schedule 4.

7.112   If companies choose to account for Government grants by deducting them from the cost of the assets, they can do so only by invoking the 'true and fair' override that is available under Section 228 of the Act. However, if a company uses the true and fair override, then it must disclose the particulars of, the reasons for, and the effect of, the departure. The particulars and reasons could be disclosed in the company's accounting policy for Government grants, and the effect could be disclosed as part of the fixed asset note.

7.113   In practice, however, many companies have merely deducted the grant without regarding that treatment as a departure from the requirements of the Act. Therefore, they have not given the particulars of, the reasons for, and the effect of, the departure. The alternative method in *(b)* above of accounting for grants using deferred credits is referred to in Chapter 9, paragraph 9.22.

Investment properties

7.114   The Act does not use the term 'investment properties'. However, SSAP 19 defines it as "an interest in land and/or buildings:

   (a) in respect of which construction work and development have been completed; and

   (b) which is held for its investment potential any rental income being negotiated at arms length."
   [*SSAP 19 para 7*].

7.115   Moreover, the Standard gives the following two examples of properties that should not be treated as investment properties:

   (a) A property that is owned and occupied by a company for its own purposes.

   (b) A property that is let to, and occupied by, another group company.
   [*SSAP 19 para 8*].

7.116   Where a property is held for its investment potential, but it is either partly occupied by the company or partly let to and occupied by another group company, it would normally be appropriate to apportion the property between an 'investment' element and a 'non-investment' element. This apportionment could, for example, be done on the basis of arm's length rentals. However, before a company apportions properties in this way, it should consider materiality. For example, if a company has a number of investment properties and one small 'split' property, all the properties could be treated as investment properties.

7.117   Investment properties (excluding leases with less than 20 years to run) should not normally be depreciated. This applies even though they have a limited useful economic life and may have a residual value less than their book amount. [*SSAP 19 para 10*].

7.118 The Standard requires also that investment properties should be included in the balance sheet at their open market value. [*SSAP 19 para 11*]. Therefore, the application of SSAP 19 will be a departure from the depreciation rules in the Act. Such a departure is, however, permitted in order for the financial statements to give a true and fair view. [*Sec 228*]. This section, in turn, requires the financial statements to show, in a note, particulars of the departure, the reasons for it, and its effect. However, if a company is to show the *effect* of *not* depreciating investment properties, it must, by implication, calculate and disclose depreciation.

7.119 There may, however, be circumstances in which the amount of depreciation cannot be identified or quantified. With this in mind, the accountancy bodies discussed with the DTI the potential conflict between SSAP 19 and the Act that arose when this provision was originally brought into company law by the 1981 Act. Issue No. 20 of the APC Bulletin 'True and Fair' stated:

> "The Department of Trade has reviewed the text of the following note and has indicated that it meets the requirements of [*Section 228 of the Act*] where SSAP 19 is applied:
>
> 'Investment Properties
>
> In accordance with SSAP 19, (i) investment properties are revalued annually and the aggregate surplus or deficit is transferred to a revaluation reserve, and (ii) no depreciation or amortisation is provided in respect of freehold investment properties and leasehold investment properties with over 20 years to run. The Directors consider that this accounting policy results in the accounts giving a true and fair view. Depreciation or amortisation is only one of many factors reflected in the annual valuation and the amount which might otherwise have been shown cannot be separately identified or quantified.' "

Accordingly, where this note is included, it will not be necessary for the financial statements to show the effect of not providing for depreciation or amortisation.

7.120 The Standard does not require the valuation of investment properties to be made by qualified or independent valuers. But it does call for the disclosure of the names or qualifications of the valuers, the bases they used, and a statement of whether the person who made the valuation is an employee or officer of the company. [*SSAP 19 para 12*].

7.121 However, where investment properties represent a substantial proportion of the total assets of a *major* company (for example, a listed company), the valuation should normally be carried out:

(a) Annually by persons holding a recognised professional qualification and having recent post-qualification experience in the location and with the category of properties concerned.

(b) At least every five years by an external valuer.
[*SSAP 19 para 6*].

7.122   The Standard requires companies to display prominently in their financial statements both the carrying value of investment properties and
the investment revaluation reserve. [*SSAP 19 para 15*]. An example of
how a company discloses its investment properties is shown in Table 26.

Table 26: Illustration of the disclosure of investment properties.

Extract from Rosehaugh PLC Report & Accounts 30 June 1984.

Accounting policy

The company's accounting policy is reproduced in Table 2 on page 25.

Notes

11.   Fixed assets
(a) The movements in the year were as follows:

	Total £'000	Investment Properties £'000	Development properties held for investment £'000	Office equipment vehicles & furniture £'000	Plant & equipment leased to customers £'000
Cost or valuation					
Beginning of year	19,894	7,979	1,254	341	10,320
Additions	1,221	—	26	221	974
Disposals	(1,101)	(139)	—	(70)	(892)
Revaluations	49	49	—	—	—
End of year	20,063	7,889	1,280	492	10,402
Depreciation and amounts written off					
Beginning of year	3,444	—	—	89	3,355
Charge	2,301	—	—	79	2,222
Disposals	(820)	—	—	(26)	(794)
End of year	4,925	—	—	142	4,783
Net book value Beginning of year	16,450	7,979	1,254	252	6,965
Net book value End of year	15,138	7,889	1,280	350	5,619

(b) Investment properties

The investment properties, all of which are long leasehold, are stated in the
balance sheet at their aggregate open market value based on valuations carried
out at 30th June, 1984 by independent professional surveyors and valuers,
Messrs. Clive Lewis & Partners and Messrs. Weatherall Hollis & Gale. These
valuations gave rise to a net revaluation surplus of £49,000 which has been
credited to the revaluation reserve (see note 19). The aggregate surplus at 30th

June, 1984 of the value at which the investment properties are stated in the balance sheet over their aggregate cost to the Group is £876,000 (1983 – £827,000).

(c) Development properties held for investment

Development properties held for investment are stated in the balance sheet at cost.

19. **Reserves**

The movements in reserves during the year were as follows:

(a) Group	Total £'000	Share premium £'000	Revaluation reserve £'000	Retained profits £'000
Beginning of year	10,834	630	827	9,377
Revaluation surplus on investment properties (see note 11(b))	49	—	49	—
Retained profit for year	657	—	—	657
End of year	11,540	630	876	10,034

7.123 The treatment of the revaluation deficits or surpluses that may arise on the revaluation of investment properties are discussed in Chapter 5, paragraphs 5.21 and 5.22.

7.124 A further problem that arises with investment properties is whether they should be treated as tangible fixed assets or as fixed asset investments. Neither the Act nor SSAP 19 gives any clear guidance on this ques-industry and practical problems of lease accounting, are explained in detail in various other books.

Leased assets

7.125 Although the Act contains no specific requirement for it, SSAP 21 requires that, where a company finances a significant amount of its capital investment through leasing, its financial statements should properly reflect the full impact of its leasing transactions. SSAP 21 became operative in respect of financial statements relating to accounting periods beginning on or after 1 July 1984. Some parts of the Standard relating to lessees and hirers, however, do not become mandatory until accounting periods that begin on or after 1 July 1987. The Standard details the accounting treatment that both lessors and lessees should adopt.

7.126 A lease is defined in SSAP 21 as a contract between a lessor and a lessee for the hire of a specific asset. The lessor retains ownership of the asset, but he conveys to the lessee the right to use the asset in return for paying specific rentals. In addition, the definition of a lease in the Standard also includes other arrangements, not described as leases, in which some party retains ownership, but conveys to another party the right to use the asset for an agreed period of time in return for specific rentals. For example, a 'bare boat charter' (that is, a charter of a boat without a crew) will normally have all the characteristics of a lease, and it should be accounted for as such.

7.127 The scope of SSAP 21 does not include either lease contracts concerning rights to explore or exploit natural resources or licensing agreements (for example, agreements to lease motion pictures, video recordings, manuscripts, plays, patents and copyrights).

7.128 Also, as with all Accounting Standards, the provisions of the Standard need not be applied where such transactions are immaterial to the financial statements. For example, a lessee need not capitalise his finance leases if doing so would have an immaterial effect on his financial statements. Materiality within this context will need to be viewed in the terms of the possible effects on the lessee's total fixed assets, total borrowings and obligations, gearing ratio and profit and loss account.

7.129 The accounting treatment that a company adopts for a leased asset (whether the company is a lessor or a lessee) will depend on whether the lease is a finance lease or an operating lease.

7.130 The Standard defines a finance lease as a lease that transfers to the lessee substantially all the risks and rewards of owning an asset. All other leases are classified as operating leases.

7.131 Because the subject of lease accounting is highly complex, the rest of this section looks only at the disclosure that SSAP 21 and the Act require in company financial statements of both lessees and lessors. The implications of SSAP 21, together with the current practices in the leasing industry and practical problems of lease accounting, are explained in detail in various other books.

Treatment and disclosure of finance leases by lessees

7.132 The Standard requires that a finance lease (including a hire purchase contract that is of a financing nature) should be recorded in a lessee's balance sheet both as an asset and as an obligation to pay future rentals. At the inception of the lease, the sum to be recorded both as an asset and as a liability should be the present value of the minimum lease payments, derived by discounting them at the interest rate implicit in the lease. [*SSAP 21 para 32*].

7.133 An asset leased under a finance lease should be depreciated over the shorter of the lease term and its useful life. With a hire purchase contract that has the characteristics of a finance lease, the asset should be depreciated over its useful life. [*SSAP 21 para 36*].

7.134 Rentals payable should be apportioned between the finance charge and a reduction of the outstanding obligation for future amounts payable. The total finance charge under a finance lease should be allocated to accounting periods during the lease term, so as to produce either a constant periodic rate of charge on the remaining balance of the obligation for each accounting period or a reasonable approximation to it. [*SSAP 21 para 35*].

7.135 In respect of finance leases (including hire purchase contracts that have the same characteristics as finance leases), SSAP 21 requires the following information to be disclosed in the lessee's financial statements:

(a) The gross amount, the related accumulated depreciation and the total depreciation allocated for the period, analysed by each major class of asset capitalised under finance leases. [*SSAP 21 para 49*].

Alternatively, this information may be included within the totals disclosed by each major class of asset for owned assets. However, where this alternative is adopted, the total of the net amount of assets held under finance leases, and the total amount of depreciation allocated for the period in respect of finance leases, need to be disclosed separately. [*SSAP 21 para 50*].

(b) The liability for net obligations under finance leases (net of finance charges allocated to future periods), shown separately from other liabilities. This liability should be disclosed either on the face of the balance sheet or in the notes to the financial statements. [*SSAP 21 para 51*].

(c) The liability for net obligations under finance leases, analysed between amounts payable in the next year, amounts payable in the second to fifth years inclusive from the balance sheet date, and the aggregate amounts payable after the fifth year. [*SSAP 21 para 52*].

Where the lessee discloses the analysis of obligations under finance leases separately, he may, as an alternative to analysing the net obligations, analyse the gross obligations, and show future finance charges as a separate deduction from the total. [*SSAP 21 para 52*]. Companies that are either listed on The Stock Exchange or traded on the USM also have to comply with the disclosure requirements that are outlined in Chapter 9, paragraph 9.05.

(d) The aggregate finance charge allocated to the period. [*SSAP 21 para 53*].

(e) The commitments under finance leases existing at the year end that have been entered into, but whose inception occurs after the year end. [*SSAP 21 para 54*]. (This requirement is analogous to the legal requirements in Schedule 4, paragraph 50(3) in respect of capital commitments for fixed assets (see Chapter 9 para 9.61).)

These disclosure requirements are illustrated in Table 27.

Table 27: *Illustration of the disclosure of finance leases in a lessee's financial statements in accordance with SSAP 21.*

Extract from The Caledonian Aviation Group plc Report and Accounts 31 October 1984.

Accounting policy extract

(b) Accounting for Tangible Fixed Assets

Expenditure on tangible fixed assets, including those subject to hire purchase agreements, is capitalised.

Tangible fixed assets operated under the terms of finance leases are also capitalised at a value equal to the cost incurred by the lessor in acquiring the relevant assets and depreciated in the same manner as owned assets. Leases are regarded as finance leases where their terms transfer to the lessee substantially all the benefits and burdens of ownership other than the right to title. The capital element of future lease payments is included under loans and term finance.

Depreciation and amortisation of tangible fixed assets is calculated to write off the cost, less any residual value, commencing in the year of purchase, by equal annual instalments as follows:

Aircraft fleet and support equipment
   Remaining estimated commercial lives, which vary between 2 and 17 years.

Freehold hotels and related equipment
   Spanish hotel buildings 33 years.
   United Kingdom hotel buildings – see below.
   Related equipment between 3 and 12 years.

Other land and buildings
   Land is not depreciated.
   Freehold buildings 50 years.
   Lesser of unexpired term of lease of expected life of leasehold buildings and fittings.

Other plant and fixtures
   Between 3 and 13 years.

Notes

3. Operating Profit	1984 £'000	1983 £'000
Operating profit is arrived at		
(a) after crediting –		
Transfers to intangible fixed assets	3,234	120
Selective financial assistance	127	331
(b) after charging –		
Depreciation and amortisation of tangible fixed assets	24,483	19,120
Amortisation of intangible fixed assets	1,039	933
Hire of aircraft and equipment	6,916	6,900
Directors' emoluments (note 4)	344	278
Auditors' fees and expenses	272	210

Table 27 continued

9. Tangible Fixed Assets (*extract*)
(a) The tangible fixed assets of the Group comprise:

	Aircraft Fleet Owned £'000	Aircraft Fleet Leased £'000
Cost or valuation at 1st November, 1983	88,511	109,441
Foreign exchange adjustments	3,458	12,625
Acquisition of subsidiaries	—	—
Additions	69,529	10,792
Disposals	(5,659)	—
Transfers	(412)	412
Transfers to Stocks	(586)	—
Revaluation adjustment	(580)	—
Cost or valuation at 31st October, 1984	154,261	133,270
Depreciation at 1st November, 1983	15,399	17,900
Foreign exchange adjustments	—	—
Acquisition of subsidiaries	—	—
Charge for the year	9,012	7,364
Disposals	(4,941)	—
Transfers	(98)	98
Transfers to Stocks	(261)	—
Revaluation adjustment	(1,479)	—
Depreciation at 31st October, 1984	17,632	25,362
Net book value at 31st October, 1984	**136,629**	**107,908**
Net book value at 31st October, 1983	73,112	91,541

(b) Cost or valuation at 31st October, 1984 comprises:

Valuations 1980	—	—
1982	—	—
1983	52,480	—
1984	1,043	—
Cost	100,738	133,270
	154,261	133,270

Table 27 continued

Extract from The Caledonian Aviation Group plc Report and Accounts 31 October 1984.

17. Loans and Term Finance

		1984 Group £'000	1984 Company £'000	1983 Group £'000	1983 Company £'000
Loan Capital	– Unsecured Loan Stock 1990/95	655	655	655	655
Secured Bank Loans					
	– Sterling	58,467	3,717	46,762	4,130
	– U.S. Dollars	80,439	—	76,620	—
	– Pesetas	15	—	38	—
Unsecured Bank Loans					
	Sterling	7,000	7,000	—	—
	– U.S. Dollars	4,279	—	446	—
Term Finance	– Wholly repayable within five years:				
	Hire Purchase Agreements				
	– Sterling	1,877	—	—	—
	– U.S. Dollars	17,509	—	—	—
	Mortgage Loan – Sterling	420	—	540	—
	Lease Finance – Sterling	5,760	—	3,956	—
	– Not wholly repayable within five years:				
	Hire Purchase Agreements				
	– Sterling	41,820	—	46,210	—
	– U.S. Dollars	—	—	16,825	—
	Mortgage Loan				
	– Sterling	64,627	—	5,094	—
	– U.S. Dollars	5,376	—	—	—
	Lease Finance – Sterling	59,556	—	67,668	—
		347,800	11,372	264,814	4,785
Deposits		(70,819)	—	(70,181)	—
		276,981	11,372	194,633	4,785

The secured bank loans and term finance are generally secured by fixed charges on the tangible fixed assets being financed or by floating charge over all assets. The deposits are pledged as security for, and their levels are geared to, the repayment of the amounts outstanding to the providers of lease finance. The term finance is at various interest rates, with the highest being 14.875%.

Group loans and the capital element of lease finance are repayable as follows:	1984 £'000	1984 £'000	1983 £'000	1983 £'000
Within one year		42,177		34,336
1 – 2 years	37,362		27,254	
2 – 3 years	32,114		33,818	
3 – 4 years	83,660		29,673	
4 – 5 years	29,989		23,634	
Over 5 years	51,679		45,918	
		234,804		160,297
		276,981		194,633

Table 27 continued

22, Future Commitments	1984		1983	
	Group £'000	Company £'000	Group £'000	Company £'000
Capital				
At 31st October there were future commitments for which contracts had been placed amounting to	183,350	—	216,550	—
and amounts authorised by the directors but not contracted for of	4,235	—	6,636	—

Revenue The Group has future·revenue commitments in the ordinary course of business for the payment of operating lease rentals as follows:	1984 £'000	1983 £'000
Within one year	4,125	4,323
1 – 2 years	2,675	2,797
2 – 3 years	1,105	1,803
3 – 4 years	756	57
4 – 5 years	229	31
Over 5 years	39	91
	8,929	9,102

7.136 It is evident from the above that the lessee has several choices regarding the way he can disclose both his obligations under finance leases and assets he holds under finance leases. For example, the lessee can show his obligations under finance leases as a separate item on the balance sheet under the heading of 'Creditors'. Alternatively, he can combine that item within the total of another liability under the same heading, and analyse it in the notes to the financial statements. Similarly, the lessee can show assets he holds under finance leases as fixed assets separately on the balance sheet under the heading 'Tangible assets'. Alternatively, he can combine those assets with other owned tangible assets on the face of the balance sheet, and disclose the appropriate information in the notes to the financial statements. All these options are available to the lessee, and they are also permitted under the Act's balance sheet formats. The lessee's choice of methods will, normally, depend on the materiality of the amounts concerned.

7.137 The Standard does not address the question of whether assets held under finance leases should be disclosed as tangible fixed assets or as intangible fixed assets. However, the fact that the Standard allows the lessee to combine such assets with owned assets gives the impression that the lessee should treat such assets as tangible fixed assets. It may seem strange that the Standard treats assets held under finance leases as tangible fixed assets when in fact it argues that it is the rights in the assets, and not the assets themselves, that are capitalised. However, there is very little difference in substance between assets held under finance leases and owned assets. Also, because the disclosure requirements leave the reader in no doubt as to the true nature of leased assets, there is little to be gained by describing such assets as intangibles. The Standard, therefore, takes a commonsense view, and it does not take too literal an interpretation of the word 'tangible'.

Treatment and disclosure of operating leases by lessees

7.138   Operating leases should not be capitalised, and the lease rentals should be charged on a straight-line basis over the lease term. Unless another systematic and rational basis is more appropriate, this applies even if the payments are not made on such a basis. [*SSAP 21 para 43*].

7.139   In respect of operating leases (including hire purchase contracts that have the same characteristics as operating leases), SSAP 21 requires the following information to be disclosed:

(a) The total of operating lease rentals charged as an expense in the profit and loss account, and analysed between amounts payable in respect of the hire of plant and machinery and in respect of other operating leases. [*SSAP 21 para 55*].

(b) The payments that the lessee is committed to make during the next year, analysed between those in which the commitment expires within that year, those in which the commitment expires within the second to fifth years inclusive, and those in which the commitment expires more than five years after the balance sheet date. This analysis should show the commitments in respect of land and buildings separately from those of other operating leases. [*SSAP 21 para 56*].

7.140   The disclosure requirements for operating leases may present particular practical problems. Under the disclosure requirements, the payments that the lessee is committed to make during the next year are analysed according to the time when the commitment expires. Two situations that have to be provided for are a rental pause during the next year (where no rentals are due), and a significant rent review that is expected during the period. In either of these situations, and in order to avoid misleading the uses of the financial statements, the basic disclosure will need to be supplemented with an explanation.

Additional disclosure required in lessees' financial statements

7.141   In respect of both finance leases and operating leases, the accounting policies that the lessee has adopted must be disclosed. [*SSAP 21 para 57*].

7.142   An example of an accounting policy that a company may adopt is as follows:

"Where assets are financed by leasing agreements that give rights approximating to ownership ('finance leases'), the assets are treated as if they had been purchased outright. The amount capitalised is the present value of the minimum lease payments payable during the lease term. The corresponding leasing commitments are shown as obligations to the lessor.

Depreciation on the relevant assets is charged to the profit and loss account on a straight-line basis to write the assets off over their expected useful lives.

Lease payments are treated as consisting of capital and interest elements, and the interest is charged to the profit and loss account using the annuity method.

All other leases are 'operating leases', and the annual rentals are charged to the profit and loss account on a straight-line basis over the lease term.''

7.143 In addition to the Standard's disclosure requirements, the Guidance Notes to the Standard indicate that other details about a company's leases may need to be disclosed in order to show a true and fair view of the company's state of affairs. These include, for example, contingent rentals, profit participation arrangements, significant restrictions on future borrowing or leasing, and contingent liabilities. The minimum material and relevant information the lessee needs to disclose within this context will depend on whether a user's appreciation of the company's state of affairs would be affected if he was aware of that information. The criteria to be applied to that information are no different to those to be applied to any other information about the company's financial affairs.

7.144 Where a lessee sub-leases assets to a third party, he will also need to consider the disclosure requirements appropriate to lessors.

Treatment and disclosure of finance leases by lessors

7.145 The amount due from the lessee under a finance lease should be recorded in the lessor's balance sheet as a debtor at the amount of the net investment in the lease, after making provisions for items such as bad and doubtful rentals receivable. [*SSAP 21 para 38*].

7.146 The lessor should normally allocate his total gross earnings under a finance lease to accounting periods to give a constant periodic rate of return on his net cash investment in the lease (after taking account of all cash flows including tax). In arriving at the constant periodic rate of return, the lessor may make a reasonable approximation. [*SSAP 21 para 39*]. A finance company will normally allocate gross earnings from a hire purchase contract to give a constant periodic rate of return on its net investment (ignoring any tax effects). This is because the tax effects of a hire purchase contract are rarely significant and so the company's net investment in a hire purchase contract will approximate to its net cash investment in that contract.

7.147 In respect of finance leases and hire purchase contracts that have similar characteristics, the following need to be disclosed:

(a) The net investment in finance leases at the balance sheet date. This figure should show separately the amount in respect of finance leases and the amount in respect of hire purchase agreements. [*SSAP 21 para 58*].

(b) The cost of assets acquired in the period (whether by purchase, finance lease or hire purchase) for the purpose of letting under finance leases or hire purchase contracts. [*SSAP 21 para 60(c)*].

(c) The accounting policy adopted for recognising finance lease income. [*SSAP 21 para 60(a)*].

These disclosure requirements are illustrated in Table 28.

Treatment and disclosure of operating leases by lessors

7.148   SSAP 21 requires that a lessor should record, as fixed assets, the assets he holds for leasing under operating leases. It also requires that he should depreciate those assets over their useful economic lives. [*SSAP 21 para 42*].

7.149   The lessor should recognise his rental income from operating leases (excluding charges for services such as insurance and maintenance) on a straight-line basis over the period of the lease, irrespective of when the payments are due. [*SSAP 21 para 43*]. This requirement does not apply, however, if another systematic and rational basis is more representative of the time pattern in which the lessor receives the benefit from the leased asset (for example, the time pattern of the related depreciation charge).

7.150   The lessor needs to disclose the gross amount and the accumulated depreciation of the assets he holds for use under operating leases or hire purchase contracts that have similar characteristics. [*SSAP 21 para 59*].

Additional disclosure required in lessors' financial statements

7.151   In respect of both finance leases and operating leases (including hire purchase contracts that have similar characteristics), the following need to be disclosed also:

(a) The policy adopted for accounting for operating leases and finance leases.

(b) The aggregate rentals receivable in the accounting period, analysed between amounts receivable under finance leases and amounts receivable under operating leases.
[*SSAP 21 para 60*].

7.152   Where a lessor adopts a policy of grossing up the amount of regional development grant (RDG) that is credited to his profit and loss account, he will need to disclose the amount by which both his profit before tax and his taxation have been increased.

Table 28: *Illustration of the disclosure of finance leases in a lessor's financial statements in accordance with SSAP21.*

Extract from Lloyds and Scottish PLC Report and Accounts 30 September 1983.

Accounting policy extract

Leased assets
Leased assets are accounted for on the basis of gross rentals receivable and related unearned income rather than on the fixed assets basis previously used. The amount of income recognised in the year is unaffected by this change in method of disclosure. Comparative figures have been restated.

Note extract

(b) Turnover
The aggregate turnover of the Group is £376,841,000 (1982—£333,958,000). Turnover is the aggregate of the amount of finance charges earned under agreements for provision of instalment and other finance, rentals earned under contracts for leasing of plant and vehicles and rental of television sets, equipment and taxicab sales, television, electrical and furniture goods sales and factoring service fees.

Balance sheet extract

	Note	1983 £'000	1982 £'000
Current and other assets			
Instalment debtors, advances, loans, debts purchased and loans on life policies		1,653,967	1,294,252
Leasing rentals receivable		471,464	402,576
Factored debts..		315,986	231,788
		2,441,417	1,928,616
Less: Unearned income	9	315,138	251,013
		2,126,279	1,677,603

Note

9 Unearned income	The Group	
	1983 £'000	1982 £'000
On instalment debtors and other advances	251,646	195,968
On leasing rentals receivable	62,013	53,938
On factored debts..	1,479	1,107
	315,138	251,013

7.153 The term 'grossing up' means that the lessor prefers to gross up the amount of RDG he credits to the profit and loss account in each period (as if he had received the RDG net of tax), and to increase the tax charge accordingly. In this way he spreads the tax benefits from the RDG over the life of the lease in the same way as the RDG itself (that is, in proportion to the net cash investment in the lease).

7.154   The Guidance Notes to SSAP 21 indicate that the lessor may also need to disclose further information about his leases and hire purchase contracts that is of particular significance to the users of the financial statements. (This includes, for example, details of arrangements that could affect his future profitability, such as contingent rentals or new-for-old guarantees.)

Implications of the Act on the disclosure made by lessors

7.155   A leasing company's financial statements will need to comply with the Act's requirements, and they must show a true and fair view. Consequently, they must comply with the specific requirements of either Schedule 4 or, if the company is a special category company, Schedule 9 (see Chapter 13).

7.156   Although some banks that are special category companies and comply with Schedule 9 may carry out leasing activities themselves, most banks prefer, for tax reasons, to carry out their leasing through a separate subsidiary. Consequently, most lessors, whether they are related to a bank or not, will be neither a recognised bank nor a licensed institution within the meaning of the Banking Act 1979. As a result, most lessors will not be special category companies, and so they will have to comply with the requirements of Schedule 4 to the Act.

7.157   Lessor companies may have various problems in following the balance sheet formats and the profit and loss account formats detailed in the Act.

7.158   The balance sheet formats set out in Schedule 4 do not show any specific category for leased assets. Paragraph 3(2) of Schedule 4, however, permits (with certain exceptions) a company's balance sheet or profit and loss account to include an item that is not otherwise covered in the formats.

7.159   Leased assets can, therefore, be shown on the face of the balance sheet as a separate item. However, leased assets will have to be shown under the heading of either fixed assets or current assets. They can be shown in one or other of the following two ways:

   (a) As a category of tangible fixed assets (for example, 'Assets out on operating leases').

   (b) As a category of debtors under current assets (for example, 'Amounts receivable under finance leases').

7.160   Schedule 4 states that a company's assets are fixed assets if the company intends to use them on a continuing basis in its activities. It states also that any assets the company does not intend to use in that way are current assets. Assets leased out under operating leases are certainly intended to be used on a continuing basis in a company's activities.

Consequently, they should be shown as tangible fixed assets. Assets leased out on finance leases are more difficult to classify, and they could be classified either as current assets or as fixed assets under the definition in the Act. However, SSAP 21 requires that amounts due under finance leases should be shown under current assets as a category of debtors. In this respect, SSAP 21's requirements are more restrictive than the Act's requirements. This means also that the amounts due under finance leases must be analysed between amounts receivable within one year and those receivable after more than one year. [*Note 5 on the balance sheet formats*].

7.161 Irrespective of whether leased assets are classified under Schedule 4 as fixed or current, a lessor will need to follow the appropriate valuation rules of Schedule 4 (discussed in Chapter 4). Therefore, unless the alternative accounting rules are applied, those leased assets that are shown as tangible fixed assets will need to be shown at purchase price or production cost, less depreciation. Those leased assets that are shown as debtors will need to be shown as amounts receivable, less (where appropriate) a provision to reduce the amount to the net realisable value.

7.162 The profit and loss account formats set out in Schedule 4 are not particularly well suited to a leasing company. For example, a leasing company has neither 'Turnover' nor 'Cost of sales' in the normal sense of these words. Paragraph 3(3) of Schedule 4, however, provides that, in any case where the special nature of the company's business requires such adaptation, the directors should adapt the arrangement and the headings of those items that are preceded by Arabic numerals. This allows the lessor to adapt the profit and loss account formats to reflect the special nature of his business. For example, a finance lessor should normally show, as his turnover, his 'gross earnings' from leasing. Similarly, where interest costs are a direct cost of leasing, these costs could be deducted from gross earnings to show 'Gross profit'. Alternatively, interest costs could be shown in their normal position in the profit and loss format (that is, below 'Administrative expenses').

CHAPTER 8

BALANCE SHEET – INVESTMENTS AND CURRENT ASSETS

Chapter 8

Balance Sheet — Investments and Current Assets

Introduction

8.01 This chapter considers the disclosure required for all types of investments, including subsidiaries. The requirements that relate to subsidiaries that are outlined below apply also to a holding company's accounts that are included in a set of group accounts. This chapter looks also at problems that arise in the disclosure and the valuation of stocks and work in progress and other current assets.

Investments

All investments

8.02 A company that has fixed asset investments has to disclose certain information in its financial statements about the purchase and sale of those investments. The required information is the same as for other fixed assets. These requirements are discussed in Chapter 7, paragraphs 7.07 to 7.10. Table 29 illustrates the disclosure requirements that are considered below for investments in subsidiary companies, associated companies and other investments.

8.03 The Act requires the notes to the financial statements to include certain information about *any* investments a company holds (irrespective of whether these are shown as fixed assets or as current assets). In particular, the notes must disclose:

(a) The amount that relates to listed investments.[*4 Sch 45(1)*].

(b) The amount in *(a)* split between the investments listed on a recognised stock exchange, and any other listed investments. [*4 Sch 45(1)*].

(c) The aggregate market value of listed investments, where it differs from the amount at which they are stated in the balance sheet. [*4 Sch 45(2)(a)*].

(d) Both the stock exchange value and the market value of any listed investments, where the latter value is taken as being higher than their stock exchange value. [*4 Sch 45(2)(b)*]. This disclosure is required because the market value and the stock exchange value may differ according to the size of the investment and its marketability. For example, a controlling stake could be worth proportionately

more than a minority interest in a company, because stock exchange prices traditionally reflect the values of small parcels of shares (see further Chapter 7 para 7.52).

Table 29: *Illustration of the disclosure of subsidiaries, associated companies and other investments.*

Extract from Rank Hovis McDougall PLC Annual report and accounts 1 September 1984.

12 Shares in subsidiary companies	The Group 1984 £000	The Company 1984 £000
At cost less amounts written off:		
At 3 September 1983	—	102,396
Additions	—	2,719
Transfers from group companies	—	11,100
Disposals and liquidations	—	(139)
Amounts written off to reserves	—	(6,102)
At 1 September 1984	—	109,974

Details of principal subsidiary companies are shown on pages 32 and 33.

13 Associated companies (all unlisted)	The Group 1984 £000	The Company 1984 £000
At cost less amounts written off:		
At 3 September 1983	4,006	—
Exchange adjustments	113	—
Additions	71	—
At 1 September 1984	4,190	—
Share of reserves	2,713	—
	6,903	—

The Group's interest in associated companies consists of attributable share of net assets £6,019,000 (1983 £6,058,000) and goodwill £884,000 (1983 £816,000).

Dividends receivable from associated companies for the year amounted to £343,000 (1983 £549,000).

In compliance with Section 4 of the Companies Act 1967 [*now paragraph 12 of Schedule 5 to the Companies Act 1985*] details of associated companies are set out in the Annual Return.

14 Other investments	The Group 1984 £000	The Company 1984 £000
At cost less amounts written off:		
At 3 September 1983	113	1
Additions	112	—
Disposals	(17)	—
At 1 September 1984	208	1
Other investments comprise:		
Listed	34	1
Unlisted	174	—
	208	1
At valuation:		
Listed	29	1
Unlisted	174	—
	203	1

The valuation of listed investments is their stock exchange value.

8.04   For this purpose, a 'listed investment' means any investment that is listed either on a recognised stock exchange or on any other reputable stock exchange outside Great Britain. [*4 Sch 84*]. All other investments are to be regarded as unlisted, including those traded on the USM, and no additional information is required to be disclosed for these investments. A 'recognised stock exchange' means any body of persons that is a recognised stock exchange for the purposes of the Prevention of Fraud (Investments) Act 1958. [*Sec 744*]. Currently, the only body designated in Great Britain as a recognised stock exchange is The Stock Exchange.

8.05   There is no definition of 'reputable stock exchange'. In practice, whether a stock exchange outside Great Britain is reputable or not will depend both on its status in its own country and on the circumstances surrounding its operation.

8.06   The disclosure requirements outlined above are best illustrated by an example (see also Table 29):

	Company	Balance sheet value £000	Market value £000	Stock exchange value £000
Listed on The Stock Exchange (A recognised stock exchange)				
	A	100	250	300
	B	150	110	110
	C	130	150	125
	D	75	25	20
		455	535	555
Listed on The New York Stock Exchange (A reputable stock exchange outside Great Britain)				
	E	190	200	225
	F	65	110	100
	G	15	25	25
		270	335	350
Listed on The Unlisted Securities Market				
	H	30	70	75
Total of investments		755	940	980

This disclosure may be summarised in the notes to the financial statements as follows:

Listed investments

	£000
Listed on a recognised stock exchange	455
Other listed investments	270
Total — balance sheet value	725
Total — market value	870 *(being £535,000 + £335,000)*

Listed investments include certain investments for which the market value is considered to be higher than the stock exchange value. The market value of these investments is £285,000 *(that is, £150,000 + £25,000 + £110,000)* and their stock exchange value £245,000 *(that is, £125,000 + £20,000 + £100,000).*

Shareholdings exceeding 10%

8.07 Where a company at the end of its financial year holds shares of any class of *equity share capital* in another body corporate (which is not its subsidiary), and their nominal value exceeds *one-tenth* of the *nominal value* of all the allotted shares of that class, the Act requires the company to disclose certain information. [*5 Sch 7*].

8.08 'Equity share capital' means, in relation to a company, its issued share capital excluding any part of that capital which, neither as regards dividends nor as regards capital, carries any right to participate beyond a specified amount in a distribution. [*Sec 744*]. Therefore, ordinary share capital will generally be included within the definition, whereas preference share capital normally will not. However, it is not possible to say specifically what will or will not be included, because this will depend on the rights attaching to the different types of shares in issue.

8.09 The notes must disclose in respect of that body corporate:

(a) Its name.

(b) Its country of registration, if it is incorporated in Great Britain and is registered in England or Wales, and the investing company is registered in Scotland (or *vice versa*).

(c) Its country of incorporation, where it is incorporated outside Great Britain.

(d) The identity of each class of shares the investing company holds.

(e) The proportion of the nominal value of the allotted shares of each class that the investing company holds.
[*5 Sch 7*].

8.10   The Act requires the same information to be disclosed in two further situations:

(a) Where a company holds *shares* in a body corporate (which is not a subsidiary), and the nominal value of the shares that it holds exceeds *one-tenth* of the nominal value of the *total allotted share capital* of that body corporate. 'Shares' include equity share capital and all other classes of share capital. [*5 Sch 8*]. Consequently, this will include a company that holds, for example, preference shares in another company. The situation in paragraph 8.07 above covers a holding only of equity shares.

(b) Where a company holds *shares* in a body corporate (which is not a subsidiary), and the amount of the investment as stated in the company's balance sheet exceeds *one-tenth* of the *company's assets* as disclosed in that balance sheet. [*5 Sch 9*].

8.11   The particulars to be disclosed may relate to (*inter alia*) either a body corporate that is incorporated outside the UK or a body corporate that is incorporated within the UK, but carries on its business outside the UK. Where, in either of these two situations, the directors believe that disclosure of the information detailed in paragraph 8.09 above would be harmful to the business of the company or that body corporate, and the company has obtained the agreement of the Secretary of State, that information need not be disclosed. [*5 Sch 10*].

8.12   Where a company has a number of investments and, in the directors' opinion, compliance with the disclosure requirements would mean that particulars of excessive length would have to be disclosed in the financial statements, the company is not required to disclose the information detailed above. In this circumstance, the directors still have to give, in the notes to the financial statements, the information relating to those investments that principally affect either the company's profit (or loss) or the amount of its assets. [*5 Sch 11*]. Also, this exemption does not apply to those investments that fall into the category detailed in paragraph 8.10*(b)* above.

8.13   Where a company takes advantage of this exemption, the financial statements must state that the information is given only for those investments that principally affect either the company's profit (or loss) or the amount of its assets. [*5 Sch 12*]. Particulars of the investments whose details are not disclosed in the financial statements must be annexed to the company's next annual return. Where a company fails to annex this information to its next annual return, the company and any officer of it who is in default is liable to a fine. [*Sec 231(3) — see Appendix IV*].

Shareholdings exceeding 20%

8.14   Where a company holds *shares* in a body corporate (which is not a subsidiary) and the nominal value of the shares that it holds exceeds *one-*

fifth of the nominal value of the *total allotted share capital* of that body corporate, the following information should be given in the financial statements in addition to the information required by paragraphs 8.07 to 8.13 above:

(a) The aggregate amount of the capital and the reserves of that subsidiary or body corporate. These are to be ascertained from those financial statements of the subsidiary or the body corporate that were prepared for the year ending with, or last before, the company's financial year.

(b) The profit or the loss of that subsidiary or body corporate as disclosed by those financial statements.
[*5 Sch 16*].

8.15   If this additional information is immaterial, it need not be disclosed. [*5 Sch 17(4)*]. Also, the exemptions in paragraphs 8.11 and 8.12 above are still available.

8.16   Moreover, this additional information does not need to be given in respect of any body corporate in either of the following two situations:

(a) The company's investment in the body corporate is stated either in, or in the notes to, the company's financial statements according to the equity method of accounting (see further para 8.34 below). [*5 Sch 17(2)*].

(b) The company's investment is in a body corporate that is not required to deliver a copy of its balance sheet to the Registrar of Companies under either Section 241 (unlimited companies) or Section 700 (overseas companies) of the Act, and that does not publish a balance sheet in Great Britain or elsewhere. Where this applies, the information need not be given, provided that the company's holding in that body corporate does not amount to 50% or more of the nominal value of that body's allotted share capital. [*5 Sch 17(3)*].

8.17   Where a company takes advantage of the exemption from disclosure mentioned in paragraph 8.12 above where compliance would involve giving particulars of excessive length, the annual return must set out both the information given in the financial statements and that which, but for the exemption, the company would have had to give in the financial statements (for example, see Table 29). [*5 Sch 18*].

8.18   The Stock Exchange's Continuing Obligations require that the following information should be given by listed companies that have interests in equity share capital that exceed 20% of another company's capital (where that company is not a subsidiary):

(a) The company's principal country of operation.

(b) Particulars of its issued capital and debt securities.

(c) The percentage of each class of debt securities attributable to the company's interest (either direct or indirect).
[*CO 21(e)*].

8.19   If the number of such investments is large and, consequently, the details to be disclosed would be excessive, then The Stock Exchange requires details of only the more material investments to be disclosed.

8.20   The USM's General Undertaking contains a similar requirement, except that it requires one further detail to be disclosed. Unless the group's interest in the company is dealt with in the consolidated balance sheet as an associated company (see below), the financial statements must disclose the total amount of the company's reserves. [*GU 10(e)*]. The General Undertaking, however, gives no exemption from disclosure if the number of such investments is large. Nevertheless, in practice, only the more material investments would be disclosed.

Related companies and associated companies

8.21   One specific category of investments that the Act outlines is 'Shares in related companies'. The definition of a related company in paragraph 92 of Schedule 4 closely corresponds to SSAP 1's definition of an associated company, although the two definitions are not identical.

8.22   A *'related company'* is defined in paragraph 92 as:

"Any body corporate (other than one which is a group company in relation to that company) in which that company holds on a *long-term* basis a *qualifying capital interest* for the purpose of securing a contribution to that company's own activities by the *exercise of any control or influence* arising from that interest."

8.23   A 'qualifying capital interest' is an interest in a class of the equity share capital of that body corporate that *carries rights to vote in all circumstances at general meetings* of that body corporate. Unless the contrary can be shown, a body corporate will be presumed to be a related company if the investing company has a qualifying capital interest of 20% or more in that body corporate. [*4 Sch 92*].

8.24   SSAP 1 defines an *'associated company'* as:

"A company not being a subsidiary of the investing group or company in which:

(a) the interest of the investing group or company is effectively that of a partner in a joint venture or consortium and the investing group or company is in a position to exercise a significant influence over the company in which the investment is made; or

(b) the interest of the investing group or company is for the *long-term* and is *substantial* and, having regard to the disposition of the other shareholdings, the investing group or company is in a position *to exercise a significant influence* over the company in which the investment is made."

8.25   Paragraph 53 of SSAP 1 points out that the definition of a related company is wider than that of an associated company. The definition of 'related company' and the definition of 'associated company' contain several points of difference. For instance, under SSAP 1, where the investing company's interest is not that of a partner, that interest has to be substantial. In contrast, it is sufficient for the purposes of the definition of 'related company' that the investing company has an interest in those equity shares that carry voting rights "for the purpose of securing a contribution to that company's own activities by the exercise of any control or influence arising from that interest".

8.26   It is also possible for an associated company not to be a related company. For example, if a company has a substantial interest in an associated company, but that interest does *not carry rights to vote in all circumstances at general meetings*, then that associated company is not a related company.

8.27   Accordingly, it is possible for a related company not to be an associated company, and *vice versa*. Companies will need to consider whether any of those of their investments that do not fall within one definition will nonetheless fall within the other.

8.28   Strictly, the term 'related company' should be used in the financial statements, and a reference to the fact that the related company is an associated company should be made where appropriate. In practice, though, many companies use only the term 'associated company' in their financial statements (for example, see Table 29). The DTI has confirmed that the use of this term is acceptable.

8.29   Further information about related companies is required to be disclosed in an investing company's financial statements in addition to the information about investments outlined in paragraphs 8.14 to 8.20 above.

8.30   'Shares in related companies' and 'Loans to related companies' appear as separate sub-headings under the fixed asset main heading of 'Investments' in both balance sheet formats. Also, both balance sheet formats require the disclosure of 'Amounts owed by related companies' under the current asset main heading of 'Debtors', and the disclosure of 'Amounts owed to related companies' under the liabilities main heading of 'Creditors'. In addition, amounts owed by and to related companies that are due for payment within one year must be shown separately from amounts due after one year. [*Notes 5 and 13 on the balance sheet formats*]. These requirements of the formats effectively prohibit companies from showing investments in associated companies as one figure, including the cost of the shares in the associates, loans to them and after deducting loans from them. The same argument applies to investments in subsidiaries. The argument is explained more fully in Chapter 17, paragraph 17.11. This disclosure also fulfils the requirements contained in paragraphs 27 and 28 of SSAP 1.

8.31   Companies that have investments in associated companies have to comply with the requirements of SSAP 1. This is so even where the associated companies are not related companies. The Standard requires that income from a company's investments in associated companies should be brought into account on the following bases:

(a) The investing company's own financial statements should show dividends received and receivable.

(b) The investing group's consolidated financial statements should show the investing group's share of the profits less losses of associated companies.
[*SSAP 1 para 18*].

8.32   SSAP 1 requires that the investing group's financial statements should indicate the nature of the associated companies' businesses. [*SSAP 1 para 49*]. The disclosure of the group's share of the results of associated companies is considered in Chapter 10, paragraphs 10.84 to 10.89. Those requirements of SSAP 1 that relate to the carrying value of the investment in associated companies are set out below.

8.33   Unless it is shown at a valuation, the amount at which the investing company's interests in associated companies should be shown in the investing company's own financial statements is the cost of the investment less any amounts written off. [*SSAP 1 para 25*].

8.34   The amount at which the investing group's interests in associated companies should be shown in the consolidated balance sheet is the value under the 'equity method of accounting' being the total of:

(a) The investing group's share of the net assets (other than goodwill) of the associated companies, stated, when possible, after attributing fair values to the net assets at the time the interests in the associated companies were acquired.

(b) The investing group's share of any goodwill in the associated companies' own financial statements.

(c) The premium paid (or the discount) on the acquisition of the interests in the associated companies, in so far as it has not already been written off or amortised.

The Standard requires that *(a)* should be disclosed separately, but *(b)* and *(c)* may be aggregated. [*SSAP 1 para 26*]. This disclosure requirement is illustrated in Table 29.

8.35   Where an investing group's interest in an associated company is material to the investing group's financial statements, more detailed information about that associate's assets and liabilities may need to be given in the group's financial statements in order that they show a true and fair view (for example, see Table 43 on page 221). [*SSAP 1 para 30*].

8.36 The investing group must disclose its share of post-acquisition reserves of associated companies and any movements in them during the year. [*SSAP 1 para 31*]. The investing group should normally also reflect its share of any deficiency in an associated company's net asset value. Where there is any permanent diminution in value of the associated company, a provision must be made against the carrying value of the investment in the associated company to reflect that decrease in its value. [*SSAP 1 paras 32, 33*]. A provision of this nature may be required in both the holding company's financial statements and the group's consolidated financial statements.

8.37 If the investing company does not prepare consolidated financial statements, then it should disclose the information outlined in paragraphs 8.31 to 8.36 above either in a separate balance sheet or by adding the information in a supplementary form to its own balance sheet. [*SSAP 1 para 35*].

8.38 Where an associated company's results are included in the investing group's consolidated financial statements, the following provisions may be relevant:

(a) The financial statements of the associated company used should be coterminous with those of the group. Alternatively, they should be made up to a date that is either not more than six months before, or shortly after, the date of the investing group's financial statements.

(b) Where non-coterminous financial statements are used, and the effect of this approach is material to the group results, the fact that they are non-coterminous and the date of the associated company's year end should be disclosed.

(c) Adjustments similar to those required for the purpose of including subsidiaries in the consolidated financial statements should be made when associated companies are incorporated into the group's consolidated financial statements (see further Chapter 17 para 17.21).

(d) The effective date of acquisition and disposal of an associated company is established in the same way as for a subsidiary company (see further Chapter 17 paras 17.51 to 17.55).

(e) If there are any restrictions on an associated company's ability to distribute its retained profits, the extent of the restrictions should be indicated (see further Chapter 17 paras 17.74 and 17.75).

(f) Where the associated company is held by a subsidiary that has a minority holding, the minority's share of the associated company's results should be shown as part of minority interests in the consolidated financial statements.

(g) Where an associated company has subsidiaries and associates, the share of the associated company's results to be disclosed will be the share of that associate's consolidated results.

(h) Where an associate ceases to qualify as an associated company, the investing group's consolidated balance sheet should include the investment at the aggregate value (outlined in para 8.34 above) on the date that its status changed. If the investment's carrying value then suffers a permanent diminution in value, provision should be made against it.
[*SSAP 1 paras 36, 37, 39, 44*]

Shareholdings exceeding 50%

8.39   Where, at the end of a financial year, a company has subsidiaries, the investing company's financial statements have to disclose the information outlined in paragraph 8.09 above. [*5 Sch 1*]. For this purpose, a company has another company as its subsidiary if any one of the following applies:

(a) It is a member of it and controls the composition of its board of directors, and has the power to remove or appoint the majority or all of the directors without the consent or agreement of any other shareholders.

(b) It holds more than one-half in nominal value of the company's equity share capital.

(c) It is a subsidiary of another subsidiary company.
[*Sec 736(1)*].

8.40   The disclosure requirement in paragraph 8.09 *(e)* above is extended to include, in addition, the proportion of shares held by any subsidiaries (or by a nominee on behalf of any subsidiary) of the investing company. [*5 Sch 2*]. Consequently, the aggregate proportion of the shares that the group holds in a subsidiary company has to be shown. It is not sufficient to show just the proportion of shares the holding company holds in the subsidiary company. This requirement is also included in SSAP 14, paragraph 33.

8.41   Except where one of the conditions below is satisfied, the information outlined in paragraph 8.14 above must be given for each subsidiary:

(a) The company is exempt from preparing group accounts by Section 229(2) of the Act (that is, where the company is the wholly-owned subsidiary of another body corporate incorporated in Great Britain). [*5 Sch 17(1)(a)*].

(b) The company prepares group accounts and these include the subsidiary's financial statements. Alternatively, the company's investment in the subsidiary is stated either in, or in the notes to, the company's financial statements according to the equity method of accounting. [*5 Sch 17(1)(b)*].

As a result of these two exemptions, most groups will not need to disclose the additional information in respect of their subsidiaries that is detailed in paragraph 8.14.

8.42   SSAP 14 requires the financial statements to give an indication of the nature of the business of the company's principal subsidiaries. [*SSAP 14 para 33*]. In addition, the Act requires the directors' report to indicate the principal activities of the company and its subsidiaries. [*Sec 235(2)*]. Listed companies and companies traded on the USM are also required to give the name of the principal country in which each subsidiary operates. [*CO 21 (d); GU 10(d)*]. This requirement is in addition to the Act's requirement for the country of incorporation to be disclosed. However, the exemptions from disclosing excessive amounts of information (outlined in para 8.12) apply also to the information that both the Act and The Stock Exchange's Continuing Obligations require in respect of subsidiaries. The exemptions do not specifically apply to that information which the USM's General Undertaking requires, but again, in practice, this information is likely to be summarised by companies traded on the USM.

8.43   Where, at the end of a financial year, a company is a subsidiary of another body corporate, the name, and the country of incorporation (if known), of the company that the directors regard as the ultimate holding company should be disclosed in the notes to the subsidiary's financial statements. [*5 Sch 20*]. This disclosure is not required if the subsidiary carries on business outside the UK, and if it would, in the opinion of the directors, be harmful to the business of its holding company or any of its holding company's subsidiaries, and the Secretary of State agrees that the name of the ultimate holding company need not be disclosed. [*5 Sch 21*]. Some companies have taken advantage of this concession where they have reason to believe that the ultimate holding company's nationality would be unacceptable or offensive to its own customers.

8.44   The requirements to prepare group accounts are considered in more detail in Chapter 17.

Own shares

8.45   The main heading of 'Investments' has a sub-heading 'Own shares'. When a company purchases its own shares, those shares are treated as cancelled on purchase. [*Sec 160(4), 162(2)*]. Thus, unlike the practice that is generally permitted both in the USA and also by the Second EC Directive, a company cannot purchase its own shares and then treat them as 'treasury shares' until the time it resells them.

8.46   A company will generally hold its own shares only where it has acquired them by forfeiture, or by surrender in lieu of forfeiture, or by way of gift. The Act sets out certain rules to govern cases where companies hold their own shares. In particular, a company that acquires shares by forfeiture must generally dispose of them within three years. Otherwise, it must cancel them and so effectively bring about a capital reduction (see also Chapter 6 para 6.19). [*Sec 146*].

Other investments

8.47   The category 'Other investments' will normally include the following
       items (other than investments in subsidiaries and related companies):

   (a) Listed and unlisted securities.

   (b) Life assurance policies.

   (c) Joint ventures and partnerships.

8.48   Building society deposits and bank deposits could be included either
       as 'Other investments' (either under fixed assets or under current assets
       — depending on the nature of the deposits) or as 'Cash at bank and
       in hand'. If the amount is material, the accounting policies should dis-
       close where such items are included.

Stocks

Disclosure

8.49   The Act requires that stocks should be analysed between the following
       four categories:

   (a) Raw materials and consumables.

   (b) Work in progress.

   (c) Finished goods and goods for resale.

   (d) Payments on account.
   [*4 Sch formats*].

8.50   A company should follow this categorisation so long as it effectively
       produces true and fair financial statements. In this context, the special
       nature of a company's business may mean that the company needs to
       adapt the formats. The requirement in SSAP 9 is that stocks and work
       in progress should be classified in any manner that is appropriate to
       the business. 'Payments on account' represent the payments a company
       makes on account of stocks, and not the payments it receives from
       customers.

8.51   SSAP 9 requires that the figure of stocks disclosed in the financial state-
       ments should be the total of the lower of cost and net realisable value
       of the separate items of stock or of groups of similar items. In addi-
       tion, the Standard requires that the accounting polices used in calculat-
       ing cost, net realisable value, attributable profit and foreseeable losses
       should be stated.

8.52   The Act allows companies to use certain methods for arriving at the
       purchase price or the production cost of stocks and other fungible items.
       For this purpose, 'fungible items' are those items that are indistinguish-

able one from another (for example, identical nuts and bolts). [*4 Sch 27(6)*]. A company may adopt any of the following methods:

(a) First-in, first-out (FIFO).

(b) Last-in, first-out (LIFO).

(c) Weighted average price.

(d) Any other similar method.
[*4 Sch 27(1) (2)*].

8.53   When choosing a method, the directors must ensure that the method they choose provides the fairest practicable approximation to 'actual cost'. SSAP 9 considers that the LIFO method does not usually bear a reasonable relationship to actual cost, and so LIFO is not an acceptable method of valuation in the UK at present.

Replacement value of stocks

8.54   Paragraph 27 of Schedule 4 says that, where the historical cost of stocks or fungible assets is calculated using a method (such as those mentioned in paragraph 8.52 above), and that valuation differs materially from the relevant alternative amount of those items, then the difference should be disclosed in the notes to the financial statements (see Tables 30 and 31). [*4 Sch 27(3)*].

Table 30: Disclosure of the replacement value of stocks. This example shows that this company has given the replacement value for all of its stocks.

Extract from The Caledonian Aviation Group PLC Report and Accounts 31 October 1984.

13. Stocks	1984	1983
	£'000	£'000
Raw materials and consumables	21,762	17,580
Work in progress	4,031	296
Finished goods and goods for resale	2,478	1,292
	28,271	19,168
Due to increases in the cost of raw materials and labour, the replacement value of stocks is estimated to be:		
Raw materials and consumables	24,123	18,788
Work in progress	4,233	312
Finished goods and goods for resale	2,478	1,292
	30,834	20,392

8.55   The 'relevant alternative amount' will normally be the amount at which the assets would have been disclosed if their value had been determined according to their replacement cost as at the balance sheet date. [*4 Sch 27(4)*]. The replacement cost of these types of assets will normally be their current cost. However, a company may instead determine the relevant alternative amount according to the most recent actual purchase price or the most recent actual production cost of assets of that class before that date. But it can do this only where this method gives a more appropriate standard of comparison for assets of the class in question. [*4 Sch 27(5)*]. The Act leaves it to the company's directors to form an opinion as to whether the method does this.

8.56   The example below illustrates the calculation of the value of stocks on both a FIFO basis and a weighted average price basis. It also considers how the replacement cost of stocks should be disclosed:

Two companies, A and B, have identical opening and closing stocks figures and purchases in a particular year, as follows:

	Units	Value
		£
Opening stocks	100	835
Purchases — March	50	500
— July	100	1,150
— September	50	600
— December	150	2,000
Closing stocks	250	

Company A chooses to determine the value of its closing stocks by the FIFO method, and Company B does so by the 'weighted average price' method.

In these circumstances, the amount to be included in the balance sheets would be calculated as follows:

Company A:

$$
\begin{array}{ll}
 & £ \\
150 \text{ at } £2,000/150 = & 2,000 \\
50 \text{ at } £600/50 \quad = & 600 \\
50 \text{ at } £1,150/100 = & \underline{575} \\
 & \underline{\underline{3,175}}
\end{array}
$$

Company B:

$$
\frac{£835 + £500 + £1,150 + £600 + £2,000}{100 + 50 + 100 + 50 + 150} \times 250 = \underline{\underline{2,825}}
$$

The value of the stocks at replacement cost is, say, £3,300.

If the difference between the balance sheet value of stocks and their replacement cost is material in the context of their balance sheet value, it must be disclosed under the requirement outlined in paragraph 8.54. The difference for Company A is £125 (£3,300—£3,175), which is unlikely to be considered material. The difference for Company B is £475 (£3,300—£2,825), which may, in certain circumstances, be considered material. If it is, it must be disclosed.

8.57   However, Counsel has advised that a 'method' is not used when stocks are valued at either their actual purchase price or their production cost. It would appear, therefore, that where companies value their stocks at actual purchase price or production cost, they do not need to disclose, in their financial statements, the difference between this value and the replacement value of those stocks.

8.58   In many situations, it is likely that some items of stocks will be valued by one of the methods mentioned above, and that other items will be valued at actual purchase price or production cost. Where a company does this, the company will need to disclose not only the difference between the figure of stocks valued by a method and their replacement cost, but also the historical cost of the stocks it has valued by that method. Otherwise, it could be misleading for the company to disclose the figure that represents the difference, without also giving an indication of the proportion of the total stock value to which this difference relates.

8.59   For those stocks valued by a 'method', the Act effectively requires two stock valuations: one for normal balance sheet purposes and the other for arriving at the relevant alternative amount. Where a company has to calculate the current replacement cost of stocks for current cost accounting purposes, this calculation should impose no additional burden on the company in complying with the Act. The current replacement cost may have been arrived at by a fairly 'broad-brush' approach (by using indices, for example), but the amount is likely to be sufficiently accurate for arriving at a disclosure figure. Although indices are not ideal, some companies use them in preparing current cost financial statements as their main statutory financial statements, and this approach is quite acceptable. Strictly, companies that apply indices to arrive at current replacement cost are contravening the Act's separate valuation principle. However, as long as a company uses indices that are sufficiently relevant to each line of its stocks, the result when it applies them globally is, in accounting terms, equivalent to the result produced when it applies them to each individual line.

Long-term contract work in progress

8.60   Paragraph 22 of Schedule 4 requires that "the amount to be included in respect of any current asset shall be its purchase price or production cost". However, paragraph 27 of SSAP 9 requires that "the amount at which long-term contract work in progress is stated in periodic financial statements should be cost plus any attributable profit, less any foreseeable losses and progress payments received and receivable".

8.61   There are two important differences between the legal requirement and the requirement of SSAP 9. First, under SSAP 9, 'attributable profit' has to be included in the carrying value of long-term contract work in progress (subject to certain limitations), whereas the Act does not permit attributable profit to be included. This conflict can arise in both the profit and loss account and the balance sheet. Secondly, SSAP 9 requires progress payments to be shown separately (perhaps in the notes to the financial statements), as a deduction in arriving at the balance sheet amount of long-term work in progress. In contrast, the Act requires progress payments to be shown separately on the face of the balance sheet, either as a deduction from stocks or as an item under creditors. The first of these two differences is considered to be more significant.

8.62   The profit and loss account conflict was considered in Technical Release No. 481, 'The determination of realised profits and disclosure of distributable profits in the context of the Companies Acts 1948 to 1981', which the CCAB issued in September 1982. Although TR 481 considers this problem in relation to the Companies Acts 1948 to 1981, it applies equally to the Companies Act 1985. TR 481 is reproduced in Appendix VIII. In particular, paragraph 3 of the Appendix to TR 481 states that:

> "An example of the principle that profit recognised in accordance with an Accounting Standard should normally be treated as realised is provided by SSAP 9, 'Stocks and work in progress'. This requires that long-term contract work in progress should be stated in periodic financial statements at cost plus any attributable profit, less any foreseeable losses and progress payments received and receivable. There was initially some concern as to whether profit thus recognised on long-term contract work in progress would be construed as realised profit within the provisions of the Companies Acts. However, the relevant principles of recognising profits in SSAP 9 are based on the concept of 'reasonable certainty' as to the eventual outcome and are not in conflict with the statutory accounting principles. Such profits should be treated as realised profits. The Department of Trade [*now the DTI*] does not dissent from this view."

From the point of view of the profit and loss account, therefore, there is no conflict between SSAP 9 and the Companies Act.

8.63   From the point of view of the balance sheet, however, there could be a conflict. When a company follows SSAP 9 for the purpose of giving a true and fair view, it must, *inter alia*, state the effect of the departure from the requirements of Schedule 4. In regard to the inclusion of attributable profit in accordance with SSAP 9, Counsel has advised, and the DTI has agreed, that the amount of attributable profit to be disclosed is the amount added to the cost of work in progress before the deduction of progress payments. This is because both SSAP 9 (paragraph 30) and Schedule 4 (format 1, items E3 and H3, and format 2, item C3) require the progress payments to be shown separately. The amount of progress payments deducted from work in progress has to be *disclosed*, because, on the true construction of Note 8 on the balance sheet formats, it is not sufficient for these payments merely to be deducted from stocks, so that only the net figure is shown in the balance sheet.

8.64   Many companies, particularly those in the construction industry, hold a view contrary to the view that Counsel and the DTI hold. They believe that the attributable profit should be judged against the amount of work in progress net of progress payments. Their arguments for holding this view are considered below:

(a) Some contracts require stage payments to be made at approximately the same rate as that at which the work is carried out and the profits are earned. With those contracts, the attributable profit that is recognised in accordance with SSAP 9 will probably be restricted to that based on work that is covered by either cash received or a debtor. Therefore, the company will not include any attributable profit in its net work in progress. By using this basis, the company will not depart from the valuation rule in paragraph 22 of Schedule 4 and so it will not need to make any special disclosures.

(b) In other contracts, stage payments do not necessarily keep pace with the value of the work done, and yet the company may recognise profit in accordance with SSAP 9 based on the work done. Probably, therefore, the company will include a profit element in the work in progress even net of progress payments. With those contracts where the amounts are material and are on this basis, companies will need to invoke the true and fair override. In doing this they will rely on Section 228 (5) of the Act, which permits a company to depart from the requirements of Schedule 4 if the special circumstances that apply to the company mean that compliance with Schedule 4 would not give a true and fair view.

Companies using this departure continue to include work in progress in the balance sheet in accordance with SSAP 9. But they should also disclose, in a note to the financial statements, particulars of the departure, the reasons for it and its effect.

(c) The disclosure of particulars, reasons and effect have been interpreted by these companies to relate to the work in progress net of progress payments. The disclosure of 'particulars' and 'reasons' would appear to present no problems. The task of interpreting the word 'effect' is slightly more complex. Although the word 'effect' is not synonymous with the word 'amount', it is clear that something more than 'particulars' is intended. In the context of a company's financial statements, there would be a strong presumption that, if it is practicable to do so, and if the effect is material, the company is required to quantify the effect.

If the disclosure relates to the gross work in progress, it is generally practicable to determine the amount of attributable profit that is included in that gross figure. Also, such attributable profit would generally be material. However, these companies argue that, whereas the attributable profit at the gross figure may be material, the amount net of progress payments may well be immaterial. In addition, it may not be practicable for a company to determine how much profit is carried forward after deducting the progress payments it received, because the latter are not allocated between cost and profit. They argue that it would be artificial for a company to make such an allocation, and that the resulting figure would not be meaningful.

8.65   The calculation of the amounts that the Act requires to be disclosed can be best explained by an example:

A company has the following long-term contract at the end of its financial year:

	£
Cost to date	1,000,000
Attributable profit	300,000
Progress payments received	500,000

The year-end work in progress figure can be analysed as follows:

	Net cost of WIP £000	Profit £000	Gross total of WIP £000
Cost to date	1,000	—	1,000
Attributable profit	—	300	300
Gross work in progress	1,000	300	1,300
Progress payments	?	?	(500)
Net work in progress	?	?	800

The Act seems to require the profit element added to the gross work in progress to be disclosed (namely, £300,000). However, the construction companies argue that the profit element of the progress payments included in the net work in progress figure cannot be analysed, and consequently the profit element included in net work in progress cannot be determined.

8.66   The above paragraphs set out two conflicting arguments. Because of this controversy, the DTI is seeking to resolve this matter with the ASC. In the meantime, some companies may choose to continue to adopt the same disclosure that they have used in the past, but others may change their approach. The two methods of presentation are shown in Table 31.

8.67   Where the company has received large progress payments, they should be shown as a deduction from work in progress to the extent of costs to date, plus attributable profit less provision for losses. Any excess of progress payments should be included in creditors as 'Payments received on account'. [*Note 8 on the balance sheet formats*].

8.68   A company should provide for all anticipated losses on long-term contracts. If anticipated losses on individual contracts exceed costs incurred to date less progress payments received and receivable, such excesses should be shown separately under 'Provisions for liabilities and charges'.

Table 31: Illustrations of a company that has disclosed the amount of attributable profit included in work in progress and of a company where it is impracticable to determine the effect of the departure from the Act.

Extract from The Plessey Company plc Report & Accounts 30 March 1984.

15 Stocks

	Group		Company	
	1984	1983	1984	1983
	£000	£000	£000	£000
Stocks comprise:				
Raw materials and consumables	**83,298**	**85,180**	—	—
Work-in-progress	**207,311**	**146,594**	—	—
Finished goods	**35,485**	**42,232**	—	13
Long term contract work-in-progress	**153,444**	**112,929**	—	—
	479,538	**386,935**	—	13
Less payments on account				
– long term contract work-in-progress	*138,121*	*98,889*	—	—
– other	*74,229*	*33,911*	—	—
	267,188	**254,135**	—	13

In accordance with the provisions of SSAP 9, attributable profit amounting to £8,668,000 (1983 – £5,626,000) has been included in the value of long term contract work-in-progress. The inclusion of this attributable profit supersedes the statutory valuation rules for current assets to enable the accounts to give a true and fair view.

The replacement cost of stocks was greater than the balance sheet value by £2,850,000 (1983 – £2,300,000).

Extract from Alfred McAlpine PLC Annual Report & Accounts 31 October 1984.

12. Stocks

	Group		Company	
	1984	1983	1984	1983
	£000's	£000's	£000's	£000's
Raw materials	**2,717**	1,896	—	—
Plant spares and consumable stores	**3,444**	2,960	—	—
Finished goods and goods for resale	**2,753**	3,332	—	—
Work in progress (see below)	**71,611**	46,833	—	—
Other stocks	**3,622**	2,764	—	—
	84,147	57,785	—	—
Work in progress				
Gross cost	**1,085,875**	926,349	—	—
Less payments on account	**1,014,264**	879,516	—	—
Net work in progress	**71,611**	46,833	—	—
Amount of net work in progress certified and unpaid	**46,189**	14,526		

The inclusion of attributable profit in long term contract work in progress in accordance with SSAP 9 constitutes a departure from the valuation rules contained in Schedule 8 to the Companies Act 1948 [*now Schedule 4 to the Companies Act 1985*]. This departure is necessary to enable the accounts to give a true and fair view, and is required by Section 149(3) of that Act [*now Section 228(5) of the Companies Act 1985*]. As it is not possible to allocate progress payments between costs and profits, it is impracticable to determine the effect of this departure on the amount attributed to long term contract work in progress in the balance sheet.

Debtors

8.69   The amount of each item to be shown under the heading 'Debtors' must be split between those receivable within one year of the balance sheet date and those receivable later than that. [*Note 5 on the balance sheet formats*]. For this purpose, a debtor is considered to be receivable on the earliest date on which payment is due, rather than on the earliest date on which payment is expected.

8.70   One problem that arises with the valuation of debtors is where a company invoices customers at provisional prices that may be higher than the prices that eventually will be agreed. The customers usually pay all or some of the amount of the provisional invoices, and the company sets up a provision for possible repayment. The provision is deducted from debtors in respect of the same customer, and the net price is recorded as sales. A similar situation may also arise where a company gives a discount to its debtors for the early settlement of debts, although this type of discount would not normally be deducted from sales, but would be included under 'Administrative expenses' as it is more in the nature of a finance charge.

8.71   This accounting treatment is basically acceptable. The provision that prohibits set-off (paragraph 5 of Schedule 4) does not inhibit normal accounting for assets and liabilities. Debts should be shown net of provisions to reduce them to their net realisable value. This treatment is not in any way affected by the fact that set-off is prohibited.

8.72   The three following situations may arise:

(a) If the customer pays only part of the provisional amount, and the part he pays is equal to the subsequently agreed price, the deduction of the provision from debtors quite properly states the debtor at the net sum. This is in accordance with the Act, which requires that current assets should be stated at the lower of cost and net realisable value.

(b) If the customer pays the whole of the provisional amount, the fact that a provision has been deducted from the debtor will cause the account, or that part of it, to be in credit. Consequently, the company's account will show, at least in part, a liability payable to the customer. Assume that the company settles this liability by either issuing a credit note or using some similar method. The account is therefore settled by a series of invoices, credit notes and cash. If, in the normal course of the company's dealing with the customer, he has one account that, in normal circumstances, will represent a net debtor at any one stage, there is no reason for the company to include the credit balance in creditors, rather than to net it against debtors.

(c) In some cases, refunds may be so substantial as to turn a normal debtor relationship into a normal creditor relationship (for example, the liability may be settled in due course by a cheque). In that case,

it would be incorrect to leave the negative amount in debtors. And in this situation it would be more appropriate to include the amount in creditors, rather than in debtors (provided that the amount concerned is material).

8.73   The company is adopting a course of trading that it is then following faithfully in its accounting. The company would not be invoking the 'true and fair' override the Act envisages. Consequently, it would not need to disclose any further information.

8.74   The Act requires that all debtors should be disclosed as current assets, no matter when they fall due for payment. The Act draws a distinction only between fixed assets and current assets. If a company intends to use assets on a continuing basis in its activities, then they are fixed assets. If the assets do not comply with this definition, they are deemed to be current assets. Consequently, long-term debts are current assets, because the company does not use them on a continuing basis in its activities. However, a situation may arise where a company has a particular long-term debt that is very material. If it has such a debt, it may be misleading to include this debt under current assets, and the company may have to insert an intermediate asset heading between 'Fixed assets' and 'Current assets'. The company may need to do this in order that its financial statements show a true and fair view.

Loans for acquisition of own shares

8.75   Where any outstanding loans made in respect of the acquisition of the company's shares under either Section 153(4)(b) or (c) or Section 155 of the Act (see Chapter 12) are included under any item in the balance sheet, these must be disclosed in aggregate for each item. [*4 Sch 51(2)*].

Cash at bank and in hand

8.76   Because the Act does not allow set-off between either assets and liabilities or income and expenditure, there has been considerable debate about the situation where there is a legal right of set-off of debit and credit bank balances. The question that arises is whether it is acceptable, in such circumstances, to offset the balances for balance sheet disclosure under the Act.

8.77   The answer to this offset question will depend on the particular circumstances of each situation. However, the following comments may provide useful guidance.

8.78   Paragraph 5 of Schedule 4 provides that:

"Amounts in respect of items representing assets or income may not be set off against amounts in respect of items representing liabilities or expenditure (as the case may be), or *vice versa.*"

As explained below, it seems that this provision does not preclude recognition of the effect of a legally-enforceable right of set-off, and the resulting net sum the company owes is the true amount of its liability for the purposes of Schedule 4.

8.79　There is no definition, for this purpose, of the word 'liability'. A reasonable definition would be that it is an amount that a company would be held liable to pay in legal proceedings, on the assumption that those proceedings are commenced on the balance sheet date.

8.80　Applying this definition, a company should, if there is no special arrangement that precludes set-off, show in its balance sheet the net amount it owes to its bank at that date in each of the following situations:

(a) Both the amount it has deposited with the bank and the amount it owes to the bank are due on demand.

(b) Both such amounts are due for payment on the same date.

(c) The amount that it owes to the bank has either fallen due for payment or will fall due for payment before the deposit it made with the bank matures. However, such deposit will either mature or can be made to mature before the expiration of the minimum period within which the bank could obtain judgment against the company, commencing on the balance sheet date.

(d) The amount the company owes to the bank will fall due for payment after the deposit it made with the bank matures.

8.81　In all these situations, it is likely that the amount that a court would find was due from the company on the date on which it gave judgment (or would be due from the company on the due date for the payment of its debt, if that is later) would be the net amount. It should be noted that the situations described above are all circumstances where the company that makes the deposit is also the company that is the debtor to the bank. It seems that it is not possible in the consolidated financial statements for an amount that one group company owes to the bank to be set off against the amount of a deposit that another member of the group has lodged.

8.82　Equally, the liability of one member of a group to a bank cannot be reduced or extinguished because the company that made the deposit has guaranteed the liability of the debtor company. However, this situation would be different if both of the following conditions applied:

(a) Each and every member of the group that borrowed money from, or deposited money with, the bank was jointly and severally liable to the bank for the amounts owed to the bank.

(b) The bank, accordingly, was liable to repay deposits to such companies jointly and severally.

In this circumstance, set-off would be acceptable.

Prepayments and accrued income

8.83   Prepayments and accrued income may be disclosed in one of two alternative positions. [*Note 6 on the balance sheet formats*]. They may be
disclosed either as a category of debtors or as a separate category in
their own right. A note to the formats requires that the amount that
will fall due after more than one year should be shown separately for
each item that is included under debtors. [*Note 5 on the balance sheet
formats*]. Consequently, where prepayments and accrued income are
disclosed under debtors, they must be analysed by age. If, however,
they are included as a separate category, no such analysis is required.

CHAPTER 9

BALANCE SHEET — LIABILITIES

Chapter 9

Balance Sheet — Liabilities

Introduction

9.01   This chapter deals with the general disclosure requirements for creditors, loans, provisions for liabilities and charges, share capital, reserves and contingent liabilities. It also considers some of the problems that arise in accounting for items such as deep discounted stock and the current developments in the information to be disclosed in respect of pension commitments.

Creditors

Disclosure

9.02   The Act specifies a considerable amount of detail that a company's financial statements must give in respect of its indebtedness.

9.03   All items included under creditors must be analysed between amounts that will fall due within one year of the balance sheet date and amounts that will fall due after more than one year. [*Note 13 on the balance sheet formats*].

9.04   In addition, the notes must, in respect of each item that is shown under the heading 'Creditors: amounts falling due after more than one year' in format 1 (or 'Creditors' in format 2) [*4 Sch 48(5)(a)*], state:

(a) The aggregate amount that is included under the item which:

(i) Is payable or repayable (other than by instalments) in more than five years, beginning with the day after the end of the financial year.

(ii) Is payable or repayable by instalments, any of which will fall due for payment after the end of that five-year period. In this situation, the aggregate amount of the instalments that will fall due for payment after the end of the five-year period must also be disclosed.

These amounts must be shown separately.
[*4 Sch 48(1)*].

(b) The terms of payment or repayment, and the applicable rate of interest, for the debts outlined in *(a)* above. Where the number of debts is such that, in the directors' opinion, this requirement would

173

result in a statement of excessive length, this information need be given only in general terms. [*4 Sch 48(2)(3)*].

9.05   A company that is either listed on The Stock Exchange or traded on the USM must analyse its liabilities still further. The Stock Exchange's Continuing Obligations and General Undertaking require bank loans and overdrafts, and other borrowings, to be analysed between amounts repayable:

(a) Within one year, or on demand.

(b) Between one year and two years.

(c) Between two and five years.

(d) After five years.
[*CO 21(f); GU 10(f)*].

Of these, *(b)* and *(c)* represent additional analysis that only a listed company or a company traded on the USM is required to give. This is because, as already explained in paragraph 9.04, the Act only requires companies to show the amounts in *(a)* and *(d)* and the aggregate of the amounts in *(b), (c)* and *(d)*. An illustration of these disclosure requirements is given in Table 32.

9.06   For the purpose of the Act, a loan falls due for repayment (or an instalment falls due for payment) on the earliest date on which the lender could require repayment (or payment) if he were to exercise all options and rights available to him. [*4 Sch 85*]. This rule would apply also for the purpose of The Stock Exchange's Continuing Obligations and the USM's General Undertaking.

9.07   Where any item that is shown under the heading 'Creditors' includes liabilities for which the company has given security, these liabilities must be disclosed in aggregate. Also, the notes must give an indication of the nature of the securities given by the company. [*4 Sch 48(4)*]. For this requirement to be meaningful, the financial statements should show some disaggregation of the relevant liabilities. This is because it could be misleading merely to disclose the aggregate of a basket of securities compared with the aggregate of a basket of liabilities.

9.08   This requirement to disclose securities does not apply to the situation where an unpaid supplier has supplied the company with stocks that are subject to a reservation of title clause. The reason for this is that, in this situation, the person who reserves title does not pass ownership in the goods, and so his rights are not in the nature of security. The ICAEW published in July 1976 an accounting statement, 'Accounting for goods sold subject to reservation of title' (V24 — now section 2.207 of the ICAEW Members Handbook). This statement recommends that, if the amount of creditors that are covered by reservation of title clauses is material, the accounting policies should describe how these creditors have been treated. Also, the financial statements should disclose, if practicable, the amount of creditors that are covered by reservation of title clauses.

Table 32: Disclosure of the group's and the company's borrowings.

Extract from BTR plc Annual Report 29 December 1984.

£ millions	BTR plc 1984	1983	Consolidated 1984	1983
18 Debenture loans, bank loans and overdrafts				
8% debenture stock 1985/90			7.9	7.9
10¾% debenture stock 1991/96				1.6
11% debenture stock 1996/2001				1.0
			7.9	10.5
Amounts payable otherwise than by instalments beyond five years			7.9	10.5
Bank loans repayable otherwise than by instalments wholly beyond five years	20.0	20.0	116.5	85.2
Bank loans repayable by instalments:				
Repayable within five years	37.5	1.8	86.9	110.3
Repayable beyond five years	142.5	178.2	162.3	239.2
Other bank loans and overdrafts			108.4	116.5
	200.0	200.0	474.1	551.2
Redeposits			(79.8)	(112.2)
	200.0	200.0	394.3	439.0

The above bank loans and overdrafts are at interest rates varying between 4.85% and 18.75%.
Bank loans and overdrafts amounting to £38.3 million (£38.1 million) are secured.
Debenture loans, bank loans and overdrafts are repayable:

	BTR plc 1984	1983	Consolidated 1984	1983
Over one and under two years			70.8	65.4
Over two and under five years	37.5	1.8	124.5	161.4
Beyond five years	162.5	198.2	286.7	334.9
	200.0	200.0	482.0	561.7
Redeposits			(79.8)	(112.2)
	200.0	200.0	402.2	449.5

Analysing creditors due

9.09　It should not be too difficult to analyse creditors on the basis outlined in paragraph 9.04. However, with a bank loan or an overdraft, it is not always obvious how that analysis should be made.

9.10　The age or the repayment term of a bank overdraft will usually be determined by reference to the terms of repayment, rather than by the facility period. If the overdraft is repayable on demand, it will clearly fall into the category of being repayable within one year. However, a company may have a medium-term bank facility for, say, five years. It uses this facility by drawing bills that the bank then discounts. When these bills become repayable, other bills are drawn, and so on. Normally, these would also fall into the category of being repayable within one year. But, if there is no way that the bank can recall the money as long as the amounts outstanding remain within the facility, the loans may be treated as medium-term borrowings (that is, loans that will fall due after more than one year). If the bank has the ability to terminate the facility and not to discount the new bills, the loans should then be shown as loans that will fall due within one year. Either way, the amounts may be shown either as 'Bank loans and overdrafts' or as 'Bills of exchange payable'.

Other creditors including taxation and social security

9.11 The line 'Other creditors including taxation and social security' must be analysed between other creditors, and taxation and social security. [*Note 9 on the balance sheet formats*]. These headings should include the following items:

(a) Other creditors
—Excise duty (which is not strictly a tax).
—Dividends (see para 9.14 below).
—Any items that cannot appropriately be analysed elsewhere.

(b) Taxation and social security
—Corporation tax.
—VAT.
—ACT payable on dividends (see para 9.16 below).
—Social security and other amounts (such as PAYE owed in respect of wages and salaries).

9.12 'Other creditors including taxation and social security' contrasts with the line under provisions for 'Taxation, including deferred taxation'. The latter item will comprise all deferred tax liabilities (see further para 9.51 below).

9.13 'Other creditors including taxation and social security', like other categories of creditors, has to be split between amounts that will fall due within one year and amounts that will fall due after more than one year. Some companies will find that they have corporation tax liabilities that will be due within one year and other companies will find that their corporation tax liabilities will be due after more than one year. These balances should be analysed and disclosed accordingly. The corporation tax balance should not be included in the heading under provisions 'Taxation, including deferred taxation'. This is because the corporation tax liability is not strictly a 'provision' as defined in the Act (see further para 9.45 below), because the amount of the liability is certain as to both its amount and the date when it is payable.

Dividends and related ACT

9.14   Dividends are not specifically referred to in either of the balance sheet formats. Schedule 4 requires the disclosure in the profit and loss account of the aggregate amount that is recommended for distribution by way of dividend. [*4 Sch 3(7)*]. Paragraph 51(3) of Schedule 4 requires the proposed dividends to be disclosed also in the balance sheet or in the related notes. A proposed dividend is not a liability in law until it has been declared, and so it would not be appropriate to include it within any of the items listed in the formats. In practice it is normally included as a separate item under 'Creditors'.

9.15   In addition, the notes to the financial statements must state:

(a) The amount of any arrears in the payment of fixed cumulative dividends on the company's shares.

(b) The period for which these dividends are in arrear. Where there is more than one class in arrear, this period must be given in respect of each class.
[*4 Sch 49*].

9.16   Furthermore, SSAP 8 requires that proposed dividends should be included in creditors without the addition of the related ACT. The ACT payable on proposed dividends (whether recoverable or irrecoverable) should be included under 'Taxation and social security'.

9.17   Where there is unrelieved ACT on proposed dividends that is deemed to be recoverable, it should be treated as an asset. Unless the unrelieved ACT can be set off against the deferred tax account (see para 9.52), it should be included in 'Prepayments and accrued income'.

9.18   This treatment complies with SSAP 8. In addition, SSAP 15 says that ACT should be carried forward only to the extent that it is foreseen that sufficient corporation tax will be assessed on the profits or income of the next accounting period, against which the ACT is available for offset. Unless the recovery of ACT is assured beyond reasonable doubt, those debit balances that arise in respect of ACT should be written off. Such recovery will normally only be assured where the debit balances are recoverable (without replacement by equivalent debit balances) out of the corporation tax that is expected to arise on the profits or income of the next accounting period. [*SSAP 15 paras 31, 32*].

9.19   The provisions of the Standard, detailed above, that apply to the carry forward of ACT are based on the same logic as the provisions that apply to the need to provide for deferred taxation. That is, ACT should be carried forward as an asset only to the extent that it is expected to be recoverable, in the same way that deferred taxation should be provided as a liability only to the extent that it is likely to become payable.

Trade creditors

9.20   'Trade creditors' could comprise either all items included in the creditors ledger or simply those items that relate to the cost of sales. Most companies classify all creditors ledger items as trade creditors, although such treatment could distort the cost of sales/trade creditors ratio. A company should ensure that, whatever treatment it adopts, it is consistent from year to year.

Accruals and deferred income

9.21   In the same way that 'Prepayments and accrued income' may be shown in either of two positions in the formats, the item 'Accruals and deferred income' may be disclosed either as a category of creditors or as a separate category in its own right. [*Note 10 on the balance sheet formats*]. Where 'Accruals and deferred income' is disclosed under creditors, it must be analysed between those amounts that will fall due within one year and those amounts that will fall due after more than one year. [*Note 13 on the balance sheet formats*]. No such analysis is required if 'Accruals and deferred income' is included as a separate category.

9.22   'Accruals and deferred income' could include government grants of a capital nature that are accounted for as deferred credits, and are not deducted from the cost of the fixed assets. (The treatment of capital-based grants is discussed in Chapter 7, paragraphs 7.110 to 7.113.)

9.23   In addition, 'Accruals and deferred income' may include that proportion of any revenue-based grants that are deferred to match against future related expenditure. SSAP 4 says that revenue-based grants should be credited to revenue in the same period in which the expenditure to which they relate is charged. Therefore, where a revenue-based grant is received before the related expenditure is incurred, the grant should be carried forward as deferred income. A proportion of the grant should be credited annually to revenue to match the related expenditure that is charged to revenue in that year. Where the amount of government grants remaining as a deferred credit is material, it should be shown separately in the balance sheet. [*SSAP 4 para 9*].

Debenture loans

9.24   A company that has debenture loans must split them between convertible and non-convertible loans. [*Note 7 on the balance sheet formats*].

9.25   The term 'debenture' is defined in Section 744 of the Act as including "debenture stock, bonds and any other securities of a company, whether constituting a charge on the assets of the company or not". This definition is very wide. It does not distinguish clearly between a debenture loan and any other loan. Whether a particular loan is a debenture or not will depend on the documentation. A formal loan agreement, whether containing security or not, may often constitute a debenture. Although a bank loan may be a debenture loan, the balance sheet formats distinguish between bank loans and other debenture loans. Consequently, the disclosure requirements that are set out in paragraphs 9.26 and 9.27 below apply only to those other debenture loans and not to bank loans.

9.26   If a company has issued any debentures during the financial year, the notes to the financial statements must disclose:

(a) The reason for making the issue.

(b) The classes of debentures issued.

(c) The amount issued, and the consideration the company received in respect of each class of debentures issued.
[*4 Sch 41(1)*].

9.27   Moreover, the notes must also disclose:

(a) Particulars of any redeemed debentures that the company has power to reissue.

(b) The nominal amount and the book value of any debentures that are held by either a nominee of, or a trustee for, the company.
[*4 Sch 41(2)(3)*].

9.28   Convertible loan stock is another form of debenture and this type of stock is considered further in paragraph 9.79 below.

9.29   In addition, the general disclosure requirements for creditors set out in paragraphs 9.02 to 9.10 above apply to all debentures (for example, see Table 32).

Discounted stock

Deep discounted stock

9.30   Deep discounted stock is a form of loan stock (that is, debenture loan) that is issued at a discount and repayable at par. In a Parliamentary written answer published on 25 June 1982, the Chancellor of the Exchequer announced that from that date companies would be able to issue deep discounted stock. The disclosure provisions outlined in paragraphs 9.24 to 9.29 above apply equally to deep discounted stock. The paragraphs that follow outline the accounting treatment that should be adopted by both the company issuing the loan stock and the company acquiring the loan stock.

The issuing company

9.31   To a company that issues this type of stock, the discount it gives when it issues the stock is effectively its cost of borrowing the money. The company should, therefore, treat the discount as interest payable, and write it off in stages as a charge against income in arriving at the company's profit or loss on ordinary activities before taxation.

9.32   The annual write-off (that is, the deemed interest) can be calculated either on a straight-line basis over the period of the loan (to give a constant charge each year), or on an actuarial basis (to give a constant rate on the amount outstanding at any one time).

9.33   Whatever the legal position may be, companies should not write the whole of the discount off against reserves (either direct, or by an appropriation from the profit and loss account, or against share premium account). This is because these methods of dealing with the discount would not normally give a true and fair view of the cost of capital the company uses. However, Section 130 of the Act specifically allows a company to write off against the share premium account the discount it allows on an issue of debentures. If a company wishes to take advantage of this provision, it should first debit the discount to the profit and loss account as interest paid, and then transfer the cost (net of tax) to the share premium account by means of an adjustment to retained profit. This adjustment should be made on the face of the profit and loss account.

9.34   If the terms of the issue are that the stock is repayable at par (either at the end of a set period or, in specific circumstances, on an earlier date), it would be appropriate to show in the balance sheet the liability at par and the unamortised discount as an asset. In accordance with paragraph 5 of Schedule 4 to the Act, a company cannot show the asset as a deduction from the liability. Where a company shows the unamortised discount as an asset, paragraph 24 of Schedule 4 requires the company either to show that asset separately on the face of the balance sheet or to disclose it in the notes to the financial statements.

9.35   If the terms of the issue specify that, for example, the stock can be repaid at a date earlier than the redemption date, but at less than par, it may be appropriate to show the liability in the balance sheet at that lower amount. In this situation, the liability may increase progressively over the years as the date of redemption at par draws closer.

9.36   In addition to making the disclosures noted in paragraphs 9.26 and 9.27 above, the company should disclose also the accounting policy that it has adopted in respect of the treatment of deep discounted stock in both the profit and loss account and the balance sheet.

The special tax rules that apply to deep discounted stock are set out in the Finance Act 1984. Generally (subject to various conditions), a company that issues this type of stock will obtain tax relief in each accounting period for the discount that accrues over that period. The accrued discount that will be allowed is determined for each income period by applying the following formula:

$$\frac{(A \times B) - C}{100}$$

In the above formula:

A is the adjusted issue price (that is, the issue price plus the accrued discount for all previous income periods).

B is the yield to maturity (that is, broadly, the rate, on a compound yield basis, at which the issue price has to grow in order to reach the redemption value at the redemption date, taking into account the amount and the frequency of any interest payments).

C is the amount of interest attributable to the income period.

The company that issues the stock must print an accrued discounts table on it.

The issuing company will also have to consider the need to provide or disclose any deferred tax that may arise from any timing difference between the amount of the discount charged in the company's profit and loss account and the amount of discount allowed in its tax computation.

The investing company

9.37   To the company that acquires the loan stock, the discount is effectively the interest it will receive on the loan. Although it does not receive the 'interest' until the stock is redeemed, the company should treat it as interest receivable on an annual basis. The company should credit it in arriving at its profit or loss on ordinary activities before taxation. It may, however, consider the amount not to be realised, and therefore not distributable, until it has actually been received.

9.38   The deep discounted stock should be included in the balance sheet as an investment loan at cost plus the amount of interest that has been credited to the profit and loss account.

9.39   However, where a company holds the deep discounted stock as a fixed asset, but it does not intend to hold the stock to redemption, and where the market value at the balance sheet date is lower than cost plus accrued interest, the company will need to make a provision if it expects the diminution in value to be permanent. Where the company holds the deep discounted stock as a current asset, and the market value is lower than cost plus accrued interest, the company will need to make a provision to ensure that the deep discounted stock is shown at the lower of cost and net realisable value.

9.40   It is important that the notes to the financial statements clearly state the company's policy in respect of deep discounted stock.

As mentioned in paragraph 9.36, the special tax rules that apply to deep discounted stock are set out in the Finance Act 1984. The investing company will be taxed only when it either redeems or disposes of the stock. The company will be taxed as if it had received investment income equal to the accrued discount over the period for which it has held the security. There will be a timing difference between the treatment of the discount in the company's profit and loss account and the treatment in its tax computation. Consequently, the company may have to account for deferred taxation on this timing difference.

Other discounted stock

9.41   As an alternative to issuing deep discounted stock, companies may issue other forms of stock at a discount. With other discounted stock, the rate of interest can be very low or it can be deferred for the first few years and become payable only over the last few years to redemption, or alternatively, the interest can be stepped. Another possibility is that stock may be redeemable at a premium. The discount on such stock will be lower than the discount on deep discounted stock, but the principles outlined above in paragraphs 9.30 to 9.40 still apply.

9.42   Traditionally, the discount on issue, and the premium on redemption, of debentures is written off to the share premium account. Section 130 of the Act specifically allows the share premium account to be used for this purpose. However, it is preferable for companies to account for such discounted stock in the way set out in paragraph 9.33 above for deep discounted stock (that is, spreading the cost over the life of the stock). Whenever the cost of writing off the discount or spreading the interest is material (either as a proportion of the total financing cost or in relation to the profit or loss on ordinary activities before taxation), it should be charged in arriving at the profit or loss on ordinary activities before taxation in order to give a true and fair view. In some situations, the company may then be able to transfer an equivalent amount from the share premium account to the profit and loss account. Again, whichever method a company uses, it is important that it should clearly state the method used in its accounting policy.

Unit trusts and investment trusts

9.43   Unit trusts and investment trusts (and some investment companies) are required, by their trust deeds and articles of association respectively, to distinguish clearly between capital and income. They are prohibited from making distributions out of their capital. Because of this, it is generally not appropriate for unit trusts and investment trusts to account for the discount as interest receivable. Instead, any increase in value should probably be treated as a capital profit that is not available for distribution.

Provisions for liabilities and charges

9.44   There is sometimes confusion whether items should be disclosed under provisions, or creditors or accruals. In this connection, the treatment of provisions for taxation has already been considered under 'Other creditors including taxation and social security' (see para 9.11 above). For some provisions (for example, those for bad and doubtful debts), it is correct to net them against the assets to which they relate. This treatment is correct because the assets have to be stated, in accordance with the statutory accounting rules, at their net realisable value. [*4 Sch 19(2), 23(1)*].

9.45   'Provisions for liabilities or charges' is defined in the Act as:

"Any amount retained as reasonably necessary for the purpose of providing for any liability or loss which is either likely to be incurred, or certain to be incurred but uncertain as to amount or as to the date on which it will arise." [*4 Sch 89*].

9.46   Creditors, by contrast, normally comprise those amounts that are actually owing to third parties, and not amounts retained that are reasonably necessary for providing for any liability or loss that is likely to be incurred. Also, accruals generally include those amounts representing costs and charges (possibly apportioned at the balance sheet date) that are not yet actually owing to third parties.

9.47   Certain information is required to be disclosed in the notes to the financial statements in respect of each provision for liabilities or charges that is shown either on the face of the balance sheet or in the notes. This information is as follows:

(a) The aggregate amount of the provision at both the beginning and the end of the financial year.

(b) Any amounts transferred either to or from the provision during the financial year.

(c) The source and the application of any amounts so transferred. [*4 Sch 46(1)(2)*].

An example of such disclosure is given in Table 33.

Table 33: Disclosure of provisions for liabilities and charges.

Extract from Tate & Lyle PLC Annual Report 29 September 1984.

Note extract

17. PROVISIONS FOR LIABILITIES AND CHARGES

	Pensions and similar obligations	Deferred taxation	Insurance funds	Other	Total
	£ million	£ million	£ million	£ million	£ million
Group					
At 1st October 1983	2.5	11.2	3.6	7.9	25.2
Differences on exchange	—	2.3	0.3	0.2	2.8
Subsidiaries acquired	—	—	—	0.6	0.6
Utilised in period	(2.5)	—	—	(3.5)	(6.0)
Charged to profit and loss account	—	4.5	1.5	7.5	13.5
Surplus Advance Corporation Tax payable for period	—	(4.4)	—	—	(4.4)
Additional provision for deferred taxation	—	9.3	—	—	9.3
At 29th September 1984	—	22.9	5.4	12.7	41.0

9.48   Where an amount is shown under 'Other provisions', and it includes any individual provision that is itself material, the information detailed above must be given in respect of each such provision. [*4 Sch 46(3)*].

9.49   Possible examples are provisions for future rationalisation, for redundancy, for dilapidations, or for warranty claims.

9.50   If the provision for liabilities and charges does include any provision for taxation (other than deferred taxation — which is discussed below), it must be disclosed separately. [*4 Sch 47*].

Deferred taxation

Actual liability

9.51   The provision for deferred taxation should be included under the balance sheet heading 'Taxation, including deferred taxation'. In addition, SSAP 15 requires the provision for deferred taxation to be shown separately. The Standard says that tax deferred or accelerated by the effect of timing differences should be accounted for to the extent that a liability or an asset will probably crystallise. The deferred tax balance, its major components, and transfers to and from the deferred tax account should be disclosed in the notes to the balance sheet (for example, see Table 34). [*SSAP 15 paras 25, 37, 38*].

Table 34: Disclosure of deferred taxation.

Extract from Arthur Guinness and Sons PLC Report and Accounts 30 September 1984.

---

27 Deferred taxation

The amounts provided and the full potential liabilities as far as holding and subsidiary companies are concerned are as follows:

	Amount provided 1984 £m	Full potential liability 1984 £m	Amount provided 1983 £m	Full potential liability 1983 £m
Excess of capital allowances over accumulated depreciation	2·0	31·6	1·1	29·3
Chargeable gains on properties	—	2·5	—	5·0
Stock appreciation relief	—	—	—	2·4
	2·0	34·1	1·1	36·7
Provision allowable for tax in future years	—	(10·1)	—	(11·7)
Advance corporation tax not immediately recoverable	—	(7·4)	—	(4·2)
	2·0	16·6	1·1	20·8

No deferred taxation liability is expected to arise in group companies from the reversal of timing differences as a result of the changes in the basis of taxation introduced by the Finance Act 1984.

9.52   The provision for deferred tax should be calculated by the liability method, and it should be reduced by any deferred tax debit balance that arises from separate categories of timing differences. It should also be reduced by any ACT that is available for offset against the deferred tax provision. [*SSAP 15 paras 24, 29*]. However, it is incorrect to offset ACT against a deferred tax balance to a greater extent than it is actually recoverable against that deferred tax liability when it becomes payable. For example, if a company has a deferred tax balance of £20,000 (excluding any deferred tax on capital gains) that has been calculated at a corporation tax rate of 35%, then the maximum amount of ACT that can currently be offset against that deferred tax balance is £17,143 (namely, £20,000 x 30%/35%). The 30% used in the calculation is the current rate of income tax.

Contingent liability

9.53   Where a company does not provide for some or all of any deferred tax (because the directors do not consider that a liability will crystallise), paragraph 40 of SSAP 15 requires that the total amount of any unprovided deferred tax should be disclosed in a note to the financial statements, analysed into its major components. In addition, where the potential amount of deferred tax on an asset that has been revalued is not shown (because the revaluation does not constitute a timing difference), this fact (but not necessarily the amount) should be stated in the financial statements (see further Chapter 5 paras 5.59 to 5.63). [*SSAP 15 para 41*].

9.54   When the value of an asset is shown in a note to the financial statements (because it differs materially from its book amount), the note should show the tax effects, if any, that would arise if the asset were realised at that value at the balance sheet date. [*SSAP 15 para 42*]. In this situation, the 'tax effect' means that the potential amount of tax should be disclosed.

9.55   The deferred tax disclosure requirements that relate to the profit and loss account are considered in more detail in Chapter 10, paragraphs 10.97 to 10.101.

Contingent liabilities

Guarantees and financial commitments

9.56   The notes to the financial statements must give details of:

(a) Any charge on the company's assets that has been given in order to secure the liabilities of any other person.

(b) The amounts so secured (where practicable).
[*4 Sch 50(1)*].

9.57   This requirement is particularly relevant for groups of companies. These requirements will include (for example) the disclosure of amounts that a holding company has secured on its assets in respect of a subsidiary's borrowings (and *vice versa*). Therefore, where (for example) a company has guaranteed a subsidiary's overdraft to the extent of £30m by way of a charge on the company's assets, the actual overdraft of the subsidiary at the year end should be disclosed (up to a maximum, in this situation, of £30m).

9.58   In respect of any other contingent liability that has not been provided for in the financial statements, the notes must disclose:

   (a) The amount, or the estimated amount, of that liability.

   (b) Its legal nature.

   (c) Whether any valuable security has been provided by the company in connection with that liability. Where this is so, details of the security provided must be given.
   [4 Sch 50(2)].

9.59   Consequently, if a company has given an unlimited guarantee for an overdraft of its subsidiary, and there is no charge on its assets, the fact that it is unlimited and that no valuable security has been provided and the actual amount of the overdraft need to be disclosed.

9.60   In addition to the Act's requirements, SSAP 18 requires a company to accrue all its material contingent losses in its financial statements. This requirement applies only if it is probable that a future event will confirm a loss that can be estimated with reasonable accuracy at the date on which the board of directors approves the financial statements. [*SSAP 18 para 15*]. For example, the company may have entered into an uncovered forward foreign currency contract during the year. If this contract matures before the date when the board approves the financial statements, and it results in a loss, the company should provide for this loss in its financial statements. In other situations, material contingent losses must merely be disclosed in the notes to the financial statements (unless the possibility of loss is remote, in which case no disclosure is required). [*SSAP 18 para 16*]. To comply with this latter requirement of SSAP 18, the notes to the financial statements must state:

   (a) The nature of the contingency.

   (b) The uncertainties that are expected to affect the ultimate outcome.

   (c) A prudent estimate of the financial effect, or a statement that such an estimate is not practicable. For this purpose, the amount to be disclosed is the potential financial effect (before taking account of taxation) after deducting any amounts accrued and the amounts of any contingencies that have only a remote possibility of loss.
   [*SSAP 18 paras 18, 19, 20*].

   Table 35 illustrates the disclosure of contingent liabilities.

Table 35: Disclosure of contingent liabilities.

Extract from Imperial Group public limited company Report and Accounts 31 October 1984.

21 Commitments and contingent liabilities

a Subsidiaries have contingent liabilities amounting to approximately £1.5m (1983 £7.0m) in respect of guarantees given for commitments in the normal course of trade.

b The Parent Company has guaranteed the listed debenture and loan stocks of Imperial Foods Ltd and Imperial Brewing & Leisure Ltd totalling £48.9m (1983 £49.3m) and has outstanding guarantees of certain other borrowings by subsidiaries amounting to £8.0m (1983 £5.4m) and former subsidiaries of £20.0m (1983 £16.4m).

c The Parent Company and certain of its subsidiaries have continuing obligations in connection with employees' pension schemes.

d Leased assets other than short and long leasehold properties are not included in the balance sheet. Annual rentals are charged to profit and loss account. The future minimum lease payments to which the Group is committed under non-cancellable finance leases are as follows:—

Parent Company £ million	Year ending 31st October	Consolidated £ million
5.2	1985	28.0
5.2	1986	26.9
5.0	1987	25.3
4.9	1988	22.1
3.8	1989	17.8
2.5	1990 and after	62.1
26.6		182.2
(3.8)	Less:— Interest	(51.4)
22.8		130.8
19.7	At 31st October 1983	101.6

9.61 The Act requires the notes to the financial statements also to disclose, where practicable, either the aggregate amount or the estimated amount of capital expenditure that:

(a) Has been contracted for, but not provided for, at the balance sheet date.

(b) Has been authorised by the directors, but not contracted for, at that date.
[*4 Sch 50(3)*].

Pension commitments

9.62 The notes to the financial statements must show separately pension commitments that have respectively been provided for and not been provided for. [*4 Sch 50(4)*]. The notes must give a separate indication of any such commitments that relate to a company's former directors. [*4 Sch 50(4)*].

9.63 'Pension commitments' is a fairly broad term. It could be interpreted as referring to pensions actually payable direct by the company (which is rare). However, the generally accepted view is that it relates to a company's commitments to ensure that a pension fund is capable of providing the pensions that are and will be payable.

9.64   The Act does not specify the basis a company should use to measure pension commitments that it has not provided for. Presumably, the Act intends the company to disclose its policy in respect of pension costs, because the mere disclosure of pension commitments that have not been provided for will, on its own, be meaningless.

9.65   Some companies publish notes on their accounting policies in respect of their contributions to pension funds. However, there is no statutory obligation for a company to do so unless its policies are significant and may affect the truth and fairness of the financial statements.

9.66   In November 1984, the ASC published a SOI that deals with both the measurement and the disclosure aspects of accounting for pension costs. It is intended that this SOI will form the basis of an exposure draft. The SOI concludes that, where a company has a commitment to provide pensions, the company's accounting objective should be to charge the cost of pensions against profits on a systematic basis over the service lives of groups of employees. The company's commitment could arise either from a specific contract or as a result of custom or practice. The SOI says that companies should account for variations from regular pension costs by charging such variations over the remaining working lives of current members. Consequently, companies need not charge such variations immediately to the profit and loss account. The ASC believes that many companies already account for their contributions in accordance with the SOI's proposals.

9.67   The information that the SOI suggests should be included in a company's financial statements is as follows:

(a) The nature of the pension schemes (for example, defined benefit or defined contribution), whether they are externally funded or internally financed, and any legal obligations on the company (for example, an undertaking to meet the balance of cost).

(b) The accounting policy, and the funding policy (if different from the accounting policy), with an indication of the basis used for allocating pension costs to accounting periods.

(c) The fact of whether or not the pension costs and liabilities are assessed in accordance with the advice of a professional qualified actuary and, if so, the date of the most recent actuarial valuation.

(d) The amount charged in the profit and loss account for pension costs, distinguishing between normal charges related to employees' pay and service in the accounting period and other charges or credits, and with explanations of such charges or credits. Other charges might include additional charges to cover the cost of post-retirement awards not covered by the normal charge, or reductions in the normal charge to take account of contribution holidays, or a temporarily reduced contribution rate resulting from overfunding.

(e) Any commitments to change the rate of contributions, or to make special contributions.

(f) Any provisions or prepayments in the balance sheet that have resulted from a difference between the accounting policy and the funding policy.

(g) The amount of any deficiency on a discontinuance actuarial valuation, or on the requirements of the Occupational Pensions Board, with an indication of the action, if any, that is being taken to deal with that deficiency in future financial statements.

(h) The amount of any material self-investment. ('Self-investment' is the investment of all or part of a scheme's assets in the shares or assets of the employer, or of a subsidiary, or of an associated company of the employer.)

(i) Where the scheme is internally financed, the amount of the provision at the balance sheet date and the amount of any identifiable fund of assets representing the provision.

(j) Expected significant effects on future financial statements of any changes that have occurred in the above, including the effects of any material improvements in benefits.

9.68 Until the ASC issues a Standard on accounting for pension costs, the disclosure requirements outlined in paragraph 9.67 above can be regarded as best accounting practice. However, the disclosure required by the Act (as outlined in paras 9.62 to 9.64 above) will normally give the minimum level of acceptable disclosure. An illustration of the type of information that companies disclose is given in Table 36.

Table 36: Disclosure of pension scheme information.

Extract from Sedgwick Group plc Annual Report 31 December 1984.

---

25 Pensions

Sedgwick Group plc and its principal subsidiaries operate pension schemes, the assets of which are independent of the group's finances. These pension schemes cover all the group's material obligations to provide pensions to its retired employees and currently eligible members of staff.

The Sedgwick Group Pension Scheme (the Scheme) provides retirement and death benefits for all eligible staff in the United Kingdom. This exempt approved scheme, which is valued by the Scheme's actuary every three years, is funded partly by contributions from members of staff and partly by contributions from group companies determined as a result of the actuary's valuation. As at 1 January 1984, that valuation disclosed an excess of assets over liabilities and the employer's contributions have accordingly been reduced for the three years ending 31 December 1986 while still leaving the assets to exceed liabilities by a prudent margin.

9.69 The treatment in group accounts should conform as far as possible to the above disclosure requirements insofar as it is practicable and material. However, it will often be excessively burdensome for a group to disclose specific information in its group accounts about each different pension scheme the group operates. Consequently, some form of summarised pension cost information will normally be sufficient.

Other financial commitments

9.70   Any other financial commitments that have not been provided for must be disclosed in the notes to the financial statements to the extent that they are relevant to a proper understanding of the company's state of affairs. [*4 Sch 50(5)*]. An example of such a commitment might be where a company has agreed in principle to enter into a major joint venture with another company. In this situation, the company should disclose the amount of money that it has agreed in principle to put into the venture. It is not envisaged that this provision of the Act will normally require the disclosure of financial commitments that relate to a company's day-to-day trading operations (such as commitments under supply contracts).

9.71   Where any of the commitments referred to in paragraphs 9.56, 9.58, 9.61, 9.62 and 9.70 above relate to group companies, these must be shown separately. In particular, they must be analysed between those relating respectively to:

(a) Any holding company or any fellow subsidiary of the company.

(b) Any subsidiary of the company.
[*4 Sch 50(6)*].

Called-up share capital

9.72   The amount of allotted share capital and the amount of paid-up capital must be shown separately. These amounts must be shown either under the heading 'Called-up share capital' in the balance sheet, or in a note to the financial statements. [*Note 12 on the balance sheet formats*]. 'Called-up share capital' means:

(a) That proportion of a company's share capital that equals the aggregate amount of the calls on its shares (whether or not those calls have been paid).

(b) Any share capital that has been paid up without being called.

(c) Any share capital that is to be paid on a specified future date under the articles of association, or under the terms of allotment, or any other arrangements for paying for those shares.
[*Sec 737(1)*].

9.73   The following example illustrates the disclosure requirements for called-up share capital:

On 30 November 1985, a company allots 100,000 ordinary shares of £1 each. By 31 December 1985, the company has made calls amounting to 75p per share. At 31 December 1985, the holders of 10,000 shares have not paid the last call of 25p per share. In the financial statements at 31 December 1985, the company would have to make the following disclosures:

Allotted share capital	£100,000
Called-up share capital	£75,000
Paid-up share capital	£72,500
Called-up share capital not paid	£2,500

9.74 Called-up share capital not paid is part of the double entry, and it will appear in the balance sheet format either as a separate item (A in format 1 or 2) or under debtors (C II 5 in format 1 or 2). Similarly, called-up share capital forms part of the double entry, and it will appear under capital and reserves (KI in format 1 or AI in format 2). Neither the allotted share capital nor the paid-up capital forms part of the double entry. However, they must still be disclosed either on the face of the balance sheet or in a note to the financial statements.

9.75 In addition, the notes to the financial statements must show the amount of a company's authorised share capital. Also, where shares of more than one class have been allotted, the notes must show the number and the aggregate nominal value of the shares of each class that have been so allotted. [*4 Sch 38(1)*].

9.76 In practice, companies will generally be able to refer to share capital that is 'allotted, called up and fully paid', because these items will often be the same amount.

9.77 Where any part of the allotted share capital consists of redeemable shares, the notes to the financial statements must show:

(a) The earliest and the latest dates on which the company may redeem those shares.

(b) Whether the company is obliged to redeem those shares, or whether the company or the shareholder merely has an option to redeem them or to require redemption.

(c) The amount of any premium payable on redemption, or the fact that no such premium is payable.
[*4 Sch 38(2)*].

9.78 Also, where a company has allotted any shares during the financial year, the notes to the financial statements must state:

(a) The reason for making the allotment.

(b) The classes of shares allotted.

(c) The number of shares allotted, their aggregate nominal value, and the consideration received in respect of each class of shares allotted.
[*4 Sch 39*].

9.79 Furthermore, information has to be given about any 'contingent rights to the allotment of shares' that may exist. These rights could be options to subscribe for shares, or rights on the conversion of loan stock or any other rights where a person may require the allotment of shares (whether, in the latter case, the rights arise on conversion of any other type of security or otherwise). The information to be given is:

(a) The number, the description and the amount of the shares in respect of which the right is exercisable.

(b) The period during which the right is exercisable.

(c) The price to be paid for the shares allotted.
[*4 Sch 40*].

This disclosure is illustrated in Table 102 on page 474.

9.80   Consequently, the financial statements have to include the rights of conversion of convertible loan stock.

Disclosure of reserves

9.81   Certain information must be included in the notes to the financial statements in respect of each reserve that is shown either on the face of the balance sheet or in the notes to the financial statements. This information is as follows:

(a) The aggregate amount of the reserve at both the beginning and the end of the financial year.

(b) Any amounts transferred to or from the reserve during the financial year.

(c) The source and application of any amounts transferred.
[*4 Sch 46(1)(2)*].

Table 37 shows how a group discloses its reserves.

Table 37: *Illustration of the disclosure of reserves. This company has also given the amount of the distributable reserves of the group.*

Extract from Fleet Holdings P.L.C. Report & Accounts 30 June 1984.

21. Reserves

	The Group			The Company	
	Revaluation reserve	Other reserves	Profit and loss account	Revaluation reserve	Profit and loss account
	£000	£000	£000	£000	£000
Balance at 1 July 1983	956	14,908	19,202	28,518	6,574
Provision for deferred taxation	—	—	(5,922)	—	(4)
Profit retained for the year	—	—	11,023	—	11,887
Foreign exchange translation difference	—	192	—	—	—
Revaluation of investments	80,051	—	—	74,071	—
Transfer to profit and loss account:					
Losses of related companies	(71)	—	71	—	—
Balance at 30 June 1984	80,936	15,100	24,374	102,589	18,457

At 30 June 1984 the distributable reserves of the group amount to £40,359,000 and of the Company to £18,457,000.

Revaluation reserve

9.82 The revaluation reserve must be disclosed on the face of the balance sheet. However, it may be described by a different name, although it is generally preferable for companies to keep to the terminology in the Act. [*4 Sch 34(2)*].

9.83 The revaluation reserve and some of the problems surrounding it are considered in the discussion on the alternative accounting rules in Chapter 5, paragraphs 5.08 to 5.63.

Other reserves

9.84 The main heading 'Other reserves' includes four sub-headings: 'Capital redemption reserve', 'Reserve for own shares', 'Reserves provided for by the articles of association' and 'Other reserves'. The last heading will include all reserves, both realised and unrealised, that do not fit elsewhere in the formats. If they are material, they should be specifically described.

Profit and loss account

9.85 Many companies do not use the wording 'Profit and loss account'. They use instead terms such as 'Revenue reserves'. The possibility of changing the wording of headings from those prescribed in the formats is discussed in Chapter 6, paragraphs 6.07 and 6.08. The general rule is that the Act does not allow different wording to be used. The term 'Revenue reserves', however, is generally accepted and understood in the UK and so there appears to be little danger that, if this term is used, it will mislead a user of the financial statements. This applies equally to those companies such as investment trusts that wish to publish a 'Revenue account', instead of a 'Profit and loss account'.

Reserves of related companies

9.86 Where a balance sheet includes a proportion of a related company's reserves, these reserves should be analysed between the various format headings (see also Chapter 8 para 8.36).

Realised and distributable reserves

9.87 The Act contains no specific requirement for reserves to be disclosed as either realised or unrealised, or as distributable or non-distributable. However, where a company has significant non-distributable reserves, it may need, in order to present a true and fair view, to disclose the amount of the reserves that it may not legally distribute under the Act (for example, see Table 37).

9.88 Realised and distributable reserves are dealt with in more detail in Chapter 19.

CHAPTER 10

THE PROFIT AND LOSS ACCOUNT

Chapter 10

The Profit and Loss Account

Introduction

10.01 The profit and loss account is one of the statements that a company must include in its financial statements. The Act requires the profit and loss account to comply with one of the four alternative formats of profit and loss account: formats 1 and 3 classify expenses by function and formats 2 and 4 classify expenses by type. These formats are set out in more detail in Chapter 6. The format a company chooses can be significant because, depending on the format, some of the information the company discloses in its profit and loss account will be different. Some of the items that are discussed below may relate only to one pair of formats. In addition, the Act lays down certain rules that relate to the disclosure of information in the notes to the profit and loss account, and also certain rules regarding the measurement of items that are included in the profit and loss account and these requirements are also considered below.

Turnover

10.02 The Act clearly defines the amount a company must include in its profit and loss account under the heading of 'Turnover'. It comprises the amounts a company derives from providing goods and services that fall within its ordinary activities, after deducting trade discounts, VAT and any other taxes based on the amounts it so derives. [*4 Sch 95*]. This definition accords with the requirement in SSAP 5 that turnover should exclude VAT on taxable outputs. However, SSAP 5 goes further: it says that, if a company wishes to show also its gross turnover, it should show the VAT relevant to that turnover as a deduction in arriving at the turnover exclusive of VAT.

An example of an accounting policy for turnover is given in Table 38.

10.03 The Act's definition does give rise to some unexpected results, particularly in specialised businesses. Four examples are given below:

Example 1

Where a company's only activity is rent collection, the rents it receives fall within the definition of turnover, because the company derives these by providing those *services* that fall within its ordinary activities.

Table 38: Example of an accounting policy for turnover.

Extract from Alfred McAlpine PLC Annual Report & Accounts 31 October 1984.

Turnover
Turnover comprises the value of work performed, land and goods sold and services provided outside the group. It includes the group's share of turnover in joint ventures but excludes the proportion of turnover of related companies attributable to the group.

Example 2

Where a company sells certain items either FOB (free on board) or CIF (cost, insurance, freight), it may wish to reduce the CIF items to FOB by deducting these expenses from turnover. However, because there is usually a profit element in the CIF charges and because there is no right of set-off of expenditure against income under the Act, the amount for turnover should include the full CIF selling price.

Example 3

With those construction companies and other companies that have long-term contract work in progress, neither SSAP 9 nor the Act defines the way in which they should calculate turnover. However, SSAP 9 does refer to the profit to be taken on long-term contracts, and it says that:

"The profit, if any, taken up [*in the profit and loss account*] needs to reflect the proportion of the work carried out at the accounting date." [*SSAP 9 para 8*].

Consequently, it seems by implication that the amount to be included in turnover is the proportion of the total contract price that relates to the work carried out to date, less any such amounts taken into account in previous years. This is the sales venue of contracts completed during the year, plus (or minus) the increase (or decrease) in the balance sheet value of gross work in progress.

Similarly, the costs of sales figure will be based on the same amounts, but will exclude the attributable profit element. The table below explains the amounts to be included in both turnover and cost of sales:

Long-term contract work in progress	Cost	Attributable profit	Gross WIP
	£000	£000	£000
Balance brought forward	700	200	900
Costs incurred in year	400	—	400
Attributable profit	—	100	100
Contracts closed	(300)	(50)	(350)
Balance carried forward	800	250	1,050

	Turnover	Cost of sales	Gross profit
	£000	£000	£000
Contracts closed	350	(300)	50
Increase in carrying value of work in progress	150	(100)	50
Total	500	(400)	100

It can be seen that the figure for turnover can just as easily be calculated by adding the attributable profit to the cost of work incurred during the year (that is, £400,000 + £100,000).

Many construction companies state, in their accounting policies, that their turnover includes the sales value of work they have carried out. The sales value of work carried out is equivalent to the figure for the cost of work incurred, plus attributable profit (as calculated above).

Example 4

Where a company acts as an agent or a dealer (for example, a commodity broker) it should not include the gross value of its contracts in turnover. It should, however, include only the commission of margin that it makes on each deal in turnover.

Disaggregated information — turnover and profit or loss before taxation

10.04 The Act requires the notes to the profit and loss account to include certain information analysed by both class of business and geographical market.

10.05 Where a company has carried on two or more classes of business during the financial year in question, and these, in the directors' opinion, differ substantially from each other, the notes must give:

(a) A description of each class.

(b) The amount of turnover that is attributable to each class.

(c) The amount of profit or loss before taxation that is, in the directors' opinion, attributable to each class.
[*4 Sch 55(1)*].

An illustration of this disclosure is shown in Table 39.

10.06 'Turnover' has the same meaning for this purpose as that given in paragraph 10.02 above.

10.07 The Act states that, in determining either the turnover or the profit or loss attributable to each class, the directors must have regard to the way in which the company's activities are organised. [*4 Sch 55(3)*]. Where classes of business do not, in the directors' opinion, differ substantially, they are to be treated as one class. Similarly, where the directors believe that markets do not differ substantially, those markets are to be treated as one market. [*4 Sch 55(4)*].

10.08 Where a company has supplied goods or services within two or more markets during the financial year in question, the turnover (but not the profit or loss before taxation) must also be disaggregated between markets (see also Table 39). This is necessary, however, only if the directors believe that the markets differ substantially. For this purpose, 'market' means a market delimited by geographical bounds. [*4 Sch 55(2)*].

10.09 It is important that companies maintain adequate records to enable them to meet these requirements.

Table 39: Disclosure of disaggregated information for turnover and profit before taxation.

Extract from B.A.T. Industries p.l.c. Annual report and accounts 31 December 1984.

Geographical analyses

Turnover	1984 £m	%	1983 £m	%
UK	2,346	16	2,167	18
Europe	3,095	21	2,367	20
North America	5,828	40	4,521	38
Latin America	1,721	12	1,601	14
Asia	939	7	725	6
Africa	411	3	398	3
Australasia	86	1	67	1
Commercial activities	14,426	100	11,846	100

The above analysis is based on the area of manufacture and figures based on location of market would not be materially different.

Profit	1984 £m	%	1983 £m	%
UK	106	7	80	8
Europe	109	7	65	7
North America	657	45	485	50
Latin America	138	10	113	11
Asia	83	6	61	6
Africa	49	3	41	4
Australasia	6		6	1
Commercial activities	1,148	78	851	87
Financial services	125	9		
Associated companies	192	13	125	13
Operating profit	1,465	100	976	100
Net interest	(60)		3	
Profit before taxation	1,405		979	

Industrial analyses

Turnover	1984 £m	%	1983 £m	%
Tobacco	6,943	48	6,138	52
Retailing	4,511	31	3,528	30
Paper	1,379	10	1,051	9
Packaging & printing	659	5	537	4
Other trading activities	934	6	592	5
Commercial activities	14,426	100	11,846	100
Financial services	1,077		—	
Share of associated companies	2,700		1,993	

Profit	1984 £m	%	1983 £m	%
Tobacco	698	48	542	56
Retailing	221	15	165	17
Paper	144	10	100	10
Packaging & printing	35	2	24	2
Other trading activities	50	3	20	2
Commercial activities	1,148	78	851	87
Financial services	125	9		
Associated companies	192	13	125	13
Operating profit	1,465	100	976	100
Net interest	(60)		3	
Profit before taxation	1,405		979	

Profit of associated companies is the Group's share of those companies' profits after interest but before taxation.

10.10 With listed companies and companies that are traded on the USM, The Stock Exchange's Continuing Obligations and the USM's General Undertaking respectively require a geographical analysis of both the net turnover and the contribution to trading results of those trading operations the company or the group carries on outside the UK and (in the case of listed companies) the Republic of Ireland. [*CO 21(c); GU 10(c)*]. Although the Act specifically refers to turnover attributable to each different geographical market that the company has supplied, and not the country of supply, the Continuing Obligations state that:

"A broad geographical analysis of net turnover by way of figures or percentages, given by market (not necessarily given country by country), will be acceptable." [*CO 21(c)*].

10.11 The disaggregated information need not be disclosed where the directors consider that its disclosure would be seriously prejudicial to the company's interests. In these circumstances, however, the fact that any such information has been omitted must be stated, although the reasons need not be given. [*4 Sch 55(5)*].

10.12 As an extreme example, if a company or a group supplies only customers in two countries that are politically opposed to each other, a published geographical split of turnover could well be prejudicial to the interests of the company or the group, and provided that the notes to the profit and loss account disclose the fact that this analysis has not been given, no further information is required. However, if a company is either listed or traded on the USM, and it considers that disclosure would be seriously prejudicial to its interests, it should seek such exemption from The Stock Exchange Quotations Department. This is because the Continuing Obligations and the General Undertaking do not give similar exemptions from disclosing disaggregated information.

10.13 In determining the split of profit or loss before taxation, a company should allocate its interest costs over the different segments. A company may be able to achieve this categorisation on a reasonable basis. For example, if a particular class of business is financed by specific loan capital, a company could allocate interest on that loan capital to the particular class of business. However, it is often difficult for a company to prepare such an analysis on a meaningful basis. If a company decides that it would be either totally impracticable or misleading to analyse its interest costs by category, it would be acceptable for it to classify the interest as, for example, unallocated head office costs.

Cost of sales, distribution costs and administrative expenses

10.14 These headings give rise to many questions concerning the allocation of costs and overheads. The following lists are intended to provide guidance as to the items that may be included under each heading.

10.15 *Cost of sales* will normally comprise:

(a) Opening (less closing) stocks and work in progress.

(b) Direct materials.

(c) Other external charges (such as the hire of plant and machinery or the cost of casual labour).

(d) Direct labour.

(e) All direct production overheads, and indirect overheads that cannot be related specifically to the distribution and administrative functions.

(f) Research and development costs.

(g) Cash discounts received on 'cost of sales' expenditure (this is *not* a set-off, but an effective reduction in the purchase price of an item).

(h) Stock provisions.

201

10.16   *Distribution costs* will normally comprise:

   (a) Payroll costs of the sales, marketing and distribution functions.

   (b) Advertising.

   (c) Salesmen's travel and entertaining.

   (d) Warehouse costs for finished goods.

   (e) Transport costs concerning the distribution of finished goods.

   (f) All costs of maintaining sales outlets.

   (g) Agents' commission payable.

10.17   *Administrative expenses* will normally comprise:

   (a) Payroll costs of the administrative function.

   (b) All costs of maintaining the administration buildings.

   (c) Bad debts.

   (d) Professional costs.

   (e) Cash discounts on sales.

10.18   As stated in Chapter 6, paragraph 6.30, if format 1 or 3 is adopted, charges for depreciation or the diminution in value of assets have to be analysed under the above headings. [*Note 14 on the profit and loss account formats*]. The type of analysis will depend on the function of the related assets.

10.19   In some specific instances, the above analyses may not be appropriate. For example, in the context of a mail order company, agents' commission payable may be regarded as a cost of sale rather than as a distribution cost.

10.20   The way in which a company analyses its costs will depend very much on the nature of its business. Where a company incurs significant operating expenses that it considers do not fall under any one of the headings 'Cost of sales', 'Distribution costs' and 'Administrative expenses', there is nothing to prevent the company including an additional heading for these expenses in formats 1 or 3. The overriding consideration is that a company should analyse its operating expenses consistently from year to year.

10.21   Some companies have adapted these headings to show additional items. However, these companies seem to be in a minority. This is probably because the headings are general enough to apply to most companies' expenditure. Examples of adaptations and additional items that companies have used in their financial statements are shown below.

Examples of adaptation of headings:

(a) Selling and distribution costs.

(b) Marketing, selling and distribution costs.

(c) Administrative and selling expenses.

(d) Selling and general administration expenses.

Examples of additional items:

(a) Research and development costs.

(b) Sales commission (shown in addition to distribution costs).

(c) Major reorganisation costs, including redundancy.

10.22 Because consolidated financial statements have to comply with the Act, they must, if format 1 or 3 is adopted, disclose the group's cost of sales, distribution costs and administrative expenses. The way in which a group analyses these costs will depend on the extent to which group companies deal both with other group companies and with third parties. If (for example) a distribution company within a group acts only for other group companies, most of those of its costs that are cost of sales in its own financial statements will be distribution costs as regards the group as a whole. If the distribution company acts solely for third parties, then its cost of sales will remain under that classification in the consolidated financial statements. Therefore, each group has to consider the nature of each group company's business. It may be acceptable in some groups to deal with all costs of manufacturing companies within the group as cost of sales, and with all costs of distribution companies as distribution costs, and so on.

10.23 Although there is no statutory obligation for a group to do so, most groups find that, from a practical point of view, it makes consolidation easier if all companies in the group adopt the same profit and loss account format.

10.24 If groups or individual companies that are primarily involved in supplying services adopt the format 1 profit and loss account (classification of expenses by function), these companies are unlikely to have any cost of sales or distribution costs. Consequently, most of their expenditure will fall under the category of administrative expenses. In these circumstances, it may be desirable for the administrative expenses to be analysed further into broad categories of expenditure.

Gross profit

10.25 The gross profit or loss has to be shown as a separate item in format 1, and it can be readily ascertained from the items that are disclosed in format 3. Formats 2 and 4 analyse expenditure in a different manner. Therefore, if a company wishes to avoid disclosing its gross profit, it should adopt either format 2 or format 4.

Own work capitalised

10.26 Where a company has constructed some of its own tangible fixed assets, and it adopts either format 2 or format 4 for its profit and loss account, it should include the costs of direct materials, direct labour and overheads it has capitalised as a credit under the heading 'Own work capitalised'. The costs of direct materials, direct labour and overheads are charged in the profit and loss account, by including these amounts under the relevant expenditure headings. The amount capitalised is then credited in the profit and loss account as own work capitalised, and it is debited to tangible fixed assets. Thus, items such as raw material costs in the profit and loss account will include the costs connected with such work.

Other operating income

10.27   'Other operating income' will include income that is associated with a company's normal activities, but that falls outside the definition of turnover. Such income could (for example) include the profit on the sale of fixed assets. However, if the profit on the sale of fixed assets is not material, it could be applied in reducing the depreciation charge.

10.28   'Other operating income' could include also rents from land (net of outgoings). In addition, the notes to the profit and loss account must disclose the amount of rents from land, after deducting ground rents, rates and other outgoings. This requirement, however, applies only if a substantial part of the company's revenue for the financial year in question consists of such rents. [*4 Sch 53(1)(5)*].

Staff costs and numbers

Employee costs

10.29   Staff costs are defined in paragraph 94 of Schedule 4 to the Act as being the costs a company incurs in respect of the persons it employs under contracts of service. A contract of *service* (or a contract of employment as it is also called) is an agreement under which the employer agrees to employ the employee for a wage or a salary in return for the employee's labour. This agreement may be made either orally or in writing. However, self-employed persons are not employed by the company but merely have contracts to perform specific *services* for that company. The costs of self-employed people should normally be excluded from staff costs, because their contracts will be contracts to perform *services*. Examples of such persons are consultants and contractors. Their costs should normally be included under 'Other external charges'.

10.30   Normally, casual employees should also be excluded from 'Staff costs'. In certain circumstances, however, it may be necessary to include casual employees in order for the financial statements to show a true and fair view. An example of such a circumstance would be where a company employs significant levels of casual staff (such as in the newspaper and hotel industries).

10.31 The item 'Staff costs' does not appear in the profit and loss account formats 1 and 3. This is because expenses are classified in these formats by function, rather than by type. However, where a company prepares its profit and loss account in the style of either format 1 or format 3, it has to disclose, in the notes to the profit and loss account, the equivalent information to that given when formats 2 and 4 are used.

10.32 In summary, either the profit and loss account format or the notes must disclose, in aggregate, each of the following amounts:

(a) The wages and salaries that were either paid to employees or are payable to them, in respect of the financial year in question.

(b) Social security costs that the company has incurred on behalf of its employees. For this purpose, social security costs are any contributions the company makes to any social security or pension scheme, or fund or arrangement that the State runs. These costs will include the employer's national insurance contributions.

(c) Other pension costs the company has incurred on behalf of its employees. For this purpose, pension costs include:

(i) Any contributions a company makes for the purposes of any non-State occupational pension scheme that is established to provide pensions for employees.
(ii) Any sums the company has set aside for that purpose.
(iii) Any amounts the company has paid in respect of pensions, without those amounts having first been so set aside.

Pension costs will, therefore, include the company's contributions to any pension scheme other than the State scheme. [*4 Sch 56(4), 94*].

An illustration of these disclosure requirements is given in Table 40.

10.33 The Act says that wages and salaries should be determined by reference to either the payments the company makes or the costs it incurs in respect of all persons it employs under contracts of service. [*4 Sch 94(3)*]. There is no definition in the Act of 'costs incurred'. However, it is unlikely that this item should include the money value of benefits in kind as applies to the disclosure of directors' remuneration under paragraph 22(3) of Schedule 5 to the Act (see further para 10.60 below).

Average number of employees

10.34 In addition to requiring that either the profit and loss account or the notes should disclose employee costs, the Act requires that the notes should include information in respect of the number of employees.

Table 40: Illustration of the disclosure of employee costs and numbers.

Extract from The Plessey Company plc Report & Accounts 30 March 1984.

Note Extract

7 Employees

	1984 £000	1983 £000
Staff costs, including directors' emoluments, were:		
Wages and salaries	369,620	321,951
Social security costs	35,249	34,312
Other pension costs	26,152	20,613
	431,021	376,876

	1984	1983
The average weekly number of persons employed by the Group was:		
Direct labour	20,461	21,285
Indirect production	10,760	11,645
Selling, marketing and distribution	2,929	3,044
Administration	2,583	2,813
Research and development	2,105	2,085
	38,838	40,872

The classification of employees has been revised and the 1983 comparatives have been restated accordingly.

10.35   The two disclosures that the notes must contain in connection with the number of employees are:

(a) The average number of employees in the financial year. [*4 Sch 56(1)(a)*]. The number must be calculated by:

(i) Ascertaining the number of persons employed under contracts of service, whether full-time or part-time, for each week in the year.

(ii) Adding together all the weekly numbers.

(iii) Dividing the resulting total by the number of weeks in the financial year.
[*4 Sch 56(2)(3)*].

The average number of employees includes persons who work wholly or mainly overseas, as well as persons who work in the UK.

(b) The average number of employees by category. This number must be calculated by applying the same method of calculation as outlined above to each category of employees. For this purpose, the categories of persons employed are to be such categories as the directors select, having regard to the way in which the company's activities are organised. [*4 Sch 56(1)(b), (2)(3)(5)*].

These disclosure requirements are illustrated in Table 40.

10.36 Because the guidance on how to select categories is rather vague, directors of companies have chosen a variety of different categories. In the Green Paper 'Company Accounting and Disclosure' (Cmnd 7654), it was suggested that the split should be between part-time employees and full-time employees. However, a more meaningful split may be between hourly-paid, weekly-paid and salaried staff, or between production, sales and administration staff.

10.37 Consolidated financial statements should include the information outlined above only for the group as a whole. This applies to all profit and loss account disclosures for a company that avails itself of the exemption not to publish its own profit and loss account (see Chapter 17 para 17.24). [*Sec 228(7)*].

10.38 There is no exemption from disclosure where the number of employees is small, or (for example) where a company is a wholly-owned subsidiary.

Directors

10.39 Directors that have a contract of service with the company are included as employees. Therefore, their salaries, their social security costs and their other pension costs must be included in the required analysis under staff costs (as illustrated in Table 40). However, directors' emoluments have also to be disclosed separately in accordance with the requirements of paragraphs 22 to 34 of Schedule 5 to the Act, but these emoluments will exclude those social security costs that the company bears (see para 10.59) and will include benefits in kind (see para 10.60). It is not appropriate to omit the directors from the detailed analysis of staff costs, even if a note is included stating that directors' emoluments are shown elsewhere.

10.40 In contrast to payments under a contract of service (where the director is employed), amounts paid to directors under contracts *for services* should not be disclosed under staff costs. But, under paragraphs 22 to 34 of Schedule 5 to the Act, they must be disclosed as directors' emoluments in the notes to the financial statements.

10.41 Whether a director's contract with the company is a contract *of service* or a contract *for services* is a question of fact in each circumstance. Usually, however, executive directors will have contracts *of service*, whereas non-executive directors will have contracts *for services*. Contracts for services might include, for example, consultancy arrangements.

Practical problems relating to employee costs

10.42 In practice, there may be problems in deciding on the employees to include in staff costs and in identifying the average number of employees. One of the most frequent problems arises where employees clearly work for one company, but their contracts of service are with another company (for example, the holding company). Also, further complications arise when that other company pays the wages and salaries of these employees.' If paragraph 56 of Schedule 4 to the Act was strictly interpreted in these situations, it could lead to the disclosure of misleading information in the financial statements. Accordingly, a company may need to depart from the strict interpretation of paragraph 56 to enable its financial statements to show a true and fair view. In those situations where a departure is necessary, the financial statements should disclose particulars of the departure, the reasons for it, and its effect. [*Sec 230(6)*].

10.43   Some of the more common problems that arise in this respect are considered below:

(a) Employees work full time for, and are paid by, a subsidiary company, but their contracts of service are with the holding company.

It would be misleading if there was no disclosure of staff costs or numbers in the subsidiary company's financial statements. Consequently, the wages and salaries the subsidiary company pays to those employees should be disclosed as 'Staff costs' in its financial statements, and those employees should be included in the calculation of the average number of staff employed.

The notes to the subsidiary company's financial statements should explain that those staff have contracts of service with another company. They should also explain why their remuneration and average number are disclosed in the financial statements.

The holding company's consolidated financial statements normally will not be affected (unless the subsidiary is not included in the group accounts), because they will show the average number of employees and staff costs of the group as a whole, but not those of the holding company separately. Consequently, no additional disclosure should be necessary in the holding company's financial statements. (However, if the contracts of service are with a fellow subsidiary company, then that fellow subsidiary company's financial statements should disclose the fact that certain employees have service contracts with the company. But those financial statements should state that, because those employees work for, and are paid for wholly by, a fellow subsidiary company, their staff costs and average number are disclosed in the fellow subsidiary company's financial statements.)

(b) Employees work full time for the subsidiary company, but they are not paid by the subsidiary company, and they do not have service contracts with it. However, the subsidiary company bears a management charge for their services from the company that pays the employees, and it can ascertain the proportion of the management charge that relates to staff costs.

Again, in this situation it could be misleading if the subsidiary company's financial statements disclosed no information about staff costs or numbers. Accordingly, the proportion of the management charge that relates to staff costs should be disclosed in the subsidiary company's financial statements as 'Staff costs'. The employees concerned should be included in the calculation of the average number of employees. The notes to the financial statements should explain that the employees do not have contracts of employment with the company, and they should also explain why their costs and average number are disclosed in the financial statements. For the reason outlined in *(a)* above, the holding company's financial statements should not be affected. (As in example *(a)* above, if the contracts of service are with, and the employees are paid by, a fellow subsidiary company, then that fellow subsidiary's financial statements should contain the information outlined in *(a)* above.)

(c) The facts are the same as in *(b)* above, except that the subsidiary company is unable to break down the management charge and ascertain the part of it that relates to staff costs.

In this situation, for the same reason as explained in *(a)* above, the holding company's consolidated financial statements will be unaffected. The notes to the subsidiary company's financial statements should explain that the employees' contracts of service are with the holding company and that their remuneration is included in the holding company's financial statements. The notes should also explain that the management charge that the holding company makes includes the cost of these employees, but that it is impossible to ascertain separately the element of the management charge that relates to staff costs. (If the employees' contracts of service are with a fellow subsidiary, rather than with the holding company, and that fellow subsidiary also pays the employees, the fellow subsidiary's financial statements should disclose the employees' remuneration in its staff costs, and should also include the employees in the calculation of average number employed. The notes should explain that these employees work for a fellow subsidiary company, and that the company recharges the cost of their employment to that fellow subsidiary as part of a management charge.)

(d) The facts are the same as in *(b)* above, except that no management charge is made for the employees' services. This will often apply where staff work either full time or part time for small companies.

In this situation, the notes to the subsidiary company's financial statements should explain that the company is not charged for the services provided by the employees that work for it. If appropriate, the notes should also indicate that the cost of these employees and their average number are included in the holding company's consolidated financial statements. For the same reason as given in *(a)* above, however, the holding company's consolidated financial statements should not be affected. (Once again, if it is a fellow subsidi-

209

ary that employs and pays the employees, its financial statements should include the cost of these employees in its staff costs, and should include these employees in the average number employed. If appropriate, the notes to the financial statements should explain that these employees work for a fellow subsidiary company, but that no management charge is made for their services to that company.)

Directors' remuneration

10.44   The disclosure of directors' remuneration can be considered under five headings:

(a) Aggregate emoluments.

(b) Banding of emoluments.

(c) Emoluments waived.

(d) Pensions.

(e) Compensation for loss of office.

These areas are considered in turn in paragraphs 10.53 to 10.75 below. First, however, certain general rules are outlined, and these apply to all forms of directors' remuneration.

General rules

10.45   A company's directors have a duty to give information about their remuneration to the company so that the information discussed below can be disclosed in the financial statements. This requirement applies also to a person who has been a director of the company within the preceding five years. If a director does not give notice of the required information to the company, he is liable to a fine. [*Sec 231(4) — see Appendix IV*].

10.46   If the required information is not disclosed in the financial statements, the auditors have a duty to include the information (so far as they are reasonably able to do so) in their audit report. [*Sec 237(5)*].

10.47   The remuneration to be disclosed should include all amounts paid to a director (whether those payments are made by the company, or by a subsidiary of the company or by any other person), unless the director has to account in turn for the receipt of the remuneration. (This provision, however, does not apply to emoluments a director has waived.) [*5 Sch 30(2)*].

For example, Mr. Smith spends part of his time as an executive director of Company A and part of his time as an employee of Company B (Company B is not connected with Company A). Company B pays Mr. Smith's salary, and it invoices Company A for an amount to cover that part of the time that Mr. Smith spends on Company A's business. Although Mr. Smith is paid by Company B (and not by Company A of which he is a director), the amount that he receives from Company B is partially in respect of his services as a director of Company A. Consequently, he should disclose to Company A, as remuneration, the proportion of his salary that relates to his services as a director of Company A. This figure may or may not be the same as the amount that Company B has invoiced Company A. This will depend on whether the invoiced amount is intended to cover an amount that is either more or less than the actual cost of the director's services (for example, it may cover in addition other management services provided by Company B to Company A).

10.48 There is also nothing in the Act to suggest that the director must receive payments personally in order that they should be subject to disclosure as remuneration. Consequently, even where a director sets up another company specifically to receive his remuneration, he cannot avoid disclosing it.

10.49 In addition, if the company has nominated the director to be a director of another company, the director's remuneration should include any amount he receives as a director of that other company (whether or not that other company is a subsidiary of the company). [5 Sch 33(2)(a)].

10.50 A director's remuneration (excluding any emoluments he waives) that needs to be disclosed in the financial statements for a particular year is the remuneration receivable by him in respect of that year, regardless of when it is paid to him. If any remuneration is not receivable in respect of a period, then it should be disclosed in the financial statements of the period in which it is paid. [5 Sch 31(1)].

10.51 If it is necessary to apportion remuneration paid to a director (for example, if the person was appointed a director part way through the year), the directors may apportion it in any way that they consider appropriate. [5 Sch 32].

10.52 If any director's remuneration is not included in the notes to the financial statements of a period on the ground that the director is to account for it to another group company, or on the ground that an expense allowance is not chargeable to UK income tax (see para 10.60 below) and that ground is not subsequently justified, the remuneration must be disclosed in a note to the first financial statements in which it is practicable for this to be done, and the remuneration must be identified separately. [5 Sch 31(2)].

Aggregate emoluments

10.53 The notes to the profit and loss account must disclose the aggregate amount of the directors' emoluments. [5 Sch 22(1)].

10.54 This amount must be split between emoluments in respect of services as a director (whether of the company or of a subsidiary), and other emoluments (for example, fees for the professional services a director has rendered to the company). [5 Sch 22(2)(b)]. An illustration of these disclosure requirements is given in Table 41.

Table 41: *Example of the disclosure of directors' emoluments. In this example the company has also shown emoluments after tax.*

Extract from Reuters Holdings PLC Report and Accounts 31 December 1984.

Note

7 Directors' emoluments	1984 £000	1983 £000
Directors' emoluments:		
Fees	138	85
Other emoluments	349	298
The emoluments of the chairman were	14	12
The emoluments of the highest paid director were	142	113

The table which follows shows the number of directors whose gross emoluments were within the bands stated. The after-tax figures indicate the net amount receivable after deducting income tax at 1984/1985 rates from the emoluments at the mid point of each band, assuming the recipient is a married man and has no other source of income.

Gross emoluments	Emoluments after tax	1984	1983
Directors:			
Up to £ 5,000	£ 2,500	2	8
£ 5,001 – £ 10,000	£ 6,196	11	—
£ 10,001 – £ 15,000	£ 9,696	1	1
£ 60,001 – £ 65,000	£33,933	—	1
£ 70,001 – £ 75,000	£37,933	1	1
£ 80,001 – £ 85,000	£41,933	1	—
£110,001 – £115,000	£53,933	—	1
£140,001 – £145,000	£65,933	1	—

10.55   For this purpose, 'emoluments' paid to or receivable by a director consist of the following:

(a) Fees and percentages.

(b) Any expense allowances (to the extent that they are chargeable to UK income tax).

(c) Contributions paid in respect of him under any pension scheme.

(d) The estimated money value of any benefits in kind.
[5 Sch 22(3)].

10.56   A director should include, in his emoluments, amounts in respect of:

(a) His services as a director of the company.

(b) His services as a director of any subsidiary of the company, during the time in which he is a director of the company.

(c) His involvement with the management of either the company or any subsidiary of the company.
[*5 Sch 22(2)(a)*].

10.57 If the director renders the service while a company is a subsidiary of the company, his emoluments in relation to that service should then be included. [*5 Sch 33(2)(b)*].

10.58 A 'pension scheme' for a director is a scheme for providing pensions in respect of his service both as a director and as an employee. A 'contribution' to a pension scheme means any payment (including an insurance premium) paid for the purposes of the scheme. However, it does not cover payments made in respect of two or more persons, if the amount paid in respect of each of them cannot be ascertained separately. [*5 Sch 33(3)(b)(c)*]. For example, if a company either makes a lump sum payment to a pension scheme or pays a premium to an insurance company for a pension scheme, and the contribution in respect of each director cannot be separately identified, no amount is required to be disclosed as directors' emoluments in respect of pension contributions.

10.59 Directors' emoluments should not include the employer's national insurance contributions, because the amounts are neither paid to the director nor paid in respect of a pension scheme.

10.60 The estimated money value of a benefit in kind that must be included in directors' emoluments should be taken as the market value of the facility that is provided for the director's private benefit, less any contribution the director pays. The amount used to assess the taxable benefit should be used only where it is not possible to ascertain the market value of the benefit. However, where a director has a contract of service with the company, the amount of his emoluments that is included in staff costs should exclude the money value of benefits in kind (see para 10.39 above).

Banding of emoluments

10.61 The directors' emoluments (*excluding* contributions paid to a pension scheme) must also be analysed in the following way:

(a) Chairman's emoluments. [*5 Sch 24*].

(b) Highest-paid director's emoluments, if different from *(a)* above. [*5 Sch 25(3)*].

(c) Banding of *all* directors' emoluments. [*5 Sch 25(2)*].

An example of these disclosure requirements is given in Table 41.

10.62 This information must be given if the company is either a holding company or a subsidiary of another company. However, other companies

need not give the information where the aggregate amount of the directors' emoluments (*including* pension scheme contributions) for the
financial year does not exceed £60,000. [*5 Sch 23*]. Consequently, where
the company is either a subsidiary or a holding company, it must still
give the information outlined above, even where the aggregate directors' emoluments are below £60,000. In this context, the 'financial year'
means the company's reporting period. [*Sec 742(1)(d)*]. Therefore, even
if the profit and loss account covers a period of, say, only nine months,
or 15 months, the limit for disclosure is still £60,000.

10.63   A 'chairman' means, in this context, the person elected to chair directors' meetings. If a chairman is not elected, then the chairman is deemed
to be the person who carries out this function at directors' meetings.
[*5 Sch 24(1)*].

10.64   If more than one person has been chairman during the year, each such
person's total emoluments for the year must be attributed to that part
of the year during which he was chairman, and these amounts must
be disclosed separately. [*5 Sch 24(3)*]. The notes do not have to disclose the emoluments of a chairman who worked either exclusively or
mainly outside the UK. [*5 Sch 24(2)(3)*].

10.65   The notes must disclose the emoluments of the highest-paid director
who did not work either exclusively or mainly outside the UK during
the year. The highest-paid director's emoluments need not be disclosed
separately if he was the chairman. [*5 Sch 25(3)(4)(5)*]. Where there has
been more than one chairman during the year, the emoluments of those
chairmen in respect of the period during which they were chairman
should be aggregated in order to determine whether another director
has received emoluments in excess of the aggregate chairmen's emoluments. [*5 Sch 25(5)*].

10.66   Also, the bands into which the emoluments of *all* directors (including
both the chairman and the highest-paid director but excluding any directors who worked either exclusively or mainly outside the UK) fall must
be disclosed in the notes to the financial statements. The Act defines
the 'bands' as 0 to £5,000, £5,001 to £10,000, and bands of £5,000
beyond that. The notes must give the number of directors whose emoluments fell within each band. [*5 Sch 25(2)*]. No matter how long the company's reporting period is, the bands do not change. For example, if
the profit and loss account covers a period that exceeds 12 months,
the bands still remain as multiples of £5,000. Companies may, however,
wish to give as additional information the numbers in bands on an annu-
alised basis. Some companies disclose also, as supplementary information, the number of directors whose emoluments net of tax (basic rate
less tax allowances) fall into the appropriate bands (for example, see
Table 41).

Emoluments waived

10.67 If any director has waived his right to receive emoluments, the notes to the financial statements must give the following information:

(a) The number of directors who have waived their rights to receive emoluments.

(b) The aggregate amount of the emoluments they have waived. [5 Sch 27(1)].

10.68 The Stock Exchange's Continuing Obligations and General Undertaking require listed companies and companies traded on the USM respectively to disclose also particulars of any arrangement under which a director has either waived or agreed to waive any future or current emoluments. This applies in respect of emoluments from either the company or any of its subsidiaries. [CO 21(n); GU 10(k)].

Pensions

10.69 The notes must disclose the aggregate amount of the present directors' pensions and any past directors' pensions. [5 Sch 28(1)]. This amount must be divided between pensions in respect of services as a director (whether of the company or of a subsidiary), and other pensions. [5 Sch 28(3)]. The term 'pension' includes any superannuation allowance, or superannuation gratuity or similar payment. [5 Sch 33(3)(a)].

10.70 If the contributions paid under a pension scheme are substantially adequate for maintaining that scheme, the amount of pensions disclosed should not include any pension paid or receivable under that scheme. In practice, this means that if the contributions a company paid under an occupational pension scheme were adequate to fund those pensions, the pensions payable under that scheme need not be disclosed. However, 'top hat' or other additional pensions that are not provided from the standard occupational scheme would have to be disclosed. Otherwise, the term 'pension' includes any pension paid or receivable by either a director or a past director in respect of services he has provided to either the company or another group company. It includes also any pension paid to or receivable by any other person (for example, a dependant) in respect of the services of either a director or a past director. [5 Sch 28(2)].

Compensation for loss of office

10.71 Disclosure must be made of the aggregate amount of any compensation paid to directors or past directors in respect of loss of office. [5 Sch 29(1)]. This amount should include not only payments made in respect of loss of the office of director of the reporting company, but also payments in respect of the loss of any other office the person concerned held. It will, therefore, include compensation for the loss of office as a director of any subsidiary or of any other office that involved the management of the company or of any subsidiary. The amount should include any compensation paid either while the person was a director, or immediately on ceasing to be so, or otherwise in connection with his ceasing to be a director of the company. [*5 Sch 29(2)(a)*]. Compensation for loss of office also includes any amount paid in connection with a director's retirement from office. That is to say, it includes any payments made when the director leaves the company, either on reaching retirement age or in any other circumstances when it is he, rather than the company, who is the prime mover in his own resignation from office. [*5 Sch 29(3)*]. Because pensions are separately disclosed, they should not be included in this category of payment. Benefits in kind given to the director in connection with his retirement and therefore loss of office (for example, the gift to the director of a car that he previously used, but that was owned by the company) may be regarded as compensation for loss of office. Alternatively, such a benefit may represent, and have to be disclosed as, emoluments of a former director.

10.72   The statutory description of 'payments made in compensation for loss of office' is widely drawn. In deciding whether a payment made to a director or a former director falls to be disclosed, regard should be had to both the nature and the circumstances of the payment, rather than to just the description the company gives to it. For example, most *'ex-gratia'* payments made on either a director's retirement or his removal from office should be regarded not as gratuitous payments, but as payments in compensation for loss of office. And, as such, they should be disclosed.

10.73   The amount of compensation for loss of office must distinguish between sums payable by or receivable from:

(a) The company.

(b) The company's subsidiaries.

(c) Any other persons.
[*5 Sch 30(3)*].

10.74   For this purpose, a subsidiary includes a company that was a subsidiary immediately before the date on which the director lost office.

10.75   Compensation paid to a director for loss of office is a category of payment different from an emolument. Consequently, it should not be included in that person's emoluments for banding purposes.

Higher-paid employees

10.76   The notes to the financial statements must disclose the bands of emoluments of higher-paid employees. The bands that the Act lays down are:

£30,001 to £35,000, £35,001 to £40,000, and similar bands of £5,000 beyond that (for example, see Table 42). [*5 Sch 35(1)*].

Table 42: Disclosure of higher-paid employees.

Extract from Imperial Group public limited company Report and Accounts 31 October 1984.

Note extract

Higher paid employees

The number of employees, other than Directors of the Parent Company, whose pre-tax emoluments exceeded £30,000, including performance-related bonuses for certain individuals, was as follows:—

	Parent Company 1984	1983	Group 1984	1983
Over £90,000 up to £95,000	1	—	1	—
,, £85,000 ,, £90,000	1	—	2	2
,, £80,000 ,, £85,000	—	2	1	2
,, £75,000 ,, £80,000	2	—	3	—
,, £70,000 ,, £75,000	—	1	—	2
,, £65,000 ,, £70,000	—	2	3	4
,, £60,000 ,, £65,000	1	1	4	2
,, £55,000 ,, £60,000	6	—	7	2
,, £50,000 ,, £55,000	9	3	14	9
,, £45,000 ,, £50,000	6	—	11	1
,, £40,000 ,, £45,000	5	7	16	10
,, £35,000 ,, £40,000	13	14	37	23
,, £30,000 ,, £35,000	17	21	53	45

10.77   Higher-paid employees include any persons whose emoluments exceed £30,000, but they exclude directors of the company and any person who worked either wholly or mainly outside the UK during the year. [*5 Sch 35(2)*].

10.78   For this purpose, emoluments are defined in almost the same way as directors' emoluments (see para 10.55). They *include* any amounts paid to or receivable by the employee in respect of his services as a person in the employment of either the company or a subsidiary. However, they *do not include* any contributions paid in respect of the employee under any pension scheme. [*5 Sch 36,37*].

10.79   In addition, the provisions outlined in paragraphs 10.50 and 10.52 above apply in a similar way to higher-paid employees' emoluments. [*5 Sch 36(3)(4)*].

Depreciation (including other amounts written off assets)

10.80   Where the company prepares its profit and loss account in accordance with either format 1 or format 3, expenses are classified by function. Consequently, any provisions for either depreciation or the diminution in value of tangible and intangible fixed assets will not be disclosed in the profit and loss account format. Accordingly, the Act requires that this information must be disclosed separately in the notes to the financial statements. [*Note 17 on the profit and loss account formats*]. The rules that relate to the calculation of depreciation contained in the Act and in SSAP 12 are discussed in more detail in Chapter 4, paragraphs 4.04 to 4.17, Chapter 5, paragraphs 5.64 to 5.83 and Chapter 7.

Other operating charges (including other external charges)

10.81   The relevant formats link 'Other external charges' with 'Raw materials and consumables'. Therefore, such charges are likely to include any production costs from external sources that are not included under other headings (for example, equipment rentals and the costs of subcontractors). 'Other operating charges' tends to be a residual class of all charges relating to the ordinary activities of a business that do not fall into any other category. 'Other external charges' may include also losses on exchange.

Income from investments (including group companies and related companies)

Dividends

10.82   The notes must disclose separately the amount of income from listed investments. [*4 Sch 53(1)(4)*]. SSAP 8 requires that dividends received from UK resident companies should be included in the profit and loss account at the amount of cash received or receivable, plus the related tax credit. The amount of the tax credit is then disclosed under UK corporation tax as 'Tax attributable to franked investment income' (see also para 10.94 below).

10.83   Dividends received and receivable from both subsidiary and fellow subsidiary companies will be included in 'Income from shares in group companies'. Traditionally, dividends are included in the receiving company's financial statements, even though they may not be declared or paid by the paying company until the subsequent year. In a group's consolidated financial statements, this line will appear only if dividends are received or receivable from subsidiaries that have not been consolidated (see Chapter 17).

Related companies

10.84   'Income from shares in related companies' will include, in most circumstances, dividends received from associated companies. This is because the definition of an associated company is very similar to that of a related company (see further Chapter 8 paras 8.21 to 8.28). Where dividends have been received solely from associated companies, the wording of the formats may be amended to read 'Income from shares in associated companies'.

Associated companies

10.85 On consolidation, SSAP 1 requires that the consolidated profit and loss account should include, in the profit or loss on ordinary activities before taxation, the investing group's share of the profits less losses of associated companies before taxation. It also says that this item should be shown separately, and that it should be suitably described (for example, as 'Share of profits less losses of associated companies'). [*SSAP 1 para 19*]. Consequently, the question arises as to where the share of the associates' results should be disclosed in the formats. Because the formats were designed for the accounts of a single company, and not for the accounts of a group of companies, the formats do not specify where these results should be disclosed. There appear to be two possible positions in formats 1 or 2 where these results could be disclosed. The first is in the same position as the item 'Income from shares in related companies'. The second is after the item 'Interest payable and similar charges'. In practice, companies commonly use both of these positions to disclose their share of the results of their associated companies. SSAP 1 requires that the consolidated financial statements should disclose also the following items that relate to the results of associated companies:

(a) The tax attributable to the share of the associated companies' profits. This should be included, and be shown separately, within the group's tax charge.

(b) The group's share of the extraordinary items dealt with in the associates' financial statements. They should be included with the group's extraordinary items, but only to the extent that they are extraordinary to the group.

(c) The group's share of the aggregate of the net profits less losses retained by associated companies.
[*SSAP 1 paras 20,21,22*].

10.86 SSAP 1 does not require that the group's financial statements should include the group's share of the associated companies' turnover or depreciation within the items disclosed in the profit and loss account. If, on the other hand, the results of one or more associated companies are so material in the context of the group's financial statements, more-detailed information about them may need to be disclosed in order that the group's financial statements show a true and fair view. Where this applies, the total turnover, the total depreciation and the total profit or loss on ordinary activities before taxation of the material associated companies should be disclosed. In addition, the share of those profits or losses on ordinary activities that are attributable to the investing group should be disclosed (for example, see Table 43). [*SSAP 1 para 23*].

10.87 Where an investing company does not prepare consolidated financial statements, SSAP 1 requires that a separate profit and loss account should be prepared. Alternatively, it requires that supplementary information showing the share of the associated company's results should be given in the notes to the financial statements. The separate profit and loss account or the supplementary note should contain the equivalent information to that outlined in paragraph 10.85 above. [*SSAP 1 para 24*].

10.88 The financial statements used for the purpose of including the results of associated companies should be either coterminous with those of the group or made up to a date that is either not more than six months before, or shortly after, the date of the investing group's financial statements. Where non-coterminous financial statements are used, and the effect is material to the group results, the facts and the dates of the year ends should be disclosed. [*SSAP 1 paras 36,37*].

10.89 If an associated company is listed on a recognised stock exchange, only published information should be disclosed in the group's financial statements. [*SSAP 1 para 36*].

10.90 The disclosure of associated companies in the balance sheet is considered in Chapter 8, paragraphs 8.29 to 8.38.

Interest payable and similar charges

10.91 The Act requires certain disclosures in respect of interest. Schedule 4 requires the disclosure of:

"The amount of the interest on or any similar charges in respect of:

(a) bank loans and overdrafts, and loans made to the company (other than bank loans and overdrafts) which:

(i) are repayable otherwise than by instalments and fall due for repayment before the end of the period of five years beginning with the day next following the end of the financial year; or

(ii) are repayable by instalments the last of which falls due for payment before the end of that period; and

(b) loans of any other kind made to the company."
[*4 Sch 53(2)*].

This paragraph can be interpreted in several different ways. However, the DTI has confirmed that it is intended that three separate amounts should be disclosed, representing *(a)*(i), *(a)*(ii) and *(b)* above respectively.

Table 43: Example of a group that has given additional information about its material associated companies.

Extract from The Rank Organisation Plc Report and Accounts 31 October 1984.

Note extract

The holdings, all through subsidiaries, of associated companies principally affecting profits are:

	Percentage voting interest	Country of incorporaton and operation	Class of capital owned	Percentage holding	Date of accounts (see note 2(i))
Rank Xerox companies					
Rank Xerox Limited	48·8	Great Britain	'B' Ordinary	96·4	31.10.84
			'D' Ordinary	96·4	
Rank Xerox Business					
Equipment Inc.	49·0	U.S.A.	'B' Common	96·4	31.10.84
Rank Xerox Holding B.V.	48·8	Holland	'B' Ordinary	96·4	31.10.84
			'C' Ordinary	96·4	
Rank Xerox Investments Limited	49·0	Bermuda	'B' Ordinary	96·4	31.10.84
Other associated companies					
Film exhibition					
Cathay Films Distribution					
Company Limited	24·2	Hong Kong	Ordinary	24·2	31.12.83
Cathay Organisation Private					
Limited	24·2	Singapore	Ordinary	24·2	31.12.83
Kerridge Odeon Corporation					
Limited	50·0	New Zealand	Ordinary	50·0	31. 3.84
Communication systems					
Telecom Plus International Inc.*	30·5	U.S.A.	Common	30·5	30. 9.84

* unaudited management accounts

The business of the **Rank Xerox** companies consists mainly of the manufacture in the United Kingdom, France and Holland of xerographic equipment for high speed document copying and duplicating, the marketing of such equipment through subsidiaries operating in Europe, Asia, Africa, the Middle East and Australasia and the manufacturing and marketing operations of Fuji Xerox Co. Ltd., a company incorporated in Japan, which is 50% owned by Rank Xerox Limited.

Under an agreement with Xerox Corporation made in 1977, the Group, through Rank RX Holdings Limited, is entitled to a share in the annual combined profits before taxation of all the associated companies owned jointly with Xerox Corporation. This share amounts to one half of such profits up to a maximum annual sum of £3,700,627 plus one third of the amount by which such profits exceed £7,401,254, from which is deducted the related taxation.

For this purpose, the combined profits before taxation are calculated after making such adjustments as are necessary to eliminate charges made by Xerox Corporation for research and development and corporate overhead costs and the effect of inter-group trading.

A summary of the combined financial statements of the Rank Xerox companies is set out below:-

Profit and Loss Account	1984 £ million	1983 £ million	Balance Sheet	1984 £ million	1983 £ million
Turnover	1,765	1,534	Fixed assets		
Less costs	1,599	1,399	Intangible assets	2	3
			Tangible assets	591	524
Trading profit	166	135	Investments	178	133
Interest	(19)	(10)			
Share of results of asssociates	55	41		771	660
			Net current assets	324	327
Profit before Xerox					
Corporation charges	202	166			
Xerox Corporation charges	(81)	(78)	Total assets less current		
			liabilities	1,095	987
			Creditors falling due after more		
Profit before tax	121	88	than one year	(178)	(183)
Tax	(37)	(40)	Provisions for liabilities and		
			charges	(23)	(28)
Profit after tax	84	48		894	776
			Share capital and reserves	882	764
			Minority interests	12	12
				894	776

10.92 The requirement does not apply to either interest or charges on loans from group companies. But it does apply to interest or charges on all other loans, whether or not these are made on the security of a debenture. [*4 Sch 53(2)*].

Table 44 illustrates these disclosure requirements.

Table 44: Disclosure of interest payable and similar charges.

Extract from Fairview Estates plc Report & Accounts 30 June 1984.

7 INTEREST PAYABLE AND SIMILAR CHARGES

	£000	£000
On loans repayable wholly or in part after 5 years:		
Bank loans	1,926	2,932
Other loans	803	831
On loans repayable within 5 years:		
Bank loans and overdrafts	1,711	1,352
Other loans	26	262
Interest received	(173)	(77)
Total charges	4,293	5,300
Less interest capitalised in the cost of investment properties	(395)	(711)
Decrease/(Increase) in the amount of interest included in the cost of land and buildings in course of development	583	(148)
Charged against profits	4,481	4,441

Taxation

10.93 The notes to the profit and loss account must disclose the following amounts in respect of taxation:

(a) The amount of the charge to UK corporation tax. Where this amount would have been greater but for double taxation relief, the gross amount must also be disclosed.

(b) The amount of the charge to UK income tax.

(c) The amount of the charge for taxation that has been imposed outside the UK on profits, income and (to the extent to which it has been charged to income) capital gains.
[*4 Sch 54(3)*].

10.94 SSAP 8 requires that the amount of UK corporation tax should specify:

(a) The charge for corporation tax on the income of the year. (Where such corporation tax includes transfers between the deferred

taxation account and the profit and loss account, and these transfers are material, they should be separately disclosed.)

(b) Tax attributable to franked investment income (see para 10.82 above).

(c) Irrecoverable ACT (see Chapter 9 paras 9.14 to 9.19).

(d) The relief for overseas taxation (that is, double taxation relief). [*SSAP 8 para 22*].

10.95 The notes to the profit and loss account must disclose the basis on which the charges to both UK corporation tax and income tax have been computed. They must disclose also details of any special circumstances that affect any liability to taxation (whether for the financial year in question or for future years, and whether in respect of profits, income or capital gains). [*4 Sch 54(1)(2)*]. 'Special circumstances' could include (for example) the effect on the tax charge (if this is material) of losses either utilised or carried forward. In addition, the rate of taxation that has been used in calculating the above figures should be disclosed. (SSAP 8 requires this disclosure only if the rate of corporation tax is not known for all or part of the financial year. [*SSAP 8 para 23*]. However, it is generally accepted accounting practice to disclose the rate in all circumstances.)

10.96 In addition to the requirement to disclose the amount in *(d)* in paragraph 10.94 above, SSAP 8 requires that the financial statements should disclose the total overseas taxation figure (including both relieved and unrelieved overseas taxation) and also that part of the unrelieved overseas taxation that arises from either the payment or the proposed payment of dividends. [*SSAP 8 para 22*].

10.97 Further to the requirements of both the Act and SSAP 8, SSAP 15 requires that the amount of deferred tax that relates to the company's ordinary activities should be disclosed separately as part of the tax on the profit or loss on ordinary activities. [*SSAP 15 para 33*]. SSAP 15 also requires that the notes to the financial statements should disclose any amounts of deferred tax that have not been provided in the year, analysed into the major components (see also Chapter 9 paras 9.51 and 9.52). [*SSAP 15 para 35*].

10.98 Where deferred tax is not provided on earnings that are retained overseas, this fact should be noted. [*SSAP 15 para 41*].

Table 45 illustrates the taxation disclosure requirements detailed above.

10.99 Where a company has incurred an extraordinary profit or loss, the notes must disclose separately the taxation on the profit or loss on ordinary activities and the taxation on the extraordinary profit or loss. [*4 Sch 54(3)*]. The profit and loss account formats also require separate disclosure of the taxation on an extraordinary item, because the formats

Table 45: Disclosure of the profit and loss account taxation charge on ordinary activities.

Extract from B.A.T. Industries p.l.c. Annual report and accounts 31 December 1984.

	1984	1983
6 Taxation on ordinary activities	£ millions	
UK Corporation Tax on profits of the period at **46·25%**		
1983 – 50·5%	198	139
Less double taxation relief	(171)	(93)
ACT written off	17	16
UK taxation	44	62
Overseas taxation	332	244
Current taxation	376	306
Deferred taxation	61	19
Taxation charge B.A.T. Industries and consolidated subsidiaries	437	325
Financial services	25	
Share of associated companies' taxation	70	48
Total taxation	532	373

The charge for taxation has been reduced in respect of accelerated depreciation and other timing differences by **£72 million** 1983 £63 million.

include the heading 'Tax on extraordinary profit or loss'. In addition, any deferred tax that relates to the extraordinary item should be shown separately as part of the taxation on the extraordinary item. [*SSAP 15 para 34*].

10.100 ED 36 suggests that the taxation attributable to extraordinary items should be calculated by computing the tax on the profit or loss on ordinary activities as if the extraordinary items did not exist. This notional tax charge may then be compared with the total estimated tax charge on the profit and loss for the financial year. Any additional tax charge or credit (including deferred tax) that arises should be attributed to the extraordinary items.

10.101 Where a deferred tax adjustment arises that is due to a change in either the rate of tax or tax allowances, it should normally be disclosed as part of the tax charge for the period and not as a prior-year adjustment. However, where an adjustment arises because of a significant change in government fiscal policy (such as the changes made to corporation tax in the 1984 Budget), it should, where it is material, be treated as an extraordinary item (for example, see Table 46 on page 230). [*SSAP 15 para 36*]. The Standard precludes such an adjustment from being treated as either a prior-year adjustment or an adjustment to opening reserves.

10.102 The Act does not indicate the type of information that must be included under the profit and loss account heading 'Other taxes not shown under the above items'. At present, no such 'other taxes' are collected in the UK, and so this heading in the formats appears to be superfluous for the time being.

Group relief

10.103 Where a company that is a member of a group is determining the amount of deferred taxation to be provided, SSAP 15 requires that it should take into account any group relief that it expects (on reasonable evidence) to be available and also any charge for that relief. Any assumptions the company has made in anticipation of either the receipt or the surrender of group relief should be noted. [*SSAP 15 para 43*]. When group relief gives rise to special circumstances that affect the liability to taxation of either the year or future years, it ought (if it has a material effect) to be disclosed to comply with paragraph 54 of Schedule 4 to the Act (see para 10.95 above).

10.104 Group relief may be obtained with or without a payment passing between the companies concerned. Where it is not proposed that the claimant company should pay the surrendering company for the tax loss, the trading loss may be financed in another way (for example, by way of a loan). However, non-payment for group relief received is not acceptable if there are minority interests in either the paying or the receiving company. The reason for this is that if a company that has minority shareholders surrenders its losses for group relief purposes without receiving an adequate compensation payment, the minority shareholders' interests will be impaired.

10.105 The claimant company may make a payment to the surrendering company of any amount that does not exceed the gross amount of the group relief that it receives. The payment may take one of the following forms:

(a) The payment may be of the gross amount of the group relief, but no more than that. Any part of a payment in excess of the gross amount of the group relief (for example, to finance the balance of a loss) is not a payment in respect of group relief, and it should not be dealt with as such in the financial statements.

(b) The payment may be of the amount of the corporation tax saving by reason of group relief. Such a payment would normally be appropriate where a partly-owned subsidiary is involved (whether as the claimant company or as the surrendering company) in order to preserve the minority shareholders' interests.

(c) The payment may be of any other amount up to a maximum of the gross amount of the group relief (as in (a) above) if it is desired to finance only part of the surrendering company's loss.

10.106 With group relief where no payment passes between the companies concerned, the companies' financial statements should normally disclose the facts and the impact.

Where a payment passes between the companies concerned, the accounting treatment will depend upon the nature of the payment. In the examples that follow, corporation tax is calculated at a rate of 35%.

(a) Where the payment is equivalent to the gross amount of group relief, and the companies adopt format 1 or 2 for the profit and loss account, it should be dealt with in arriving at the profit before taxation, and it should be disclosed as shown below:

    (i) **The claimant company:**

	£000
Profit on ordinary activities	110
Amount payable to holding company (subsidiary or fellow subsidiary) in respect of group relief	(60)
Profit before taxation	50
Tax on profit on ordinary activities *(being, £50,000 x 35%)*	18
Profit for the financial year	32

    (ii) **The surrendering company:**

	£000
Loss on ordinary activities	(70)*
(*of which £10 disallowed for tax purposes)	
Amount receivable from subsidiary (holding company or fellow subsidiary) in respect of group relief	60
Loss for the financial year	(10)

In this instance, a note as in *(c)*(ii) below may be necessary.

(b) Where the payment represents the amount of the tax saving, it should be dealt with as part of the tax charge to bring this into proper relationship with the profits, and it should be disclosed as shown below:

(i) **The claimant company:**

	£000	£000
Profit on ordinary activities before taxation		110
Tax on profit on ordinary activities	18	
Amount payable to holding company (subsidiary or fellow subsidiary) in respect of tax saved by group relief	21	
(that is, £110,000 x 35%)		39
Profit for the financial year		71

(ii) **The surrendering company:**

	£000
Loss on ordinary activities before taxation	(60)
Amount receivable from subsidiary (holding company or fellow subsidiary) in respect of tax saved by group relief	21
Loss for the financial year	(39)

(c) Where the payment is of any other amount up to a maximum of the gross amount of the group relief, it should be dealt with in arriving at the profit before taxation, and it should be suitably described and amplified by a note, as shown below:

(i) **The claimant company:**

	£000
Profit on ordinary activities	110
Contribution towards loss of holding company (subsidiary or fellow subsidiary) payable by way of group relief	(40)
Profit before taxation	70
Tax on profit on ordinary activities (see note below) *(being, (£70,000 x 35%) – £7,000)*	18
Profit for the financial year	52

Note: The charge for taxation has been reduced by £7,000 *(being (£60,000 – £40,000) x 35%)* by reason of group relief receivable in addition to that appropriate to the contribution towards the loss of the holding company (subsidiary or fellow subsidiary) that is charged against the company's profits.

(ii) **The surrendering company:**

	£000
Loss on ordinary activities	(60)
Contribution towards loss receivable from subsidiary (holding company or fellow subsidiary) by way of group relief	40
Loss for the financial year	(20)

Note: The whole of the company's losses for taxation purposes have been absorbed by way of group relief claimed by a subsidiary (the holding company or a fellow subsidiary). Consequently, they are not available to be set off against the company's future profits in computing the liability to taxation on those profits.

(d) Where the group relief payment is for an amount that is less than the amount of the tax saving, the disclosure in the company's financial statements should be as follows:

	£000
Profit on ordinary activities	110
Tax on profit on ordinary activities *(being, (£110,000 x 35%) – £10,000)*	29
	81

Note: The charge for taxation has been reduced by £10,000 by reason of group relief receivable from the holding company for which no payment has been made.

In this situation, the treatment in the surrendering company would be similar to that shown in (c)(ii) above.

ACT can also be surrendered from one group company to another for a payment of any amount up to the amount of the ACT surrendered. Where the payment is for an amount that is less than the ACT surrendered, then the difference should be credited to the tax charged in the profit and loss account. A note similar to that shown above should explain the treatment that has been adopted.

(e) Where a payment for group relief is brought into account in a year subsequent to that to which it relates, it should be appropriately described (depending upon the nature of the payment) as set out in *(a)* to *(d)* above, with the addition of words indicating that it relates to previous years. If the tax relief appropriate to the payment is brought into account at the same time, that too should be described appropriately.

10.107 The claimant company's profit that is available for group relief may include capital gains that have been taken to extraordinary items, rather than to the profit before taxation. Without a claim for group relief, the corporation tax on the capital gain would normally be charged to extraordinary items as a deduction from the gain. If a claim for group relief is made in these circumstances, the claimant company's accounting treatment should normally be as follows:

(a) The loss that is being surrendered should be applied to the profits on the following basis. In accordance with ED 36, the tax charge should be calculated with and without including extraordinary items, and the difference between these two amounts will then be effectively due to the extraordinary items. The loss surrendered should be apportioned first to the profit on ordinary activities up to the extent of the attributable tax charge and any remaining relief to the tax charge on the extraordinary items. The *payment* for the relief given should then be dealt with by apportioning that payment between ordinary and extraordinary items on the same basis as the relief surrendered.

(b) If the amount of corporation tax chargeable on extraordinary items is reduced by a claim for group relief, and no payment is made for this, it may be desirable, on consolidation, for a transfer to be made (equivalent to the amount of that reduction) from extraordinary items to reduce the tax charge on ordinary activities in the profit and loss account.

Provided that some other group companies are making profits, such a transfer would have the effect, on consolidation, of bringing the group tax charge into proper relationship with the group profit on ordinary activities before taxation as shown in the consolidated profit and loss account. At the same time, it would leave a charge which, in the consolidated profit and loss account, will represent corporation tax on the capital gain.

(c) Where the charge to extraordinary items in respect of corporation tax on a capital gain is reduced by group relief, and no compensating set-off against the tax charge is made on consolidation, a note explaining the treatment should be appended to extraordinary items.

(d) Certain types of company whose articles of association contain restrictions on the distribution of capital profits (for example, invest-

ment companies), need to take care that they do not effectively pay away a capital gain as a group relief payment to a subsidiary or a fellow subsidiary, because this would defeat the purpose of their articles. There is, however, nothing to prevent payment being made of an amount equivalent to the tax that would otherwise have been paid on the gain.

Other profit and loss account disclosure items

10.108 In addition to the items required to be disclosed by the formats, the following three further amounts require to be disclosed:

(a) Any amounts that have been set aside for redeeming either share capital or loans. [*4 Sch 53(1)(3)*].

(b) Any amounts that have been charged to revenue in respect of the hire of plant and machinery. [*4 Sch 53(1)(6)*].

(c) The amount of the auditors' remuneration (including any expenses the auditors incurred and the company reimbursed). [*4 Sch 53(1)(7)*].

Extraordinary and exceptional items

10.109 The notes to the profit and loss account must disclose particulars of any amounts that:

(a) Are extraordinary.

(b) Fall within the company's ordinary activities, but are exceptional by virtue of either their size or their incidence. Examples of such items are abnormal charges for bad debts or stock write-offs, abnormal provisions for losses on long-term contracts, and significant adjustments of prior-year taxation provisions.

(c) Are included under any item in the profit or loss account, but relate to a previous financial year.
[*4 Sch 57*].

Extraordinary items

10.110 The Act does not define the term 'extraordinary'. But SSAP 6 defines it as those items that derive from events or transactions outside the ordinary activities of the business and that are both material and expected not to recur either frequently or regularly.

10.111 The profit and loss account formats require extraordinary items to be analysed under the four headings of: 'Extraordinary income', 'Extraordinary charges', 'Extraordinary profit or loss' and 'Tax on extraordinary profit or loss'. It is not correct simply to list all such items under one main heading 'Extraordinary items'. However, the detailed breakdown may be given in a note, rather than on the face of the profit and loss account, and in practice, many companies adopt this form of disclosure (for example, see Table 46).

Table 46: Disclosure of extraordinary items. In this example deferred taxation has arisen from the revisions of the rates of UK corporation tax and taxation allowances contained in the Finance Act 1984. This adjustment has been made as an extraordinary item and this treatment accords with the requirements of SSAP 15.

Extract from Grand Metropolitan Public Limited Company Annual Report 30 September 1984.

Profit and loss account extract

	Notes	£m	1984 £m	£m	1983 £m
Profit Attributable to Ordinary Shareholders before Extraordinary Items			235.2		200.6
Deferred taxation	10	(20.0)			—
Other extraordinary items	10	(4.2)		(1.1)	
			(24.2)		(1.1)
Profit for the financial year			211.0		199.5
Ordinary dividends	11		67.1		58.0
Transferred to Reserves			143.9		141.5

Note

10 Extraordinary Items

(i) The charge of £20.0m in respect of deferred taxation arises from the revisions to the rates of UK corporation tax and taxation allowances on capital expenditure contained in the Finance Act 1984.

(ii) Other extraordinary items	£m	1984 £m	£m	1983 £m
Extraordinary income				
Profits less losses (including provisions) on sales of property and investments		17.4		11.8
Extraordinary charges				
Cost of total closures and other material capacity reductions		(23.0)		(19.2)
Extraordinary loss for the year		(5.6)		(7.4)
Tax relief relating to extraordinary items				
UK corporation tax	(6.0)		4.0	
Overseas taxation	(0.4)		(0.6)	
Deferred taxation	7.8		2.9	
		1.4		6.3
		(4.2)		(1.1)

10.112 The above disclosure requirements correspond with those of SSAP 6, except that SSAP 6 requires only the net amount of extraordinary items to be disclosed.

10.113 The ASC issued ED 36 in February 1985, and this proposes certain revisions to SSAP 6. If these proposals are accepted, they will not change the disclosure requirements for extraordinary items in the profit and loss account. ED 36 does, however, propose certain changes in the way in which revaluation surpluses should be treated, and these are discussed in more detail in Chapter 5.

10.114 Whether or not particular items are classified as extraordinary will depend on the particular circumstances. Items that are extraordinary in one company will not necessarily be extraordinary in another. Subject to this, ED 36 gives some examples of items that may be classified as extraordinary. They are:

(a) The discontinuance of a significant business segment, either through termination or disposal.

(b) The sale of an investment that was not acquired with the intention of resale (such as an investment in a subsidiary or in an associated company).

(c) Provision made for the permanent diminution in value of a non-current asset because unusual events or developments have occurred during the period.

(d) The expropriation of assets.

10.115 Where a significant business segment has been discontinued, the extraordinary item will usually include some or all of the following items:

(a) Redundancy provisions (net of government contributions).

(b) Retention payments to key personnel during the run-down period.

(c) Profits or provisions for losses that arise from disposing of assets (including anticipated ongoing costs such as rent, rates and security).

(d) Pension costs.

(e) Bad and doubtful debts that arise from the decision to close.

(f) All debits and credits that arise from trading after the commencement of the closure.

(g) Any losses caused by penalty clauses in contracts.

10.116 Where such provisions occur over a number of periods, they are not prevented from being treated as extraordinary. Also, it does not matter whether the costs result from a single decision or a number of separate unrelated decisions. In these situations, these costs may be treated as extraordinary over a number of years. However, reorganisation programmes do not represent a discontinuance of a business segment. They are part of the normal business process and so their related costs should be included in the results of the company's ordinary activities. The effect of a change in the basis of taxation or of a significant change in Government fiscal policy (for example, the changes in tax rates and allowances announced in the 1984 Budget—illustrated in Table 46) should be treated as an extraordinary item. [*SSAP 15 para 36*].

Exceptional items

10.117 Formats 2 and 4 have a specific position for the item 'Exceptional amounts written off current assets'. However, the Act does not indicate the place where other exceptional items should be shown, although in accordance with the requirements set out in paragraph 10.109 above, they must be disclosed in the notes to the financial statements.

10.118 SSAP 6 does not define exceptional items, but the proposals in ED 36 do contain a definition that follows closely the description in paragraph 57 of Schedule 4 to the Act (see para 10.109 *(b)* above). The definition in ED 36 says that exceptional items are those items that arise from a company's ordinary activities, but that (because of their size or incidence) need to be disclosed in order that the financial statements should show a true and fair view.

10.119 ED 36 gives the following examples of items that may be classified as exceptional if they are material:

(a) Redundancy costs that relate to continuing business segments.

(b) Reorganisation costs that are unrelated to the discontinuance of a business segment.

(c) Previously capitalised development expenditure written off other than as part of a process of amortisation.

(d) Profits appropriated to employee share schemes.

(e) Profits or losses on the disposal of fixed assets.

(f) Abnormal charges for bad debts and write-offs of stocks and work in progress. (These items would be included in 'Exceptional amounts written off current assets' in formats 2 and 4.)

(g) Abnormal provisions for losses on long-term contracts. (This item would also be included in 'Exceptional amounts written off current assets' in formats 2 and 4.)

(h) Surpluses that arise when insurance claims are settled.

(i) Amounts received in settlement of insurance claims for consequential loss of profits.

10.120 ED 36 proposes that it should be acceptable to relegate exceptional items of this nature to a note to the profit and loss account. However, the proposals require that where the profit before exceptional items needs to be shown separately in order to give a true and fair view, exceptional items should be disclosed as a separate item on the face of the profit and loss account.

10.121 Until SSAP 6 is revised, the proposals contained in ED 36 outlined above in respect of exceptional items can be regarded as best accounting practice.

Dividends

10.122 'Dividends' is not an item that is found in the detailed profit and loss account formats. However, paragraph 3(7) of Schedule 4 to the Act requires that a company's profit and loss account shall show separately the aggregate amount of any dividends paid and proposed. Dividends cannot be relegated to the notes to the profit and loss account: they must be disclosed on the face of it. The amount of dividends paid and proposed that is disclosed should exclude any amount of related ACT. [*SSAP 8 para 14*].

10.123 A question arises as to where dividends should be disclosed in the profit and loss account formats. For example, there is the question of whether dividends can be shown directly after 'Profit or loss on ordinary activities after taxation' in the profit and loss account format (that is, before 'Extraordinary income'). Counsel has advised that this particular disclosure would be possible if the amount of 'Profit or loss for the financial year' before dividends was disclosed somewhere on the face of the profit and loss account. However, in this respect, ED 36 requires also that dividends should be shown after, and be deducted from, the profit or loss for the financial year.

10.124 In practice, dividends are normally disclosed as a deduction from 'Profit or loss for the financial year', after tax and extraordinary items, but before accounting for amounts to be set aside to, or withdrawn from, reserves (see further para 10.130 below).

10.125 The example below illustrates this treatment:

Extract from profit and loss account:

	£
Profit for the financial year	X
Dividends	(X)
Retained profit for the year	X

10.126 The disclosure of dividends outlined below is equally acceptable, and it is often used by companies that have made losses during the year, but have sufficient distributable reserves to pay a dividend:

Extract from profit and loss account:

	£
Loss for the financial year	(X)
Profit and loss account balance brought forward	X
	X
Dividends	(X)
Profit and loss account balance carried forward	X

10.127 However, if the proposals in ED 36 become standard accounting practice, then the disclosure shown immediately above will not be allowed. This is because paragraph 35 of the exposure draft says that dividends should be shown after and deducted from the profit or loss for the financial year.

10.128 In order to pay a dividend, a company has to have sufficient distributable reserves. Distributable reserves are considered in detail in Chapter 19.

10.129 In addition to the Act's requirements regarding dividends, The Stock Exchange's Continuing Obligations for listed companies and General Undertaking for companies traded on the USM require particulars to be disclosed of any arrangements under which a shareholder has either waived or agreed to waive any dividends. [*CO 21(o); GU 10(l)*].

Reserve movements

General disclosure

10.130 The Act requires that any amounts set aside to, or proposed to be set aside to, or withdrawn from, or proposed to be withdrawn from, reserves should be shown separately in the company's profit and loss account. [*4 Sch 3(7)(a)*]. As with dividends, reserve movements of this type should not be shown in the notes to the profit and loss account. They must be shown on the face of the profit and loss account. In practice, profit and loss account reserve movements are normally found after the line 'Profit or loss for the financial year'. An example of an acceptable disclosure is shown in paragraph 10.125 above. However, there are a number of other ways of disclosing these types of reserve transfers that are equally acceptable. Two further examples are given below:

(a) **Extract from profit and loss account:**

	£
Profit for the financial year	X
Dividends	(X)
	X
Transfer from revaluation reserve	X
	X
Profit and loss account balance brought forward	X
Profit and loss account balance carried forward	X

234

(b) **Extract from profit and loss account:**

	£
Profit for the financial year	X
Profit and loss account balance brought forward	X
	X
Transfer to fixed asset replacement reserve	(X)
Dividends	(X)
Profit and loss account balance carried forward	X

This latter example does not comply with ED 36's proposals, because the dividend is not deducted from the profit or loss for the financial year.

Prior-year adjustments

10.131 'Prior-year adjustments' is not a statutory expression. However, SSAP 6 defines it as those material adjustments applicable to prior years that arise either from changes in accounting policies or from the correction of fundamental errors. It does not include the normal recurring corrections and adjustments of accounting estimates made in previous years.

10.132 One of the fundamental accounting concepts is that there should be consistency of treatment of like items from one accounting period to the next. [*SSAP 2 para 14*]. A change in accounting policy should, therefore, not be made unless the new policy can be justified as being preferable to the one that it replaces. Where a company changes an accounting policy, SSAP 6 requires that those cumulative adjustments that apply to previous years that have no bearing on the current year's results should be accounted for by restating those previous years. The object of this restatement is to adjust the opening balance of retained profits on to the new basis of accounting. Where it is practicable to do so, the effect of the change should be disclosed, by showing the amount involved separately in the restatement of the previous year (for example, see Table 47). [*SSAP 6 para 16*].

10.133 A fundamental error is an error that is significant enough to affect the truth and fairness of a company's financial statements. It has to be so fundamental that it would have led to the withdrawal of those financial statements if the error had come to light before those financial statements had been laid before the members at a general meeting. The correction of such an error should not be included in the current year's profit and loss account. Instead, it should be adjusted by restating previous years' results.

10.134 Where either a change in accounting policy or a correction of a fundamental error affects the corresponding profit and loss account and balance sheet for the immediately preceding period, that profit and loss

Table 47: Illustration of the disclosure of a prior-year adjustment.

Extract from Racal Electronics PLC Annual Report & Accounts 31 March 1984.

Profit and loss account extract

Note	Statement of Group Retained Profits for the year ended March 31st 1984		1984 £000		1983 £000
	Retained Profits for the Year		60,124		58,562
	Retained Profits at March 31st 1983 As previously reported	143,769		112,876	
10	Prior Year Adjustment	4,773		2,488	
	As restated		148,542		115,364
	Capitalisation on August 16th 1983		(33)		—
	Amortisation of Revaluation Reserve		154		—
	Transfer to Revaluation Reserve in respect of properties sold during the year		(384)		—
	Goodwill written off		(3,102)		(25,384)
	Retained Profits at March 31st 1984		205,301		148,542

Note

10   Prior Year Adjustment
The policy followed in accounting for profits and losses resulting from changes in exchange rates, which in prior years were transferred to Currency Equalisation Reserve, was changed during the year ended March 31st 1984 to comply with Statement of Standard Accounting Practice No. 20. All such profits and losses on exchange are now taken to the profit and loss account, other than those arising on the retranslation of overseas subsidiary and associated companies accounts and differences on long term foreign currency loans which relate to investments in the overseas companies. In restating the results for the year ended March 31st 1983 on the basis of the new policy the profit has been increased by £3,644,000 less attributable taxation £1,359,000. The profits and losses on exchange relating to earlier years, amounting to £2,488,000 net of taxation has resulted in the restatement of retained profits at March 31st 1982.

account and balance sheet should be adjusted onto the same basis as for the current period.

10.135 The example that follows illustrates how a prior-year adjustment may be presented.

Consolidated profit and loss account	1985 £000	£000	1984 £000	£000
Turnover		115		102
Cost of sales		90		82
Profit on ordinary activities before taxation		25		20
Tax on profit on ordinary activities		10		8

Profit on ordinary activities after taxation	15	12
Extraordinary items	2	1
Profit for the financial year	13	11
Dividends	5	4
Retained profit for the financial year	8	6

Statement of retained profits

Retained profit for the financial year		8	6
Profit and loss account balance at the beginning of the year as previously reported	45	38
Prior-year adjustment (Note X)	(3)	(2)
As restated	42	36
Profit and loss account balance carried forward	50	42

Note X: During the financial year, the group changed its accounting policy regarding the treatment of goodwill in its financial statements. In accordance with SSAP 22, the group now amortises goodwill on consolidation to the profit and loss account over its estimated useful life. Consequently, the group wrote off goodwill of £3,000 in 1985 as a prior-year adjustment. £1,000 of this balance arose in 1984, and the corresponding profit and loss results have been adjusted accordingly.

10.136 The example outlined above shows the statement of retained profits on the face of the profit and loss account. ED 36 proposes that companies should be able to choose where they disclose their reserve movements. It proposes that financial statements should include a single statement showing all movements on reserves. This statement may either follow the profit and loss account immediately, or form a separate statement within the financial statements, or be included as a note to the financial statements. However, where this statement does not immediately follow the profit and loss account, reference is required on the face of the profit and loss account as to the place in the financial statements where it may be found.

Earnings per share

10.137 The Act does not require information to be given in respect of earnings per share. However, SSAP 3 requires listed companies and companies traded on the USM to show the figure of earnings per share on the face of the profit and loss account (for example, see Table 48). This requirement does not apply, however, to some special category companies (as defined in Chapter 13 para 13.03). [*SSAP 3 para 13*].

10.138 The earnings per share is the profit or loss in pence that is attributable to each equity share. The profit or loss to be used in this calculation is the consolidated profit or loss for the period both after tax and after deducting minority interests and preference dividends, but before taking into account extraordinary items. It should also include associated companies' earnings. The earnings figure should be divided by the number of equity shares that are in issue and that rank for dividend in respect of the period. Both of these figures should be shown in a note to the profit and loss account.

Table 48: Illustration of the calculation and disclosure of earnings per share.

Extract from Rothmans International p.l.c. Annual Report and Accounts 31 March 1984.

Profit and loss account extract

Earnings per Share	References 9	1984	1983
Fully diluted		24.6p	23.9p
Basic, following bond conversions in the year		34.6p	
before bond conversions			42.6p

Note

9 Earnings per Share

The fully diluted earnings per share is based on adjusted earnings of £77,616,000 (1983: £75,526,000) and 18,259,456 Ordinary and 297,163,999 "B" Ordinary shares. This allows for full conversion into 83,868,899 (1983: 157,957,787) "B" Ordinary shares of the remaining convertible bonds (note 19) issued by Rothmans International p.l.c.

The basic earnings per share is calculated by reference to:

(a) earnings, after deducting preference dividends, of £73,767,000 (1983: £67,135,000), and

(b) 18,259,456 (1983: 18,259,456) Ordinary shares and, following bond conversions during the year (note 20), a weighted average of 194,772,878 (1983: 139,206,212) "B" Ordinary shares calculated by reference to 30th June 1983, the date to which interest was payable in respect of the bonds converted.

If the shares issued as a result of bonds converted during the year to 31st March 1984 had been in issue throughout 1984 and 1983 the earnings per share would have been 32.0p (1983: 30.8p).

10.139 The earnings per share figure disclosed on the face of the profit and loss account for both the period under review and the corresponding previous period should be calculated using the 'net basis'. [*SSAP 3 para 14*]. On this basis, the charge for taxation used in determining the earnings figure should include:

(a) Any irrecoverable ACT.

(b) Any unrelieved overseas tax that arises from the payment or the proposed payment of dividends.
[*SSAP 3 para 11*].

10.140 The profit and loss account tax charge should be used even where it has been reduced by losses brought forward. However, where this has a material effect on the earnings per share figure that is disclosed, an explanation of the effect should be given. Also, SSAP 3 considers the effect of using the 'nil basis' for calculating earnings per share. Under this basis, the charge for taxation that should be used excludes *(a)* and *(b)* above, except in so far as they arise in respect of preference dividends. SSAP 3 says that, if there is a material difference between the earnings calculated using the nil basis and the earnings calculated using the net basis, then it is desirable to disclose the earnings per share calculated on both bases. [*SSAP 3 para 12*].

10.141 ED 36 suggests that, in order to be consistent with the 'all-inclusive' concept adopted in the proposed revision to SSAP 6, the earnings per share figure should show earnings before and after extraordinary items on a pence per share basis. The ASC believes that this disclosure would improve presentations and also would dissuade users from focusing on a single figure that cannot encapsulate all aspects of a company's performance. Although this requirement is not yet standard accounting practice, it can now be considered best practice to include the earnings per share figure calculated on a figure of earnings both before and after extraordinary items.

Treatment of changes in equity share capital

10.142 Where there is only one class of equity share capital, and this remains constant throughout the period, the calculation of the earnings per share is simple. If, however, there is more than one class of equity shares or (perhaps) some of the shares are not fully paid, the calculation becomes more difficult. In these circumstances, the earnings should be apportioned over the different classes of shares in issue in accordance with either their dividend rights or other rights that they may have to participate in profits.

10.143 If new equity shares are issued during the year, either for cash at full market price or as consideration for the acquisition of an asset, the earnings should be apportioned over the average number of shares that rank for dividend during the period, and weighted on a time basis. When a subsidiary is acquired for shares, the new shares should be taken into account from the day on which the new subsidiary's profits are included in the group's earnings. Where a company makes a bonus issue (or subdivides the shares into shares of a smaller nominal value), the earnings should be apportioned over the number of shares that rank for dividend after the capitalisation. The corresponding earnings per share figure disclosed for the previous year should be recalculated using the new number of shares in issue.

10.144 Where equity shares are issued during the year by way of a rights issue at less than full market price, SSAP 3 recommends that the factor used to adjust the earnings per share for the previous period (and all earlier periods) should be based on the closing price on the last day of quotation of the shares cum rights. The factor it recommends is:

$$\frac{\text{Theoretical ex rights price}}{\text{Actual cum rights price on the last day of quotation}}$$

An adjustment is necessary to correct the earnings per share figure of previous years to reflect the effective bonus element in the rights issue. For the earnings per share of the current year, it is necessary to adjust the weighted average share capital. This can be done by adding the proportion of the capital in issue before the rights issue (after applying the reciprocal of the factor set out above) to the proportion of the capital in issue after the rights issue.

Fully diluted earnings per share

10.145 Companies often have equity shares in issue that do not rank for a dividend in the period, although they may do so in the future. They may also have debentures, or loan stock or preference shares that are convertible into the company's equity shares. Furthermore, there may be options or warrants to subscribe for shares in the company.

10.146 Where these situations exist, SSAP 3 requires that the fully diluted earnings per share (calculated on the basis outlined in paragraph 10.148 below) should be shown also on the face of the profit and loss account (for example, see Table 48). [*SSAP 3 para 16*]. Where this figure is disclosed, SSAP 3 requires that:

(a) The basis of calculation should be disclosed.

(b) The corresponding amount should be given (unless the assumption on which the calculation is based did not exist in the previous period).

(c) Equal prominence should be given to the basic and fully diluted earnings per share figures.

10.147 The fully diluted earnings per share figure need not be given if either the dilution amounts to less than 5% of the basic earnings per share figure or the basic earnings per share figure is negative. [*SSAP 3 para 16*].

10.148 The fully diluted earnings per share should be calculated in the following ways:

(a) Where equity shares exist that will rank for a dividend in the future, the fully diluted earnings per share figure should be calculated using the assumption that these shares ranked for dividend from the beginning of the period (or from the date of their issue, if this was during the period). [*SSAP 3 para 29*].

(b) Convertible loan stock should be brought into the calculation as if it had been converted into the maximum number of new equity shares at the beginning of the period (or on the date of the issue of the loan stock, if this was during the period). Also, the earnings for the period should be adjusted to take account of the saving of

interest on the stock (net of corporation tax) that would have arisen if the conversion had occurred. [*SSAP 3 para 30*].

(c) Where options or warrants exist, the calculations should be made using the maximum number of equity shares that would have been in issue if the options and warrants had been exercised on the first day of the period (or on the date of issue, if this was during the period). The earnings for the period should also be adjusted using the assumption that the proceeds of subscription were invested in 2½% Consolidated Stock on the day on which the options or warrants were exercised. [*SSAP 3 para 31*].

10.149 For both convertible loan stock and options and warrants, the fully diluted earnings per share figure will still have to be given in the year in which either the loans are converted or the options and warrants are exercised. This will be necessary unless the conversion or the exercise was carried out on the first day of the period.

CHAPTER 11

DIRECTORS' AND OFFICERS' LOANS AND TRANSACTIONS

Chapter 11

Directors' and Officers' Loans and Transactions

Introduction

11.01 By making certain transactions and arrangements unlawful, the Act imposes restrictions on dealings between a company and its directors. The purpose of these restrictions is to prevent a conflict of interest arising between the directors and the company. In addition (and whether they are lawful or not), the Act requires that most transactions and arrangements that may favour directors should be disclosed. The Act also requires certain transactions with officers of the company to be disclosed.

11.02 The Act's requirements relating to transactions between the company and its directors or officers are, perhaps, the main legal safeguard there is against directors or officers abusing their position in a company. The disclosure requirements, in particular, ensure that shareholders and others that have an interest in the company (for example, creditors) will be informed about all the significant transactions the company enters into with those responsible for the company's management that might (either directly or indirectly) benefit those individuals. The intention is to encourage directors and officers to take care before entering into such transactions, because the shareholders will be fully informed of them.

11.03 Appendix VII contains decision tables that determine whether a loan to a director is prohibited by the Act. These tables should be read in conjunction with this chapter.

Definitions

11.04 The definitions of a 'relevant company' and a 'connected person' are considered below. They are essential to an understanding of the types of transaction that the Act prohibits.

Relevant company

11.05 A 'relevant company', for the purpose of the provisions of the Act that relate to directors' transactions, is either of the following types of

245

company:

(a) A public company.

(b) A company that belongs to a group in which either the holding company or any subsidiary is a public company.
[*Sec 331(6)*].

Connected person

11.06 A 'connected person' is a person who is connected with a director and is either an individual or a legal person (for example, a company). A connected person includes any of the following:

(a) The director's wife or husband or child (including an illegitimate child), or step-child, but excluding any child who is at least 18 years of age. [*Sec 346(2)(a),(3)(a)*].

(b) A company with which the director is associated. [*Sec 346(2)(b)*]. For this purpose, a company is 'associated' with the director if, and only if, the director, together with the persons connected with him, either are *interested* in at least 20% of the equity share capital or are able to *exercise or control* at least 20% of the voting power at any general meeting. [*Sec 346 (4)*].

In the definition of 'associated', the director's interest in shares, or his control of the voting power, may be either direct (that is, he himself owns the shares or controls the votes) or indirect (that is, a company that he controls owns the shares or controls the votes). For this purpose, the director will be regarded as controlling an intermediary company if he (and his connected persons), together with his fellow directors, either are interested in more than 50% of the intermediary company's equity share capital or control more than 50% of its votes at a general meeting. This is provided that the director and his connected persons are interested in some of the shares or control some of the votes. It is not possible for a director and his connected persons to control a company where they are not interested in, or do not control any voting power attached to, any shares in that company, even though his fellow directors may be interested in shares or control the votes of the company concerned. [*Sec 346(5)*].

Under the above provisions, the interests of a director must be aggregated with those of his connected persons. The rules that the Act lays down for determining whether a person is interested in shares provide, *inter alia,* that a person is to be treated as interested in shares if a company is interested in them and the person is entitled to exercise, or control the exercise of, more than 50% of that company's voting power at general meetings. [*13 Sch 4*]. To avoid taking the same interest into account twice when determining whether a director is associated with a company, the Act provides that companies with which he is associated are not treated as his connected persons, unless they are persons connected with him by virtue of either *(c)* or *(d)* below. For the same reason, in determining whether a third company is associated with a director, a trustee of a trust whose beneficiaries include, or may include, a company that is associated with that director are not to be treated as a connected person of his by reason only of that fact. [*Sec 346(6)(b)*].

The following two examples illustrate these principles:

(i) Mr. Jones owns 2% of Company A's equity share capital, and he also owns 51% of Company B's equity share capital. Company B owns 19% of Company A's equity share capital.

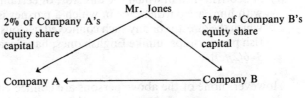

Mr. Jones

2% of Company A's equity share capital

51% of Company B's equity share capital

Company A ← Company B

19% of Company A's equity share capital

Mr. Jones is connected with Company B, because he has a controlling interest in that company. However, when determining whether Mr. Jones is connected with Company A, Company B's interest in Company A's shares should be ignored. [*Sec 346(6)(a)*]. However, Mr. Jones is taken to be interested in the shares of Company A held by Company B, because he is entitled to exercise, or control the exercise of, more than 50% of the voting power of Company B. [*13 Sch 4*]. Consequently, Company A is connected with Mr. Jones via the operation of Section 346(4)(a), because he has an interest in 21% (that is, greater than 20%) of Company A's equity share capital.

(ii) Mr. Williams owns 2% of Company C's equity share capital and he also owns 100% of Company D's £1 non-voting 'A' equity shares and 26% of Company D's £1 'B' equity shares, which represent in total 26% of the voting power and 63% of the share capital of Company D. Company D owns 80% of Company C's equity share capital (which represents 80% of Company C's votes).

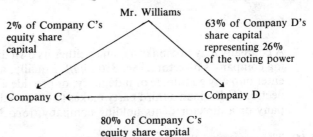

Mr. Williams

2% of Company C's equity share capital

63% of Company D's share capital representing 26% of the voting power

Company C ← Company D

80% of Company C's equity share capital

As in the previous example, Mr. Williams is connected with Company D, because he has an interest in more than 20% of the share capital of that company. In accordance with Section 346(6)(a), the interest of Company D in the shares of Company C should be disregarded. However, unlike in example (i) above, Mr. Williams is also not interested in the shares in Company C held by Company D via the operation of paragraph 4 of Schedule 13, because he is only entitled to exercise, or control the exercise of, 26% of the voting power of Company D. But, under Section 346(8), Mr. Williams is able to exercise effective control of more than 20% of the voting power of Company C, because he controls the voting power of Company D. Accordingly, Company C is associated with Mr. Williams by the operation of Section 346(4)(b).

(c) A person acting in his capacity as a trustee of any trust that either includes as a beneficiary the director or one of his connected persons, or confers a power on the trustees to benefit either the director or certain of those with whom he is connected. [*Sec 346(2)(c)*]. However, trustees of either an employee share scheme or a pension scheme are not to be regarded as connected with a director merely by virtue of that trusteeship. [*Sec 346(3)(b)*].

(d) A partner of either the director or certain of his connected persons. [*Sec 346(2)(d)*].

(e) A Scottish firm in which the director, or certain persons connected with him, are partners, or in which a partner is a Scottish firm in which the director or any such connected persons are partners. (Scottish partnerships, unlike English ones, have legal personality.) [*Sec 346(2)(e)*].

However, none of the above persons are connected if they themselves are also directors of the company. [*Sec 346(2)*].

Prohibited transactions with directors

11.07   Section 330 of the Act prohibits companies from entering into certain transactions, such as loans and credit transactions, for the benefit of their directors or persons connected with those directors. The extent of these restrictions varies according to whether or not the company concerned is a relevant company. The Act also includes certain exemptions from these restrictions that are available in certain circumstances, and these are considered in detail in paragraphs 11.28 to 11.32 below.

Loans

11.08   A company may not make a loan to either its own directors or its holding company's directors. [*Sec 330(2)(a)*]. Equally, a company may not enter into any guarantee or indemnity, or provide any security, in connection with a loan a third party makes to either a director of the company or a director of its holding company. [*Sec 330(2)(b), 331(2)*].

11.09   The expression 'loan' is not defined in the Act. However, it was interpreted in a case brought under the Companies Act 1948. In that case it was held that the dictionary definition should be applied. The dictionary definition of a loan is "a sum of money lent for a time to be returned in money or money's worth". (*Champagne Perrier-Jouet S.A. v H.H. Finch Ltd. [1982] 1 WLR 1359.*)

11.10   A holding company is not prohibited from making loans to a director of its subsidiary. Similarly, a subsidiary may lend to a director of a fellow subsidiary.

11.11   Non-relevant companies may make a loan to a person who is connected with a director. Such a loan is unlawful, however, if a relevant company makes it. [*Sec 330(3)(b)*]. Also, a relevant company may not enter into any guarantee, or provide any security, in connection with any loan that a third party makes to either a director or a person who is connected with a director. [*Sec 330(3)(c)*].

11.12   But a relevant company may make a loan (or enter into a guarantee, or provide any security in connection with a loan) to another company within the same group. This applies even where a director of the relevant company is associated with that other group company. [*Sec 333*].

11.13   There is a general exemption for small loans. Any company (whether relevant or non-relevant) may make a loan to a director of either the company or its holding company, provided that the aggregate of the 'relevant amounts' immediately after the loan is made to him does not exceed £2,500. The amounts to be aggregated are:

(a) The value of the proposed transaction.

(b) The amount outstanding under any other transaction that was made under the same exception.

(c) The value of any existing arrangement within Section 330(6) or (7) (described in paras 11.23 and 11.26 below), that was made under the same exception.
[*Sec 339(2)*].

The amounts outstanding and the values that have to be taken into account under *(b)* and *(c)* respectively are those made by the *company or any subsidiary* to the following people:

(i)   The director in question (or, where the proposed transaction is to be made for a connected person of a director, the director with whom that person is connected).
(ii)   Any person connected with the director.
[*Sec 339(3)*].

Where the proposed transaction is to be made by a company for a director of its holding company or a person connected with such a director, there must also be taken into account the amounts outstanding and the values under *(b)* and *(c)* respectively that were made by the *holding company or any subsidiary* for the persons mentioned in (i) and (ii) above. [*Sec 339(2)*].

11.14   The small loans exemption does not apply, however, to loans that relevant companies make to persons who are connected with a director. It also does not apply to guarantees, or indemnities or securities that such companies provide to directors or their connected persons. [*Sec 334*]. The value of a loan for these purposes is the amount of its principal. [*Sec 340(2)*].

249

Quasi-loans

11.15   Quasi-loans are transactions where one party (the creditor) either agrees to pay, or pays, a sum for another (the borrower). It also covers transactions where the creditor agrees to reimburse, or reimburses, expenditure another party incurs for the borrower. A quasi-loan will exist where either of the following two conditions applies:

(a) The transaction's terms are such that the borrower (or a person on his behalf) will reimburse the creditor.

(b) The circumstances surrounding the transaction give rise to a liability on the borrower to reimburse the creditor.
[*Sec 331(3)*].

The value of a quasi-loan is the amount, or maximum amount, that the person to whom it is made is liable to reimburse the creditor. [*Sec 340(3)*].

11.16   A common example of a quasi-loan arises where a director uses a company credit card to buy goods, and he does so on the understanding that the company will settle the liability and he will reimburse the company at a later date. Another example is the type of arrangement whereby companies in a group pay for goods and services for the personal use of a director of the holding company, on the basis that he will reimburse those companies at a later date.

11.17   Non-relevant companies may make quasi-loans of any amount to either the company's directors or its holding company's directors, or to the connected persons of such directors. They may also guarantee or provide security in respect of a quasi-loan to such a person.

11.18   Relevant companies are prohibited from making quasi-loans to either the company's directors or its holding company's directors, or to a director's connected persons. [*Sec 330(3)(a)(b)*]. However, relevant companies may make quasi-loans to a director (but not to his connected persons), provided that the total amount of quasi-loans outstanding in favour of that director does not exceed £1,000, and provided also that he is required to repay each quasi-loan within two months. [*Sec 332(1)*]. The total amount of quasi-loans will include such loans made by the relevant company or by any of its subsidiaries, or, if the director is a director of a holding company of that relevant company, by any other subsidiary of the holding company.

11.19   Relevant companies may not enter into a guarantee or provide security for a quasi-loan a third party makes to either a director or a person connected with him. [*Sec 330(3)(c)*]. However, where a relevant company is a member of a group, it is not prohibited either from making a quasi-loan to another member of that group, or from entering into a guarantee or providing security for any such quasi-loan, by reason only that a director of one of the group companies is associated with another group company. [*Sec 333*].

Credit transactions

11.20 The Act does not permit a relevant company to enter into credit trans-actions for the benefit of a director of either the company or its hold-ing company, or of a person connected with such a director. [*Sec 330(4)(a)*] Also, a relevant company may not either guarantee such a transaction that somebody else enters into, or provide security in respect of such a transaction. [*Sec 330(4)(b)*]. Non-relevant companies are not affected by the rules relating to credit transactions.

11.21 A credit transaction is any transaction where a creditor:

(a) Supplies any goods or any land under either a hire purchase agree-ment or a conditional sale agreement.

(b) Leases any land or hires any goods in return for periodic payments.

(c) Disposes of land, or supplies goods or services, on the understand-ing that the payment (whatever form it takes) is to be deferred. [*Sec 331(7)*].

'Services' means anything other than goods or land. [*Sec 331(8)*].

11.22 An exemption is available to relevant companies, provided that the aggregate of the relevant amounts (see para 11.13) does not exceed £5,000.[*Sec 335(1)*]. The value of this type of transaction is the price that it would be reasonable to expect could be obtained for the goods, land or services to which the transaction relates if they had been sup-plied in the ordinary course of the company's business and on the same terms (apart from price). [*Sec 340(6)*]. If the value of the transaction cannot be ascertained, then it is deemed to exceed £50,000. [*Sec 340(7)*]. There is another exemption available for credit transactions of any amount made by a relevant company where:

(a) The company enters into the transaction in the ordinary course of its business.

(b) The value and the terms on which the company offers the credit transaction to the director are no more favourable than the value and the terms the company would have offered to a person who was of similar financial standing, but was unconnected with the company.
[*Sec 335(2)*].

Assignment or assumption of rights, or obligations or liabilities

11.23 Both relevant companies and non-relevant companies are not permit-ted to arrange to have assigned to them, or to assume responsibility for, any rights, or obligations or liabilities under loans, or quasi-loans or credit transactions (or any guarantee or provisions of security in respect of such loans or transactions). This applies if the transactions concerned would have been unlawful had the company itself entered into them. For the purpose of this section, the transaction will be treated as having been entered into on the date of the arrangement. [*Sec 330(6)*]. The value of this type of arrangement is the value of the transaction to which the arrangement relates less any amount by which the person's liability has been reduced. [*Sec 340(5)*]. If the value of the transaction cannot be ascertained, then it is deemed to exceed £50,000. [*Sec 340(7)*].

11.24 An example of an 'assignment' is where a third party makes a loan to a director of a company and, subsequently, the director's company purchases the third party's rights to the loan. In this situation, the company has (illegally) paid out resources to acquire an asset, and it becomes a creditor of the director just as if it had advanced the loan itself.

11.25 An example of an 'assumption of liabilities' is where a third party guarantees a loan that a fourth party makes to a director of a company and, subsequently, the director's company enters into an arrangement with the third and the fourth parties, whereby the third party is released from his guarantee, and the company assumes the liability. Again, in this situation, the company's resources are (illegally) tied up by a contingent liability when the company assumes the guarantee on behalf of the director.

Indirect arrangements

11.26 The Act prohibits those indirect arrangements whereby another person enters into a transaction that would have been unlawful had the company itself entered into it. This prohibition applies only if that person has obtained, or is to obtain, under the arrangement any benefit from the company, or its holding company, or its subsidiary or its fellow subsidiary. [*Sec 330(7)*]. This provision is designed to prevent a company's resources from being used to procure another person to provide one of the various forms of prohibited credit without the company itself either entering into, or subsequently becoming a party to, the transaction. The value of an indirect arrangement is ascertained in the same way as the value of an assignment or an assumption of rights considered in paragraph 11.23 above.

11.27 This provision is very widely drafted, and it is intended to cover the wide variety of forms that these types of arrangement can take. For example, it covers the situation where a company agrees to make a loan to another company's director in return for that other company making a loan to one of the first company's directors. It also covers the situation where a director persuades a bank to make a loan on favourable terms to him in return for his company placing business with the bank.

Exemptions from prohibited transactions

11.28 In addition to the exemptions that apply only to particular types of transaction (for example, the *de minimis* exemption for a loan of less than £2,500), the Act includes more general exemptions in respect of:

(a) Transactions between a subsidiary and its holding company.

(b) Directors' business expenditure.

Transactions between a subsidiary and its holding company

11.29 The following transactions between a subsidiary and its holding company are not affected by the restrictions that the Act imposes on loans, quasi-loans and credit transactions:

(a) A loan or a quasi-loan a company makes to its holding company, or a company's guarantee or provision of security to a third person who has made a loan or quasi-loan to the company's holding company.

(b) A credit transaction a company enters into as creditor for its holding company, or a guarantee or security that a company provides in connection with a credit transaction a third party makes for the company's holding company.
[*Sec 336*].

These types of transactions are, therefore, lawful.

Directors' business expenditure

11.30 The Act permits a company to give a director funds to enable him to perform his duties properly as an officer of the company. [*Sec 337(1)*]. The company may provide these funds by way of a loan, or a quasi-loan or a credit transaction, or by any other similar arrangement. This exemption applies, however, only if one of the following two conditions is satisfied:

(a) The transaction has been approved in advance by the company in general meeting. [*Sec 337(3)(a)*]. At that general meeting, the purpose of the expenditure, the amount of funds to be provided, and the extent of the company's liability under the transaction must all be made known. [*Sec 337(4)*].

(b) It is a condition of the transaction that, if the company does not subsequently approve the transaction at or before the next annual general meeting, the director will discharge, within six months, any liability that arises under the transaction. [*Sec 337(3)(b)*].

A relevant company may not enter into such a transaction if the aggregate of the relevant amounts (see para 11.13 above) exceeds £10,000. [*Sec 337(3)*]. However, with non-relevant companies there is no upper limit on transactions of this type.

11.31   The most common form of transaction of this nature is a bridging loan a company gives to a director who changes location within the company, and so is required to move house.

11.32   Section 337 of the Act does not restrict advances of an appropriate amount a company makes to a director for business expenditure. Consequently, these types of transaction are permitted without first needing to be approved in general meeting. This is because the funds the company provides to the director in this way are not lent to him.

Money-lending companies and recognised banks

11.33   Those provisions of the Act that prevent companies from making loans and quasi-loans to directors or their connected persons are relaxed to some extent for money-lending companies and recognised banks. The special rules that cover the legality of these transactions for such companies are set out in Section 338 of the Act.

11.34   A 'recognised bank' is a company that is recognised as a bank under the Banking Act 1979. [*Sec 331(5)*]. (The Bank of England's annual report gives a full list of recognised banks.) However, this definition does not include 'licensed institutions', but these companies do fall within the definition of 'money-lending companies'. The Act defines a 'money-lending company' as "a company whose ordinary business includes the making of loans or quasi-loans, or the giving of guarantees in connection with such loans". [*Sec 338(2)*].

11.35   Section 338(1) of the Act permits money-lending companies to make loans or quasi-loans, or to guarantee such transactions, to any director or his connected persons, subject to the following two conditions:

(a)   The company makes the transaction in the ordinary course of its business. [*Sec 338(3)(a)*].

(b)   The amount involved is not greater than, and the terms of the contract are not more favourable than, those that the company might reasonably be expected to have offered to, or in respect of, a person who was unconnected with the company, but who had a similar financial standing to that of the director. [*Sec 338(3)(b)*].

11.36   A further condition applies to a money-lending company that is a relevant company. Such a company may not enter into a transaction if the aggregate of the relevant amounts (see para 11.13 above) concerned exceeds £50,000. [*Sec 338(4)*]. In determining that aggregate, loans to companies that the director is connected with, but that he does not control, may be excluded. [*Sec 338(5)*]. However, this restriction does not apply to a recognised bank. Consequently, there is no limit on the size of transaction that a recognised bank may enter into, except in respect of house mortgages (see para 11.38 below).

11.37   Provided that the loans are on commercial terms and are disclosed to shareholders, recognised banks can generally lend to their directors without limit. Moreover, the problems that might have arisen in relation to loans a bank makes to companies connected with any of the bank's directors are alleviated by Section 338(5). This section exempts, from the definition of a 'connected person' for this particular purpose, companies that a director does not control (see para 11.06 above). This provision is necessary because such a broad restriction might otherwise significantly inhibit a bank's normal business. It would also be very difficult for a bank to keep constant track of all the many transactions between the bank and the large number of companies that may be connected with its directors. This would apply particularly where many of a bank's transactions are arranged at branch level.

11.38   Loans that recognised banks make to directors for house purchase and house improvement are permitted in certain instances. A recognised bank may make loans to either its directors or its holding company's directors, even though those loans are greater in amount than, or are on more favourable terms than, those that the bank would normally give in its ordinary course of business. Provided that all the following conditions are satisfied, loans for the above purposes will be allowed:

(a) The loan is to assist the director either to purchase or to improve his only or main residence. This type of loan will also include a loan a bank has made to take over any similar loan that any other person has made to the director.

(b) The bank makes similar loans of that type available to its employees on no less favourable terms.

(c) The aggregate of the relevant amounts (see para 11.13 above) does not exceed £50,000.
[*Sec 338(6)*].

11.39   However, money-lending companies and recognised banks do not benefit from any special provisions that apply to the following types of transaction:

(a) The provision of security in connection with a loan or a quasi-loan.

(b) Credit transactions, or the provision of a guarantee or security in connection with them.

(c) The assignment of rights, or obligations or liabilities under any transaction.

(d) Indirect arrangements under any transaction.

In all these situations, money-lending companies and recognised banks are in the same position as any other company, and the rules detailed in Sections 330 to 337 of the Act (as outlined in paras 11.07 to 11.32 above) apply to them.

Criminal sanctions and civil remedies

11.40   The penalties the Act imposes on a company that contravenes those of the Act's provisions that relate to the legality of directors' transactions, vary according to whether or not the company is a relevant company. A relevant company will incur both criminal and civil liability, whereas a non-relevant company will incur only civil liability.

11.41   As regards criminal liability, a relevant company that contravenes Section 330 of the Act will be guilty of an offence. [*Sec 342(2)*]. A director will also be guilty of an offence if he either authorises or permits the transaction concerned. This provision will also apply to any other person who causes the company to enter into such a transaction. [*Sec 342(1)(3)*]. In this situation, the director's or the other person's *state of mind* is relevant in deciding whether an offence has been committed. To be guilty of an offence, he must have known, or have had reasonable cause to believe, that the transaction contravened Section 330. A relevant company may escape liability if it can prove that it did not know of the facts at the time it entered into the transaction. [*Sec 342(5)*]. The criminal penalty is imprisonment or a fine, or both. [*Sec 342(4) — see Appendix IV*].

11.42   A company may choose to regard an unlawful transaction as voidable. [*Sec 341(1)*]. This means that a company does not need to regard itself as bound by any agreement that it has entered into with the director or any other person. However, because a transaction is not actually void, a company may wish to elect to affirm the agreement instead. Also, the company will not be entitled to treat the transaction as voidable if the subject matter of the transaction cannot be restored (for example, where the sum a company has lent has been used to buy goods which have been consumed), or if the person who benefited under the transaction has indemnified the company. [*Sec 341(1)(a)*].

11.43   Similarly, a transaction will not be voidable if a third party has, *bona fide* and without actual notice, acquired rights under the agreement, and these rights would be affected if the company avoided the liability. [*Sec 341(1)(b)*].

11.44   The person who benefited from the unlawful transaction may not himself elect to treat it as voidable. Moreover, he, and any other director who authorised the transaction, are (without prejudice to any other liability imposed by law) liable to account to the company for any gain they have made (whether directly or indirectly) and also to indemnify the company for any loss or damage it incurs as a result of the transaction. [*Sec 341(2)(3)*]. Where a director took all reasonable steps to ensure that the transaction did not contravene the Act, he need not either account to the company or indemnify it, if the transaction in question was made for a person connected with him. [*Sec 341(4)*]. A connected person (and a director who authorised the transaction) will avoid civil liability if they can show that, at the time the company entered into the agreement, they did not know of the circumstances that amounted to a contravention. [*Sec 341(5)*].

Prohibited transactions with shadow directors

11.45 The restrictions on directors' dealings in Sections 330 to 346 of the Act (including the penalties that attach if the Act is contravened) apply to shadow directors and their connected persons, as well as to ordinary directors. [*Sec 330(5)*]. A 'shadow director' is a person who is not himself a director of the company, but in accordance with whose instructions the directors are accustomed to act. [*Sec 741(2)*].

Interests in contracts

11.46 Where a director has an interest in a contract that involves the company, Section 317 of the Act imposes a specific obligation on the director to disclose his interest in the contract at a meeting of the company's directors. This applies whether the director is either directly or indirectly interested in the contract, or the proposed contract, with the company. A director must disclose his interest in a proposed contract at the directors' meeting at which the contract is first considered. If, however, the director acquires an interest in the contract at a later date, he must disclose his interest at the next subsequent meeting. [*Sec 317(2)*]. A contract for this purpose includes any transaction or arrangement made on or after 22 December 1980.

11.47 When a director is, for example, a member of another company that may enter into significant transactions with the company, then he can give a general notice that he is interested in that other company. If he does this, it will be regarded as giving sufficient notice to cover all further transactions with that company. [*Sec 317(3)*]. The director must either give the notice at a meeting of the directors or take reasonable steps to ensure that it is brought up and read at the next directors' meeting. [*Sec 317(4)*].

11.48 These notification requirements apply to those transactions and arrangements favouring directors or their connected persons that are covered by Section 330 (see paras 11.07 to 11.27). [*Sec 317(6)*]. Consequently, a director, for example, must declare at a directors' meeting his interest in any loan that he, or one of his connected persons, receives from the company. Again, a general notice of an interest may be given.

11.49 These requirements also apply to substantial property transactions and arrangements of a kind described in paragraphs 11.53 to 11.59 below. The requirements apply irrespective of whether the transactions and arrangements have been approved by the company in general meeting.

11.50 If a director fails to disclose an interest in accordance with Section 317 of the Act, this will be a criminal offence, and he will be liable to a fine. [*Sec 317(7)* — *see Appendix IV*]. Also, this section does not prejudice the operation of any rule of law that may restrict a director from being interested in contracts with the company. [*Sec 317(9)*]. This means that the contract may be voidable, and the director may be liable to account to the company for any gain he has made as a result of the transaction, and to indemnify the company for any loss it incurs.

11.51 The general principles of Section 317 apply also to shadow directors. However, a shadow director must disclose his interest by notice, in writing, to the directors, not at a meeting of the directors. Such notice can be in either one of the following forms:

(a) Specific, and given before the date of the meeting at which he would have been required to declare his interest, had he been a director.

(b) General (as described in para 11.47 above).
[*Sec 317(8)*].

11.52 In addition to the statutory requirement to disclose interests in contracts, the company's articles of association may also contain other specific requirements for the disclosure of interests in contracts. For example, the revised Table A deals, in regulations 85 and 86, with directors' material interests in contracts. The requirements of these regulations are as follows:

"Subject to the provisions of the Act, and provided that he has disclosed to the directors the nature and extent of any material interest of his, a director notwithstanding his office—

(a) may be a party to, or otherwise interested in, any transaction or arrangement with the company or in which the company is otherwise interested;

(b) may be a director or other officer of, or employed by, or a party to any transaction or arrangement with, or otherwise interested in, any body corporate promoted by the company or in which the company is otherwise interested; and

(c) shall not, by reason of his office, be accountable to the company for any benefit which he derives from any such office or employment or from any such transaction or arrangement or from any interest in any such body corporate and no such transaction or arrangement shall be liable to be avoided on the ground of any such interest or benefit.

For the purposes of [*the above*] regulation 85—

(a) a general notice given to the directors that a director is to be regarded as having an interest of the nature and extent specified in the notice in any transaction or arrangement in which a specified person or class of persons is interested shall be deemed to be a disclosure that the director has an interest in any such transaction of the nature and extent so specified; and

(b) an interest of which a director has no knowledge and of which it is unreasonable to expect him to have knowledge shall not be treated as an interest of his.''

Substantial property transactions

General requirements

11.53 Unlike transactions such as loans, quasi-loans and credit transactions that (for relevant companies at least) are *prima facie* unlawful, the Act does not prohibit a company from entering into contracts with directors or their connected persons for the sale of non-cash assets. The Act does require, however, that an interest of a director or his connected person in such a contract should first be approved by the *company* in *general meeting*. If, alternatively, the contract is with a director of the holding company or a person connected with him, it must also be first approved by a general meeting of the holding company. [*Sec 320(1)*]. The arrangements that this section of the Act covers are those where:

(a) A director of either the company or its holding company, or a person connected with such a director, acquires (or is to acquire) a non-cash asset from the company.

(b) A company acquires (or is to acquire) a non-cash asset from a director of either the company or its holding company, or from a person connected with such a director.
[*Sec 320(1)*].

11.54 The same rules also apply to those transactions of this nature that involve a shadow director or his connected persons. [*Sec 320(3)*].

11.55 In this context, 'non-cash asset' means any property, or any interest in property other than cash. (For this purpose, 'cash' includes foreign currency.) The acquisition of a non-cash asset also includes the creation of an interest in property (for example, a lease) and the discharge of any person's liability other than a liability for a liquidated sum. [*Sec 739(1)(2)*].

11.56 One of the effects of Section 320 of the Act is that a director may sell a non-cash asset to his company, or buy a non-cash asset from it, if it is of the requisite value only with the shareholders' approval.

11.57 Section 320 also affects certain intra-group transactions. Where, for example, a director of a company owns or controls a certain percentage of the shares in another group company, that other group company may fall within the definition of a connected person (see para 11.06 above). In these circumstances, and unless the company in general meeting first approves them, all dealings between the company and any company that falls within the definition of a connected person will require approval (but see para 11.58).

11.58 However, although the company will still have to comply with the disclosure requirements set out in paragraph 11.77 below, the shareholders' approval is not required for an arrangement of the type described in paragraph 11.53 above where one of the following conditions is satisfied:

(a) The value of the non-cash asset at the time of the arrangement is less than £1,000 (or, if the value is greater than £1,000, it is less than the lower of £50,000 and 10% of the company's asset value). For this purpose, 'asset value' means the value of the company's net assets as disclosed in its latest financial statements. Alternatively, where there are no such financial statements, 'asset value' means the amount of the company's called-up share capital (as defined in Section 737(1)). [*Sec 320(1)(2)*].

(b) The body corporate in question is neither a company within the meaning of the Act, nor a body registered under Section 630. [*Sec 321(1)*].

(c) The company in question is a wholly-owned subsidiary of any company, wherever incorporated. In these circumstances, in practice, the holding company's directors have control over the subsidiary's directors. [*Sec 321(1)*].

(d) The non-cash asset is to be acquired:

   (i) By a holding company from any of its wholly-owned subsidiaries.
   (ii) By a wholly-owned subsidiary from its holding company.
   (iii) By a wholly-owned subsidiary from a fellow wholly-owned subsidiary.
   [*Sec 321(2)(a)*].

In effect, this exemption relieves companies that would otherwise be required by Section 320 of the Act to obtain approval at a general meeting for intra-group transactions that take place in a wholly-owned group.

(e) The arrangement is entered into by a company that is being wound up, and the winding-up is not a members' voluntary winding-up. [*Sec 321(2)(b)*].

(f) The following two conditions are satisfied:

   (i) A member of the company acquires an asset from the company.
   (ii) The arrangement was made with that person in his capacity as a member of the company.
   [*Sec 321(3)*].

11.59 The Stock Exchange's requirements that relate to substantial property transactions (and other transactions with directors) are considered in paragraphs 11.99 to 11.103 below.

Penalties

11.60 A director who contravenes Section 320 of the Act is not guilty of a criminal offence, but he may incur civil penalties. The arrangement (and any transaction pursuant thereto) may be treated as voidable by the company unless at least one of the following three conditions is satisfied:

(a) It is impossible to obtain restitution of the subject matter of the transaction, or else the company has been indemnified for any loss or damage it has suffered.

(b) A third party has acquired rights, *bona fide* and for value, and without having notice of the contravention.

(c) The arrangement is affirmed by the company in general meeting (and/or by the holding company, as the case may be) within a reasonable period of the arrangement being made. [*Sec 322(1)(2)*].

11.61 The director who entered into the arrangement, or a person connected with him, or a director who authorised it may all be liable to account to the company for any gain they have received. They may also be liable to indemnify the company from any resultant loss or damage it has incurred. [*Sec 322(3)*]. However, a director will not be liable if the arrangement was made with a person connected with him, and if he himself took all reasonable steps to ensure that the company obtained the required approval. [*Sec 322(5)*]. This liability is without prejudice to any other liability which may have been incurred and arises whether or not the arrangement has been avoided. [*Sec 322(4)*]. A connected person or a director who authorised the transaction will not be liable if they can show that they did not know the relevant circumstances that formed the contravention. [*Sec 322(6)*].

Transactions to be disclosed

11.62 So far, this chapter has considered the legality of directors' transactions. The Act also requires considerable detail to be disclosed, either in the group accounts, or in the financial statements of any company other than a holding company, regarding transactions with directors whether they are lawful or not. [*Sec 232(1)(2)*]. These disclosure requirements are dealt with below.

11.63 Details of the transactions that require to be disclosed must be given in the notes to the financial statements. Such transactions are required to be disclosed for shadow directors as well as for other directors. [*Sec 232(3)*]. Where a company with subsidiaries has not prepared group accounts (either because it is a wholly-owned subsidiary or because its subsidiaries are not dealt with in those accounts for one of the reasons given in Chapter 17, paragraph 17.60), the notes to the financial statements must give the equivalent information that would have been given if those group accounts had been prepared. [*Sec 232(4)*].

11.64 The Act requires that the following two broad categories of directors' transactions should be disclosed:

(a) Any transaction of a type described in Section 330 of the Act that the company or its subsidiary has entered into, or has agreed to enter into, for a person who was a director of either the company or its holding company at any time during the financial year (for example, see Table 49). This requirement applies also to a person who was connected with such a director. [*6 Sch 1(a)(b), 2(a)(b)*].

(b) Any other transaction involving the company or its subsidiary in which a person who was, at any time during the financial year, a director of either the company or its holding company had, either directly or indirectly, a material interest (for example, see Tables 49 and 50). [*6 Sch 1(c), 2(c)*]. This requirement also applies if a person who is connected with a director has an interest in such a transaction. [*6 Sch 3(1)*].

Section 330 transactions

11.65 Unless they are specifically exempted from being disclosed (see para 11.80), all transactions specified in Section 330 of the Act have to be disclosed in the notes to the financial statements. This applies to unlawful transactions, as well as to lawful transactions. [*6 Sch 6(a)*].

11.66 Accordingly, the details outlined in paragraph 11.77 below must be given where any company:

(a) Makes a loan, or a quasi-loan, or enters into a credit transaction, either to one of its directors or to a director of its holding company. [*Sec 330(2)(a),(3)(a),(4)(a)*].

(b) Enters into any guarantee (including an indemnity [*Sec 331(2)*]), or provides any security, in connection with any loan, quasi-loan, or credit transaction that any person made to such a director. [*Sec 330(2)(b),(3)(c),(4)(b)*].

(c) Arranges to have assigned to it, or to assume, any rights or obligations or liabilities under a transaction that would have been prohibited if the company had initially entered into it. The financial limits relating to disclosure apply to such a transaction as if it had been entered into on the date of the arrangement (see further para 11.23). [*Sec 330(6)*].

(d) Takes part in any arrangement where another person enters into a transaction that would have been prohibited had the company entered into it. [*Sec 330(7)*].

These types of transactions and their legality are discussed in paragraphs 11.07 to 11.32 above.

11.67 Also, where any transaction listed in *(a)* to *(d)* above is made by a relevant company in favour of a connected person of either a director of the company or a director of the company's holding company, the company must disclose details of that transaction.

Table 49: Disclosure of transactions with directors.

Extract from Marks & Spencer p.l.c. Reports and Financial Statements 31 March 1984.

24 Transactions with directors

1 During the year the Company was the lessee of the two properties listed below, each of which was sub-let to a director at a rent equal to the annual value of the property concerned as part of the arrangements, details of which are set out below. Mr. Sacher surrendered his sub-lease on 20th March 1984.

Name of director	Property Cost (nearest £'000)	Company's Tenure	Acquired From: Date of Acquisition	Length of sub-lease to director	Annual Rental Payable £
Lord Rayner	121,000	Leasehold to 2013	Open Market 23rd June 1978	7 years from 28th November 1978.	2,650
Mr. M. M. Sacher	239,000	Leasehold to 2040 (note a)	Open Market 22nd May 1980	5 years from 24th June 1980 with option to extend for further 5 years* but subject to option on the tenant's part to determine on one month's notice at any time. *Option surrendered for nil consideration on 28th March 1983.	2,000

NOTES:—

a In the case of Mr. Sacher:

(i)   The property cost included the leasehold of an adjoining garage which was included in the sub-lease and option to him. The tenure of the Company in this garage is leasehold to the year 2000.

(ii)   The Company, as a separate transaction, had also acquired on the open market for the sum of £47,500 a leasehold interest to 1998 in a property close to that shown above as occupied by Mr. Sacher, for use by him in connection therewith. This property was sub-let to Mr. Sacher for a term of 9¾ years from 29th September 1980 at the market rental of £2,000 p.a., subject to an option to Mr. Sacher to determine on 24th June 1985 by not less than three months' notice.

Mr. Sacher did not have an option to purchase this property and surrendered his sub-lease on 18th November 1983.

b Each of the properties listed was sub-let to the director at a rent equal to the annual value for rating purposes of the property concerned at the date of the sub-letting, as shown above.

c Property cost shown above is the purchase price paid for the property, excluding acquisition costs, with the addition, where applicable, of the cost of subsequent capital expenditure.

d In the opinion of Gerald Eve & Co., who have been consulted by the Board, it is not possible to attribute a market value to the various Leases and Option at the time they were granted by reason, *inter alia*, of the restrictions thereon. Since the value of each arrangement is not capable of being expressed as a specific sum of money, it is a requirement of Section 65(5) of the Companies Act 1980 [*now Section 340(7) of the Companies Act 1985*] that the value is deemed in each case to exceed £50,000, regardless of its actual value.

2   Interest-free house purchase loans were made by the Company to the following, prior to their appointments as directors. These loans were made under the employees' loan scheme and are being repaid by equal monthly instalments:

Director	Date of loan	Balance outstanding at year end	
		This year	Last year
Mr. N. L. Colne	1980	**£9,720**	£11,160
Mr. D. G. Trangmar	1979 – 1982	**£11,960**	£13,760

3   An interest-free loan to Mr. Orton of C$83,250 (*last year C$83,250*) was outstanding in respect of the Canadian Stock Purchase Scheme – see note 8(d)(ii).

Other transactions and arrangements

11.68 Certain other transactions are required to be disclosed under the Act (for example, contracts between a director and a company for the sale of non-cash assets—see also Tables 49 and 50). These transactions are in addition to those specified in Section 330 of the Act. The test of whether these other transactions have to be disclosed will depend on whether the director had a material interest (either directly or indirectly) in the transaction concerned. If he did have a material interest, then the transaction must be disclosed. [*6 Sch 1(c), 2(c)*].

Table 50: Example of the disclosure of substantial contracts with directors.

Extract from R. P. Martin p.l.c. Report & Accounts 30 June 1984.

Directors' emoluments and substantial contracts note extract

Substantial contracts with Directors and former Directors:

(i) Messrs. P. M. Endres and W. Struck are shareholders in BBMP Beteiligungsgesellschaft mbH ("BBMP") which is the minority partner in Bierbaum & Co. GmbH & Co. oHG, Dusseldorf. Under the terms of the R. P. Martin/Bierbaum merger agreement dated 10th July 1981, at any time after 30th June 1986, R. P. Martin may exercise a call option and the shareholders of BBMP may exercise a put option over the ordinary share capital of BBMP at an independent valuation which may, at the option of R. P. Martin, be satisfied either in cash or by the issue of Ordinary Shares of R. P. Martin.

(ii) Mr. E. W. Will is a Director of Bear Stearns International Limited, which acted as financial advisers to Bierbaum in respect of the merger with R. P. Martin. Bear Stearns International Corporation will, in the event of R. P. Martin acquiring any shares in BBMP, receive a fee not exceeding £30,000.

(iii) Mr. M. H. Renfer was a profit-participating partner in Bierbaum & Co. Depot oHG, Frankfurt, up to and including 30th June 1984 when the partnership was dissolved and the assets and liabilities converted into a company.

(iv) Mr. A. Griffiths is a Director and shareholder in Aljermik Exchange Inc. a company which provides brokerage services to, and has a profit sharing agreement expiring on 30th June 1986 with, Bierbaum-Martin Inc. Under an agreement dated 2nd July 1981 as amended by an agreement dated 1 July 1983, R. P. Martin may exercise a call option and the shareholders of Aljermik Exchange Inc. may exercise a put option over all the share capital of Aljermik Exchange Inc. at an independent valuation, at any time between 30th June 1986 and 30th June 1991.

11.69 Consequently, if a director has a material interest in either contracts or substantial property transactions (as outlined in paras 11.46 to 11.52 and 11.53 to 11.61 respectively), these have to be disclosed in the company's financial statements.

Interpretation of 'material interest'

11.70 In practice, the interpretation of the words 'material interest' has caused considerable debate. Although the test of materiality is not clear, two tests, the 'relevant' test and the 'substantial' test, are regarded as having some authority. The 'relevant' test considers a transaction to be material if it is likely to be of interest or relevance either to the shareholders or to the other users of the financial statements. The 'substantial' test considers a transaction to be material if the director's interest in the transaction is substantial.

11.71 The 'substantial' test can be illustrated by the following example. Where a director buys a bar of chocolate in the company's shop, he is the other party to the contract, and accordingly his interest in the transaction (his purchase of the bar of chocolate from the company) is *material.*

11.72 The expression 'material' has not yet been interpreted in case law in the context of directors' transactions. However, of the two tests referred to above, Counsel has advised that the 'relevant' test is to be preferred. Counsel has said that the correct approach should be to find out whether the existence of the arrangement would be significant to a shareholder. And it could be significant either because it is one of importance to the company or because it is one of importance to the individual director. Where the transaction is of importance either to the company or to the individual director, then a material interest does exist, and it should be disclosed. On the other hand, it should be borne in mind that other Counsel have advised that the substantial test is preferred.

11.73 Because of this confusion, the Law Society's Standing Committee on Company Law proposed an amendment to paragraph 3(2) of Schedule 6 to the Act to try to clarify the meaning of 'material interest'. It suggested that the definition should be altered to include the following:

> "An interest is material if, and only if, knowledge thereof might reasonably be expected to influence the judgement:
>
> *(a)* of a person in determining whether he will enter into any transaction or arrangement with the relevant company and, if so, upon what terms or whether he will deal in securities of the company; or
>
> *(b)* of a member of the company in determining whether he will exercise any of his rights in that capacity."

11.74 Although no amendment on these lines has yet been adopted, the rules on the disclosure of material interests in transactions as they affect transactions in groups of companies were relaxed in 1984. These changes have been included in the Act and are those described in paragraph 11.80*(g)* and *(h)* below.

11.75 Consequently, it can be seen that there is still considerable uncertainty about the meaning of this term. Therefore, if a director has an interest in a transaction that may or may not be material, legal advice should be taken.

11.76 Certain other types of transaction involving a director (or his connected persons) and the company may not be regarded as material, and if so, they do not have to be disclosed in the financial statements. These are considered in paragraph 11.80*(f)* below.

Disclosure requirements

11.77 Where a company has entered into a transaction of one of the types described in paragraph 11.64 above that is required to be disclosed in the financial statements, the financial statements must contain the following information:

(a) Particulars of the transaction's principal terms. [*6 Sch 9(1)*]. The 'principal terms' will include those terms that relate to the provision of either the cash or the non-cash asset, and also the arrangements for repaying the value of that asset (including any interest component, together with any related security or guarantees).

(b) A statement that the transaction either was made during the financial year or existed during that period. [*6 Sch 9(2)(a)*].

(c) The name of the director concerned in the transaction. Where a transaction is made for a director's connected person, the name of the connected person and the director concerned have to be given. [*6 Sch 9(2)(b)*].

(d) The name of the director who has the material interest in the transaction, and the nature of the interest. [*6 Sch 9(2)(c)*].

(e) The following details of any loan, or of any arrangement relating to a loan:

    (i) The amount of the liability (including both principal and interest), at both the beginning and the end of the financial year.

    (ii) The maximum amount of the liability during that period.

    (iii) The amount of any unpaid interest.

    (iv) The amount of any provision that the company has made against the failure or the anticipated failure of the borrower to repay the whole, or any part, of the principal or interest. [*6 Sch 9(2)(d)*].

The 'value' of such loans is considered in paragraph 11.13.

(f) The following details of any guarantee or security, or of any arrangement relating to any guarantee or security:

    (i) The amount of the company's or its subsidiary's liability, at both the beginning and the end of the financial year.

(ii) The maximum amount for which the company or its subsidiary may become liable.

(iii) Any amount the company or its subsidiary has paid, and any liability it has incurred, either in fulfilling the guarantee or in discharging the security.
[*6 Sch 9(2)(e)*].

The 'value' of such guarantees or securities is the amount guaranteed or secured. [*Sec 340(4)*].

(g) The value of any other transaction, or of any transaction that any other agreement relates to. [*6 Sch 9(f)*]. The effect of this provision is to require, for example, the disclosure of:

(i) The amount to be reimbursed where a company buys goods on behalf of a director, or the maximum amount to be reimbursed in respect of quasi-loans (for example, see Table 51). [*Sec 340(3)*].

(ii) The arm's length value of any goods and services purchased in credit transactions. [*Sec 340(6)*].

(iii) The value of arrangements for assignments and back-to-back deals. [*Sec 340(6)*].

The meaning of 'value' for these types of transactions is considered in paragraphs 11.18, 11.23 and 11.26.

Many of these disclosure requirements are illustrated in Tables 49 to 51 and Table 53.

Table 51: Illustration of the disclosure of quasi-loans with directors.

Extract from The Caledonian Aviation Group plc Report and Accounts 31 October 1984.

Note

21. Directors' and Officers' Loans and Transactions
(a) In accordance with the requirements of Section 54 of the Companies Act 1980 [*now Section 232 of the Companies Act 1985*], the following information is given for directors and persons connected with directors. As a result of sundry transactions and the use of credit cards, balances exist with directors. These sums are repaid within two months but qualify as Quasi-Loans under the Act.

There were no balances outstanding at either the beginning or end of the financial year but in the course of the year maximum amounts existed for Sir Adam Thomson £840, Mr T. E. Boud £518 and Mr A. T. Pugh £56. There were no credit transactions with directors during the period.

(b) During the year, £146,185 was paid to Knapp-Fishers in respect of legal and regulatory advice and reimbursement of related out of pocket expenses in connection with the Group's activities. Mr D. A. Beety is a partner in this firm. £236,719 was similarly paid to Leonard N. Bebchick, P.C. Mr L. N. Bebchick is President of this professional corporation.

(c) There were no loans to officers at 31st October, 1984 to be disclosed under the requirements of Section 56 of the Companies Act, 1980 [*now Section 233 of the Companies Act 1985*].

11.78   The details outlined above must be disclosed, irrespective of whether or not:

(a) The transaction is either prohibited by Section 330 of the Act, or falls within one of the exemptions given in Sections 332 to 338.

(b) The person for whom the transaction was made was a director, or was a person connected with a director, at the time the transaction was made. This is provided, however, that the person has subsequently become a director, or has become connected with a director (see Table 53).

(c) The company that entered into the transaction was a subsidiary of the company of which the person was a director at the time the transaction was made.
[*6 Sch 6*].

11.79   There is one other partial exemption from the requirement to disclose the information outlined in *(a)* to *(g)* of paragraph 11.77 above. The information outlined in *(d)* to *(g)* of paragraph 11.77 above need not be disclosed for loans and quasi-loans where a company makes them to another wholly-owned company in the same group, or to the holding company where the company is wholly owned, and where the information would otherwise have been disclosable only on the grounds that the director of the company that made the loan was also associated with the company that received the loan. [*6 Sch 10*]. But, where this type of transaction does exist, the financial statements still have to give particulars of the transaction's principal terms, a statement that the transaction was made or existed during the year, and the name of the company concerned (see para 11.77 *(a)* to *(c)* above). This exception means that, where certain *intra-group loans* are made by the company, only those details are required to be disclosed.

Exemptions from disclosure

11.80   The disclosure requirements set out in paragraph 11.77 above do not apply to:

(a) A transaction between two companies, where a director of one of the companies (or of its subsidiary or its holding company) is interested only by virtue of the fact that he is also a director of that other company. [*6 Sch 5(a)*]. This exemption means that, among other things, details of many general *intra-group trading* transactions between companies are not required to be disclosed.

(b) A contract of service between a company and one of its directors, or between a company and a director of its holding company, or between a director of the company and any of its subsidiaries. [*6 Sch 5(b)*]. A listed company must disclose details of service contracts under the requirements of The Stock Exchange's Continuing Obligations. This requirement is considered in Chapter 12, paragraph 12.42.

(c) A transaction that was not entered into during the period to which the financial statements relate, and that did not exist at any time during that period. *[6 Sch 5(c)]*.

(d) The following transactions that a company or its subsidiary has made for a person who was a director of the company or its holding company, or was connected with any such director, at any time during the financial year, provided that the outstanding aggregate value of the transactions did not exceed £5,000 at any time during that period:

(i) Credit transactions.
(ii) Guarantees or security relating to credit transactions.
(iii) Assignments, or assumptions or arrangements of the type referred to in Section 330(6) and (7) of the Act that relate to credit transactions (see para 11.66 *(c)* and *(d))*.
(iv) Agreements to enter into credit transactions.
[6 Sch 11(1)(2)].

The reference to 'aggregate value' in *(d)* above means the value of all transactions for the particular director, including those made to a person connected with him. In addition, the amount by which the liability of the person for whom the transaction was made has been reduced should be deducted. *[6 Sch 11(1)]*.

Without this threshold limit, a company's financial statements would sometimes contain an excessive amount of information about directors' transactions. Petty transactions involving deferred payment by directors are very common, and it is not the Act's intention to prevent these. The Act intends that disclosure should prevent abuse only where the transactions involve larger sums.

(e) Certain transactions in which a director has a material interest. This exception applies if the value of each such transaction which was made after the commencement of the financial year, and the value of each such transaction that was made before the commencement of the financial year, less the amount (if any) by which the liability of the person for whom the transaction was made has subsequently been reduced, did not exceed £1,000 at any time *during* the relevant period. These transactions include any transactions with the company or any of its subsidiaries. Alternatively, if that value did exceed £1,000, it did not exceed the lower of £5,000 and 1% of the value of the company's net assets *at the end* of the relevant period. *[6 Sch 12]*. For this purpose, 'net assets' are the aggregate of the company's assets less the aggregate of its liabilities (including provisions for liabilities and charges). This minimum figure is flexible in order that it should take account of the needs of different sizes of company.

(f) Transactions that, in the opinion of the board, are not material. 'The board' means the directors of the company who prepare the financial statements, but it excludes the particular director who has the interest in the transaction. *[6 Sch 3(2)]*.

As mentioned in paragraph 11.76 above, Schedule 6, paragraph 3(2) to the Act provides that "an interest in... a transaction or arrangement is not 'material' ... if in the board's opinion it is not so; but this is without prejudice to the question whether or not such an interest is material in a case where the board have not considered the matter".

Although the Act does not say so explicitly, it is, of course, implicit that the directors' opinion on the materiality of a transaction must have been formed in good faith. Where the directors have not considered the question of materiality, the materiality of a transaction will be a matter of fact. This does not mean that the transaction will be regarded as material. It simply means that, in the absence of an opinion from the directors, it cannot be presumed not to be material.

(g) Transactions involving other members of the same group which are entered into by those group companies in the ordinary course of their business and at arm's length and which would otherwise be disclosable under Schedule 6, paragraphs 1(c) or 2(c) (that is, those transactions outlined in para 11.64 *(b)* above). [*6 Sch 7*].

(h) A transaction or arrangement that would otherwise be disclosable under paragraph 1(c) or 2(c) of Schedule 6 because the director had a material interest, but only on account of the fact that he was associated with the company. ('Associated' is defined in paragraph 11.06.) This exemption applies only if the company is a member of a group of companies and if one of the following situations exists:

   (i) The company is a wholly-owned subsidiary.
   (ii) No company within the same group, other than the company itself or one of its subsidiaries, was a party to the transaction or arrangement.
   [*6 Sch 8*].

These conditions mean that the exemption from disclosure is available only if minority interests in the company are not affected. The effect of this provision is that, provided the conditions are satisfied, a director who is associated with the company and who would therefore have an interest in every contract that the company is party to that may be disclosable, does not have to disclose that interest.

11.81 The Secretary of State has power to increase by statutory instrument the financial limits mentioned in *(d)* and *(e)* in paragraph 11.80 above. [*6 Sch 13*].

Penalty for failure to disclose

11.82 The Act imposes a penalty on the company's directors for failure to disclose information about directors' transactions in the company's financial statements by the implementation of Section 245. If the company's financial statements that are either laid before the company in general meeting or delivered to the Registrar of Companies do not disclose the required information, then any person who at the time when the financial statements are laid or delivered is a director of the company is guilty of an offence and is liable to a fine. [*Sec 245(1) — see Appendix IV*]. Moreover, where the financial statements do not disclose the information required, the auditors must include, in their report (so far as they are reasonably able to do so), a statement giving the details that have been omitted. [*Sec 237(5)*]. The auditors are not required to draw attention to an unlawful transaction by stating that it either is illegal or contravenes the Act, but they should, of course, consider the effect of any illegal transaction on the truth and fairness of the financial statements. This consideration will include the question of whether the debt is recoverable.

Special provisions relating to recognised banks

General disclosure requirements

11.83   A recognised bank, or a recognised bank's holding company, is exempted from some of the disclosure requirements that apply to other companies. [*Sec 234(1)*]. It does, however, have to give the same information about a transaction where a director or his connected person has, directly or indirectly, a material interest if the recognised bank is a party to the transaction (see para 11.77 above). [*6 Sch 4*]. A money-lending company (unless it is a recognised bank's holding company) is bound by the same disclosure requirements as any other company.

11.84   A recognised bank, or a recognised bank's holding company, must maintain a register that contains a copy of every transaction whose particulars would have been disclosed in the financial statements had the company not been a recognised bank. The register must contain this information for the current year and for the ten preceding years. If the transaction is not recorded in writing, the register must contain a written memorandum setting out the transaction's terms. [*Sec 343(1)(2)(3)*].

11.85   In addition, unless the recognised bank is a wholly-owned subsidiary of another UK company [*Sec 344(2)*], it must prepare a statement that includes particulars of those transactions for the financial year preceding its annual general meeting. This statement must be made available for inspection by the company's members for at least 15 days before the annual general meeting, and also at the meeting itself. [*Sec 343 (4)(5)*]. The auditors must examine this statement. They must also submit a report to the shareholders stating whether or not all the particulars the Act requires have been included in it. [*Sec 343(6)*]. Where any required particulars have been omitted, the auditors must include a statement of the required particulars in their report (so far as they are reasonably able to do so). [*Sec 343(7)*]. Their report must be annexed to the company's statement. [*Sec 343(6)*].

11.86   Where the outstanding aggregate value of transactions of this type (described in para 11.84) for a director or a connected person does not exceed £1,000 at any time during the financial year, then the requirements of Section 343 of the Act do not apply. [*Sec 344(1)*].

11.87   But Section 234(1) does require the group accounts (or the holding company's financial statements, if group accounts are not prepared), or the company's financial statements (if the recognised bank is not part of a group), to comply with the disclosure requirements outlined in paragraph 11.88 below for the following transactions with a company's directors or their connected persons:

   (a) Loans (including any guarantees or security for loans), or arrangements of the types described in Section 330(6) or (7) of the Act that relate to loans, or agreements to enter into any such transactions (see *(c)* and *(d)* of para 11.66).

   (b) Quasi-loans (including guarantees or security for quasi-loans), or arrangements of the types described in Section 330(6) or (7) relating to quasi-loans, or agreements to enter into any such transactions (see *(c)* and *(d)* of para 11.66).

   (c) Credit transactions (including guarantees or security for credit transactions), or arrangements of the types described in Section 330(6) or (7) that relate to credit transactions, or agreements to enter into any such transactions (see *(c)* and *(d)* of para 11.66).
   [*6 Sch 15(a)-(c)*].

11.88   The details to be disclosed are as follows:

   (a) The aggregate amounts outstanding (as defined in Schedule 6, paragraph 21(c)) at the end of the financial year, analysed under the categories of transactions specified in *(a),(b)* and *(c)* of paragraph 11.87 above that the recognised bank made for directors or their connected persons.

   (b) The number of persons for whom the bank made those transactions.
   [*6 Sch 19*].

An illustration of this disclosure is given in Table 52.

11.89   For the purpose of these provisions insofar as they relate to loans and quasi-loans, a company that a person does not control should not be treated as being connected with him. [*Sec 343(9); 6 Sch 20*].

Liability for contravention

11.90   Where a recognised bank fails to comply with the requirements set out in paragraphs 11.84 and 11.85, any person who is a director at the time (other than a shadow director) is both guilty of an offence and liable to a fine. In these circumstances, however, it will be a sufficient defence for a person to show that he took all reasonable steps to ensure that the bank complied with the requirements. [*Sec 343(8) — see Appendix IV*].

Table 52: Illustration of the disclosure of loans made to directors and officers of a banking company.

Extract from Midland Bank plc Annual Report and Accounts 31 December 1984.

Note

35 Directors' and officers' loans

In accordance with the requirements of Section 56 of the Companies' Act 1980 [*now Section 234 of the Companies Act 1985*], the aggregate amounts outstanding at 31 December 1984 from persons who were directors (or connected with directors) or officers during the year, and the number of persons concerned, were as follows:

	Aggregate amount outstanding		Number of persons	
Directors	1984	1983	1984	1983
	£m	£m		
Loans	0.5	0.4	13	12
Quasi-loans	*	*	15	17
Credit transactions	—	—	—	—
Officers				
Loans	0.8	0.6	2	1
Quasi-loans	—	—	—	—
Credit transactions	—	—	—	—

*aggregate amount outstanding was £6,467 (1983 £6,872)

Disclosure requirements regarding shadow directors

11.91 The disclosure requirements of paragraphs 1 to 14 of Schedule 6 to the Act apply not only to transactions with directors but also to transactions with shadow directors. [*Sec 232(3)*].

Transactions with officers

11.92 In contrast to its substantial number of provisions that relate to transactions with directors, the Act does not prohibit a company from entering into transactions with its officers other than directors. However, the Act does require that certain disclosures should be made in the company's financial statements regarding such transactions. [*Sec 233(1)(2)*].

11.93 For this purpose, the term 'officer' should be interpreted as including the company secretary and the company's senior managers. [*Sec 744*].

Disclosure of transactions

11.94 The types of transactions to be disclosed are those outlined in paragraph 11.87 above.

11.95 In respect of the transactions to be disclosed, the group accounts, or (if group accounts are not prepared) the holding company's financial statements, or the financial statements of any company other than a holding company, must disclose:

(a) The aggregate amounts outstanding at the end of the financial year under such transactions, made by either the company or (if it is a holding company) its subsidiaries. The aggregate amounts must relate to each category of transaction.

In this respect, 'amounts outstanding' means the amount of the outstanding liabilities of the person for whom the transaction was made. With a guarantee or a security, it means the amount guaranteed or secured. [*6 Sch 17*].

(b) The number of officers with whom the company made those transactions.
[*6 Sch 16(1)*].

An illustration of these disclosure requirements is given in Tables 52 and 53.

Table 53: Example of the disclosure of loans that a company has made to its officers.

Extract from Imperial Chemical Industries PLC Annual Report 31 December 1984.

Note

27 Other statutory information
Included in debtors are interest-free loans totalling £119,500 (1983 £116,839) to officers of the Company, comprising £35,000 in total to 3 directors and £84,500 in total to 5 other officers. The loans to directors were made, prior to their joining the Board, in accordance with the Company's policy of providing housing assistance to staff who have been transferred. The amounts outstanding throughout the year were £10,000 each from Sir Robin Ibbs and Dr C H Reece and £15,000 from Mr D H Henderson. The loans to the other officers were in respect of housing loans.

Exemptions from disclosure

11.96 Transactions made by recognised banks for their officers or for officers of their holding company need not be disclosed. [*Sec 233(3)*]. However, this relaxation does not apply to money-lending companies.

11.97 Also, the transactions outlined in paragraph 11.87 above need not be disclosed where the aggregate amount outstanding at the end of the financial year for an officer of the company does not exceed £2,500. [*6 Sch 16(2)*]. The Secretary of State has power to increase this limit by statutory instrument. [*6 Sch 16(3)*].

Penalty for failure to disclose

11.98 There is a penalty on the company's directors if they fail to make the disclosure the Act requires in respect of a company's officers (see para 11.82 above). [*Sec 245(1)*]. In addition, the auditors must include a statement in their audit report giving the required particulars, so far as they are reasonably able to do so. [*Sec 237(5)*].

The Stock Exchange's requirements

11.99 The Stock Exchange's Continuing Obligations for listed companies and its General Undertaking for companies traded on the USM contain further disclosure requirements that relate to substantial property transactions and other transactions with directors. The principal requirement that relates to the disclosure of a company's transactions with its directors and former directors is that the company is obliged to circulate to its shareholders information about, and usually to obtain their prior approval of, those transactions that fall within the definition of Class 4 transactions. 'Class 4' transactions are defined in Chapter 1 of Section 6 of the 'Admission of Securities to Listing'. A 'Class 4' transaction is any transaction that involves a director, or any associate of a director, or a past director (or certain other persons stipulated in that section).

11.100 Although the proposed transaction may be legal within the meaning of the Act, The Stock Exchange may, nevertheless, require that the company should observe certain additional formalities. The basic requirement is stated in paragraph 14 of The Stock Exchange's Continuing Obligations. That paragraph requires, *inter alia*, that details of any acquisitions or realisations of assets that fall within the definition of a Class 4 transaction, must be notified to The Stock Exchange and to the shareholders.

11.101 The USM's General Undertaking contains a similar requirement. Note 1(d) to the General Undertaking requires that "transactions which involve, or involve an associate of, a director ... should be subject to prior approval of the company in general meeting and the issue of an explanatory circular".

275

Table 54: Disclosure of transactions required by The Stock Exchange's Continuing Obligations.

Extract from Arthur Guinness and Sons PLC Report and Accounts 30 September 1984.

Stock Exchange Listing Agreement Transactions

The following transactions involving directors of subsidiary companies have been entered into:

Jackel International (Asia) Limited (incorporated in Hong Kong)

In January 1984 the Group sold its 93·5% interest in Jackel International (Asia) Limited to Miss Pansy Chan Shun Kwai, the minority shareholder and a director of the company.

The consideration amounted to HK$749,000 for the net assets denominated in Hong Kong dollars and US$778,000 for the net assets denominated in United States dollars, a total of approximately £624,000, which represents a discount against the net assets at 30 September 1983 of HK$1,200,000 (approximately £110,000 using the exchange rate prevailing at the date of the agreement).

In the year ended 30 September 1983 the company reported a profit before taxation of HK$3,543,000 (approximately £278,000 at 30 September 1983 exchange rates).

GBR Educational Limited

In February 1984 the Group acquired the 49% minority shareholding in GBR Educational Limited from Mr. AA. Shipton, a director of that company, for a nominal consideration of £1. Mr. AA. Shipton resigned as a director from the date of the agreement.

The net liabilities of the company at 30 September 1983 amounted to £43,000 and the loss before taxation for the year then ended amounted to £16,000.

Kyko Internacional S.A. (incorporated in Spain)

In July 1984 the Group sold its 60% interest in Kyko Internacional S.A., to the ten minority shareholders in the company, of whom two, Sr. Alfredo Serratosa Ridaura and Sr. Francisco Tamarit Montesinos, were directors. The consideration amounted to Pts 22 million (approximately £100,000). At 30 September 1983 the company had net assets attributable to the Group's interest of approximately £350,000 and reported a loss before taxation for the year then ended of £110,000.

Idées Photo Ciné S.A. and AICO France Sarl (incorporated in France)

In September 1984 the Group sold its 55% interest in the above companies to M. Raymond Visciano, the minority shareholder and a director of both companies. The consideration for the shares amounted to FF100 (approximately £8) and in addition debt owing to the Group of FF1,850,000 (approximately £160,000) will be repaid over a period of 10 years commencing on 1 October 1985.

The Group has entered into certain financing arrangements, in exchange for which, the purchaser has agreed to take over substantial bank guarantees which had been made by the Group.

At 30 September 1983 the two companies had combined net assets attributable to the Group's interest of approximately £260,000 and reported a profit before taxation for the year then ended of £17,000.

11.102 In addition to the statutory disclosure requirements (outlined in paras 11.62 to 11.89 above), The Stock Exchange's Continuing Obligations require listed companies to give particulars in their statutory financial statements of any contract of significance (including substantial property transactions) that existed during the financial year and that a director was materially interested in (for example, see Table 54). [*CO 21(k)*]. In this context, a 'contract of significance' is one that represents a sum equal to 1% or more of:

(a) The company's net assets, for a capital transaction.

(b) The company's net assets, for a transaction whose principal purpose is the granting of credit.

(c) The total purchases, sales, payments or receipts of the company, for other transactions.

11.103 Where a listed company's directors have not had a material interest in any significant contracts of the company during the financial year, they must disclose this fact in the financial statements (for example, see Table 55). [*CO 21(k)*].

Table 55: *Example of the disclosure required by The Stock Exchange's Continuing Obligations where there were no contracts of significance with the directors of the company.*

Extract from Globe Investment Trust P.L.C. Annual Review Report and Accounts 31 March 1984.

Directors' report extract

Contracts

There were no contracts subsisting during or at the end of the financial year in which a Director of the Company is or was materially interested and which is or was significant in relation to the Group's business.

CHAPTER 12

DIRECTORS' REPORT

Directors' Report

Introduction

12.01 The principal objective of the directors' report is to supplement the financial information in the profit and loss account and the balance sheet with certain narrative information about the company's activities and its future. The purpose of that narrative information is to give the user of the financial statements a more complete picture of the company than he would otherwise obtain.

12.02 A 'special category company' (as defined in Chapter 13) does not have to include in its directors' report all the information stipulated in this chapter. The directors' report of a special category company is considered in Chapter 13, paragraphs 13.85 to 13.102.

The company's activities and its future

12.03 The directors must include in their report a fair review of the development of the business of the company and its subsidiaries during the financial year (for example, see Table 56), and of their position at the end of it. [*Sec 235(1)(a)*]. The Act goes on to require the directors' report also to give particulars of any *important events* affecting the company or any of its subsidiaries that have occurred *since the end of the financial year* [*7 Sch 6(a)*], and to indicate likely *future developments* in the business of the company and its subsidiaries. [*7 Sch 6(b)*]. The Act also requires the directors' report to indicate the activities (if any) of the company and its subsidiaries in the field of *research and development*. [*7 Sch 6(c)*].

12.04 The Act does not indicate the form that this review of the business should take, nor does it indicate the detail the directors must include in their review. This provision is expressed in broad terms only, so as to allow directors as much freedom as possible to decide how best to meet the requirement.

12.05 Many public companies do not, in practice, include in their directors' report the review of the business and indications of likely future developments. Instead, they include the required information either in the chair-

man's statement or in a detailed review of operations. Provided that
the directors' report refers to the place where the information appears,
it still complies with the Act.

***Table 56: Illustration of the type of information required to be given
in the directors' report about the group's business during
the year.***

*Extract from Arthur Guinness and Sons PLC Report and Accounts
30 September 1984.*

---

4 Review of the business

During the year the Group has significantly extended its retailing interests with the
acquisition of Martin the Newsagent plc ("Martins"), and the subsequent formation
of the Martin Retail Group with over 650 shops.

In the brewing division, work has continued on brand revitalisation and extensive new
product development programmes. Investment in new plant and improved efficiency
is beginning to show through as savings in operating costs.

The results for the year show profit before taxation increasing by 20%, although the
full financial effects of management's actions have yet to be reflected. The Group
has now positively entered into an expansion phase.

Important post-balance-sheet events

12.06 SSAP 17 also covers the disclosure of any important events that have
occurred since the end of the financial year (see also Chapter 21 para
21.12).

12.07 SSAP 17 distinguishes between events that require changes in the
amounts to be disclosed in the financial statements ('adjusting events')
and events that only require to be disclosed ('non-adjusting events').
Basically, a material post-balance-sheet event requires changes in the
amounts disclosed in the financial statements where either of the following applies:

(a) It is an adjusting event (that is, it is an event that provides additional evidence relating to conditions that existed at the balance sheet
date).

(b) It indicates that it is not appropriate to apply the going concern
concept to either the whole or a material part of the company.

12.08 On the other hand, a material post-balance-sheet event does not require
changes in the financial statements (but it does require to be disclosed
in the notes to the financial statements) in either of the following cases:

(a) It is a non-adjusting event. That is, it is an event that arises after
the balance sheet date, and it concerns conditions that did not exist

at that time. But it is of such materiality that its non-disclosure would affect the ability of users of the financial statements to reach a proper understanding of the financial position.

(b) It is either a reversal or a maturity after the year end of a transaction entered into before the year end, and the substance of that transaction was primarily to alter the appearance of the company's balance sheet (that is, window dressing).

12.09 In such cases, the information to be disclosed is the nature of the event and an estimate of its financial effect. Where it is not possible to make such an estimate, that fact must be disclosed.

12.10 However, an important difference between the Act and SSAP 17 is that the Act requires material post-balance-sheet events to be disclosed in the *directors' report* (as illustrated in Table 57), whereas SSAP 17 requires that either the financial statements must be adjusted or the effect must be disclosed in the *notes to the financial statements*. If a company decides to disclose the information only in one place, there should be a cross-reference from the directors' report to the notes, or *vice versa*.

Table 57: Illustration of the type of information required in the directors' report on significant post-balance-sheet events.

Extract from Alfred McAlpine PLC Annual Report & Accounts 31 October 1984.

Post Balance Sheet Events

Since 31st October, 1984 the group's South African subsidiary, Alfred McAlpine & Son Limited, acquired a 60% interest in the share capital of Severin Minerals Corporation (Proprietary) Limited, which is involved in coal mining and the reclamation of gold from mine dumps. The consideration for this acquisition was Rand 2.159 million which was settled as to Rand 1.109 million in cash and the balance in shares of Alfred McAlpine & Son Limited. As a consequence the group's holding in Alfred McAlpine & Son Limited was reduced by 1.7 per cent to 68.3 per cent.

In the United States the group acquired R & S Materials Inc., a company engaged in sand and gravel extraction in Alabama.

Likely future developments

12.11 The Act requires the directors' report to contain an indication of likely future developments in the business of the company and its subsidiaries. [*7 Sch 6(b)*]. As with the provisions relating to a review of the company's business during the year, the Act contains no amplification as to the extent and the scope of this commentary on likely business developments. The reason why this provision is expressed in broad terms only is to allow directors as much freedom as possible to decide how best to meet the requirement (for example, see Table 58).

> **Table 58: Illustration of the information to be disclosed in the directors' report on the future developments of the group.**
>
> *Extract from Debenhams PLC Annual Report 28 January 1984.*
>
> **3. Future developments**
>
> The Group intends to continue its policy of developing and improving the profitability of its principal businesses. Suitable opportunities for growth will be pursued with continuing investment in businesses which have performed well and have sound future prospects. Contraction or divestment will be undertaken where necessary. The Board considers that the improvements in productivity and efficiency resulting from the policy of decentralisation and tighter cost control have put the Group in a strong position to take advantage of improved trading conditions in the High Street and in the economy as a whole.

12.12   With either listed companies or companies that are traded on the USM, the wording for the note on future developments will have to be chosen very carefully. Otherwise, there is the danger that the note could, at some later stage, be construed as a profit forecast. This could have the following consequences for such companies:

(a) The Council of The Stock Exchange issued a statement in August 1975 that stated that "Whenever it becomes possible, by using [*the wording of any statement*] in conjunction with published data, to arrive at an approximate figure for future profits by an arithmetical process, the Council will take the view that a forecast has been made and require it to be reported upon". This means that, if the directors' report is construed as including a profit forecast, accountants must report on that forecast.

(b) The following year's financial statements will have to explain any material differences (if any exist) between the actual results and the forecast. [*CO 21(b); GU 10(b)*].

(c) The City Code on Take-Overs and Mergers states that, if a company has issued any statement that constitutes a profit forecast, and that forecast relates to a period during which a takeover bid arises, then that forecast must be repeated in any offer or defence document, and accountants must report on it.

Research and development activities

12.13   The requirement to give an indication of the research and development activities of the company and its subsidiaries does not mean that the accounting policy for research and development should be disclosed in the directors' report. This should remain as part of the financial statements. The Act requires instead a narrative statement that considers the commercial aspects of the research and development, and that supplements the accounting policy and the information that SSAP 13 requires (see also Chapter 7 para 7.15). Some companies may be reluctant to disclose too much information on research and development to competitors. However, the Act does not indicate how much detail needs to be given, and so a broadly-worded note should be sufficient to comply with the Act's requirements. An illustration of this disclosure is shown in Table 59.

Table 59: *Illustration of the type of information required to be given in the directors' report about the group's research and development activities.*

Extract from The Plessey Company plc Report & Accounts 30 March 1984.

Research and development
The Group maintains extensive laboratories and other facilities, and devotes considerable resources to research and development aimed at new products and processes. The Group holds 752 United Kingdom and 1,498 foreign patents. The following table shows the amounts spent by the Group, and the amounts funded by customers of the Group.

	Group funded £000	Customer funded £000	Total £000
1983/84	66,424	149,575	215,999
1982/83	45,065	121,687	166,752
1981/82	31,672	103,439	135,111
1980/81	25,518	102,892	128,410
1979/80	19,595	89,247	108,842

The company's acquisition of its own shares

12.14 The directors' report of a UK listed company must give particulars of any authority given by the shareholders in general meeting for the company to purchase its own shares that is still effective at the year end (for example, see Table 60). [*CO 21(p)*].

12.15 If the company has acquired its own shares, Part II of Schedule 7 to the Act requires the directors' report to include certain information. The directors' report must contain the details set out in paragraph 12.16 below where any of the following circumstances occur:

(a) A company acquires its own shares by purchase, or by forfeiture, or by surrender in lieu of forfeiture, or by way of a gift, or in a reduction of capital duly made, or by order of the court. [*7 Sch 7(a); Sec 143(3)*].

(b) A nominee of a public company acquires shares in the company from a third party without the company providing any financial assistance, and the company has a beneficial interest in those shares. [*7 Sch 7(b); Sec 146(1)(c)*].

(c) Any person acquires shares in a *public* company with the financial assistance of the company, and the company has a beneficial interest in those shares. [*7 Sch 7(b); Sec 146(1)(d)*].

(d) A company takes a lien or a charge (either express or implied) on its own shares for any amount that is payable in respect of those shares. [*7 Sch 7(c); Sec 150(2)*].

(e) A company that remained an 'old public company' (as defined in Chapter 13 para 13.59) after 22 March 1982, and did not apply before that date to be re-registered under section 8 of the Companies Act 1980 as a public company, holds a lien or a charge (either express or implied) on its own shares, and that lien or charge existed on 22 March 1982. [*7 Sch 7(c); CC(CP) s 6(3)*].

(f) A company that either existed on 2 November 1862 or was formed after that date in pursuance of either any Act of Parliament (other than the 1985 Act) of letters patent, or was otherwise legally constituted, and that was not registered under any previous Companies Act and has registered under Section 680 of the 1985 Act as a public company, holds a lien or a charge (either express or implied) on its own shares, and that lien or charge existed immediately before the company was registered as a public company. [*7 Sch 7(c); Sec 150(4)*].

Table 60: Illustration of a company's directors seeking power to purchase the company's own shares.

Extract from The General Electric Company, p.l.c. Report and Accounts 31 March 1984.

Directors' report extract

AUTHORITY FOR COMPANY TO PURCHASE ITS OWN SHARES

11. The Companies Act 1981 enables a company to purchase its own shares if it is authorised by its Articles of Association to do so, and has obtained the requisite authority from shareholders. The directors believe that it is in the Company's best interests to take powers to purchase its own shares in accordance with these provisions. Shareholders' approval is being sought to the requisite alteration to the Articles of Association of the Company and to give a general authority for the Company to make market purchases of its own shares. The general authority will last for 18 months from the date of shareholders' approval, and authorises market purchases of up to 250 million Ordinary Shares of 5p each at not more than 300p and not less than 5p per share respectively. Accordingly, the following resolutions will be proposed as Special Business at the forthcoming Annual General Meeting, number 3 as a Special Resolution and number 4 as an Ordinary Resolution.

"3 THAT the Articles of Association of the Company be and they are hereby amended by the insertion after Article 9 thereof of a new Article as follows:

"9A   Subject to and in accordance with the provisions of the Companies Act 1981, the Company may purchase any of its own shares of any class at any price (whether at par or above or below par), and any shares to be so purchased may be selected in any manner whatsoever. All shares so purchased shall be cancelled immediately upon completion of the purchase and the amount of the Company's issued share capital (but not authorised share capital) shall be reduced by the nominal amount of the shares so purchased and the authorised but unissued share capital resulting from such purchase and cancellation shall be designated as Ordinary Shares of 5p each (regardless of the nominal amount of any share so purchased and cancelled)." "

"4 THAT the Company be and it is hereby authorised to make market purchases (within the meaning of Section 49(2) of the Companies Act 1981 [*now Section 163 of the Companies Act 1985*]) on The Stock Exchange of up to an aggregate of 250 million Ordinary Shares of 5p each in its capital at not more than 300p per share and not less than 5p per share (in each case exclusive of expenses) and that the authority conferred by this Resolution shall expire on 13th March 1986 (except in relation to the purchase of shares the contract for which was concluded before such date and which might be executed wholly or partly after such date)."

12.16 Where any of the above circumstances has occurred, the directors' report must state the following details:

(a) The number and the nominal value of the shares that the company has purchased in the financial year.

(b) The aggregate consideration the company paid and the reasons it purchased the shares.

(c) The number and the nominal value of the shares the company has at any time either acquired or charged as mentioned in (a) to (f) in paragraph 12.15 (excluding any shares the company has purchased).

(d) The maximum number and the nominal value of shares the company has at any time either acquired or charged as mentioned in (a) to (f) in paragraph 12.15 (excluding any shares the company has purchased) that the company or the other person held at any time during the financial year.

(e) The number and the nominal value of shares the company has at any time either acquired or charged as mentioned in (a) to (f) in paragraph 12.15 (excluding any shares the company has purchased) that, during the financial year, either the company or the other person has disposed of or the company has cancelled.

(f) The percentage of the total called-up share capital that the shares of that description represent, if the number and the nominal value of shares of any particular description are disclosed pursuant to (a) to (e) immediately above.

(g) The amount of any charge.

(h) The amount or the value of any consideration for any shares that either the company or the other person disposed of during the financial year that the company or the other person acquired for money or money's worth.
[7 Sch 8].

The directors should take care in drafting the note that explains the reason for any purchase by the company of its own shares (as required by (b) above). The reason should be consistent with that put forward for tax purposes.

12.17 The directors' report of a UK listed company must give the following additional information concerning purchases or proposed purchases of the company's own shares:

(a) In relation to purchases other than either through the market or by tender or by partial offer to all shareholders, the names of the sellers of the shares that have been purchased, or are to be purchased, by the company.

287

(b) If the company has purchased any of its own shares since the year end, or has either been granted an option or entered into a contract to purchase its own shares since the year end, then the directors' report should disclose the equivalent information to that detailed in paragraph 12.16 above.
[*CO 21(p)*].

Employee information

12.18   Parts III, IV and V of Schedule 7 require the directors' report to contain information regarding the company's policy in respect of the employment of disabled persons, of the health, safety and welfare at work of employees, and of the involvement of employees in the management of the company.

12.19   If a company is required to prepare group accounts, the directors' report needs to contain the employee information required by Schedule 7 only in respect of the holding company. However, in practice, most holding companies include the required employee information in respect of the whole group.

Employment of disabled persons

12.20   If the company employed, on average, 250 or more employees in the UK in each week of the financial year, the directors' report must contain a statement that describes the company's policy during the year in respect of the following:

(a) Giving full and fair consideration (having regard to the persons' particular aptitudes and abilities) to applications for employment that disabled persons (as defined in the Disabled Persons (Employment) Act 1944) make to the company.

(b) Continuing the employment of, and arranging appropriate training for, any of the company's employees who have become disabled during the period in which the company employed them.

(c) Otherwise providing for the training, the career development and the promotion of those disabled persons the company employs.
[*7 Sch 9*].

An illustration of this disclosure is given in Table 61.

Health and safety of employees

12.21   The Secretary of State may make regulations that require certain classes of company to include in their directors' report information concerning employees' health and safety. [*7 Sch 10(1)(3)*]. The information should include details of the arrangements in force in the financial year both for securing the health, safety and welfare at work of employees of the company and its subsidiaries, and for protecting other persons against risks to their health or safety connected with the work of those employees. [*7 Sch 10(1)*].

> **Table 61: Illustration of the information required in the directors' report on the employment of disabled persons.**
>
> Extract from Imperial Group public limited company Report and Accounts 31 October 1984.
>
> **Employment of disabled people**
> In considering applications for employment from disabled people in the UK, the Group seeks to ensure that full and fair consideration is given to the abilities and aptitudes of the applicant against the requirements of the job for which he or she has applied. Employees who become unable to carry out the job for which they are employed are given individual consideration. Depending on the nature, severity and duration of the disability, individuals may be considered for alternative work, including retraining if necessary.
> Training, career development and promotion opportunities are available to all employees on the basis of individual aptitude and abilities and the business requirements of the organisation. Disabled employees may be eligible for special training if there is a particular individual need.

12.22 To date, July 1985, the Secretary of State has not made any such regulation, and so there is no requirement at present for companies to disclose in the directors' report information on employees' health and safety. Nevertheless, some companies do so on a voluntary basis.

Employee involvement

12.23 Paragraph 11 of Schedule 7 requires the directors' report to describe the action the company has taken during the financial year to introduce, maintain, or develop arrangements aimed at:

(a) Providing employees systematically with information on matters of concern to them as employees.

(b) Consulting employees or their representatives on a regular basis, so that the company can take the views of employees into account in making decisions that are likely to affect their interests.

(c) Encouraging the involvement of employees in the company's performance through (for example) an employees' share scheme.

(d) Achieving a common awareness on the part of all employees of the financial and the economic factors that affect the company's performance.
[7 Sch 11(3)].

Table 62 gives an example of the information to be shown.

12.24 This requirement applies only to the directors' report of a company that employs, on average, more than 250 employees in the UK each week during the financial year. [7 Sch 11(1)].

> **Table 62: Illustration of the information required in the directors'
> report on employee involvement.**
>
> *Extract from Crown House plc Annual Report 31 March 1984.*
>
> **Employees**
> Within the bounds of commercial confidentiality, information is disseminated to all levels
> of staff about matters that affect the progress of the group and are of interest and con-
> cern to them as employees. Each group company, where relevant, encourages employees
> to meet on a regular basis to discuss matters affecting employees, and progress was made
> during the year in creating employee committees and quality circles.

Political and charitable gifts

12.25   If a company that is not the wholly-owned subsidiary of another company incorporated in Great Britain has given money for either political purposes or charitable purposes during the year, and the amount
given for both purposes exceeds £200 in aggregate, the company must
disclose certain information in its directors' report. [7 Sch 3(1)(2)].

12.26   The information that must be disclosed is as follows:

(a) The amount given for both political purposes and charitable purposes. These amounts must be disclosed separately. [7 Sch 3(2)(a)].

(b) If the company has given money for political purposes (including
a subscription to a political party), the name of each person or political party to whom the company has donated more than £200 during the year, together with the actual amount donated. [7 Sch
3(2)(b)].

12.27   With a group, the holding company directors' report needs to give the
information in paragraph 12.26 above in respect of the group as a whole.
It has to give the information only if the amount the company and its
subsidiaries have given for both political purposes and charitable purposes exceeds £200 in aggregate. [7 Sch 4].

12.28   Money a company gives for 'charitable purposes' means any money
it gives for purposes that are exclusively charitable. [7 Sch 5(4)]. Donations for purposes that include either a political or a commercial element do not come within the definition. The definition also excludes
charitable donations a company gives to a person who, at the time of
the gift, was ordinarily resident outside the UK. [7 Sch 5(3)].

Directors' interests

12.29   The financial statements must disclose information about the directors'
interests in the company's shares or debentures. For this purpose, an

interest in shares or debentures includes any interest of any kind what-soever in shares or debentures. [*13 Sch 1(1)*]. The information on directors' interests may be disclosed either in the directors' report or in the notes to the financial statements. [*7 Sch 2(3)*].

12.30 The notes to the financial statements or the directors' report must state whether or not anyone who was a director of the company at the end of the financial year was interested, at the end of the financial year, in any shares in, or any debentures of, the company, or any subsidiary, or any holding company or any fellow subsidiary. This statement should be based on the information contained in the register the company maintains in accordance with Sections 324 to 328 of the Act (director's obligation to notify his interests in the company and in companies in the same group). [*7 Sch 2(1)(a)*].

12.31 If any director had such an interest at the end of the financial year, the financial statements must give also the following information:

(a) The number of shares in, and the amount of debentures of, each company (that is, the company itself, or a subsidiary, or a holding company or a fellow subsidiary) in which the director was interested at the end of the financial year. The name of the company in question must be specified.

(b) A statement as to whether or not the director had an interest in either that company or any other group company at the beginning of the financial year and if so, the number of shares in, and the amount of debentures of, such company in which the director had an interest at the beginning of the year. Again, the name of the company in question must be specified.
[*7 Sch 2(1)(b)*].

12.32 If a person was appointed a director of the company during the financial year, the information required under *(b)* above is the information that applied at the date of his appointment as a director, rather than the information that applied at the beginning of the year. [*7 Sch 2(1)(b)*]. If a person was appointed a director on more than one occasion during the year, the information should be given as at the date he was first appointed. [*7 Sch 2(2)*]. This requirement covers a situation where, for example, a person is appointed a director between the end of the preceding financial year and the date of the annual general meeting. Under regulation 79 of Table A (if applicable), this person would have to be reappointed as a director at the annual general meeting. However, the financial statements should give the information required under paragraph *(b)* above as at the date he was first appointed.

12.33 The financial statements must disclose information about the interests of the company's directors in the company's shares, where such interests take the form of a 'put' or a 'call' option that a director holds otherwise than under a trust. [*13 Sch 6(1)*].

12.34 However, it is not clear from the Act whether the financial statements should contain particulars of an option that a director (or his spouse or infant child) holds to subscribe for shares in the company or in another company in the same group. Such an option must be shown in the register the company maintains in accordance with Sections 324 to 328 of the Act. [*Sec 325(3)*]. The uncertainty arises because it is not entirely clear from the Act whether an option to subscribe for shares is an 'interest in shares'. However, paragraph 1(1) of Schedule 13 to the Act does say that "an interest in shares ... is to be read as including any interest of any kind whatsoever in shares". It seems, therefore, that an option that a director holds to subscribe for the company's shares may be covered by the Act, and may require to be disclosed.

12.35 In any event, the Stock Exchange's Continuing Obligations specifically require all listed companies to disclose such options [*CO 21(h)*], and so, whatever the statutory position may be, listed companies' financial statements must contain the relevant particulars.

12.36 The information that the financial statements should disclose in respect of a director's option to subscribe for shares (if such an option is required to be disclosed) consists of the number of shares that the director has an option over and the name of the company to which the shares relate. However, the financial statements do not have to disclose the price at which the director can exercise his option. But, the *notes* to the financial statements must disclose, in summary, both the option price at which, and the period during which, *any* options are exercisable in respect of the company's shares (see Chapter 9 para 9.79). [*4 Sch 40*].

12.37 Where a director of a wholly-owned subsidiary is also a director of the holding company, The Companies (Disclosure of Directors' Interests) (Exceptions) Regulations 1985 (SI 1985/802) give relief from the disclosure requirements in paragraphs 12.29 to 12.34 above. In this situation, the director's interest needs to be disclosed only in the holding company's financial statements, and not in the subsidiary's.

12.38 In addition, a company that is either listed on The Stock Exchange or traded on the USM must disclose any change in the directors' interests between the end of the financial year and a date not more than one month before the date of the notice of the general meeting at which the financial statements are to be presented. Where there has been no such change, this fact should be stated in the directors' report. Also, the interests that are disclosed for these companies must distinguish between beneficial interests and non-beneficial interests. [*CO 21(h); GU 10(h)*].

An illustration of how a company discloses its director's interests is given in Table 63.

Table 63: Illustration of the disclosure of the directors' interests and other major interests in the capital of the company.

Extract from The Savoy Hotel PLC Directors' Report & Annual Accounts 31 December 1984.

Interests at 31st December, 1984, and (shown in italics) at 1st January, 1984.

Directors' Beneficial Interests	Ordinary Share Capital			
	A Shares		B Shares	
Sir Hugh Wontner	144,425	*144,425*	4,616	*4,616*
Dame Bridget D'Oyly Carte	1,044,758	*1,044,758*	4,515	*4,515*
M. B. Radcliffe	3,033	*2,933*	—	—
G. R. C. Shepard	11,652	*11,652*	11	*11*
Sir Antony Part	275	*275*	22	*22*
M. J. de R. Richardson	1,500	*1,500*	—	—
R. S. Wilkins	1,500	*1,500*	—	—
V. S. Emery	130,087	*130,087*	90,913	*90,913*
Sir Anthony Tuke	500	*500*	—	—
H. Morton Neal	5,324	*5,324*	—	—
Interests as Trustees				
Sir Hugh Wontner	390,410	*390,410*	842,210	*841,900*
Dame Bridget D'Oyly Carte	390,410	*390,410*	841,580	*841,570*
M. B. Radcliffe	390,110	*390,110*	597,240	*597,240*
G. R. C. Shepard	—	—	630	

	Debenture and Loan Stocks					
	4% First		8¼%		8½%	
Directors' Beneficial Interests	£	£	£	£	£	£
Sir Hugh Wontner	2,800	*2,800*	1,000	*1,000*	4,500	*4,400*
Dame Bridget D'Oyly Carte	1,000	*1,000*	—	—	18,835	*18,835*
V. S. Emery	—	—	—	—	50	*50*
Interests as Trustees						
Sir Hugh Wontner	600	*600*	2,000	*2,000*	—	—
G. R. Shepard	600	—	2,000	—	—	—

Sir Hugh Wontner, Dame Bridget D'Oyly Carte and Mr. V. S. Emery have beneficial interests of £4,200 *(£3,850)*, £16,400 *(£16,400)* and £100 *(£100)* respectively in the 4% First Mortgage Debenture Stock of Savoy Theatre Limited. Sir Hugh Wontner also has an interest as a trustee in £500 *(£500)* of this Debenture Stock.

Between the end of the year and 26th March, 1985, the interests as trustees of Sir Hugh Wontner and Dame Bridget D'Oyly Carte have increased by 1,278,124 A Ordinary Shares and 1,479 B Ordinary Shares, and the beneficial interests of Mr. G. R. C. Shepard and Mr. M. B. Radcliffe have increased by 371 A Ordinary Shares and 200 A Ordinary Shares respectively.

Other Major Interests at 26th March, 1985

Apart from the interests of the Directors, the Company has been notified of one holding in excess of 5 per cent.

	Ordinary Share Capital				Issued	Total
	A Shares		B Shares		Capital	Votes
Trusthouse Forte PLC	19,479,880	70.35%	164,960	12.63%	69.02%	42.32%

Under the terms of the Companies Act, 1948, The Savoy Hotel PLC is a subsidiary of Trusthouse Forte PLC, but Trusthouse Forte does not control The Savoy Hotel PLC.

Other information to be disclosed in the directors' report

12.39   The directors' report must disclose also the following information:

(a) The amount (if any) that the directors recommend should be paid as a dividend, and the amount (if any) that they propose to carry to reserves. [*Sec 235(1)(b)*].

(b) The name of anyone who was a director of the company at any time during the financial year. [*Sec 235(2)*].

(c) The principal activities of both the company and of its subsidiaries during the year, and details of any significant change in those activities. [*Sec 235(2)*].

(d) Particulars of any significant changes in the fixed assets of both the company and any of its subsidiaries that have occurred during the year. [*7 Sch 1(1)*].

(e) The difference (with such degree of precision as is practicable) between the market value and the balance sheet value of any interest in land and buildings, if the market value of the interest differs substantially from the value at which it is included in the balance sheet, and if, also, the directors are of the opinion that the difference is of such significance that it should be brought to the shareholders' attention (for example, see Table 64). [*7 Sch 1(2)*].

Table 64: Illustration of the type of information required to be given in the directors' report about the value of the group's properties.

Extract from The Great Universal Stores P.L.C. Annual Report 31 March 1984.

Market value of properties
The group's freehold, heritable and leasehold properties in the United Kingdom and overseas (with the exception of certain leasehold properties and specialised mail order warehouses with a net book value of £32 million) were professionally valued at 31st March, 1984 on the basis of their open market value and within their existing use. The valuation was carried out by Edward Erdman with the exception of certain overseas properties where local firms of professional valuers were employed. The valuation resulted in a surplus of approximately £400 million over the net book value, subject to any capital gains tax in the event of disposals. Of this surplus £290 million related to properties occupied by the group for trading purposes and £110 million to investment properties. In accordance with SSAP 19 the surplus relating to investment properties has been incorporated in the consolidated balance sheet.

Failure to comply with the requirements of the Act

12.40   Every person who was a director of the company at the end of the period within which (under Section 242) the company's financial statements must be laid before the company in general meeting and must be delivered to the Registrar of Companies (see Chapter 21), is guilty of an offence if the directors' report fails to comply with the Act's requirements. In addition, every such person is liable to a fine. [*Sec 235(7)* — see Appendix IV].

12.41 It is a defence in such a situation for a director to prove that he took all reasonable steps to ensure that the directors' report complied with all the Act's requirements. [*Sec 235(7)*].

Additional requirements for listed companies and USM companies

12.42 The Stock Exchange's Continuing Obligations and its General Undertaking for USM companies require the directors' report of listed companies and companies traded on the USM respectively to give information on further matters in addition to those the Act covers. These are as follows:

(a) The directors should state whether, so far as they are aware, the company is a 'close company' for taxation purposes. They should also state whether there has been any change in that respect since the end of the financial year. [*CO 21 (j); GU 10(j)*].

(b) The directors' report should disclose particulars of any substantial interest in the company's share capital that any person other than a director holds as at a date not more than one month before the date of notice of the meeting at which the financial statements are to be presented. For this purpose, a 'substantial interest' is any holding of 5% or more of the nominal value of any class of share capital that carries voting rights. [*CO 21 (i); GU 10(i)*]. This information should be contained in the register the company maintains in accordance with Sections 198 to 220 of the Act (for example, see Table 63).

(c) The directors' report *for listed companies only* should state the unexpired period of any service contract of more than one year's duration of any director who is proposed for re-election at the annual general meeting. If the director has a service contract for a term of less than one year, the directors' report must state that fact. [*CO 43(c)*].

If a director's service contract does not specify a term, the term can be ascertained in one of the following ways:

(i) If the contract is determinable on the giving of notice, the expiration of the notice period will indicate the earliest date at which the contract could end.

(ii) If no notice period is stated in the contract, the term may be implied. This implication may be given either by custom and practice, or by the company's articles of association, or in some other way.

(iii) If the contract contains no express or implied provision as to notice, there would be a presumption that the term is for a period of five years. A longer period cannot be agreed without the approval of the company in general meeting.

Where the length of the unexpired period of a director's service contract has been determined in one of the ways above, the details should be fully disclosed in the directors' report. The notice convening the annual general meeting of companies listed on The Stock Exchange and also of companies traded on the USM must give the place where, and the time at which, copies of service contracts can be examined (for example, see Table 65). If there are no such contracts, the notice must state that fact. [CO 43(b); GU 11].

(d) The directors' report should disclose particulars of any contract of significance between the company (or one of its subsidiaries) and a corporate substantial shareholder. [CO 21(1)]. For this purpose, a 'contract of significance' is one which represents in value a sum equal to 1% or more of:

   (i) The company's net assets, for a capital transaction or for a transaction of which the principal purpose is the granting of credit.

   (ii) The company's total purchases, sales, payments or receipts, as appropriate, for other transactions.

Where the company has subsidiaries these comparisons should be made on a group basis.

Also, a 'corporate substantial shareholder' is defined as any body corporate who either is entitled to exercise, or control the exercise of, at least 30% of the voting power at the company's general meetings or is in a position to control the composition of a majority of the company's board of directors. [CO 21(1)].

(e) In addition, the directors' report should disclose details of any contract with a corporate substantial shareholder (as defined in *(d)* above) to provide services to the company or to one of its subsidiaries. This information is not required if the shareholder is providing services that it normally provides as part of its principal business and it is not a contract of significance that *(d)* above requires to be disclosed. [CO 21(m)].

Table 65: Illustration of the requirement for the inspection of directors' service contracts.

Extract from Imperial Chemical Industries PLC Annual Report 31 December 1984.

The following information, which is available for inspection during business hours at the Company's Registered Office, will, on the day of the Annual General Meeting, be available for inspection at the Royal Lancaster Hotel, Lancaster Terrace, London W2, from 10.45 a.m. until the conclusion of the meeting:

(1) A statement of transactions of Directors (and of their family interests) in the share capital and debentures of the Company and any of its subsidiaries.

(2) Copies of all contracts of service under which Directors of the Company are employed by the Company or any of its subsidiaries.

Auditors' consideration of the directors' report

12.43   The auditors have a statutory duty to carry out such investigations during the course of their audit of the financial statements as are necessary for them to form an opinion on whether or not the information that the directors' report contains is consistent with the financial statements on which they are reporting. The Act requires auditors to draw attention in their report to any inconsistency they find between the directors' report and the company's financial statements for the year in question. [*Sec 237(6)*]. However, the Act does not require the directors' report to be audited as such. If the information contained in the directors' report is consistent with that in the financial statements, the audit report does not have to include any specific comment.

12.44   The directors' report does not form part of the financial statements on which the auditors report. Consequently, the pages referred to in the 'scope' paragraph of the audit report should not include the pages on which the directors' report is printed.

12.45   Where companies choose to disclose in some other statement certain of the statutory information that is required to be included in the directors' report (see para 12.05 above), the auditors have to consider whether all of the financial information that is contained in that other statement is consistent with the information disclosed in the financial statements. If the auditors are to do this, they may have to perform considerably more work than if they merely reviewed the limited information that the directors' report should give.

12.46   The Auditing Guideline, 'Financial information issued with audited financial statements', includes the following example of an audit report qualified on the grounds of inconsistency between the directors' report and the audited financial statements:

> "In our opinion, the information given in the directors' report is not consistent with the company's financial statements for the financial year. Paragraph 7 of the directors' report states without amplification that the company's trading resulted in a profit before tax of £X. The profit and loss account, however, states that the company incurred a loss before tax for the year of £Y and, as an extraordinary item, a profit from the sale of land of £Z."

12.47   Auditors should also review the chairman's statement and any other supplementary financial information that is disclosed (for example, five-year summaries), in order to ensure that the information disclosed is neither misleading nor incompatible with the financial statements on which they are reporting.

CHAPTER 13

SPECIAL CATEGORY COMPANIES

Chapter 13

Special Category Companies

Introduction

13.01 The Act *permits* certain types of companies (that is, banking companies, insurance companies and shipping companies) that are described as 'special category companies' to prepare their financial statements in accordance with Sections 258 to 262 of, and Schedule 9 to, the Act. This means that such companies have two choices as to the way in which they may prepare their financial statements. They can decide to adopt the standard rules that apply to the majority of companies set out in Section 228 of, and Schedule 4 to, the Act. Alternatively, they can prepare them in accordance with the rules specifically provided for special category companies.

13.02 The rules that apply to special category companies are intended to be only temporary. The EC is developing Directives that set out the accounting requirements for banking companies and insurance companies (see Appendix III). These Directives will eventually form part of UK legislation, and this legislation will supersede those rules set out in the 1985 Act that relate to these types of companies. Shipping companies were specifically exempted from the requirements of the EC Fourth Directive (and, consequently, from certain of the requirements of the 1985 Act), but only for a period of *ten years* from the date of adoption of the Directive, which was 25 July 1978. Consequently, from July 1988, shipping companies will be required to comply with the standard rules contained in Schedule 4.

Definitions

13.03 'Special category companies' are banking companies, insurance companies and shipping companies. For this purpose, the following definitions apply:

—A 'banking company' is a company that is recognised as a bank, or is a licensed institution, under the Banking Act 1979.

—An 'insurance company' is a company to which Part II of the Insurance Companies Act 1982 applies.

—A 'shipping company' is a company that satisfies two conditions in respect of either itself or one of its subsidiaries:

(a) It owns ships, or it includes either the management of, or the operation of, ships among its activities.

(b) It satisfies the Secretary of State that it ought, in the national interest, to be treated as a shipping company for the purposes of Part VII of the 1985 Act.
[*Sec 257(1)*].

The format of special category companies' financial statements

13.04 Special category companies *may* prepare their financial statements in accordance with the requirements of Sections 258 to 262 of, and Schedule 9 to, the Act. In addition, the group accounts of a holding company that is, or has as its subsidiary, a special category company, *may* be prepared under Section 259 of, and Schedule 9 to, the Act. [*Sec 257(3)*]. The scope of this latter concession is very wide. It covers the consolidated financial statements of any group, provided that at least one company within the group is a special category company. However, where it is a subsidiary that is the special category company, then, although the consolidated financial statements may be prepared under Section 259 of, and Schedule 9 to, the Act, the holding company's balance sheet must still be prepared in accordance with Schedule 4 (see para 13.83 below). Some groups that include a special category company do not make use of this provision, because all of the group companies' individual financial statements (other than those of the special category company) are prepared in accordance with the requirements as to form and content that are set out in Schedule 4 to the Act. Therefore, it may be easier in practice for some groups to prepare consolidated financial statements under Schedule 4, rather than under Schedule 9.

13.05 Financial statements prepared in accordance with Schedule 9 must contain a statement that they are prepared in compliance with Chapter II of Part VII of, and Schedule 9 to, the Act. [*Sec 257(3)*]. Appropriate wording for a note to a single entity's financial statements that have been drawn up in accordance with the Schedule 9 rules would be:

"The company is not required to comply with the accounting and disclosure provisions of Part VII, Chapter I of the Companies Act 1985. These financial statements are drawn up in accordance with Part VII, Chapter II of, and Schedule 9 to, the Companies Act 1985."

13.06 Appropriate wording for a note to group accounts (or consolidated financial statements) that have been drawn up in accordance with the Schedule 9 rules would be:

"Neither the group nor the holding company is required to comply with the accounting and disclosure provisions of Part VII, Chapter I of the Companies Act 1985. The group accounts are drawn up in accordance with Part VII, Chapter II of, and Schedule 9 to, the Companies Act 1985.

Also, Table 70 on page 325 gives an example of the note required where the holding company is not a special category company, but the group prepares its consolidated financial statements in accordance with Section 259 of, and Schedule 9 to, the Act.

13.07 Special category companies are still bound by the overriding requirement that the balance sheet and the profit and loss account must give a true and fair view of the company's state of affairs and profit or loss for the financial period. [*Sec 258(1)*]. In addition, the Act says that the requirement that the balance sheet and the profit and loss account must comply with the provisions of Schedule 9 is without prejudice to any other requirements of the Act. [*Sec 258(3)*].

13.08 Certain types of special category company are exempted from many of the requirements even of Schedule 9. Where these exemptions are adopted in the preparation of a special category company's financial statements, these financial statements will not be deemed not to give a true and fair view as required by the Act by reason only that they do not give the information required by the provisions of Schedule 9 from which they are exempt. [*9 Sch 27(4),28(2),29(2)*]. These exemptions are very wide in their application, and some special category companies can, if they wish, restrict the information that they are required to disclose under Schedule 9. However, although a special category company may be entitled to take advantage of these exemptions, it may decide to take advantage only of some of them or it may decide to ignore them completely. Consequently, all of the requirements for special category companies are considered below in paragraphs 13.12 to 13.66, and the exemptions that may be taken up by some special category companies are then considered in paragraphs 13.67 to 13.82.

13.09 The Secretary of State may also modify any of the disclosure requirements that apply to special category companies in order to adapt them to a particular company's circumstances. This modification may be made either on the application of the company's directors or with their consent. However, the Secretary of State cannot waive the requirement that the financial statements must show a true and fair view. [*Sec 258(4)*].

13.10 A special category company is exempt only from those requirements of Part VII, Chapter I of, and Schedule 4 to, the Act that govern the preparation of financial statements. It normally has to comply with the other provisions contained in Part VII, Chapter I (for example, the directors' duty to prepare annual financial statements).

13.11 Also, many of the disclosure requirements imposed by other parts of the Act that apply to other companies apply to special category companies. For example, Schedule 5 (matters to be dealt with in the notes), Schedule 6 (details of loans and other transactions favouring directors and officers) and Schedule 7 (matters to be dealt with in the directors' report) still apply to special category companies, subject to certain exemptions. These exemptions are highlighted in this chapter.

The balance sheet

General

13.12 Schedule 9 does not detail formats that a special category company's balance sheet must follow. However, it does require the financial statements to disclose certain information for balance sheet items. An illustration of a consolidated balance sheet of a group prepared in accordance with Schedule 9 is given in Table 66.

Table 66: Illustration of the balance sheet of a banking company prepared in accordance with Schedule 9.

Extract from Lloyds Bank Plc Report and Accounts 31 December 1984.

Consolidated balance sheet

	Note	1984 £ million	1983 £ million
Assets employed			
Cash and short-term funds	9	5,398	5,412
Cheques in course of collection		740	517
Investments	10	1,423	1,134
Advances and other accounts	11	35,248	30,300
		42,809	37,363
Trade investments	14	150	195
Premises and equipment [see Table 67]	16	1,050	874
		44,009	38,432
Financed by			
Liabilities			
Current, deposit and other accounts		40,545	35,523
Current and deferred taxation	17	492	188
Dividend		40	35
		41,077	35,746
Loan capital	18	865	386
Minority interests		15	107
Share capital and reserves			
Issued share capital of Lloyds Bank Plc	19	235	194
Reserves	20	1,817	1,999
		2,052	2,193
		44,009	38,432

13.13 The balance sheet should show amounts for share capital, reserves, provisions, assets and liabilities. These amounts should be classified under headings appropriate to the company's business, except that:

(a) If the amount for a particular class is not material, it may be included with another class.

(b) If assets of one class are not separable from assets of another class, then both these classes may be included under the same heading. [*9 Sch 4*].

13.14 In addition, the financial statements should give details that explain the general nature of the assets and liabilities. [*9 Sch 2,4(1)*].

13.15 Assets should be split between fixed assets, current assets and assets that are neither fixed nor current. [*9 Sch 4(2)*].

13.16 Schedule 9 does not define the terms 'fixed assets' and 'current assets', but it is reasonable that, in deciding which assets to include under each category, special category companies should look to the definition of fixed assets in Schedule 4 (see further Chapter 7 para 7.03). However, special category companies do have the alternative of classifying assets as another category other than fixed or current.

13.17 Unlike the provisions that relate to Schedule 4 companies, special category companies may capitalise, as assets, the following items if they have not been written off:

(a) Preliminary expenses.

(b) Expenses incurred in connection with any issue of share capital or debentures.

(c) Any commission paid in respect of any shares or debentures.

(d) Any amount allowed by way of discount in respect of debentures.

(e) The amount of the discount allowed on any issue of shares at a discount.

The balance sheet must show such assets separately. [*9 Sch 3*].

Corresponding amounts

13.18 The balance sheet, or the related notes, or a statement or report annexed to the financial statements, should include the corresponding amount for the preceding financial year in respect of each item included. However, corresponding amounts do not need to be given for:

(a) The amount of additions and disposals of fixed assets (see para 13.27).

(b) The movements on reserves and provisions (see para 13.53). [*9 Sch 13(18)*].

Fixed assets

13.19 The financial statements must state the method used to arrive at the amount included in the balance sheet for each category of fixed assets. [*9 Sch 4(3)*]. This disclosure normally forms part of the company's accounting policies. In addition, SSAP 12 requires that the method should be stated.

13.20 In general, any fixed asset should be included in the balance sheet at its original cost (or, if it has been revalued, at the amount of the valuation), less any amounts provided for depreciation or diminution in value. [*9 Sch 5(1)*].

13.21 Certain fixed assets are exempted from the general principle outlined in paragraph 13.20 above. The assets that are exempted are:

(a) Assets acquired before or during the accounting period beginning with 1 July 1948, where their cost cannot be ascertained without unreasonable expense or delay.

(b) Assets whose replacement will be provided for either wholly or partly in one of the following ways:

  (i) By setting up a provision for renewal and charging the cost of the replacement against that provision (see para 13.22).
  (ii) By charging the cost of the replacement direct to revenue.

(c) Listed investments.

(d) Unlisted investments, provided that the directors have estimated their value, and provided also that this estimated value is either included in the balance sheet or disclosed in the notes to the financial statements.

(e) Goodwill, patents or trade marks.
[*9 Sch 5(2)*].

13.22 Schedule 9 to the Act permits an alternative to a depreciation charge in respect of an asset that has a limited useful economic life. This alternative is to set up a provision for the renewal of the asset by transferring an amount to this provision from the profit and loss account each year. If a company does set aside an amount for the replacement of fixed assets in this way, then Schedule 9 requires that the financial statements must disclose both the aggregate amount set aside and the means by which their replacement has been provided for. [*9 Sch 5(4)*]. The amount charged to revenue to provide for the renewal of fixed assets must also be disclosed separately. [*9 Sch 14(3)*].

13.23 However, SSAP 12 requires that any asset that has a finite useful life *must be depreciated*. In addition, if the proposals in ED 37 are accepted, the new Standard will specifically state that companies should not charge supplementary depreciation in their profit and loss accounts. However, it will still allow a company to set up a reserve for the replacement of fixed assets by an *appropriation* from retained profits.

13.24 Consequently, a company *must* provide depreciation on the carrying amount of its fixed assets in the balance sheet and it *may* also set aside an additional amount for the replacement of fixed assets by an appropriation from retained profits.

13.25 Where an amount has been provided for the renewal or the diminution in value of an asset, and the directors consider that the amount provided is excessive, they must treat the excess as a reserve, rather than as a provision (see also para 13.51). [*9 Sch 32(2)*].

13.26 In respect of all fixed assets, other than those that are exempted from complying with the general principle stated in paragraph 13.20 above, the financial statements must disclose:

(a) The aggregate cost (or the valuation) of the fixed assets.

(b) The aggregate accumulated amount that has been provided for depreciation or diminution in value.
[*9 Sch 5(3)*].

13.27 In addition, the financial statements must show the amount of any additions and disposals during the year of each category of fixed assets (other than investments). [*9 Sch 13(10)*].

13.28 Land and buildings must be subdivided, in the financial statements, between freehold property, long leasehold property and short leasehold property. [*9 Sch 13(11)*]. For this purpose, a lease includes an agreement for a lease, and a long lease is a lease in respect of which the unexpired portion is 50 years or more at the end of the financial year. [*9 Sch 34*].

13.29 If any fixed assets are included in the balance sheet at a valuation, as opposed to being included at their original cost, the financial statements must show:

(a) The year in which each valuation was made (so far as the directors know them).

(b) The amount of the valuations, analysed according to the years when each valuation was made.
[*9 Sch 13(9)*].

An illustration of the disclosure of fixed assets by a banking company is given in Table 67.

13.30 Furthermore, where any assets are valued during the financial year, then the notes to the financial statements should state the names of the valuers (or the valuers' qualifications) and the bases of valuation that they used. [*9 Sch 13(9)*]. SSAP 19 requires similar disclosure where investment properties are revalued (see Chapter 7 para 7.120).

13.31 The balance sheet must include the aggregate net amount of any goodwill, patents and trade marks that have not been written off. This figure should include any goodwill arising on consolidation. [*9 Sch 10(1)(b), (2)*]. SSAP 22 applies also to the disclosure and the accounting treatment of goodwill and requires the disclosure of both the cost and amortisation of goodwill. The rules contained in SSAP 22 are considered in Chapter 7, paragraphs 7.39 to 7.94.

Table 67: Example of the disclosure of fixed assets by a banking company.

Extract from Lloyds Bank Plc Report and Accounts 31 December 1984.

Note

16 Premises and equipment

	The Group		Lloyds Bank Plc	
	Premises £m	Equipment £m	Premises £m	Equipment £m
Cost or valuation:				
At 31 December 1983	702	356	454	244
Exchange adjustments	9	15	—	—
Additions	48	88	20	49
Disposals	(15)	(41)	(2)	(17)
Surplus on revaluation of premises	112		72	
Less: Accumulated depreciaton written back	(43)		(22)	
	69		50	
At 31 December 1984	813	418	522	276
Accumulated depreciation	—	(181)	—	(125)
Net book amount at 31 December 1984	813	237	522	151
		1,050		673
Net book amount at 31 December 1983	673	201	439	136
		874		575

Net book amount of premises comprises:	The Group		Lloyds Bank Plc	
	1984 £m	1983 £m	1984 £m	1983 £m
Freeholds	650	530	397	324
Leaseholds 50 years and over unexpired	117	107	104	92
Leaseholds less than 50 years unexpired	46	36	21	23
	813	673	522	439
At valuation – 1981	—	407	—	406
– 1982	—	18	—	—
– 1983	—	167	—	—
– 1984	765	—	519	—
At cost	48	81	3	33
	813	673	522	439

The majority of valuations were carried out by professionally qualified staff.

13.32 The financial statements should state the amount of any proposed capital expenditure that has been:

(a) Contracted for, but not provided for, at the balance sheet date.

(b) Authorised by the directors, but not contracted for, at the balance sheet date.

[*9 Sch 13(8)*].

Investments

13.33 The aggregate amount of investments should be split between listed investments and unlisted investments (defined in the same way as for other companies — see Chapter 8 paras 8.04 and 8.05). [*9 Sch 10(1)(a),33*]. In addition, listed investments should be subdivided between investments listed on a recognised stock exchange and other listed investments. [*9 Sch 10(3)*].

13.34 If the company is listed or traded on the USM, The Stock Exchange's Continuing Obligations and its General Undertaking respectively require certain additional information to be disclosed about the company's investments. These additional requirements are set out in Chapter 8, paragraphs 8.18 to 8.20.

13.35 The financial statements must state the aggregate market value of listed investments (unless they are included at that value in the balance sheet). Where the market value of any investments is considered to be higher than the stock exchange value of those investments, their stock exchange value should also be stated (see further Chapter 8 para 8.03). [*9 Sch 13(13)*].

13.36 If a company has investments in the form of equity share capital in unlisted companies, the directors may estimate the value of these investments (either individually or collectively) and disclose this value either in the balance sheet, or, alternatively, in the notes to the financial statements. [*9 Sch 6*].

13.37 Where the directors have not valued unlisted investments, the information set out below should be disclosed about the unlisted companies concerned. Either the notes to the financial statements or a statement annexed to the financial statements should disclose:

(a) The aggregate amount of income the company received from them during the year.

(b) The total of the company's share of their profits less losses before and after taxation.

(c) The company's share of their accumulated post-acquisition undistributed profits less losses.

(d) The manner in which any losses the unlisted companies have incurred have been dealt with in the company's financial statements. [*9 Sch 6*].

Current assets

13.38 The financial statements must disclose the aggregate amount outstanding as a result of the following:

(a) Money the company has provided under an employees' share scheme for the purchase of fully-paid shares in the company or its holding company.

(b) Loans the company has made to employees (other than directors) to enable them to acquire, for their own benefit, fully-paid shares in the company or its holding company.

(c) Financial assistance a private company has given to assist the acquisition of shares in either the company or its holding company (if that holding company is a private company). (Financial assistance of this nature can be given only if the conditions in Sections 155 to 158 of the Act are satisfied.)
[*9 Sch 10(1)(c)*].

13.39 Where the directors consider that the value included in the balance sheet for any current asset is greater than the amount that it would realise in the ordinary course of the company's business, they should state that fact in the notes. [*9 Sch 13(12)*]. However, in this type of situation, best accounting practice, and in particular the concept of prudence outlined in SSAP 2, requires that the current asset should be written down to its net realisable value.

Liabilities

13.40 The balance sheet or the notes to the financial statements must disclose the following:

(a) The aggregate amount of bank loans and overdrafts. [*9 Sch 10(1)(d)*].

(b) The aggregate amount of loans (other than bank loans and overdrafts) that are repayable either wholly or partly in more than five years after the balance sheet date [*9 Sch 10(1)(d)*], together with the terms on which each such loan is repayable and the rate of interest on each loan. However, if the latter part of this requirement would require a statement of excessive length to be included in the notes to the financial statements, then the information may be given in general terms. [*9 Sch 10(4)*]. (Loans or loan instalments are deemed to fall due for repayment or payment on the earliest date on which the lender can require repayment or payment if he exercises all options and rights available to him. [*9 Sch 35*].)

(c) The amount of any proposed dividends. [*9 Sch 10(1)(e)*].

13.41 Listed companies and companies that are traded on the USM have to comply also with the requirements that relate to loans that are outlined in The Stock Exchange's Continuing Obligations and in its General Undertaking respectively. These requirements are discussed in Chapter 9, paragraph 9.05.

13.42 If the company has used any of its assets to secure a liability, its financial statements should indicate that the liability is secured. However, the company does *not* need to indicate the assets that have been charged as security. [*9 Sch 11*]. In addition, the notes to the financial statements must give details of any charge there is on the company's assets to secure the liabilities of any other person. If it is practicable, the amount of the liability that is secured in this way should also be stated. [*9 Sch 13(6)*].

13.43   Furthermore, the financial statements should disclose the general nature of any other contingent liabilities that have not been provided for, together with (if this is practicable) the actual amount of, or an estimate of, the liabilities. [*9 Sch 13(7)*]. In this respect, the financial statements should comply with the requirements of SSAP 18 also. These requirements are set out in Chapter 9, paragraph 9.60.

Share capital

13.44   The authorised share capital and the issued share capital must be shown either on the face of the balance sheet or in the notes to the financial statements. [*9 Sch 2*].

13.45   If any part of the issued share capital includes redeemable shares, the following information must be given:

(a) The identity of the part of the issued share capital that includes redeemable shares.

(b) The earliest and the latest dates on which the company has power to redeem those shares.

(c) A statement of whether the shares must be redeemed in any event, or whether redemption is exercisable either at the company's option or at the shareholder's option.

(d) The amount of any premium that is payable on redemption or, if none is payable, a statement to that effect.
[*9 Sch 2(a)*].

13.46   Where a person has an option to subscribe for any of the company's shares, the financial statements must show the number, the description and the amount of those shares. Also, the following information must be given in respect of options granted:

(a) The period during which the option is exercisable.

(b) The option price to be paid for the shares.
[*9 Sch 13(2)*].

The requirement to disclose directors' interests in share options is considered in Chapter 12, paragraphs 12.33 to 12.36.

13.47   Where a company is in arrears in paying any fixed cumulative dividends on its shares, this fact should be noted in the financial statements, together with the period for which the dividends are in arrears. [*9 Sch 13(5)*].

311

Reserves and provisions

13.48   The term 'provision' is defined in Schedule 9 to the Act for special category companies as:

> "Any amount written off or retained by way of providing for depreciation, renewals or diminution in value of assets or retained by way of providing for any known liability of which the amount cannot be determined with substantial accuracy."

The expression 'liability' includes in this context all liabilities in respect of expenditure contracted for, and all disputed or contingent liabilities. [*9 Sch 32(1)(a)*].

13.49   Although the definition of a provision in Schedule 4 is expressed in different terms to those used in the definition given above that applies to special category companies, there is little, if any, difference in the meaning of the two definitions. However, the definition given in Schedule 9 does include provisions for renewals, whereas this item is not included in the definition of a provision given in Schedule 4.

13.50   The term 'reserve' is not defined in Schedule 4, but, in respect of special category companies, it is stated in Schedule 9 as *excluding*:

> "Any amount written off or retained by way of providing for depreciation, renewals or diminution in value of an asset or retained by way of providing for any known liability or any sum set aside for the purpose of its being used to prevent undue fluctuations in charges for taxation." [*9 Sch 32(1)(b)*].

13.51   Where an amount has been provided for depreciation of an asset (including provisions for renewals or diminution in value), or an amount has been provided for a liability, and the directors consider that the amount provided is excessive, they must treat the excess as a reserve, rather than as a provision. [*9 Sch 32(2)*].

13.52   The aggregate amount of reserves and provisions, other than provisions for depreciation, or renewals or the diminution in value of assets, must be stated separately. If either of these amounts is immaterial, it may be combined with the other amount. In addition, a separate statement of provisions is not necessary if the Secretary of State is satisfied that the public interest does not require a separate statement, and that, if one were given, it would be disadvantageous to the company. Where this statement is omitted,the financial statements must identify any heading that includes a provision that has *not* been separately disclosed. [*9 Sch 7*].

13.53   The financial statements must disclose the following movements on reserves and provisions unless they are provisions for depreciation, or renewals or the diminution in value of assets:

(a) The source of the increase or application of the decrease, where

the amount of *reserves* shown in the financial statements has increased or decreased since the previous financial year end.

(b) The source of the increase, where the amount of *provisions* has increased since the previous financial year end.

(c) The application of any amount that has not been used for the purposes for which the *provisions* were set up. This need only be disclosed where the amount of provisions at the previous year end exceeds the aggregate of the amounts applied during the year for the purposes of the provisions and the amounts still retained for the same purposes.

This information must be given separately for each sub-heading of reserves and provisions. [*9 Sch 8*].

13.54 If the company has a share premium account, this must be shown separately. [*9 Sch 2(c)*].

13.55 Any provision for deferred taxation must be disclosed to comply with both the Act and SSAP 15 (see further Chapter 9 paras 9.51 to 9.54). [*9 Sch 9*]. If a provision for deferred taxation that has previously been set up is applied during the year to some other purpose, both this fact and the amount that has been applied must be stated. [*9 Sch 13(14)*].

The profit and loss account

General disclosure

13.56 Schedule 9 does not detail formats that a special category company's profit and loss account must follow. However, the profit and loss account (or the related notes) must disclose the information that is outlined below. An illustration of a consolidated profit and loss account prepared in accordance with Schedule 9 is given in Table 68.

(a) The aggregate amount of provisions for depreciation, or renewals or the diminution in value of fixed assets that has been charged in the profit and loss account. [*9 Sch 14(1)(a)*]. If provision has been made both for depreciation or diminution in value and for the renewal of a particular asset, the amount of the provision for renewal should be disclosed separately. [*9 Sch 14(3)*]. Where the amount charged in the profit and loss account to provide for any fixed asset's depreciation or diminution in value is based on a value other than the value at which that asset is included in the balance sheet, this fact must be stated. [*9 Sch 14(4)*]. This latter provision specifically allows a special category company to use the method of 'split depreciation' discussed in Chapter 5, paragraphs 5.64 to 5.83, although ED 37 proposes to prohibit it.

Table 68: *Illustration of the profit and loss account of a banking company prepared in accordance with Schedule 9.*

Extract from Barclays PLC Report and Accounts 31 December 1984.

Consolidated profit and loss account

Note		1984 £m	1983 £m
3	**Operating profit**	737	582
	Share of profit of associated companies	87	77
	Total Group profit	824	659
	Interest on loan capital and undated capital notes	169	102
	Profit before taxation and extraordinary items	655	557
4	Taxation	342	220
	Profit after taxation	313	337
	Profit attributable to miniority interests in subsidiary companies	22	48
		291	289
5	Extraordinary items:	£m	
	Special provisions for deferred taxation	(543)	
	Transfer from reserves	543	
		—	
	Surplus on reduction of holdings in Group companies	7	
		7	—
6	**Profit attributable to members of Barclays PLC**	298	289
7	Dividends:	£m	£m
	Interim	43	39
	Second interim (1983 final)	46	43
		89	82
8	**Profit retained**	209	207
9	**Earnings per £1 Ordinary stock**	85·1p	84·8p

Table 68 continued.

Note

---

3. Operating profit

Operating profit is arrived at in accordance with the accounting policies explained in note 1, and takes account of the following:

	1984 £m	1983 £m
Income:		
Income, including amortisation of dated securities, from investments (other than associated companies and trade investments):		
Listed	202	219
Unlisted	31	29
Profits on realisation of investments (other than associated companies and trade investments)	14	19
Income from trade investments:		
Listed	1	1
Unlisted	2	3
Charges:		
Interest on deposits and other accounts	5,466	4,615
Interest on long-term borrowings of overseas subsidiary companies	85	58
Amount allocated to trustees for profit sharing schemes	25	20
Depreciation of property and equipment	134	118
Auditors' remuneration, of which £0·3m relates to the Bank (1983 £0·3m)	3	3

(b) The amount of interest on bank loans, overdrafts and other loans that are *wholly* repayable within five years of the balance sheet date. [9 Sch 14(1)(b)].

(c) The amount of interest on any other loans not included in *(b)* above. [9 Sch 14(1)(b)].

(d) The amount of the UK corporation tax charge and the basis used in computing it. Where the UK corporation tax charge would have been greater if double taxation relief had not been received, the gross amount must be disclosed. [9 Sch 14(1)(c), 18(3)]. The disclosure requirements of SSAP 8 must also be complied with. These are considered in Chapter 10, paragraphs 10.94 to 10.96.

(e) The amount of the UK income tax charge and the basis used in computing it. [9 Sch 14(1)(c), 18(3)].

(f) The amount of the taxation charge that has been imposed outside the UK on profits, income and (to the extent to which it has been charged to income) capital gains. [9 Sch 14(1)(c)].

(g) Details of any special circumstances that affect any liability to taxation (whether for the financial year in question or for future years, and, also, whether in respect of profits, or income or capital gains). [9 Sch 18(4)].

(h) Any amount that has been set aside for the redemption of either share capital or loans. [9 Sch 14(1)(d)].

(i) The amount that has been, or is proposed to be, set aside to, or withdrawn from, reserves. [9 Sch 14(1)(e)].

(j) The amount that has been set aside to provisions, or withdrawn from provisions (and not applied for the purpose for which the provision was set up). This applies to provisions other than provisions for depreciation, or renewals, or the diminution in value of fixed assets. [*9 Sch 14(1)(f)*]. The Secretary of State may waive this requirement if the disclosure of this information would be detrimental to the company and the public interest does not require it to be disclosed. Where this requirement is waived, the financial statements must indicate any amount that is stated after taking account of any amount that has been set aside but that, because of this requirement, has not been separately disclosed. [*9 Sch 14(2)*].

(k) The amount of investment income. This must be split between income from listed investments and income from unlisted investments. [*9 Sch 14(1)(g)*].

(l) The amount of rents from land, after deducting ground rents, rates and other outgoings. This information has to be disclosed only if a substantial part of the company's income for the year consists of such rent. [*9 Sch 14(1)(h)*].

(m) The amount that has been charged to revenue in respect of the hire of plant and machinery. [*9 Sch 14(1)(j)*].

(n) The aggregate amount of any dividends that either have been paid or are proposed. [*9 Sch 14(1)(k)*].

(o) The amount of any charge or credit that has arisen because of an event that occurred in a preceding financial year. [*9 Sch 15*].

(p) The amount of the auditors' remuneration (including any expenses the auditors incurred and the company reimbursed). [*9 Sch 16*].

(q) The turnover for the year, and the method used to arrive at the figure for turnover. However, a company does not have to disclose all of its turnover in the following two situations:

   (i) Where some or all of the company's turnover is attributable to the business of banking or discounting, only that part of the turnover that is not attributable to the business of banking or discounting has to be disclosed. Where an amount of turnover has been omitted for this reason, the fact that it has been omitted must be stated.
   (ii) Where the company is neither a holding company nor a subsidiary of another company, and the company's turnover does not exceed £1 million, then it need not disclose its turnover in its financial statements.
   [*9 Sch 17*].

(r) Details of any exceptional or extraordinary items and of the effect of any changes in accounting policy. [*9 Sch 18(6)*]. Compliance with SSAP 6 will ensure that the profit and loss account complies with this requirement of the Act.

Corresponding amounts

13.57 The profit and loss account must include the corresponding amount for the preceding year for every amount shown either in the profit and loss account or in the related notes. [*9 Sch 18(5)*].

Other information to be disclosed in the financial statements

General disclosure

13.58 The financial statements must disclose particulars of any redeemed debentures that the company has power to reissue. [*9 Sch 2(d)*]. Also, if any of the company's debentures are held by a nominee of, or a trustee for, the company, the financial statements must disclose both the nominal amount of those debentures and the amount at which they are stated in the company's books. [*9 Sch 12*].

13.59 Where a *public* special category company has either purchased or acquired its own shares, the notes to the financial statements must disclose certain information. The circumstances in which disclosure must be made, and the details to be disclosed, are exactly the same for a special category company as they are for other companies, except that:

(a) The requirements apply only to *public* special category companies whereas they apply to all Schedule 4 companies (whether public or private). However, these requirements do not apply to 'old public companies'. An 'old public company' is a company that existed on 22 December 1980 (or was incorporated after that date pursuant to an application made before that date) and was not a private company within section 28 of the Companies Act 1948, and that has not subsequently been re-registered as a public company or become a private company. [*CC(CP) s 1(1)*].

(b) Schedule 4 companies must disclose the required information in the directors' report, whereas a special category company may disclose it either in the notes to its financial statements, or in the directors' report, or in some other statement or report annexed to its financial statements.

The circumstances in which disclosure must be made and what must be disclosed (including The Stock Exchange's requirements) are outlined in Chapter 12, paragraphs 12.14 to 12.17. [*9 Sch 13(3)*].

13.60 A special category investment company (as defined in Chapter 14 para 14.03) must give details of any distribution that reduces the amount of the company's net assets to less than the aggregate of its called-up share capital and its undistributable reserves (see Chapter 19 paras 19.89 to 19.93). [*9 Sch 13(4)*].

Accounting policies

13.61   Where the figures concerned are material, the Act requires the accounting policies for the following two areas to be explained:

(a) Stocks and work in progress.

(b) The conversion of foreign currency amounts into sterling.
[9 Sch 13(15)(16)].

13.62   Also, SSAP 2 requires *any* significant accounting policies a company has adopted in preparing its financial statements to be stated in the notes (see also Chapter 6 para 6.37).

13.63   In addition, the notes to the financial statements should disclose the basis used to compute the UK corporation tax liability. [9 Sch 13(17)].

Information not required

13.64   Special category companies are not required to include, in the notes to their financial statements, the following information that is detailed in Schedule 5 to the Act:

(a) Information about companies (that are not subsidiaries) in which the company holds more than 10% of the nominal value of the allotted share capital (as required by paragraph 8 of Schedule 5). However, the information required still has to be given where the company either holds more than 10% of a company's *equity* share capital of any class or holds shares in a body corporate and the amount of the investment as stated in the company's balance sheet exceeds one-tenth of the company's assets as disclosed in that balance sheet (see Chapter 8 paras 8.07 to 8.13).

(b) Financial information about subsidiaries (as required by Part III of Schedule 5 — see Chapter 8 paras 8.39 to 8.43).
[Sec 260(1)].

Corresponding amounts

13.65   It has already been stated in paragraphs 13.18 and 13.57 that, with certain exceptions, corresponding amounts for the preceding financial year must be given for all the amounts that are included in the financial statements in compliance with Schedule 9. This applies also to any information that is included in the notes to the financial statements to comply with Parts V or VI of Schedule 5 (chairman's and directors' emoluments, pensions, compensation for loss of office, and details of higher-paid employees). [Sec 260(2)]. The detail of the information these Parts require to be disclosed is discussed in Chapter 10, paragraphs 10.44 to 10.79.

Merger relief

13.66 If the company has allotted shares in consideration for the issue, or transfer or cancellation of shares in another company, it may be able to take advantage of the statutory provisions relating to 'merger relief' (see further Chapter 18). If a company uses merger relief, it does not have to credit any premium on the shares that it allots to a share premium account. Where a company takes advantage of the merger relief provisions, it must disclose certain additional information in accordance with paragraph 31 of Schedule 9 to the Act in the year the merger takes place and in the two subsequent years. This information is identical to the information that other companies must disclose in accordance with paragraph 75 of Schedule 4. This additional information is detailed in Chapter 18, paragraphs 18.85 to 18.91.

Exemptions available to certain special category companies

13.67 As mentioned in paragraph 13.08, Part III of Schedule 9 to the Act exempts certain types of special category company from many of the provisions of Schedule 9. These exemptions are explained below.

13.68 Although these exemptions are given in the Act, special category companies may still have to comply with some of the provisions to the extent that they form part of standard accounting practice codified in SSAPs. However, the explanatory foreword to SSAPs says that "where accounting standards prescribe specific information to be contained in accounts, such disclosure requirements do not override exemptions from disclosure requirements given to and utilised by special classes of companies under Statute". Consequently, special category companies may, without contravening any requirements of SSAPs, take advantage of those exemptions in Part III of Schedule 9 that relate to *disclosure*.

13.69 However, although these companies do not need to comply with those *disclosure* requirements of SSAPs that conflict with the exemptions given in the Act, they are expected still to comply with the *measurement* requirements of all SSAPs (such as the requirement to provide depreciation on fixed assets that have a limited useful life).

13.70 Much of the information that Part III of Schedule 9 to the Act exempts special category companies from giving would normally be considered essential if the financial statements are to show a true and fair view. Therefore, the Act specifically states that a company's financial statements will not be deemed not to give a true and fair view as required by the Act merely because the company has taken advantage of some or all of the exemptions given in Part III of Schedule 9. [*9 Sch 27(4), 28(2), 29(2)*].

Banking companies

13.71 Before a banking company can take advantage of the exemptions detailed below, it must satisfy the Secretary of State that it ought to benefit from them. [*9 Sch 27(1)*]. The references given in brackets below are to the paragraphs in Schedule 9 to the Act that banking companies need *not* comply with.

Balance sheet exemptions

13.72 In respect of its balance sheet, a banking company need not:

(a) Classify reserves, provisions and liabilities under suitable headings (see para 13.13). (9 Sch 4 except in so far as it relates to assets).

(b) Include fixed assets in the balance sheet at cost (or valuation) less any provisions for depreciation or diminution in value, or disclose the cost and accumulated depreciation of fixed assets (see paras 13.20 to 13.26). (9 Sch 5).

(c) Give the information regarding unlisted investments detailed in paragraph 13.37. (9 Sch 6).

(d) Show the aggregate amounts of reserves and provisions and the movements on such reserves and provisions during the year (see paras 13.52 and 13.53). (9 Sch 7,8).

(e) Disclose the amount of any provision for deferred taxation. (9 Sch 9).

(f) Give details of the aggregate amount of bank loans and overdrafts and the aggregate amount of other loans that are repayable (either wholly or partly) more than five years after the balance sheet date, and of the repayment terms and rates of interest applicable to such loans (see para 13.40). (9 Sch 10(1)(d),(4)).

(g) Give the information detailed in paragraph 13.29 that must normally be stated if any fixed assets are shown at a valuation. (9 Sch 13(9)).

(h) Give details of additions and disposals of fixed assets (see para 13.27). (9 Sch 13(10)).

(i) Analyse land between freehold, long leasehold and short leasehold (see para 13.28). (9 Sch 13(11)).

(j) Show the aggregate market value, and the stock exchange value (if applicable) of listed investments (see para 13.35). (9 Sch 13(13)).

(k) Give details of any amount that has previously been provided for deferred tax but has been used for an alternative purpose during the year (see para 13.55). (9 Sch 13(14)).

[*9 Sch 27(2)(a)*].

Profit and loss account exemptions

13.73   In respect of its profit and loss account, a banking company need not:

(a) Disclose the amount of any depreciation charge and any amount provided for either renewals or the diminution in value of fixed assets (see para 13.56*(a)*). (9 Sch 14(1)(a),(3)).

(b) Show the amount of interest on loans, giving the analysis described in paragraph 13.56*(b)* and *(c)*. (9 Sch 14(1)(b)).

(c) Disclose details concerning the tax charge and how it is computed (see para 13.56*(d)* to *(g)*). (9 Sch 14(1)(c), 18(3)(4)).

(d) Disclose any amount set aside for the redemption of either share capital or loans. (9 Sch 14(1)(d)).

(e) Give details of the amount set aside to, or proposed to be set aside to, or withdrawn from, reserves or provisions (see para 13.56*(i)* and *(j)*). (9 Sch 14(1)(e)(f), (2)).

(f) Disclose the amounts of income from both listed investments and unlisted investments. (9 Sch 14(1)(g)).

(g) Show any amount charged to revenue for the hire of plant and machinery. (9 Sch 14(1)(j)).

(h) State, if this is so, that an amount charged for either depreciation or the diminution in value of any asset has been based on a value other than the value at which that asset is included in the balance sheet (see para 13.56*(a)*). (9 Sch 14(4)).

(i) Show the turnover for the year or the method used to compute turnover (see para 13.56*(q)*). (9 Sch 17).

(j) Give details of either any exceptional or extraordinary items or any items that have been affected by a change in accounting policy (see para 13.56*(r)*). (9 Sch 18(6)).
[*9 Sch 27(2)(b)*].

13.74   If a company takes advantage of the exemption that allows reserves and provisions not to be stated separately and described as such (para 13.72*(a)* above), then the financial statements must identify any heading in the balance sheet that contains such a reserve or provision. They must also explain how these reserves and provisions have been treated in the profit and loss account. [*9 Sch 27(3)*].

An example of a group that takes advantage of some of these exemptions is given in Table 69.

Table 69: *Illustration of a group that takes advantage of the exemptions from disclosure available to banking companies.*

Extract from The Union Discount Company of London, p.l.c. Annual Report 31 December 1984.

Accounting policies extract

Neither the Group nor the Company is required to comply with the accounting and disclosure provisions of Part 1 of the Companies Act 1981 [*now Part VII, Chapter I of the Companies Act 1985*]. The Financial Statements are drawn up in accordance with Sections 149A and 152A of, and Schedule 8A to, the Companies Act 1948 [*now, Part VII, Chapter II of, and Schedule 9 to, the Companies Act 1985*].

Notes

2   The Group is not required to disclose its turnover.

3   The profit for the year of £7,940,953 is arrived at after providing for rebate, taxation and making a transfer to Inner Reserve.

4   The additional provision of £3,600,000 has been made as a result of the changes in rates of corporation tax and capital allowances introduced by the Finance Act 1984. After making this charge and taking into account the sums already set aside, the Directors consider that the Group has adequate provisions to meet its likely future tax liabilities.

Balance sheet extract

	Note	1984 £	1983 £
FIXED ASSETS			
Freehold premises	1 and 14	11,750,000	11,500,000
Equipment, fixtures and fittings	1	1,177,462	1,097,818

Accounting policies extract

1 *(f)* i Freehold property is included at a professional valuation dated 31st December, 1984. Depreciation is provided at the rate of 2%.

ii Equipment, fixtures and fittings are stated at cost less accumulated depreciation. Depreciation is provided on a straight line basis at the following rates: ancillary plant 5%, fixtures and fittings 10%, and other equipment 20% and 33%.

Note

14 A professional valuation has been made as at 31st December, 1984 of the Company's freehold property, 39-42 Cornhill, by Messrs. St. Quintin, Chartered Surveyors, on an open market basis. The property has been included in the Financial Statements at its updated valuation of £11,750,000 resulting in an increase to the Revaluation Reserve of £349,662. No account has been taken of any capital gains tax liability that would arise if the property were disposed of at this valuation.

Insurance companies

13.75 Subject to any directions by the Secretary of State (see para 13.79 below), any insurance company that is a special category company may take advantage of the following exemptions.

Balance sheet exemptions

13.76 In respect of its balance sheet, an insurance company need not:

(a) Classify reserves, provisions, liabilities *or assets* under suitable headings (see para 13.13). (9 Sch 4(1)).

(b) Analyse assets between fixed assets, current assets and those that are neither fixed nor current (see para 13.15). (9 Sch 4(2)).

(c) State the method that has been used to arrive at the amount for each category of fixed asset. (9 Sch 4(3)).

(d) Include fixed assets in the balance sheet at cost (or valuation) less any provisions for depreciation or diminution in value, or disclose the cost and accumulated depreciation of fixed assets (see paras 13.20 to 13.26). (9 Sch 5).

(e) Give the information detailed in paragraph 13.29 that must normally be stated if any fixed assets are shown at a valuation. (9 Sch 13(9)).

(f) Give details of additions and disposals of fixed assets (see para 13.27). (9 Sch 13(10)).

(g) Analyse land between freehold, long leasehold and short leasehold (see para 13.28). (9 Sch 13(11)).

(h) Analyse investments between listed investments (including further analysis between those listed on a recognised stock exchange and other listed investments) and unlisted investments (see para 13.33). (9 Sch 10(1)(a), (3)).

(i) Show the aggregate market value, and the stock exchange value (if applicable) of listed investments (see para 13.35). (9 Sch 13(13)).

(j) Give the information regarding unlisted investments detailed in paragraph 13.37. (9 Sch 6).

(k) Show the aggregate amounts of reserves and provisions and the movements on such reserves and provisions during the year (see paras 13.52 and 13.53). (9 Sch 7,8).

(l) Give particulars of any charge on the company's assets given to secure the liabilities of any other person. (9 Sch 13(6)).

(m) Give details of any other contingent liabilities. (9 Sch 13(7)).

(n) State, if this is so, that the directors consider that the realisable value of some current assets is less than the value at which they are included in the balance sheet (see para 13.39). (9 Sch 13(12)).
[*9 Sch 28(1)(a)*].

Profit and loss account exemptions

13.77 In respect of its profit and loss account, an insurance company need not:

(a) Disclose the amount of any depreciation charge and any amount provided for either renewals or the diminution in value of fixed assets (see para 13.56*(a)*). (9 Sch 14(1)(a),(3)).

(b) Give details of the amount set aside to, or proposed to be set aside to, or withdrawn from, reserves or provisions (see para 13.56*(i)* and *(j))*. (9 Sch 14(1)(e)(f),(2)).

(c) Disclose the amounts of income from both listed investments and unlisted investments. (9 Sch 14(1)(g)).

(d) Disclose the amount of rent received (see para 13.56*(l)*). (9 Sch 14(1)(h)).

(e) Show any amount charged to revenue for the hire of plant and machinery. (9 Sch 14(1)(j)).

(f) State, if this is so, that an amount charged for either depreciation or the diminution in value of any asset has been based on a value other than the value at which that asset is included in the balance sheet (see para 13.56*(a)*). (9 Sch 14(4)).
[*9 Sch 28(1)(b)*].

An illustration of an insurance company that takes advantage of some of these exemptions is given in Table 70.

13.78 As with banking companies, if an insurance company takes advantage of the exemption that allows it not to state its reserves and provisions separately or to describe them as such, its financial statements must identify any heading in the balance sheet that contains such a reserve or provision. The financial statements must also explain how such reserves and provisions have been treated in the profit and loss account. [*9 Sch 28(1)*].

13.79 The Secretary of State may direct that an insurance company whose business includes a substantial amount of business *other than* insurance business, will not be entitled to benefit from all or some of the exemptions detailed above. Alternatively, he may direct that the company may benefit from the exemptions in respect of some of its business (for example, its insurance business), but may not benefit in respect of the remainder of its business. [*9 Sch 28(1)*].

> **Table 70: Illustration of an insurance group that prepares its con-
> solidated balance sheet and profit and loss account in ac-
> cordance with Schedule 9 and its holding company's balance
> sheet in accordance with Schedule 4.**
>
> *Extract from Prudential Corporation plc Annual Report and Accounts
> 31 December 1984.*
>
> **Accounting policy**
>
> **(a) Disclosure requirements**
> The consolidated accounts are prepared in accordance with the provisions of sections
> 149A and 152A of and schedule 8A to the Companies Act 1948 [*now, Part VII, Chapter
> II of, and Schedule 9 to, the Companies Act 1985*]. They are not required to comply
> with the accounting and disclosure provisions of the Companies Act 1981. The balance
> sheet of the Company on page 32 is prepared in accordance with section 149 of and
> schedule 8 to the Companies Act 1948 [*now, Part VII, Chapter I of, and Schedule 4
> to, the Companies Act 1985*].
>
> The Company has taken advantage of the exemption from presenting its own profit and
> loss account.
>
> As most of the Company's subsidiaries are insurance companies, the group accounts
> do not disclose certain information, some relating to provisions and reserves, which they
> are exempt from disclosing under the provisions of the Companies Acts 1948 to 1981.

Shipping companies

13.80   Any shipping company that is a special category company may take
advantage of those exemptions that are detailed below.

Balance sheet exemptions

13.81   In respect of its balance sheet, a shipping company need not:

(a) Classify reserves, provisions and liabilities under suitable headings
(see para 13.13). (9 Sch 4 except in so far as it relates to assets).

(b) Include fixed assets in the balance sheet at cost (or valuation) less
any provisions for depreciation or diminution in value, or disclose
the cost and accumulated depreciation of fixed assets (see paras
13.20 to 13.26). (9 Sch 5).

(c) Show the aggregate amounts of reserves and provisions and the
movements on such reserves and provisions during the year (see
paras 13.52 and 13.53). (9 Sch 7,8).

(d) Give the information detailed in paragraph 13.29 that must normally be stated if any fixed assets are shown at a valuation. (9 Sch
13(9)).

(e) Give details of additions and disposals of fixed assets (see para
13.27). (9 Sch 13(10)).
[*9 Sch 29(1)(a)*].

Profit and loss account exemptions

13.82 In respect of its profit and loss account, a shipping company need not:

(a) Disclose the amount of any depreciation charge and any amount provided for either renewals or the diminution in value of fixed assets (see para 13.56*(a)*). (9 Sch 14(1)(a),(3)).

(b) Give details of the amount set aside to, or proposed to be set aside to, or withdrawn from, reserves or provisions (see para 13.56*(i)* and *(j)*). (9 Sch 14(1)(e)(f),(2)).

(c) State, if this is so, that an amount charged for either depreciation or the diminution in value of any asset has been based on a value other than the value at which that asset is included in the balance sheet (see para 13.56*(a)*). (9 Sch 14(4)).

(d) Show the turnover for the year or the method used to compute turnover (see para 13.56(q)). (9 Sch 17).
[*9 Sch 29(1)(b)*].

Special category group accounts

13.83 As mentioned in paragraph 13.04, a group that includes a special category company may, if it so wishes, prepare its group accounts in accordance with Schedule 9 to the Act rather than in accordance with Schedule 4. [*Sec 257(3)*]. However, if the holding company is not a special category company, its own balance sheet and related notes must be prepared in accordance with Schedule 4.

13.84 With certain exceptions, the requirement to prepare group accounts, the methods that should be used to produce them, and the form and the content of both the holding company's own accounts and the group accounts are exactly the same for a special category group as for a normal group. Consequently, they generally follow the requirements set out in Chapter 17. However, the differences from these requirements are as follows:

(a) Special category group accounts should comply, so far as practicable, with the requirements of Schedule 9, as opposed to the requirements of Schedule 4, both as to their form and content and as to the information that they must disclose in the notes. They should comply as if they were the financial statements of an actual special category company (as outlined earlier in this chapter). [*Sec 259(3); 9 Sch 22*].

(b) A holding company of a special category group that takes advantage of the same exemption that is available to a normal group not to include its own profit and loss account in the consolidated financial statements it prepares in accordance with Schedule 9 (see Chapter 17 paras 17.24 to 17.26) does not have to state, in a note, that it has taken advantage of this exemption. [*Sec 258(5)*]. However,

this note still has to be given where the holding company's balance sheet is prepared in accordance with Schedule 4 to the Act. [*Sec 228(7)*].

(c) If the holding company (including any intermediary holding company) is a special category company, the aggregate amount of its assets that consist of shares in, or amounts owing from, the company's subsidiaries should be shown separately from all other assets in the holding company's balance sheet. Shares should be shown separately from indebtedness. Similarly, the aggregate amount owing to the company's subsidiaries should be shown separately from all the company's other liabilities. [*9 Sch 19(2)*]. However, the holding company may show its investment in, and loans to and from, its subsidiaries as one aggregate figure. But, this is provided that the aggregate figure is analysed in the notes to the financial statements in such a way as to give the information required above. This type of disclosure is not acceptable for a normal holding company (see Chapter 17 para 17.11). The above requirements apply also where the subsidiary is excluded from consolidated financial statements. [*9 Sch 25(a)*]. The general requirements of Schedule 9 regarding the valuation and disclosure of investments do not apply to investments in subsidiaries. [*9 Sch 19(2)(a)(b)*].

(d) A special category company that is a subsidiary of another company (whether or not it is itself a holding company), must show separately, in its balance sheet, the aggregate amount that it owes to any holding company or any fellow subsidiaries, and also the aggregate amount that such companies owe to it. Each of these two amounts should be split between indebtedness in respect of debentures and otherwise. The balance sheet should also disclose the aggregate amount of any shares in fellow subsidiaries. [*9 Sch 20*].

(e) Where subsidiaries are not consolidated or where group accounts are not submitted (see Chapter 17 paras 17.60 to 17.62), certain information has to be given in respect of the excluded subsidiaries. A statement must be annexed to the holding company's balance sheet and that statement must show separately the aggregate amounts of post-acquisition profits of those subsidiaries that are both *dealt with* and *not dealt with* in the holding company's financial statements. These aggregate amounts must be split between:

(i) The amount for the respective financial years of the subsidiaries excluded, ending with or during the holding company's financial year.

(ii) The amount for the previous financial years of the subsidiaries excluded, from the time they became subsidiaries of the holding company.

[*9 Sch 19(4)(b)(c),(5), 25(b)*].

This requirement compares with that in Schedule 4 to the Act for the aggregate investment in such companies to be stated in the holding company's financial statements by the equity method of valuation (see Chapter 17 para 17.70). However, this information is not required to be given where the subsidiary is wholly owned and there is annexed to the balance sheet a statement that in the directors' opinion the aggregate value of the investment in the subsidiary (including amounts due from the subsidiary) is not less than the subsidiary's net assets. [*9 Sch 19(6)*].

The directors' report

13.85   The directors' report of a special category company does not have to include a fair review of the development of the business of the company and its subsidiaries during the year, and of their position at the end of the year. Instead, the directors have to report on the 'state of the company's affairs'. As with other companies, the directors must state, in their report, the amount that they recommend should be paid as a dividend, and the amount that they propose to carry to reserves. [*Sec 261(2)*].

13.86   The directors' report of special category companies is allowed to contain information that would otherwise be given elsewhere in the financial statements. The directors' report must show the corresponding amount for any such item, unless it would not have been necessary to disclose the corresponding amount if the item had been included elsewhere in the financial statements. In addition, if an item is included in the directors' report that would normally have been included elsewhere in the financial statements, the directors' report must be treated as forming part of the financial statements. Consequently, it must be audited, but only to the extent that it gives information that would otherwise be shown elsewhere in the financial statements. [*Sec 261(3)(4)*].

13.87   The directors' report of a special category company must contain the same information that other companies are required to disclose in respect of the following matters:

(a) Directors' interests in the shares in, or the debentures of, the company or another group company (see Chapter 12 paras 12.29 to 12.38). Although other companies may give this information either in the directors' report or in the notes to the financial statements, a special category company *must* give the information in the directors' report. [7 Sch 2].

(b) Political and charitable gifts (see Chapter 12 paras 12.25 to 12.28). [*7 Sch 3*].

(c) Employment of disabled persons (see Chapter 12 para 12.20). [*7 Sch 9*].

(d) Health, safety and welfare at work of the company's employees (see Chapter 12 paras 12.21 and 12.22). [*7 Sch 10*].

(e) Employee involvement (see Chapter 12 paras 12.23 and 12.24). *[7 Sch 11]*.

[Sec 261(5)].

13.88 A special category banking company that has *not* satisfied the Secretary of State that it ought to be exempt from certain of the requirements of Part I of Schedule 9 to the Act (see para 13.71) must give details also of the following:

(a) Significant changes in fixed assets (see Chapter 12 para 12.39*(d)*). *[7 Sch 1(1)]*.

(b) The difference between the book value and the market value of interests in land (see Chapter 12 para 12.39*(e)*). *[7 Sch 1(2)]*.

[Sec 261(5)].

13.89 In addition, Schedule 10 to the Act sets out certain information that the directors' report of *all* special category companies must contain. This information is considered below.

Issues of shares or debentures

13.90 If the company has issued any shares or debentures during the year, the directors' report must state:

(a) The reason for making the issue.

(b) The classes of shares or debentures issued, and, in respect of each class of shares or debentures issued:

   (i) The number of shares or the amount of debentures issued.
   (ii) The consideration the company received for the issue.
   [10 Sch 1(1)(2)].

Disaggregated information

13.91 A special category company whose turnover for the year exceeds £1 million, or a special category company that is either the holding company or the subsidiary of another body corporate (but is not a company with subsidiaries that prepares consolidated financial statements) must disclose, in the directors' report, the information set out below. However, this requirement applies only if the company carries on business of two or more classes that, in the directors' opinion, are substantially different. The information required is:

(a) A description of each class of business.

(b) The proportion of turnover for the year that is attributable to each class of business.

(c) The amount of profit or loss before taxation that is, in the directors' opinion, attributable to each class of business.

13.92 The disclosure required above excludes turnover and profit that is attributable to the classes of banking or discounting. [*10 Sch 2*].

13.93 If the special category company is a company with subsidiaries, and if it prepares consolidated financial statements, then the directors' report should give the information required in paragraph 13.91 above in total in respect of the companies that are dealt with in the consolidated financial statements. [*10 Sch 3*].

13.94 If, in the directors' opinion, two classes of business do not differ substantially from each other, they should be treated as one class. [*10 Sch 4*].

13.95 If the special category company is either listed on The Stock Exchange or traded on the USM, it will have to comply also with The Stock Exchange's Continuing Obligations or its General Undertaking as appropriate as to the disclosure of disaggregated information for turnover and profit. This requirement is discussed in Chapter 10, paragraph 10.10.

Employees and their remuneration

13.96 The directors' report of a special category company must disclose:

   (a) The average number of people the company employed in Great Britain during each week of the year. This figure should be calculated by first adding up the total number of people employed under contracts of service for each week of the year. These weekly totals should then be added, and the total should be divided by the number of weeks in the year.

   (b) The total remuneration paid or payable in respect of the year to these people. For this purpose, remuneration is the gross remuneration, including bonuses, that was paid or was payable.
   [*10 Sch 5,7*].

13.97 If, at the end of the financial year, the company has subsidiaries, the directors' report should give the same information as above. But the information it gives should relate to both the company and its subsidiaries and not the company alone. [*10 Sch 6*].

13.98 However, none of this information has to be given if either the company is a wholly-owned subsidiary of another company incorporated in Great Britain or the company (together with subsidiaries, if applicable) employs on average fewer than 100 people each week in Great Britain. [*10 Sch 8*].

Other matters

13.99 The directors' report must contain details of any other matters that, although not specifically required, are material to the shareholders' appreciation of the state of the company's affairs. But the directors do not have to disclose any matters that, in their opinion, would be harmful to the business of the company or any of its subsidiaries. [*10 Sch 9*].

Mixed groups

13.100 A situation may arise where a holding company prepares its financial statements in accordance with Schedule 4 to the Act, but the group accounts are prepared in accordance with Schedule 9 (because one or more subsidiaries are special category companies).

13.101 Because the directors' report is attached to the holding company's balance sheet, it should comply with the requirements of Schedule 7 to the Act. However, because the group accounts are prepared in accordance with Schedule 9, the directors' report should contain also the information required by paragraphs 2 to 6 of Schedule 10. These paragraphs require the disaggregation of turnover and profit or loss before taxation by class of business, and also the disclosure of the average number of employees and their aggregate remuneration (for example, see Table 71). [*Sec 235(6)*]. The information to be disclosed is outlined in paragraphs 13.91 to 13.98 above.

Table 71: Illustration of the additional information required to be given in the directors' report.

Extract from Prudential Corporation plc Annual Report and Accounts 31 December 1984.

Directors' report extract

Number of employees
The average number of persons employed by the Company and its subsidiaries in the United Kingdom in each week of 1984 was 22,464 and the total remuneration was £244·4m.

Auditors' consideration of the directors' report

13.102 Auditors are not required to consider the directors' report of a special category company. Consequently, they do not have to report if, in their opinion, the directors' report is inconsistent with the financial statements. [*Sec 261(7)*]. Nevertheless, it is generally accepted that auditors should review the directors' report to ensure that the views it gives are neither misleading nor incompatible with the financial statements. Also, as stated in paragraph 13.86 above, where information that would normally be shown in the company's financial statements is included in the directors' report, the auditors' report should cover that information.

Auditors' report

13.103 In respect of the financial statements of a special category company (other than one that is not entitled to benefit from, or that has not taken advantage of, the exemptions from Part I of Schedule 9 to the Act that are set out in Part III of that Schedule), the auditors are *not* required to report whether, in their opinion, the balance sheet and the profit and loss account give a true and fair view both of the state of the company's affairs at the end of the year and of the company's profit or loss for the period. However, they must still report whether, in their opinion, the balance sheet and the profit and loss account have been properly prepared in accordance with the Act. [*Sec 262*].

Distributable profits of a special category company

13.104 Distributable profits are determined by reference to a company's *relevant accounts* (as discussed in Chapter 19). However, a special category company's *relevant accounts* will normally not be prepared in accordance with the rules in Schedule 4 to the Act (in particular, as regards the balance sheet formats).

13.105 Consequently, certain of the amounts that are normally used to determine distributable profits either may not appear in a special category company's *relevant accounts*, or may not comply with the definitions given in Schedule 4. For example, fixed assets are not defined in Schedule 9, and the definition of provisions in Schedule 9 differs slightly from that in Schedule 4.

13.106 Schedule 11 to the Act modifies the rules for determining distributable profits when the *relevant accounts* are those of a special category company. [*Sec 279*]. The principal provisions of Schedule 11 are set out below:

(a) If an asset is included in a special category company's *relevant accounts* as neither a fixed asset nor a current asset, then it shall be treated as a fixed asset for the purpose of:

(i) Determining the distributable profits of a special category investment company (see Chapter 19 paras 19.89 to 19.93). [*11 Sch 2(b)*].

(ii) Determining whether a provision for the diminution in value of an asset is realised or unrealised (see Chapter 19 paras 19.34 to 19.52). [*11 Sch 7(b)*].

(b) Development costs that have been capitalised and included as an asset in the balance sheet do not have to be treated as a realised revenue loss (see Chapter 19 para 19.76). [*11 Sch 3*].

(c) Provisions stated in accordance with the definition in Schedule 9 to the Act should be used to calculate the distributable profits of a special category company (as opposed to provisions stated in accordance with the tighter definition in Schedule 4 — see para 13.48 and Chapter 9 para 9.45). [*11 Sch 1,2(a),4(a),7(a)*].

(d) The requirement that the *relevant accounts* should be properly prepared (whether they be annual financial statements, or interim accounts or initial accounts) does not prevent a special category company from taking advantage of the exemptions in Part III of Schedule 9 in preparing those financial statements (see paras 13.67 to 13.82). [*11 Sch 5(a),6(b)*].

13.107 Realised and distributable profits are considered in more detail in Chapter 19.

CHAPTER 14

INVESTMENT COMPANIES AND APPROVED INVESTMENT TRUSTS

Chapter 14

Investment Companies and Approved Investment Trusts

Introduction

14.01 This chapter considers the special provisions of the Act that relate to investment companies. If an investment company is listed, it must also comply with the further requirements set out in The Stock Exchange's Continuing Obligations.

14.02 An approved investment trust is a particular type of investment company that has satisfied the Inland Revenue that it complies with certain conditions. Investment trusts have an advantage over other investment companies in that they are entitled to various tax concessions. However, the Continuing Obligations impose additional requirements on investment trusts that are more onerous than those imposed on other investment companies.

Definition of an investment company

14.03 The Act defines an investment company as a *public* company that has given notice in the prescribed form to the Registrar of Companies of its intention to carry on business as an investment company. In addition, it has, since the date of that notice, complied with the following requirements [*Sec 266(1)*]:

(a) The company's business consists of investing its funds principally in securities, with the aim of spreading the investment risk and of giving its members the benefit of the results of its management of its funds. [*Sec 266(2)(a)*].

(b) None of the company's holdings in companies (other than in approved investment trusts — see para 14.11 below) represents more than 15% of its total holdings. [*Sec 266(2)(b), (4)*]. This requirement does not apply where an investment's value exceeds the 15% limit only because it has been revalued.

(c) The distribution of the company's capital profits is prohibited by either its memorandum or its articles of association. [*Sec 266(2)(c)*].

(d) The company has not retained (during any accounting reference period) more than 15% of its investment income, unless it was prohibited from making a distribution under the provisions of the Act. [*Sec 266(2)(d)*].

337

14.04   The Act requires that investment companies must indicate their status both on their letters and on their order forms. [*Sec 351(1)(c)*].

14.05   The Secretary of State has specific powers to introduce regulations that extend the provisions relating to investment companies to other companies whose principal business consists of investing their funds in securities, or land or other assets, with the aim of spreading their investment risk and of giving their members the benefit of the results of their management of the assets. [*Sec 267(1)*]. In this connection, he may make regulations applying:

   (a) Different provisions for different classes of companies. [*Sec 267(2)(a)*].

   (b) Any transitional and supplemental provisions that he thinks necessary. [*Sec 267(2)(a)*].

14.06   A company will cease to be an investment company if it revokes the notice that it has previously given to the Registrar of Companies. It may do this by giving notice to him, in the prescribed form, that it no longer wishes to be an investment company. [*Sec 266(3)*].

Special provisions that apply to investment companies

14.07   The Act specifies four provisions that apply to investment companies:

   (a) Any profit or loss that arises from including investments in an investment company's balance sheet, either at their market value or at some appropriate valuation other than historical cost, does not need to be either credited or debited to a revaluation reserve, but may be either credited or debited to any other reserve. [*4 Sch 71(1)*]. The effect of this provision is to exempt any such profits or losses from the restrictions that the Act places on the uses of the revaluation reserve (see Chapter 5 para 5.08). However, the use of these profits or losses will usually be restricted by the company's articles of association.

   (b) Where an investment company writes down the value of its fixed asset investments to account for either a temporary or a permanent fall in value, the amount of this write-down need not be charged in the profit and loss account. This applies, however, only if either the write-down is charged to a reserve account to which revaluation surpluses that arose on the revaluation of investments have been credited, or the write-down is disclosed separately in the balance sheet under the sub-heading 'Other reserves'. [*4 Sch 71(2)(3)*]. It appears, therefore, that in this situation it is acceptable for an investment company to have a debit balance on either of these reserves.

   (c) An investment company must disclose, in the notes to its financial statements, the amount of any distribution it makes that reduces the amount of its net assets to less than the aggregate of its called-up share capital and its undistributable reserves. For this purpose, 'undistributable reserves' are defined in the same way as they are for the purpose of determining distributable profits (see Chapter 19 para 19.07). 'Net assets' are defined as the aggregate of the company's assets less the aggregate of its liabilities. 'Liabilities' include any provision for liabilities or charges (as defined in Chapter 9 para 9.45). [*4 Sch 72*].

The Act permits investment companies that are listed on a recognised stock exchange to make distributions either on the basis of the same capital maintenance test that applies to all public companies, or on the basis of an asset ratio test. [*Sec 265(1)*]. These provisions and the way in which they apply to investment companies are considered in detail in Chapter 19, paragraphs 19.89 to 19.93.

The effect that the above provision has on an investment company is that where it makes a distribution on the basis of the asset ratio test, it must disclose, in its financial statements, the amount of any distribution it has lawfully made, but that would have been unlawful if any other public company had made it.

(d) Where the holding company of a group of companies is an investment company, the consolidated financial statements (or the group accounts) can be prepared taking advantage of those exemptions available to investment companies that are outlined in *(a)* and *(b)* above. [*4 Sch 74*].

Where an investment company wishes to take profits or losses on the sale of its investments to a capital reserve, SSAP 6 requires that they should first be taken to the profit and loss account and then transferred from that account to the capital reserve. However, this requirement does not apply to investment trusts (see para 14.14*(e)* below). [*SSAP 6 para 10*].

Listed investment companies

14.08 An investment company must be a public company, but it may be either listed or unlisted. If an investment company seeks a listing on The Stock Exchange, then it must comply with certain conditions that are set out in section 10, Chapter 3 of the book, 'Admission of Securities to Listing' (the 'Yellow Book'), before it will be admitted for listing.

14.09 The main conditions which an investment company must comply with are as follows:

(a) The company must undertake not to take legal control or management control of any of its investments (except in so far as the investments take the form of partnerships, or joint ventures or other forms of non-corporate investment).

(b) Not more than 20% of the group's assets (before deducting borrowed money) may be invested in the securities of any one company.

(c) Dividends must be paid only out of income received from investments.

(d) Shareholders' approval must be sought to realise any investment that has a directors' valuation amounting to 50% or more of the investment portfolio.

(e) Where the company has a policy to subscribe for shares in another company or fund which itself invests in a portfolio of securities, it must ensure that its directors comprise a majority of the directors of that company or fund. This is to ensure that the investment company's directors control that company's or fund's underlying policies. [*CO 44*].

14.10 When an investment company receives a listing on The Stock Exchange, it must give the following additional information in its financial statements:

(a) A summary of (at least) the investment company's ten largest investments, with corresponding amounts. In addition, the investing company should summarise any other investments that it owns that have a value greater than 5% of its assets. The type of information that is required to be summarised is as follows:

    (i) A brief description of the business.
    (ii) The proportion of the company's share capital that is owned.
    (iii) The cost of the investment.
    (iv) The directors' valuation of the investment.
    (v) The dividends received during the year (with an indication of any abnormal dividends).
    (vi) The dividend cover or the underlying earnings.
    (vii) Any extraordinary items.
    (viii) The net assets attributable to the investment (that is, the company's share of the net assets of the company that it has invested in).

An illustration of these disclosure requirements is given in Table 72.

(b) An analysis of any provision for the diminution in value of its investments. The notes should state which investments have been provided against, and also:

    (i) The original cost of the investment concerned.
    (ii) The amount of the provision made against the investment.
    (iii) The book value of the investment after the provision has been made.

(c) An analysis of realised and unrealised surpluses, with a separate statement of profits and losses (whether realised or not) split between listed and unlisted investments.
[*CO 21(r)*].

Table 72: Illustration of a summary of the information required by The Stock Exchange's Continuing Obligations of an investment company's largest investments.

Extract from Abingworth plc Annual Report six months ended 30 June 1983.

Fifteen largest investments extract

Holding	Percentage of equity	Cost	Valuation as at 30th June 1983
Penta Systems Inc.			
140,000 shares of common stock	3·4%	$490,000	$1,679,125

Penta is a quoted U.S. company involved in the development and marketing of computer turnkey systems based upon the company's applications software for composition, processing and electronic pagination of printed material.

For the 15 month period to 31 December 1982 sales were $16·2 million and net income $1·5 million (including an extraordinary gain of $206,000) or $0·44 per share compared with sales of $10·4 million and net income of $1·2 million or $0·35 per share for the twelve months to 30 September 1981. In the six months to 30 June 1983, sales amounted to $8·5 million against $6·2 million in the previous year and net income was $420,000, or $0·11 per share, against $292,000 or $0·08 per share.

J. N. Nichols (Vimto) plc			
237,200 25p ordinary shares	4·5%	£297,956	£1,079,260

J. N. Nichols (Vimto) is a listed UK company involved in the manufacture, packing and sale of soft drinks. Its principal product is Vimto, which is sold as a cordial or aerated in bottles or cans. Abingworth first invested in the company in 1978.

For the year ended 31 December 1982 sales were £16·3 million and pre tax profit was £2·7 million against £12·1 million and £2·6 million in 1981. Earnings per share were 26·2 pence per share compared with 25·5 pence per share.

For the six months to 30 June 1983 sales rose to £10·0 million from £8·3 million in the comparable period in 1982 while pre-tax income was £2·2 million (including £153,000 profit on sale of investments) compared to £1·6 million. Earnings per share were 19·4 pence per share compared with 14·6 pence per share. During the period to 30 June a gross dividend of £20,331·43 was received.

Approved investment trusts

14.11 An investment company may become an 'approved investment trust' by satisfying the Inland Revenue that it complies with the conditions that are set out in the Income and Corporation Taxes Act 1970, section 359 (as amended by the Finance Act 1972, section 93(6)). These can be summarised as follows:

(a) It is resident in the UK.

(b) Its income is derived either wholly or mainly from shares or securities.

(c) No investment represents more than 15% of the value of the investing company's assets (unless that investment is in another investment trust). This requirement does not apply where an investment exceeds the 15% limit only because it has been subsequently revalued.

(d) It is a public company and its shares are listed.

(e) Its memorandum or its articles of association prohibit the distribution by way of dividend of capital profits realised on the sale of investments.

(f) It retains no more than 15% of its income.

(g) It is not a 'close' company.

14.12   These conditions are very similar to those that a company must satisfy in order to qualify as an investment company under the Companies Act. However, an investment trust must satisfy the Inland Revenue that it complies with these conditions. The main advantage of qualifying as an 'approved investment trust' is that chargeable capital gains are not taxable.

14.13   The Stock Exchange imposes certain additional conditions in section 10, Chapter 3 of the Yellow Book that an approved investment trust must comply with before it will be accepted for listing as an approved investment trust. The conditions that apply to the investment policy of newly-formed investment trusts are as follows:

(a) Not more than 10% of the group's assets (before deducting borrowed money) may be either lent to or invested in the securities of any one company (other than another approved investment trust). (This restricts the condition in paragraph 14.11*(c)* above).

(b) Not more than 25% of the group's assets (before deducting borrowed money) may be invested in total in securities not listed on any recognised stock exchange (as defined in Chapter 8 para 8.04) or quoted on the NASDAQ system in the US or Canada.

(c) Not more than 25% of the group's assets (before deducting borrowed money) may be invested in total in holdings in which the group's interest amounts to 20% or more of the total equity capital (including any capital that has an element of equity) of any one listed company. However, this restriction does not apply if such investments are in other approved investment trusts.

14.14   For such an investment trust, The Stock Exchange's Continuing Obligations require the trust's financial statements to give the following information:

(a) A statement that the Inland Revenue has approved the company as an approved investment trust, specifying the last accounting period in respect of which such approval has been given, and confirming that the company has subsequently conducted its affairs in such a way that it will continue to be approved (for example, see Table 73). A new investment trust must state that it will direct its affairs so as to enable it to seek approval.

Table 73: Disclosure of an investment trust's status.

Extract from Globe Investment Trust P.L.C. Annual Review Report and Accounts 31 March 1984.

Directors' report extract

Review of the business
The Inland Revenue has approved the Company as an investment trust for the purposes of Section 359 of the Income and Corporation Taxes Act 1970 (as amended) for the year ended 31st March 1983 and its affairs have been directed so as to enable it to continue to seek such approval.

(b) An analysis of the investment portfolio:

   (i) By broad geographical area (based on the countries of incorporation of the companies that the investment trust has invested in).
   (ii) By broad industrial or commercial sector.
   (iii) Between equity capital, securities that have an equity element (for example, convertible loan stock) and fixed income securities.

   A graphical analysis of this type of information is given in Table 74.

(c) A list of the investment trust's largest investments by market value, stating the market value for each such investment. An illustration of this disclosure is given in Table 75.

(d) An analysis of income between:

   (i) Dividends.
   (ii) Interest.
   (iii) Other income (distinguishing, where material, between underwriting income and the results of subsidiaries' dealings).

   An example of this disclosure is given in Table 76.

(e) An analysis, where material to an appreciation of the investment trust's financial position, of realised and unrealised profits and losses, split between listed and unlisted investments. In addition, SSAP 6 says that it may not be appropriate to deal with such realised or unrealised surpluses and deficits in the profit and loss account and that where this is so, they should be shown prominently either in the balance sheet or in a note to the financial statements (for example, see Table 77). [*SSAP 6 para 10*].

(f) The name of the group or company that manages the investment portfolio, together with an indication of the terms and duration of its appointment and the basis for its remuneration.
[*CO 21(q)*].

343

Table 74: Disclosure of the classification by sector and the geographical distribution of an investment trust's portfolio of investments shown graphically. A more detailed analysis by investment is also given in the financial statements.

Extract from Globe Investment Trust P.L.C. Annual Review Report and Accounts 31 March 1984.

Classification by sector

Fixed Interest 6.72%

Capital Goods 14.48%

Consumer Goods 21.10%

Other Groups 16.02%

Commodities 3.38%

Financial 14.24%

Oil 14.44%

Convertibles 9.62%

Geographical distribution

Great Britain
67.48%

North America
19.77%

Other Markets
1.69%

Far East
11.06%

344

Table 75: Disclosure of an investment trust's largest investments.

Extract from Globe Investment Trust P.L.C. Annual Review Report and Accounts 31 March 1984.

Twenty largest investments of the Company

Convertibles and all classes of equity in any one company are treated as one investment.

Tyndall Group Limited, the Company's wholly-owned financial services subsidiary, valued at £30m in the Consolidated Balance Sheet, has been excluded from the table.

Position 1983	Position 1984		Market Value 31st March 1984	Portfolio
			£'000	%
1	1	Mercantile House Holdings	49,339	8.74
3	2	British Petroleum	45,355	8.04
2	3	Electra Investment Trust	39,999	7.09
—	4	U.S. Treasury Bonds	20,025	3.55
11/16	5	Argyll Group (formerly Argyll Food/Amalgamated Distilled Products)	16,340	2.90
5	6	Clyde Petroleum	12,358	2.19
9	7	House of Fraser	10,605	1.89
15	8	Rank Organisation	10,250	1.82
—	9	Dee Corporation	10,240	1.81
20	10	Hanson Trust	10,080	1.79
8	11	Harrisons & Crosfield	9,169	1.63
18	12	Debenhams	8,550	1.52
10	13	British Electric Traction	7,366	1.30
—	14	Extel Group	6,969	1.24
19	15	Ferranti	6,930	1.23
7	16	Imperial Group	6,510	1.15
14	17	European Ferries	6,416	1.14
—	18	U.S. Steel Corporation	6,298	1.12
—	19	Bowater Corporation	6,070	1.08
—	20	Saxon Oil	5,840	1.03

The above investments total £294,709,000 which represents 52.2 per cent. of the investment portfolio of the Company. At 31st March 1984, 230 separate investments were held in 216 different companies.

Commentaries on and lists of investments held by the Company appear on pages 11 to 13 (United Kingdom), 14 to 16 (North America) and 17 to 20 (Far East, Australia and other markets).

Table 76: Illustration of the disclosure of the analysis of an investment trust's income.

Extract from Globe Investment Trust P.L.C. Annual Review Report and Accounts 31 March 1984.

Consolidated profit and loss account extract

	Note	1984 £'000	1983 £'000
Income of the investment trust from fixed asset investments	2		
Listed investments: Great Britain		16,742	12,959
Overseas		3,499	6,249
		20,241	19,208
Unlisted investments: Great Britain		3,362	1,866
Overseas		222	264
Electra Investments (Zimbabwe) Limited		448	691
Interest receivable and other income		3,039	3,752
		27,312	25,781

Other matters

Investment income

14.15   Some investment companies have, in the past, accounted for their investment income in their financial statements on a 'cash received' basis, whereas other investment companies have accrued dividends. Dividends could be accrued from the time when any one of the following occurs:

(a) The dividends are declared.

(b) The paying company's shares are quoted ex-dividend.

(c) The dividends are due and payable.

14.16   Investment companies should *not* account for dividends on a 'cash received' basis, because the Act requires all income to be brought into account without regard to the date of receipt or payment. [*4 Sch 13*].

14.17   In practice, the difference between accounting for investment income under the three accruals bases outlined above can be significant. Generally, investment companies account for dividends receivable on the date when they become due for payment. An example of an investment trust's accounting policy for investment income is given in Table 78.

Table 77: Illustration of the disclosure of an investment trust's reserves between realised and unrealised reserves.

Extract from Globe Investment Trust P.L.C. Annual Review Report and Accounts 31 March 1984.

Note

20. Reserves

	Group £'000	Company £'000
Share premium account		
Balance at 1st April 1983	11,247	11,247
Premiums less expenses on conversion of loan stocks	94	94
Balance at 31st March 1984	**11,341**	**11,341**
Other reserves – non distributable		
Realised profits		
Balance at 1st April 1983	226,542	234,694
Adjustment to reflect non consolidation of Tyndall Group Limited	1,632	—
Restated balance at 1st April 1983	228,174	234,694
Net profits on realisation of investments	58,544	58,033
Balance at 31st March 1984	**286,718**	**292,727**
Unrealised profits		
Balance at 1st April 1983	144,693	138,818
Adjustment to reflect non consolidation of Tyndall Group Limited	1,403	—
Restated balance at 1st April 1983	146,096	138,818
Increase in valuation of investments	38,516	38,375
Surplus on revaluation of properties	3,840	—
Surplus on revaluation of Tyndall Group Limited	18,844	—
Current year profits of Tyndall Group Limited included in the consolidated profit and loss account	(1,537)	—
Deficit on revaluation of Electra Investments (Zimbabwe) Limited	(351)	—
Provision for loss on forward currency contracts	(686)	(686)
Balance at 31st March 1984	**204,722**	**176,507**
Profit and loss account – distributable		
Balance at 1st April 1983	17,531	14,781
Adjustment to reflect non consolidation of Tyndall Group Limited	(3,035)	—
Restated balance at 1st April 1983	14,496	14,781
Transfer from profit and loss account	396	1,201
Balance at 31st March 1984	**14,892**	**15,982**
Total Reserves at 31st March 1984	**517,673**	**496,557**
Total Reserves at 1st April 1983	400,013	399,540

Table 78: Example of an accounting policy for investment income.

Extract from Globe Investment Trust P.L.C. Annual Review Report and Accounts 31 March 1984.

Accounting policy

---

5. Income and expenses
All income and expenses are treated on the accruals basis; investment income being included in revenue in the year in which the due date for payment of the dividend arises, with the exception of fixed coupon investment income, where the investment is financed by borrowings.

Format headings

14.18   Many investment companies use the term 'Revenue account' instead of the term 'Profit and loss account' in their financial statements. The legality of using the former term is discussed in Chapter 9, paragraph 9.85.

14.19   It has also been questioned whether an investment company can show investment income under the heading 'Turnover' in the profit and loss account formats. On the grounds that such income is the company's principal source of revenue, this disclosure appears to be acceptable. In practice, several investment companies have adopted this approach.

Associated companies

14.20   Where an investment trust owns more than 20% of another company's equity share capital, it will not normally be appropriate for the investment trust to account for that other company under the equity method of accounting in accordance with SSAP 1 (for example, see Table 79). This is because the special distribution rules that apply to investment trusts make it inappropriate to include a share of the associated company's results in the investment trust's profit and loss account.

14.21   Any revaluation of such an investment to an amount above cost will normally be taken to a revaluation reserve and is undistributable. Even where the investment is subsequently sold, an investment trust is prohibited from distributing this surplus by its memorandum and articles of association.

Table 79: Example of the treatment of associated companies by an investment trust.

Extract from Globe Investment Trust P.L.C. Annual Review Report and Accounts 31 March 1984.

Accounting policy

11. Associated companies

Globe Investment Trust P.L.C. holds 20 per cent. or more of the equity capital of certain companies. Only the dividends received from such companies have been included in the Consolidated Profit and Loss Account since in the opinion of the Directors it would be misleading for an investment trust to include its share of the undistributed earnings of such companies in its Consolidated Profit and Loss Account. Such holdings are included in the Balance Sheets at valuation.

Details of the associated companies are shown on pages 43 and 44.

14.22 Where an investment company is listed on The Stock Exchange, it will have agreed not to take management control of the company that it has invested in. Therefore, to comply with both SSAP 1 and the Act, it cannot treat those companies as either associated companies or related companies in its financial statements.

CHAPTER 15

SMALL AND MEDIUM-SIZED COMPANIES

Small and Medium-sized Companies

Introduction

15.01 The Act includes certain concessions that permit small and medium-sized companies to file modified financial statements. Companies that take advantage of these concessions will be able to file financial statements that do not comply with all the detailed provisions of the Act as to their form and content.

15.02 It is important to appreciate that the available concessions relate only to the financial statements that a company must deliver to the Registrar of Companies under Section 241(3)(a) of the Act. [*Sec 247(1)(5)*]. The concessions do not affect the financial statements that a company must provide to its shareholders. Accordingly, even if a small or a medium-sized company wishes to take advantage of the concessions in respect of the financial statements that it must file, it must still prepare full financial statements. These full financial statements must comply with all the provisions of the Act. In addition, the company must give those financial statements to the shareholders and also lay them before the company in general meeting in accordance with Sections 240(1) and 241(1) of the Act.

15.03 The practical result of these concessions is that, if a company chooses to file modified financial statements, it must prepare *two* sets of financial statements: one for the Registrar of Companies and one for the shareholders. Consequently, it is hardly a concession.

15.04 The concessions relating to modified financial statements are not available to any company that is, or was at any time during the financial year that the financial statements relate to, one of the following types of company:

(a) A public company.

(b) A banking company (as defined in Chapter 13 para 13.03).

(c) An insurance company (as defined in Chapter 13 para 13.03).

(d) A shipping company (as defined in Chapter 13 para 13.03).

(e) A member of an ineligible group. An ineligible group is a group in which any of its members is one of the following:

   (i) A company of the types described in *(a)* to *(d)* above.
   (ii) A body corporate (other than a company) that has power under its constitution to offer its shares or debentures to the public, and that may lawfully exercise that power.
   (iii) A body corporate (other than a company) that is a recognised bank, or a licensed deposit-taking institution or an insurance company.

   (f) A private company that is a subsidiary of an overseas body corporate that has power under its constitution to offer its shares to the public, and that may lawfully exercise that power.
   [*Sec 247(2)(3), 257(1)*].

15.05 With the exception of dormant companies (see Chapter 16), the 'unmodified' financial statements (that is, those financial statements prepared under Section 227 of the Act and sent to shareholders) of small and medium-sized companies must be audited.

Definitions of small and medium-sized companies

15.06 A company qualifies as a small company for a financial year if it satisfies any two of the following three conditions during that year:

   (a) The amount of its turnover did not exceed £1,400,000.

   (b) The balance sheet total (see para 15.09) did not exceed £700,000.

   (c) The average number of employees the company employed in the financial year (as defined in Chapter 10 para 10.35) did not exceed 50.
   [*Sec 248(1)*].

15.07 A company qualifies as a medium-sized company for a financial year if it fails to satisfy the criteria for a small company, but satisfies any two of the following three conditions during that year.

   (a) The amount of its turnover did not exceed £5,750,000.

   (b) The balance sheet total (see para 15.09) did not exceed £2,800,000.

   (c) The average number of employees the company employed in the financial year (as defined in Chapter 10 para 10.35) did not exceed 250.
   [*Sec 248(2)*].

15.08 The turnover limits and the balance sheet total limits are based on the limits given in the EC Fourth Directive. The EC Commission may review this Directive from time to time, and may amend these limits. If it does so, the limits in the Act will be brought into line (see Appendix III).

15.09 Where a company adopts format 1 (see Chapter 6) for its balance sheet, the 'balance sheet total' is the aggregate of the amounts shown under the headings that are preceded by the letters A to D inclusive. Where a company adopts format 2 for its balance sheet, the 'balance sheet total' is the aggregate of the amounts shown under the general heading 'Assets'. [*Sec 248(3)*]. In either case, the effect is to equate 'balance sheet total' to gross assets.

15.10 The Act lays down the following four rules that must be applied in determining whether a company may file modified financial statements:

(a) In respect of a company's first financial year, the company will qualify to deliver the modified financial statements that apply to a small or a medium-sized company, provided that it satisfies the appropriate size conditions in respect of that year. [*Sec 249(2)*].

(b) In subsequent years, a company will be able to file modified financial statements, provided that it satisfies the appropriate size qualifications under Section 248 both in the year in question and in the preceding year. [*Sec 249(3)(4)*].

(c) A company that qualifies to be treated as either a small or a medium-sized company in one year, may file modified financial statements in the following year, even if it does not satisfy the conditions in that year. However, if it does not satisfy the conditions in the year after that, then, at that time, it must file the kind of financial statements in that subsequent year that are appropriate to the company's size. If, on the other hand, the company reverts to satisfying the conditions in that year, then it may continue to file modified financial statements. [*Sec 249(5)(6)*].

(d) Where a company has not prepared its financial statements in respect of a 12-month period, the turnover threshold must be proportionately adjusted in order to establish whether the appropriate condition has been satisfied. [*Sec 248(5)*]. For example, if a company prepares financial statements for a nine-month period, the turnover threshold will be £1.05m (that is, 9/12 x £1.4m) for a small company, and £4,312,500 (that is, 9/12 x £5.75m) for a medium-sized company.

15.11 The application of these provisions is complicated and, perhaps, is best illustrated by an example. Consider the following details relating to two companies (A and B). Company A has existed for many years, and in the year immediately before year 1 it qualified as a medium-sized company. Company B is incorporated on the first day of year 2.

	Year 1	Year 2	Year 3	Year 4
Company A:				
Turnover	£5.7m	£5.8m	£5.8m	£6.0m
Gross assets	£2.0m	£2.0m	£2.2m	£2.3m
Average number of employees	240	255	255	250
Company B:				
Turnover	—	£1.3m	£1.5m	£1.3m
Gross assets	—	£0.7m	£0.8m	£0.7m
Average number of employees	—	55	60	63

In year 1, Company A satisfies all the criteria that enable it to be treated as a medium-sized company. It is assumed that it did so also in the previous year. Consequently, it can file financial statements modified for a medium-sized company for year 1.

In year 2, Company A ceases to qualify as a medium-sized company because both its turnover and its number of employees exceed the criteria. However, it can still file the modified financial statements of a medium-sized company, because the Act permits it to do so if it was able to file the modified financial statements in the preceding year. Also, in year 2 (which is its first year after incorporation), Company B qualifies as a small company. Therefore, under the Act, it can file 'small company' financial statements, because the Act permits it to do so if it satisfies the criteria in its first financial year. (It satisfies the criteria both for turnover and gross assets, but not for number of employees.)

In year 3, Company A ceases to qualify as a medium-sized company for a second consecutive year. Consequently, it is no longer entitled to file 'medium-sized company' financial statements. In this year, Company B also ceases to qualify as a small company, because it has exceeded all the three conditions. However, it can still file 'small company' financial statements, because it qualified to do so in the preceding year.

In year 4, Company A reverts to satisfying the criteria of a medium-sized company. However, it is not entitled to take advantage of the concessions. This is because it must satisfy the criteria for two consecutive years before it changes its classification. By contrast, Company B reverts in this year to qualifying as a small company. Despite the fact that it did not satisfy the criteria in respect of year 3, it can still continue to file 'small company' financial statements, because it failed to satisfy the criteria for only one year.

Exemptions for small companies

15.12 Where a company qualifies as a small company, its directors need deliver only modified financial statements to the Registrar of Companies. These modified financial statements need to contain only a modified balance sheet and modified notes. [*8 Sch 2(1),5*].

15.13 The directors of a small company need not deliver either a profit and loss account, or a directors' report, or any information relating to the emoluments of directors or higher-paid employees. [*8 Sch 3,4*].

15.14 The modified balance sheet referred to in paragraph 15.12 is a balance sheet that discloses only those items that are preceded in the appropriate format by either a letter or a Roman numeral. [*8 Sch 2(2)*]. However, the aggregate amounts of debtors and creditors must be split between the amounts receivable or payable within one year and the amounts receivable or payable in more than one year. The split must be disclosed either on the face of the balance sheet or in the notes. [*8 Sch 6*].

15.15 Only the requirements of Schedule 4 relating to the following matters apply in respect of the notes to the financial statements of a small company:

(a) Accounting policies.

(b) Share capital.

(c) Particulars of allotments.

(d) Particulars of creditors payable in more than five years, and particulars of securities given.

(e) The basis used in translating foreign currency amounts into sterling.

15.16 Corresponding amounts for the previous year must also be given in respect of each of the above items. [*8 Sch 5*].

15.17 However, disclosure requirements imposed by other sections of, and schedules to, the Act still apply (for example, Schedule 6 — particulars of transactions with directors and officers).

15.18 A small company's modified financial statements will not disclose the amount of its profit for the year. The nearest that a user of the financial statements can get to this figure will be the difference between the 'profit and loss account' in the balance sheet at both the beginning and the end of the period that the financial statements cover. This amount may be very misleading, because it is arrived at not only after the deduction of undisclosed directors' fees, but also after the deduction of undisclosed dividends. This means that the detail of profit will not be placed on public record with the Registrar of Companies, and so it will not be available to the company's competitors. However, this detail will be disclosed to shareholders, because the company must give shareholders 'unmodified' financial statements even though it files modified financial statements.

15.19 An example of a modified vertical balance sheet for a small company (based on format 1 — see Chapter 6 para 6.16) is set out on the next page.

Exemptions for medium-sized companies

15.20 The modifications that the Act permits regarding the financial statements that a medium-sized company must deliver to the Registrar of Companies relate principally to the profit and loss account. They allow the following items to be combined and shown as one item under the heading of 'Gross profit or loss':

(a) In the formats where expenses are classified by function: turnover, the cost of sales, gross profit or loss and other operating income.

(b) In the formats where expenses are classified by type: turnover, the change in stocks of finished goods and in work in progress, own work capitalised, other operating income, raw materials and consumables, and other external charges.
[*8 Sch 7(2)*].

15.21 In addition, the notes to the financial statements may omit the disaggregated information in respect of both turnover and profit or loss before taxation that would otherwise be required. [*8 Sch 8*].

Modified balance sheet for a small company

	£	£
Fixed assets		
Intangible assets		X
Tangible assets		X
Investments		X
		X
Current assets		
Stocks	X	
Debtors	X	
Investments	X	
Cash	X	
	X	
Creditors (amounts falling due within one year)	X	
Net current assets		X
Total assets less current liabilities		X
Creditors (amounts falling due after more than one year)		(X)
Provisions for liabilities and charges		(X)
Net assets		X
Capital and reserves		
Called-up share capital		X
Share premium account		X
Revaluation reserve		X
Other reserves		X
Profit and loss account		X
		X

Directors' statement on modified financial statements

15.22 For small companies, each modified balance sheet a company delivers to the Registrar of Companies must be signed by the directors in accordance with Section 238 of the Act. [*8 Sch 2(3)*]. Moreover, where the directors of either a small company or a medium-sized company have relied on the exemptions for individual financial statements in delivering any documents to the Registrar of Companies, they must include a statement immediately above their signatures to the effect that:

(a) They have relied on the exemptions set out in Sections 247 to 249 of the Act that entitle them to deliver modified financial statements.

(b) They have done so because the company is entitled to benefit from those exemptions as a small or a medium-sized company (as appropriate).
[*8 Sch 9*].

15.23 With a small company the directors' statement could take the following form:

"We have relied on the exemptions for individual financial statements contained in Sections 247 to 249 of the Companies Act 1985 because, under that Act, the company is entitled to benefit from those exemptions as a small company."

A medium-sized company's directors must include a similar statement.

Auditors' responsibilities

15.24 Where the directors propose to rely on the exemptions that entitle them to deliver modified financial statements, the auditors must provide the directors with a report that states whether:

(a) In the auditors' opinion, the directors are entitled to deliver modified financial statements.

(b) The documents to be delivered as modified financial statements have been properly prepared in accordance with the Act.
[*8 Sch 10(3)*].

15.25 The directors must also include, with the documents that they deliver to the Registrar of Companies, a special auditors' report. This report must state that, in the auditors' opinion:

(a) The directors are entitled to deliver modified financial statements.

(b) The modified financial statements have been properly prepared in accordance with Schedule 8.
[*8 Sch 10(1)*].

15.26 The special auditors' report must also reproduce the full text of the auditors' report under Section 236 that was made in respect of the full financial statements the company prepared for shareholders. [*8 Sch 10(2)*].

15.27 An example of a special report is as follows:

Auditors' report to the directors of Small Company Limited

In our opinion, the directors are entitled by Sections 247 to 249 of the Companies Act 1985 to deliver modified financial statements in respect of the year ended 31 August 1985 and, in particular, the modified financial statements have been properly prepared in accordance with Schedule 8 to that Act. We are not required to express an audit opinion on the truth and fairness of these modified financial statements.

We reported, as auditors of Small Company Limited, to the members on 31 December 1985 on the company's financial statements prepared under Section 227 of the Companies Act 1985 for the year ended 31 August 1985, and our audit opinion was as follows:

"We have audited the financial statements on pages ... [*insert full text of audit opinion*] ... and comply with the Companies Act 1985."

Chartered Accountants

(Address)

(Date)

15.28 For the purpose of making the two required auditors' reports, it will usually be sufficient if the auditors perform their normal audit work on the main financial statements and also review the modified financial statements. Auditors are not required to perform an audit as such of the modified financial statements. Such financial statements are, anyway, unlikely to show a true and fair view.

15.29   Where the auditors have qualified their report on the main financial statements, they will need to ensure that the subject matter of their qualification is not relevant in assessing the criteria for exemption. Where the effect of the subject matter of the qualification cannot take either the turnover or the total assets over the exemption limits, then there is no problem, and the auditors can issue a standard special report that contains the text of the qualified report.

15.30   The importance of a qualification in the auditors' report on the financial statements the company has prepared for its shareholders may not be obvious from the modified financial statements themselves. For instance, the qualification in question may refer to a note to the financial statements given to shareholders, but this note may not be reproduced in a small company's modified financial statements. In this situation, the auditors' report should include some further information that makes it clear that the note concerned has not been reproduced.

15.31   If modified financial statements were delivered to the Registrar or Companies with a *qualified special report*, it would appear that the directors would be in breach of the Act.

Special provisions relating to groups

15.32   The Act contains special provisions that must be applied where the company that is seeking to file modified financial statements is a holding company that Section 229 requires to prepare group accounts. Such a holding company will be entitled to take advantage of the concessions only if the group (consisting of the holding company and its subsidiaries), taken as a whole, satisfies the conditions. [*Sec 250(1)(2)*].

15.33   Therefore, where the holding company would otherwise qualify as a small company, but the group satisfies the conditions to qualify only as a medium-sized group, the holding company must itself be treated as a medium-sized company.

15.34   In addition, the two rules detailed in paragraph 15.10*(b)* and *(c)* do not apply in determining whether a holding company may file modified financial statements. Section 250(2) of the Act says that "the directors of the holding company may not under section 249... deliver accounts modified as for a small company unless the group ... is *in that year* a small group". There is a similar statement in respect of medium-sized groups. The Act does not apply the exemptions in paragraph 15.10*(b)* and *(c)* to a holding company. Consequently, the group must satisfy the criteria in the particular year for the holding company to be able to take advantage of the appropriate concessions.

15.35 For these purposes, it is necessary to look at the aggregate figures for the group. These will normally be ascertained by reference to the group accounts. These will be either the consolidated financial statements or (where the group accounts are not prepared as consolidated financial statements) the corresponding figures given in those group accounts, with such adjustments as would have been made if the group accounts had been prepared in consolidated form. However, where the group accounts do not include one or more of the subsidiaries, those accounts will have to be adjusted to take account of the relevant figures for the subsidiaries that were omitted from the group accounts. The subsidiaries' relevant figures should be ascertained from the financial statements prepared for the year ending with, or last before, the holding company's year end. This adjustment will not be required, though, where the subsidiary in question was omitted on the ground that it was impracticable to deal with it in the group accounts (see Chapter 17). [*Sec 250(3)(4)(5)*].

15.36 If a group satisfies the appropriate size conditions, the directors may deliver to the Registrar of Companies modified group accounts in respect of that period, instead of the complete group accounts. [*Sec 250(6)*]. The modifications permitted by the Act correspond to those permitted in respect of the financial statements of an individual company. And they apply to either the consolidated financial statements or the group accounts that give information equivalent to the information in the consolidated financial statements. [*Sec 250(6); 8 Sch 12 to 19*].

15.37 Where the directors deliver modified group accounts under the provisions outlined above, the balance sheet must contain a statement by the directors to the effect that the documents delivered to the Registrar include modified group accounts. [*8 Sch 21*]. This statement could be the same as that set out in paragraph 15.23, but with the following additional sentence:

> "By virtue of Section 250 of the same Act, the documents delivered to the Registrar include modified group accounts."

15.38 Also, there must be a special auditors' report on the modified group accounts. This report must be the same as the report required for modified individual financial statements (see para 15.27), except that the text of the full audit report will refer also to the group accounts. [*8 Sch 22*].

Power of the Secretary of State

15.39 The Act gives the Secretary of State the power to modify the accounting exemption provisions by statutory instrument. [*Sec 251(1)*]. However, both Houses of Parliament must approve a draft of the statutory instrument before the Secretary of State can either reduce the classes of company that are entitled to benefit from the accounting exemption provisions or make the requirements of those provisions more onerous. [*Sec 251(2)*].

CHAPTER 16

DORMANT COMPANIES

Dormant Companies

Introduction

16.01 Sections 252 and 253 of the Act make certain provisions regarding dormant companies. In particular, Section 252 allows a company to resolve not to appoint auditors when it becomes dormant.

16.02 For this purpose, a 'dormant company' is defined as a company that had no significant accounting transaction during the period in question. A 'significant accounting transaction' is defined as any transaction that Section 221 requires the company to enter into its accounting records (for example, receiving or expending money, or buying or selling goods), except for one that results from a subscriber to the memorandum taking shares in the company under his undertaking given in the memorandum. [*Sec 252(5)*].

16.03 Where a company has been dormant for any period, it ceases to be dormant if any significant accounting transaction occurs. [*Sec 252(5)(b)*].

Exemption available

16.04 A dormant company may exclude the application of Section 384 of the Act (company to appoint auditors at general meeting) by passing a special resolution resolving that auditors shall not be appointed. This resolution may be passed only at a general meeting of the company at which copies of its latest financial statements (which have been prepared in accordance with Section 227) are laid before the company. [*Sec 252(2)*].

16.05 A company may only pass such a resolution provided that the following three conditions are satisfied:

(a) The financial statements that are being laid must not be required under Section 229 to include group accounts for the year in question.

(b) The directors must have been entitled during the year to take advantage of the exemptions available to small companies when preparing the company's financial statements (see Chapter 15 paras 15.04 to 15.11). The only exception to this relates to a company that was not entitled to benefit from those exemptions solely because it was a member of an ineligible group (see Chapter 15 para 15.04*(e)*). In this situation, the company will be treated for the purpose of this part of the Act as if it had been so qualified.

(c) The company must have been dormant since the end of the financial year.
[*Sec 252(2)*].

16.06   If, for example, a company has reserves that it pays up to its holding company, it will have a significant accounting transaction in any year in which it accounts for the dividend. This means that it cannot then be dormant, and it must appoint auditors.

16.07   Although Section 252 of the Act empowers dormant companies to pass a special resolution enabling them to avoid the statutory requirement to appoint auditors, it is important also that they check that the resolution would not contravene any provision in the company's articles of association. Companies that have adopted Table A (other than in the new form which took effect from 1 July 1985) as their articles, and many other companies (especially those incorporated before 1967), will have a clause in their articles that requires them to appoint auditors. Section 252 does not automatically override such a clause, because it relates only to the statutory requirement in Section 384 to appoint auditors.

16.08   In this situation, the company should, in addition to passing the special resolution under Section 252, first pass a special resolution amending its articles by removing the clause concerning the appointment of auditors.

16.09   If a company has not appointed auditors in previous financial years by relying on the exemption in Section 252, but it has overlooked its articles, the company should:

(a) Ratify, by special resolution, its previous decision not to appoint auditors.

(b) Amend, by special resolution, its articles, and remove the clause that requires it to appoint auditors.

(c) Pass a new special resolution resolving not to appoint auditors. This resolution will then be effective until such time as the company ceases to be dormant.

16.10   Where a company has not yet held its first general meeting at which financial statements are laid, it may exempt itself from the obligation to appoint auditors by passing a special resolution at any time before that general meeting. It can do this only if it has been dormant from the time it was formed until the time the resolution is passed. [*Sec 252(3)*]. A company may not take advantage of this exemption if it is either a public company or a special category company (see Chapter 13). [*Sec 252(4)*].

16.11   The resolution need be passed only in the first year in which the company wishes to take advantage of the exemption. The company does not have to repeat the resolution in subsequent years. It will, however, have both to appoint auditors and to have financial statements audited in a year when the company ceases to qualify as a dormant company (see para 16.19 below).

16.12   Any company wanting to take advantage of these provisions of the Act should include a statement, such as the one set out below, either in the notice of the meeting or in the directors' report attached to the financial statements that are to be laid before the next general meeting of the company.

"Auditors

In accordance with Section 252 of the Companies Act 1985, a special resolution resolving that auditors shall not be appointed will be put to the annual general meeting."

Additional matters relating to dormant companies

16.13   There are three additional points that are relevant to a dormant company that is exempt from the obligation to appoint auditors. These points apply whether the company was so exempt throughout the relevant financial year, or became so exempt by passing a resolution during that year. [*Sec 253(1)*].

16.14   The first point is that a dormant company's directors remain under an obligation to prepare financial statements under Section 227 of the Act, and also to ensure that those financial statements contain those documents that Section 239 requires (that is, the company's profit and loss account and balance sheet and the directors' report). The only difference is that a dormant company is not required to include an audit report in its financial statements. [*Sec 253(2)*].

16.15   The best way in which a dormant company can satisfy the requirement to prepare a profit and loss account is to include a note in its financial statements on the following lines:

"Profit and loss account

The company did not trade during the year and, accordingly, it made neither a profit nor a loss. Therefore, no profit and loss account is attached."

16.16   However, Schedule 4 to the Act provides that a company may omit headings and sub-headings from the formats only where there is no relevant amount for both the current year and the preceding year. Consequently, if a company trades in the year before it becomes dormant, it must prepare a profit and loss account in the year that it becomes dormant. This will apply even though there will be no current year figures.

16.17 The second point is that, if the company takes advantage of the exemption, the directors must include a statement immediately above their signatures on the balance sheet to the effect that the company was dormant throughout the financial year in question. [*Sec 253(3)(a)*]. The directors' statement could take the following form:

> "The company was dormant (within the meaning of Section 252 of the Companies Act 1985) throughout the year ended 31 December 1985."

16.18 The third point is that, if the company takes advantage of the exemption for dormant companies, and the directors decide to deliver modified financial statements applicable to a small company to the Registrar (see para 16.05), then the following are not required:

(a) The directors' statement that is required under Schedule 8, paragraph 9 (company is entitled to rely, and has relied, on exemptions for small and medium-sized companies) (see Chapter 15 paras 15.22 and 15.23).

(b) The special report of the auditors required by Schedule 8, paragraph 10 (see Chapter 15 paras 15.25 to 15.27).
[*Sec 253(3)(b)*].

Ceasing to qualify as a dormant company

16.19 Where a company ceases, for any reason, to qualify as a dormant company, the directors may appoint auditors at any time before the next general meeting at which the company's financial statements prepared under Section 227 of the Act are laid before the company. Where this applies, those auditors hold office until the conclusion of that meeting. [*Sec 252(7)*].

16.20 If the directors fail to appoint any auditors in such circumstances, the company in general meeting may appoint them. [*Sec 252(7)*].

Agency companies

16.21 An agency company that acts for either a disclosed or an undisclosed principal may be able to take advantage of the exemption for dormant companies. Because a company may be treated as dormant only if it is not required to record any transaction in its accounting records, it may not qualify as a dormant company if it is involved in any one or more of the following activities:

(a) Receiving and expending monies.

(b) Disposing of assets.

(c) Dealing in goods or stocks that it holds.

16.22 With any of the activities set out above, it will be a matter of fact as to whether a particular agency company performs any such activity.

In the first instance, it is necessary to look to the agency agreement for guidance. This agreement defines the relationship between the principal company and the agency company, and it sets out the tasks the respective companies are to perform.

16.23 When considering the agreement, the following points may assist in determining whether the agency company is in fact 'dormant':

(a) Receiving and expending monies

An agency company that is merely required to account to its principal for the amount (or the net amount) equal to the monies it has received for its principal in the course of the agency, is the owner of the monies it receives when acting as agent. The agency company should enter such receipts in its own accounting records. Where, however, the agency company is obliged to hand over to its principal the very monies it receives as agent, it will receive those monies as a trustee for its principal. It will then not be obliged to record those receipts in its own accounting records. Where the agent is a trustee, the agency company must pay the monies it receives on behalf of the principal into a separate bank account belonging to the principal.

As regards expenditure, it is not sufficient that the principal indemnifies the agency company against any liabilities the company incurs in the course of acting as agent. The agency company must contract with third parties solely in its capacity as agent, and without assuming any liability on the resultant contract. It does not so contract if it does not disclose its principal. If the agency company does assume a liability on the contract, it would have a significant accounting transaction, and so it would not qualify as dormant.

(b) Disposing of assets

An agency company might not, in fact, own any assets. However, care should be taken in situations where the agency company remains the legal owner of property. Provided that the agency agreement passed all the beneficial interests in freehold or leasehold property to the principal, and left only the legal title to that property in the name of the agency company, the subsequent transfer of that title would not constitute a transfer of assets. This is because a bare legal title that is held to the order of the principal cannot be said to be an asset of the agent.

(c) Dealing in goods or stocks that the agency company holds

If the agent's sole business is that of trading for and on behalf of the principal, the agent is unlikely to *hold* any stocks of its own.

16.24 It would, therefore, appear that there is no reason in principle why agency companies, in appropriate circumstances, should not qualify to be treated as dormant companies. Whether the agency company actually qualifies for the exemption available to dormant companies will, however, be a matter of fact in the light of both the appropriate agency agreement and the actual relationship between the two parties. Suppose, for example, that a holding company owns an agency company, but there is no formal agency agreement. The agency company may be able to avoid an audit if there was a minute that confirmed its status. Although there would be no formal documentation between the companies, the arrangement as minuted would be both effective and clear.

CHAPTER 17

GROUP ACCOUNTS

Chapter 17

Group Accounts

Introduction

17.01 The Act includes accounting provisions that apply to group accounts. In general, these provisions correspond to those that apply to an individual company's financial statements. Consequently, group accounts must normally comply with most of the requirements of Schedule 4 to the Act (Form and content of company accounts). One exception to this rule is that if any member of a group is a special category company, the group may prepare its group accounts in accordance with Schedule 9. Special category companies are considered in Chapter 13.

17.02 This chapter deals primarily with the requirements to prepare group accounts, and with the information that has to be disclosed in those accounts. The method of determining goodwill and the principles of both acquisition accounting and merger accounting are dealt with in Chapter 7 and Chapter 18 respectively.

Status of EC Seventh Directive

17.03 In addition to those provisions of the Companies Act 1985 that relate to group accounts, the EC Seventh Directive specifies requirements for the preparation, the content and the publication of group accounts. The EC adopted this Directive in 1983. However, the Directive does not have to be incorporated into the law of Member States until the end of 1987, and its provisions do not have to be effective until 1 January 1990. The UK has not yet introduced legislation implementing the Directive, but it is not expected that the enactment of this Directive will have any major effect on the content of group accounts. This is because the 1985 Act requirements relating to groups largely conform to those of the Seventh Directive.

Requirement to produce group accounts

17.04 If, at the end of the financial year, a company has one or more subsidiaries, group accounts must be prepared in addition to the holding company's individual financial statements. The group accounts should deal with the state of affairs and the profit or loss of the company and its subsidiaries taken as a whole. [*Sec 229(1)*]. The group accounts form part of the company's accounts. Consequently, they are required to be included with the other documents that must be both laid before the company and delivered to the Registrar of Companies (see Chapter 21). [*Sec 239*].

17.05   Group accounts need not be prepared if the holding company was itself, at the end of the financial year, a wholly-owned subsidiary of another company incorporated in Great Britain. [*Sec 229(2); SSAP 14 para 19*].

17.06   However, this exemption does not extend to the content of the directors' report. This is because it is a requirement of an *individual* company's directors' report that it should, for example, contain "a fair review of the development of the business of the company *and its subsidiaries*". [*Sec 235(1)(a)*]. Accordingly, even where group accounts are not prepared (for example, where the company itself is a wholly-owned subsidiary), the directors' report still has to include information in respect of the company and its subsidiaries.

17.07   SSAP 14 specifies additional rules that groups must comply with. It requires that a holding company should prepare group accounts in the form of a single set of consolidated financial statements covering the holding company and its subsidiary companies (both at home and overseas). The only exceptions to this general rule are outlined in paragraph 17.63 below. [*SSAP 14 para 15*].

Provisions relating to the financial statements of both the holding company and subsidiaries

17.08   The balance sheet formats detailed in Schedule 4 to the Act specify the place where the aggregate amounts should be shown of any amounts owed to and from, and any interests in, any holding company, or any subsidiary or any fellow subsidiary.

17.09   These items in format 1 (see Chapter 6) are as follows:

    B Fixed assets
        III   Investments
            1 Shares in group companies
            2 Loans to group companies

    C Current assets
        II   Debtors
            2 Amounts owed by group companies

        III   Investments
            1 Shares in group companies

    E Creditors: amounts falling due within one year
            6 Amounts owed to group companies

    H Creditors: amounts falling due after more than one year
            6 Amounts owed to group companies

17.10 In addition to the disclosure the formats require, a holding company or a subsidiary must disclose separately (either on the face of the balance sheet or in the notes to the financial statements) the amounts detailed above, split between the amounts owed to or from, and any interests in:

(a) Any holding company or any fellow subsidiary.
(b) Any subsidiary.
[*4 Sch 59*].

17.11 Because amounts owed by and to group companies have to be shown in specific positions in the formats, it is not acceptable for companies to net these balances off and to disclose the net balance in the balance sheet as 'Investment in subsidiaries'. This applies even where a note to the financial statements gives additional information that explains the net balance. For example, the disclosure that follows is *not* acceptable:

Investment in subsidiaries

Shares in subsidiaries	X
Amounts owed by subsidiaries	X
Amounts owed to subsidiaries	(X)
	X

17.12 Moreover, the amounts owed and owing have to be ascertained on a company-by-company basis. [*4 Sch 5*]. Consequently, for accounting disclosure purposes in a holding company's financial statements, amounts that one subsidiary owes to the holding company cannot be offset against amounts the holding company owes to another subsidiary. Set-off can be allowed only in circumstances where there is a *legal* right of set-off between the loans. Such a *legal* right may exist, for example, if it is included as a clause in a loan agreement.

An example of the correct way in which to disclose this information is given in Table 80.

17.13 Companies have to analyse amounts owed by, and to, group companies between amounts that will fall due within one year and amounts that will fall due after more than one year. [*Notes 5 and 13 on the balance sheet formats*]. The results of this analysis will largely depend both on the way in which group companies are financed and on the terms of any formal and informal agreements between the companies.

17.14 In addition, The Stock Exchange's Continuing Obligations and the USM's General Undertaking require listed companies and companies that are traded on the USM respectively also to analyse amounts due to subsidiary companies between the aggregate amounts repayable:
(a) In one year or less, or on demand.

(b) Between one and two years.

(c) Between two and five years.

(d) In five years or more.
[*CO 21(f); GU 10(f)*].

Table 80: Illustration of the disclosure of investments and loans to and from subsidiaries.

Extract from The Rank Organisation Plc Report and Accounts 31 October 1984.

Notes

14 Investments in subsidiaries

	Shares at cost or valuation £ million	Loans and advances £ million	Provisions £ million	Net book amount £ million
Balances at 31st October 1983	285·8	307·6	(38·8)	554·6
Additions	3·6	78·6	—	82·2
Disposals/repayments	(28·0)	(55·7)	2·4	(81·3)
Increase in provisions	—	—	(4·2)	(4·2)
Reduction of provisions	—	—	7·7	7·7
Surplus on revaluation	13·6	—	—	13·6
Balances at 31st October 1984	275·0	330·5	(32·9)	572·6

The Company's 60% directly owned holding in Rank Precision Industries (Holdings) Plc was revalued by the directors on 31st October 1984 at £120·9m being an amount equal to the historical cost of £3·3m plus the appropriate share of post acquisition retained reserves. The surplus on revaluation has been taken to revaluation reserve.

Of the loans and advances to subsidiaries £46·2m (1983 £61·6m) has been subordinated to other creditors as an alternative to increasing the share capital of certain subsidiaries.

18 Debtors

	Group		Company	
Amounts falling due within one year	1984 £ million	1983 £ million	1984 £ million	1983 £ million
Trade debtors	76·9	83·7	7·3	7·6
Amounts owed by group companies	—	—	62·5	27·7
Other debtors	12·8	9·3	7·3	6·7
Fixed assets held for disposal	7·1	14·2	1·5	1·8
Prepayments and accrued income	17·4	16·7	6·9	5·1
Dividends receivable from associated company	11·2	10·8	—	—
	125·4	134·7	85·5	48·9

20 Other creditors

	Group		Company	
Amounts falling due within one year	1984 £ million	1983 £ million	1984 £ million	1983 £ million
Payments received on account	7·4	4·9	—	0·1
Trade creditors	60·2	54·3	18·9	16·8
Interest payable to group companies	—	—	2·1	1·9
Amounts owed to group companies	—	—	86·3	73·8
United Kingdom corporation tax	3·3	1·6	0·2	0·2
Overseas taxation	2·0	1·6	—	—
Advance corporation tax	10·7	8·5	10·7	8·5
Development land tax	4·5	1·4	4·3	1·3
Social security	4·3	4·1	2·0	1·7
Other creditors	15·0	14·1	4·7	6·5
Accruals and deferred income	36·6	40·4	12·3	11·5
Dividends				
Accrued on preference shares	0·2	0·2	0·2	0·2
Payable and proposed on ordinary shares	24·2	20·2	24·2	20·2
Minority shareholders of subsidiaries	0·7	0·9	—	—
	169·1	152·2	165·9	142·7

17.15 The notes to a holding company's financial statements must disclose the number, the description and the amount of any of its shares or debentures that subsidiaries or their nominees hold. [*4 Sch 60(1)*]. This information is not required, however, where the subsidiary is concerned only as a personal representative. Nor is it required where the subsidiary is concerned only as a trustee, provided that either of the following applies:

(a) Neither the company nor any subsidiary is beneficially interested in the trust.

(b) Any beneficial interest arises only as security under a transaction that a money-lending company has entered into in the ordinary course of its business.
[*4 Sch 60(2)*].

17.16 The general disclosure requirements in respect of investments in subsidiaries are discussed in more detail in Chapter 8, paragraphs 8.39 to 8.43.

Consolidated financial statements

17.17 Consolidated financial statements are the most common form of group accounts. The term 'consolidated financial statements' is defined in SSAP 14 as a form of group accounts that presents the information contained in the separate financial statements of a holding company and its subsidiaries as if they were a single entity's financial statements. However, group accounts need not be in the form of consolidated financial statements. If the directors consider that the information about the group's state of affairs and profit or loss would be better presented in some other form (in particular, so as to make the information more understandable), they may present it in that form (for example, see Table 81). The Act gives the following alternative forms of group accounts:

(a) More than one set of consolidated financial statements, where one set deals with the company and one group of subsidiaries, and other sets deal with other groups of subsidiaries.

(b) Separate financial statements dealing with each of the subsidiaries.

(c) Statements expanding the information about the subsidiaries in the company's individual financial statements.

(d) Any combination of the forms outlined in (a), (b) and (c).
[*Sec 229(6)*].

17.18 The group accounts may also be incorporated, either wholly or partly, into the holding company's individual balance sheet and profit and loss account. [*Sec 229(7)*].

> *Table 81: An example of subsidiaries excluded from consolidation, but where their results are presented separately in the group accounts.*
>
> *Extract from Schroders Public Limited Company Annual Report 31 December 1984.*
>
> **Accounting policies extract**
>
> (b) Basis of consolidation:
> The accounts of subsidiary companies are co-terminous with those of Schroders plc apart from those of the life assurance and certain related subsidiaries which are made up to 31st October to avoid undue delay in the preparation of the Group accounts.
>
> The consolidated accounts include the assets, liabilities and results of all subsidiary companies other than those of the life assurance subsidiaries for which, in the opinion of the Directors, the information is better provided by being presented separately. A summary of the assets, liabilities and results of those subsidiaries is given in Note 22.
>
> The earnings of the life assurance subsidiaries are included in the consolidated profit and loss account on the basis of dividends declared. The value of the Group's investment is included in the consolidated balance sheet at Directors' valuation as described in Note 22; changes in this valuation are taken directly to non-distributable consolidated reserves, as set out in Note 11.
>
> **Note**
>
> **Investment in Life Assurance Subsidiaries**
>
> 22 (a) Valuation
> In order to reflect the increase in the value of the in-force business of the life assurance companies, the Directors have revalued the investment in these unconsolidated subsidiaries which was stated previously at cost less provisions. Accordingly, the amount at which the investment in the unconsolidated life assurance subsidiaries is stated, £21,500,000, represents the Directors' valuation of the Group's investment in the life assurance subsidiaries at 31st October, 1984, determined on independent actuarial advice provided by Tillinghast, Nelson & Warren Limited. The valuation comprises the shareholders' funds of those subsidiaries together with the present value, net of tax, of the future profits of the in-force business. Goodwill is not included in this valuation.
>
> The investment in unconsolidated life assurance subsidiaries in the Consolidated Balance Sheet of the Group at 31st December, 1984 comprised:
>
> | | £'000 |
> |---|---|
> | Book value of investment in life assurance subsidiaries at 31st December, 1983 | 5,719 |
> | Additional investment during 1984 | 4,000 |
> | | 9,719 |
> | Surplus arising on revaluation – see Note 11 | 11,781 |
> | | 21,500 |

Table 81 continued.

Surplus arising on revaluation includes non-distributable reserve of the life assurance subsidiaries of £533,000.

The issued share capital of the United Kingdom life assurance subsidiary was increased by £4,000,000 during the year ended 31st October, 1984 to meet in full the margin of solvency required under the Insurance Companies Act 1982. The historical cost of the investment was £11,532,000 of which £1,813,000, principally representing goodwill on acquisition, was written off in prior years.

If the investment in life assurance subsidiaries were to be realised at the Directors' valuation at 31st October, 1984 a liability for taxation would have arisen of an estimated amount of £2,778,000 for which no provision has been made.

No dividends were declared by the life assurance subsidiaries in respect of 1984 or 1983.

(b) Accounts

The net assets of the life assurance subsidiaries based on the accounts for the years ended 31st October are summarised as follows:

	1984	1983
	£'000	£'000
Investments		
Listed securities	64,522	81,646
Unlisted investments	1,038	335
Unit trusts	140,804	55,730
Properties	23,537	18,914
Mortgages and loans	11,054	16,069
Deposits with local authorities and banks	24,651	22,756
	265,606	195,450
Net current assets (liabilities)	1,038	(570)
	266,644	194,880
Deferred taxation	(256)	—
Insurance funds	(256,136)	(189,362)
	10,252	5,518
Representing:		
Share capital	9,500	5,500
Capital reserve	19	19
Non-distributable reserve	533	—
Profit and loss account	—	(201)
	10,052	5,318
Subordinated loan capital	200	200
	10,252	5,518

The turnover of the life assurance subsidiaries, represented by net premiums, was £81,016,000 (£62,496,000).

Table 81 continued.

The movements on profit and loss account of the life assurance subsidiaries were:

	1984	1983
	£'000	£'000
Net transfer of surplus from (to) insurance funds	869	(62)
Taxation	(135)	—
	734	(62)
Brought forward	(201)	(139)
	533	(201)
Transfer to non-distributable reserve	(533)	—
Carried forward	—	(201)

Other Group companies act as bankers and investment advisers for the life assurance subsidiaries, as a result of which an amount of £1,591,000 (£7,679,000) due to the life assurance subsidiaries is included in deposit and other accounts in the Consolidated Balance Sheet.

(c) Principal accounting policies
  (i) In determining the liability to policyholders represented by the balance on insurance funds, the directors of the life assurance subsidiaries, on the advice of the Actuary, make allowance for a deferral of a proportion of the expense of acquiring new business in order to match such expenses more closely against future revenue from in-force business.

  (ii) On the advice of the Actuary, any surplus disclosed by annual actuarial valuations is allocated by the directors of the life assurance subsidiaries between policyholders and shareholders.

  (iii) Investments are included at market value except for mortgages, loans and deposits which are stated at cost or estimated net realisable value in the normal course of business, whichever is lower.

  (iv) All income and expenditure is dealt with through the insurance funds account.

17.19   Where a company is listed on The Stock Exchange, and it has subsidiaries, the group accounts that it issues must be in consolidated form. [*CO 20*].

17.20   Where a holding company does not prepare group accounts as consolidated financial statements, the group accounts must still give either the same or equivalent information as the company would have disclosed if it had prepared consolidated financial statements. [*4 Sch 68*]. SSAP 14 requires the directors to state, in addition, the reasons why they consider the group accounts give a fairer view of the group's financial position than those statements would have done had they been prepared as consolidated financial statements. [*SSAP 14 para 22*]. SSAP 14 also requires that, where consolidated financial statements are presented, a description should be given of the bases on which those statements have dealt with subsidiary companies. [*SSAP 14 para 15*]. This disclosure would normally form part of the group's accounting policies.

17.21 When preparing consolidated financial statements, the group should follow uniform accounting policies. Where a subsidiary does not follow the group's uniform policies when it is preparing its own financial statements, appropriate adjustments should be made in the consolidated financial statements. The need for such consolidation adjustments should not arise frequently in a group that operates wholly within the UK, because all UK companies are expected to follow SSAPs. Also, if a new subsidiary is acquired that applies an accounting policy that differs from the group's policy, the new subsidiary has a sufficient reason to change its policy and make a prior-year adjustment in accordance with SSAP 6 (see also para 17.28 below).

17.22 Where a subsidiary does not adopt the same accounting policies as the group when preparing its own financial statements, and it is impracticable to make adjustments on consolidation, this will be acceptable provided that:

(a) The policies are generally acceptable.

(b) They are disclosed in the consolidated financial statements.

(c) The consolidated financial statements indicate the amounts of assets and liabilities involved.

(d) The consolidated financial statements indicate, where practicable, the effect the different policy has had on the group's results and net assets.

(e) The consolidated financial statements give the reasons for the different treatment.
[*SSAP 14 para 16*].

17.23 Where group accounts are prepared in the form of consolidated financial statements, the financial statements will include the following:

(a) The directors' report (see further Chapter 12).

(b) The consolidated balance sheet and related notes. [*Sec 229(5)(a)*].

(c) The consolidated profit and loss account and related notes. [*Sec 229(5)(b)*].

(d) The holding company's balance sheet and related notes. [*Sec 228(1)(2)(7)*].

(e) The group's statement of source and application of funds (see Chapter 6 para 6.44). [*SSAP 10 para 12*].

(f) The auditors' report on the statements covered by *(b)* to *(e)* above. [*Sec 236*].

17.24 When a holding company is preparing consolidated financial statements, it is not required to include its own profit and loss account and related notes if the financial statements satisfy the following requirements:

(a) The consolidated profit and loss account complies with the Act's disclosure requirements.

(b) The consolidated profit and loss account shows how much of the consolidated profit or loss for the financial year the holding company's profit and loss account deals with.

(c) The notes to the financial statements disclose the fact that the holding company has taken advantage of this exemption.
[*Sec 228(7)*].

17.25 Suitable wording for a note to be included in the financial statements would be:

> "As permitted by Section 228(7) of the Companies Act 1985, the holding company's profit and loss account has not been included in these financial statements."

An illustration of this type of note is given in Table 82.

Table 82: Illustration of the disclosure required where a holding company has not reproduced its own profit and loss account in the financial statements.

Extract from Rowntree Mackintosh plc Annual Report 29 December 1984.

7 Profit attributable to Rowntree Mackintosh plc
The group accounts do not include a separate profit and loss account for Rowntree Mackintosh plc (the parent company) as permitted by Section 149(5) of the Companies Act 1948 [*now Section 228(7) of the Companies Act 1985*]. The amount of group profits attributable to Rowntree Mackintosh plc dealt with in the accounts of the parent company is £48·3 million (1983 £21·9 million).

17.26 Where the group accounts are prepared in a form other than consolidated financial statements, but the profit and loss account is framed as a consolidated profit and loss account, and it deals with all or any of the company's subsidiaries, the above exemption still applies. [*Sec 228(7)*].

Application of the general provisions of the Act to group accounts

17.27 Irrespective of the form in which group accounts are presented, the following general principles apply:

(a) The group accounts must give a true and fair view, so far as they concern the holding company's shareholders, of the state of affairs and the profit or loss of the company and those of its subsidiaries that the financial statements as a whole deal with. As with individual financial statements, this is an overriding requirement (see Chapter 3 para 3.09). [*Sec 230(2)(3)*]. If strict compliance with the Act does not enable group accounts to show a true and fair view, then

additional information must be given in the notes to the group accounts to ensure that such a view is shown. [*Sec 230(4)*]. If the provision of additional information is not sufficient to ensure that a true and fair view is shown, then the directors must depart from the Act's requirement. [*Sec 230(5)*]. If they do so, they must disclose, in a note to the group accounts, the details of the departure, the reason for it and its effect. [*Sec 230(6)*].

(b) The group accounts must comply, so far as is practicable, with the requirements of Schedule 4 to the Act (to the extent that this Schedule applies to those accounts) both as to their form and content and as to the information they must disclose in the notes. The group accounts must also comply, subject to certain exceptions discussed in paragraphs 17.45 and 17.46 below, with the other requirements of the Act, as if they were the accounts of an actual company. [*Sec 230(1); 4 Sch 62, 63, 68*]. This provision applies without prejudice to any provisions of the Act that relate specifically to group accounts. [*4 Sch 64, 68*]. However, the Secretary of State is empowered to modify the requirements of Schedule 4 as they apply to group accounts, to take account of any special circumstances that apply to a particular company. He may do so either on the application of the company's directors or with their consent. [*Sec 230(8)*].

(c) The group accounts must combine the information that is contained in the separate balance sheets and profit and loss accounts of the holding company and the subsidiaries that the group accounts deal with. However, the directors must make any adjustments that they think necessary. [*4 Sch 61, 68*].

17.28 Problems can arise with overseas subsidiaries in applying uniform accounting policies. Where the subsidiaries are subject to either company law or tax law that is different from that in the UK, it may not always be practicable for the holding company to insist that the subsidiaries change their accounting policies to bring them into line with the group's accounting policies. For example, under the tax law of a number of European countries, provisions for accelerated depreciation and other items have to be incorporated in the statutory financial statements in order to qualify for tax relief. In these circumstances, it would obviously not be in the group's best interests for the UK holding company to insist that the foreign subsidiary company should depreciate, in its statutory financial statements, its fixed assets over their estimated useful lives, in accordance with the Act and SSAP 12. Therefore, to comply with the provisions of SSAP 14, an appropriate consolidation adjustment should be made (for example, see Table 83).

17.29 There are other reasons for making consolidation adjustments. Consolidation adjustments are required, for example, to eliminate preacquisition reserves and the effects of intra-group trading and to deal with goodwill on consolidation (see Chapter 7 para 7.39).

> **Table 83: Illustration of a company that consolidates subsidiaries with non-coterminous year ends and of an accounting policy that explains unusual consolidation adjustments.**
>
> *Extract from Grand Metropolitan Public Limited Company Annual Report 30 September 1984.*
>
> **Basis of consolidation**
> The consolidated profit and loss account and balance sheet include the financial statements of the company and all its subsidiaries. Because of seasonal trading the financial statements of several subsidiaries are made up to 30th June; the financial statements of the company and all other subsidiaries are made up to 30th September. As the company's results are included in the consolidated profit and loss account, a separate profit and loss account is not presented.
>
> **Overseas subsidiaries**
> The financial statements of some overseas subsidiaries do not conform with the group's accounting policies because of the legislation and accounting practices of the countries concerned. Appropriate adjustments are made on consolidation in order to present the group financial statements on a uniform basis.

17.30   A consolidation adjustment may be necessary also where a material 'subsequent event' occurs in a subsidiary between the date when the subsidiary's directors sign the subsidiary's own financial statements and the date when the holding company's directors sign the group accounts. If the subsequent event is material to the group and is an 'adjusting event' as defined in SSAP 17 — see Chapter 12 para 10.07), a consolidation adjustment should be made for it in the group accounts.

17.31   It is debatable, however, whether some other adjustments that are made 'on consolidation' and do not relate to the process of consolidation are legitimate. For example, if a group were to set up a provision on consolidation against possible doubtful debts in a subsidiary, it would be unlikely that the subsidiary's financial statements could show a true and fair view without that provision being included in them.

17.32   The holding company's directors have a duty to ensure that the financial year end of each of its subsidiaries coincides with the company's own financial year. This applies unless the directors consider that there are good reasons why subsidiaries should not have coterminous year ends. [*Sec 227(4)*].

17.33   This requirement reinforces SSAP 14, which requires that all subsidiaries' financial statements should, wherever practicable, be prepared:

(a) To the same accounting date as the holding company.

(b) For identical accounting periods as the holding company. [*SSAP 14 para 17*].

17.34   Where a subsidiary's financial year does not coincide with its holding company's financial year, the subsidiary's financial statements that should be used in preparing the group accounts are those that were prepared for the year ending with, or last before, the end of the holding company's financial year. This will apply unless the Secretary of State directs otherwise. [*Sec 230(7)*]. Also, in this situation, the notes to the group accounts must disclose:

(a) The reason why the directors consider it inappropriate for the subsidiary's financial year to coincide with the holding company's financial year.

(b) The balance sheet date of the subsidiaries involved or the earliest and the latest of those dates.
[*4 Sch 70; SSAP 14 para 18*].

Illustrations of the required disclosure are given in Tables 81 and 83.

17.35 This information must still be given even if the subsidiary in question is not dealt with in the group accounts, or if the group accounts are not prepared as consolidated financial statements. [*4 Sch 70*]. In addition, SSAP 14 requires that the notes should disclose, for each principal subsidiary that has a different accounting date, its name and its accounting date. If a principal subsidiary's accounting period is of a different length from that of the holding company, this accounting period should also be stated. [*SSAP 14 para 18*].

17.36 The group accounts may use the equity method of accounting for an investment in another body corporate if, in the opinion of the holding company's directors, that body corporate is so closely associated with a member of the group that the use of the equity method is justified. [*4 Sch 65(1)*]. The Act does not give any guidance on what is meant by either 'so closely associated with' or 'the equity method of accounting'. However, it is likely that one company will be 'so closely associated' with another if it is an associated company within the terms of SSAP 1.

17.37 The phrase 'equity method of accounting' refers to the method used to account for associated companies in accordance with SSAP 1. However, the definition of 'equity accounting' can only be found in SSAP 14. It is defined as:

"A method of accounting under which the investment in a company is shown in the consolidated balance sheet at:

(a) the cost of the investment; and

(b) the investing company or group's share of the post-acquisition retained profits and reserves of the company; less

(c) any amounts written off in respect of *(a)* and *(b)* above;

and under which the investing company accounts separately in its profit and loss account for its share of the profits before tax, taxation and extraordinary items of the company concerned."
[*SSAP 14 para 14*].

SSAP 1 has been revised since SSAP 14 was introduced. The revised SSAP 1 requires the value of the investment determined in accordance with the equity method of accounting to be disclosed differently (see Chapter 8 para 8.34). However, the aggregate value to be disclosed is the same. Examples of groups that use this method are given in Tables 84 and 88.

Table 84: Illustration of a holding company that has used the equity method to value its investment in subsidiaries.

Extract from The Savoy Hotel PLC Directors' Report and Annual Accounts 31 December 1984.

Accounting policy

Subsidiaries

The Company accounts for its investments in subsidiary companies by the equity method, whereby the original cost of the investment is adjusted for changes since the date of acquisition in the applicable underlying net assets.

Note

14 Fixed Asset Investments	Consolidated £'000	The Savoy Hotel PLC £'000
Investment in Subsidiary Companies – unlisted		
Shares at net asset value at 31st December, 1983..	—	9,697
Revaluation surplus (Note 22)	—	60
Shares at net asset value at 31st December, 1984	—	9,757
Unlisted Investment		
Additions in 1984..	53	53
Shares at cost at 31st December, 1984	53	53
	53	9,810
On an historical cost basis the above investments would be included at:	53	2,865

17.38   With associated companies, this figure will then be analysed between the investing company's share of the other company's net assets (including any goodwill that exists in that company) together with any goodwill that arose on the acquisition. However, generally the investment will be included in the investing company's own balance sheet at cost, and not on the equity basis. Accounting for associated companies is considered further in Chapter 8, paragraphs 8.21 to 8.38 and in Chapter 10, paragraphs 10.85 to 10.89.

17.39   On consolidation, consolidation goodwill often arises. The Act specifically excludes such goodwill from the general requirement that goodwill should be written off over a period that does not exceed its useful economic life. [4 Sch 66]. However, SSAP 22 removes this exception. It requires that goodwill that arises on consolidation (like any other purchased goodwill) should be written off either immediately or over a period that does not exceed the goodwill's useful economic life. Goodwill is discussed in detail in Chapter 7, paragraphs 7.39 to 7.94.

Minority interests

17.40   Outside interests or minority interests in the share capital and reserves of the companies consolidated should be disclosed as a separate amount in the consolidated balance sheet. 'Minority interests' is not an item that is found in either of the balance sheet formats detailed in Schedule 4 to the Act, because that schedule relates principally to an individual company's financial statements. Consequently, minority interests, at present, can be disclosed in a variety of positions in the formats. However, paragraph 34 of SSAP 14 says that they should *not* be shown as part of shareholders' funds.

17.41   In contrast, Article 12(2) of the EC Seventh Directive on group accounts says that minority interests should be shown as a separate item (with an appropriate heading 'Shares held by persons outside the group') in the company's capital, reserves and results brought forward. There will, consequently, be a conflict between SSAP 14 and the EC Seventh Directive when the latter is enacted into UK law. In practice, however, minority interests are generally disclosed in one of two positions: either as a deduction from net assets or as an additional item next to capital and reserves.

17.42   Even where there is a minority interest, the group's consolidated profit and loss account should include all of the profits and losses that are attributable to a subsidiary. The minority's share of these profits and losses is then either deducted from or added to the group's consolidated profit or loss. Again, there is no item for minority interests in the profit and loss account formats of Schedule 4. However, SSAP 14 requires that the minority's share of these profits or losses should be either deducted from or added to the group's profit or loss after tax, but before extraordinary items. [*SSAP 14 para 35*]. Consequently, the item 'Minority interests' will normally appear in the formats after 'Profit or loss on ordinary activities after taxation' (for example, see Table 16 on page 87).

17.43   The minority interest in extraordinary items should be either deducted from or added to the related amounts in the consolidated profit and loss account. [*SSAP 14 para 35*].

17.44   A situation may arise where the minority interest in a subsidiary's net assets becomes a debit balance. This will occur where the company's liabilities (after including holding company loans) exceed its assets. In this situation, the group should include a debit minority interest in the consolidated financial statements only if there is a binding obligation on the minority shareholders to make good the losses incurred. Where there is no such agreement, the consolidated profit and loss account should provide for the minority's share (in addition to the group's share) of the losses the subsidiary made. Consequently, no amount should be added back in the profit and loss account for the minority interest. [*SSAP 14 para 34*]. The above process should be reversed when profits attributable to the minority start to make good the losses that were made earlier.

Provisions not applicable to group accounts

17.45   Certain provisions in the Act do not apply to group accounts. These are as follows:

(a) Part II of Schedule 5 (statement in a company's financial statements of the identities and the places of incorporation of companies other than subsidiaries whose shares it holds, and particulars of those shares).

(b) Part III of Schedule 5 (disclosure of financial information in respect of subsidiaries and other bodies corporate in which the company holds shares).

(c) Part V of Schedule 5 (particulars in financial statements of chairman's and directors' emoluments, pensions and compensation for loss of office).

(d) Part VI of Schedule 5 (particulars in financial statements of higher-paid employees).

(e) Sections 232 to 234 and Schedule 6, so far as they relate to accounts other than group accounts (disclosure of transactions etc. with directors and officers).
[4 Sch 63, 68].

17.46   The effect of these exemptions is to exclude, from the group accounts, details of directors' emoluments and transactions and also details of significant shareholdings. But such details are still required in respect of the holding company in its own financial statements. However, in respect of higher-paid employees, many groups of companies go further than the Act requires, and they give details, in their consolidated financial statements, of higher-paid employees not only for the holding company, but also for the group as a whole (for example, see Table 85).

Changes in the composition of the group

17.47   Goodwill that arises on consolidation and accounting for business combinations are considered in more detail in Chapter 7 and Chapter 18 respectively.

17.48   There are no requirements in the Act as to information that must be given in the financial statements relating to material additions to, or disposals from, the group. However, SSAP 14 requires that consolidated financial statements should contain sufficient information about the results of the subsidiaries acquired or sold to enable shareholders to appreciate the effect these results have had on the consolidated results. In addition, SSAP 10 requires that the statement of source and application of funds should show the effects of additions to, and disposals from, the group. These requirements in SSAP 10 are considered in Chapter 6, paragraphs 6.51 and 6.52 (see also Table 86).

Table 85: *Illustration of a group that has shown the number of senior employees of the group whose remuneration exceeds £30,000.*

Extract from Extel Group PLC Report and Accounts 31 March 1984.

Note extract

Higher paid employees
The number of senior employees of the group other than directors whose remuneration was in the following ranges:

	1984	1983
£30,001 – £35,000	13	7
£35,001 – £40,000	6	3
£40,001 – £45,000	1	1
£60,001 – £65,000	1	—

Number of employees
The average number of persons employed by the group during the year was:

	1984	1983
Monthly paid	1,970	2,056
Weekly paid	963	910
	2,933	2,966

17.49 When there is an addition to the group, the consolidated profit and loss account should include the subsidiary's results from the date the group acquired it. When there is a material disposal, the consolidated profit and loss account should include the following:

(a) The subsidiary's results up to the date of disposal.

(b) The gain or loss on the sale of the investment. This gain or loss is the difference, at the time of the sale, between the sale proceeds and the holding company's share of the subsidiary's net assets, together with either any premium (less any amounts written off) or any discount on acquisition.
[*SSAP 14 para 31*].

17.50 The calculation of the gain or loss on sale can be illustrated by the following example:

A holding company purchased an 80% interest in a subsidiary for £80,000 during 1980, when the fair value of the subsidiary's net assets was £87,500. Goodwill on consolidation that arose on the acquisition is being amortised over its estimated useful life of ten years, and a full year's charge for amortisation was made in the group accounts to 31 December 1980. The holding company sold its investment in the subsidiary on 31 December 1984 for £100,000. The fair value of the subsidiary's net assets on the date of the sale was £112,500.

The holding company's profit and loss account for 1984 would show a gain on the sale of the investment of £20,000 calculated as follows:

	£
	£
Sale proceeds	100,000
Less: Cost of investment in subsidiary	(80,000)
Gain on sale to the holding company	20,000

However, the group's profit and loss account for 1984 would show a gain on the sale of the subsidiary of £4,000 calculated as follows:

	£
	£
Sale proceeds	100,000
Less: Share of net assets at date of disposal (£112,500 x 80%)	(90,000)
Less: Goodwill on consolidation unamortised at date of sale*	(6,000)
Gain on sale to the group	4,000

*The unamortised goodwill on consolidation is calculated as follows:

	£
Fair value of consideration at date of acquisition	80,000
Less: Fair value of net assets of subsidiary at date of acquisition (£87,500 x 80%)	70,000
Goodwill arising on consolidation	10,000
Amortisation (4 years x £1,000)	4,000
Unamortised goodwill at 31.12.1984	6,000

The difference between the gain in the holding company's profit and loss account and the gain reported in the group's consolidated profit and loss account is £16,000 (that is, £20,000—£4,000).

This difference represents the share of post-acquisition profits retained in the subsidiary of £20,000 (that is, (£112,500—£87,500) x 80%) that have been reported in the group's profit and loss account up to the date of sale, less goodwill of £4,000 that has been written off in the group's profit and loss account.

17.51 The date upon which a holding company should account for either the acquisition or the disposal of a subsidiary should be the earlier of the two dates that follow:

(a) The date on which consideration passes.

(b) The date on which an offer becomes, or is declared, unconditional.

This applies even where the acquiring company has the right, under the purchase agreement, to share in the profits of the acquired business from an earlier date. [*SSAP 14 para 32*].

17.52 The application of paragraph 32 of SSAP 14 still causes problems in practice. Paragraph 17.51 *(b)* above reflects the legal (and more usual) position as to when a company either becomes or ceases to be a subsidiary. Paragraph 17.51 *(a)* covers the more unusual situation where the whole of the consideration passes at an earlier date. In the latter situation, the acquiring company would almost certainly take effective management control of the acquired company as soon as the whole of the consideration passes. Sometimes a proportion, say 10%, of the consideration passes as a deposit when contracts are exchanged. This payment of a deposit gives the acquiring company a beneficial interest in the company it is acquiring. It would not, however, be deemed to represent a change in ownership.

17.53　If there is a provision in a purchase agreement that the acquiring company has a right to share in the profits of the acquired business before the effective date of its acquisition, this provision cannot override the accounting treatment required by paragraph 32 of SSAP 14. A company is purchased at a particular date, and the acquirer has the right to the company's net assets at that date. This applies irrespective of the way in which these assets are derived, and regardless of whether they are distributable in law or otherwise. For accounting purposes, the acquired company's retained earnings at the *date of the purchase* are pre-acquisition to the acquirer. (The treatment of pre-acquisition profits is considered further in Chapter 18, paragraphs 18.92 to 18.98.) Even where the purchase agreement refers to the net assets at the previous balance sheet date, the acquirer, in arriving at the purchase price, will have taken into account changes in those net assets between that date and the date of acquisition.

17.54　In practice, the effective date of acquisition or disposal (particularly where an unlisted company is involved) may differ from that originally intended by the management of both the vendor and the purchaser. Negotiations to either purchase or sell a subsidiary often take place over a considerable period of time. There can also be a delay between the time when agreement is reached in principle and the time when the formal contracts and other necessary legalities are completed. Conditions, such as the receipt of third parties' consent, may take time to be satisfied. Until such time as agreement is reached and all the conditions are satisfied, the transaction cannot be regarded as 'unconditional'. In a simple case where the agreement is between only two parties, it is reasonable to interpret 'the date on which an offer becomes, or is declared, unconditional' as being the date on which agreement is reached in principle and evidenced in writing (for example, in the form of heads of agreement). This is provided, however, that the consideration also passes at that time. This applies even though the shares may not be formally transferred until a later date.

17.55　To a lesser extent, the behaviour of the respective parties to the transaction may also give some indication as to the effective date. If they both act as if the control of the company concerned had changed hands, this would normally indicate that the acquisition was effective. However, if there was some major matter that was still unresolved between the parties, or if there was some important condition that had still to be satisfied under the agreement, it is unlikely that the acquirer would become involved in the management of the company.

17.56 Paragraph 32 of SSAP 14 does not apply to those cases where the acquisition is treated as a merger (see Chapter 18 para 18.56).

17.57 SSAP 1 includes a paragraph in respect of the effective date of acquisition or disposal of an interest in an associated company that is similar to paragraph 32 of SSAP 14. SSAP 1 is considered in Chapter 8, paragraph 8.21.

17.58 Sometimes a company may decide, before its accounting year end, to sell one of its subsidiaries, but the actual disposal does not take place until early in the next accounting period.

17.59 The question then arises as to how the company's current year's consolidated financial statements should reflect the disposal. Under SSAP 17, the disposal of the subsidiary is a non-adjusting event. Consequently, despite the company's decision to sell, the company should still include the subsidiary in its current year's consolidation. In addition, if the sale is material, the fact of the sale and its financial effect should be shown in the notes to the company's consolidated financial statements. Although the control of the subsidiary could now be said to be only temporary (see para 17.63*(d)* below), the subsidiary should not be excluded from consolidation. This is because, unless a subsidiary has been purchased with the intention that it will subsequently be sold, control should not be considered to be temporary simply because the subsidiary is due to be sold in the near future. Where the directors have decided to dispose of a subsidiary, they may wish to disclose its results separately in the group's consolidated profit and loss account.

Exclusion of a subsidiary from group accounts

17.60 The Act says that group accounts *may* exclude a subsidiary if the company's directors are of the opinion that one of the following situations exists:

(a) It would be either *impracticable* or *of no real value* to the holding company's shareholders to include the subsidiary, because the amounts involved are immaterial.

(b) It would involve *expense or delay* out of proportion to the value to the company's shareholders to include the subsidiary (for example, see Table 86).

(c) The group accounts, if the subsidiary was included, would either be *misleading* or be *harmful* to the business of either the company or any of its subsidiaries (provided that, in a situation where it would be *harmful*, the directors obtain the approval of the Secretary of State to exclude the subsidiary).

(d) The *business* of the holding company and that of the subsidiary are *so different* that they cannot reasonably be treated as a single undertaking (provided that the directors obtain the approval of the Secretary of State to exclude the subsidiary).
[*Sec 229(3)(4)*].

Table 86: *Illustration of a subsidiary that has been excluded from consolidation because it would have caused expense and delay in the preparation of those consolidated financial statements.*

Extract from The Caledonian Aviation Group plc Report and Accounts 31 October 1984.

Directors' report extract

Acquisition and Investment

In October 1983, the Group acquired the Jetsave group of companies which have been accounted for as subsidiaries since 1st November 1983. In July 1984, a further three travel shops were acquired with Robin Edwards Travel (WGC) Limited.

Note extract

10. Investments (a) The Group's investments comprise:	Subsidiary not Consolidated Unlisted Shares £'000	Related Unlisted Shares £'000	Companies Share of Profits £'000	Trade Investments Unlisted Shares £'000	Total £'000
Cost at 1st November, 1983	1,384	1,063	92	549	3,088
Reclassifications	(1,384)	—	—	—	(1,384)
Additions	—	—	15	27	42
Disposals	—	—	—	(3)	(3)
	—	1,063	107	573	1,743

(b) Subsidiary not Consolidated

On 10th October, 1983, the Company contracted to purchase for £1,384,000 the entire share capital of Jetsave Limited and its wholly owned subsidiary Jetsave Travel Limited, both incorporated in England, and Jetsave Travel Inc., incorporated in the United States. Completion took place on the purchase of the English companies on 14th October, 1983 and of the U.S. company on 1st November, 1983. The accounts of these companies were not consolidated into the 1983 Group accounts as the directors believed them to be of no real value to the members in view of the insignificant amounts involved and that the expense and delay in their production would have been out of proportion to the value of those accounts. The subsequent incorporation of these companies into the 1984 Group accounts has been dealt with in note 10(f) below.

(f) Acquisition of Subsidiaries

An analysis of the consolidation of the Jetsave companies and the acquisition of Robin Edwards (W.G.C.) Limited is as follows:

Net Assets Acquired	£'000	Discharged by	£'000
Tangible Fixed Assets	346	Cash paid	1,697
Goodwill	1,387		
Debtors	1,379		
Cash	2,872		
Creditors – short term	(4,287)		
	1,697		1,697

The £1,697,000 has been dealt with in the Movement of Funds Statement as £348,000 in Acquisition of Subsidiaries and £1,349,000 included in Expenditure on Intangible Fixed Assets.

17.61 If the directors consider that each of the company's subsidiaries should be excluded from the group accounts for any of the reasons stated above, then they need not prepare group accounts. [*Sec 229(3)*].

17.62   SSAP 14 also states that where a subsidiary has been excluded from the group accounts, for any of the reasons outlined in paragraph 17.60 above, the reason for the exclusion must be given in the group's financial statements. However, it also says that where a subsidiary has been excluded in this way, the resulting financial statements will need to be considered to determine whether they give a true and fair view of the position of the group as a whole. [*SSAP 14 para 20*].

Exclusion of a subsidiary from consolidation

17.63   In contrast to the Act's requirements outlined above, SSAP 14 sets out various situations where it *requires* that a subsidiary should be excluded from *consolidation*. There is some overlap between the situations described in SSAP 14 and those outlined by the Act. The ones described in SSAP 14 are more restrictive, but all of them are likely also to fall under one or more of the circumstances outlined in *(a)* to *(d)* in paragraph 17.60 above. The situations outlined in SSAP 14 are as follows:

(a)   *Dissimilar activities*. The subsidiary's activities are *so different* from those of the other group companies that consolidated financial statements including that subsidiary would be misleading. The information would be better presented to the holding company's shareholders by including separate financial statements for the subsidiary in the group accounts (for example, see Table 87). This is a combination of situations *(c)* and *(d)* outlined in paragraph 17.60 above.

(b)   *Lack of effective control*. The holding company *does not control* the subsidiary. This situation would arise where the holding company (although it owns more than one-half of the subsidiary's equity share capital) either does not own share capital that carries more than one-half of the voting rights, or is restricted in some way from appointing the majority of the directors (for example, see Table 88). The reason for excluding this type of company from consolidation may equally result from the situations described in *(a)*, *(b)* and *(c)* of paragraph 17.60 above.

(c)   *Severe restrictions*. The subsidiary operates under *severe restrictions* that significantly restrict the holding company's control, and that are expected to last for the foreseeable future. Situation *(c)* in paragraph 17.60 above may also cover this type of subsidiary.

(d)   *Temporary control*. The holding company's directors intend that its *control* over the subsidiary should be only *temporary*. This situation may also be covered by *(a)* and *(c)* in paragraph 17.60.
[*SSAP 14 para 21*].

Accounting treatment where a subsidiary is not consolidated

17.64   SSAP 14 details the accounting treatment that should be followed where (for any of the reasons given above in paragraph 17.63) a subsidiary has not been *consolidated*.

Table 87: Example of a subsidiary not consolidated because its activities are so dissimilar from those of other companies within the group.

Extract from J. Hepworth & Son, PLC Report and Accounts 31 August 1983.

Accounting policies extract

Basis of consolidation

The group accounts consolidate the accounts of the company and its subsidiaries except Club 24 Limited, the Hepworth share in the profits of which is shown in the profit and loss account. The accounts of each company in the group have been prepared to 31st August 1983. The results of subsidiaries sold during any year are included to the date of sale. All unrealised intra-group profits are eliminated on consolidation.

Profit and loss account extract

Notes		1983 £000	1982 £000
2	**Turnover**	98,603	83,370
	Cost of sales	85,542	73,387
	Gross profit	13,061	9,983
	Distribution costs	2,308	2,361
	Administrative expenses	5,285	5,018
2		5,468	2,604
2	Share of profits, including interest, from non-consolidated subsidiary, Club 24 Limited	3,806	3,644
	Operating profit	9,274	6,248

Investments note extract

The directors consider that comprehension of the group results is improved by not consolidating the accounts of Club 24 Limited because of its different trade. The group's share of the profit of Club 24 Limited is included in the profit and loss account and a summary of the investment in Club 24 Limited attributable to J. Hepworth & Son, plc is given below:

Club 24 Limited Summary balance sheet	1983 £000	1982 £000
Fixed assets	718	—
Current assets – debtors	75,345	57,313
Current liabilities	33,826	21,603
Net assets	42,237	35,710
Less unsecured loans and minority shareholding	17,245	13,915
Investment in Club 24 Limited attributable to J. Hepworth & Son, plc	24,992	21,795

Club 24 Limited provides retail credit card facilities for the customers of group retail companies and other companies outside the group.

Under the terms of the financing agreement with Forward Trust Limited, the company's minority shareholder, the whole of the post tax profits of Club 24 Limited amounting to £662,000 (1982 £111,000) is distributable. The dividend of £439,000 (1982 £85,000) receivable by the group together with interest receivable amounting to £3,276,000 (1982 B3,467,000) in respect of loans made by the group to Club 24 Limited is included in the group profit and loss account.

Dissimilar activities

17.65   The consolidated financial statements should include the subsidiary
under the equity method of accounting (see para 17.37 above). The
group accounts should include the subsidiary's separate financial statements. These financial statements may be combined with the financial
statements of those other subsidiaries that have similar operations. The
subsidiary's financial statements should include the following:

   (a) Details of the holding company's interest.

   (b) Details of intra-group balances.

   (c) The nature of the subsidiary's transactions with the rest of the
   group.

   (d) A reconciliation with the amount included in the consolidated financial statements for the group's investment in the subsidiary.
   [*SSAP 14 para 23*].

Lack of effective control

17.66   If the subsidiary satisfies all of the criteria given in SSAP 1 to allow
it to be treated as an associated company, it should be included in the
consolidated financial statements under the equity method of accounting (see para 17.37 above). Otherwise, it should be included in the consolidated financial statements as an investment at cost or valuation,
less any provision required (for example, see Table 88). [*SSAP 14 para
24*].

Severe restrictions

17.67   The amount of the group's investment in the subsidiary should be stated
in the consolidated balance sheet, under the equity method of accounting (see para 17.37 above), at its value at the date when the severe restrictions came into force. No further accrual should be made for its
profits or losses after that date. However, if the directors consider that
there has been a permanent fall in the value of the investment from
the value determined under the equity method, then they should provide for the loss through the consolidated profit and loss account. For
this purpose, they should consider each investment individually. [*SSAP
14 para 25*].

17.68   In addition, the group accounts should give the following information
in respect of the subsidiary:

   (a) The net assets.

   (b) The profits or losses for the period.

   (c) Any amounts included in the consolidated profit and loss account
   for dividends received or for the write-down of the investment.
   [*SSAP 14 para 26*].

Table 88: *Illustration of the treatment of subsidiaries that have been excluded from consolidation because of lack of effective control or because to consolidate would involve expense and delay out of proportion to the value to shareholders.*

Extract from Trusthouse Forte PLC Report & Accounts 31 October 1984.

Notes

1 ACCOUNTING POLICIES
Basis of consolidation
(a) Acquisitions and disposals: The Group balance sheet includes all the assets and liabilities of subsidiary companies including those acquired during the year. The Group profit after taxation includes only that proportion of the results arising since the effective date of control, or in the case of companies or interests disposed of, for the period of ownership.

As explained in note 12, the accounts of The Savoy Hotel PLC and its subsidiaries, and Luncheon Vouchers Limited have not been consolidated.

12 FIXED ASSETS – INVESTMENTS
Subsidiaries
Company
Shares in subsidiary companies have been revalued on the basis of the Company's share of the book value of the net assets of the subsidiaries at 31st October, 1984.

Group
The principal subsidiary companies in the Group are shown on pages 26 and 27.

At 31st October, 1984 the Group owned 69% of the equity of The Savoy Hotel PLC ('Savoy') representing 42·3% of the voting rights. The accounts of Savoy have not been consolidated as the Group plays no part in the management or direction of Savoy. The Group's investment in Savoy has been treated as a long-term trade investment and included at cost. To comply with the Companies Act 1948 concerning group accounts the Savoy accounts for the year ended 31st December, 1983 which are the latest available audited accounts, are set out on pages 28 to 33.

The Group owns 56% of the equity of Luncheon Vouchers Limited ('L.V.'). The Articles of Association of L.V. do not allow any one company to control its Board of Directors. Therefore in accordance with the provisions of SSAP 14 and because the Directors of the Group believe that to consolidate the accounts would involve expense and delay out of proportion to the value to the Shareholders, L.V. has been dealt with in the accounts as an unlisted investment.

Temporary control

17.69 The investment should be included in the consolidated balance sheet as a current asset at the lower of cost and net realisable value. [*SSAP 14 para 27*].

Disclosure where a subsidiary is excluded from group accounts

17.70 Where group accounts are not prepared, or where a subsidiary is excluded from the group accounts, the notes to the holding company's financial statements (or where these are prepared, the consolidated financial statements [*4 Sch 69(7)*]) must disclose:

(a) The reasons why the subsidiary or the subsidiaries are not dealt with in the group accounts. [*4 Sch 69(2)(a); SSAP 14 para 20*].

(b) Any qualification contained in the auditors' report on the subsidiary's or the subsidiaries' financial statements that cover the period that ends with or during the holding company's financial year. This applies to the extent that the qualification is not covered by the report on the holding company's own financial statements, and to the extent that it is material from the point of view of the holding company's shareholders.

(c) The aggregate amount of the holding company's total investment in the excluded subsidiaries' shares, determined according to the equity method of accounting (see para 17.37 above). This information need not be disclosed, however, where both the following conditions are satisfied:

(i) The company is itself the wholly-owned subsidiary of another company incorporated in Great Britain.
(ii) The financial statements include a note stating that, in the directors' opinion, the aggregate value of shares in subsidiaries and of amounts owing from subsidiaries is not less than the aggregate of the amounts at which those assets are stated or included in the company's balance sheet.

[*4 Sch 69(1)-(4)(7)*].

17.71 However, provided that the fact is stated in the notes to the holding company's financial statements or (where they are prepared) the consolidated financial statements, the information referred to in paragraph 17.70 above need not be disclosed if it is unobtainable. Also, it need not be disclosed if the Secretary of State directs that all or some of the information need not be given. The Secretary of State may so direct either on the application of the company's directors or with their consent. [*4 Sch 69(5)(6)*]. An example of an occasion when it would be allowable not to disclose this information would be when a company has trading subsidiaries in two countries, and those two countries either are at war, or have trading embargoes between them. In these two situations the disclosure of the UK group's investment in each subsidiary might impair its trading ability in those countries.

Disclosure where a subsidiary is excluded from consolidation

17.72 SSAP 14 requires that the following information should be disclosed in the group accounts in respect of those subsidiaries that are excluded from consolidation:

(a) The reasons for excluding the subsidiaries from consolidation.

(b) The names of the principal subsidiaries excluded.

(c) Any premium or discount on acquisition (determined by comparing the purchase consideration and the fair value of the assets acquired) to the extent that it has not been written off.
[*SSAP 14 para 28*].

17.73 In addition, where a subsidiary has been excluded from consolidation as outlined in paragraph 17.63 above, the Act requires the information outlined in paragraph 17.70 to be given. [*4 Sch 69(7)*]. Also, where a holding company prepares consolidated financial statements, the information set out in paragraphs 17.08 and 17.16 above (details of intercompany balances, etc.) must be given in respect of any subsidiaries that are not consolidated. [*4 Sch 67*].

Realised and distributable reserves

17.74 Realised and distributable reserves are discussed in detail in Chapter 19. The restrictions on distributions contained in the Act apply to individual companies, and not to groups. This is because individual companies make distributions, whereas groups do not. However, users of group accounts may quite possibly wish to know the amount the holding company could distribute if all the group's subsidiaries were to pay up their realised profits by way of dividend to the holding company. The figure of consolidated realised reserves gives an approximate indication of this potential distribution. Many groups specifically disclose the amount of consolidated realised reserves (for example, see Table 37 on page 192). If this information is not disclosed, users of the group accounts may reasonably interpret the consolidated profit and loss account balance and any other reserve balance as representing realised reserves, and the consolidated revaluation reserve balance as representing unrealised reserves. The amount of the consolidated realised reserves can be a very important figure to users of the group accounts. Also, if it is not disclosed, it may affect the truth and fairness of those financial statements in certain situations.

17.75 In addition, SSAP 14 requires that where there are significant restrictions on the holding company's ability to distribute the group's retained profits (other than those shown as non-distributable) because of statutory, or contractual or exchange control restrictions, the extent of the restrictions should be indicated.

17.76 The holding company's ability to distribute pre-acquisition reserves of its subsidiaries is discussed in Chapter 18, paragraphs 18.92 to 18.98.

Translation of overseas subsidiaries' financial statements

17.77 The Act does not deal with the translation of foreign currency financial statements of a UK holding company's overseas subsidiaries. Translation is necessary so that the financial statements of overseas subsidiaries may be consolidated with the holding company's sterling financial statements. SSAP 20 deals with translation, and it covers also the translation of the results of overseas associated companies and foreign branches. Normally, a company should use the closing rate/net investment method for such translations. [*SSAP 20 para 52*].

17.78 The 'closing rate/net investment' method recognises that a company's investment is in the net worth of its foreign enterprise, rather than being a direct investment in that enterprise's individual assets and liabilities. The net investment that a company has in a foreign enterprise is its effective equity stake, and it comprises its proportion of that enterprise's net assets. In appropriate circumstances, intra-group loans and deferred balances may be regarded as part of the effective equity stake. [*SSAP 20 para 43*].

17.79 Under the closing rate/net investment method, a company should use the closing rate of exchange when translating the amounts in the balance sheets of its overseas enterprises. The company should record, as a movement on consolidated reserves, the exchange differences that arise when it retranslates its opening net investment in a foreign enterprise to the closing rate. [*SSAP 20 para 53*]. (SSAP 20 does not require companies or groups to maintain a separate reserve for exchange differences, but some companies do so.)

17.80 Under the closing rate/net investment method, a company should translate the profit and loss accounts of its foreign enterprises either at the closing rate or at an average rate for the period.

17.81 The company should record, as a movement on consolidated reserves, the difference between translating the profit and loss account at the average rate and translating it at the closing rate. [*SSAP 20 para 54*].

Table 89 illustrates a group's treatment of foreign currency amounts.

17.82 SSAP 20 defines the 'closing rate' as the exchange rate for spot transactions that was ruling at the balance sheet date. It is the mean of the buying rate and the selling rate at the close of business on the day for which the rate is to be ascertained. [*SSAP 20 para 41*].

17.83 Where the balance sheet date of an overseas subsidiary differs from that of the holding company, the closing rate for the purposes of preparing consolidated financial statements is the rate ruling at the overseas subsidiary's balance sheet date.

Table 89: Illustration of a group's treatment of amounts recorded in foreign currencies.

Extract from Bass PLC Annual Review 30 September 1984.

Accounting policy

d) Foreign currencies
Assets and liabilities in foreign currencies together with the trading results of overseas subsidiaries are translated into sterling at the relevant rates of exchange ruling at the balance sheet date.

Exchange differences whether realised or unrealised:

i) on overseas net assets are taken to retained earnings.

ii) on foreign currency borrowings of the investing company are taken to retained earnings to the extent that these differences match those in (i) above but are included as part of cost of borrowing where these differences are unmatched.

All other exchange differences are dealt with in arriving at the trading profit.

The Company's investment in overseas subsidiaries is translated into sterling at the rate of exchange ruling at the date of acquisition.

Note

17 Reserves

	Share premium account £m	Revaluation reserve £m	Group Other reserves £m	Company Share premium account £m
a) Undistributable reserves				
At 30th September 1983	88·2	237·5	5·2	88·2
Exchange adjustment (17b)	—	·4	—	—
Premium on allotment of ordinary shares	5·6	—	—	5·6
Revaluation surplus on intangible fixed assets (note 9)	—	·6	—	—
Realised revaluation surpluses transferred to profit and loss account	—	(1·8)	—	—
Revaluation element in depreciation charge (17b)	—	(1·4)	—	—
At 30th September 1984	93·8	235·3	5·2	93·8

	Group £m	Company £m
b) Profit and loss account		
Retained earnings at 30th September 1983	731·7	219·2
Exchange adjustment on revaluation reserves (17a)	(·4)	—
Exchange adjustment on assets, less borrowings	·3	—
Revaluation element in depreciation charge (17a)	1·4	—
Premium on acquisition of subsidiaries	(1·3)	—
Retained earnings for the year	91·4	5·8
Retained earnings at 30th September 1984	823·1	225·0
The amount of exchange losses on foreign currency borrowings offset above using the matching concept is	4·3	

17.84 However, where the rate ruling at the holding company's balance sheet date would give significantly different figures, the holding company will need to consider whether (in accordance with the provisions of SSAP 17) to disclose, or to adjust for, that difference in the consolidated financial statements.

17.85   Where a company uses an average rate, it should calculate it by the method it considers is most appropriate to the foreign enterprise's circumstances. [*SSAP 20 para 54*]. It can use any reasonable method, but the objective of the method must be to calculate a weighted average that reflects changes both in exchange rates and in the volume of business.

17.86   Where the foreign enterprise's trade depends more on the economic environment of the investing company's currency than on its own reporting currency, the company should use the temporal method of translation. [*SSAP 20 para 55*]. The mechanics of the temporal method are identical to those that an individual company uses when preparing its financial statements. For example, the foreign enterprise's fixed assets are translated at the rates ruling at the date when it acquired each asset. As a result, the foreign enterprise's financial statements are included in the consolidated financial statements as if the investing company itself had entered into the enterprise's transactions in its own currency.

In practice, however, there will be few occasions when companies should use the temporal method. One example of a situation where the temporal method might be appropriate is where a foreign enterprise acts as a selling agency that receives stocks of goods from the investing company and remits the proceeds back to the investing company. Another example of a situation where the temporal method might be appropriate is where a foreign enterprise is located overseas for tax, or exchange control or similar reasons, or to act as a means of raising finance for, or for holding surplus funds on behalf of, other group companies.

17.87   The closing rate/net investment method is illustrated by the following example:

A UK company has a wholly-owned subsidiary in France. At 31 March 1984, the UK company's net investment (share capital and reserves) in the French subsidiary amounted to FF 1,250,000, and the exchange rate was £1 = FF 11.5. During the year ended 31 March 1985, the French subsidiary made a profit of FF 75,000. The subsidiary made no distribution to the holding company during the year.

At 31 March 1985, the UK company's net investment in the French subsidiary amounted to FF 1,325,000 (FF 1,250,000 + FF 75,000), and the exchange rate was £1 = FF 11.7.

The loss on the retranslation of the opening net investment is:

	£
FF 1,250,000 at 11.5	108,696
FF 1,250,000 at 11.7	106,838
Loss on retranslation	1,858

The UK company would include the loss on the retranslation of the opening net investment as a movement on its consolidated reserves.

The French subsidiary's profit for the year ended 31 March 1985 at the closing rate would be £6,410 (that is, FF 75,000 at 11.7).

The UK company's net investment in the French subsidiary at 31 March 1985 can be reconciled as follows:

	£
At 31 March 1984	
FF 1,250,000 at 11.5	108,696
Loss on retranslation to closing rate	(1,858)
Profit for the year	6,410
At 31 March 1985	
FF 1,325,000 at 11.7	113,248

If the UK company had used a weighted average rate of £1 = FF 11.6 to translate the profit and loss account of its French subsidiary, it would have had an additional movement on its consolidated reserves. This additional movement would represent the difference between the use of the closing rate and the use of an average rate to translate the French subsidiary's profit for the year. The difference is:

	£
FF 75,000 at 11.7	6,410
FF 75,000 at 11.6	6,466
Difference	56

The net investment in the subsidiary at 31 March 1985 would then reconcile as follows:

	£
At 31 March 1984	
FF 1,250,000 at 11.5	108,696
Loss on retranslation to closing rate:	
of opening net investment	(1,858)
of profit for the year	(56)
Profit for the year	6,466
At 31 March 1985	
FF 1,325,000 at 11.7	113,248

17.88 Where a subsidiary operates in a country that either has experienced or is experiencing hyperinflation, the normal translation rules will not be applicable. Paragraph 26 of SSAP 20 states that where a foreign enterprise operates in a country where a very high rate of inflation exists, the group may not present fairly, in its historical cost financial statements, the foreign enterprise's financial position, if the group merely uses a translation process. Where this applies, the local currency financial statements should be adjusted, where possible, before the translation process is undertaken, to reflect current price levels.

CHAPTER 18

SHARE PREMIUMS AND ACCOUNTING FOR BUSINESS COMBINATIONS

Share Premiums and Accounting for Business Combinations

Introduction

18.01 Chapter III of Part V of the Act sets out rules that relate to the creation of share premium on an issue of shares, and also to the way in which that premium may be used. The basic rule is detailed in Section 130(1), which says that, where a company issues shares at a premium (whether for cash or otherwise), a sum equal to the aggregate amount or value of the premium must be transferred to a share premium account. This section is derived from section 56 of the Companies Act 1948 and, until the Companies Act 1981 came into effect, there was no relief from the provisions of that section. The Companies Act 1981 introduced certain merger relief provisions that modified the effect of section 56 of the Companies Act 1948. These merger relief provisions are now set out in Sections 131 and 132 of the Companies Act 1985 and section 12 of the Companies Consolidation (Consequential Provisions) Act 1985.

18.02 Chapter 17 considers the necessity to produce group accounts. This chapter looks at the two accounting methods a company may use when preparing group accounts, namely, *acquisition accounting* and *merger accounting*. However, before these two methods are considered, the provisions of the Act that relate to share premiums are explained.

Share premium account

18.03 Where a company issues shares at a value that exceeds their nominal value, a sum equal to the difference between the issue value and the nominal value must be transferred to a share premium account. [*Sec 130(1)*]. For example, if a company issues 100,000 £1 shares at £1.50 each, then it must credit £50,000 to a share premium account. An illustration of how a company treats a premium on the issue of its shares is given in Table 90.

18.04 Once a share premium account has been established, it may only be used to:

(a) Pay up fully paid bonus shares.

(b) Write off preliminary expenses.

(c) Write off expenses of any issue of shares or debentures.

(d) Write off commission paid or discount allowed on any issue of shares or debentures.

(e) Provide for the premium payable on any redemption of debentures. [*Sec 130(2)*].

Table 90: Illustration of how a company treats a premium on the issue of its shares.

Extract from Dalgety PLC Report to shareholders 30 June 1984.

Directors' report extract

Capital
Shares
During the year 164,381 ordinary shares were issued at a premium of 288p per share as part consideration for the purchase of British Soya Products Ltd.

Note

19 Parent company reserve movements	Share premium account £m	Other reserves £m	Profit and loss account £m
At 30 June 1983	98.8	(3.7)	22.3
Exchange rate variations	—	(1.1)	—
Premium on shares issued in year	0.6	—	—
Attributable profit for year	—	—	37.1
Dividends	—	—	(19.0)
Other	—	—	0.1
At 30 June 1984	99.4	(4.8)	40.5

18.05 Apart from these specific uses, the share premium account has to be treated as if it were part of the paid-up share capital of the company. Consequently, the provisions of the Act that apply to the reduction of share capital apply also to the share premium account. [*Sec 130(3)*].

Implications of *Shearer v Bercain Ltd.*

18.06 The tax case of *Shearer v Bercain Ltd.* [*1980*] *3 AER 295* questioned the construction of section 56 of the Companies Act 1948, which is now Section 130 of the Companies Act 1985.

18.07 Before *Shearer v Bercain Ltd.*, it was widely thought that there were two legally acceptable methods of accounting for certain types of business combinations:

(a) The first method, the acquisition method, which the majority of companies used, required that the shares transferred to the purchasing company should be recorded in that company's books at the value of the consideration given. Where the value ascribed to any shares that the purchasing company issued in exchange exceeded their nominal value, the excess had to be recorded as a share premium (in accordance with the requirements of section 56 of the 1948 Act). This treatment had the effect of treating the acquired company's reserves as pre-acquisition and, therefore, as undistributable.

(b) The second method, the merger method, which few companies used, required that the shares transferred to the purchasing company as part of a merger should be recorded in the purchasing company's books at the nominal value of the shares that it issued in exchange. Consequently, the only difference that had to be dealt with on consolidation was the difference between the nominal value of the shares issued as consideration and the nominal value of the shares transferred to the purchasing company. With the exception of any adjustment required to account for this difference, the distributable reserves of all the companies involved in the merger remained distributable.

18.08 The merger method was seldom used in practice, because its legality was uncertain. However, it was more attractive than acquisition accounting because it gave companies freedom to distribute both companies' distributable reserves.

18.09 In *Shearer v Bercain Ltd.*, the court had to consider whether company law permitted companies to use the merger method as an alternative to the acquisition method. The facts before the court were as follows:

An investment holding company (a 'close' company for tax purposes) acquired the share capital of two limited companies by an issue of its own shares. The value of the shares acquired in the two companies exceeded the nominal value of the shares the issuing company issued in exchange. Consequently, the issuing company created a share premium account in respect of this excess. Some time later, the two acquired companies paid dividends out of their pre-acquisition profits and, when the investment company received those dividends, it wrote down the value of its investments in the two companies. Subsequently, the investment company was assessed to tax on the basis that there was a shortfall in its distributions equal to the amount of the dividends that it had received from the two companies.

When the investment company appealed against the assessment, it was common ground between the parties that, if the investment company was obliged to create a share premium account equal in amount to the excess of the value of the shares it acquired over the nominal value of the shares it issued in exchange, this would constitute a 'restriction imposed by law' (within section 290(4) of the Income and Corporation Taxes Act 1970) as regards the distribution of the dividends that it had received from the acquired companies. As a result, the shortfall assessment would have to be discharged.

18.10 In the circumstances, the court held that where shares were issued at a premium, whether for cash or otherwise, section 56 of the 1948 Act *required the premium* to be carried into a share premium account in the issuing company's books, and the premium could be distributed only if the procedure for reducing capital was carried through. Consequently, the shortfall assessment was discharged.

18.11 This judgment gave authority to the interpretation of section 56 of the 1948 Act that required a company to set up a share premium account in any transaction where it acquired another company's shares in return for the allotment of its own shares, and the fair value to it of the shares it acquired exceeded the nominal value of the shares it issued.

18.12 *Shearer v Bercain Ltd.* was not directly concerned with the actual accounting treatment of acquisitions. But the effect of requiring that a share premium account should be set up in such circumstances was to legally prohibit the merger method of accounting. It meant that it was also not lawful for the acquiring company to distribute the acquired company's pre-acquisition profits. Consequently, companies that had previously used merger accounting, and had then regarded the acquired company's pre-acquisition profits as distributable, had contravened the law.

18.13 Following the court's decision, the Government made it known that it considered that there were certain circumstances in which a company's failure to set up a share premium account was unobjectionable.

18.14 Accordingly, the Government introduced legislation that relieved companies, in certain circumstances, from the obligation to carry any share premium to a share premium account. The provisions that give this relief now appear in Sections 131 and 132 of the 1985 Act.

Merger relief

18.15 The essence of merger relief is that, where appropriate conditions are met, the application of Section 130 of the 1985 Act (that is, the equivalent section to section 56 of the 1948 Act) is restricted.

18.16 The situations in which companies can obtain merger relief are those in which the merger satisfies the following three conditions:

(a) A company (which is known as either the issuing company or the acquiring company) secures at least 90% of the nominal value of each class of the equity share capital of another company (the acquired company) as a result of an arrangement.

(b) The arrangement provides for the allotment of equity shares in the issuing company. (Such allotment will normally be made to the acquired company's shareholders.)

(c) The consideration for the shares so allotted is either the issue or the transfer to the issuing company of equity shares in the acquired company or the cancellation of those of the equity shares in the acquired company that the issuing company does not already hold. [*Sec 131(1)(5)*].

18.17 In determining whether a particular merger satisfies the above conditions, the following rules apply:

(a) Any shares in the acquired company that are held by other companies in the same group (other than associates) as the issuing company, or their nominees, should be treated as being held by the issuing company. [*Sec 131(6)*].

(b) An 'arrangement' means any agreement, or scheme or arrangement, including any arrangement that is sanctioned under either Section 425 of the Act (company compromise with creditors and members) or Section 582 of the Act (liquidator accepting shares, etc., as consideration for the sale of the company's property). [*Sec 131(7)*].

(c) A company will be treated as having secured a 90% holding in another company as part of an arrangement, irrespective of whether or not it actually acquired, under that arrangement, all the equity shares that it holds. [*Sec 131(4)*]. This rule means that, in determining whether or not a company has obtained a 90% holding in another company, prior holdings can be taken into account.

(d) 'Company' includes any body corporate, except where reference is made to either the issuing company or the acquiring company. [*Sec 133(4)*].

(e) In any provisions that relate to a company's acquisition of shares in another company, shares that a nominee of a company acquired are to be treated as having been acquired by the company itself. Similarly, the issue, or the allotment or the transfer of any shares to or by a company's nominee is to be regarded as if the shares were issued, or allotted or transferred to or by the company itself. [*Sec 133(2)*].

(f) 'Equity share capital' is a company's issued share capital, excluding any part that (as regards both dividends and capital) does not carry a right to participate beyond a specified amount in a distribution. 'Non-equity shares' are all other shares. [*Sec 744, 131(7)*]. In particular, preference shares do not form part of a company's equity share capital.

(g) The transfer of a company's shares includes the transfer of a right to be included in the company's register of members in respect of those shares. [*Sec 133(3)*].

18.18   The examples that follow illustrate the application of these provisions:

(a) Company A acquires 90% of Company B's equity shares in a share-for-share exchange. This is the most obvious application of the provisions. In these circumstances, Company A is entitled to the relief from Section 130 of the Act.

(b) Company C owns 60% of Company D's equity shares. The members of Company D agree to the cancellation of the equity shares that Company C does not hold, in return for the allotment to them of equity shares in Company C. In this case, also, Company C is entitled to the relief from Section 130. There are two reasons for this:

(i) The effect of cancelling the remaining shares is to increase Company C's 60% holding to a 100% holding (and so over the 90% threshold).

(ii) The consideration for the allotment of Company C's equity shares is the cancellation of those of Company D's shares that it does not already hold.

For this purpose, it is irrelevant that the acquiring company did not acquire the original 60% holding as part of the arrangement. To be entitled to the relief, a company (whether newly formed or otherwise) needs only to acquire shares sufficient to either secure or increase its holding to at least 90%. However, Company C is entitled to the relief only on the shares it is now issuing in consideration for the cancellation of the shares in Company D that it does not hold. It cannot retrospectively write back any share premium that it set up on any shares it issued when it acquired the 60% holding.

(c) Company E acquires all of Company F's 'A' equity shares. Company F also has 'B' equity shares in issue, but Company E holds none of these. In this situation, Company E is not entitled to the relief from Section 130 of the Act, because Section 131 requires a 90% holding of each class of equity shares in the acquired company. This applies even if the 'B' shares represent in total only 10% or less of the nominal value of Company F's equity share capital.

(d) Company G acquires 95% of Company H's equity shares. The consideration for these shares is, in equal proportions, equity shares in Company G and cash. In this situation, Company G is entitled to the relief from Section 130. This is because there is no 'cash limit' criterion in the merger conditions. The section states only that the consideration that the acquiring company provides should include shares. It does not stipulate any minimum proportion of the consideration that should consist of shares.

Application of merger relief

18.19   Where a merger satisfies the conditions referred to in paragraph 18.16, the Act provides relief from the application of Section 130. In these circumstances, Section 130 will not apply to any premium that attaches to the shares that the issuing company allots as part of the arrangement. [*Sec 131(2)*].

18.20   In addition, the relief is extended to cover an arrangement that provides for the allotment of any shares in the issuing company in return for either of the following:

(a) The issue or the transfer to the issuing company of non-equity shares in the acquired company.

(b) The cancellation of any such shares that the issuing company does not hold.

In such circumstances, Section 130 will not apply to any premium that attaches to the shares that the issuing company allots for this purpose. [*Sec 131(3)*].

18.21 In this connection, it is important to note that:

(a) Unless there is also a merger that satisfies the conditions referred to in paragraph 18.16, the relief will not extend to shares issued for either the acquisition or the cancellation of non-equity shares.

(b) Where a merger satisfies those conditions, the issuing company can allot any of its shares in return for either the acquisition or the cancellation of non-equity shares in the acquired company. This means that the issuing company may itself allot non-equity shares for such acquisition or cancellation.

Relief in respect of group reconstructions

18.22 The decision in *Shearer v Bercain Ltd.* made it clear also that the issuing company should transfer any premium on the issue of its shares to a share premium account, not only where a *third party* acquisition occurs, but also where a group reconstruction occurs. The Act provides some relief from this requirement. But it does not dispense altogether with the requirement to set up a share premium account. The merger relief provisions of Section 131 (which have been discussed in paras 18.15 to 18.21 above) are not available for group reconstructions. [*Sec 132(8)*]. The relief in respect of group reconstructions is contained in Section 132 of the Act. The group reconstructions to which the Act applies are those that satisfy the following conditions:

(a) A wholly-owned subsidiary (the issuing company) allots some of its shares either to its holding company or to another wholly-owned subsidiary of its holding company.

(b) The allotment is in consideration for the transfer to it of any assets (other than cash) of its holding company or of another wholly-owned subsidiary of its holding company.
[*Sec 132(1)*].

18.23 For example, the allotment may be in consideration for the transfer to the issuing company of shares in another subsidiary (which is not necessarily wholly-owned) that the holding company holds. Diagrammatically, the situation before and after such a reconstruction would be as follows:

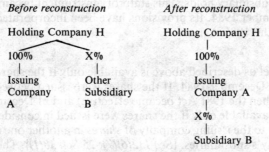

In practice, the holding company, Company H, will often be liquidated after the reconstruction has taken place.

18.24   Where those shares in the issuing company that relate to the transfer are issued at a premium, the issuing company need only transfer to the share premium account an amount equal to the minimum premium value. [*Sec 132(2)*].

18.25   For this purpose, the following definitions apply:

   (a) The 'minimum premium value' is the amount, if any, by which the base value of the consideration that the issuing company received exceeds the aggregate nominal value of the shares that it allots in consideration for the transfer. [*Sec 132(3)*].

   (b) The 'base value' of the consideration that the issuing company received is the amount by which the base value of the assets transferred to it exceeds the base value of any liabilities that the issuing company assumes as part of that consideration. [*Sec 132(4)*].

   (c) The 'base value of the assets transferred' is the lower of:

   (i) The cost to the transferor company of those assets.
   (ii) The amount at which the assets are stated, immediately before the transfer, in the transferor company's accounting records. [*Sec 132(5)(a)*].

   (d) The 'base value of the liabilities' assumed is the amount at which those liabilities are stated, immediately before the transfer, in the transferor company's accounting records. [*Sec 132(5)(b)*].

   (e) 'Company' and 'transfer of shares' have the same meaning as in paragraph 18.17.

18.26   The relief in respect of group reconstructions was originally given in section 38 of the Companies Act 1981. However, the relief given in that section was narrower than it is now under Section 132 of the 1985 Act. The 1981 Act gave relief only where the issuing company's allotment of shares was in consideration for the transfer to it of *shares* in another one of the holding company's subsidiaries. This relief was extended by the Companies (Share Premium Account) Regulations 1984 (SI 1984/2007) to cover the transfer to the issuing company of *any assets* (other than cash) that either the holding company or another wholly-owned subsidiary holds. This statutory instrument became effective on 21 December 1984. Its provisions have been incorporated into Section 132 of the 1985 Act.

18.27   The relief as described above is available only if the shares were issued after 21 December 1984. If the shares were issued between 4 February 1981 (when the 1981 Act became effective) and 21 December 1984, the relief is available only if the shares were issued in consideration for the transfer to the issuing company of *shares* in another one of the holding company's subsidiaries. [*Sec 132(6)(7); 25 Sch 38(1)*]. The relief available in this situation is the same as that outlined in paragraphs 18.24 and 18.25 above. [*Sec 132(7)*].

18.28 The following two examples illustrate the method of calculating the relief available:

(a) An issuing company (Company Y) allots 1,200 £1 ordinary shares (valued at £5 per share) to its holding company (Company X). In consideration of this allotment, Company X agrees to transfer to Company Y its 75% holding in a fellow subsidiary (Company Z). Company X originally paid £3,000 for its 75% holding in Company Z. Immediately before the reconstruction, the amount at which that holding was stated in Company X's accounting records was £2,000.

In these circumstances, the base value of the shares in Company Z is £2,000. This amount is the lower of the cost of the shares to Company X (that is, £3,000) and the amount at which the shares are stated in Company X's accounting records (that is, £2,000).

The nominal value of the shares that Company Y allots in respect of the transfer is £1,200.

Therefore, the minimum premium value is £800. This amount is calculated as the base value of the shares in Company Z (that is, £2,000) less the nominal value of the shares Company Y allots (that is, £1,200). Consequently, the amount of £800 must be transferred to Company Y's share premium account. (Without the relief given by Section 132, the company would have had to transfer £4,800 to its share premium account. This amount is calculated as the difference between the value of £5 and the nominal value of £1 for each of the 1,200 shares.)

(b) A holding company (Company H) has a wholly-owned subsidiary (Company S). Company H has, as part of its assets, land that originally cost £110,000. This land has subsequently been revalued, and it is currently included in the company's accounting records at £175,000. In addition, the purchase of the land was partly financed by a loan of £40,000 that is secured on the land and is still outstanding. The land is currently valued at £200,000.

It is proposed that Company S allots to Company H 25,000 of its ordinary £1 shares in consideration for the transfer to it of the land that Company H currently owns. In addition, Company S will assume the liability for the loan of £40,000 that is secured on the land.

If the Act did not provide relief from Section 130 in respect of group reconstructions such as the above, Company S would need to transfer £135,000 to a share premium account. This premium is calculated as follows:

	£	£
Nominal value of shares allotted		25,000
Fair value of the consideration received:		
Current value of the land	200,000	
Less: liability assumed	40,000	
		160,000
Premium on the shares allotted		135,000

However, because of the relief from Section 130 that Section 132 of the Act gives, the company needs only to transfer £45,000 (which is the 'minimum premium value') to a share premium account. This minimum premium value is calculated as follows:

	£
Base value of the land transferred (being the lower of the original cost of £110,000 and the amount at which it currently stands in Company H's books, £175,000)	110,000
Base value of the liability that Company S assumes	40,000
Base value of the consideration that Company S receives for the shares it allots	70,000
Nominal value of the shares that Company S allots	25,000
'Minimum premium value'	45,000

415

18.29   The principal difference between the relief that relates to group reconstructions and the relief that relates to mergers is that, with group reconstructions, the need may arise to set up a share premium account: with mergers, there is no such requirement.

Retrospective relief

18.30   Before the Companies Act 1981 came into force, many companies had failed to establish a share premium account (as required by section 56 of the Companies Act 1948) after a merger or a group reconstruction. Some companies also subsequently distributed the pre-acquisition reserves of the company that they had acquired.

18.31   The court's judgment in *Shearer v Bercain Ltd.* made it clear that such actions were unlawful.

18.32   However, the Companies Act 1981 gave retrospective relief in certain circumstances. This relief is now contained in the Companies Consolidation (Consequential Provisions) Act 1985. It provides retrospective relief where all the following circumstances exist:

   (a) A company (the issuing company) has issued shares at a premium before 4 February 1981.

   (b) The company has allotted the shares as part of an arrangement.

   (c) The consideration under the arrangement for the shares allotted was one of the following:

   (i) The issue or the transfer of shares in another company (the acquired company) to the issuing company.
   (ii) The cancellation of any shares in that other company that the issuing company did not already hold.

   (d) The acquired company was either a subsidiary or a fellow subsidiary of the issuing company at the time of the arrangement, or it became a subsidiary or a fellow subsidiary of the issuing company as a result of the arrangement.

   (e) The premium on the shares that the issuing company issued was not credited to a share premium account.
   [*CC(CP) s 12(1)-(3)*].

18.33   The meaning of 'company', 'arrangement' and 'transfer of shares' in this context is the same as that defined in paragraph 18.17. [*CC(CP) s 12(5)*].

18.34   In such circumstances, section 56 of the Companies Act 1948 is deemed never to have applied to that part of the premium that arose when the issuing company issued the shares, and was not transferred to the company's share premium account. Therefore, there is no need to have regard to that section in order to determine whether that part of the premium ought to have been included in that company's share premium account. [*CC(CP) s 12(4)*].

18.35 This retrospective relief from section 56 of the Companies Act 1948 is wider than the relief available under Section 131 of the Companies Act 1985. In particular, a company is entitled to the retrospective relief even where:

(a) It does not, as a result of the arrangement, hold 90% or more of the shares in the acquired company.

(b) It does not allot its own *equity* shares in consideration for the shares acquired.

Accounting treatment of the investment in an acquired company

18.36 The Companies Act 1985 clarifies the accounting treatment of an investment in an acquired company that should be used in an issuing company's balance sheet where there is:

(a) A merger under Section 131.

(b) A group reconstruction under Section 132.

(c) Retrospective relief under section 12 of the Companies Consolidation (Consequential Provisions) Act 1985.

18.37 In these circumstances, the cost of the issuing company's investment in the acquired company that has to be shown in the issuing company's balance sheet does not need to include an amount corresponding to the premium (or the part of the premium) that the issuing company has not credited to its share premium account. [*Sec 133(1)*]. The value of the investment to be shown in the holding company's balance sheet is considered further in paragraphs 18.79 to 18.91 below. Although the Act says that the value of the investment shown in the balance sheet need not include the premium, it is debatable whether the investment should be described as being at cost, because the amount shown in the balance sheet may be quite different from the actual cost. It could be argued that the 'true' cost of the shares issued is their fair value, and not their nominal value. Consequently, the company may need to choose some appropriate wording other than 'cost' to describe the investment (for example, 'at nominal value of shares issued').

Other provisions

18.38 The Secretary of State has the power to make regulations for the following purposes:

(a) To make provision for further relief from Section 130 in respect of premiums other than cash premiums.

(b) To modify or to restrict any relief from Section 130 that Sections 131 to 133 give.
[*Sec 134(1)*].

18.39   Any regulations that the Secretary of State makes under Section 134 may make either different provisions for different companies or different provisions for different classes of company. They may also include any incidental and supplementary provisions that he believes are necessary. [*Sec 134(2)*].However, both Houses of Parliament must approve any such regulation. [*Sec 134(3)*]. The Secretary of State's power in this matter is principally designed to deal with any changes that will be required as a result of the UK's adoption of the EC Seventh Directive on group accounts (see further Chapter 17 para 17.03).

Acquisition accounting and merger accounting

18.40   In April 1985, the ASC issued SSAP 23. This Standard is the end result of a long debate on acquisition and merger accounting that has taken place since the ASC originally published ED 3, 'Accounting for acquisitions and mergers', in 1971. The ASC published ED 3 to try to standardise the method of merger accounting that was developing at the time. However, some people believed at that time that merger accounting might conflict with the requirement in section 56 of the Companies Act 1948 to set up a share premium account (see paras 18.06 to 18.14 above). On the grounds that there was insufficient agreement on the legal implications of merger accounting, the ASC decided not to convert ED 3 into an Accounting Standard.

18.41   During the consideration at the Committee Stage of the merger relief provisions that were incorporated into the Companies Act 1981, the Government indicated that a future Accounting Standard should prescribe the accounting treatment that companies should adopt where they obtained merger relief. In response to the Government's comments, the ASC issued ED 31, 'Accounting for acquisitions and mergers', in October 1982. In drafting ED 31, the ASC took into account the merger relief provisions in the Companies Act 1981.

18.42   It is important to remember that the Act contains provisions where *merger relief* may be applied to individual companies, but not to groups. SSAP 23, on the other hand, deals only with *acquisition accounting* and *merger accounting* in consolidated financial statements, and it does not apply to individual companies' financial statements. There is, however, a significant overlap between the concept of *merger relief* and *merger accounting*.

18.43   SSAP 23 lays down rules that determine whether a holding company should use acquisition accounting or merger accounting in its consolidated financial statements. SSAP 23 came into effect in respect of business combinations that groups account for in financial statements of periods beginning on or after 1 April 1985. The Standard briefly describes the circumstances where each accounting method may be appropriate, and it sets out the main differences between acquisition accounting and merger accounting.

18.44 In general, merger accounting may be an appropriate method of accounting for a business combination where the consideration given for the shares acquired in the business combination does not cause substantial resources to leave the group.

Merger accounting conditions

18.45 If a business combination satisfies all of the conditions outlined in SSAP 23, then the group *may* use either acquisition accounting or merger accounting to account for the business combination. If the business combination fails to satisfy any of the conditions, then the group *must* use acquisition accounting to account for the business combination. [*SSAP 23 para 15*]. The four conditions that have to be satisfied if a group is to use merger accounting are as follows:

(a) Offer to shareholders

The business combination must result from *an* offer both to the holders of all those equity shares that the offeror does not already hold, and to the holders of all those voting shares that the offeror does not already hold.

Therefore, a group may use merger accounting only if the business combination arises from a single offer. 'Step-by-step' business combinations (in which the offeror acquires an increasing percentage of the offeree's share capital as a result of several separate offers) will normally not qualify for merger accounting. One exception to this rule is where the first few offers a company makes result in the company acquiring less than 20% of the offeree's share capital (but see *(c)* below), and the final offer secures a holding of at least 90%. Another exception is where the separate offers are effectively a single composite transaction.

(b) 90% holding

As a result of the offer, the offeror must secure a holding of at least 90% of each class of the offeree's equity shares, and must secure at least 90% of the offeree's votes.

An offer that secures at least 90% of the total equity shares might not satisfy this merger condition, because the offeror must secure at least 90% of *each class* of equity shares. Alternatively, the offeree might have voting non-equity shares, and so the offeror might not satisfy the requirement that it must secure at least 90% of the offeree's votes.

(c) Prior holdings

Immediately before the offer, the offeror must not hold 20% or more of any class of the offeree's equity shares, and also must not hold 20% or more of the offeree's votes.

The ASC decided on a 20% prior holdings limit because the offeror would generally have accounted for a larger holding in the offeree as an associated company in accordance with SSAP 1. SSAP 1 requires the investing company to ascribe fair values to the relevant share of the associated company's assets (see further Chapter 8 paras 8.34 to 8.38). Because fair value accounting is inconsistent with merger accounting, the ASC decided on a 20% limit on prior holdings (but see paras 18.46 and 18.47 below).

(d) 10% cash limit

The following two conditions apply:

   (i) Equity share capital must form not less than 90% of the fair value of the total consideration that the offeror gives for the offeree's equity share capital.
   (ii) Equity share capital and/or voting non-equity share capital must form not less than 90% of the fair value of the total consideration that the offeror gives for the offeree's voting non-equity share capital.

The fair value of the total consideration that the offeror gives should include also the fair value of the consideration that the offeror gave for shares that it held before the offer.
[*SSAP 23 para 11*].

18.46 If the offeror has previously acquired a holding of just less than 20% of the offeree's shares entirely for cash, it is still possible that the fourth condition in paragraph 18.45 above may be satisfied. Consider the following example:

Company B has share capital of 1,000 £1 ordinary shares. Company A has previously acquired 180 shares in Company B for £1,800 (that is, £10 per share). These shares were acquired entirely for cash. Company A now wishes to acquire the remaining 820 shares in Company B. Because the value of Company B has increased since Company A acquired its previous holding, and because the 820 shares are valued as a controlling interest (as opposed to a minority interest), the 820 shares are valued at £50 per share. The consideration for these 820 shares is to be given entirely by an issue of Company A's ordinary shares.

The fair value of the total consideration that Company A will have given is:

		£
Cash		1,800
Fair value of shares		
(namely, 820 x £50)		41,000
Total consideration		£42,800

This satisfies the fourth merger condition, because the cash element represents only 2% of the fair value of the total consideration.

18.47 If the cost per share of the prior holding (purchased for cash) is close to the price per share of the holding that the offeror is currently acquiring, it may be that the 20% limit on prior holdings is effectively restricted to nearer 10% (which is the allowable cash element of the total consideration).

18.48 The *fair value* of the shares issued has an effect on whether or not the business combination satisfies the merger conditions. For example, if the total consideration consists of equity shares with a nominal value of £75,000 plus cash of £25,000, then the merger conditions are, at first sight, not satisfied. This is because the equity share capital forms less than 90% of the total of the *nominal* value of the shares issued plus the cash element of the consideration. However, if the shares' fair value is £275,000, the business combination satisfies the fourth merger condition in paragraph 18.45 above, because the equity share capital's fair value is not less than 90% of the total of the issued shares' *fair* value plus the cash element of the consideration.

18.49 In this respect, there is a significant difference between the provisions of SSAP 23 and the provisions of the EC Seventh Directive on group accounts (see Chapter 17 para 17.03). Under the Seventh Directive, merger accounting will be available only if the arrangement does not include a cash payment that exceeds 10% of the *nominal* value (not, as in SSAP 23, the *fair* value) of the shares that the holding company issues under the terms of the arrangement.

18.50 Any convertible stock that is outstanding at the time of the offer should not normally be regarded as equity for the purposes of satisfying the merger conditions. The only exception to this is where the convertible stock is converted into equity as a result of, and at the time of, the business combination. [*SSAP 23 para 12*].

18.51 References to 'the offeror' in the merger conditions include not just the offeror itself, but also the following:

(a) A holding company of the offeror.

(b) A subsidiary of the offeror.

(c) A fellow subsidiary of the offeror.

(d) A nominee or nominees of either the offeror or any of *(a)* to *(c)*. [*SSAP 23 para 13*].

18.52 References in the merger conditions to voting shares relate to *full* voting shares. They do not include shares that carry votes only in special circumstances (for example, when dividends are in arrears). [*SSAP 23 para 14*].

Differences between merger accounting conditions and merger relief conditions

18.53   There are several differences between the *merger accounting* conditions in SSAP 23 and the conditions for *merger relief* in Section 131 of the Act (outlined in para 18.16 above). These differences are:

(a) Under SSAP 23, the offeror must secure a holding of at least 90% of each class of equity shares, and it must also secure a holding of the shares that carry at least 90% of the offeree's votes. To qualify for merger relief under Section 131, the issuing company must secure a holding of at least 90% of each class of equity shares. However, the issuing company does not need to secure shares that carry at least 90% of the offeree's votes.

(b) Under SSAP 23, at least 90% of the fair value of the total consideration that the issuing company gives for equity shares must itself be in the form of equity shares. The Act imposes no such condition.

(c) SSAP 23 stipulates that the offeror's prior holding in the offeree must not exceed 20%. Again, the Act imposes no such condition.

18.54   The conditions for merger accounting in SSAP 23 are more restrictive than the conditions for merger relief in the Act.

18.55   There may be occasions, therefore, where a *holding company* qualifies for merger relief, but the *group* must use acquisition accounting on consolidation. In these circumstances, the Act allows the company to record its investment in the subsidiary at nominal value. But SSAP 23 requires the group to use fair values on consolidation. [*SSAP 23 Appendix para 1(a)*]. Consequently, the holding company must record its investment in the subsidiary at the fair value of the consideration given. However, the difference between the fair value of the shares issued and the nominal value of those shares need not be credited to a share premium account. Instead, it can be credited to a special merger reserve (see paras 18.82 to 18.84 below).

Differences between acquisition accounting and merger accounting

18.56   SSAP 23 highlights the following three main differences between acquisition accounting and merger accounting:

(a) In acquisition accounting, the consolidated financial statements reflect the acquired company's results from the date of acquisition only. However, in merger accounting, the consolidated financial statements incorporate the combined companies' results as if the companies had always been combined. Consequently, under merger accounting, the consolidated financial statements reflect both companies' full year's results, even though the business combination may have occurred part of the way though the year. Under

merger accounting, the corresponding amounts in the consolidated financial statements for the previous year should reflect the results of the combined companies, even though the business combination did not occur until the current year.

(b) In acquisition accounting, the acquiring group should account for the assets it acquired at the cost to the acquiring group. The acquiring group determines that cost by attributing a fair value to the assets and liabilities that it acquires. However, in merger accounting, the group does not restate any assets and liabilities at their fair values. Instead, the group incorporates the assets and liabilities at the amounts recorded in the books of the combined companies. As in *(a)* above, merger accounting shows the position of the combined companies as if the companies had always been combined.

(c) Acquisition accounting may give rise to goodwill on consolidation. However, goodwill does not arise in merger accounting. Merger accounting may lead to differences in values on consolidation. For example, in merger accounting, there may be a difference between the nominal value of the shares issued together with the fair value of any additional consideration given, and the nominal value of the other company's shares that have been acquired (see paras 18.66 to 18.70). However, such differences are not goodwill as defined in SSAP 22, because they are not based on the fair values of both the consideration given and the separable net assets acquired.

18.57 The following example illustrates the difference between acquisition accounting and merger accounting:

Company H (the issuing company) acquires the whole of Company A's equity share capital. The effect of the acquisition will be to merge the interests of Company H and Company A.

Company A's shareholders accept an offer from Company H of one share in Company H for each share in Company A as at 31 December 1984. The value at 31 December of the 400,000 of Company H's £1 shares that are offered to Company A's shareholders is £6,400,000, (that is, £16 per share). The fair value of Company A's net assets is £6,100,000 (that is, £100,000 above their net book value). The difference of £300,000 is attributable to goodwill.

On 31 December 1984, before the acquisition, the summarised balance sheets of the two companies are as follows:

	Company H	Company A
	£000	£000
Share capital (shares of £1 each)	500	400
Reserves	4,500	5,600
	5,000	6,000
Net assets	5,000	6,000

423

The summarised consolidated balance sheets of the issuing company and its subsidiary under the two methods of accounting are as follows:

	Acquisition accounting £000	Merger accounting £000
Share capital	900 (a)	900 (a)
Distributable reserves	4,500 (b)	10,100 (c)
Undistributable reserves:		
Share premium account	6,000 (b)	—
	11,400	11,000
Goodwill on consolidation	300 (d)	—
Net assets	11,100 (e)	11,000 (e)
	11,400	11,000

Notes to the example above:

(a) The share capital consists of the 500,000 shares originally in issue, together with the 400,000 shares allotted when Company H combined with Company A.

(b) The amount credited to the share premium account in accordance with Section 130 of the Act is £6,000,000 (that is, 400,000 shares issued at a premium of £15 per share). The amount of distributable reserves represents Company H's reserves.

(c) Section 131 of the Act contains no requirement to transfer, to a share premium account, the premium on the shares allotted to the acquired company's shareholders. Consequently, both companies' distributable reserves are pooled. In accordance with paragraph 18 of SSAP 23, the excess of the fair value of Company A's net assets over their book value (that is, £100,000) need not be incorporated into the consolidated financial statements (see para 18.62 below).

(d) Goodwill on consolidation is the amount by which the purchase consideration (that is, 400,000 shares at £16, or £6,400,000) exceeds the fair value of the underlying net assets acquired (that is, £6,100,000) (see further Chapter 7 paras 7.39 to 7.94).

(e) Net assets are the two companies' total net assets. In acquisition accounting, the assets are included at their fair value, as required by SSAP 14 (see also para 18.59).

Thus, the main effect of the provisions of Section 131 of the Act is to treat the premium of £6,000,000 as part of other reserves. Consequently (and subject to those provisions of the Act on distributions that are considered in Chapter 19), the premium is distributable.

18.58   The principles of acquisition accounting and merger accounting are considered in greater detail below.

General consolidation principles

Acquisition accounting principles

18.59   Where a group accounts for a business combination as an acquisition, the group should, in accordance with the requirements of SSAP 14, incorporate into its consolidated financial statements the fair values of the various net tangible and intangible assets (other than goodwill) that it has acquired. There may be a difference between the fair value of the purchase consideration and the aggregate of the fair values of the net tangible and intangible assets (other than goodwill). Any such difference represents goodwill (for example, see Table 91). The group should account for this goodwill in accordance with the provisions of SSAP 22.

> **Table 91: Example of an accounting policy of a company that has adopted the acquisition method of accounting for its business combinations.**
>
> *Extract from Rosehaugh Public Limited Company Report & Accounts 30 June 1984.*
>
> **Accounting policy extract**
>
> **1. Basis of consolidated accounts**
>
> The consolidated accounts have been prepared under the historical cost convention, as modified by the accounting policies, and include the accounts of the Company and all of its subsidiaries, together with the Group's share of the results of associated companies (see accounting policy 8). The accounts of subsidiary and associated companies are all made up to 30th June, 1984. The results of subsidiary companies acquired during the year are included from their date of acquisition. Subsidiaries that were acquired have been recorded on the basis of the purchase method of accounting, whereby the consideration given and the net assets acquired are recorded at fair value. The excess of consideration over the fair value of the net assets acquired is written off to retained profits. The surplus of the fair value of the net assets acquired over consideration is credited to capital reserve.

18.60 Both the method of determining goodwill and its accounting treatment are considered in detail in Chapter 7, paragraphs 7.39 to 7.94. Chapter 17 considers also other consolidation principles that relate to acquisition accounting.

18.61 As mentioned in paragraph 18.56*(a)*, when a group accounts for a business combination as an acquisition, the consolidated financial statements should incorporate the acquired company's results from the date of acquisition only.

Merger accounting principles

18.62 When a group uses merger accounting to account for a business combination, the group does not need to incorporate into its consolidated financial statements the fair values of the subsidiary's assets and liabilities. [*SSAP 23 para 18*]. Therefore, the group may incorporate into its consolidated financial statements the assets and liabilities at the amounts at which the subsidiary recorded them in its books before the combination.

18.63 One exception to this principle is that a group should adopt uniform accounting policies throughout the group in accordance with SSAP 14. Consequently, if the acquired company's accounting policies are not the same as the acquiring company's, then the acquired company should change its policies to achieve uniformity. It should, therefore, restate the amount of its assets and liabilities in its books to reflect the change in accounting policy. Alternatively, if it is not practicable for the acquired company to change its accounting policies (for example, for the reason discussed in Chapter 17 para 17.21), adjustments may need to be made on consolidation to the values of the acquired company's assets and liabilities that are stated in its books.

18.64   The group's consolidated financial statements for the period in which the business combination takes place should include the subsidiary's results for the entire period. [*SSAP 23 para 19*]. That is to say, they should include the subsidiary's results for the part of the period *before* the business combination, as well as the results of the subsidiary for the part of the period *after* the business combination. In addition, the corresponding amounts in the consolidated financial statements should reflect the position that would have arisen if the companies had been combined throughout the previous period and also at the previous balance sheet date.

18.65   The aim of the consolidated financial statements in merger accounting is to show the combined companies' results and financial positions as if they had always been combined. An illustration of a group that has used merger accounting to account for a business combination is given in Tables 92 to 95.

Table 92: Background to the merger between Extel Group PLC and Benn Brothers plc.

Extract from Extel Group PLC Report and Accounts 31 March 1984.

Directors' report extract

Results and dividends
The results have been drawn up on merger accounting principles to include Benn Brothers plc ("Benn") as explained in note 2 on page 24.

Mergers, acquisitions and disposals
Benn became a wholly owned subsidiary of the company on 18th November 1983. The fair value of the 4,782,682 ordinary shares of the company issued to acquire Benn, based on 336 pence per share, being the middle market price of the ordinary shares of the company on 30th June 1983, the date of the offer, was £16,070,000.

Note

2. Merger

The provisions of the proposed Statement of standard accounting practice relating to mergers [*now SSAP 23*] and section 37 of the Companies Act 1981 [*now Section 131 of the Companies Act 1985*] have been applied to the acquisition of Benn Brothers plc. No share premium arises from the acquisition and the results of Benn Brothers plc have been consolidated as though the companies had been combined since 1st April 1982.

Table 93: Example of an accounting policy of a company that has adopted the merger method of accounting for some business combinations while it has adopted acquisition accounting for other business combinations.

Extract from Extel Group PLC Report and Accounts 31 March 1984.

Accounting policy extract

Consolidation
Subsidiaries are consolidated as follows:—

Merger accounting principles are applied to those subsidiaries where the transaction meets the requirements of section 37 of the Companies Act 1981 [*now Section 131 of the Companies Act 1985*] and conforms to current accounting practice on mergers.

Other subsidiaries are consolidated from the effective date of acquisition. The purchase consideration is allocated to each class of asset on the basis of fair value at the date of acquisition. The surplus of cost over the fair value of the net assets of subsidiaries at date of acquisition is charged against reserves.

All companies of the group have accounting years ending 31st March.

Table 94: Disclosure of the merged share capital.

Extract from Extel Group PLC Report and Accounts 31 March 1984.

Note extract

	(in thousands of pounds)	
	Company 1984	Company 1983
18. Share capital		
Extel Group PLC		
Authorised:		
24,000,000 ordinary shares of 25p each	**6,000**	4,450
838,198 10½% cumulative preference shares of £1 each	**838**	—
	6,838	4,450
Allotted, called-up and fully paid:		
17,362,051 ordinary shares of 25p each	**4,341**	3,122
838,198 10½% cumulative preference shares of £1 each	**838**	—
	5,179	3,122

Allotments of 4,872,125 ordinary shares of 25p each, having a nominal value of £1,218,031, were made during the year as follows:

On 26th July 1983, 33,037 ordinary shares in the company were allotted to the trustees of the Profit Sharing Scheme.

On 28th October 1983, 55,352 ordinary shares in the company were allotted in settlement of the consideration payable for the acquisition of MGE Limited.

On various dates up to 18th November 1983, 4,782,682 ordinary shares and 838,198 10½% Cumulative Preference Shares of £1 each in the company were allotted in respect of the acquisition of Benn Brothers plc.

Table 95: Disclosure of merged share capital.

Extract from Extel Group PLC Report and Accounts 31 March 1984.

Note extract

Restatement of merged share capital	Merged Called-up Number	Merged Called-up Amount
Ordinary shares of 25p each as previously reported at 31st March 1983	12,489,926	3,122
Increase in ordinary share capital and shares issued in connection with merger with Benn Brothers plc	4,782,682	1,196
As restated at 31st March 1983	17,272,608	4,318
10½% Cumulative preference shares of £1 each issued in connection with merger with Benn Brothers plc	838,198	838
As restated at 31st March 1983	838,198	838
		5,156

18.66 In merger accounting, the holding company's balance sheet will show the holding company's investment in the subsidiary at the nominal value of the shares that the holding company issued as consideration, plus the fair value of any additional consideration. A difference may then arise on consolidation between the value at which the holding company carries its investment in the subsidiary, and the nominal value of the subsidiary's shares that the holding company acquires. SSAP 23 says that the group should adjust these differences on consolidation against the consolidated reserves. [*SSAP 23 para 20*].

18.67 Where the investment's carrying value is *less than* the nominal value of the shares that the holding company has acquired, the group should treat the difference as a reserve that arises on consolidation. Where the investment's carrying value is *greater than* the nominal value of the shares acquired, the difference represents the extent to which the group has effectively capitalised its reserves as a result of the merger. Consequently, the group should reduce its reserves by the amount of the difference.

18.68 The two examples that follow show how these consolidation differences arise and how they should be treated:

(a) The carrying value is less than nominal value

Company A acquires all of Company B's £200,000 nominal share capital. The purchase consideration consists of new shares that Company A issues, and these have a nominal value of £190,000. The business combination satisfies all the merger conditions, and the group decides to use merger accounting.

The respective balance sheets, after the merger, of the individual companies and the group are as follows:

	Company A £000	Company B £000	Group £000
Net tangible assets	1,500	200	1,700
Investment in subsidiary	190	—	—
	1,690	200	1,700
Share capital	1,190	200	1,190
Profit and loss account	500	—	500
Difference on consolidation	—	—	10
	1,690	200	1,700

The difference on consolidation of £10,000 is calculated as follows:

	£000
Nominal value of shares acquired	200
Holding company's carrying value of investment	190
Difference on consolidation	10

The group should treat the difference on consolidation as a reserve that arises on consolidation, because the investment's carrying value is *less than* the nominal value of the shares acquired.

(b) The carrying value is greater than nominal value

The facts in this example are the same as those in *(a)* above, except that the purchase consideration consists of new shares with a nominal value of £250,000. In this example, the respective balance sheets, after the merger, of the individual companies and the group are as follows:

	Company A £000	Company B £000	Group £000
Net tangible assets	1,500	200	1,700
Investment in subsidiary	250	—	—
	1,750	200	1,700
Share capital	1,250	200	1,250
Profit and loss account	500	—	500
Difference on consolidation	—	—	(50)
	1,750	200	1,700

The difference on consolidation of £50,000 is calculated as follows:

	£000
Nominal value of shares acquired	200
Holding company's carrying value of investment	250
Difference on consolidation	(50)

The investment's carrying value is greater than the nominal value of the shares acquired, and so the group should reduce its reserves by the amount of the difference.

18.69   Where the difference on consolidation arises because the investment's carrying value is *less than* the nominal value of the shares that the holding company has acquired, paragraph 20 of SSAP 23 says that the group should treat the difference as a reserve that has arisen on consolidation. Where the difference is material, the group should treat the difference as a separate reserve, in order to show a true and fair view. The most appropriate place to disclose the difference is under 'Other reserves'. Where the difference is not material, the group may treat the difference by adjusting any of its consolidated reserves.

18.70   However, where the difference on consolidation arises because the investment's carrying value is *greater than* the nominal value of the shares that the holding company has acquired, paragraph 20 of SSAP 23 says that the group should reduce its reserves by the amount of the difference on consolidation. The Standard does not specify the reserves against which the group should adjust this type of difference. However, because of the restrictions on the use of a share premium account detailed in paragraph 18.04, a group may not write such a difference off against a share premium account. It appears also that a group may not be able to write such a difference off against a revaluation reserve. The uses of the revaluation reserve are discussed in Chapter 5, paragraphs 5.51 to 5.53.

Disclosure

General

18.71   The acquiring company or the issuing company should disclose certain information in respect of *all material* business combinations, whether accounted for under the merger method or the acquisition method. The company must disclose this information in the consolidated financial statements that deal with the period in which the business combination occurs. The information that a company needs to show is as follows:

(a) The names of the combining companies.

(b) The number and the class of the securities that the company issued in respect of the combination.

(c) Details of any other consideration that the company gave in respect of the combination.

(d) The accounting treatment that the company adopted for the business combination. That is to say, the company should disclose whether it accounted for the business combination as an acquisition or as a merger.

(e) The nature and the amount of any significant accounting adjustments that the combining companies made to achieve consistent accounting policies.

[*SSAP 23 para 21*].

Additional disclosure for acquisitions

18.72 The consolidated financial statements should contain sufficient information about the results of any subsidiaries the group has acquired during the year. In this context, 'sufficient information' means enough information to enable shareholders to appreciate the effect that the results of the subsidiaries have had on the consolidated results. SSAP 14 requires similar disclosure also. [*SSAP 14 para 30*]. In addition, the group should disclose the date from which it has brought the results of major acquisitions into the financial statements. This date will be the effective date of the acquisition (see further Chapter 17 paras 17.51 to 17.57). [*SSAP 23 para 22*].

Additional disclosure for mergers

18.73 The issuing company should disclose the following information in the financial statements that deal with a year in which a merger occurs:

(a) The fair value of the consideration that the issuing company gave in respect of the business combination (for example, see Table 92 on page 426). Therefore, although in merger accounting the holding company will carry the investment in the subsidiary at the *nominal value* of the shares that the holding company issued as consideration plus the fair value of any additional consideration, the holding company must disclose the *fair value* of the total consideration.

(b) The amount of the current year's attributable profit before extraordinary items that relates to the part of the year *before* the merger, and also the amount that relates to the part of the year *after* the merger. It is likely, although SSAP 23 does not specifically state it, that the 'current year's attributable profit before extraordinary items' refers to the profit of the group attributable to the holding company's shareholders, and not merely to the issuing company's profit. Consolidated financial statements disclose the group profit before extraordinary items, but they do not normally disclose the holding company's profit before extraordinary items. Consequently, it seems more logical that the figure that the Standard requires to be disaggregated is the group figure, rather than the holding company's figure.

(c) An analysis of the attributable profit before extraordinary items of the current year up to the effective date of the merger between that of the issuing company and that of the subsidiary. Again, although SSAP 23 does not specifically state it, the 'issuing company' for this purpose presumably includes any existing subsidiaries other than the newly 'merged' subsidiary.

(d) An analysis of the attributable profit before extraordinary items of the previous year between that of the issuing company and that of the subsidiary.

(e) An analysis of extraordinary items between those extraordinary items that relate to the period before the merger's effective date, and those extraordinary items that relate to the period after the merger's effective date.

(f) An analysis of extraordinary items that indicates to which party to the merger the extraordinary items relate. It is likely that the group should analyse the current year's extraordinary items in this way, and should also analyse the previous year's extraordinary items in this way, in order to show a true and fair view.

[*SSAP 23 para 23*].

Further disclosure requirements that may apply if a merger has occurred are set out in paragraphs 18.87 to 18.89. Many of these disclosure requirements are illustrated by the extracts from the Argyll Group PLC Report & Accounts for the year ended 31 March 1984 that are reproduced in Tables 96 to 98.

Table 96: Background to the merger of Argyll Group PLC with Argyll Foods PLC and Amalgamated Distilled Products PLC.

Extract from Argyll Group PLC Report & Accounts 31 March 1984.

Directors' report—group results extract

This report covers the results for the year to 31 March 1984. Following the merger of the Company with Argyll Foods and Amalgamated Distilled Products, which became effective on 11 November 1983, the Company has adopted the merger relief provisions of the Companies Act 1981. Accordingly, the results of the Company, Argyll Foods and Amalgamated Distilled Products have been combined for the whole of the year ended 31 March 1984, and the comparative results for the previous year have been presented on the same basis.

Table 97: *Illustration of the basis used for the presentation of a group's financial statements where the merger method of accounting for business combinations has been used.*

Extract from Argyll Group PLC Report & Accounts 31 March 1984.

Accounting policy extract

PRINCIPLES OF CONSOLIDATION

The group accounts comprise the accounts of the Company and its subsidiaries made up to 31 March 1984.

The results of subsidiaries acquired or disposed of in the year are included in the group profit and loss account as from or up to their effective date of acquisition or disposal. The principles of merger accounting have been applied to account for the merger with Argyll Foods PLC ('Argyll Foods') and Amalgamated Distilled Products PLC ('Amalgamated Distilled Products'), as described in Note 1.0.

Goodwill arising in connection with the acquisition of subsidiaries and businesses has been written off against reserves as described in Note 10.1.

No profit and loss account is presented for the Company, as provided by Section 149 of the Companies Act 1948 [*now Section 228(7) of the Companies Act 1985*].

Note

1.0 BASIS OF PRESENTATION

On 11 November 1983, the Company merged with Argyll Foods and Amalgamated Distilled Products. Full details of the Schemes of Arrangement under Section 206 of the Companies Act 1948 [*now Section 425 of the Companies Act 1985*] through which the merger was effected were set out in a circular to the ordinary shareholders, preference shareholders and warrant holders of Argyll Foods, and the ordinary shareholders and loan stock holders of Amalgamated Distilled Products, dated 9 September 1983.

As a result of the merger the Company acquired 129,967,653 ordinary shares of 10p each and 616,986 8 per cent convertible redeemable cumulative preference shares of £1 each of Argyll Foods and 32,924,430 ordinary shares of 10p each and 32,924,430 deferred shares of 10p each of Amalgamated Distilled Products which the Company or its subsidiaries did not already own.

The Company also acquired the minority shareholdings in its subsidiaries, Gulliver Foods Limited ('Gulliver Foods') and Gulliver Vintners Limited ('Gulliver Vintners'). These comprised 1,551,706 ordinary shares and 266,115 deferred shares of £1 each of Gulliver Foods and 367,500 ordinary shares and 245,000 deferred shares of £1 each of Gulliver Vintners.

The Company has adopted the merger relief provisions of the Companies Act 1981 and has recorded its acquisition of the shares of Argyll Foods, Amalgamated Distilled Products, Gulliver Foods and Gulliver Vintners at the nominal value of the new shares issued by the Company. Full details of the shares issued in connection with the merger and their fair value are set out in Note 19.2.

The group accounts have been prepared in accordance with the principles of merger accounting. Consequently, in the group profit and loss account the results of the Company (which includes Gulliver Foods and Gulliver Vintners), Argyll Foods and Amalgamated Distilled Products have been combined for the whole of the year ended 31 March 1984 and the comparative results for the previous year have been presented on the same basis.

Table 97 continued.

Profit before extraordinary items and extraordinary items are analysed between Argyll Foods, Amalgamated Distilled Products and the Company and between the periods before and after the date of the merger (11 November 1983) below:

| | 1984 | | | |
	Pre Merger £'000	Post Merger £'000	Total £'000	1983 £'000
PROFIT BEFORE EXTRAORDINARY ITEMS				
Argyll Foods	17,155	12,721	29,876	19,534
Amalgamated Distilled Products	4,725	2,173	6,898	3,851
The Company	(2,357)	(675)	(3,032)	(132)
	19,523	14,219	33,742	23,253
EXTRAORDINARY ITEMS				
Argyll Foods	—	(4,500)	(4,500)	2,988
Amalgamated Distilled Products	—	—	—	230
The Company	956	—	956	373
	956	(4,500)	(3,544)	3,591

The Company's loss before extraordinary items for the year ended 31 March 1984 comprises net management expenses of £30,000, interest expense of £247,000 and a taxation charge of £2,755,000 principally relating to advance corporation tax written off.

In the group balance sheet at 31 March 1984, the assets, liabilities and revenue reserves of the Company, Argyll Foods and Amalgamated Distilled Products have been combined without adjustment. Corresponding amounts for the previous year in the group balance sheet have been presented on the same basis, adjusted as though the ordinary shares issued in connection with the merger had been in issue throughout the whole of that year.

No significant accounting adjustments have been required by the Company, Argyll Foods or Amalgamated Distilled Products in order to achieve consistency of accounting policies.

Group reconstructions

18.74 SSAP 23 refers mainly to business combinations in which either an acquiring company or an issuing company issues shares in consideration for the transfer to it of another company's shares. Paragraph 24 of SSAP 23 says that the Standard applies also to any other arrangements that achieve similar results to the above-mentioned business combination. Such an arrangement might set up a new holding company that issues shares to the shareholders of two other companies, as consideration for the transfer to it of shares in both those other companies.

18.75 Whatever the nature of the arrangement, the group may account for the business combination as a merger only if the business combination complies with all of the merger accounting conditions that are outlined in paragraph 18.45 above.

Table 98: Illustration of the disclosure of a merger capital reserve.

Extract from Argyll Group PLC Report & Accounts 31 March 1984.

Note

22.2 Merger capital reserve

As explained in Note 1.0, on 11 November 1983 the Company completed the acquisition of the whole of the issued share capital of Argyll Foods and Amalgamated Distilled Products, and also acquired the minority shareholdings in Gulliver Foods and Gulliver Vintners. The Company has followed the merger relief provisions of the Companies Act 1981 and has recorded these investments at the nominal value of the new ordinary shares issued.

The group accounts have been prepared in accordance with the principles of merger accounting and the merger capital reserve in the group balance sheet is set out below:

	£'000
Nominal value of 174,823,221 ordinary shares issued to acquire the issued share capital of Argyll Foods and Amalgamated Distilled Products	(43,706)
Nominal value of 6,793,215 ordinary shares issued to acquire the minority interests in Gulliver Foods and Gulliver Vintners	(1,698)
Fair value of 2,449,451 ordinary shares issued to acquire warrants of Argyll Foods and 10 per cent unsecured convertible loan stock of Amalgamated Distilled Products	(3,117)
Cost of original investment in Argyll Foods and Amalgamated Distilled Products	(6,102)
	(54,623)
Issued share capital, convertible loan stock and capital reserves of Argyll Foods and Amalgamated Distilled Products and minority interests in Gulliver Foods and Gulliver Vintners	72,385
Prior year adjustment in respect of goodwill written off (Note 10.1)	(5,218)
Merger capital reserve at 31 March 1983	12,544
Merger expenses	(983)
Net proceeds from share issues in subsidiaries	4,584
Net transfer from profit and loss account in respect of redemption of preference shares and convertible loan stock in subsidiaries	779
Merger capital reserve at 31 March 1984	16,924

18.76 Consequently, where a group reconstruction is eligible for the relief that Section 132 of the Act gives in respect of group reconstructions (as discussed in paras 18.22 to 18.29 above), it may also be possible to use merger accounting. But this will be possible only if the reconstruction complies with all of the merger accounting conditions (see para 18.45).

18.77 The example that follows illustrates the differences between using acquisition accounting and using merger accounting in a group reconstruction:

In 1979, Company A acquired all of Company C's issued share capital (100,000 £1 shares) for £390,000. Company C had no reserves at that time.

On 31 December 1984, another wholly-owned subsidiary (Company B) allots 100,000 £1 shares to Company A. In return for the allotment, Company A transfers to Company B the shares in Company C that it owns. Subsequently, Company A is to be liquidated, and its shareholders will receive shares in Company B. At the time of the reconstruction, Company B's shares that are issued to Company A are worth £400,000 (that is, £4 per share), and the fair value of Company C's recorded net assets is £360,000 (the difference of £40,000 being attributed to goodwill). The fair value of Company A's and Company B's net assets is equal to their book value.

Diagrammatically, the reconstruction is as follows:

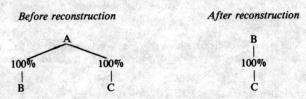

Before reconstruction   *After reconstruction*

The individual balance sheets of the three companies as at 31 December 1984 before the reconstruction are as follows:

	Company A £000	Company B £000	Company C £000
Share capital (shares of £1 each)	150	200	100
Reserves	380	500	250
	530	700	350
Investment in B*	210	—	—
Investment in C*	320	—	—
Net assets	—	700	350
	530	700	350

*The investments are stated at the cost of shares to Company A, reduced for Company A's investment in Company C by a write-down of £70,000 made in 1982.

After the reconstruction, the summarised consolidated balance sheet of Company B and its subsidiary Company C is as follows:

	Acquisition accounting £000	Merger accounting £000
Share capital	300 (a)	300 (a)
Share premium account	300 (b)	220 (c)
Other reserves	500 (d)	530 (d)
	1,100	1,050
Goodwill on consolidation	40 (e)	—
Net assets	1,060 (f)	1,050
	1,100	1,050

Notes to the example above:

(a) The share capital consists of the 200,000 shares originally in issue, together with the 100,000 shares allotted on Company B's acquisition of Company C.

(b) The amount credited to the share premium account in accordance with Section 130 of the Act is £300,000 (that is, 100,000 shares issued at a premium of £3 per share).

(c) Under Section 132 of the Act, the issuing company is required to transfer to the share premium account only an amount equal to the minimum premium value (see para 18.24). The minimum premium value is calculated as the amount by which the base value of the shares in Company C that are transferred from Company A to Company B exceeds the aggregate nominal value of the shares that Company B allots in consideration for the transfer. The amount of the transfer to the share premium account is calculated as follows:

	£000	£000
The base value of shares in Company C is the lower of:		
—The cost of those shares to Company A	390	
—The amount at which those shares are stated in Company A's accounting records immediately before the transfer	320	
		320
Less: Nominal value of the shares Company B allotted in respect of the transfer		100
Transfer to the share premium account		220

(d) Under acquisition accounting, the amount to be included in other reserves is the amount of Company B's reserves (that is, £500,000). Under Section 132 of the Act (which gives the relief in respect of group reconstructions), other reserves are made up as follows:

	£000
Reserves of Company B	500
Reserves of Company C less minimum premium value (that is, £250,000 — £220,000)	30
	530

(e) Goodwill on consolidation is the amount by which the purchase consideration (that is, 100,000 shares at £4, or £400,000) exceeds the fair value of the underlying assets acquired (that is, £360,000). Under merger accounting, goodwill does not arise, because the net assets' fair value need not be incorporated in the consolidated financial statements (see para 18.62 above).

(f) Company C's net assets are included at their fair value when they are accounted for as an acquisition. But when they are accounted for as a merger, they are included at their book value.

18.78 The main effect of the provisions of Section 132 of the Act is to reduce the amount of the premium that must be taken to the share premium account. Subject to the provisions of the Act on distributions (which are considered in Chapter 19), the balance of the premium, included in other reserves, is then distributable.

The holding company's financial statements

18.79 Although the Appendix to SSAP 23 does not form part of the Standard, it does provide guidance on how an offeror should normally account for a business combination in its own financial statements.

Acquisition accounting

18.80 Where the offeror accounts for a business combination as an acquisition, it should normally record its investment in the new subsidiary at cost. The cost of the investment will be the fair value of the consideration that the offeror gives (see further Chapter 7 paras 7.46 to 7.58).

18.81 If the fair value of any shares that the offer includes in the consideration exceeds their nominal value, and if merger relief is *not* available under Sections 131 and 132 of the Act, then the offeror should credit, to a share premium account, the excess of the shares' fair value over their nominal value. In the consolidated financial statements, in these circumstances, the group would not generally be able to write off against the share premium account any consolidation goodwill that arises on the acquisition. However, it is possible for a company to apply to the court to release share premium, by means of a capital reduction, to create reserves against which the goodwill can be written off.

18.82 As explained in paragraph 18.55 above, there are situations where a company may claim merger relief under the Act, but may not use merger accounting in accordance with SSAP 23. In such a situation, the offeror's balance sheet should normally show its investment in the subsidiary at the fair value of the consideration given. The fair value of any shares that the offeror includes in the consideration may exceed their nominal value. If so, and if merger relief is available under Sections 131 or 132 of the Act, then the offeror should credit the amount by which the fair value exceeds the nominal value to a separate merger reserve, and not to a share premium account. [*SSAP 23 Appendix para 2*]. This treatment has an advantage in that a merger reserve may be used in ways that a share premium account cannot be. The merger reserve will appear also in the consolidated financial statements.

18.83 Paragraph 2 of the Appendix to SSAP 23 does not specifically comment on whether this merger reserve is realised or unrealised. However, paragraph 4 of the Appendix discusses the possibility that part of the merger reserve can legally be regarded as realised when the subsidiary makes a distribution to the holding company from pre-combination profits. Consequently, this paragraph implies that the merger reserve is unrealised when the offeror establishes that reserve.

18.84 If a group establishes a merger reserve in the consolidated financial statements for the reasons set out in paragraph 18.82, it may then write off against that merger reserve any consolidation goodwill that arises on the acquisition.

Merger accounting

18.85 The Appendix to the Standard says that where the offeror accounts for a business combination as a merger, it should record its investment in the new subsidiary at the *nominal* value of the shares that it issues, plus the *fair* value of any consideration other than shares.

18.86 Cash is probably the most common form of consideration other than shares, and loan stock is another form. For example, part of the consideration may be loan stock that bears an interest rate above the current market rate. Or it may be loan stock that can be subsequently converted into shares. The fair value of either type of loan stock may differ from its nominal value.

18.87 Where a company takes advantage of the merger relief provisions in the Act, it must disclose in its financial statements:

(a) The name of the other company.

(b) The number, the nominal value and the class of shares allotted.

(c) The number, the nominal value and the classes of shares of the other company that were either issued, or transferred or cancelled.

(d) Details of the accounting treatment the company has adopted in its financial statements.

(e) If the company prepares group accounts, particulars of how and to what extent the group's profit or loss for the year as shown in the group accounts is affected by the other company's (or any of its subsidiaries') profit or loss that arose before the merger.
[4 Sch 75(1)].

18.88 Where the company has used merger accounting on consolidation, most of the information to be disclosed above is also required by SSAP 23 (see para 18.71 above).

18.89 If the company has, during the financial year or during either of the two preceding financial years, allotted shares taking advantage of merger relief, then the notes to the financial statements may need to disclose further information in the following two circumstances:

(a) The holding company or any of its subsidiaries disposes of either of the following:

(i) Shares in the merged company.
(ii) Fixed assets that, at the time of the merger, were assets of either the merged company or any of its subsidiaries.

If the holding company or any of its subsidiaries realises a profit or loss on such a disposal, and that profit or loss is included in the consolidated profit and loss account (or in the holding company's profit and loss account — if it has not prepared a consolidated profit and loss account), the amount of that profit or loss has to be disclosed. [4 Sch 75(3)(a)].

(b) The holding company or any of its subsidiaries disposes of shares uin any company (*other than* the merged company), and the profit or loss it makes on this disposal is to some extent attributable to the fact that the company whose shares have been sold (or one of its subsidiaries) owned as assets either of the following:

(i) Shares in the merged company.

(ii) Fixed assets that, at the time of the merger, were assets of either the merged company or any of its subsidiaries.

In this situation, the profit or loss attributable to the sale of those assets that is included in the company's consolidated profit and loss account (or its own profit and loss account — if it has not prepared a consolidated profit and loss account) has to be disclosed. [*4 Sch 75(3)(b)*].

18.90   In both the above situations, the notes to the financial statements must give an explanation of the transaction. These provisions are explained by the example that follows:

Company A has two subsidiaries, Company B and Company C. Company C also owns a minority interest in Company B. In 1984, Company A merged with another company, Company D. At the time of the merger, Company D owned a particular fixed asset. Consider the following two situations:

(a) After the merger, Company D transferred the asset to Company A. In 1985, Company A sells the asset for a profit of £50,000. This profit of £50,000 will be included in the consolidated profit and loss account Company A prepares for the year ended 31 December 1985. The notes to these financial statements must disclose the profit of £50,000 and explain how it has arisen. This is because of the requirement in *(a)* in paragraph 18.89 above.

(b) After the merger, Company D transferred the asset to Company B. In 1986, Company C sells its minority interest in Company B, and realises a profit of £200,000. Company A's directors consider that £30,000 of this profit is attributable to the fact that Company B owned the asset. The profit of £200,000 will be included in the consolidated profit and loss account of Company A for the year ended 31 December 1986. The notes to these financial statements must disclose the fact that £30,000 is attributable to the asset. They must also explain what has happened. This is because of the requirement in *(b)* in paragraph 18.89 above.

18.91   At first sight, it is difficult to see why these provisions are necessary. However, this type of disclosure will alert those shareholders who have acquired shares in a new company in exchange for their shares in another company, of any substantial disposals of the assets of the company that they originally owned. This type of disclosure may also alert shareholders to situations where a group's management are pursuing a policy of 'asset stripping'. Such a policy would conflict with the basic concept of a merger as outlined in paragraph 18.44 in this chapter.

Pre-combination profits

18.92   Paragraph 15(5) of the pre-1981 Schedule 8 to the Companies Act 1948 implied that a subsidiary's pre-acquisition profits were not to be treated as the holding company's profits. However, the Companies Act 1981 specifically amended this requirement so that a company that wishes to claim the benefit of the merger relief provisions is able to distribute to its shareholders the subsidiary's pre-combination profits. If the 1981 Act had not included this amendment, one of the principal advantages of *merger relief* would have been lost, because the distributability of the subsidiary's pre-combination profits would still have been restricted. The impact of this change is considered in more detail below.

Acquisition accounting

18.93 In acquisition accounting, the subsidiary's pre-combination profits are normally frozen (that is, they are normally not available for eventual distribution to the holding company's shareholders). In some circumstances, however, the subsidiary's pre-combination profits *may* be available for eventual distribution to the holding company's shareholders. Where a new subsidiary pays a dividend out of its pre-combination profits, the holding company should apply the dividend to reduce the investment's carrying value. But it should do this only to the extent that is necessary in order to provide for a diminution in that carrying value. [*SSAP 23 Appendix para 3*]. The following example illustrates the way in which companies that use acquisition accounting should apply this rule.

A holding company (Company H) is to acquire a subsidiary (Company S). Before the acquisition, the balance sheets of Company H and Company S are as follows:

	Company H £000	Company S £000
Net tangible assets	1,300	140
Share capital	1,000	100
Profit and loss account	300	40
	1,300	140

Company H makes an offer for all of Company S's shares. The consideration is new shares in Company H that have a nominal value of £120,000 and a fair value of £150,000. The fair value of Company S's net tangible assets equals their book value. The holding company takes advantage of the merger relief provisions in Section 131 of the Act. However, although the group could take advantage of the merger accounting provisions of SSAP 23, it chooses to adopt acquisition accounting.

After the acquisition, the balance sheets of Company H, Company S and the group are as follows:

	Company H £000	Company S £000	Group £000
Goodwill	—	—	10 (a)
Net tangible assets	1,300	140	1,440
Investment	150	—	—
	1,450	140	1,450
Share capital	1,120	100	1,120
Merger reserve	30 (b)	—	30 (b)
Profit and loss account	300	40	300
	1,450	140	1,450

Notes to the example above:

(a) The goodwill arising on consolidation represents the difference between the fair value of the consideration that Company H gives (namely, £150,000) and the fair value of Company S's net tangible assets (namely, £140,000).

(b) The merger reserve represents the difference between the fair value of the consideration that Company H gives (namely, £150,000) and the nominal value of the shares that it issues (namely, £120,000) (see para 18.82 above).

If Company S now distributes its profit and loss account balance of £40,000 to Company H, it is left with net tangible assets of £100,000 and share capital of £100,000. After the distribution, the value of Company H's investment in Company S is £110,000 (that is, net tangible assets of £100,000, plus goodwill of £10,000), which compares with its carrying value of £150,000. Paragraph 3 of the Appendix to SSAP 23 indicates that Company H should use the whole £40,000 dividend that it receives from Company S to provide for the diminution in the carrying value of its investment in Company S. Therefore, none of the dividend represents realised profits to Company H.

The balance sheets of Company H, Company S and the group after the distribution are as follows:

	Company H £000	Company S £000	Group £000
Goodwill	—	—	10
Net tangible assets	1,340	100	1,440
Investment	110	—	—
	1,450	100	1,450
Share capital	1,120	100	1,120
Merger reserve	30	—	30
Profit and loss account	300	—	300
	1,450	100	1,450

18.94 In the above example, the subsidiary's pre-combination profits were frozen. However, in some circumstances, the subsidiary's pre-combination profits might not be frozen.

18.95 The example that follows illustrates a situation in which pre-combination profits may be treated as realised in the holding company's financial statements.

The facts are the same as in the previous example (before the distribution of Company S's profit and loss account balance to Company H). In the year after the acquisition, Company S makes a trading profit of £10,000, and revalues its fixed assets upwards by £20,000. Company H makes neither a profit nor a loss. Company S then distributes its profit and loss account balance (now £50,000) to Company H. After the distribution, the balance sheets of Company H, Company S and the group are as follows:

	Company H £000	Company S £000	Group £000
Goodwill	—	—	10
Net tangible assets	1,350	120	1,470
Investment	130	—	—
	1,480	120	1,480
Share capital	1,120	100	1,120
Revaluation reserve	—	20	20
Merger reserve	30	—	30
Profit and loss account	330	—	310
	1,480	120	1,480

The value of Company H's investment in Company S is £130,000 (that is, net assets of Company S of £120,000 plus goodwill of £10,000). Therefore, Company H should use £20,000 of the dividend that it receives to provide for the diminution of the carrying value in its investment in Company S. The remaining £30,000 of the dividend (which amount includes £20,000 of the pre-combination profits) represents realised profits to Company H.

However, it could be argued that it is imprudent to treat the £20,000 revaluation in Company S as increasing the profit and loss account of Company H. It could be argued that it would be more prudent of Company H to credit a revaluation reserve with £20,000, rather than crediting the profit and loss account with £20,000. This more prudent approach would mean that only £10,000 of the dividend represents realised profits to Company H.

18.96 There has so far been no firm legal ruling on distributions from pre-combination profits, although, as mentioned in paragraph 18.93 above, SSAP 23 takes the view that, to the extent that a dividend received from a subsidiary is not utilised in writing down the investment, it does represent a realised profit. However, there is still some uncertainty about how a company should account for the receipt of a dividend from a subsidiary out of that subsidiary's pre-combination profits. But it does now seem that a company may, as suggested in SSAP 23, need to apply only part of the dividend received to write down the investment in that subsidiary. It then appears acceptable to take the excess of the dividend to realised reserves. However, because there is still some uncertainty as to whether this excess is realised and, therefore, distributable, where a holding company wishes to make a distribution to its members from *these* reserves, it may wish to seek legal advice before doing so. Pre-combination profits are considered also in Chapter 19, paragraphs 19.77 to 19.81.

Merger accounting

18.97 In merger accounting, the subsidiary's pre-combination profits are normally available for eventual distribution to the holding company's shareholders. However, in some circumstances, the subsidiary's pre-combination profits may be frozen (and may, therefore, *not* be available for distribution to the holding company's shareholders). Where the new subsidiary pays a dividend out of its pre-combination profits, the holding company should apply the dividend to reduce the carrying value of its investment to the extent that it is necessary in order to provide for a diminution in that carrying value. [*SSAP 23 Appendix para 3*]. The following example illustrates the way in which companies that use merger accounting should apply this rule:

The abbreviated balance sheets of Company H and Company S before the merger are as follows:

	Company H £000	Company S £000
Net tangible assets	1,000	135
Share capital	800	10
Profit and loss account	200	125
	1,000	135

Company H issues shares with a nominal value of £100,000 in exchange for the shares in Company S. The abbreviated balance sheets of Company H, Company S and the group after the merger are as follows:

	Company H £000	Company S £000	Group £000
Net tangible assets	1,000	135	1,135
Investment	100	—	—
	1,100	135	1,135
Share capital	900	10	900
Profit and loss account	200	125	235*
	1,100	135	1,135

*The group profit and loss account balance is made up as follows:

	£000
Profit and loss account balance of Company H	200
Profit and loss account balance of Company S	125
	325
Excess of carrying value of investment over nominal value of shares acquired (that is, £100,000 — £10,000)	(90)
	235

If Company S then pays up all of its profit and loss account balance of £125,000 as a dividend to Company H, Company S will be left with share capital of £10,000 and net tangible assets of £10,000.

If the £10,000 of net tangible assets represents the value of Company H's investment in Company S, then Company H should reduce the carrying value of its investment in Company S to £10,000. Paragraph 3 of the Appendix to SSAP 23 indicates that Company H should use £90,000 of the dividend that it receives, in order to provide for the diminution in the carrying value of its investment in Company S. The remaining £35,000 of the dividend represents realised profits to Company H. The abbreviated balance sheets of Company H, Company S and the group after the distribution are then as follows:

	Company H £000	Company S £000	Group £000
Net tangible assets	1,125	10	1,135
Investment	10	—	—
	1,135	10	1,135
Share capital	900	10	900
Profit and loss account	235	—	235
	1,135	10	1,135

However, the £10,000 of net tangible assets might not represent the value of Company H's investment in Company S, because Company S may have substantial hidden reserves. For example, Company S's fixed assets might have a net book value of £5,000 but a current value of £35,000. Company S would then have a hidden reserve of £30,000, and the value of Company H's investment in Company S would be £40,000 — not £10,000. Consequently, Company H need use only £60,000 of the dividend that it receives, in order to provide for the diminution in the carrying value of its investment in Company S. The remaining £65,000 of the dividend represents realised profits to Company H. The abbreviated balance sheets of Company H, Company S and the group are then as follows:

	Company H £000	Company S £000	Group £000
Net tangible assets	1,125	10	1,135
Investment	40	–	–
	1,165	10	1,135
Share capital	900	10	900
Profit and loss account	265	–	235 *
	1,165	10	1,135

*Company H's profit and loss account is greater than the group's profit and loss account. The group profit and loss account balance is made up as follows:

	£000
Profit and loss account balance of Company H	265
Profit and loss account balance of Company S	–
	265
Excess of carrying value of investment over nominal value of shares acquired (that is, £40,000 - £10,000)	(30)
	235

18.98 The above example illustrates the fact that, when the investment's carrying value exceeds the nominal value of the shares that the holding company acquires, some pre-combination profits may effectively be frozen in merger accounting.

Vendor placing

18.99 In a business combination, some or all of the target company's shareholders may prefer to receive cash, rather than shares in the acquiring company. However, the acquiring company may want to use merger accounting on consolidation. Consequently, it may prefer to pay for the target company by issuing shares, rather than by paying cash. In these circumstances, a vendor placing (technically known as a 'Vendor consideration placing') can reconcile the apparently conflicting objectives of the target company's shareholders and the acquiring company.

18.100 A vendor placing could work as follows. An acquiring company that must be listed will offer its shares to the target company's shareholders in exchange for their shares in that company. If there are any shareholders of the target company who do not wish to retain the consideration shares of the acquiring company, then the acquiring company will arrange for its financial advisor (for example, a merchant bank) to act as a broker to place those consideration shares. The financial advisor will put together a placing list (that will normally include institutions such as pension funds and insurance companies) so that the target company shareholders may dispose of their consideration shares in the acquiring company for cash.

18.101 So, after the vendor placing has occurred, cash has been transferred from the institutions, via the financial advisor (acting in his capacity as a broker) to some or all of the target company's shareholders. In return, the institutions now own shares in the acquiring company, and the acquiring company now owns the target company. The acquiring company has issued shares, rather than paying cash, for the target company, and, as long as the offer complies with SSAP 23's merger conditions, the acquiring company can use merger accounting on consolidation.

18.102 On the grounds that the substance of a vendor placing is a cash takeover, there is an argument that vendor placings do not comply with the spirit of SSAP 23. If this were the case, the acquiring company would have to account for the business combination as an acquisition, rather than as a merger.

18.103 However, SSAP 23's main criterion for merger accounting is whether material resources leave one or other of the combining companies. In a vendor placing, the acquiring company issues shares, and so material resources do not leave the group. Consequently, SSAP 23 allows a group, in this situation, to use merger accounting to account for the business combination.

Vendor rights

18.104 The vendor rights method of financing a business combination is a variation of a vendor placing (see paras 18.99 to 18.103 above). In a vendor placing, the financial advisor normally arranges to place the consideration shares in the acquiring company to institutional investors. Consequently, the acquiring company's other shareholders find that their shareholdings become diluted. However, the vendor rights method limits the dilution of these shareholders' interests in the acquiring company.

18.105 The vendor rights method could work as follows. The acquiring company, which must be listed, will offer its shares to the target company's shareholders in exchange for their shares in that company. If any shareholders of the target company do not wish to retain the consideration shares of the acquiring company, then the acquiring company will arrange for its financial advisor to act as a broker and to place those consideration shares. Up to this point, the vendor rights method is the same as a vendor placing. However, as part of the placing agreement, the acquiring company's shareholders will have an option to buy ('claw back') some of the consideration shares from the placees. They will be entitled to buy back at the placing price a certain proportion of the placed shares on a pro-rata basis.

18.106 Therefore, after the vendor rights method is completed, cash has been transferred from the acquiring company's shareholders, via its financial advisor (acting as a broker), to some or all of the target company's shareholders. In return, the acquiring company's shareholders now have a stake in a larger group, because the acquiring company now owns the target company. The acquiring company has issued shares, rather than paying cash, for the target company, and so it can use merger accounting on consolidation.

18.107 The method is referred to as 'vendor rights' because it is similar to a rights issue. In both the vendor rights method and a rights issue, the existing shareholders pay cash to acquire more shares in the company. The shares are issued on a pro-rata basis. However, although there are similarities between vendor rights and a rights issue, there are significant differences in the accounting implications. If a company finances a business combination both by making a rights issue and then using the cash to buy the target company, then it must use acquisition accounting on consolidation. However, if a company finances a business combination by using the vendor rights method, then as long as the offer complies with SSAP 23's merger conditions, the acquiring company may use merger accounting on consolidation.

18.108 As with vendor placings, there is an argument that the vendor rights method does not comply with the spirit of SSAP 23.

18.109 However, as mentioned in paragraph 18.44, the main criterion for merger accounting in SSAP 23 is whether material resources leave one or other of the combining companies. In the vendor rights method, the acquiring company *issues shares* to acquire the other company, and so material resources do not leave the group. Consequently, SSAP 23 allows the group to use merger accounting to account for the business combination.

CHAPTER 19

REALISED AND DISTRIBUTABLE PROFITS

Chapter 19

Realised and Distributable Profits

Introduction

19.01 Companies may make a distribution to their shareholders only out of profits that are available for distribution. Part VIII of the Act, 'Distribution of profits and assets', imposes conditions that companies must satisfy before they can make distributions. Some of these conditions apply only to public companies. Also, special provisions apply to investment companies and insurance companies, and these provisions are considered in paragraphs 19.89 to 19.99 of this chapter.

19.02 The statutory rules in Part VIII of the Act supplement the common law requirements as to distributions. For example, under common law, a distribution can be made only in accordance with any conditions in a company's memorandum or articles of association.

Definition of distribution

19.03 For the purposes of Part VIII of the Act, 'distribution' is defined as any distribution of a company's assets to its shareholders (whether or not it is made in cash), *other than* a distribution that is made by way of any one of the following:

(a) The issue of either fully-paid or partly-paid bonus shares.

(b) The redemption or the purchase of any of the company's own shares, either out of capital, or out of the proceeds of a fresh issue of shares, or out of unrealised profits in accordance with Part V, Chapter VII of the Act.

(c) The reduction of share capital by either of the following means:

  (i) Extinguishing or reducing the liability in respect of share capital that is not paid up.
  (ii) Paying off paid-up share capital.

(d) The distribution of assets to shareholders on a winding-up.
[*Sec 263(2)*].

451

Basic conditions applying to all companies other than investment companies and insurance companies

19.04   Any company (whether public or private) may make a distribution only out of 'profits available for the purpose'. [*Sec 263(1)*].

19.05   For any company other than an investment company or an insurance company, profits available for distribution are the company's accumulated realised profits that have not previously been either distributed or capitalised, less its accumulated realised losses (insofar as they have not been previously written off in either a reduction or a re-organisation of capital). [*Sec 263(3)*]. The origin of these profits and losses may be either revenue or capital. [*Sec 280(3)*].

Additional condition that public companies have to satisfy

19.06   In addition to the condition that it can make a distribution only out of profits available for the purpose, a *public* company can make a distribution only to the extent that the distribution does not reduce the amount of the company's net assets below the aggregate of its called-up share capital (defined in Chapter 9 para 9.72) plus its undistributable reserves. [*Sec 264(1)*].

19.07   In this context, 'undistributable reserves' include:

(a) The share premium account.

(b) The capital redemption reserve.

(c) The excess of accumulated unrealised profits that have not previously been capitalised over accumulated unrealised losses that have not previously been written off by a reduction or a re-organisation of capital. For this purpose, capitalisation includes the issuing of bonus shares, but it excludes transfers of profits to the capital redemption reserve that have been made after 22 December 1980.

(d) Any reserve that the company, for any other reason, is prohibited from distributing.
[*Sec 264(3)*].

19.08   The effect of this additional condition is that whereas a *private* company can make a distribution provided only that it has realised profits available, a *public* company can do so only if it has profits available after it has provided for any net unrealised losses.

19.09   The example below, which sets out extracts from the balance sheets of four companies, gives examples of the method of calculating distributable profits as outlined in paragraphs 19.04 to 19.06 above:

	Company 1		Company 2		Company 3		Company 4	
	£	£	£	£	£	£	£	£
A Share capital		1,000		1,000		1,000		1,000
B Unrealised profits	150		150		150		—	
C Unrealised losses	—		(200)		(200)		(200)	
D Net unrealised profits		150		—		—		—
E Net unrealised losses		—		(50)		(50)		(200)
F Realised profits	300		300		300		300	
G Realised losses	—		—		(120)		(120)	
H Net realised profits		300		300		180		180
I Share capital and reserves		1,450		1,250		1,130		980
Maximum distributable profit:								
Private company (H)		300		300		180		180
Public company (H — E)		300		250		130		Nil

The relevant accounts

19.10 The Act states that, in order to determine whether a company has profits available, and (if it is a public company) whether the additional condition in paragraph 19.06 above has been satisfied, reference must be made to certain items in the company's *relevant accounts*. [*Sec 270(2)*].

19.11 The items to be referred to in the relevant accounts are:

(a) Profits, losses, assets and liabilities.

(b) Provisions as defined in Chapter 9, paragraph 9.45.

(c) Share capital and reserves (including undistributable reserves). [*Sec 270(2)*].

19.12 The 'relevant accounts' are normally the company's latest audited financial statements that have been laid before the company in general meeting. [*Sec 270(3)*]. However, *interim accounts* must be prepared and used where a distribution would exceed the amount that is distributable according to the latest audited financial statements. [*Sec 270(4)(a)*]. And *initial accounts* must be prepared and used where a company proposes to make a distribution during its first accounting reference period (see further Chapter 2 para 2.28) or before the date on which it lays its first audited financial statements before the shareholders. [*Sec 270(4)(b)*].

19.13 The Act lays down requirements in respect of the relevant accounts. Failure to comply with these requirements will mean that the distribution will be illegal. [*Sec 270(5)*]. The shareholders cannot agree to waive these requirements. *(Re Precision Drippings Ltd.* [*1985*] *Court of Appeal.)* These requirements do not apply to a *private company's interim* or *initial accounts*. However, the Act still requires a private company to prepare such accounts to enable the directors to make a reasonable judgement as to the profits available for distribution. [*Sec 270*].

19.14 The requirements for relevant accounts, including *interim* and *initial accounts* of public companies, are as follows:

(a) They must be properly prepared, or they must be so prepared at least to the extent that is necessary in order to decide whether or not a proposed distribution is legal. In particular, the items referred to in paragraph 19.11 above must be determined. [*Sec 271(2), 272(2), 273(2)*].

For annual financial statements, 'properly prepared' means that they must comply with Part VII of the Act. For either *interim* or *initial accounts*, it means that they must comply with Section 228 of the Act (that is, both the form and the content must comply with Schedule 4). It also means that the balance sheet comprised in those accounts has to be signed by the directors in accordance with Section 238 of the Act. [*Sec 272(3), 273(3)*].

(b) They must give a true and fair view of both the state of the company's affairs and its profit or loss. [*Sec 271(2), 272(3), 273(3)*].

(c) They must not include, for a public company, any uncalled share capital as an asset. [*Sec 264(4)*].

(d) With annual financial statements, the auditors must have given their opinion on them in accordance with Section 236 of the Act. [*Sec 271(3)*]. So far as *initial accounts* are concerned, the auditors must have reported whether, in their opinion, those accounts have been properly prepared. [*Sec 273(4)*]. *Interim accounts* need not be audited.

(e) If the auditors have qualified their opinion, they must state, in writing, whether the subject matter of their qualification is material in determining the legality of the proposed distribution. [*Sec 271(3)(4), 273(4)(5)*]. With annual financial statements, this statement will suffice if it relates to other distributions, provided that it covers, *inter alia*, distributions of the same description as the distribution proposed (see para 19.64 below). [*Sec 271(5)*].

(f) With annual financial statements, the statement referred to in (e) above must have been laid before the shareholders in general meeting. [*Sec 271(4)*]. With *interim accounts*, it is required only that a copy of the accounts should be delivered to the Registrar of Companies. [*Sec 272(4)*]. Similarly, with *initial accounts*, a copy of those accounts, together with a copy of the auditors' report and accompanying statement (where applicable), must have been delivered to the Registrar of Companies. [*Sec 273(6)*].

19.15 If any document in a set of accounts that must be delivered to the Registrar is in a foreign language, a certified translation of that document must also be delivered to the Registrar. [*Sec 241(3)(b), 272(5), 273(7)*]. However, the Registrar will, by concession, accept financial statements in a currency other than sterling, provided that they include the exchange rate between that currency and sterling at the balance sheet date.

19.16 Both *interim* and *initial accounts* delivered to the Registrar in accordance with the above requirements are unlikely to need to include a directors' report in order to show a true and fair view.

19.17 A company may find that it does not have sufficient distributable reserves shown in its last relevant accounts to justify paying an interim dividend. Where this is so, the company will have to prepare *interim accounts* and, with a public company, will have to deliver them to the Registrar of Companies (in the way outlined above) to justify the payment of the interim dividend. In this situation, if the company is listed on The Stock Exchange, it is advisable that the company should also release the interim accounts to The Stock Exchange. This is because the interim accounts may contain price-sensitive information, and the Continuing Obligations include a general requirement that such information should be released to The Stock Exchange as soon as it is available. A similar requirement in the General Undertaking makes it advisable that a company traded on the USM should do the same.

19.18 A particular set of financial statements may have been used to determine whether a distribution can be made. If it is proposed to determine the legality of a subsequent distribution by reference to the same financial statements, the amount of the proposed distribution must be notionally increased by the amount of the earlier distribution. [*Sec 274(1)*]. The object of this requirement is to prevent a company avoiding the restrictions by making several small distributions that are permissible individually, but which, when taken in aggregate, exceed the amount available for distribution.

19.19 Consider the two situations below:

	A	B
Distributable profits, per relevant accounts	£30,000	£20,000
Distribution already made by reference to those accounts	£15,000	£15,000
Proposed further distribution	£10,000	£10,000

If the proposed further distribution is considered in isolation, then it is permissible in both situations. However, Section 274(1) of the Act requires the proposed distribution to be added to those distributions that have already been made by reference to the same financial statements. This means that, in both situations, the amount to be compared with the profits available for distribution is £25,000 (that is, £15,000 + £10,000). In situation A, this is less than the distributable profits (£30,000) and so the further distribution is permissible. In situation B, however, the distributable profit is only £20,000. Consequently, the proposed further distribution of £10,000 is not permissible, and only £5,000 remains to be distributed.

Distinction between realised and unrealised profits and losses

19.20 Although Section 263(3) of the Act provides that a company's available profits for distribution are "its accumulated, *realised* profits ... less its accumulated, *realised* losses", the exact meaning of the term 'realised' is not defined in the Act. Paragraph 91 of Schedule 4 to the Act merely gives an indication of the interpretation of the term. Paragraph 91 says that "references ... to realised profits ... are to such profits ... as fall to be treated as realised profits ... in accordance with principles generally accepted with respect to the determination for accounting purposes of realised profits at the time when those accounts are prepared".

19.21 Moreover, there is little indication in case law of what is meant by 'realised'. The few cases that there have been mainly relate to tax law, rather than to company law. All that can really be derived from those cases is that the judges have interpreted 'realised' as meaning something wider than 'realised in cash', and also that they, like the legislature, see realisation as an accounting, rather than a strictly legal, concept.

19.22 Because of these difficulties of interpretation, the CCAB issued, in September 1982, the following guidance statements:

> TR 481 — The determination of realised profits and the disclosure of distributable profits in the context of the Companies Acts 1948 to 1981.

> TR 482 — The determination of distributable profits in the context of the Companies Acts 1948 to 1981.

These two guidance statements are reproduced as Appendix VIII. Although they both refer to the Companies Acts 1948 to 1981, they apply equally to the Companies Act 1985, and all references below refer to the equivalent sections of the 1985 Act.

Technical release 481

19.23 The main purpose of TR 481 is to give guidance on the interpretation of the term 'principles generally accepted', as used in paragraph 91 of Schedule 4 to the Act. The phrase is not defined in the Act. But it has been given a judicial interpretation, as being "principles which are generally regarded as permissible or legitimate by the accountancy profession. That is sufficient even though only one company actually applies it in practice". *(*Lord Denning, MR, in *Associated Portland Cement Manufacturers Ltd. v Price Commission [1975] ICR 27.)*

19.24 The main conclusions that TR 481 arrives at are as follows:

(a) Unless an Accounting Standard specifically indicates that a profit should be treated as unrealised, a profit that is required by an Accounting Standard to be recognised in the profit and loss account should normally be treated as a realised profit. For example, SSAP 9, 'Stocks and work in progress', requires that attributable profit should be included in the value of long-term contract work in progress (see Chapter 8 para 8.60). Consequently, this attributable profit should be treated as realised.

(b) A profit may be recognised in the profit and loss account in accordance with an accounting policy that is not the subject of an Accounting Standard, or (exceptionally) that is contrary to a Standard. Such a profit will normally be a realised profit if the accounting policy is consistent with the two concepts of accruals and prudence as set out in both SSAP 2 and Schedule 4 to the Act (see Chapter 3 paras 3.25 to 3.30).

(c) Where, in special circumstances, a company could not give a true and fair view (even if it provided additional information) without including an unrealised profit in its profit and loss account, the Act requires a company to include that unrealised profit. Moreover, where the directors have special reasons for doing so, Schedule 4 allows them to include an unrealised profit in the profit and loss account. Where unrealised profits are thus recognised in the profit and loss account, a note to the financial statements must give particulars of this departure from the statutory accounting principles, the reasons for it, and its effect (see Chapter 3 para 3.18). [*4 Sch 15*].

19.25 In February 1983, the ASC requested the ICAEW's Research Board to commission a research project on the practical implications for Accounting Standards of the concept of realised profits as set out in the EC Fourth Directive (and hence in the Companies Act 1985). The research was carried out by Professor Bryan Carsberg (the ICAEW's director of research) and Christopher Noke (of the London School of Economics). They reported their findings to the ASC in December 1984. Their research paper entitled 'The reporting of profits and the concept of realisation' will be published shortly. Their findings are, of course, as relevant to the Companies Act 1985 as to the Fourth Directive, because the Act includes the provisions that implemented the Directive into UK law.

19.26 First, they surveyed and analysed existing academic literature. This analysis led them to conclude that "no single definition of the term 'realised profits' commands general acceptance". They went on to say that "The British standard SSAP 2 contains definitions that are unclear. The US literature refers to variability of practice and avoids taking a firm position to end that variability".

19.27 Secondly, they used ideas from their survey of the literature to identify possible meanings of the term 'realisation' and to analyse the relative merits of those meanings. This work identified the following six possible meanings of 'realisation':

(a) Conversion into cash.

(b) Conversion into one of a set of specific assets.

(c) Resulting from an exchange.

(d) Earned by undertaking services.

(e) Measurable with acceptable reliability.

(f) Represented by a freely disposable store of wealth.

19.28   They established a preference for the approach in *(e)*, that is one based on the reliability of measurement. This approach would mean that a surplus or a gain should be included in profit only if its occurrence can be established from sufficiently reliable measurements. Their overall conclusion was that they had failed to identify any currently accepted clear meaning of realisation. Consequently, they recommended that the ASC should prepare a statement that would produce a general definition of realisation (probably by revising SSAP 2). They considered that the main purpose underlying the concept of realisation is to secure reliability of measurement to ensure that profits are recognised only when they can be said to have occurred with reasonable certainty. They also considered that a definition based on this concept should be explored. They suggested that, once realisation has been defined generally, individual Standards should indicate the application of this general definition to specific situations. In addition, they considered that the traditional profit and loss account should be limited to legally distributable profits, and also that companies should be encouraged to publish an additional statement (perhaps a statement of 'Total gains') to indicate the overall financial performance by bringing together all profits and gains. Finally, they recommended that the ASC should consider expressing a view about whether financial capital maintenance or physical capital maintenance is the preferable concept to form the basis for profit measurement in the main financial statements.

19.29   Until the ASC revises Accounting Standards to take account of Carsberg and Noke's research, TR 481 is the principal guidance available on determining which profits are realised and which are not.

Technical release 482

19.30   TR 482 gives guidance on the way in which a company should determine distributable profits in the context of current legislation. It states that, in general, companies are allowed to make distributions only out of realised profits, less realised losses (as outlined in para 19.05). In addition, a public company must deduct any net unrealised losses from net realised profits before making a distribution.

19.31   When determining the profits from which a company is allowed to make distributions, the starting point (the 'accumulated realised profits ... less accumulated realised losses') will normally be the accumulated balance on the profit and loss account. This figure may need adjusting to take into account any items that the company is required to exclude in determining its distributable profits (such as the additional restriction imposed on public companies referred to above).

19.32   Increasingly, there are differences between the balance on a company's profit and loss account and the amount that is realised (and so is distributable in law). A company may or may not need to highlight, in its financial statements, the fact that there is a difference between the balance on the profit and loss account and the amount that is legally distributable. Where the difference is material, the financial statements may need to disclose the amounts of distributable and undistributable reserves respectively, in order to show a true and fair view (for example, see Table 9 on page 68 and Table 37 on page 192).

19.33 This requirement may also apply when the size of a dividend paid or proposed is substantial, as compared to the total of distributable reserves, and there is the risk that the shareholders may be under the mistaken impression that the same level of dividends can be maintained in the future without unrealised profits being turned into realised profits. In these circumstances, companies should disclose the difference between the balance on the profit and loss account and the amount that is legally distributable, in order that their financial statements should show a true and fair view.

Effect that revaluations of fixed assets have on distributable profits

19.34 An example of an adjustment that may be necessary to arrive at the profit available for distribution arises when fixed assets have been revalued. Consider the following situations.

19.35 First, provisions for the depreciation of revalued fixed assets require special treatment to the extent that they *exceed* the amounts that would have been provided if the assets had not been revalued. For the purpose of calculating the amount of profit that is legally available for distribution, a company is required to treat an amount equivalent to the excess depreciation on the revaluation surplus as a realised profit. [*Sec 275(2)*]. In this way, the provision for depreciation that is charged in the profit and loss account is reduced to the amount that would have been charged on the asset's original cost.

19.36 As a result, when fixed assets have been revalued, the depreciation of the 'surplus element' will not normally affect the amount of a company's accumulated distributable profits. However, it will affect its annual profits as stated in the published financial statements (see also Chapter 5 paras 5.64 to 5.83).

19.37 The example that follows (which ignores the effects of taxation) illustrates the implications of Section 275(2):

	Cost	Valuation	Difference between cost and valuation
	£	£	£
Fixed assets	1,000	2,500	1,500
Profit before depreciation	5,000	5,000	N/A
Depreciation at 10% a year	100	250	150
Profit after depreciation	4,900	4,750	N/A

459

If the Act did not contain Section 275(2), the distributable profit for the period would be £4,750, because the profit that the financial statements disclosed would be the profit after charging depreciation on the revalued amount. The effect of Section 275(2) is to add back the additional depreciation of £150 (that arises because the assets have been revalued) in determining the profits available for distribution. Without this provision, companies might be discouraged from revaluing their fixed assets, because the extra depreciation to be charged on the resulting surplus would have the effect of reducing their profits available for distribution.

This provision is illustrated in Table 99.

Table 99: *Example of a company that transfers an amount equivalent to the amount of excess depreciation charged on revalued assets from the revaluation reserve to the profit and loss account.*

Extract from Tate & Lyle PLC Annual Report 29 September 1984.

Notes

19. REVALUATION RESERVE

The revaluation reserve arises as a consequence of carrying certain tangible fixed assets in the balance sheet at valuations determined in years up to 1981. The movement on the reserve is analysed below:

	Tate & Lyle PLC	Subsidiary companies	Related companies	Total
	£ million	£ million	£ million	£ million
At 1st October 1983	—	21.6	0.3	21.9
Differences on exchange	—	0.2	—	0.2
Transfer to profit and loss account	—	(2.4)	—	(2.4)
At 29th September 1984	—	19.4	0.3	19.7

21. PROFIT AND LOSS ACCOUNT

	Tate & Lyle PLC	Subsidiary companies	Related companies	Total
At 1st October 1983	72.3	76.9	13.9	163.1
Differences on exchange	—	8.2	0.4	8.6
Transfer from revaluation and other reserves	—	2.2	—	2.2
Additional provision for deferred taxation	—	(9.2)	(0.1)	(9.3)
Retained profit for the period	(3.2)	25.0	2.6	24.4
At 29th September 1984	69.1	103.1	16.8	189.0

The amount of depreciation provided in the period on the book value of tangible fixed assets which represents revaluation surpluses has been transferred from revaluation reserve to profit and loss account. This is in accordance with section 39(5) of the Companies Act 1980 [*now Section 275(2) of the Companies Act 1985*].

19.38   Secondly, adjustments will be required for any items taken to reserves that may properly be included in the determination of distributable profits. For example, an unrealised profit on an asset revaluation will originally be credited direct to a revaluation reserve. When the asset is subsequently disposed of, the whole profit is clearly realised, notwithstanding the fact that all or part of it may not have been passed through the profit and loss account. In addition, where a revalued asset is disposed of, any deficit from cost that has previously been treated as unrealised (see para 19.41 below) should be redesignated as a realised loss.

19.39 Where an asset's original cost is not known, or where it is not possible to ascertain it without unreasonable delay or expense, its cost is taken to be the value shown in the company's earliest available record of its value. [*Sec 275(3)*].

19.40 The CCAB guidance statement TR 482 discusses also the writing-back of past depreciation when an asset is revalued. However, opinion is divided as to whether the amount of depreciation written back represents a realised or an unrealised surplus, and the guidance statement gives no firm guidance. Where a company places reliance on such a profit being realised in order to make a distribution, the directors may consider it appropriate to seek legal advice (see further Chapter 5 paras 5.30 to 5.36). (ED 37 comments that this depreciation should not be written back to the profit and loss account. However, this comment does not necessarily answer the question of whether the profit is realised or not.)

19.41 Thirdly, unless it offsets a previous unrealised surplus on the same asset, a deficit on the revaluation of an asset gives rise to a provision, and that deficit must normally be treated as a realised loss. Such a realised loss cannot be reduced by being offset (either wholly or in part) against revaluation surpluses on other assets (whether or not they are of the same class). There is, however, an exception to this: the Act says that where a provision for the diminution in value of a fixed asset arises on a revaluation of *all* the fixed assets, such a provision may be treated as unrealised. [*Sec 275(1)*]. A revaluation of all of the company's fixed assets may exclude the revaluation of goodwill. [*Sec 275(1)*]. Furthermore, in this connection, the directors may *consider* the value of a fixed asset and treat that consideration as a revaluation of that asset. [*Sec 275(4)*]. This means that the directors do not need to have all of the fixed assets professionally valued in order to take advantage of the provision in Section 275(1). But they must consider the value of all those assets that have not been revalued, and they must comply with the other conditions that are listed in paragraphs 19.46 and 19.47 below.

Treatment of revalued assets in relevant accounts

19.42 The interpretation of the provisions in Section 275 has caused numerous problems. Some guidance on some of these problems is set out in paragraph 19.50 below. However, this guidance needs to be read with an understanding of Sections 275(1), 275(4), 275(5) and 275(6) of the Act. These sections are, therefore, summarised in paragraphs 19.43 to 19.49 that follow.

19.43 Section 275(1) of the Act states that a diminution in value of a fixed asset that appears when all the company's fixed assets are revalued, need not be treated as a realised loss. (This applies even if goodwill is not revalued, notwithstanding that goodwill is to be treated as a fixed asset in the balance sheet.)

19.44 In determining whether a revaluation of a company's fixed assets has taken place for the purposes of Section 275(1), the directors' *consideration* of the value at any particular time of any fixed asset may be treated as a revaluation (for example, see Table 100). [*Sec 275(4)*]. However, a company may, in such circumstances, take advantage of the exemption contained in Section 275(1) only where the conditions in paragraphs 19.46 and 19.47 below are satisfied.

Table 100: Example of a company whose directors have 'considered' the value of its fixed assets in order to treat a provision for the diminution in value of some of its investments as unrealised for distribution purposes.

Extract from The Rank Organisation Plc Report and Accounts 31 October 1984.

Capital and reserves note extract

In presenting the figures for the Company's investments in subsidiary and associated companies the directors have adopted the alternative accounting rules under the terms of Schedule I Part II Section C of the Companies Act 1948 [*now Schedule 4 Part II Section C to the Companies Act 1985*] and have revalued an investment in a subsidiary company at 31st October 1984. The valuation surplus of £13·6m arising thereon in the year has been take to revaluation reserve.

The directors also consider that a permanent diminution in value has occurred in a number of subsidiary companies and consequently have made a charge of £4·2m to the profit and loss account of the Company during the year.

The directors have considered the value at 31st October 1984 of the remaining fixed assets of the Company without actually revaluing them, and are satisfied that these remaining assets are worth in total not less than the aggregate amount at which they are stated in these accounts.

Accordingly, and as provided in Section 39(4) and (4A) of the Companies Act 1980 [*now Section 275 of the Companies Act 1985*], the provisions for diminution in value of investments in subsidiaries of £4·2m charged in arriving at the surplus for the year of £45·9m in the Company's profit and loss account do not fall to be treated as realised losses and therefore are not regarded as reducing distributable reserves.

19.45 For this purpose, 'consideration' does not necessarily mean the directors' valuation of the asset as an individual item. It simply means that the directors should have addressed themselves to the question of the asset's value for the purpose of determining the legitimacy of distributions.

19.46 The conditions referred to in paragraphs 19.42 and 19.44 above that must be satisfied are as follows:

(a) All the company's fixed assets (or all those other than goodwill) have been revalued, either by an actual revaluation or by the directors' consideration of their value.

(b) The directors are satisfied that the aggregate value of the fixed assets that they have treated as having been revalued only because they considered the assets' value at the time in question, is not less than the aggregate amount at which those assets are, for the time being, stated in the company's financial statements. [*Sec 275(5)*]. However, the directors will not be able to use this consideration to justify treating a provision as unrealised unless the notes to the relevant accounts state that:

   (i) The directors have considered the value of some of the company's fixed assets, without actually revaluing those assets.

   (ii) The directors are satisfied that the aggregate value of those assets whose value they have considered was not less than the aggregate amount at which those assets are or were stated in the company's accounts.

   (iii) The asset or assets that have diminished in value are recorded in the company's relevant accounts after providing for that diminution in value.

  [*Sec 275(6)*].

19.47 In addition, the directors' consideration of the value of those fixed assets that have not been revalued must take place at the same time as, and must consider the value at the same date as, the revaluation that recognised the particular asset's diminution in value. The notes must also state this fact. [*Sec 275(6)(c)*]. For example, if, in December 1985, a professional valuer values as at 30 June 1985 a company's land and buildings, then the directors must, also in December 1985, consider the value of all the other fixed assets (with the possible exception of goodwill) as at 30 June 1985. This means that where, to justify a distribution in (say) early 1987, the directors prepare relevant accounts (the last relevant accounts being those to December 1985), they are not allowed to consider retrospectively the value as at 30 June 1985 of all the company's assets that were not revalued in December 1985.

19.48 Surprisingly, where a company revalues all of its fixed assets, then even where this revaluation shows an overall deficit, the diminution in value of the asset that is being accounted for can still be treated as an unrealised loss. This interpretation appears to be inconsistent with normal accounting convention. However, the diminution in value of the asset that is being accounted for will reduce a public company's distributable profits if, as a result of the provision, there is a net deficit on the revaluation reserve. This is because a public company's distribution must not reduce its net assets to less than its share capital plus undistributable reserves (see para 19.06 above).

19.49 The information that follows is used to illustrate four possible situations that may arise when directors consider the value of a company's assets:

	Book value £000	Market value £000	Deficit £000
Land and buildings	1,000	750	250
Plant and machinery	50	40	10
	1,050	790	260

The four situations are as follows:

(a) The market value of all the fixed assets has been determined by a professional valuation. The diminutions in value may, therefore, be treated as unrealised losses, even though there is an overall deficit of £260,000. The reason for this is that the deficit results from a revaluation of *all* the fixed assets. [*Sec 275(1)*].

(b) The market value of the land and buildings has been determined by a professional valuation, but the market value of the plant and machinery results from the directors' consideration of its value. Because the aggregate value of the assets that the directors have considered is £40,000, which is less than their book value of £50,000, the directors cannot claim to be satisfied that those assets' aggregate value is not less than their book value. The directors are, therefore, not able to rely on the exemption in Section 275(1) and so they must treat the deficit on the revaluation of the land and buildings as a realised loss. [*Sec 275(5)*].

(c) If the directors considered that the plant and machinery's market value was £60,000 (not £40,000), then they would be able to treat the deficit on the land and buildings of £250,000 as unrealised. This applies even though the fixed assets have an overall deficit of £240,000.

(d) However, in both situation *(a)* and situation *(c)* above, if the company was a public company, it might still be prevented from making a distribution even if it could treat the loss as unrealised. This is because a distribution must not reduce the amount of a public company's net assets below the aggregate of its called-up share capital plus its undistributable reserves. [*Sec 264(1)*].

Interpretation of the provisions of Section 275

19.50 Paragraph 19.42 above refers to the fact that these provisions of Section 275 have caused many problems when companies determine their distributable profits. The responses to the problems discussed below are based on guidance given by Counsel.

(a) Where a provision has been charged to realised profits, and it is subsequently released, does this restore the realised profits in question?

Where an asset has been either written down or provided against and it is then written up again, the initial reaction may be that the write-up constitutes a profit that *prima facie* appears to be unrealised. However, it seems correct that the write-up should be treated as a realised profit to the extent that the previous reduction was charged to realised profits. (This view is supported by *Bishop v Smyrna and Cassaba Railway Co.* [1895] *2 Ch 596*, in particular at 601, and by *Stapley v Read Bros.* [1924] *2 Ch 1*.)

(b) In what order should releases of provisions be applied where provisions have been made in previous years, and where some of these have been treated as realised losses and some as unrealised losses?

The principle expressed in *(a)* above is easy enough to apply when all provisions have been charged against the same reserve, and where the whole of a particular provision is restored at the same time. It seems that there is no established authority or principle that lays down any rule where the position is less simple. The best solution would seem to be to apply common sense. This solution leads to the conclusion that the more recent parts of the provision should normally be regarded as being released before the earlier parts.

(c) What is the meaning of the words 'value' and 'the company's accounts' in Section 275(5)?

It seems clear that the word 'value' in Section 275(5) means market value, and not book value.

The question arises whether 'the company's accounts' that are referred to in Section 275(5) are those financial statements (to, say, 30 September 1985) which are in the course of preparation and in which the directors have adjusted the assets' book values (by taking into account depreciation, for example) or the previous financial statements (that is, those to 30 September 1984).

When Section 275(4) is relied on, Section 275(6) deals with the contents of the note to the financial statements where the directors have considered the value of any of the company's fixed assets, without actually revaluing those assets. Section 275(6)(b) requires the notes to state:

> "That they [*the directors*] are satisfied that the aggregate value of those assets at the time in question is or was not less than the aggregate amount at which they are or were for the time being stated in the company's accounts".

This note makes it clear that the company's accounts for the purposes of Section 275(5) are those in which the revaluation is incorporated. Thus the directors must compare actual values with the values at which the relevant assets are to be incorporated into the accounts being prepared.

This view is supported by the fact that the Section 275(4) procedure, including the requirement for a Section 275(6) note, applies also to *initial accounts*.

(d) If no dividend is to be paid by reference to the relevant accounts, but the directors have considered the value of the company's fixed assets in accordance with Section 275(6), does that section require

that the note that is needed if a distribution is to be made should be included in those relevant accounts?

Relevant accounts are those financial statements that contain the entries that justify a particular distribution, either because they show adequate distributable profits or because they have been specially prepared in order to justify the distribution. (This interpretation seems clear from Section 270 generally and, in particular, from subsections (2) and (3) and the introductory words of Sections 271(1), 272(1) and 273(1).)

Consequently, it appears to follow that, if a company does not propose to justify a particular distribution by reference to a particular set of financial statements, Section 275(6) does not require those financial statements to contain the special note, because those financial statements are not *relevant accounts*.

Accordingly, it seems that the note that Section 275(6) requires need not appear in the financial statements either for the year in which the Section 275(4) revaluation took place, or for a subsequent year, unless those financial statements are to be relied upon for the purpose of justifying a distribution.

However, if the note is excluded from the financial statements, the directors cannot use those financial statements to justify a distribution in the future. Although the directors may have no plans at that time to make a distribution, they may wish to do so at some time before the next audited financial statements are prepared. If they have not included the note required by Section 275(6) in the last set of financial statements, then they will need to prepare *interim accounts* to justify the proposed distribution. Consequently, it will be sensible to include in the financial statements the note that Section 275(6) requires, even where the directors do not intend at that time to make a distribution.

However, for a private company, the note need not appear in the *interim* or the *initial accounts* that the directors rely upon to justify making a distribution. This is because Sections 272 and 273 do not apply to private companies.

(e) Where the note that Section 275(6) requires is not included in a company's financial statements, does this omission convert a provision on a revaluation that is made in those financial statements into a realised loss for all future financial statements that are to be used as relevant accounts?

It appears that any financial statements that are used to justify a distribution are *relevant accounts*. And, for the purposes of Section 275(6), they are *the* relevant accounts, even if the directors do not need to rely on the particular Section 275(4) revaluation in order to justify a current distribution. Accordingly, if a set of financial statements that does not contain a note relating to a Section 275(4) revaluation that took place in either that year or a previous year, become *relevant accounts* (because they are used to justify a distribution), it seems that the provision that is made on that revaluation becomes, and must remain, a realised loss. Where it becomes necessary to rely on Section 275(4) to justify a subsequent distribution, it will be too late to include the Section 275(6) note in a subsequent set of financial statements.

This last point, however, is a difficult issue, and it is still the subject of debate. Consequently, this is another reason why it is advisable to include in any financial statements the note that Section 275(6) requires, even where a distribution is not to be made by reference to those financial statements.

Summary of desirable action

19.51 To summarise, therefore, when the directors have some of the company's assets valued, and the deficits that arise on this revaluation affect the company's ability to pay a dividend, the directors should:

(a) Consider the value as at the same date of all other assets (excluding goodwill) at the same time that the valuation of the assets that shows the deficit is made.

(b) Include the note referred to in paragraph 19.46 above in the financial statements for the year in which the valuation took place. The directors should do this even if they do not intend to make a distribution by reference to those financial statements.

(c) Repeat that note in all subsequent financial statements, because they may become *relevant accounts* for the purpose of making a distribution in the future.

19.52 If the directors take these three steps, any deficits that arise from a revaluation of the company's assets may be treated as unrealised for the purpose of making distributions.

Effect that foreign currency translation has on distributable profits

19.53 SSAP 20 requires that a company should translate those of its currency transactions that are outstanding at the end of the year (for example, creditors for fixed assets purchased from overseas and currency loans) using the rate of exchange at the balance sheet date (that is, the closing rate). Where, however, the rate of exchange is fixed under the terms of the relevant transaction, the company should use that rate. Where an outstanding trading transaction is covered by a related or a matching forward contract, the rate specified in that contract may be used. [*SSAP 20 para 48*].

19.54   Exchange gains and losses will arise both on the currency transactions a company completes during the year and on its currency transactions outstanding at the end of the year. The company should include all such exchange differences in its profit or loss for the year from ordinary operations. The only exception to this rule is that an exchange difference on a currency transaction that is itself treated as an extraordinary item should be included as part of that item. [*SSAP 20 para 49*].

19.55   However, not all exchange gains on the translation of currency transactions that are included in the profit and loss account are realised. There is a conflict here with paragraph 12 of Schedule 4 to the Act, because this paragraph states that "only profits realised at the balance sheet date shall be included in the profit and loss account".

19.56   Where exchange gains arise on short-term monetary items, their ultimate cash realisation can normally be assessed with reasonable certainty. 'Monetary items' are defined in SSAP 20 as money held and amounts to be either received or paid in money. Where a company is not an exempt company (as defined in SSAP 20), monetary items should be categorised as either short-term items or long-term items. 'Short-term monetary items' are those that fall due within one year of the balance sheet date. [*SSAP 20 para 44*]. Therefore, such gains are realised in accordance with the prudence concept defined in SSAP 2. Accordingly, if they are included in the profit and loss account, this treatment does not conflict with paragraph 12 of Schedule 4 to the Act.

19.57   Exchange gains that arise on long-term monetary items are not realised, but there is a *special reason* for a company to include these gains in its profit and loss account. The special reason is that the company should treat exchange gains and exchange losses symmetrically. Exchange gains can be determined just as objectively as exchange losses. Consequently, it would be illogical to account for adverse movements in exchange rates and then not to account also for favourable movements. [*SSAP 20 para 10*]. Paragraph 15 of Schedule 4 to the Act states that, where there is a special reason, companies may depart from the accounting principles in Schedule 4. Where a company does include exchange gains on long-term monetary items in its profit and loss account, it must state, in its financial statements, the particulars of, the reasons for, and the effect of, the departure from the Act (see Table 3 on page 27). [*4 Sch 15*].

19.58   However, SSAP 20 does recognise that, in exceptional circumstances, it may be prudent for a company to restrict the amount of the exchange gain on long-term monetary items (or the amount by which the gain exceeds past losses on the same items) that it recognises in the profit and loss account. This restriction would be appropriate where the company has doubts about either the convertibility or the marketability of the currency in question. [*SSAP 20 para 50*].

19.59 Where exchange gains on long-term monetary items are included in the profit and loss account, they will be unrealised to the extent that they exceed past losses on the same items. Where exchange losses on long-term monetary items are included in the profit and loss account, they will be realised to the extent that they exceed past unrealised gains on the same items.

To illustrate this, consider the following example. In 1984, a UK company took out a long-term US dollar loan. It did not use the loan to finance a foreign equity investment. Consequently, the company must include in its profit and loss account the exchange gains and losses that arise when the loan is retranslated at the closing rate. (There are no doubts as to either the convertibility or the marketability of US dollars.)

Assuming that the exchange differences were as shown below, they should be treated either as unrealised or as realised in the way indicated below.

Year ended 31 December	Exchange gain/(loss) included in profit and loss account £	Unrealised £	Realised £	Note
1984	250,000	250,000		(a)
		250,000		
1985	(300,000)	(250,000)	(50,000)	(b)
		—	(50,000)	
1986	75,000	25,000	50,000	(c)
		25,000	—	
1987	50,000	50,000		(d)
		75,000		

Notes to the example above:

(a) The company must treat the whole of the exchange gain as unrealised.
(b) On the basis that the exchange loss reverses the previous exchange gain on the loan, it would appear equitable that the company can treat £250,000 of the loss as unrealised. The company must treat the balance of the loss as realised.
(c) The company can treat the gain as realised to the extent that it reverses a past loss on the loan. It must treat the balance of the gain as unrealised.
(d) The company must treat the whole of the exchange gain as unrealised.

19.60 In order to identify unrealised exchange gains on the translation of long-term monetary items, a company will need to keep detailed records of the exchange gains and losses that arise over the life of each long-term monetary item.

19.61 Where a company has used foreign currency borrowings either to finance, or to provide a hedge against, its foreign equity investments, and where, also, the conditions set out in paragraph 19.62 below apply, the company may denominate its equity investments in the appropriate foreign currency. This means that the investment will be regarded as a currency investment, and the company will need to translate the carrying amount at the closing rate each year for inclusion in its financial statements. Where a company treats investments in this way, it should take to reserves any exchange differences that arise when the investments are retranslated. It should also take the exchange differences on the related foreign currency borrowings to reserves. It would then offset the exchange differences as a net increase or a net decrease to unrealised reserves. [*SSAP 20 para 51*]. (SSAP 20 does not require companies to maintain a separate reserve for exchange differences.)

19.62 The conditions for offset, all of which must apply, are:

(a) In any accounting period, a company may offset the exchange differences on its borrowings only to the extent of the exchange differences that arise when the investments (being financed by those borrowings) are retranslated.

(b) The borrowings must not exceed, in aggregate, the total amount of cash that the investments are expected to be able to generate from profits or otherwise.

(c) A company should apply consistently the accounting treatment it adopts.
[*SSAP 20 para 51*].

19.63 Consequently, where the exchange difference on a borrowing is a loss, it can be argued that the loss is not a provision because it is not a loss "either likely to be incurred, or certain to be incurred but uncertain as to amount or as to the date on which it will arise". [*4 Sch 89*]. On the basis of this argument, a company would not have to take such a loss into account when determining its distributable profits. Because of the uncertainty that exists, the ASC's technical release that accompanies SSAP 20 suggests that, if sufficient distributable profit exists only as a result of the company offsetting a loss on its currency borrowings against a gain on its related foreign equity investments, it may be appropriate for the directors to obtain legal advice. Foreign currency translation is also considered in Chapter 17, paragraphs 17.77 to 17.88

Qualified audit reports and distributions

19.64 As mentioned in paragraph 19.14*(e)* above, if the auditors have qualified their opinion, they must state in writing whether the subject matter of their qualification is material in determining the legality of the proposed distribution. [*Sec 271(3)(4), 273(4)(5)*].

19.65 Therefore, where auditors qualify their report on the annual financial statements of a company that is proposing to pay a dividend, they will need to make an additional statement to the shareholders. This statement must be laid before the company in general meeting. [*Sec 271(4)*].

19.66 Many companies pay interim dividends, and the annual financial statements that the auditors report on will constitute the *relevant accounts* for the purposes of those interim dividends. Accordingly, auditors should, whenever possible, word their report in the annual financial statements to cover any future distributions.

19.67 The implication of a qualified audit report may be either *favourable* or *unfavourable*. An audit qualification may be material for distribution purposes, but in a favourable sense. For example, it may be possible to say that if any adjustment was to be made to eliminate the need for the qualification, it could have the effect only of increasing the company's net assets or realised profits. In this situation, the qualification is regarded as *favourable* for distribution purposes. An *'unfavourable'* qualification means that the profits available for distribution could be less than the amount included in the financial statements.

19.68 Where the effect of the auditors' qualification is *favourable*, the auditors could include the following additional statement in their report:

> "In our opinion, the qualification is not material for the purpose of determining whether any distribution payable by reference to these financial statements is permitted under the Companies Act 1985."

19.69 Where the auditors can quantify the effect of an audit qualification that is *unfavourable* but not material for this purpose, they could word the additional statement in their report as follows:

> "In our opinion, the qualification is not material for the purpose of determining whether distributions not exceeding £X in total payable by reference to these financial statements are permitted under the Companies Act 1985."

19.70 If the auditors can word their statement on these lines, and not restrict it to the legality of the proposed final dividend only, they will not need to make a further statement in respect of the next interim dividend (for example, see Table 101). If, however, the auditors do have to make a further statement, the company will have to hold a general meeting to lay the statement before the shareholders.

Other matters

Bonus issues

19.71 Some companies have found that they have utilised past revaluation reserves for bonus issues (as illustrated in Table 102). The question has then arisen as to whether, in order to comply with the Act, they need to reinstate the revaluation reserve out of distributable reserves.

19.72 Although the position is not entirely clear, there is a strong argument against the need to reinstate the revaluation reserve. Section 264(3) of the Act defines a company's undistributable reserves as including "the amount by which the company's accumulated unrealised profits, so far as not previously utilised by capitalisation ... exceed its accumulated, unrealised losses (so far as not previously written off in a reduction or reorganisation of capital duly made)". Capitalisation is defined as including every description of capitalisation except a transfer of the company's profits to its capital redemption reserve on or after 22 December 1980. This definition implies that a company may utilise its undistributable reserves, such as a revaluation reserve, for bonus issues. In addition, there is no specific provision in the Act that requires the revaluation reserve to be reinstated if it has been utilised in a manner the law permits (see further Chapter 5 para 5.51).

Table 101: Example of a qualified audit report that has been worded in a way to avoid restricting profits that are available for distribution.

Extract from George Wimpey PLC Annual report 31 December 1983.

Auditors' report

We have audited the accounts on pages 35 to 58 in accordance with approved Auditing Standards.

As explained in the directors' report on page 30:
(a) exceptional losses have been incurred and provisions have been made on contracts and for reducing the activities of a company in Saudi Arabia in which the group has a 49% interest.
(b) the directors believe that the losses have now been contained and adequate provisions have been made but the outcome will remain uncertain until contracts are completed and contractual claims settled.

We concur with the directors' view as to the uncertainty of the outcome until final settlement.

Subject to adjustments, if any, that may be necessary in respect of these matters, in our opinion the accounts give a true and fair view of the state of affairs of the company and the group at 31 December 1983 and of the profit and source and application of funds of the group for the year then ended and comply with the Companies Acts 1948 to 1981.

In our opinion this qualification is not material for the purpose of determining whether the distributions payable by reference to these accounts are permitted under the Companies Act 1980 (see note 24).

The accounts do not contain the current cost accounts required by Statement of Standard Accounting Practice No. 16.

Deloitte Haskins & Sells
CHARTERED ACCOUNTANTS
LONDON, 26 APRIL 1984

Directors' report extract

EXCEPTIONAL ITEMS
In February 1984 shareholders were informed of profits arising from a major programme of disposals of partly owned property investments and the inclusion of exceptional losses in the accounts for 1983.

The accounts for 1983 include exceptional profits of £42.1 million realised on the disposal of the group's interests in Euston Centre Properties PLC and eight other property companies. As a result of these disposals revaluation reserves of £41.5 million have been converted into realised profits.

Table 101 continued.

The exceptional losses arise from three unrelated situations:

(a) Losses incurred on a contract to construct a hydro electric scheme in Swaziland amount to £9.6 million. Both the ground conditions and eventual design were markedly different from those in the tender documents and substantial claims have been lodged but not anticipated in the accounts although they are being pursued.

(b) A joint venture high rise residential property development in central Hong Kong has ceased due to the considerable reduction in property values there. The group has honoured its financial obligations and written off its original investment resulting in a loss of £9.2 million. The group has renegotiated its position so that, depending on the extent that property values in Hong Kong recover, it may recoup some of the loss.

(c) The group has a 49% interest in an electrical and mechanical engineering company in Saudi Arabia which is in financial difficulty and is being supported by its shareholders. Losses of £16.4 million have been incurred on contracts and a further £6.5 million on overheads and the costs of reducing the company's activities. The directors believe that the losses have now been contained and adequate provisions made. The outcome will remain uncertain until contracts are completed and contractual claims settled. This uncertainty is reflected in the report of the auditors on page 34.

Note

24 PROFIT AND LOSS ACCOUNT	PARENT	SUBSIDIARY COMPANIES	ASSOCIATED COMPANIES	1983 GROUP	1982 GROUP
1 January 1983	158.9	170.8	17.9	347.6	308.9
Exchange adjustments	(0.1)	6.3	0.4	6.6	9.8
Capitalisation issue of shares	(6.4)	—	—	(6.4)	—
Adjustment in respect of former associated companies	—	2.4	(2.4)	—	—
Cost of control of new subsidiaries	—	(1.1)	—	(1.1)	(2.0)
Retained profit for year	10.8	11.8	(5.3)	17.3	30.9
31 December 1983	163.2	190.2	10.6	364.0	347.6

These accounts are the relevant accounts for the purposes of section 43(2) of the Companies Act 1980 [*now Section 270 of the Companies Act 1985*].

The amount of the retained profits of George Wimpey PLC that may not be legally distributed under section 40 of the Companies Act 1980 [*now Section 264 of the Companies Act 1985*] is £1.1 million (1982 £0.4 million).

Distributions up to £162.1 million made by reference to these accounts (which are after charging an exceptional loss and provision of £22.9 million referred to in the report of the directors on page 31) will not contravene section 39 of the Companies Act 1980 [*now Section 263 of the Companies Act 1985*]. To the extent that such provision is inadequate this figure will be reduced and any balance would remain available for distribution pursuant to section 39.

Table 102: Illustration of a company that has capitalised its revaluation reserve by issuing fully paid bonus shares.

Extract from Trusthouse Forte PLC Report & Accounts 31 October 1984.

Directors' report extract

Capital: On 27th April, 1984 389,748,133 Ordinary Shares and 390,000 Trust Shares of 25p each, fully paid, were issued by way of a one for one Capitalisation Issue.

Notes

20 SHARE CAPITAL	*Shares of 25p*	*£m*
Authorised		
Ordinary	999,220,000	
Trust	780,000	
	1,000,000,000	250·0

The authorised capital was increased during the year from £125m to £250m by the creation of an additional 499,610,000 Ordinary Shares and 390,000 Trust Shares of 25p each.

Allotted and fully paid		*Shares of 25p*	
		Trust	*Ordinary*	*£m*
At 31st October, 1983		390,000	389,748,133	
1 for 1 capitalisation issue		390,000	389,748,133	
At 31st October, 1984		780,000	779,496,266	195·1

The Company has granted options in respect of the following shares:

	Options granted	*Number of shares*	*Period of option*	*Price per share*
Senior executive share option scheme	1983	2,168,566	Nov 1985-Nov 1989	70p
	1984	575,696	Feb 1987- Feb 1991	98·25p
Employee savings related share option scheme	1984	2,344,703	Oct 1989- Apr 1990	97·2p

Up to 27,282,369 Ordinary Shares of 25p each, being part of authorised share capital, may be issued under these option schemes.

21 RESERVES	*Total*	*Share premium*	*Revaluation reserve*	*Profit and loss account*
Group	*£m*	*£m*	*£m*	*£m*
At 31st October, 1983	533·0	68·9	273·8	190·3
Profit retained for year	21·7	—	—	21·7
Surplus on revaluation of properties	132·2	—	132·2	—
Revaluation surplus realised on disposals	(4·0)	—	(4·0)	—
Goodwill on the acquisition of businesses	(2·0)	—	—	(2·0)
Capitalisation issue and expenses	(97·7)	(0·1)	(97·6)	—
Currency translation differences:				
Overseas fixed assets	58·6	—	21·1	37·5
Foreign currency loans	(28·5)	—	—	(28·5)
Overseas net current assets	5·9	—	—	5·9
Reserves at 31st October, 1984	619·2	68·8	325·5	224·9
Company				
At 31st October, 1983	477·5	68·9	324·5	84·1
Profit retained for year	1·4	—	—	1·4
Surplus on revaluation of subsidiaries	238·0	—	238·0	—
Capitalisation issue and expenses	(97·7)	(0·1)	(97.6)	—
Reclassification	—	—	(3·2)	3·2
Reserves at 31st October, 1984	619·2	68·8	461·7	88·7

19.73 Companies may not make bonus issues unless their articles of association expressly permit them to do so. Therefore, newly-incorporated companies must take express power in their articles to make bonus issues out of unrealised profits (for example, as detailed in regulation 110 of Table A). However, companies that existed before 22 December 1980 need not alter their articles to do this if immediately before that date they had power under their articles to capitalise unrealised profits. With companies that existed at 22 December 1980, this means that a power in the articles to make bonus issues out of profits available for dividend will be deemed to include a power to make bonus issues out of unrealised profits. [*Sec 278*].

Amounts unpaid on debentures and shares

19.74 A company may not apply an unrealised profit to pay up debentures or any amounts that are unpaid on its issued shares. [*Sec 263(4)*]. The purpose of this prohibition is to prevent profits that are not available for distribution being made available indirectly for dividend purposes.

Profits and losses made before 22 December 1980

19.75 Where the directors are unable to determine whether a profit or a loss that was made before 22 December 1980 is realised or unrealised, they may treat the profit as realised and the loss as unrealised. [*Sec 263(5)*].

Capitalisation of development costs

19.76 Where development costs are capitalised and are shown as an asset in a company's balance sheet (see Chapter 7 paras 7.15 to 7.34), any amount capitalised *must* nevertheless be treated as a realised (revenue) loss. [*Sec 269(1)*]. This does not apply to any part of the amount in the balance sheet that represents an unrealised profit on a revaluation of the development costs. It does not apply also if there are special circumstances that justify the directors deciding not to treat the capitalised development costs as a realised (revenue) loss. In this situation, the note that states the reasons for capitalising development costs must state also that the development costs have not been treated as a realised (revenue) loss. In addition, the note must state the justification the directors used for adopting this treatment. [*Sec 269(2)*].

Consolidated financial statements

19.77 Where group accounts are presented in the form of consolidated financial statements, the relevant distributable profits will be the holding company's realised profits. This is because distributable profits must be established for individual companies, and by definition, groups of companies are not individual companies. (However, some groups disclose also the aggregate distributable reserves of the group—see Table 103.)

Table 103: Illustration of a group that discloses the reserves that are distributable for the holding company and of a group that discloses the reserves that are distributable for both the group and the holding company.

Extract from S&W Berisford PLC Annual Report & Accounts 30 September 1984.

Note

24. **Total reserves**	Group £000	Company £000
Retained by—group companies	298,430	
—associated companies	450	
	298,880	
Distributable reserves		10,457
Non-distributable reserves		27,119
		37,576

Extract from First National Finance Corporation p.l.c. Report and Accounts 31 October 1984.

Note

18 Reserves	Share Premium account £000's	Revaluation reserve £000's	Profit and Loss account £000's	Total reserves £000's
Group				
Balance at 1 November, 1983	8,602	—	(4,439)	4,163
Retained profit for the year	—	—	17,604	17,604
Balance at 31 October, 1984	8,602	—	13,165	21,767
Company				
Balance at 1 November, 1983	8,602	2,784	(7,223)	4,163
Movement arising from revaluation of subsidiary companies	—	2,198	—	2,198
Retained profit for the year	—	—	15,406	15,406
Balance at 31 October, 1984	8,602	4.982	8,183	21,767

Analysis of Group reserves:

Share premium	8,602
Other undistributable reserves	13,394
Net deficiency of distributable reserves	(229)
Surplus at 31 October, 1984	21,767

Table 103 continued.

Included in the net deficiency of distributable reserves above are total positive reserves within subsidiaries of £23,389,000 which have not yet been distributed to the Company and such total includes £17,450,000 the distribution of which by First National Securities (Holdings) p.l.c. is currently subject to restrictions, including the prior establishment of a Sinking Fund of £3,486,000 within that Company in respect of its 12½% Convertible Unsecured Loan Stock 1987.

First National Securities (Holdings) p.l.c. and its subsidiaries are not permitted to make loans to or give guarantees in respect of companies elsewhere within the Group.

19.78 Consequently, a situation may arise where the group has sufficient distributable profits in aggregate to make a desired distribution, but the holding company itself has insufficient distributable profits. In this situation, a distribution may not be made to the holding company's shareholders without distributions first being made from the subsidiaries to the holding company to pass the distributable profits to the holding company. The holding company must then prepare *relevant accounts* that account for the receipt of these distributions in order to justify a distribution to its shareholders (see further paras 19.10 to 19.19). However, these relevant accounts need only include the holding company's financial statements (not the group accounts), because it is the holding company that will make the distribution.

19.79 If a holding company or a subsidiary has assets that have been revalued in accordance with the alternative accounting rules, the revaluation reserve is unrealised. However, if the company concerned sells these revalued assets to another company within the same group, the revaluation reserve becomes realised. It then appears *prima facie* that these reserves are available for distribution. Similarly, a holding company could sell one of its subsidiaries to another subsidiary to create distributable reserves. If these transactions are carried out at arm's length and are supported by proper legal documentation, the resulting surpluses appear to be realised. The fact that a transaction is undertaken between companies in the same group need not prevent the profit on the transaction being realised, and therefore distributable. If the transaction is entirely artificial, however, it may be unlawful to make a distribution from the resulting profit. This point has not yet been tested in the courts. As an example, however, Counsel has advised that, where the consideration is left outstanding because the group company that was purchasing the asset did not have sufficient funds to complete the transaction, then the transaction would not be legally valid for the purpose of creating realised profits. Where a company wishes to create distributable profits by an intra-group transaction, it would be wise for it to seek legal advice if it has any doubts about the legality of the proposed distribution.

19.80 Such transactions create problems on consolidation. Consider the following two examples:

(a) A subsidiary has a property that originally cost £100,000 but it has been revalued in the subsidiary's books to £500,000. Ignoring any depreciation, the revaluation reserve balance is £400,000. The subsidiary then sells the property to a fellow subsidiary in an arm's length transaction for £500,000 (its open market value). Consequently, the subsidiary will show in its profit and loss account the surplus on disposal of the property of £400,000. If the transaction is legally valid, the subsidiary may then distribute this realised profit to its holding company. However, as far as the group is concerned, there is no disposal. Therefore, on consolidation, the revaluation surplus that has been realised should be reinstated as an unrealised revaluation reserve. An additional problem may arise if the holding company decides to distribute these funds to its shareholders. In these circumstances, funds have left the group, and the transaction may need to be explained further if the consolidated financial statements are to show a true and fair view.

(b) The situation is similar to that described above, except that the realised profit in the subsidiary represents pre-acquisition reserves. Pre-acquisition reserves are a company's retained earnings at the date on which that company becomes a subsidiary of another company. Before the enactment of the Companies Act 1981, where a subsidiary paid a dividend to its holding company out of its pre-acquisition profits, the holding company would treat the dividend received as a reduction of the cost of its investment in that subsidiary. Consequently, dividends the subsidiary paid to the holding company out of pre-acquisition profits were *not* available for distribution to the holding company's shareholders.

The Companies Act 1981 amended paragraph 15(5) of the then Schedule 8 to the Companies Act 1948. This change has had the effect that where a subsidiary now pays a dividend to its holding company out of pre-acquisition profits, that dividend need not necessarily be applied as a reduction in the cost of the investment in the subsidiary. [*SSAP 23 Appendix para 3*]. Such a dividend should now be applied to reduce the carrying value of the investment to the extent that it is necessary to provide for a diminution in value of the investment in the subsidiary as stated in the holding company's financial statements. To the extent that this is not necessary, it appears that the amount received will be a realised profit in the hands of the holding company. However, in this example, on consolidation any part of the dividend received by the holding company that has not been applied to reduce the cost of the investment, will need to be adjusted on consolidation by taking out of the holding company's realised reserves an amount that will cause the goodwill on consolidation to remain the same as in previous years. If, as in example *(a)*, the holding company decides to distribute these funds to its shareholders, the transaction may need to be explained further if the consolidated financial statements are to show a true and fair view.

19.81 The consequences of these provisions are discussed in more detail in Chapter 18, paragraphs 18.92 to 18.98.

Memorandum and articles of association

19.82 Distributions are not only influenced by the provisions of the Act: they may also be subject to any enactment, or any rule of law or any provision in the memorandum or articles of association that may restrict either the amounts available for distribution or the circumstances in which a distribution may be made. [*Sec 281*].

19.83 For example, investment companies are restricted by their memorandum and articles of association from distributing realised capital profits (see Chapter 14 para 14.03*(c)*).

19.84 It is important, therefore, for the directors to have regard to the memorandum and articles, as well as to the statutory rules, before making a distribution. Also, a company cannot lawfully pay a dividend if, as a result, the company would either become insolvent, or have insufficient working capital to carry on its business.

Distributions in kind

19.85 A company may make a distribution that includes a non-cash asset.

19.86 Where the asset to be distributed has been included in the relevant accounts, and part of the amount at which it is stated represents an unrealised profit, the Act allows that profit to be treated as realised for the purpose of the distribution. [*Sec 276(a)*]. The Act also allows that unrealised profit to be taken to the profit and loss account if this is done for the purpose of making the distribution. [*Sec 276(b)*]. However, the company's articles must contain a power to make such distributions. Table A contains this power in regulation 105, and it requires the dividend to be approved at a general meeting. The dividend is declared as a cash amount, and it is for the directors to satisfy themselves as to the asset's value.

19.87 The directors may have difficulty in determining a value to be placed on the asset that is being distributed. They should value the asset that is being distributed at its fair value in order to show the dividend at its fair value. The asset's fair value would, in most situations, be its open market value and the asset should, therefore, be valued at arm's length. Consequently, a surplus or a deficit (which is the difference between the asset's net book value and its fair value) may have to be accounted for in the company's financial statements. This surplus (or deficit) should be recorded as an extraordinary item in the company's profit and loss account.

19.88 Consider the following example. A company wishes to distribute to its shareholders an asset that has a net book value of £9,000. The directors have obtained an independent open market valuation of the asset that assesses its value as £10,000. In order to show the true cost of the dividend, the company should record the unrealised profit of £1,000 (namely, £10,000 — £9,000) as an extraordinary item in its profit and loss account, and it should increase the asset's recorded value by £1,000. The company should then disclose a dividend of £10,000 in the profit and loss account and show the asset as having been disposed of. The company is not permitted to show the dividend as a deduction from reserves, because paragraph 3(7)(b) of Schedule 4 to the Act requires it to be shown in the company's profit and loss account.

Provisions relating to investment companies

19.89   Special provisions apply to distributions that investment companies make. The definition of an investment company is given in Chapter 14, paragraph 14.03. Section 265(1) permits investment companies to make a distribution either on the basis of the capital maintenance test, which applies to all public companies (see para 19.06) or on the basis of an asset ratio test (see para 19.92 below). However, where an investment company's distribution has reduced the amount of the company's net assets below the aggregate of its called-up capital and its undistributable reserves, this fact must be disclosed in the notes to the financial statements. [*4 Sch 72(1), 9 Sch 13(4)*].

19.90   Subject to the conditions listed in paragraph 19.91 below, an investment company may make a distribution at any time out of those of its accumulated realised revenue profits that have not previously been either distributed or capitalised, less its accumulated revenue losses (whether or not these are realised, and only insofar as they have not previously been written off in either a reduction or a re-organisation of capital). [*Sec 265(1)*].

19.91   The conditions that must all be satisfied before an investment company may make a distribution under Section 265(1) are:

(a) The company's shares must be listed on a recognised stock exchange (defined in Section 744 of the Act — see Chapter 8 para 8.04). [*Sec 265(4)(a)*].

(b) During the period beginning with the first day of the accounting reference period immediately preceding the accounting reference period in which the proposed distribution is to be made (or, where the distribution is proposed to be made during the company's first accounting reference period, the first day of that period) and ending with the date of the distribution, the company must not have:

(i) Distributed any of its capital profits.
(ii) Applied any unrealised profits or any capital profits (whether or not these are realised) in paying up debentures or any amounts unpaid on any of its issued shares. This means that companies may not distribute indirectly any amounts that are not available for distribution directly.
[*Sec 265(4)(5)*].

(c) The company must have given the Registrar of Companies the notice that Section 266(1) of the Act requires (see Chapter 14 para 14.03). It must have done this at one of the following times:

(i) Before the beginning of the period referred to in *(b)* above.
(ii) As soon as reasonably practicable after the date on which the company was incorporated.
[*Sec 265(6)*].

This condition is necessary in order to prevent the possibility that companies may adopt investment company status merely for the purpose of a particular distribution, and then revoke that status, only to adopt it again for the purpose of the next distribution.

(d) The amount of the company's assets must be at least 50% greater than the aggregate of its liabilities. [*Sec 265(1)(a)*]. In this context, 'liabilities' includes any provision other than those for depreciation or diminution in value of assets. [*Sec 265(2); 4 Sch 89*]. Moreover, the company must not include any uncalled share capital as an asset in those financial statements that are used in order to determine the legality of any distribution. [*Sec 265(3)*].

19.92 Where all these conditions are satisfied, an investment company may make a distribution, but only to the extent that the distribution does not reduce the amount of the company's assets below 150% of the aggregate of its liabilities. [*Sec 265(1)(b)*].

19.93 The following example sets out extracts from the balance sheets of four companies. The example shows how investment companies calculate their distributable profits and contrasts this with how other companies calculate their distributable profits:

		Company 1	Company 2	Company 3	Company 4
		£	£	£	£
A	Share capital	1,000	1,000	1,000	1,000
B	Share premium	100	100	100	100
C	Unrealised capital profits	600	600	600	600
D	Unrealised revenue profits	—	—	100	100
E	Unrealised capital losses	—	(700)	(700)	(700)
F	Unrealised revenue losses	—	(250)	(250)	(250)
G	Net unrealised reserves	600	(350)	(250)	(250)
H	Realised revenue profits	1,200	1,200	1,200	1,200
I	Realised capital profits	—	—	100	100
J	Realised capital losses	—	—	—	(600)
K	Realised revenue losses	—	—	(150)	(150)
L	Net realised reserves	1,200	1,200	1,150	550
M	Share capital and reserves	2,900	1,950	2,000	1,400
N	Total liabilities	1,300	1,300	1,300	1,300
O	Total assets	4,200	3,250	3,300	2,700

Maximum distributable
profits of an investment
company:

(i) per Section 265 (special rules for an investment company) (The lower of O—(1½ x N) and H—(K + F))	1,200	950	800	750
(ii) per Section 264 (normal rules for a public company) (The lower of L and (L + G))	1,200	850	900	300

Provisions relating to insurance companies

Definition of an insurance company

19.94 The Act introduces certain exceptions that relate only to those insurance companies that carry on long-term business. 'An insurance company', for this purpose, means an insurance company to which Part II of the Insurance Companies Act 1982 applies. [*Sec 268(1)*].

Special provisions in respect of insurance companies

19.95 In general, the provisions that relate to the distributable profits of companies, other than investment companies, apply also to those insurance companies that have long-term business. However, both the amounts that have been properly transferred to the profit and loss account of an insurance company from a surplus on its long-term business funds and the amount of any deficit on those funds should be treated as a realised profit or a realised loss. Subject to this, any additional profit or loss that may arise in that business fund after such transfers are made must be left out of account for the purposes of determining the realised profits of such a company. [*Sec 268(1)*].

19.96 For this purpose, the following definitions apply:

(a) 'Long-term business' means insurance business of any kind specified in Schedule 1 to the Insurance Companies Act 1982. It includes, *inter alia,* life and annuity and permanent health insurance business. [*Sec 268(3)(b); Insurance Companies Act 1982 s 1*].

(b) 'Surplus' in a fund of an insurance company means the excess of those assets that represent the fund over the liabilities that are attributable to its long-term business. The amounts concerned should be those shown either in an actuarial investigation under section 18 of the Insurance Companies Act 1982 (periodic actuar-

ial investigation of company with long-term business) or under section 42 of that Act (actuarial investigation required by the Secretary of State). [*Sec 268(2)(a), (3)(a)*].

(c) 'Deficit' in any such fund means the excess of those liabilities over those assets, as shown by an actuarial investigation. [*Sec 268(2)(b)*].

Liability for an unlawful distribution

19.97   Any shareholder of a company who receives an unlawful distribution is liable to repay it to the company if, at the time he received it, he knew, or he had reasonable grounds to believe, that it was made in contravention of the Act. [*Sec 277(1)*]. This provision is without prejudice to any other liability of a shareholder to repay distributions that have been unlawfully made to him. [*Sec 277(2)*].

19.98   Even where a distribution has been made that is apparently permitted by the relevant accounts, the directors may be personally liable in respect of payments made out of undistributable reserves. This situation may arise where the company makes a distribution that is covered by the distributable reserves shown in the last relevant accounts, but, to the knowledge of the directors, the company no longer has distributable reserves because they have been consumed by losses the company has made since those accounts were drawn up.

19.99   In these circumstances, the creditors may seek to have the company wound up. The liquidator may then sue the directors for making a distribution out of capital. Consequently, the directors should not only refer to the relevant accounts when they authorise a dividend; they should also take into account the company's results since the date on which those accounts were drawn up.

CHAPTER 20

OVERSEAS COMPANIES

Chapter 20

Overseas Companies

Introduction

20.01 An overseas company is any company that is incorporated outside Great Britain and has established a place of business in Great Britain. [*Sec 744*]. This definition includes a company that is incorporated in Northern Ireland, or in the Isle of Man, or in the Channel Islands, and has a place of business in Great Britain.

20.02 All overseas companies must prepare financial statements in respect of each accounting reference period. The basic rule is that these financial statements must contain the same information that would have been required if the company was, in fact, a company registered under the Act. [*Sec 700(1)*]. The Secretary of State may, however, make certain exemptions from this rule (see para 20.10 below). [*Sec 700(4)*].

20.03 An overseas company's financial statements must be delivered to the Registrar of Companies. If the financial statements are in a language other than English, the company must attach a certified translation of them to the financial statements that it files. [*Sec 700(2)*].

20.04 None of these requirements apply to an overseas company that would be exempt under Section 241(4) (see Chapter 21 para 21.23) from the requirement to file financial statements if it was a company registered under the Act (that is, an independent unlimited company that satisfies certain conditions). [*Sec 700(3)*].

Place of business

20.05 There is no comprehensive statutory definition of what constitutes a place of business. But Section 744 of the Act makes it clear that a share transfer office and a share registration office will be regarded as a 'place of business' for the purposes of the Act.

20.06 Guidance on what is meant by a 'place of business' can be found in decided cases. The company must have set up a place of business at a specific location.

20.07   A hotel that a director frequently stays in and from which he transacts the company's business may be a place of business. *(re Tovarishestvo Manufactur Liudvig-Rabenek [1944] Ch 404.)* However, a company will not be regarded as having established a place of business if it carries on its activities through an agent. *(Lord Advocate v Huron & Erie Loan Co. [1911] SC 612.)*

20.08   It is sufficient that the company carries on some business activity at its place of business. It does not matter if the business it carries on there does not form a substantial part of its activities. *(South India Shipping Corporation Limited v Export-Import Bank of Korea [1985] 1 WLR 585.)* The mere presence of the directors in their private residence will not make the residence a place of business. *(re Oriel Limited [1985] Financial Times 2 July 1985.)*

20.09   A foreign company that operates in Great Britain through a subsidiary will not, simply by virtue of that fact, have a place of business in Great Britain. *(Deverall v Grant Advertising Inc. [1954] 3 AER 389.)*

Financial statements of overseas companies

20.10   Although the Act states that the financial statements prepared by an overseas company must contain the same information that would have been required if the company was formed and registered under the Act [*Sec 700(1)*], the Act gives the Secretary of State power to modify this requirement by statutory instrument. [*Sec 700(4)(a)*]. The Act gives the Secretary of State power also to exempt any class of overseas company from any or all of the Act's requirements. [*Sec 700(4)(b),(5)*].

20.11   The Secretary of State has taken advantage of the power to modify the Act's requirements. The Oversea Companies (Accounts) (Modifications and Exemptions) Order 1982 (SI 1982/676) exempts overseas companies from many of the Act's accounting requirements. This statutory instrument refers to the Companies Acts 1948 to 1981. However, it is not being remade in the light of the 1985 Act, and so the exemptions it gives to overseas companies remain in force.

20.12   Overseas companies must prepare their financial statements in accordance with the requirements of Section 258 or 259 of, and Schedule 9 to, the Act, in so far as those requirements apply. [*SI 1982/676 para 2(1)(a)*]. Furthermore, overseas companies are not required to refer to the fact that their financial statements are drawn up in compliance with Section 258 or 259 of, and Schedule 9 to, the Act. Overseas companies are, of course, permitted to give additional information, including that required by Schedule 4.

20.13 Any information that an overseas company must include in its financial statements may alternatively be disclosed in a statement annexed to the financial statements.

20.14 Overseas companies may not take advantage of the exemptions available to small, or medium-sized or dormant companies. [*SI 1982/676 para 2(2)*].

Reporting requirements from which overseas companies are exempt

20.15 Overseas companies are not required to provide the following information:

(a) An audit report. In addition, an overseas company's financial statements do not have to be audited, because the requirement for a company to appoint auditors does not apply to overseas companies.

(b) A directors' report. This exemption covers all the information that a company that prepares its financial statements in accordance with Schedule 9 is required to disclose in its directors' report (such as disaggregated information in respect of turnover and profit before tax, particulars of the average number of employees and their remuneration).

(c) The basis of computation of the amount, if any, that is set aside for UK corporation tax.

(d) The amount of the charge to revenue for UK corporation tax, or the amount that such charge would have been but for the relief against double taxation.

(e) The amount of the charge for UK income tax and the amount of the charge for taxation imposed outside the UK of profits, income and capital gains (to the extent that capital gains are credited to revenue).

(f) The basis on which the charge for UK corporation tax and UK income tax is computed.

(g) The amount of turnover (even if this exceeds £1,000,000), and the method by which it is arrived at.

(h) Details in the holding company's financial statements of the identities of, and the place of incorporation of, subsidiaries, and also particulars of the company's shareholdings in the subsidiaries.

(j) Details of investments that exceed one-tenth of the nominal value of any class of the issued equity share capital of another body corporate, and details of any investment that exceeds one-tenth of the company's own assets.

(k) Details of the name and place of incorporation of the company's ultimate holding company.

(l) Particulars of the chairman's and the highest-paid director's emoluments, and of the banding of all directors' emoluments (as required by paragraphs 24 to 26 of Schedule 5 to the Act).

(m) Details of any emoluments that directors have waived (as required by paragraph 27 of Schedule 5).

(n) Particulars of higher-paid employees' emoluments (as required by paragraphs 35 to 37 of Schedule 5).

(o) Particulars of transactions with directors and officers of the company (as required by Schedule 6 to the Act).

[*SI 1982/676 Sch paras 2 to 7*].

20.16   Notwithstanding these modifications and exemptions, any overseas company that has obtained a listing on The Stock Exchange is bound by the requirements of The Stock Exchange's Continuing Obligations to circulate annual audited financial statements to its members. The Continuing Obligations state that "In the case of a company incorporated in a non-member state [*of the EC*] which is not required to draw up its accounts so as to give a true and fair view but is required to draw them up to an equivalent standard, the latter may be sufficient. Reference must, however, be made to the [*Quotations*] Department [*of The Stock Exchange*]". [*CO 20.1*]. Consequently, depending on the requirements that the Quotations Department imposes, a listed overseas company may be unable to take advantage of many of the above exemptions from the reporting requirements. This will also apply to any overseas companies that are traded on the USM.

20.17   Where an overseas company avails itself of the above exemptions, the content of its financial statements will be substantially different from the content of the financial statements of a company incorporated in Great Britain. Consequently, it is recommended that any overseas company that takes advantage of the provisions of the regulation should disclose this fact in the notes to its financial statements. This recommendation applies whether or not those financial statements are audited.

Accounting reference period

20.18   An overseas company's accounting reference period is determined in the same way as for a company registered under the Act. For this purpose, the date of incorporation of a company registered under the Act is equivalent to the date on which an overseas company establishes a place of business in Great Britain. [*Sec 701*]. Accounting reference periods are discussed further in Chapter 2, paragraphs 2.28 to 2.38.

Filing of financial statements

20.19   All overseas companies must deliver a copy of their financial statements for each accounting reference period to the Registrar of Companies within 13 months from the end of the relevant accounting reference period. [*Sec 702(1)*].

20.20   If the company's first accounting reference period exceeds 12 months, the period of 13 months that would otherwise be allowed for delivering the financial statements is reduced by the number of days by which the first accounting reference period exceeds 12 months. [*Sec 702(2)*].

20.21   If an overseas company fails to file financial statements for any accounting reference period within the permitted time, then the company and every officer or agent of the company who knowingly and wilfully authorises or permits the default to occur are guilty of an offence and will be liable to a fine. [*Sec 703(1) — see Appendix IV*].

CHAPTER 21

COMPLETION OF FINANCIAL STATEMENTS AND THEIR PUBLICATION

Chapter 21

Completion of Financial Statements and their Publication

Introduction

21.01 When a company has prepared its annual financial statements in accordance with the provisions of the Act, Sections 238 to 246 govern the way in which the company should approve those financial statements, and the time allowed for delivering those statements to both the shareholders and the Registrar of Companies. These procedures are considered in more detail in paragraphs 21.03 to 21.23 below.

21.02 The publication of a company's full financial statements is considered in paragraphs 21.34 to 21.37. In addition, paragraphs 21.38 to 21.48 discuss those provisions of the Act that relate to companies that publish accounts that are not full financial statements, but that, nevertheless, reproduce either a balance sheet or a profit and loss account that either relates to, or purports to deal with, that company's full financial year. Such accounts are known as 'abridged accounts'.

Directors' duties

21.03 The directors have a duty to prepare annual financial statements for the company [*Sec 227(1)*], and this obligation is discussed in Chapter 2. The directors also have a duty to present those financial statements to the shareholders each year at a general meeting of the company [*Sec 241(1)*], and to send to the Registrar of Companies a copy of those financial statements. [*Sec 241(3)(a)*]. Where that copy of the financial statements is not in English, a certified translation of the financial statements also has to be delivered to the Registrar of Companies. [*Sec 241(3)(b)*]. In addition (and provided that the appropriate rate of exchange to sterling on the balance sheet date is disclosed in the financial statements), the Registrar of Companies will accept, for filing, a UK company's financial statements that have been prepared in a foreign currency.

21.04 The financial statements do not necessarily have to be laid before the shareholders at the *annual* general meeting; another general meeting will suffice. In practice, however, most companies do lay their annual financial statements before the shareholders at their annual general meeting. The financial statements presented at that meeting should include:

495

(a) The company's profit and loss account and balance sheet.

(b) The directors' report.

(c) The auditors' report.

(d) The company's group accounts (if the company has subsidiaries and is required to produce group accounts).
[*Sec 239*].

21.05   The auditors' report has to be read to the shareholders at the general meeting and has also to be available for inspection by the shareholders. [*Sec 241(2)*].

21.06   Two directors are required to sign, on behalf of the board of directors, every copy of the company's balance sheet that either is presented at the meeting or is to be delivered to the Registrar of Companies. However, where the company only has one director, his signature alone is required. [*Sec 238(1)*].

21.07   The board of directors has to approve the company's financial statements before the balance sheet is signed on its behalf. [*Sec 238(4)*]. SSAP 17 requires that the financial statements should disclose the date on which the board of directors approved the financial statements. The determination of the date on which the directors approved the company's financial statements will depend on the company's management structure and the procedures followed in preparing and finalising the company's financial statements. However, the date of approval will normally be the date on which the board of directors formally approves a set of documents as the financial statements.

21.08   The date of approval for group accounts is the date on which the holding company's directors formally approve them.

21.09   The requirements of both the Act and SSAP 17 will be satisfied if the directors minute their approval of the financial statements at a board meeting and include, at the foot of the balance sheet, a note along the following lines:

"The financial statements on pages X to Y were approved by the board of directors on (*date*) and are signed on its behalf by:

Name }
Name }   Directors"

21.10   The pages of the financial statements that the directors approve should normally include, where applicable, any supplementary accounts or other financial statements (such as a value added statement or current cost information). The reason for this is that the directors should acknowledge their responsibility for any such financial information that is presented.

21.11   Alternatively, a similar statement to that in paragraph 21.09 may be included in the directors' report (for example, see Table 104). But when this alternative presentation is adopted, the Act still requires two directors to sign the balance sheet of the company.

> **Table 104: *Illustration of a company that includes the note of approval by the board of directors of the financial statements in its directors' report.***
>
> *Extract from The Savoy Hotel PLC Directors' Report and Annual Accounts 31 December 1984.*
>
> *Approval of Accounts*
>
> The accounts on pages 4 to 15 were approved on 16th April, 1985, by the Board of Directors, who authorised two Directors to sign the accounts on behalf of the Board.

Subsequent events

21.12   As discussed in Chapter 12, paragraphs 12.06 to 12.10, the directors' report must give details of any significant events that occur between the end of the financial year and the date on which the directors approve the financial statements. SSAP 17 contains a similar requirement.

21.13   SSAP 17 says that it relates only to those events that occur before the date on which the directors approve the financial statements. However, the Standard goes on to say that, "If [*events occurring after that date*] are material the directors should consider publishing the relevant information so that users of financial statements are not misled". [*SSAP 17 para 4*]. Also, if the company is either listed on The Stock Exchange or traded on the USM, The Stock Exchange's Continuing Obligations or its General Undertaking (as appropriate) require the company to inform the Quotations Department of The Stock Exchange of any significant events that occur at any time that affect the company.

21.14   If the auditors become aware of any significant event that has occurred between the date on which the directors approve the financial statements and the date of the relevant general meeting, they should advise the company's directors to consider disclosing that event.

Persons entitled to receive the financial statements

21.15   Every member of the company and every debenture holder of the company is entitled to receive a copy of the annual financial statements. [*Sec 240(1)(a)(b)*]. A copy must be sent to them not less than 21 days before the date of the meeting at which the financial statements are to be presented. [*Sec 240(1)*]. This requirement applies even if the person is not entitled to receive notice of general meetings. However, it does not apply if the company is not aware of the person's address. [*Sec 240(3)(a)*].

21.16   A copy of the financial statements must also be given at the same time to all other persons who are entitled to receive copies of the financial statements. [*Sec 240(1)(c)*]. For example, a copy must be given to the auditors. [*Sec 387(1)*]. In addition, the company's bankers may require that they should receive copies of the company's financial statements, and this requirement could be an enforceable term of either a loan agreement or a facility agreement.

21.17   In addition to the right that a member has to be sent a copy of the annual financial statements (as mentioned in para 21.15), *every* member of the company is entitled (on demand and without charge) to be given, within seven days, a copy of the company's last financial statements that were laid before the company in general meeting. [*Sec 246*].

21.18   Where two or more people jointly hold shares or debentures, and where none of them are entitled to receive notice of general meetings, a copy of the financial statements need be sent only to one of them. Where some of the joint holders are entitled to receive notice of general meetings, but others are not so entitled, then a copy of the financial statements needs to be sent only to those of them that are entitled to receive notice of general meetings. [*Sec 240(3)(b)(c)*].

21.19   If the company does not have a share capital, copies of the financial statements are not required to be sent to those members or debenture holders who are not entitled to receive notice of the company's general meetings. [*Sec 240(2)*].

21.20   If all of the members who are entitled to vote at the general meeting are in agreement, the financial statements may be sent to members and others less than 21 days before the general meeting. [*Sec 240(4)*].

21.21   If the company is either listed on The Stock Exchange or traded on the USM, the financial statements must be given to the members within six months from the end of the relevant accounting period. [*CO 20; GU 8*].

Period allowed for filing

21.22   Generally, a public company is allowed seven months to file a copy of its financial statements with the Registrar of Companies. [*Sec 242(2)(b)*]. This period runs from the end of the company's accounting reference period that is being reported upon (see Chapter 2 para 2.28). [*Sec 242(1)*]. This period is extended to ten months for private companies. [*Sec 242(2)(a)*]. However, the period allowed for filing may be extended or shortened in the following situations:

   (a) If the directors of a company that carries on part of its business overseas or has interests overseas (that is, the business is carried

on outside the UK, the Channel Islands and the Isle of Man) have notified the Registrar of Companies of this business, then they may claim an extension to the period allowed for filing. This extension is for a further three months.

However, the Registrar will permit this extension only if he is notified within the filing period stipulated immediately above. [*Sec 242(3)*].

(b) The period for filing a company's financial statements in respect of its first accounting reference period after incorporation will be shortened if the company's first accounting reference period exceeds 12 months. Where it does, the period allowed for filing is reduced by the amount by which the first accounting period exceeds 12 months. However, the period allowed for filing cannot be reduced below three months. [*Sec 242(4)*].

Consider, for example, a public company that is incorporated on 1 August 1985, and its first accounting reference period ends on 31 December 1986 (that is, 17 months later). The company must deliver its financial statements to the Registrar of Companies by 31 March 1987. This is because, although the accounting reference period exceeds 12 months by five months, the relevant filing period of seven months cannot be reduced below three months.

(c) A company may shorten its accounting reference period by notifying the Registrar of Companies. Section 225 of the Act sets out the procedures a company must follow to shorten its accounting reference period (see Chapter 2 para 2.33 to 2.38).

Where a company takes advantage of Section 225 and shortens its accounting reference period, the period it is allowed for filing its financial statements that cover this shortened period will be the longer of:

(i) The period allowed by the preceding provisions of this paragraph.

(ii) Three months after the date on which the notice was given to the Registrar of Companies to change the accounting reference date.

[*Sec 242(5)*].

(d) The Secretary of State may also, for any reason, extend the period a company is allowed for filing its financial statements. He can do this by notifying the company, in writing, of the period of the extension. [*Sec 242(6)*].

21.23 An unlimited company's directors are not required to file a copy of the company's financial statements with the Registrar of Companies unless the company was, at any time during the financial year, any one of the following:

(a) A subsidiary of a limited company.

(b) A company that would effectively have been a subsidiary of a limited

company if, at any time during the year, the shares or voting powers held or exercisable in the company by other limited companies (or their nominees) were combined.

(c) A holding company of a limited company.

(d) A company carrying on a business as the promoter of a trading stamp scheme (under the Trading Stamp Act 1964).
[*Sec 241(4)*].

Implications of not complying with the procedures on completion of financial statements

Liability if the balance sheet is not signed

21.24 The company and those of its officers that are in default will be liable to a fine if either of the following applies:

(a) The directors have not signed a copy of the balance sheet that has been either laid before the company or delivered to the Registrar of Companies.

(b) Copies of the balance sheet have been circulated or published, and the balance sheet has not been signed by the directors or the copies do not include copies of the directors' signatures.
[*Sec 238(2) — see Appendix IV*].

Liability for not sending financial statements to those people entitled to receive them

21.25 Where the company does not comply with the requirements set out in paragraphs 21.15 and 21.16 above, the company and any officer who is in default will be liable to a fine. [*Sec 240(5) — see Appendix IV*].

Liability for not laying and delivering financial statements

21.26 If a company's directors either fail to present the financial statements at a general meeting or fail to file the financial statements with the Registrar of Companies within the period allowed (as set out in para 21.22 above), then those persons who were the directors of the company immediately before the end of that period will be both guilty of an offence and liable to a fine. If they continue to contravene, they will also be liable to a daily default fine. [*Sec 243(1) — see Appendix IV*]. As a defence, a director in this situation may use proof that he took all reasonable steps to ensure that the filing requirements had been complied with in time. However, it is no defence that the financial statements had not been prepared. [*Sec 243(2)(5)*].

Additional penalty the Secretary of State may impose

21.27 The Act details another penalty that the Secretary of State may bring into force at any time by statutory instrument. This penalty may arise where a company does not comply with the filing requirements set out in Section 241(3), when it will be liable to a penalty recoverable in civil proceedings by the Secretary of State. At the time of writing, however, the Secretary of State has not issued such a statutory instrument. [*Sec 243(3)(6)*].

Directors' duty to comply with a default order

21.28 If a company has not complied with the filing requirements of Section 241(3) of the Act within the period allowed for filing financial statements, then any member of the company, or any creditor of the company, or the Registrar of Companies may serve notice on the company requiring the company to comply with the filing requirements. If the company's directors fail to make good the default within 14 days after this notice has been served, then the person who served the notice may apply to the court to make an order instructing the directors to comply with the filing requirements within a time the court specifies. [*Sec 244(1)*]. The court order may also require the directors to bear any costs of the order and any costs that are incidental to it. [*Sec 244(2)*].

Liability for laying or delivering defective financial statements

21.29 All financial statements (including group accounts) that are either laid before the shareholders at a general meeting or delivered to the Registrar of Companies, must comply with the requirements of the Act.

21.30 However, if those financial statements do not comply with the Act, then every director who was a director at the time the financial statements were laid or delivered will be both guilty of an offence and liable to a fine. [*Sec 245(1)(2) — see Appendix IV*].

21.31 If a director can prove that he took all reasonable steps to secure compliance with the relevant requirements of the Act, then he will not be guilty of an offence. [*Sec 245(3)*].

Liability for not giving copies of financial statements to shareholders on demand

21.32 If a shareholder has asked for a copy of the company's last financial statements in accordance with Section 246(1) (see para 21.17), and he does not receive a copy within seven days, the company and any officer of it who is in default will be liable to a fine. [*Sec 246 — see Appendix IV*].

Current concern over apparent non-compliance with the filing requirements

21.33 In 1984, a report by the Committee of Public Accounts severely criticised the DTI for failing to ensure that the Companies Register is maintained to a standard that fulfils Parliament's intentions. The Committee found that there was widespread non-compliance with the filing requirements, and that this had developed over a number of years. The report made a number of recommendations for increasing the level of compliance and making the Register 80% complete by 1986. The implication of the Committee's recommendations is that there will be a more rigorous pursuit of those companies that are in default in filing returns and financial statements. Consequently, the penalties outlined above are likely to be more strictly enforced.

Publication of financial statements

Full financial statements

21.34 Section 254 of the Act sets out the requirements that companies have to comply with when they publish their financial statements. Section 254 applies to the publication of a company's annual financial statements that are both laid before the company at a general meeting and delivered to the Registrar of Companies in accordance with Section 241 (discussed earlier in para 21.03).

21.35 Any individual company's financial statements (whether modified or not) that are to be published should include both the directors' report (unless this is not required because of the exemption that paragraph 3 of Schedule 8 gives to small companies) and the auditors' report. Also, if Section 229 requires the company to prepare group accounts, then the published financial statements should include those group accounts. [*Sec 254(1)(2)(3)*].

21.36 If the financial statements that are being published are 'modified' (that is, the company is small or medium-sized and is taking advantage of the relevant exemptions), they should include the auditors' special report that paragraph 10 of Schedule 8 requires. This report is discussed further in paragraph 15.25 of Chapter 15. [*Sec 254(5)*].

21.37 If any of these requirements of Section 254 are not complied with, then the company and any officer of it who is in default will be liable to a fine. [*Sec 254(6) — see Appendix IV*].

Abridged accounts

21.38 Where a company publishes abridged accounts, those accounts must be accompanied by a statement that indicates:

(a) That the abridged accounts are not full financial statements.

(b) Whether or not the full financial statements have been delivered to the Registrar of Companies.

(c) Whether or not the auditors have reported on the full financial statements.

(d) Whether or not the auditors' report was qualified.
[*Sec 255*].

21.39 Abridged accounts are, in effect, any accounts that are not full financial statements, but nevertheless reproduce either a balance sheet or a profit and loss account that either relates to, or purports to deal with, a company's full financial year. [*Sec 255(1)*]. This means that where a full-year's figures and a narrative explanation of those figures are recognisable as either a balance sheet or a profit and loss account, the rules that relate to abridged accounts are likely to apply. [*Sec 255(2)*].

21.40 Interim statements that either a listed company or a company traded on the USM must issue are *prima facie* not considered to be abridged accounts. The reason for this is that the information they give relates to a six-month period, and not to a full year. Where, however, the interim statement includes, for comparative purposes, figures that relate to a full year, the company needs to consider the rules relating to abridged accounts. In these circumstances, much depends on whether the full year's comparative information is sufficiently comprehensive to be recognisable as either a balance sheet or a profit and loss account. Where the information can be so recognised, the provisions that relate to abridged accounts apply.

21.41 In contrast to interim statements, preliminary results that either listed companies or companies traded on the USM must issue are *prima facie* considered to be abridged accounts. This is because the preliminary results either relate to, or purport to deal with, a company's full financial year. Furthermore, the information that The Stock Exchange's Continuing Obligations and General Undertaking respectively require listed companies and companies traded on the USM to give on a preliminary basis is capable of being recognised as a balance sheet or a profit and loss account. The historical cost form of the statement includes (for example) figures for turnover, profit before and after extraordinary items and dividends, as well as "any supplementary information which in the opinion of the directors is necessary for a reasonable appreciation of the results of the period" (see further Chapter 6 paras 6.59 to 6.62). Consequently, where either a listed company or a company traded on the USM publishes a preliminary statement, the provisions that relate to abridged accounts apply.

21.42 A company will be regarded as 'publishing' financial statements if it either publishes, or issues or circulates them, or otherwise makes them available for public inspection in a manner calculated to invite members of the public to read them. [*Sec 742(5)*]. Consequently, another possible example of abridged accounts is the special report that some companies prepare for employees. Much depends on whether the report either relates to, or purports to deal with, the company's activities during a full financial year, and also on whether it takes the form of a balance sheet or a profit and loss account.

21.43   It is not likely, however, that either five-year or ten-year summaries would be considered to be abridged accounts. The reason for this is that the purpose of such a summary is not to deal with a company's activities for any particular year. Rather its purpose is to put the company's current position in a larger perspective and to provide pointers for the future.

21.44   In several instances, holding companies have published full group accounts in a form other than consolidated financial statements. For example, some companies merely bind together information on individual subsidiaries. This information should not normally be treated as abridged accounts because the Act states that abridged accounts are "any balance sheet or profit and loss account relating to a financial year of the company or purporting to deal with any such financial year, *otherwise than as part of full accounts* (individual or group)". [*Sec 255(1)*].

21.45   Where a company publishes abridged accounts, a statement along one or the other of the following lines should be included in those accounts:

> "The abridged balance sheet/income statement for the year 1985 is an extract from the latest published financial statements that have been delivered to the Registrar of Companies, and on which the auditors' report was unqualified."

> "The abridged balance sheet/income statement for the year 1985 is an extract from the latest financial statements. These financial statements have not yet been delivered to the Registrar of Companies, nor have the auditors yet reported on them."

Table 105 shows an example of a statement included in an interim statement and Table 106 shows an example of a statement included in a report to staff.

Table 105: Illustration of the disclosure in an interim statement where the comparative figures are abridged.

Extract from TI Group plc Interim statement 6 months to 30 June 1984.

Note

3 The figures for the twelve months to 31st December 1983 have been abridged from the full Group accounts for that period which received an unqualified auditors' report and which have been delivered to the registrar of companies.

21.46   Where published abridged accounts deal with more than one year (for example, preliminary announcements that must include comparative figures for the previous year), the one document may contain two sets of abridged accounts. Where this applies, the wording of the above statements should be adapted to cover both sets of accounts.

21.47 Published abridged accounts should not include the auditors' report that has been made in connection with the full financial statements in accordance with Section 236 (see Chapter 2 para 2.09). [*Sec 255(4)*].

Table 106: Example of the disclosure in a report to staff where abridged accounts have been included in the report.

Extract from Royal Insurance plc Report to Staff 31 December 1983.

The results for 1983 shown in this report are abridged from the Report and full Accounts for 1983 on which the report of the auditors was unqualified and which will be delivered to the Registrar of Companies following the Annual General Meeting.

21.48 A company that does not comply with the requirements for the publication of abridged accounts outlined above and any officer who is in default will be liable to a fine. [*Sec 255(5) — see Appendix IV*].

Aide-memoire to the Requirements of UK GAAP for the Measurement and Disclosure of Information in Financial Statements

This aide-memoire is designed to assist a company or group to ensure that the statutory measurement and disclosure requirements of the Companies Act 1985 have been complied with. It covers also the measurement and disclosure requirements of all SSAPs, The Stock Exchange's Continuing Obligations for listed companies, and The Stock Exchange's General Undertaking for companies traded on the USM.

Whilst every effort has been made to make the aide-memoire comprehensive, reference should be made to the source documents on any point of doubt or difficulty.

The aide-memoire is not applicable to special category companies or groups entitled to prepare their financial statements under the rules in Schedule 9 to the Act. (Chapter 13 explains the rules that apply to special category companies.) Also, the aide-memoire does not cover the special provisions for investment companies that are laid down by Part V of Schedule 4 to the Act. (Chapter 14 explains these special provisions.)

To comply with the Act, a company or group must adopt one of the balance sheet formats and one of the profit and loss account formats that are set out in Schedule 4 to the Act. Unless additional disclosures are required, an item that appears in those formats is not specifically referred to in this aide-memoire.

Reference should be made also to the company's articles of association for any special requirements regarding the presentation of financial statements. Furthermore, a company or group may be subject to other legislation that contains accounting requirements (for example, see Chapter 2 para 2.02).

Each step in the aide-memoire is accompanied by a reference to the appropriate provision or regulation. The abbreviations used are the same as those in the main text of the book. (A list of abbreviations is given on page xviii.)

The contents of this aide-memoire are divided into the eight sections shown below:

1. General requirements.
2. Accounting policies.
3. Profit and loss account and related notes.
4. Balance sheet and related notes.
5. Statement of source and application of funds.
6. Directors' report.
7. Foreign currency translation.
8. Group accounts and accounting for business combinations.

A more detailed list of the contents is given on the pages that follow.

Contents

1. General Requirements

1.1 Accounting principles

		Reference
1.1.1	Have the amounts to be included in the financial statements been determined in accordance with the following accounting principles:	4 Sch 9
	(a) Going concern?	4 Sch 10 SSAP 2 para 14
	(b) Consistency?	4 Sch 11 SSAP 2 para 14
	(c) Prudence?	4 Sch 12 SSAP 2 para 14
	(d) Accruals?	4 Sch 13 SSAP 2 para 14
	(e) Separate valuation of assets and liabilities?	4 Sch 14
1.1.2	If not, because the directors consider that there are special reasons for departing from them, are particulars of, their reasons for, and the effect of,the departure given?	4 Sch 15 SSAP 2 para 17

1.2 A true and fair view

1.2.1	The overriding requirement is that the profit and loss account must give a true and fair view of the profit or loss for the year and the balance sheet must give a true and fair view of the state of affairs at the end of the year.	Sec 228(2)(3), 230(2)(3)
	Therefore: (a) Where information additional to that which the Companies Act requires is needed for the financial statements to give a true and fair view, has such extra information been given?	Sec 228(4), 230(4) CO 20
	(b) Where the circumstances of the company or group are such that compliance with a requirement of the Companies Act would not result in a true and fair view even if additional information was given, has the company or group departed from that requirement?	Sec 228(5), 230(5)
1.2.2	If 1.2.1(b) applies, then are particulars of, the reasons for, and the effect of, the departure given?	Sec 228(6), 230(6)

1.3 Format of the financial statements

Note: The format of the company's financial statements and, where applicable, the consolidated financial statements should comply with the following requirements.

1.3.1	Have one of the profit and loss account formats and one of the balance sheet formats set out in Schedule 4 to the Companies Act 1985 been adopted?	4 Sch 1(1)

		Reference

1.3.2 Are the format for the profit and loss account and the format for the balance sheet the same as those used in the preceding year? — 4 Sch 2(1)

If not, does a note disclose both that the directors have adopted a different format and their special reasons for doing this? — 4 Sch 2(2)

1.3.3 Are the items in both the profit and loss account and the balance sheet shown in the order and under the headings and sub-headings set out in the chosen format? — 4 Sch 1(1)

Notes:
(a) Greater detail is permitted. — 4 Sch 3(1)

(b) Additional headings and sub-headings are permitted except that preliminary expenses, expenses of, and commission on, any issue of shares or debentures, and costs of research may not be treated as assets in the balance sheet. — 4 Sch 3(2) SSAP 13 para 20

(c) Headings and sub-headings are not required where there is no relevant amount in both the current and the preceding year. — 4 Sch 3(5), 4(3)

(d) Items preceded in the formats by an Arabic numeral may be combined if immaterial, or if combination results in greater clarity and the breakdown is given in the notes. — 4 Sch 3(4)

(e)The directors shall adapt the arrangement and the headings and sub-headings of items preceded by an Arabic numeral where the special nature of the business requires such adaptation. — 4 Sch 3(3)

(f)The letters, Roman numerals and Arabic numerals that appear in the formats set out in the Act are not required to be shown in published financial statements. — 4 Sch 1(2)

1.3.4 Are assets not offset against liabilities and *vice versa*, and is income not offset against expenditure and *vice versa*? — 4 Sch 5

1.4 Corresponding amounts

1.4.1 Are corresponding amounts for the immediately preceding year given for all items in the financial statements except where corresponding amounts are specifically not required? — 4 Sch 4(1), 58(2)(3)

Note: Corresponding amounts are specifically not required for the following items:

(a) Particulars of the company's subsidiaries and its other shareholdings detailed in Parts I and II of Schedule 5.

(b) Particulars of loans and transactions with directors and officers.

(c) Particulars of additions, disposals, transfers of fixed assets and their depreciation charge.

(d) Particulars of amounts transferred to and from reserves and provisions.

1.4.2 Where the corresponding amount is not comparable with the current amount: — 4 Sch 4(2), 58(2)

(a) Has the corresponding amount been adjusted?

(b) Have particulars of, and the reason for, the adjustment been disclosed?

	Reference

1.5 Disclosure in the event of non-compliance with a SSAP

If there is a departure from a SSAP, and if its effect is material, is such a departure referred to in:

(a) The financial statements (or, in the absence of a reference in the financial statements, in the audit report)?	SSAP's explanatory foreword
(b) The audit report, in all cases where the auditors do not concur with the departure?	Auditing Standard 103 paras 1,10

1.6 The auditors' statutory duties

1.6.1	Where the details required by steps 3.5, 3.6, 4.9 and 4.10 are not disclosed in the financial statements, have the auditors included in their audit report, so far as they are reasonably able to do so, a statement giving the required particulars?	Sec 237(5)
1.6.2	If the auditors have qualified their opinion on the financial statements and if the company proposes to pay a dividend, have the auditors made an additional statement to the members of the company as to whether the subject matter of the qualification is material in determining the legality of the proposed dividend?	Sec 271(3)(4)
1.6.3	Is the information in the directors' report consistent with the financial statements?	Sec 237(6)
	If not, is that fact stated in the audit report?	
1.6.4	Have the auditors stated the fact in their report if they are not satisfied that:	Sec 237(1)(2)

(a) The company has kept proper accounting records?

(b) They have been provided with proper returns adequate for their audit from branches they did not visit?

(c) The financial statements are in agreement with the accounting records?

2.   Accounting Policies

	Reference
Have the significant accounting policies adopted been stated?	4 Sch 36 SSAP 2 para 18
In particular, the policies in respect of:	
(a) Depreciation and diminution in value of assets (including, for each major class of depreciable fixed asset, the depreciation method used)?	4 Sch 36 SSAP 12 para 22
(b) Deferred development expenditure?	SSAP 13 para 29
(c) The calculation of cost, net realisable value and attributable profit/foreseeable loss for stocks and long-term contract work in progress ?	SSAP 9 para 28
(d) Deferred taxation?	SSAP 15
(e) The basis of translating amounts denominated in foreign currencies?	4 Sch 58(1) SSAP 20 para 59
(f) Accounting for finance leases and for operating leases by lessors and lessees ?	SSAP 21 para 57
(g) Accounting for finance leases and operating leases by lessors and, in detail, the policy for accounting for finance lease income?	SSAP 21 para 60(a)
(h) Goodwill?	SSAP 22 para 39

3. Profit and Loss Account and Related Notes	Reference

Note: If a holding company prepares a consolidated profit and loss account that complies with the requirements of the Companies Act and shows how much of the consolidated profit or loss for the year is dealt with in the financial statements of the company, it need not prepare a profit and loss account itself (but see step 3.17).

Reference: Sec 228(7)

3.1 Turnover

3.1.1 Is turnover stated exclusive of trade discounts, VAT and other taxes?

4 Sch 95
SSAP 5
para 8

3.1.2 Does turnover exclude the investing group's share of any turnover of associated companies?

SSAP 1
para 23

Note: The associated company's turnover should not be aggregated with the company's turnover, but where it is material, it should be disclosed separately. See also steps 4.7.5 to 4.7.21.

3.2 Expenditure

Do all items of expenditure include any irrecoverable VAT on that expenditure?

SSAP 5
para 9

3.3 Disaggregated information

3.3.1 Where two or more classes of business are carried on that, in the opinion of the directors, differ substantially, are the following disclosed:

4 Sch 55(1)
(3)(4)

(a) A description of each class?
(b) The amount of turnover attributable to each class?
(c) The amount of the profit or loss before taxation that the directors consider is attributable to each class?

3.3.2 Where geographically defined markets are supplied that, in the opinion of the directors, differ substantially, is the amount of turnover attributable to each market disclosed?

4 Sch 55 (2)
(3)(4)
CO 21(c)
GU 10(c)

3.3.3 If the company is listed, or if it is traded on the USM, and the contribution to profit or loss from a specific market is substantially out of line with the normal ratio of profit to turnover, is the geographical analysis of contribution to trading results disclosed?

CO 21(c)
GU 10(c)

3.3.4 Where the directors consider that disclosure of disaggregated information would be seriously prejudicial to the interests of the company or group, is there a statement that the information is not disclosed?

4 Sch 55(5)

Note: The reason for non-disclosure is not required.

3.4 Employees

3.4.1 Is the average number of employees (including directors, and employees working wholly or mainly outside the UK) in the year disclosed both in total and by category of employee?

4 Sch 56(1)
(2)(3)

	Reference

Note: The directors may select whatever categories they consider appropriate, but in doing so they should have regard to the manner in which the company's or group's activities are organised.

4 Sch 56(5)

3.4.2 Is the aggregate of each of the following amounts disclosed in respect of the employees included in step 3.4.1:

4 Sch 56(4), 94

(a) Wages and salaries paid or payable?

(b) Social security costs incurred?

(c) Other pension costs incurred?

3.5 Higher-paid employees' emoluments

Is the number of employees (excluding directors, and employees working wholly or mainly outside the UK) whose emoluments fall into each of the bands £30,001-£35,000, £35,001-£40,000, etc. in multiples of £5,000 disclosed?

5 Sch 35,36,37

Notes:
(a) Exclude contributions to pension schemes and expenses not charged to UK income tax.

5 Sch 36(2)

(b) In consolidated financial statements, the provisions apply only to employees of the holding company.

4 Sch 63(a)

3.6 Directors' emoluments

3.6.1 Are directors' emoluments (divided in each case between amounts receivable in respect of services as directors and amounts receivable in respect of other offices) disclosed as follows:

5 Sch 22, 28, 29,30

(a) Aggregate emoluments?

(b) Aggregate directors' and past directors' pensions?

(c) Aggregate of compensation paid to directors or past directors for loss of office, divided between that receivable from the company, its subsidiaries and any other persons?

Note: In consolidated financial statements, the provisions apply only to directors of the holding company.

4 Sch 63(a)

3.6.2 Are the following disclosed:

(a) The number of directors whose emoluments fall into each of the bands £0-£5,000, £5,001-£10,000, etc. in multiples of £5,000?

5 Sch 25(1) (2), 26

(b) The chairman's emoluments, or the emoluments of each person for the period during which he acted as chairman?

5 Sch 24,26

(c) The emoluments of the highest-paid director (or directors, if equal) if in excess of the chairman's emoluments?

5 Sch 25(3) (4)(5), 26

(d) The number of directors who have waived rights to receive emoluments during the year, and the aggregate amount waived?

5 Sch 27

(e) If the company is listed, or if it is traded on the USM, particulars of any arrangement under which a director has waived or agreed to waive, emoluments from the company or any of its subsidiaries. This applies both to emoluments which accrued during the year and to future emoluments?

CO 21(n) GU 10(k)

	Reference

Notes:

(a) The Companies Act requirements do not apply to those companies that are neither holding companies nor subsidiaries and the aggregate directors' emoluments do not exceed £60,000. · 5 Sch 23

(b) Exclude from (a) to (c) above directors whose duties were wholly or mainly discharged outside the UK.

(c) In calculating emoluments, exclude contributions to pension schemes. · 5 Sch 26

(d) In consolidated financial statements, the provisions apply only to directors of the holding company. · 4 Sch 63(a)

3.7 Depreciation

3.7.1 Where profit and loss account format 1 or 3 is adopted:

(a) Are 'cost of sales', 'distribution costs' and 'administrative expenses' stated after deducting provisions for depreciation and diminution in value of related assets? · 4 Sch Note 14

(b) Is the amount of the provisions for depreciation and diminution in value of tangible and intangible fixed assets disclosed? · 4 Sch Note 17 SSAP 12 para 22

3.7.2 Are the following amounts of provisions for diminution in value disclosed:

(a) The amount in respect of a temporary diminution in value of fixed asset investments? · 4 Sch 19(1)

(b) The amount in respect of a permanent diminution in value of any fixed asset? · 4 Sch 19(2)

(c) The amount written back because it is no longer required? · 4 Sch 19(3)

3.7.3 Where a fixed asset has been revalued but the depreciation charge included in the profit and loss account is based on its historical cost, is the difference between that charge and the charge based on the asset's value either shown separately in the profit and loss account or disclosed in the notes? · 4 Sch 32(3)

3.7.4 Does depreciation exclude the investing group's share of any depreciation of associated companies? · SSAP 1 para 23

Note: See also steps 4.7 to 4.7.21.

3.8 Other income and expenditure items

3.8.1. Are the following disclosed:

(a) Income and interest derived from group companies separately from income and interest derived from other sources? · 4 Sch Note 15

(b) For lessors, the aggregate amount of rentals receivable in the year in respect of finance leases (including hire purchase contracts that have similar characteristics to a finance lease) and operating leases? · SSAP 21 para 60(b)

Note: See also step 4.6.

	Reference

(c) Interest and similar charges payable to group companies separately from other interest and similar charges payable?

> 4 Sch
> Note 16

(d) Interest payable on and any similar charges in respect of:
  (i) Bank loans and overdrafts, and other loans that are repayable:
    — otherwise than by instalments wholly within 5 years of the balance sheet date?
    — by instalments wholly within 5 years of the balance sheet date?
  (ii) Loans of any other kind made to the company?

> 4 Sch 53(2)

Note: Not applicable to interest and similar charges payable on loans from other group companies.

(e) The amount of income from listed investments?

> 4 Sch 53(4)

(f) The amount, where substantial, of the revenue from rents (after deduction of ground rents, rates and other outgoings)?

> 4 Sch 53(5)

(g) Auditors' remuneration including expenses?

> 4 Sch 53(7)

(h) For lessees, the total operating lease rentals (including rentals in respect of hire purchase contracts that have similar characteristics to an operating lease) charged as an expense in the profit and loss account analysed between hire of plant and machinery and other operating leases?

> 4 Sch 53(6)
> SSAP 21
> para 55

Note: See also step 4.6.

(i) For lessees, the aggregate amount of finance charges allocated to the profit and loss account in respect of finance leases and hire purchase contracts?

> SSAP 21
> para 53

Note: See also step 4.6.

(j) The amounts set aside for the redemption of:
  (i) Share capital?
  (ii) Loans?

> 4 Sch 53(3)

3.8.2 Are dividends receivable from UK resident companies stated at the amount of cash received or receivable plus the tax credit?

> SSAP 8
> para 25

3.9 Income and share of results of associated companies

3.9.1 Is income from investments in associated companies brought into account on the following bases:

> SSAP 1
> para 18

(a) In the investing company's own financial statements — dividends received and receivable?

(b) In the investing group's consolidated financial statements — its share of profits less losses of associated companies?

Note: These bases need not be applied to those interests in partnerships and non-corporate joint ventures where it is appropriate to account for a proportionate share of individual assets and liabilities as well as profits or losses.

3.9.2 Do the investing group's consolidated financial statements disclose, in profit before tax, its share of profits less losses of associated companies?

> SSAP 1
> para 19

517

	Reference

3.9.3 If the results of one or more associated companies are very material in the context of the investing group, is there separate disclosure of items such as total turnover, total depreciation charges and total profits less losses before taxation of the associated companies concerned?

Note: When judging materiality, regard should also be had to the scale of the associated companies' operations in relation to those of the investing group.

SSAP 1 para 23

3.9.4 Except where it is a wholly-owned subsidiary, has an investing company that does not prepare consolidated financial statements shown the information required either by preparing a separate profit and loss account, or by adding the information in supplementary form to its own profit and loss account in such a way that its share of the profits of the associated companies is not treated as realised for the purposes of the Companies Act 1985?

SSAP 1 para 24

3.10 Profit or loss before taxation

Is the amount of the profit or loss on ordinary activities before taxation disclosed?

4 Sch 3(6)

3.11 Taxation

3.11.1 If the rate of corporation tax is not known for the whole or part of the year, has the latest known rate been used, and disclosed?

SSAP 8 para 23

3.11.2 Are the following elements of the taxation charge separately disclosed:

4 Sch 54(1)(3) SSAP 8 paras 33, 22

(a) UK corporation tax, and the amount which it would have been but for the relief from double taxation, and the basis of computation?

(b) Transfers to or from the deferred taxation account?

SSAP 15 para 33

(c) UK income tax, and the basis of computation?

(d) Tax attributable to franked investment income?

(e) Irrecoverable ACT?

(f) Taxation imposed outside the UK on profits, income and (so far as charged to revenue) capital gains?

(g) The amount, if any, of (f) that is unrelieved as a result of the payment or proposed payment of dividends?

Note: Elements (a),(b),(c) and (f) must be stated separately in respect of ordinary activities and extraordinary items.

4 Sch 54(3) SSAP 15 para 34

3.11.3 Do the investing group's consolidated financial statements disclose, in taxation, the tax attributable to its share of profits of associated companies?

SSAP 1 para 20

3.11.4 Has deferred taxation been provided on the liability method to the extent that it is probable that a liability (or asset) will crystallise?

SSAP 15 paras 24,25

	Reference

3.11.5 Is tax deferred or accelerated because of the effect of timing differences not accounted for to the extent that it is probable that a liability (or asset) will not crystallise? — SSAP 15 paras 26 to 28

3.11.6 Is the provision for deferred tax liabilities reduced by any deferred tax debit balances arising from separate categories of timing differences and any ACT that is available for offset against those liabilities? — SSAP 15 para 29

Note: See also steps 4.12.4 to 4.12.10.

3.11.7 Is the amount of unprovided deferred tax in respect of the year disclosed in a note and analysed into its major components? — SSAP 15 para 35

3.11.8 Where the company is a member of a group, does it take account when accounting for deferred tax of any group relief that may be available to it and any charge that may be made for that relief and are these assumptions stated? — SSAP 15 para 43

3.11.9 Are adjustments to the deferred taxation account that result from a change in the rate of taxation separately disclosed as part of the taxation charge for the year? — SSAP 15 para 36

Note: This will be so unless the change in rate is associated with a fundamental change in the basis of taxation, or with a significant change in government fiscal policy, when the adjustment should be treated as an extraordinary item.

3.11.10 Is deferred tax in respect of the remittance of overseas earnings accounted for in accordance with the provisions noted above? — SSAP 15 para 44

If not, is there a statement that deferred tax is not provided on earnings retained overseas?

3.11.11 Are any special circumstances disclosed that affect the liability in respect of taxation of profits, income or capital gains either for the year or for succeeding years (for example, tax losses utilised or carried forward)? — 4 Sch 54(2)

Note: SSAP 15 (revised) is effective in respect of financial statements relating to accounting periods beginning on or after 1 April 1985.

3.12 Dividends

3.12.1 Is the aggregate amount disclosed of any dividends paid or proposed? — 4 Sch 3(7)(b)

3.12.2 Do these dividends exclude the related ACT or the attributable tax credit? — SSAP 8 para 24

Notes:
(a) A company cannot pay a dividend unless it has profits available for the purpose. — Sec 263(1)

(b) Profits available for the purpose are accumulated realised profits less accumulated realised losses, less (in the case of a public company) accumulated net unrealised losses. (Such profits and losses may be either revenue or capital in origin.) — Sec 263(3), 264(1), 280(3)

		Reference

(c) The Companies Act 1985 does not define 'realised' and 'unrealised' but it does give some guidance in specific cases. (See Sec 263(5), 269, 276.)

3.12.3 If the company is listed, or if it is traded on the USM, are particulars of any arrangement under which a shareholder has waived, or agreed to waive, any dividends (including future dividends) disclosed?
CO 21(o)
GU 10(1)

3.13 Reserves

Are any amounts that are set aside to, or proposed to be set aside to, or withdrawn from, or proposed to be withdrawn from, reserves disclosed?
4 Sch 3(7)(a)

3.14 Exceptional and extraordinary items

3.14.1 Are the nature and size disclosed of material amounts charged or credited that relate to any preceding year (for example, the normal recurring corrections and adjustments of accounting estimates made in prior years)?
4 Sch 57(1)
SSAP 6
para 16

3.14.2 Are items of an abnormal size or incidence that are derived from the ordinary activities of the business included in arriving at the profit for the year before taxation and extraordinary items? Are their nature and size disclosed?
4 Sch 57(3)
SSAP 6
para 14

3.14.3 Do extraordinary items comprise only those items that derive from events or transactions outside the ordinary activities of the business and that are both material and expected not to recur frequently or regularly? Are their nature and size disclosed?
4 Sch 57(2)
SSAP 6
paras 11,15

3.14.4 Are extraordinary items disclosed net of attributable taxation?
SSAP 6
para 15
SSAP 15
para 34

3.14.5 Do extraordinary items in the consolidated profit and loss account include the investing group's share of the aggregate extraordinary items of associated companies (unless this amount would not be classified as extraordinary in the context of the investing group)? Where material, is the amount included separately disclosed?
SSAP 1
para 21

Note: See also steps 4.7.5 to 4.7.21.

3.15 Prior-year adjustments

3.15.1 Do prior-year adjustments comprise only those material adjustments applicable to prior years that arise from changes in accounting policies or from the correction of fundamental errors?
SSAP 6
paras 12,16

3.15.2 Are prior-year adjustments (less attributable taxation) accounted for by restating prior years, with the result that the opening balance of retained profits is adjusted accordingly?
SSAP 6
para 16

3.15.3 Is the effect of the change disclosed, where practicable, by showing the amount involved separately in the restatement of the previous year?
SSAP 6
para 16

3.15.4 Is there a statement (immediately following the profit and loss account for the year) of retained profits/reserves that shows any prior-year adjustments?
SSAP 6
para 17

	Reference

3.16 Earnings per share

Notes:
(a) SSAP 3 applies only to listed companies. Companies traded on the USM are now required also to disclose their earnings per share. — SSAP 3 para 13

(b) Appendix 1 to SSAP 3 contains guidelines for the determination of earnings per share.

3.16.1 Are earnings per share shown on the face of the profit and loss account on the net basis? — SSAP 3 para 14

3.16.2 Where materially different, are earnings per share shown also on the nil distribution basis? — SSAP 3 paras 9,14

3.16.3 Is the basis of calculating earnings per share disclosed? (In particular, the amount of the earnings and the number of equity shares used in the calculation.) — SSAP 3 para 15

3.16.4 Where a company has, at the balance sheet date, contracted to issue further shares after the end of the year, or where it has already issued shares that do not rank for dividend until future years, and the effect will be to dilute basic earnings per share by 5% or more, are fully diluted earnings per share also shown on the face of the profit and loss account, and is the basis of their calculation disclosed? — SSAP 3 para 16

3.16.5 Is equal prominence given to basic and fully diluted earnings per share? — SSAP 3 para 16

Notes:
(a) A company has 'contracted to issue further shares after the end of the year' where it has issued debentures, loan stock or preference shares that are convertible into equity shares or where it has granted options or it has issued warrants to subscribe for equity shares. — SSAP 3 para 16

(b) The corresponding amount for fully diluted earnings per share is required only if the assumptions on which the amount was based still apply. — SSAP 3 para 16

3.17 Consolidated profit and loss account

3.17.1 Is the extent to which the consolidated profit or loss is dealt with in the financial statements of the holding company disclosed? — Sec 228(7)(b)

3.17.2 Is the investing group's share of the aggregate net profits less losses retained by associated companies separately disclosed? — SSAP 1 para 22

3.17.3 Where a holding company has taken advantage of the provisions not to prepare its own profit and loss account, is there a statement to that effect in the consolidated financial statements? — Sec 228(7)

4. Balance Sheet and Related Notes

4.1 Assets — fixed and current

		Reference
4.1.1	Does the purchase price of an asset comprise the actual price paid together with any expenses incidental to its acquisition?	4 Sch 26(1) SSAP 9 para 18
4.1.2	Does the production cost of an asset comprise the purchase price of raw materials and consumables used, together with the amount of costs incurred that are directly attributable to the production of that asset?	4 Sch 26(2) SSAP 9 paras17,19,20
4.1.3	Where the production cost of an asset includes a reasonable proportion of costs incurred that are only indirectly attributable to the production of that asset, are these included only to the extent that they relate to the period of production?	4 Sch 26(3)
4.1.4	Where the production cost of an asset includes interest on capital borrowed to finance the production of that asset, is the fact that interest is included, and the amount of interest included, disclosed?	4 Sch 26(3)
4.1.5	If the company is listed, or if it is traded on the USM, is the amount of interest capitalised during the year, and an indication of the amount and treatment of any related tax relief, disclosed?	CO 21(g) GU 10(g)
4.1.6	Where any of the alternative accounting rules have been adopted, are the following disclosed: (a) The items affected and the basis of valuation adopted? (b) In respect of each balance sheet item affected (except stocks) one of the following: 　(i) The aggregate cost and aggregate accumulated depreciation on an historical cost basis? 　(ii) The difference between the aggregate cost and aggregate accumulated depreciation as stated and what they would have been on an historical cost basis?	4 Sch 33
4.1.7	Where any of the alternative accounting rules have been adopted, has the profit or loss on revaluation been transferred to the revaluation reserve?	4 Sch 34(1) SSAP 6 para 13
	Note: The revaluation reserve may be shown under another name.	4 Sch 34(2)
4.1.8	Where the amount repayable on any debt owed by a company is greater than the value of the consideration received, and the difference is treated as an asset: (a) Is the difference being written off by reasonable amounts each year so that it will be completely written off before the debt is repaid? (b) Is the amount of the difference at the year end separately disclosed?	4 Sch 24
4.1.9	Does the cost of an asset include any irrecoverable VAT on that asset?	SSAP 5 para 9
4.1.10	Where there is no record of the purchase price or production cost of an asset (or such record can be obtained only with unreasonable expense or delay), is the asset included at its earliest known value?	4 Sch 28

	Reference

4.1.11   Where the purchase price or production cost is determined by using 'the earliest known value' for the first time, are particulars given?   **4 Sch 51(1)**

4.2   Assets included at a fixed amount

Are assets under the items 'Tangible assets' and 'Raw materials and consumables' included at a fixed quantity and value, only if they are constantly being replaced and only where both their overall value is not material to assessing the state of affairs and their quantity, value and composition are not subject to material variation?   **4 Sch 25**

4.3   Fixed assets

Cost and valuation

4.3.1   Unless any of the alternative accounting rules are adopted, are fixed assets included at purchase price or production cost less any provisions for depreciation or diminution in value?   **4 Sch 16,17**

4.3.2   Where any of the alternative accounting rules are adopted, have fixed assets been valued on the following bases:

(a) Intangible fixed assets (except goodwill) at their current cost?   **4 Sch 31(1)**

(b) Tangible fixed assets either at market value as at the date of their last valuation or at their current cost?   **4 Sch 31(2)**

(c) Fixed asset investments either at market value as at the date of their last valuation or at a value determined on any basis that the directors consider is appropriate in the circumstances?   **4 Sch 31(3)**

If the latter basis is adopted, are particulars of the method adopted and the reasons for adopting it disclosed?

4.3.3   Where any fixed assets (other than listed investments) are included at a valuation, are the following disclosed:

(a) The years (so far as they are known to the directors) in which the assets were valued?   **4 Sch 43**

(b) The respective values?   **4 Sch 43**

(c) In the case of assets valued during the year: **4 Sch 43**
    (i) Either the names or the qualifications of the valuers?   **SSAP 19**
    (ii) The bases of valuation used?   **para 12**

Depreciation

4.3.4   Where any fixed asset has a limited useful economic life, is the purchase price or production cost or valuation, less the estimated residual value, written off systematically over that life?   **4Sch18,32(1)** / **SSAP 12** / **paras 17,21** / **SSAP 13** / **para 24**

Note: Leasehold investment properties should be depreciated at least over the period when the unexpired term of the lease is 20 years or less. Other investment properties should not be depreciated. (Steps 4.5.3 to 4.5.8 cover investment properties.)   **SSAP 12** / **para 16** / **SSAP 19** / **para 10**

		Reference

4.3.5   If the estimated useful life of an asset is revised, is the unamortised cost/ valuation being charged over the revised remaining useful life?   *SSAP 12 para 18*

4.3.6   In the year in which assets are revalued, is the effect on the depreciation charge disclosed, if material?   *SSAP 12 para 21*

4.3.7   If there is a change from one method of providing depreciation to another, is the unamortised cost/valuation of the asset being written off on the new basis over the remaining useful life of the asset?   *SSAP 12 para 20*

4.3.8   In the year of change, is the effect disclosed, if material?   *SSAP 12 para 20*

4.3.9   If there has been a diminution in value of any fixed asset and this diminution is expected to be permanent, has provision been made and disclosed?   *4 Sch 19(2) SSAP 12 para 19 SSAP 13 para 25*

4.3.10   Where the reasons for any provision for a diminution in value of a fixed asset cease to exist to any extent, has the provision been written back to that extent and disclosed?   *4 Sch 19(3)*

Note: Development costs once written off should not be reinstated even though the uncertainties that led to the write-off no longer apply.   *SSAP 13 para 26*

4.3.11   For each major class of depreciable fixed asset, are the useful lives or the depreciation rates used disclosed?   *SSAP 12 para 22*

Government grants

4.3.12   Are grants relating to fixed assets credited to revenue over the expected useful life of the asset by one of the following methods: *SSAP 4 para 9*

(a) Reducing the cost of the asset by the amount of the grant?

(b) Treating the grant as a deferred credit and making annual transfers to revenue?

If method (b) is adopted, is the amount of the deferred credit shown separately in the balance sheet (under the heading 'Accruals and deferred income')?

Movements

4.3.13   In respect of the cost/valuation of fixed assets under any heading, are the following disclosed:
(a) The aggregate cost/valuation at the beginning of the year?   *4 Sch 42(1)(2) SSAP 13 para 27*

(b) Any revisions to the amount in respect of a valuation during the year?

(c) Acquisitions during the year?

(d) Disposals during the year?

(e) Any reclassification of assets to, or from, that heading during the year?

(f) The aggregate cost/valuation at the end of the year?   *SSAP 12 para 22*

Note: Corresponding amounts are not required.   *4 Sch 58(3)*

		Reference

4.3.14 In respect of provisions for depreciation or diminution in value of fixed assets under any heading, are the following disclosed: *4 Sch 42(3) / SSAP 13 / para 27*

   (a) The cumulative provisions at the beginning of the year?

   (b) Any such provisions made during the year?

   (c) Any adjustments made as a result of disposals of assets during the year?

   (d) Any other adjustments made during the year?

   (e) The cumulative provisions at the end of the year?   *SSAP 12 / para 22*

Note: Corresponding amounts are not required.   *4 Sch 58(3)*

4.4 Intangible fixed assets

Development costs

4.4.1 Are development costs capitalised only where all of the following conditions apply: *4 Sch 20(1) / SSAP 13 / para 21*

   (a) There is a clearly defined project?

   (b) The related expenditure is separately identifiable?

   (c) The outcome of the project has been assessed with reasonable certainty as to both its technical feasibility and its ultimate commercial viability?

   (d) All costs (including future costs to be incurred) are reasonably expected to be more than covered by related future revenues?

   (e) Adequate resources exist, or are reasonably expected to be available, to enable the project to be completed, and to provide any consequential increases in working capital?

4.4.2 Are development costs capitalised only to the extent that their recovery can reasonably be regarded as assured?   *SSAP 13 / para 22*

4.4.3 Have the criteria for determining whether development costs may be capitalised been applied consistently?   *SSAP 13 / para 23*

4.4.4 In respect of capitalised development costs, are the following disclosed: *4 Sch 20(2)*

   (a) The period over which the costs are being, or are to be, written off?

   (b) The reasons for capitalising the costs?

   (c) Where appropriate, a statement that the directors have decided not to treat unamortised development costs as a realised loss when calculating distributable profits, and the special circumstances that justify their decision?   *Sec 269(2)(b)*

Concessions, patents, etc.

4.4.5 Are amounts in respect of concessions, patents, licences, trade marks and similar rights and assets included in the balance sheet only if one of the following applies: *4 Sch / Note 2*

	Reference

(a) The assets were acquired for valuable consideration and do not represent goodwill?

(b) The assets were created by the company?

Goodwill

		Reference
4.4.6	Is goodwill capitalised only to the extent that it was acquired for valuable consideration?	4 Sch Note 3
4.4.7	Where the company or group has recognised amounts of goodwill as a result of acquisitions during the year, do the financial statements disclose separately, where material, the goodwill arising from each acquisition?	SSAP 22 para 40
4.4.8	Where the company or group amortises purchased goodwill, does the company or group show purchased goodwill as a separate item under intangible fixed assets in the balance sheet until the company or group has fully written off the purchased goodwill?	4 Sch formats SSAP 22 para 41

Note: 4 Sch 3(4) permits a company or group to combine goodwill with another intangible asset sub-heading in either of the two following circumstances:

(a) Where the individual amounts combined are not material to an assessment of the state of affairs of the company or group.

(b) Where the combination facilitates the assessment of the state of affairs of the company or group. (A note to the financial statements must disclose the individual amounts of any items combined in this way.) SSAP 22 does not specifically permit a company or group to combine goodwill with another item in either of these two circumstances. However, the preliminary paragraph of SSAP 22 says that a company or group need not apply the Standard to immaterial items.

		Reference
4.4.9	Where the company or group amortises purchased goodwill, does the company or group disclose the movement on the goodwill account during the year? Does this disclosure include the following:	4 Sch 42 SSAP 22 para 41(a)

(a) The cost of goodwill at the beginning and at the end of the year?

(b) The accumulated amortisation at the beginning and at the end of the year?

(c) The net book value of goodwill at the beginning and at the end of the year?

(d) The amount of goodwill that the company or group has amortised through the profit and loss account during the year?

		Reference
4.4.10	Where the company or group amortises purchased goodwill, does the company or group disclose the period it has selected for amortising the goodwill that relates to each major acquisition?	4 Sch 21(4) SSAP 22 para 41(b)

Note: 4 Sch 66 exempts consolidation goodwill from the requirement in 4 Sch 21(4). However, consolidation goodwill is still subject to this requirement because of SSAP 22 para 41(b).

		Reference
4.4.11	Where the company or group amortises purchased goodwill, does the company or group disclose the reasons for choosing the period that it has selected for amortising the goodwill?	4 Sch 21(4)

	Reference

Note: Consolidation goodwill is exempt from this requirement. — 4 Sch 66

4.4.12 Where a company's or group's accounting treatment of goodwill that existed at the time the Standard came into effect differs from the policy it has followed in respect of all other goodwill, does the company or group disclose the following: — SSAP 22 para 42

(a) The accounting treatment of goodwill that existed at the time the Standard came into effect?

(b) The amounts involved?

Note: SSAP 22 is effective in respect of financial statements relating to accounting periods beginning on or after 1 January 1985.

4.5 Tangible fixed assets

Research and development

4.5.1 Is the cost of fixed assets acquired or constructed to provide facilities for research and development activities over a number of years capitalised and written off over the useful life of those assets? — SSAP 13 para 19

Land and buildings

4.5.2 Is the division of the net book amount of land and buildings between freehold, long leases (50 or more years to run) and short leases disclosed? — 4 Sch 44, 83

Investment properties

Note: SSAP 19 does not apply to investment properties owned by charities. — SSAP 19 para 9

4.5.3 Are investment properties (as defined in SSAP 19 paras 7 and 8) included in the balance sheet at their open market value? — SSAP 19 para 11

4.5.4 Are changes in the value of investment properties disclosed as a movement on an investment revaluation reserve? — SSAP 19 para 13

Note: Not applicable to the long-term business of insurance companies where changes in value are dealt with in the relevant fund account. — SSAP 19 para 14

4.5.5 If a deficit on revaluation exceeds the balance on the investment revaluation reserve, has the excess been charged in the profit and loss account? — SSAP 19 para 13

Note: For investment trust companies and property unit trusts it may not be appropriate to deal with deficits in the profit and loss account. In such cases they should be shown prominently elsewhere in the financial statements.

4.5.6 If the persons making the revaluation are employees or officers of the company or group that owns the property, is this fact disclosed? — SSAP 19 para 12

4.5.7 Are both the carrying value of investment properties and the investment revaluation reserve displayed prominently? — SSAP 19 para 15

4.5.8 Are particulars given of the departure from the specific requirement in the Act to provide depreciation on any fixed asset that has a limited useful economic life together with the reasons for, and the effect of, the departure? — SSAP 19 para 17 Sec 228(6), 230(6)

	Reference

Note: The DTI has agreed the text of a note that meets the requirements of Section 228 of the Act (see Chapter 7 para 7.119).

4.6 Leases and hire purchase contracts

Notes:
(a) Hire purchase contracts that are of a financing nature should be accounted for on a similar basis to finance leases. Other hire purchase contracts should be accounted for on a similar basis to operating leases.

SSAP 21
para 31

(b) Effective date of SSAP 21 for lessees and hirers. The accounting practices are mandatory for accounting periods beginning on or after 1 July 1987. However, the disclosure provisions, steps 2(f), 3.8.1(h), 4.13.3 and 4.13.4 are mandatory for accounting periods commencing on or after 1 July 1984.

SSAP 21
para 62

(c) Effective date of SSAP 21 for lessors and finance companies. The accounting practices are mandatory for accounting periods commencing on or after 1 July 1984. However, the provisions of the Standard need not be applied to leases that had less than 5 years to run on 1 July 1984, provided lessors disclose both the amount of gross earnings from such leases and the principal bases used.

SSAP 21
para 61

Lessees

4.6.1   Are finance leases recorded in the balance sheet as an asset and as an obligation to pay future rentals? At the inception of the lease, are both the asset and the liability recorded at the present value of the minimum lease payments derived by discounting them at the interest rate implicit in the lease?

SSAP 21
para 32

Notes:
(a) In practice, the fair value of the asset will often be a sufficiently close approximation to the present value of the minimum lease payments.

SSAP 21
para 33

(b) Where the minimum lease payments are less than the fair value of the asset because of the benefit to the lessor of regional development and other grants and capital allowances, the amount capitalised should be restricted to the minimum lease payments.

SSAP 21
para 34

4.6.2   Are finance lease rentals payable apportioned between the finance charge and a reduction of the outstanding obligation for future amounts payable?

SSAP 21
para 35

4.6.3   Is the total finance charge for each finance lease allocated to accounting periods during the lease term so as to produce a constant periodic rate of charge on the remaining balance of the obligation for each accounting period (or a reasonable approximation thereto)?

SSAP 21
para 35

4.6.4   Is an asset leased under a finance lease depreciated over the shorter of the lease term and its useful life?

SSAP 21
para 36

Note: The lease term includes the optional secondary rental period where it is reasonable to assume that the lessee will exercise the option.

SSAP 21
para 19

528

	Reference

4.6.5   Is an asset under a hire purchase contract, which has the characteristics of a finance lease, depreciated over its useful life? — SSAP 21 para 36

4.6.6   Is the rental under operating leases charged on a straight-line basis over the lease term, unless another systematic and rational basis is more appropriate? — SSAP 21 para 37

4.6.7   Are the gross amount of assets held under finance leases and the related accumulated depreciation disclosed by each major class of asset? — SSAP 21 para 49

If not (because the amounts are integrated with owned fixed assets), is the net amount of assets held under finance leases disclosed? — SSAP 21 para 50

4.6.8   Is the total depreciation allocated for the period in respect of assets held under finance leases disclosed by each major class of asset? — SSAP 21 para 49

4.6.9   If not (because the amounts are integrated with owned fixed assets), is the total depreciation allocated for the period in respect of assets held under finance leases disclosed? — SSAP 21 para 50

Note: See also steps 2(f), 3.8.1(h) and (i), 4.11.17, 4.11.18, 4.13.3 and 4.13.4.

Sale and leaseback transactions — lessees

4.6.10 Where the sale and leaseback transaction results in the seller/lessee entering into a finance lease, is any apparent profit or loss deferred and amortised over the shorter of the lease term and the useful life of the asset? — SSAP 21 para 46

4.6.11 Where the sale and leaseback transaction results in the seller/lessee entering into an operating lease: — SSAP 21 para 47

(a) If the sale price is at fair value, is any profit or loss recognised immediately?

(b) If the sale price is below fair value but future rentals are set at market rates, is any profit or loss recognised immediately?

If the sale price is below fair value, and the future rentals are below market price, is any loss arising deferred to the extent that it represents a reduction of future rentals and amortised over the shorter of the remainder of the lease term and the period during which reduced rentals are chargeable?

(c) If the sale price is above fair value, is the excess deferred and amortised over the shorter of the remainder of the lease term and the period to the next rent review?

Sale and leaseback transactions — lessors

4.6.12 Has the sale and leaseback transaction been accounted for by the buyer/lessor in the same way as for other leases (see steps 4.6.13 to 4.6.21)? — SSAP 21 para 48

Lessors

4.6.13 Is the amount due from the lessee under a finance lease recorded in the balance sheet as a debtor at the amount of the net investment in the lease after making provisions for such items as bad and doubtful rentals receivable? — SSAP 21 para 38

		Reference
4.6.14	Have the total gross earnings for finance leases been allocated to accounting periods to give a constant periodic rate of return on the lessor's net cash investment in the lease in each period?	SSAP 21 para 39
4.6.15	As an alternative to 4.6.14, has an allocation first been made out of gross earnings of an amount equal to the lessor's estimated cost of finance included in the net cash investment calculation with the balance being recognised on a systematic basis?	SSAP 21 para 40

Notes:
(a) In the case of a hire purchase contract, allocation of gross earnings so as to give a constant periodic rate of return on the finance company's net investments will in most cases be a suitable approximation to an allocation based on the net cash investment in the lease. — SSAP 21 para 39

(b) In arriving at the constant periodic rate of return a reasonable approximation may be made. — SSAP 21 para 39

4.6.16	Have tax free grants available to the lessor against the purchase price of assets acquired for finance leasing been spread over the period of the lease? Have such grants been dealt with in one of the following ways:	SSAP 21 para 41

(a) By treating the grant as non-taxable income?

(b) By grossing up the grant and including the grossed-up amount in arriving at profit before tax?

If (b) has been adopted, is the amount by which the profit before tax and the tax charge have been increased as a result of grossing up the grant disclosed?

Notes:
(a) In the case of a finance lease, the tax free grants are effectively spread on a constant rate of return basis.

(b) In the case of an operating lease, the tax free grants are spread on a straight-line basis.

4.6.17	Are assets held for use as operating leases recorded as fixed assets and depreciated over their useful lives?	SSAP 21 para 42
4.6.18	Is rental income (excluding charges for services such as insurance and maintenance) recognised for operating leases on a straight-line basis over the period of the lease (even if the payments are not made on such a basis), unless another systematic and rational basis is more representative of the time pattern in which the benefit from the leased asset is receivable?	SSAP 21 para 43

Note: Initial direct costs incurred by a lessor in arranging a lease may be apportioned over the period of the lease on a systematic and rational basis. — SSAP 21 para 44

4.6.19	In respect of assets held for use under operating leases, are the following disclosed:	SSAP 21 para 59

(a) The gross amount?

(b) The accumulated depreciation charge?

4.6.20	For a manufacturer or dealer lessor, is the selling profit under a finance lease restricted to the excess of the fair value of the asset over the manufacturer's or dealer lessor's cost less any grants receivable by the manufacturer or dealer towards the purchase, construction or use of the asset?	SSAP 21 para 45

Note: A manufacturer or dealer lessor should not recognise a selling profit under an operating lease.

	Reference

4.6.21 For lessors and finance companies, if the Standard is not applied retroactively to all leases and hire purchase contracts existing at 1 January 1984, is the amount of gross earnings from finance leases and hire purchase contracts disclosed for the current year and the corresponding period under each of the principal bases used?

SSAP 21
para 61

Note: See also steps 2(f) and (g), 3.8.1(b), 4.8.14 and 4.8.15.

4.7 Investments

Fixed asset investments and current asset investments

4.7.1 In respect of investments under any heading, are the following disclosed:

4 Sch 45,84

(a) The amount that is attributable to investments listed on a recognised stock exchange?

(b) The amount of other listed investments?

(c) The total amount of all listed investments?

(d) The aggregate market value (unless the investments are included in the balance sheet at market value)?

(e) Both the market value and the stock exchange value of any investments where the market value is higher?

Note: The only 'recognised stock exchange' in Great Britain is The Stock Exchange.

4.7.2 If the company is holding any of its own shares, is the nominal value of those shares disclosed?

4 Sch
Note 4

Significant shareholdings (excluding subsidiaries)

4.7.3 For shareholdings in a company at the balance sheet date where:

5 Sch 7,8,9

(i) The nominal value of the investing company's holding in any class of the equity share capital of that company exceeds 10% of the nominal value of the allotted shares of that class, or
(ii) The investing company's holding (whether or not equity shares) in the share capital of that company exceeds 10% of the nominal value of the total allotted share capital of that company, or
(iii) The aggregate amount of the shareholding in that company exceeds 10% of the total assets as stated in the investing company's balance sheet, are the following disclosed:

(a) The name of the company?

(b) Its country of incorporation, if outside Great Britain?

(c) Its country of registration (England and Wales or Scotland) if different from the country of incorporation?

(d) The identity of, and the proportion of, the nominal value of the allotted shares of each class (whether equity or not) held?

(e) A statement, where appropriate, that the information given deals only with the companies within (i) and (ii) whose results principally affect the profit or loss, or amount of assets, of the investing company?

5 Sch 11, 12

	Reference

Notes:
(a) Corresponding amounts are not required. — 4 Sch 58(3)

(b) In consolidated financial statements, the provisions apply only to investments by the holding company. — 4 Sch 63(a)

(c) A company need not disclose particulars in respect of bodies corporate incorporated, or carrying on business, outside the UK if it would be harmful to the business of the company or the other body corporate and the Secretary of State agrees to the non-disclosure. — 5 Sch 10

4.7.4 For shareholdings in a company (other than a subsidiary) at the balance sheet date where the investing company's holding exceeds in nominal value 20% of the allotted share capital of that company, are the following disclosed (if material): — 5 Sch 15,16, 17(4)

(a) The aggregate amount of the capital and reserves of that company as at the end of its financial year ending with, or last before, the financial year of the investing company?

(b) The profit or loss of that company for its financial year ending with, or last before, the financial year of the investing company?

Notes:
(a) Not required if the investment is included in, or in a note to, the investing company's financial statements by way of the equity method of valuation. — 5 Sch 17(2)

(b) In consolidated financial statements, the provisions apply only to investments by the holding company. — 4 Sch 63(a)

(c) Not required if immaterial. — 5 Sch 17(4)

(d) A company need not disclose particulars in respect of bodies corporate incorporated, or carrying on business, outside the UK if it would be harmful to the business of the company or the other body corporate and the Secretary of State agrees to the non-disclosure. — 5 Sch 10

(e) If the requirement would result in a statement of excessive length, the information needs to be given only for those companies whose results principally affect the profit or loss, or amount of assets, of the investing company. — 5 Sch 11

4.7.5 If the company is listed, or if it is traded on the USM, and the group has an interest of 20% or more in the equity capital of another company (not being a subsidiary), are the following disclosed in respect of each such company: — CO 21(e) GU 10(e)

(a) The principal country of operation?

(b) Particulars of its issued share capital and debt securities?

(c) The percentage of each class of debt securities attributable to the company's interest (direct or indirect)?

(d) The total amount of its reserves if the company is traded on the USM?

Notes:
(a) If the number of such holdings is large, particulars in respect of those of less importance may be omitted if the company is listed.

(b) 'Debt securities' means debenture or loan stock, debentures, bonds and notes, whether secured or unsecured. — Yellow book definitions

	Reference

Associated companies

Note: If a company or group has investments in associated companies (as defined in paragraphs 13-16 of SSAP 1), the financial statements must comply with the accounting and the disclosure requirements set out in steps 4.7.5 to 4.7.22. Paragraph 65(1) of Schedule 4 to the Companies Act 1985 permits the equity method of accounting in consolidated financial statements where the directors consider that a body corporate is so closely associated with the holding company, or any subsidiary, as to justify the use of the method in respect of that investment.

4.7.6   Where the interest of the investing group or company is not effectively that of a partner in a joint venture or consortium and it amounts to 20% or more of the equity voting rights but it is not treated as an associated company, are the accounting treatment adopted and the reasons for adopting this treatment stated?   *SSAP 1 para 38*

Note: The Standard specifies that "in those cases where disclosure of the reason would be harmful to the business, the directors may omit the information, after consultation with their auditors".

4.7.7   Where the interest of the investing group or company amounts to less than 20% of the equity voting rights but the interest is treated as an associated company, is the basis on which significant influence is exercised stated?   *SSAP 1 para 38*

4.7.8   In respect of each of the principal associated companies, are the following disclosed: *SSAP 1 para 49*

(a) Its name?

(b) The proportion of its issued shares of each class held by the investing group?

(c) An indication of the nature of its business?

4.7.9   Is the interest in associated companies shown on the following bases:

(a) In the investing company's own financial statements — either at a valuation or at cost less amounts written off?   *SSAP 1 para 25*

(b) In the investing group's consolidated financial statements — at the total of: *SSAP 1 para 26*

     (i) Its share of the net assets other than goodwill of the associated companies stated, where possible, after attributing fair values to the net assets at the time each interest was acquired?

     (ii) Its share of any goodwill in the associated companies' own financial statements?

     (iii) The premium paid, or discount, on the acquisition of the interest (to the extent that it has not been written off)?

Note: Item (i) must be disclosed separately, but items (ii) and (iii) may be combined.

4.7.10   Where there has been a permanent impairment in the value of items (ii) and (iii) in step 4.7.9(b), have they been written down and is the amount written off in the period separately disclosed?   *SSAP 1 para 32*

	Reference
4.7.11 Where an associated company has a deficiency of net assets but is still regarded as a long-term investment and is supported in some way by its shareholders, is the investing group's share of the deficiency of net assets reflected in the consolidated financial statements?	SSAP 1 para 33
4.7.12 Where an investment is made in an unincorporated entity and a liability could arise in excess of that resulting from taking account only of the investing group's share of net assets (for example, as a result of joint and several liability in a partnership), has the investing group considered whether it would be prudent either to include an additional provision or to recognise a contingent liability for this excess?	SSAP 1 para 34
4.7.13 Except where it is a wholly-owned subsidiary, has an investing company that does not prepare consolidated financial statements shown the information required either by preparing a separate balance sheet or by adding the information in supplementary form to its own balance sheet?	SSAP 1 para 35
4.7.14 If the interests in associated companies are very material in the context of the group, is more detailed information given about the associated companies' tangible assets, intangible assets and liabilities? *Note: See note to step 3.9.3.*	SSAP 1 para 30
4.7.15 Do the associated companies prepare their financial statements either to the same date as, or to a date that is not more than six months before, or shortly after, the date of the investing group's financial statements?	SSAP 1 para 36
4.7.16 If financial statements not coterminous with those of the investing group are used and the effect is material, are the facts and the dates of the year ends disclosed?	SSAP 1 para 37
4.7.17 If the investing group has used financial statements already issued by the associated company, has it ensured that later information has not materially affected the view shown by those financial statements? *Note: If the associated company is listed on a recognised stock exchange, only published financial information should be disclosed.*	SSAP 1 para 37 SSAP 1 para 36
4.7.18 Where the effect is material, has the investing group made consolidation adjustments to exclude such items as unrealised profits on stocks transferred to or from associated companies and to achieve reasonable consistency with group accounting policies?	SSAP 1 para 39
4.7.19 Where an associated company has subsidiary or associated companies, is the investing group's share of the results and net assets based on the group financial statements of the associated company?	SSAP 1 para 42
4.7.20 Where the investment in an associated company is held by a subsidiary in which there are minority interests, do the minority interests in the investing group's consolidated financial statements include the minority share of the subsidiary's interest in the results and net assets of its associated companies?	SSAP 1 para 41

	Reference

4.7.21 Has the effective date for both the acquisition and the disposal of an interest, or part interest, in an associated company been taken as the earlier of either the date on which consideration passes or the date on which an offer becomes unconditional? — SSAP 1 para 44

4.7.22 When an investment in a company ceases to fall within the definition of an associated company, is it stated in the consolidated balance sheet at the carrying amount under the equity method at that date? — SSAP 1 para 43

Note: The carrying amount should be adjusted if dividends are subsequently received out of profits earned prior to the change of status or if there is any impairment in value.

4.7.23 Have steps 3.1.2, 3.7.4, 3.9.1 to 3.9.4, 3.11.4, 3.14.5 and 3.17.2 been completed?

Investments in subsidiaries

4.7.24 For each subsidiary at the balance sheet date, are the following disclosed: — 5 Sch 1,2 / SSAP 14 para 33

(a) The name of the subsidiary?

(b) Its country of incorporation, if outside Great Britain?

(c) Its country of registration (England and Wales or Scotland) if different from the country of incorporation?

(d) The identity, and proportion of the nominal value of the allotted shares, of each class held by:

    (i) The company and its nominees?
    (ii) Subsidiaries and their nominees?

(e) If the company is listed, or if it is traded on the USM, the name of the principal country in which each subsidiary operates? — CO 21(d) / GU 10(d)

(f) A statement, where appropriate, that the information in (a) to (e) is given only for those companies whose results principally affect the profit or loss or the amount of the assets of the group? — 5 Sch 4,5 / CO 21(d)

(g) The aggregate amount of the capital and reserves of the subsidiary as at the end of its financial year ending with, or last before, the financial year of the holding company? — 5 Sch 16

(h) The profit or loss of the subsidiary for its financial year ending with, or last before, the financial year of the holding company? — 5 Sch 16

(i) For each principal subsidiary, an indication of the nature of its business? — SSAP 14 para 33

Notes:
(a) Comparative amounts are not required for the information in (a) to (f). — 4 Sch 58(3)

(b) A company need not disclose the information required by (a) to (d) in respect of subsidiaries incorporated, or carrying on business, outside the UK if it would be harmful to the business of the company or subsidiary and the Secretary of State agrees to the non-disclosure. — 5 Sch 3

	Reference

(c) The information in (g) and (h) is not required if one of the following applies: — 5 Sch 17(1)

(i) The holding company is exempt from preparing group accounts because it is the wholly-owned subsidiary of another company incorporated in Great Britain.

(ii) The financial statements of the subsidiary are included in the group accounts.

(iii) The investment of the company in the shares of the subsidiary is included in, or in a note to, the company's financial statements by way of the equity method of valuation.

(d) In consolidated financial statements, the provisions in (g) and (h) apply only to investments by the holding company. — 4 Sch 63(a)

4.7.25 Are the aggregate amounts of each of the following disclosed: — 4 Sch 59

(a) Amounts owed to or by, and any interests in, any holding company or fellow subsidiary?

(b) Amounts owed to or by, and any interests in, any subsidiary?

Note: In consolidated financial statements, these provisions apply to subsidiaries not consolidated. — 4 Sch 67

Group accounts

4.7.26 If the company has subsidiaries, have steps 8.1.1 to 8.7.3 been completed where they are relevant?

4.8 Current assets

4.8.1 Unless any of the alternative accounting rules are adopted, is each current asset included at the lower of purchase price or production cost and net realisable value? — 4 Sch 16,22, 23(1) SSAP 9 para 26

4.8.2 Does production cost exclude distribution costs? — 4 Sch 26(4)

4.8.3 Where the reasons for a provision to reduce purchase price or production cost to net realisable value cease to exist to any extent, has the provision been written back to that extent? — 4 Sch 23(2)

4.8.4 If current assets are not included at the lower of purchase price or production cost and net realisable value, then where any of the alternative accounting rules are adopted, have current assets been valued on the following bases:

(a) Current asset investments at their current cost? — 4 Sch 31(4)

(b) Stocks at their current cost? — 4 Sch 31(5)

Stocks and fungible assets

4.8.5 Is the purchase price or production cost of stocks and fungible assets determined using FIFO, weighted average price or any other similar method? — 4 Sch 27(1)(2) SSAP 9 para 4, Appendix paras 11 to 15

4.8.6 Is the method chosen one which appears to the directors to be appropriate in the circumstances of the company? — 4 Sch 27(1)

Note: Fungible assets are assets that are substantially indistinguishable from one another (for example, identical shares in a particular company). — 4 Sch 27(6)

		Reference

4.8.7   Where the purchase price or production cost of stocks and fungible assets is determined using one of the methods referred to in step 4.8.5 and it is materially different from the replacement cost (or, if more appropriate, the most recent actual purchase price or production cost) of those stocks or fungible assets, is the amount of the difference disclosed for each category? — 4 Sch 27(3)(4)(5)

Long-term contract work in progress

4.8.8   Is long-term contract work in progress stated at cost plus attributable profit less any foreseeable losses and progress payments received and receivable? — SSAP 9 para 27

4.8.9   If anticipated losses on a contract exceed costs incurred to date less progress payments received and receivable, is the excess shown separately as a provision? — SSAP 9 para 27

4.8.10   If progress payments on a contract exceed costs incurred to date plus attributable profit, is the excess included in payments received on account under the heading 'Creditors'? — 4 Sch Note 8

4.8.11   If long-term contract work in progress includes attributable profit, are particulars given of the departure from the statutory valuation rules for current assets, together with the reason for, and the effect of, the departure? — Sec 228(6), 230(6)

4.8.12   In respect of long-term contracts, are the following disclosed: (a) The amount of work in progress at cost plus attributable profit, less foreseeable losses? — SSAP 9 para 30

(b) The progress payments received and receivable on account of contracts in progress?

Debtors

4.8.13   For each item included under debtors, is the amount falling due after more than one year separately disclosed? — 4 Sch Note 5

4.8.14   Is a lessor's net investment at the balance sheet date in the following disclosed: — SSAP 21 para 58

(a) Finance leases?

(b) Hire purchase contracts?

Note: See steps 4.6.13 to 4.6.21.

4.8.15   Is the cost of assets acquired by a lessor, whether by purchase or by finance lease (including hire purchase contracts), for the purpose of letting under finance leases disclosed? — SSAP 21 para 60(c)

Note: See steps 4.6.13 to 4.6.21.

4.8.16   Do the consolidated financial statements disclose the total of loans to associated companies from the group? — SSAP 1 para 27

Are trading balances between the group and associated companies included under debtors and disclosed separately if they are material? — SSAP 1 para 29

Note: See steps 4.7.6 to 4.7.23.

Loans for acquisition of own shares

4.8.17   Is the aggregate amount of any outstanding loans in respect of financial assistance for acquisition of own shares and authorised by Sections 153(4)(b) or (c) or 155 disclosed? — 4 Sch 51(2)

	Reference

4.9 Loans and transactions with directors

Notes: Special provisions apply to recognised banks and to money-lending companies, but these provisions are not dealt with below (see Chapter 11).

If loans or other transactions with directors and connected persons have been entered into, or subsisted, during the course of the year, the notes to the financial statements must contain the disclosures set out below in respect of:

(a) Any transaction of a kind described in Sec 330 (see notes below) entered into by the company (or, in the case of a holding company, by a subsidiary of the company) for a person who at any time during the year was a director of the company, or of its holding company, or was connected with such a director. — 6 Sch 1(a), 2(a)

(b) An agreement by the company (or, in the case of a holding company, by a subsidiary of the company) to enter into such a transaction or arrangement. — 6 Sch 1(b), 2(b)

(c) Any other transaction with the company (or, in the case of a holding company, with a subsidiary of the company) in which a person, who at any time during the year was a director of the company or of its holding company, had directly or indirectly a material interest. — 6 Sch 1(c), 2(c)

(A director is also treated as being interested in a transaction between a company and any of his connected persons.) — 6 Sch 3(1)

4.9.1 Do the notes contain the following particulars: — 6 Sch 1,2

(a) The principal terms of the transaction? — 6 Sch 9(1)

(b) A statement that the transaction was made during the year, or that it subsisted during the year? — 6 Sch 9(2)(a)

(c) The name of the person for whom the transaction was made and, where that person is connected with a director, the name of the director? — 6 Sch 9(2)(b)

(d) If the transaction is one in which the director has a material interest, the name of the director and the nature of that interest. — 6 Sch 9(2)(c)

(e) In respect of a loan, or an agreement for a loan, or an arrangement within Sec 330(6) or (7) relating to a loan: — 6 Sch 9(2)(d)

  (i) The amount of the liability for both the principal and the interest outstanding at both the beginning and the end of the year?
  (ii) The maximum amount of the liability during the year?
  (iii) The amount of interest which, having fallen due, has not been paid?
  (iv) The amount of any provision that the company has made against the failure of the borrower to repay the whole, or any part, of the principal or the interest?

(f) In respect of a guarantee, or security, or an arrangement within Sec 330 (6) relating to a guarantee or security: — 6 Sch 9(2)(e)

	Reference

(i) The amount for which the company (or its subsidiary) was liable under the guarantee, or in respect of the security, both at the beginning and at the end of the year?

(ii) The maximum amount for which the company (or its subsidiary) may become liable?

(iii) Any amount paid, and any liability incurred, by the company (or its subsidiary) in fulfilling the guarantee or discharging the security?

(g) In the case of any other transaction the value of the transaction or the value of any transaction to which the agreement relates? — 6 Sch 9(2)(f)

Notes:

(a) The transactions of the kind described in Sec 330 include:

(i) A loan.

(ii) A quasi-loan.

(iii) A credit transaction.

(iv) A guarantee or provision of security in connection with a loan, quasi-loan or credit transaction.

(v) An assignment of any rights, obligations or liabilities to the company under a transaction which, if it had been entered into by the company, would have fallen within (i), (ii), (iii) or (iv) above.

(vi) An arrangement by the company for another person to enter into such a transaction.

(b) The disclosure requirements do not apply to the following transactions:

(i) A transaction between one company and another company in which a director of the first company or its subsidiary or holding company is interested only by virtue of his being a director of the other. — 6 Sch 5(a)

(ii) A contract of service between a company and one of its directors or a director of its holding company or between a director of a company and any of that company's subsidiaries. — 6 Sch 5(b)

(iii) A transaction which was not entered into during the year in question and which did not subsist at any time during that year. — 6 Sch 5(e)

(iv) Any credit transaction, guarantee, security, agreement or arrangement falling within Sec 330 (6) or (7) that is made in connection with a credit transaction, where the aggregate amount outstanding in respect of all such transactions does not exceed £5,000 for the director and his connected persons during the year. — 6 Sch 11(1)(2)

(v) A transaction (covered by 6 Sch 1(c) or 2(c)) between a company and a director of the company or of its holding company or a person connected with such a director in which the director has an interest and the majority of the directors (other than the director) of the company which is preparing the financial statements in question are of the opinion that the interest is not material. — 6 Sch 3(2)

(vi) A transaction involving other members of the same group that is entered into by those group companies in the ordinary course of their business and at arm's length and which would otherwise be disclosable under 6 Sch 1(c) or 2(c). — 6 Sch 7

	Reference

(vii) A transaction or arrangement that would otherwise be disclosable under 6 Sch paras 1(c) or 2(c) because the director had a material interest, but only on account of the fact that he was associated with the company. This exemption applies only if the company is a member of a group of companies and if one of the following situations exists: — 6 Sch 8
   (i) The company is a wholly-owned subsidiary.
   (ii) No company within the same group, other than the company itself or one of its subsidiaries, was a party to the transaction or arrangement.

(viii) A transaction (covered by 6 Sch 1(c) or 2(c)) and in which a director has a material interest if (a) the value of each such transaction made in that year in which the director had a material interest, and (b) the value of each such transaction previously made less the amount by which the liabilities of the person for whom the transaction was made have been reduced, at no time during the year exceeded £1,000 or, if more, the lower of £5,000 and 1% of the value of the net assets of the company preparing the financial statements as at the end of the year. — 6 Sch 12

(c) Corresponding amounts are not required. — 4 Sch 58(3)(b)

(d) In consolidated financial statements, the above provisions apply only to directors of the holding company and its holding company. — 4 Sch 63(b)

4.9.2 If the company is listed, are particulars of any contract of significance subsisting during, or at the end of, the year in which a director of the company is, or was (for Stock Exchange purposes), materially interested, or the fact that there are no such contracts, disclosed? — CO 21(k)

Notes:
(a) When complying with this requirement, companies should have regard to the relevant provisions of the Companies Act.

(b) For Stock Exchange purposes, a 'contract of significance' is one which represents in amount or value a sum equal to 1% or more of: — CO 21(l)

   (i) In the case of a capital transaction of which the principal purpose is the granting of credit, the net assets of the company.
   (ii) In other cases, the total purchases, sales, payments or receipts, as the case may be, of the company.

4.10 Loans and transactions with officers

In respect of transactions, arrangements and agreements made by the company, and, in the case of a holding company, by its subsidiary, for persons who were, at any time during the year, officers, but not directors, of the company, do the notes contain the following particulars: — Sec 233(1)(2) 6 Sch 15, 16(1)

(a) The aggregate amounts outstanding at the end of the year of:
   (i) Loans (including guarantees, securities, arrangements and agreements relating to loans)?
   (ii) Quasi-loans (including guarantees, securities, arrangements and agreements relating to quasi-loans)?
   (iii) Credit transactions (including guarantees, securities, arrangements and agreements relating to credit transactions)?

	Reference

(b) The number of officers that each of the aggregate amounts in (a) cover?

Notes:

(a) Where the aggregate amount outstanding at the end of the year under transactions, arrangements and agreements made for the officer does not exceed £2,500, the amount may be excluded from the aggregate amounts disclosed under (a).   6 Sch 15(2)

(b) Corresponding amounts are not required.   4 Sch 58(3)

(c) In consolidated financial statements, the provisions apply only to officers of the holding company.   4 Sch 63(b)

4.11 Creditors and other liabilities

General disclosure

4.11.1 If balance sheet format 2 is used, is the amount falling due within one year and after more than one year shown separately for each item included under creditors and in aggregate for all items?   4 Sch Note 13

4.11.2 In respect of each item included under creditors, are the following disclosed: 4 Sch 48(1)

(a) The aggregate amount of debts that are payable or repayable otherwise than by instalments more than five years after the balance sheet date?

(b) The aggregate amount of debts that are payable or repayable by instalments, any of which fall due more than five years after the balance sheet date?

(c) The aggregate amount of the instalments in (b) that fall due more than five years after the balance sheet date?

4.11.3 In relation to each debt within step 4.11.2, is one of the following disclosed: 4 Sch 48(2) (3)

(a) The terms of payment or repayment and the rate of interest payable?

(b) If the above statement would be excessively long, a general indication of the terms of payment or repayment and the rates of interest payable?

4.11.4 If the company is listed, or if it is traded on the USM, is a statement included detailing the aggregate amounts repayable: CO 21(f) GU 10(f)

(a) In one year or less, or on demand.

(b) Between one and two years.

(c) Between two and five years.

(d) In five years or more.
In respect of:
    (i) Bank loans and overdrafts?
    (ii) Other borrowings?

4.11.5 In respect of each item shown under creditors, are the following disclosed: 4 Sch 48(4)

(a) The aggregate amount in respect of which any security has been given?

(b) An indication of the nature of the securities given?

	Reference
4.11.6 Is the amount for creditors in respect of taxation and social security shown separately from the amount for other creditors?	4 Sch Note 9

Debentures

4.11.7 Is there separate disclosure of the amount of convertible debenture loans?	4 Sch Note 7
4.11.8 In respect of debentures issued during the year, are the following disclosed:	4 Sch 41(1)

(a) The reason for making the issue?

(b) The classes of debentures issued?

(c) For each class:
(i) The amount issued?
(ii) The consideration received by the company?

4.11.9 Are particulars disclosed of any redeemed debentures that the company has power to reissue?	4 Sch 41(2)
4.11.10 In respect of any of the company's debentures held by a nominee of, or trustee for, the company, are the following disclosed:	4 Sch 41(3)

(a) The nominal amount of the debentures?

(b) The book value of the holding?

4.11.11 Are the number, description and amount of the company's debentures held beneficially by subsidiaries or their nominees disclosed?	4 Sch 60
Note: In consolidated financial statements, this provision applies to subsidiaries not consolidated.	4 Sch 67

Dividends

4.11.12 Is the aggregate amount that is recommended for distribution by way of dividend disclosed?	4 Sch 51(3)
4.11.13 Do proposed dividends and dividends declared but not yet payable exclude the related ACT?	SSAP 8 para 26
4.11.14 Is the ACT on proposed dividends (whether recoverable or irrecoverable) only carried forward to the extent that it is foreseen that sufficient corporation tax will be assessed on the profits or income of the next accounting period against which the ACT is available for offset?	SSAP 15 para 31
Note: SSAP 15 (revised) is effective in respect of financial statements relating to accounting periods beginning on or after 1 April 1985.	
4.11.15 If the ACT on proposed dividends is regarded as recoverable, has it been deducted from the deferred taxation account, or, in the absence of such an account, shown under 'Prepayments and accrued income'?	SSAP 8 para 27
4.11.16 For arrears of fixed cumulative dividends, are the following disclosed:	4 Sch 49

(a) The amount of the arrears?

(b) The period for which the dividend on each class of shares is in arrears?

	Reference

Leasing obligations

4.11.17 Is the amount for lessees of obligations related to finance leases (net of finance charges allocated to future periods) disclosed separately from other obligations and liabilities either on the face of the balance sheet or in the notes to the financial statements? — SSAP 21 para 51

4.11.18 Are net obligations for lessees under finance leases analysed between amounts payable: — SSAP 21 para 52

(a) In the next year?

(b) In the second to fifth years inclusive?

(c) In more than five years?

If not (because obligations under finance leases are combined on the balance sheet with other obligations and liabilities), is the analysis given in respect of the combined total?

Note: Where net obligations are not combined on the balance sheet with other obligations and liabilities, the gross obligations can be analysed and the future finance charges separately deducted from the total. See also steps 4.6.1 to 4.6.9.

Associated companies

4.11.19 Do the consolidated financial statements disclose the total of loans from associated companies to the group? — SSAP 1 para 28

Are trading balances between the group and associated companies included under creditors and disclosed separately if they are material? — SSAP 1 para 29

Note: See steps 4.7.6 to 4.7.23.

4.12 Provisions for liabilities and charges

General disclosure

4.12.1 In respect of provisions under any heading or sub-heading where there has been a transfer to the provision, or from the provision otherwise than for the purpose for which the provision was established, are the following disclosed: — 4 Sch 46

(a) The amount of the provision at the beginning of the year?

(b) The amount and the source of transfers to the provision?

(c) The amount and the application of transfers from the provision?

(d) The amount of the provision at the end of the year?

Note: Corresponding amounts are not required. — 4 Sch 58(3)

4.12.2 Are particulars disclosed separately of each material provision that is included under the heading 'Other provisions'? — 4 Sch 46(3)

4.12.3 Is the amount of any provision for taxation other than deferred taxation disclosed? — 4 Sch 47

Deferred taxation

4.12.4 Are the deferred tax balance and its major components disclosed? — SSAP 15 para 37

4.12.5 Are transfers to and from deferred tax disclosed in a note? — SSAP 15 para 38

543

	Reference
4.12.6 Is the total amount of any unprovided deferred tax disclosed in a note analysed by its major components?	SSAP 15 para 40
4.12.7 Where amounts of deferred tax arise that relate to movements on reserves, are the amounts transferred to or from deferred tax shown separately as part of such movements?	SSAP 15 para 39
4.12.8 Are debit balances on the deferred taxation account carried forward only to the extent that they are expected to be recoverable without replacement by equivalent debit balances?	SSAP 15 para 30
Note: Debit balances in respect of ACT other than on dividends payable or proposed at the balance sheet date (see step 3.11.2) should be written off unless recovery is assured beyond reasonable doubt. Such recovery will normally only be assured where the debit balances are recoverable out of corporation tax arising on profits or income of the next accounting period, without replacement by equivalent debit balances.	SSAP 15 para 32
4.12.9 Where the financial statements disclose the value of an asset by way of note and that value differs from the book value of the asset, does the note also disclose the tax implications that would result if the asset was sold at that value?	SSAP 15 para 42
4.12.10 Where the potential amount of deferred tax on a revalued asset is not shown because the revaluation does not constitute a timing difference, is this fact, and the fact that the tax has not been quantified, disclosed?	SSAP 15 para 41
Note: SSAP 15 (revised) is effective in respect of financial statements relating to accounting periods beginning on or after 1 April 1985.	SSAP 15 para 45

4.13 Guarantees and other financial commitments

4.13.1 Are particulars (including the amount secured, where practicable) of any charge on the assets to secure the liabilities of any other person disclosed?	4 Sch 50(1)
4.13.2 Are the following amounts of capital expenditure disclosed:	4 Sch 50(3)
(a) Contracted but not provided for?	
(b) Authorised but not contracted for?	
4.13.3 Is the amount for lessees of any commitments at the balance sheet date in respect of finance leases which have been entered into but where inception occurs after the year end disclosed?	SSAP 21 para 54
Note: See also steps 4.6.1 to 4.6.9.	
4.13.4 Are the payments that the lessee is committed to make in respect of operating leases during the next year disclosed? Is this amount analysed between payments where the commitment expires:	SSAP 21 para 56
(a) In that year?	
(b) In the second to fifth years inclusive?	
(c) In more than five years?	
Is this analysis given separately for leases of land and buildings and for other operating leases?	
Note: See also steps 4.6.1 to 4.6.9.	

	Reference

4.13.5 Are particulars of the following pension commitments disclosed: — 4 Sch 50(4)

(a) Those included under any provision in the balance sheet?

(b) Those for which no provision has been made?

(c) Those in (a) and (b) in respect of pensions payable to past directors?

4.13.6 Are particulars disclosed of any other financial commitments that have not been provided for and that are relevant to the assessment of the state of affairs? — 4 Sch 50(5)

4.13.7 Is there separate disclosure of commitments in steps 4.13.1, 4.13.2, 4.13.5 and 4.13.6 that are undertaken on behalf of or for the benefit of: — 4 Sch 50(6)

(a) Any holding company or fellow subsidiary?

(b) Any subsidiary?

4.14 Contingencies

4.14.1 Have material contingent losses been accrued where it is probable that a future event will confirm a loss that can be estimated with reasonable accuracy at the date on which the financial statements are approved by the board of directors? — SSAP 18 para 15

4.14.2 Except where the possibility of loss is remote, have material contingent losses not accrued been disclosed? — SSAP 18 para 16

4.14.3 Have material contingent gains been disclosed only where it is probable that the gain will be realised? — SSAP 18 para 17

4.14.4 In respect of each contingency (or group of similar transactions) that require disclosure, are the following disclosed: — SSAP 18 paras 18, 21 / 4 Sch 50(2)

(a) The nature of the contingency?

(b) The uncertainties that are expected to affect the ultimate outcome?

(c) A prudent estimate of the financial effect (made at the date on which the financial statements are approved by the board of directors), or a statement that it is not practicable to make such an estimate?

4.14.5 In addition, in respect of any contingent liability not provided for, are the following disclosed: — 4 Sch 50(2)

(a) Its legal nature?

(b) Whether any valuable security has been provided and if so, what?

4.14.6 If an estimate of the financial effect of a contingency is disclosed, does this take into account the probable outcome of any related counter-claim or claim by or against a third party such that only the potential financial effect is disclosed? — SSAP 18 paras 6, 19

4.14.7 In the case of a contingent loss, has the potential financial effect that is disclosed been reduced by: — SSAP 18 para 19

(a) Any amounts accrued?

(b) Any amounts where the possibility of loss is remote?

		Reference
4.14.8	Has the estimate of the financial effect been disclosed before taking account of taxation, and have the taxation implications of the contingency crystallising been explained where this is necessary for a proper understanding of the financial position?	SSAP 18 para 20
4.14.9	Is there separate disclosure of contingent liabilities that are undertaken on behalf of or for the benefit of: (a) Any holding company or fellow subsidiary? (b) Any subsidiary?	4 Sch 50(6)

4.15 Share capital

4.15.1	Is the authorised share capital disclosed?	4 Sch 38(1) (a)
4.15.2	Where more than one class of shares has been allotted, are the number and the aggregate nominal value of each class of shares allotted disclosed?	4 Sch 38(1) (b)
4.15.3	Are the amount of allotted share capital and the amount of called-up share capital that has been paid up separately disclosed?	4 Sch Note 12
4.15.4	In respect of allotted redeemable shares, are the following disclosed: (a) The earliest and the latest dates on which the company has power to redeem them? (b) Whether they must be redeemed in any event or at the option of the company or of the shareholder? (c) The premium, if any, payable on redemption (or, if none, a statement to that effect)?	4 Sch 38(2)
	Where a class of preference shares (or participating or preferred ordinary shares) was issued before 6 April 1973 and indicates a fixed rate of dividend, is the new effective rate of dividend that is paid to shareholders also incorporated in the description of the shares?	SSAP 8 para 28

4.15.5	In respect of shares allotted during the year, are the following disclosed:
	
	(a) The reason for making the allotment?
	
	(b) The classes of shares allotted?
	
	(c) For each class:
	    (i) The number allotted?
	    (ii) The aggregate nominal value?
	    (iii) The consideration received by the company?
		4 Sch 39

4.15.6	In respect of any option to subscribe for shares and of any other right to require the allotment of shares to any person, are the following disclosed: (a) The number, description and amount of shares involved? (b) The period during which the option or right is exercisable? (c) The price to be paid for the shares?	4 Sch 40
4.15.7	Are the number, description and amount of the company's shares held beneficially by subsidiaries or their nominees disclosed?	4 Sch 60
	Note: In consolidated financial statements, these provisions apply also to subsidiaries not consolidated.	4 Sch 67

	Reference

4.15.8 Are the name of the company's ultimate holding company, and its country of incorporation, disclosed? — 5 Sch 20

Note: A company that carries on business outside the UK does not have to disclose this information if the directors consider that it would be harmful to the business of the company or the ultimate holding company, and the Secretary of State agrees to the non-disclosure. — 5 Sch 21

4.16 Reserves

4.16.1 In respect of reserves under any heading or sub-heading where there has been a transfer to or from the reserve, are the following disclosed: — 4 Sch 46

(a) The amount of the reserve at the beginning of the year?

(b) The amount and the source of transfers to the reserve?

(c) The amount and the application of transfers from the reserve?

(d) The amount of the reserve at the end of the year?

Note: Corresponding amounts are not required. — 4 Sch 58(3)

4.16.2 Do the consolidated financial statements disclose the following in respect of associated companies:

(a) The investing group's share of the post-acquisition accumulated reserves of the associated companies and any movements on those reserves (including amounts that have not passed through the profit and loss account)? — SSAP 1 para 31

(b) Where applicable, the fact that the accumulated reserves of overseas associated companies would be subject to further tax on distribution? — SSAP 1 para 31

(c) The extent of any significant restrictions on the ability of an associated company to distribute its retained profits (other than those shown as non-distributable)? — SSAP 1 para 40

Note: See steps 4.7.6 to 4.7.23.

4.16.3 Is the treatment for taxation purposes of amounts credited or debited to the revaluation reserve disclosed? — 4 Sch 34(4)

4.16.4 Are any amounts transferred to or from the deferred taxation account shown separately as part of such movements? — SSAP 15 para 38

4.16.5 Has the revaluation reserve been reduced to the extent that amounts standing to the credit of the reserve are in the opinion of the directors no longer necessary for the purpose of the accounting policies adopted? — 4 Sch 34(3)

4.16.6 Has an amount been transferred from the revaluation reserve to the profit and loss account only where one of the following applies: — 4 Sch 34(3)

(a) It was previously charged to the profit and loss account?

(b) It represents realised profit?

4.17 Post-balance-sheet events

Note: Financial statements should be prepared on the basis of conditions existing at the balance sheet date. — SSAP 17 para 21

		Reference
4.17.1	Do amounts included in the financial statements take account of a material post-balance-sheet event where:	SSAP 17 para 22
	(a) It is an adjusting event?	
	(b) It indicates that the application of the going concern concept to the whole or a material part of the company is inappropriate?	
4.17.2	Has a material post-balance-sheet event been disclosed where:	SSAP 17 para 23
	(a) It is a non-adjusting event of such materiality that its non-disclosure would affect the ability of the users of the financial statements to reach a proper understanding of the financial position?	
	(b) It is 'window dressing'?	
4.17.3	In respect of each material post-balance-sheet event that requires disclosure, are the following disclosed:	SSAP 17 para 24
	(a) The nature of the event?	
	(b) An estimate of the financial effect, or a statement that it is not practicable to make such an estimate?	
4.17.4	Has the estimate of the financial effect been disclosed before taking account of taxation, and have the taxation implications been explained where this is necessary for a proper understanding of the financial position?	SSAP 17 para 25

4.18 Date of approval

	Is the date on which the financial statements were approved by the board of directors disclosed and have the directors signed the company's balance sheet?	Sec 238(1) SSAP 17 para 26

5.   Statement of Source and Application of Funds

		Reference
5.1	Where an entity has turnover or gross income of £25,000 or more per annum, do the financial statements include a statement of source and application of funds?	SSAP 10 paras 9,10
	Note: Where group accounts are prepared, the statement should reflect the operations of the group.	SSAP 10 para 12
5.2	Does the statement show the profit or loss for the year together with the adjustments required for items that did not use (or provide) funds in the year?	SSAP 10 para 11
5.3	Are the following other sources and applications of funds also shown where material:	SSAP 10 para 11
	(a) Dividends paid?	
	(b) Acquisitions and disposals of fixed assets?	
	(c) Funds raised by increasing, or expended in repaying or redeeming, medium or long-term loans or the issued capital of the company?	
	(d) The increase or decrease in working capital sub-divided into its components, and movements in net liquid funds?	
	Notes: *(a) There should be a minimum of 'netting off'. The figures should generally be identifiable in the profit and loss account, or in the balance sheet or in the related notes. If adjustments to those figures are necessary, details should be given to enable the related figures to be located.*	SSAP 10 para 4
	(b) The effects of acquiring, or disposing of, a subsidiary should be reflected. (See the example in Chapter 6 para 6.52.)	SSAP 10 para 5

6. The Directors' Report

		Reference
	Does the directors' report contain the following information:	
6.1	A description of the principal activities of the company (and its subsidiaries) during the year and of any significant changes in those activities?	Sec 235(2)
6.2	A fair review of the development of the business of the company (and its subsidiaries) during the year and of their position at the end of the year?	Sec 235(1)(a)
6.3	An indication of likely future developments in the business of the company (and its subsidiaries)?	7 Sch 6(b)
6.4	Particulars of any important events affecting the company (or its subsidiaries) that have occurred since the end of the year?	7 Sch 6(a)
6.5	An indication of any activities of the company (and its subsidiaries) in the field of research and development?	7 Sch 6(c)
6.6	The amount, if any, the directors recommend should be paid by way of dividend?	Sec 235(1)(b)
6.7	The amount, if any, the directors propose to transfer to reserves?	Sec 235(1)(b)
6.8	If the company is listed, or if it is traded on the USM, an explanation of any material difference between the trading results for the year and any published forecast made by the company?	CO 21(b) GU 10(b)
6.9	Particulars of any significant changes in the fixed assets of the company (and its subsidiaries) during the year?	7 Sch 1(1)
6.10	The difference (as precisely as practicable) at the year end between the market value and the balance sheet value of an interest in land if, in the opinion of the directors, the difference is of such significance that it should be drawn to the attention of the members or the debenture holders?	7 Sch 1(2)
	Note: Under section 3 of the Interpretation Act 1889, 'land' means 'land and buildings'.	
6.11	The amount of money given by the company and its subsidiaries to UK charities and the amount given for political purposes (if together they exceed £200)?	7 Sch 3,4
6.12	In the case of any individual amount exceeding £200 for political purposes, the name of the recipient or political party concerned and the amount given?	7 Sch 3,4
	Note: Not applicable to directors' reports of wholly-owned subsidiaries of companies incorporated in Great Britain.	7 Sch 3(1)
6.13	If the company is listed, or if it is traded on the USM, a statement by the directors as to the reasons for any significant departure from applicable standard accounting practices?	CO 21(a) GU 10(a)
6.14	If the company is listed, or if it is traded on the USM, a statement of whether or not, so far as the directors are aware, the company is a close company for taxation purposes and whether there has been any change in that respect since the end of the year?	CO 21(j) GU 10(j)

		Reference
6.15	In respect of purchases by the company of its own shares during the year:	7 Sch 8(a)(e)

(a) The number and nominal value of shares purchased?

(b) The percentage of the called-up capital that shares of the description purchased represent?

(c) The aggregate consideration paid?

(d) The reasons for the purchase?

6.16	In respect of acquisitions (other than purchases) by the company of its own shares:	7 Sch 8(b)-(g)

(a) The number and nominal value of shares acquired or charged during the year, and the percentage of called-up capital that shares of the description acquired or charged represent?

(b) The maximum number and nominal value of shares acquired or charged that were held at any time during the year?

(c) The number and nominal value of shares acquired or charged that were disposed of or cancelled during the year?

(d) The consideration received in respect of disposals during the year where the shares were originally acquired for money or money's worth?

(e) The amount of any charge?

Note: Acquisitions (other than purchases) by the company of its own shares comprise: 7 Sch 7

(a) Shares acquired by forfeiture, by surrender in lieu of forfeiture or by way of gift.

(b) In the case of a public company, shares any person acquires with the financial assistance of the company and in respect of which the company has a beneficial interest.

(c) Shares that a nominee of the company acquires from a third party without the company providing any financial assistance and in respect of which the company has a beneficial interest.

(d) Shares over which the company takes a lien or a charge (express or implied) for any amount payable in respect of those shares.

(e) Shares on which the company held a charge immediately before applying to re-register or register as a public company under the Companies Act 1980.

(f) In the case of an old public company, shares on which the company held a charge immediately before the end of the re-registration period if it had not by then applied to re-register as a public company.

6.17	If the company is listed, particulars of any shareholders' authority existing at the year end for the purchase by the company of its own shares?	CO 21(p)
6.18	In the case of such purchases made otherwise than through the market or by tender or partial offer to all shareholders, the names of the sellers of such shares purchased, or proposed to be purchased, by the company during the year?	CO 21(p)

		Reference
6.19	Particulars of purchases or options or contracts to make purchases entered into since the end of the year?	CO 21(p)
6.20	The names of persons who were directors of the company at any time during the year?	Sec 235(2)
6.21	If the company is listed, the unexpired period (if greater than one year) of any service contract of each director proposed for re-election at the annual general meeting (or, if he does not have a service contract of more than one year's duration, a statement to that effect)?	CO 43(c)
6.22	The interests of each person who was a director at the end of the year in shares or debentures of either the company or any other company in the group at both the beginning of the year (or date of appointment, if later) and the end of the year?	7 Sch 2 CO 21(h) GU 10(h)

Notes:

(a) Details to be according to the register kept by the company.

(b) If a director has no such interests at the end of the year, there should be a statement to that effect.

(c) If a director has no interests at the end of the year, no details are required of any interests at the beginning of the year (whether or not he had any), unless the company is listed or it is traded on the USM.

(d) The main exemptions are:

	(i) Directors' nominee shareholdings in wholly-owned subsidiaries.	Sec 324(6)
	(ii) Interests of directors of wholly-owned subsidiaries of companies incorporated in Great Britain who are also directors of the holding company.	SI 1985/802
	(iii) Interests of directors of wholly-owned subsidiaries of companies incorporated outside Great Britain in companies incorporated outside Great Britain.	SI 1985/802

(e) Other exemptions are set out in SI 1985/802

	(f) Directors' interests may be given in the notes to the financial statements.	7 Sch 2(3)
	(g) If the company is listed, or traded on the USM, interests in shares in the company and its subsidiaries should distinguish between beneficial and non-beneficial interests and particulars should be given of the extent of any duplication that occurs.	CO 21(h) GU 10(h)
	(h) If a director has an interest in the company's shares in the form of an option, this interest should be disclosed.	13 Sch 6(1) Sec 324(2)(d), 328(2)(a)
6.23	If the company is listed, or if it is traded on the USM, any changes in directors' interests between the end of the year and a date not more than one month prior to the date of the notice of meeting, or the fact that there have been no changes?	CO 21(h) GU 10(h)
6.24	If the company is listed, or if it is traded on the USM, particulars of, and the amount of, an interest of any person (other than a director) in 5% or more of the nominal value of any class of voting capital at a date not more than one month prior to the date of the notice of meeting, or the fact that there are no such interests?	CO 21(i) GU 10(i)

Note: Details to be according to the register kept by the company under Sec 211.

		Reference
6.25	If the company is listed, particulars of any contract of significance between the company, or one of its subsidiaries, and a corporate substantial shareholder?	CO 21(l)

Notes:
(a) A 'contract of significance' is one which represents in amount or value a sum equal to 1% or more of:

(i) In the case of a capital transaction or a transaction of which the principal purpose is the granting of credit, the net assets of the company.
(ii) In other cases, the total purchases, sales, payments or receipts, as the case may be, of the company.

Where the company has subsidiaries, then comparison should be made on a consolidated basis.

(b) A 'corporate substantial shareholder' means any body corporate entitled to exercise or control the exercise of 30% or more of the voting power at general meetings of the company, or one which is in a position to control the composition of a majority of the board of directors.

		Reference
6.26	If the company is listed, particulars of any contract for the provision of services to the company or any of its subsidiaries by a corporate substantial shareholder except in the circumstances given below?	CO 21(m)

Note: Such a contract need not be disclosed if it is a contract for the provision of services which it is the principal business of the shareholder to provide and it is not a 'contract of significance'.

		Reference
6.27	If the company is listed, particulars of the participation of the company's parent company in any vendor consideration placing made during the year?	CO 22
6.28	A statement of the company's policy during the year in respect of:	7 Sch 9

(a) Applications for employment from disabled persons?

(b) Persons that become disabled during their employment?

(c) Training, career development and promotion of disabled persons?

Notes:
(a) Not applicable to employees who work wholly or mainly outside the UK.

(b) Not applicable to directors' reports of companies that employ on average 250 or fewer persons in the UK.

		Reference
6.29	A statement that describes the action that the company has taken during the year to introduce, maintain or develop arrangements aimed at:	7 Sch 11

(a) Providing employees systematically with information on matters of concern to them as employees?

(b) Consulting employees or their representatives on a regular basis so that the views of employees can be taken into account in making decisions that are likely to affect their interests?

Reference

(c) Encouraging the involvement of employees in the company's performance through an employees' share scheme or by some other means?

(d) Achieving a common awareness on the part of all employees of the financial and economic factors that affect the performance of the company?

Notes:
(a) Not applicable to employees who work wholly or mainly outside the UK.

(b) Not applicable to directors' reports of companies that employ on average 250 or fewer persons in the UK.

7. Foreign Currency Translation

7.1 Individual companies

		Reference

7.1.1   Have foreign currency transactions completed during the year been translated at one of the following rates: **SSAP 20 para 46**

(a) If the transaction is to be settled at a contracted rate, that rate?

(b) At the rate ruling on the date the transaction occurred?

Notes:
(a) See step 7.1.6 for special provisions that may be applied to foreign equity investments financed by foreign currency borrowings.   **SSAP 20 para 47**

(b) Subject to the special provisions covered by step 7.1.6, non-monetary assets once translated and recorded should not normally be retranslated.

(c) If rates do not fluctuate significantly, an average rate for the period may be used instead of the rate ruling on the date the transaction occurred.

(d) A trading transaction that is covered by a related or matching forward contract may be translated either at the rate specified in the contract or at the rate ruling on the date the transaction occurred. (A company should, however, apply consistently the policy it adopts in respect of such trading transactions.)

7.1.2   Have foreign currency monetary assets and liabilities outstanding at the balance sheet date been translated at one of the following rates: **SSAP 20 para 48**

(a) The rate fixed under the terms of the relevant transaction?

(b) The closing rate?

Note: If there is a related or matching forward contract in respect of a trading transaction, translation may be either at the rate specified in the contract or at the closing rate. (A company should, however, apply consistently the policy it adopts in respect of such trading transactions.)

7.1.3   Have exchange gains and losses on foreign currency transactions completed in the year and on foreign currency monetary assets and liabilities outstanding at the balance sheet date been reported as part of the profit or loss for the year from ordinary activities?   **SSAP 20 para 49**

Note: Exchange gains and losses that result from transactions that themselves fall to be treated as extraordinary items should be included as part of such items.

7.1.4   In the exceptional cases where there are doubts as to the convertibility or marketability of the currency of a long-term monetary item outstanding at the balance sheet date, has the company considered whether, on the grounds of prudence, it should restrict the amount of the exchange gain (or the amount by which the gain exceeds past exchange losses on the same items) that it recognises in the profit and loss account?   **SSAP 20 para 50**

7.1.5   If the profit and loss account includes unrealised gains on long-term monetary items outstanding at the balance sheet date, are particulars of, the reasons for, and the effect of, the departure from the valuation principles of the Act given?   **4 Sch 15**

	Reference
	SSAP 20 para 51

7.1.6 Where a company has used foreign currency borrowings to finance, or to provide a hedge against, its foreign equity investments and it denominates the equity investments in the appropriate foreign currency, is the offset procedure used only where both of the following conditions are met:

(a) In any year, exchange gains and losses on the translation of the borrowings are offset as a reserve movement only to the extent of the exchange differences arising on the retranslation of the equity investments?

(b) The foreign currency borrowings used in the offset process do not exceed in aggregate the total amount of cash that the investments are expected to be able to generate from profits or otherwise?

7.1.7 If the company has chosen to use the offset procedure, has it applied it consistently from year to year unless the above two conditions cease to apply? — SSAP 20 para 51

Note: Under the offset procedure, exchange gains/losses on the translation of the foreign equity investments are taken to reserves, and exchange losses/gains on the translation of the foreign currency borrowings are offset as a reserve movement against these exchange gains/losses.

7.2   Consolidated financial statements

7.2.1 If the trade of a foreign enterprise (that is, subsidiary, associated company or branch) is more dependent on the economic environment of the investing company's currency than that of its own reporting currency, have that foreign enterprise's financial statements been translated using the temporal method? — SSAP 20 para 55

7.2.2 In all other circumstances, have foreign enterprises' financial statements been translated using the closing rate/net investment method? — SSAP 20 para 52

7.2.3 Has the method of translating each foreign enterprise's financial statements been applied consistently from year to year unless there has been a change in its financial and other operational relationships with the investing company? — SSAP 20 para 56

7.2.4 Where the closing rate/net investment method is used, has the foreign enterprise's profit and loss account been translated at either the closing rate or an average rate for the year? — SSAP 20 para 54

7.2.5 If an average rate is used, has it been calculated by the method considered most appropriate to the circumstances of the foreign enterprise? — SSAP 20 para 54

Where an average rate is used, has the difference between translating the profit and loss account at that rate and translating it at the closing rate been recorded as a movement on reserves?

7.2.6 Have exchange differences that arise from retranslating the opening net investment in a foreign enterprise at the closing rate been recorded as a movement on reserves? — SSAP 20 para 53

7.2.7 Where foreign currency borrowings have been used to finance, or to provide a hedge against, group equity investments in foreign enterprises, is the offset procedure used only where all of the following conditions are met: — SSAP 20 para 57

	Reference

(a) The relationship between the investing company and the foreign enterprises concerned justifies the use of the closing rate method for consolidation purposes?

(b) In any year, exchange gains and losses on the foreign currency borrowings are offset as a reserve movement only to the extent of exchange differences arising on the net investments in foreign enterprises?

(c) The foreign currency borrowings used in the offset process do not exceed in aggregate the total amount of cash that the net investments are expected to be able to generate from profits or otherwise?

If the group has chosen to use the offset procedure, has it applied it consistently from year to year unless the above three conditions cease to apply?

Notes:
(a) Under the offset procedure, exchange losses/gains on the translation of the foreign currency borrowings are offset as a movement on consolidated reserves against exchange gains/losses on the translation of the net investments in the foreign enterprises.

(b) If, in an investing company's financial statements, the offset procedure has been applied to a foreign equity investment that is neither a subsidiary nor an associated company, the same offset procedure may be applied in the consolidated financial statements. — SSAP 20 para 58

7.3 Disclosure requirements

7.3.1 Are the following disclosed:

(a) The methods of translating the financial statements of foreign enterprises? — SSAP 20 para 59

(b) The treatment of exchange differences? — SSAP 20 para 59

(c) The net movement on reserves that arises from exchange differences? — SSAP 20 para 60

7.3.2 If the company or group is not an exempt company or group, are the following disclosed: — SSAP 20 para 60

(a) The net amount of exchange gains and losses on foreign currency borrowings less deposits?

(b) The amount of (a) that is offset in reserves under the offset procedure?

(c) The net amount of (a) that is charged or credited to the profit and loss account?

Note: An exempt company is one that does not prepare its financial statements in accordance with Section 228 or Section 230 of, and Schedule 4 to, the Companies Act 1985. — SSAP 20 para 35

8. Group Accounts and Accounting for Business Combinations

	Reference
Notes:	
If the company has subsidiaries, the financial statements must include group accounts. Group accounts are not required, however, where the company is itself the wholly-owned subsidiary of another company incorporated in Great Britain (but see section 8.6 below for information to be disclosed in the notes to the holding company's financial statements).	Sec 229(1)(2) SSAP 14 para 19
Group accounts should cover the holding company and all its subsidiaries at home and overseas unless one, or more, of the circumstances in step 8.1.1 apply.	Sec 229(3)
Group accounts should be in the form of a single set of consolidated financial statements, unless one, or more, of the circumstances in step 8.1.2 apply.	Sec 229(5) (6)(7) SSAP 14 paras15,19-22

This part of the checklist is divided into seven sections that cover standard and non-standard situations. The sections are as follows:

8.1 Consolidated financial statements.

8.2 Subsidiaries excluded from consolidation.

8.3 Group accounts other than consolidated financial statements.

8.4 Subsidiaries excluded from group accounts.

8.5 Group accounts not prepared.

8.6 Acquisition and merger accounting.

8.7 Merger relief.

8.1 Consolidated financial statements

		Reference
8.1.1	Has a subsidiary been excluded from group accounts only where one of the reasons permitted by Sec 229(3) applies?	Sec 229(3)
	Notes: *(a) The reasons permitted are:*	
	(i) It is impracticable, or it would be of no real value to members of the company, because of the insignificant amounts involved, or it would involve expense or delay out of all proportion to the value to the members of the company. *(ii) The result would be misleading, or harmful to the business of the company or any of its subsidiaries.* *(iii)The business of the holding company and that of the subsidiary are so different that they cannot reasonably be treated as a single undertaking.*	
	(b) The Secretary of State's approval is necessary for exclusion on the ground that the result would be harmful or on the ground that the businesses differ (points (ii) or (iii) above).	Sec 229(4)

		Reference
8.1.2	Has a subsidiary been excluded from consolidation where one of the following applies:	SSAP 14 para 21
	(a) Its activities are so dissimilar from those of other companies in the group that consolidated financial statements would be misleading?	
	(b) The holding company, although owning directly or through other subsidiaries more than half the equity share capital of the subsidiary, is in one of the following situations:	
	(i) It does not own share capital that carries more than half the votes? (ii) It has contractual or other restrictions imposed on its ability to appoint the majority of the board of directors?	
	(c) It operates under severe restrictions that significantly impair control by the holding company over the subsidiary's assets and operations for the foreseeable future?	
	(d) Control of the subsidiary is intended to be only temporary?	
8.1.3	Where group accounts are prepared in a form other than consolidated financial statements in circumstances different from those set out in step 8.1.2, have the directors justified and stated the reasons for reaching the conclusion that the resulting group accounts give a fairer view of the financial position of the group as a whole?	SSAP 14 para 22
8.1.4	Except where provisions specifically do not apply to consolidated financial statements, do the consolidated financial statements combine the information contained in the separate financial statements of the holding company and the subsidiaries consolidated with such adjustments, if any, that the directors think necessary?	4 Sch 61
8.1.5	Do the consolidated financial statements, in giving the information required by step 8.1.4, comply so far as practicable with the requirements of Schedule 4 and with the other requirements of the Companies Act as if they were the financial statements of an actual company?	4 Sch 62
	Note: This requirement does not override any requirements of the Act that apply specifically to group accounts.	4 Sch 64
8.1.6	Is there a description of the bases on which subsidiaries have been dealt with in the consolidated financial statements?	SSAP 14 para 15
8.1.7	When preparing the consolidated financial statements has the holding company used uniform accounting policies?	SSAP 14 para 16
8.1.8	Where group accounting policies have not been adopted in the financial statements of a subsidiary, have appropriate adjustments been made in the consolidated financial statements?	SSAP 14 para 16
8.1.9	Where it is impracticable to make appropriate adjustments and different accounting policies are used:	SSAP 14 para 16
	(a) Are they generally acceptable policies?	
	(b) Is there disclosure of:	

	Reference

(i) The different policies used?

(ii) An indication of the amounts of the assets and liabilities involved?

(iii) Where practicable, an indication of the effect on results and net assets of the adoption of different policies?

(iv) The reasons for using different policies?

8.1.10 Wherever practicable for the purposes of consolidated financial statements, have the financial statements of all subsidiaries been prepared:

    SSAP 14 para 17 Sec 227(4)

(a) To the same accounting date as the holding company?

(b) For identical accounting periods as the holding company?

8.1.11 If a subsidiary does not prepare its formal financial statements to the same date as the holding company, and if it is not practicable to use for consolidation purposes special financial statements drawn up to the same date as those of the holding company, have appropriate adjustments been made to the consolidated financial statements for any abnormal transactions in the intervening period?

    SSAP 14 para 18

8.1.12 In addition, where the financial year of any subsidiary does not coincide with that of the company, are the following disclosed:

    4 Sch 70

(a) The date on which the year of each such subsidiary ending last before that of the company ended or the earliest and latest of those dates?

(b) The reasons why the company's directors consider that the financial year of any such subsidiary should not end with that of the company?

(c) The names of the principal subsidiaries that have different year ends?

    SSAP 14 para 18

Note: This disclosure is required whether or not the subsidiary is dealt with in the group accounts.

8.1.13 If special financial statements drawn up to the same date as those of the holding company have been used for consolidation purposes, has the Secretary of State's consent been obtained?

    SSAP 14 para 18 Sec 230(7)

8.1.14 Where the accounting period of a principal subsidiary is of a different length from that of the holding company, is the accounting period involved stated?

    SSAP 14 para 18

8.1.15 Where a subsidiary has been purchased, has the purchase consideration been allocated between the underlying net tangible and intangible assets (other than goodwill) on the basis of fair value to the acquiring company?

    SSAP 14 para 29

8.1.16 If this is not done by means of adjusting the values in the books of the acquired company, has it been done on consolidation?

    SSAP 14 para 29

Note: Any difference between the purchase consideration and the fair value ascribed to net tangible assets and identifiable intangible assets (e.g. trade marks, patents or development expenditure) will represent premium or discount on acquisition. See also steps 4.4.6 to 4.4.12.

8.1.17 In the case of material additions to, or disposals from, the group, do the consolidated financial statements contain sufficient information about the results of the subsidiaries acquired or sold to enable shareholders to appreciate the effect on the consolidated results?

    SSAP 14 para 30

	Reference

8.1.18 Where there is a material disposal, does the consolidated profit and loss account include: — SSAP 14 para 31

(a) The subsidiary's results up to the date of disposal?

(b) The gain or loss on the sale of the investment (that is, the difference, at the time of the sale, between the proceeds of the sale and the holding company's share of the subsidiary's net assets together with any premium (less any amounts written off) or discount on acquisition)?

8.1.19 Has the effective date for either the acquisition or the disposal of a subsidiary been taken as the earlier of the date on which consideration passes and the date on which an offer becomes or is declared unconditional? — SSAP 14 para 32

Note: This applies irrespective of whether the acquiring company has the right under the agreement to share in profits from an earlier date.

8.1.20 Have outside or minority interests in the share capital and reserves of subsidiaries consolidated been disclosed as a separate amount in the consolidated balance sheet, and not shown as part of shareholders' funds? — SSAP 14 para 34

8.1.21 Are debit balances recognised only if there is a binding obligation on minority shareholders to make good losses incurred, and they are able to meet this obligation? — SSAP 14 para 34

8.1.22 Have the profits or losses attributable to outside or minority interests been shown separately in the consolidated profit and loss account after arriving at the group profit or loss after tax but before extraordinary items? — SSAP 14 para 35

8.1.23 Have minority interests in extraordinary items been deducted from the related amounts in the consolidated profit and loss account? — SSAP 14 para 35

8.1.24 Is the extent of any significant restrictions on the ability of the holding company to distribute the retained profits of the group (other than those shown as non-distributable) disclosed? — SSAP 14 para 36

8.2 Subsidiaries excluded from consolidation

8.2.1 Where a subsidiary is excluded from consolidation because of dissimilar activities (step 8.1.2(a)), do the group accounts include separate financial statements for that subsidiary? — SSAP 14 para 23

8.2.2 Do these separate financial statements include the following: — SSAP 14 para 23

(a) A note of the holding company's interest?

(b) Particulars of intra-group balances?

(c) The nature of transactions with the rest of the group?

(d) A reconciliation with the amount included in the consolidated financial statements for the group's investment in the subsidiary (which should be stated under the equity method of accounting)?

Note: Separate financial statements of subsidiaries with similar operations may be combined if appropriate.

		Reference
8.2.3	Where a subsidiary is excluded from consolidation because of lack of effective control (step 8.1.2(b)), is it dealt with in the consolidated financial statements on one of the following bases:	SSAP 14 para 24
	(a) Under the equity method of accounting if, in all other respects, it satisfies the criteria for treatment as an associated company under SSAP 1?	
	(b) If the criteria are not met, as an investment at cost or valuation less any provision required?	
8.2.4	Where a subsidiary is excluded from consolidation because of severe restrictions (step 8.1.2(c)), is the amount of the group's investment in the subsidiary stated in the consolidated balance sheet at the amount at which it would have been included under the equity method of accounting at the date the restrictions came into force?	SSAP 14 para 25
8.2.5	In respect of the type of subsidiary described in step 8.2.4, have no further accruals been made for its profits or losses?	SSAP 14 para 25
8.2.6	If the amount at which the investment in step 8.2.4 is stated has been impaired by a permanent diminution in value of the investment, has provision for the loss been made through the consolidated profit and loss account?	SSAP 14 para 25
8.2.7	When determining any necessary provision for step 8.2.6, were investments considered individually and not in aggregate?	SSAP 14 para 25
8.2.8	Where a subsidiary is excluded from consolidation because of severe restrictions (step 8.1.2(c)), are the following disclosed in the group accounts:	SSAP 14 para 26
	(a) Its net assets?	
	(b) Its profits or losses for the period?	
	(c) Any amounts included in the consolidated profit and loss account in respect of:	
	(i) Dividends received? (ii) Writing down of the investment?	
8.2.9	Where a subsidiary is excluded from consolidation because control is intended to be only temporary (step 8.1.2(d)), is the temporary investment in the subsidiary stated in the consolidated balance sheet as a current asset at the lower of cost and net realisable value?	SSAP 14 para 27
8.2.10	In respect of subsidiaries excluded from consolidation, are the following disclosed in the group accounts:	SSAP 14 para 28 4 Sch 69(2) (3)
	(a) The reasons for excluding the subsidiaries?	
	(b) The names of the principal subsidiaries excluded?	
	(c) Any premium or discount on acquisition (see step 8.1.16) to the extent that it is not written off?	
	(d) A statement of any qualifications in the auditors' reports on the subsidiaries' financial statements for the year ending with or during the year of the company that are material from the point of view of members of the company?	
	(e) The aggregate amount of the total investment in the subsidiaries under the equity method of valuation?	

	Reference

(f) If the information required by any one of (a), (d) or (e) above is not obtainable, a statement to that effect? — 4 Sch 69(5)

Notes:
(a)The information required in (d) above should include details of any notes to the subsidiaries' financial statements without which the auditors' report would have been qualified. — 4 Sch 69(2)

(b) The information in (e) is not required where the company is the wholly-owned subsidiary of another company incorporated in Great Britain, and a note to the financial statements includes a statement that, in the opinion of the directors, the value of the company's interests in the subsidiaries is not less than the amount at which the interests are stated in the balance sheet. — 4 Sch 69(4)

8.3 Group accounts other than consolidated financial statements

8.3.1 Where group accounts are not prepared as consolidated financial statements, do they give the same or equivalent information as that required to be given in consolidated financial statements? — 4 Sch 68

8.3.2 Is there a description of the bases on which subsidiaries have been dealt with in the group accounts? — SSAP 14 para 15

8.3.3 Where a group prepares group accounts in a form other than consolidated financial statements in circumstances different from those set out in step 8.1.2, have the directors justified and stated their reasons for reaching the conclusion that the resulting group accounts give a fairer view of the financial position of the group as a whole? — SSAP 14 para 22

8.4 Subsidiaries excluded from group accounts

8.4.1 Where a subsidiary has been excluded from group accounts for one of the reasons permitted by Sec 229(3) (step 8.1.1), do the resulting financial statements give a true and fair view of the position of the group as a whole? — SSAP 14 para 20

8.4.2 In respect of subsidiaries excluded from group accounts, is the information required by step 8.2.10(a), (d), (e) and (f) disclosed? — 4 Sch 69

8.5 Group accounts not prepared

Where a holding company does not prepare group accounts, is the information required by step 8.2.10(a), (d), (e) and (f) disclosed? — 4 Sch 69

8.6 Acquisition and merger accounting

8.6.1 Do the financial statements of the acquiring or issuing company which deal with the period in which the combination takes place disclose the following: — SSAP 23 para 21

(a) The names of the combining companies?

(b) The number and class of the securities issued in respect of the combination?

(c) Details of any other consideration given?

	Reference

(d) The accounting treatment adopted for the business combination (that is, whether it has been accounted for as an acquisition or as a merger)?

(e) The nature and amount of significant accounting adjustments by the combining companies to achieve consistency of accounting policies?

Note: The above information should be disclosed in respect of all business combinations, whether accounted for as acquisitions or as mergers.

8.6.2 Do the consolidated financial statements disclose the following in respect of all material acquisitions during the year: **SSAP 23 para 22**

(a) Sufficient information about the results of subsidiaries acquired to enable shareholders to appreciate the effect on the consolidated results?

(b) The date from which the results of major acquisitions have been brought into the accounts (that is, the effective date of those acquisitions)?

8.6.3 Do the financial statements of the issuing company disclose the following in respect of all material mergers during the year: **SSAP 23 para 23**

(a) The fair value of the consideration that the issuing company gave?

(b) An analysis of the current year's attributable profit before extraordinary items between that before and that after the effective date of the merger?

(c) An analysis of the attributable profit before extraordinary items of the current year up to the effective date of the merger between that of the issuing company and that of the subsidiary?

(d) An analysis of the attributable profit before extraordinary items of the previous year between that of the issuing company and that of the subsidiary?

(e) An analysis of extraordinary items so as to indicate:

(i) Whether each individual extraordinary item relates to pre-merger or post-merger?
(ii) To which party to the merger the item relates?

8.7 Merger relief

8.7.1 If during the year the company entered into an arrangement to which Sec 131(2) applied, are the following disclosed: **4 Sch 75(1)**

(a) The name of the company acquired?

(b) The number, the nominal value and the class of shares allotted for the acquisition?

(c) The number, the nominal value and the class of shares the acquired company issued or transferred to the company, or cancelled, as part of the arrangement?

(d) Particulars of the accounting treatment that the company adopted in respect of the issue, transfer or cancellation referred to in (c)?

Reference

(e) Where the company prepares group accounts, particulars of the extent to which, and the manner in which, the group profit or loss for the year is affected by any profit or loss of the acquired company (and any of its subsidiaries) that arose before the allotment?

Note: Where shares are allotted on different dates, the time of allotment will be one of the following:

(a) Where the other company becomes a subsidiary, the date on which the fulfilment of a condition in the arrangement makes it binding, or, where there is no such condition, the date on which the other company becomes a subsidiary.

(b) Where the other company is a subsidiary when the arrangement is proposed, the date of the first allotment that is made in accordance with that arrangement.

8.7.2   If during the year, or during either of the two immediately preceding years, the company entered into an arrangement to which Sec 131(2) applied, is there disclosure of any amounts in (a) to (c) below that are included in the company's consolidated profit and loss account (or, where consolidated financial statements are not prepared, in its own profit and loss account):   **4Sch75(2)(3)**

(a) The net amount of any profit or loss that the company (or any of its subsidiaries) realised on the disposal of shares in the acquired company?

(b) The net amount of any profit or loss that the company (or any of its subsidiaries) realised on the disposal of any assets that were fixed assets of the acquired company (or any of its subsidiaries) at the date of the acquisition and that were subsequently transferred to the company (or any of its subsidiaries)?

(c) Any net profit or loss (or part thereof) that the company (or any of its subsidiaries) realised on the disposal of shares in a company (X) other than the acquired company where the amount was attributable to the fact that, at the time of the disposal, the assets of X (or any of its subsidiaries) included one or both of the following:

(i) Shares in the acquired company?
(ii) Assets that had been fixed assets of the acquired company (or any of its subsidiaries) at the date of the acquisition but which had been subsequently transferred to X (or one of its subsidiaries)?

8.7.3   Where any amount is disclosed under step 8.7.2, is there an explanation of the transaction that gave rise to the amount?   **4 Sch 75(2)**

565

Model set of Financial Statements under UK GAAP

The financial statements that follow are the consolidated financial statements of the GAAP UK plc group of companies.

These financial statements, prepared under Schedule 4 to the Companies Act 1985, illustrate the more common disclosure requirements of the Act. They also include many of the disclosure requirements contained in Statements of Standard Accounting Practice, The Stock Exchange's Continuing Obligations for listed companies and The Stock Exchange's General Undertaking for companies traded on the USM.

The suggested disclosure throughout is intended for guidance only, and would not necessarily be applicable to all groups of companies.

The abbreviations used in this Appendix are notated in the same way as they have been throughout the book, except that the notation for a 'Section' of the Companies Act 1985 is 's'. All of the references given in the Appendix are discussed in detail elsewhere in the book. The Table of legislation and of other regulations indicates where in this book these references are considered. In many places it would be misleading to give a specific example of wording. Consequently, in these situations a description of the requirements is given in italics.

GAAP UK plc
Report and Financial Statements
For the year ended 31 December 1985

Contents

Directors' Report

---

s 235
:   The directors present their report and the consolidated financial statements of GAAP UK plc for the year ended 31 December 1985.

Principal activities and business review

This review should include:

s 235(2)
:   (a) *A description of the principal activities of the company and its subsidiaries during the year and of any significant changes in those activities.*

s 235(1)(a)
:   (b) *A fair review of the development of the company's and its subsidiaries' business during the year and of their position at the end of the year.*

7 Sch 6(b)
:   (c) *An indication of likely future developments in the business of the company and its subsidiaries.*

Results and dividends

s 235(1)(b)
:   The profit for the year after taxation and extraordinary items amounted to £   . It is recommended that this amount be dealt with as follows:

                                                                £

    Preference dividends
    Ordinary dividends- Interim paid
                     Final proposed
    Transfer to reserves   £
                                                                _____

    The directors recommend a final dividend of   p per ordinary share.

CO 21(b)
GU 10(b)
:   *This section must include (where applicable) an explanation of any material difference between the trading results and any published forecast made by the company.*

Post-balance-sheet events

7 Sch 6(a)
:   *Particulars of any important events affecting the company and its subsidiaries that have occurred since the end of the year must be given.*

Research and development

7 Sch 6(c)
:   *The report must include an indication of any activities of the company and its subsidiaries in the field of research and development.*

Significant changes in fixed assets

7 Sch 1(1)
:   *Particulars have to be given of any significant changes in the fixed assets of the company and its subsidiaries during the year.*

Market value of land and buildings

7 Sch 1(2) *If, in the directors' opinion, the difference between the book amount and the market value of land and buildings is of such significance that it should be drawn to the members' and debenture holders' attention, it must be disclosed.*

Directors

s 235(2) *The names must be given of persons who were directors of the company at any time during the year.*

Custom *This section will also probably include the director's title (for example, chairman, managing director), changes in the board of directors since the end of the year and the rotation of directors at the annual general meeting.*

Directors' service contracts

CO 43(c) The unexpired period of the service contract of each director of the company proposed for re-election at the annual general meeting is as follows:

Unexpired period

Name of director
OR

There are no directors' service contracts in existence.

Directors' interests in shares and debentures

7 Sch 2(1)
(2)
CO 21(h)

The directors of the company who held office at 31 December 1985 had the following interests in (including options to subscribe for) the shares and the debentures of group companies:

Name of and description of shares or debentures	31 December 1985		31 December 1984 (or date of appointment if later)	
	No. of Shares	Debentures £	No. of Shares	Debentures £

Name of each director

CO 21(h)
GU 10(h)

Beneficial
  interests
Non-beneficial
  interests

7 Sch 2(3) *The particulars set out above may alternatively be included in the notes to the financial statements.*

CO 21(h)
GU 10(h)

Between 31 December 1985 and (*a date not more than one month prior to the date of the notice of the meeting*) there have been the following changes in the interests of the directors in the shares of the company:

OR

Between 31 December 1985 and (*a date not more than one month prior to the date of the notice of the meeting*) there have been no changes in the interests of the directors in the shares of the company.

Substantial shareholders

CO 21(i)
GU 10(i)

On (*a date not more than one month prior to the date of the notice of the meeting*), the following were interested in 5% or more of the company's ordinary share capital:

	Number of shares	Percentage
Name		

OR

As at (*a date not more than one month prior to the date of the notice of the meeting*), no person has reported to the company an interest in 5% or more of its ordinary share capital.

Contracts of significance with corporate substantial shareholders

CO 21(c)

Particulars must be given of any contract of significance between the company or one of its subsidiaries and any corporate substantial shareholder.

Acquisition of the company's own shares

7 Sch 8

The report should include in respect of purchases during the year:

(a) *The number and the nominal value of shares purchased.*
(b) *The percentage of the called-up capital that shares of the description purchased represent.*
(c) *The aggregate consideration paid.*
(d) *The reasons for the purchase.*

7 Sch 8

The report should include in respect of other acquisitions by the company, and of acquisitions by persons with financial assistance from the company where the company has a beneficial interest in those shares:

(a) *The maximum number and the nominal value of shares acquired that were held at any time during the year.*
(b) *The number and the nominal value of shares acquired that were either disposed of or cancelled during the year.*
(c) *The consideration received in respect of disposals during the year where the shares involved were originally acquired either for money or money's worth.*
(d) *The percentage of the called-up capital that shares of the description acquired or charged represent.*
(e) *The amount of any charge.*

CO 21(p) *Details should also be included of particulars of any shareholders' authority for the purchase by the company of its own shares existing at the end of the year. For such purchases made otherwise than through the market or by tender or by partial offer to all shareholders, the names of the sellers of the shares purchased should be given also.*
For such purchases, or options or contracts to make such purchases that have been entered into since the end of the year covered by this report, the equivalent information to that required by paragraph 8 of Schedule 7 to the Act (detailed above) must be disclosed.

Charitable and political contributions

7 Sch 3 During the year, the group has made the following contributions:

United Kingdom charitable organisations   £
                                                    _____

                                                           £

United Kingdom political organisations
    (*state name of party concerned*)
Individuals (*state names*)
Total of other contributions
    under £200 each   _____

                                                           £
                                                    _____

The details outlined above are not required if charitable and political contributions in the UK do not exceed £200 in aggregate.

Employment of disabled persons

7 Sch 9 *A statement must be given of the company's policy in respect of*:

(a) *Applications for employment from disabled persons.*
(b) *Employees who become disabled.*
(c) *The training, career development and promotion of disabled persons.*

This statement is not required, however, if the company employs on average 250 or fewer persons in the UK.

Employee involvement

7 Sch 11 *The report should describe the action that the company has taken during the year to introduce, maintain or develop arrangements aimed at employee involvement. However, this statement is not required if the company employs on average 250 or fewer persons in the UK.*

Taxation status

CO 21(j) The company is not a close company within the provisions of the Income
GU 10(j) and Corporation Taxes Act 1970.

Auditors

Custom   In accordance with Section 384 of the Companies Act 1985, a resolution proposing the reappointment of (*name*) as auditors to the company will be put to the annual general meeting.

BY ORDER OF THE BOARD

Name

Secretary

Date

Auditors' Report
To the members of GAAP UK plc

Auditing
Standard
102

We have audited the financial statements on pages   to   in accordance with approved Auditing Standards.

s 236
SSAP 10

In our opinion the financial statements give a true and fair view of the state of affairs of the company and the group at 31 December 1985 and of the profit and source and application of funds of the group for the year then ended and comply with the Companies Act 1985.

Name

Chartered Accountants

Address

Date

s 237(2)(4)

The auditors must state the relevant facts in their audit report where they are of the opinion that:

(a) *The company has not kept proper accounting records.*

(b) *They have not received adequate returns from branches they did not visit.*

(c) *The financial statements are not in agreement with the accounting records and returns.*

(d) *They have not obtained all the information and explanations they considered necessary for their audit.*

s 237(5)

Where the relevant details are not disclosed in the financial statements, the auditors must include in their report, so far as they are able to do so, a statement that gives the required particulars of:

(a) *Emoluments of directors.*

(b) *Emoluments of higher-paid employees.*

(c) *Transactions with directors and officers.*

s 237(6)

If the auditors are of the opinion that the information relating to the year given in the directors' report is not consistent with the financial statements, they must state that fact in their audit report.

s 271(3)

Where the auditors qualify their audit report, and the company proposes to pay a dividend, they will have to state in writing whether the subject matter of their qualification is material in determining whether the company can lawfully make the proposed distribution. (They could give this additional statement to the members of the company as a separate statement. But that statement would have to be laid before the company at a general meeting.)

Statement of Accounting Policies

4 Sch 36
SSAP 2
para 18

The accounting policies that the group has adopted to determine the amounts included in respect of material items shown in the balance sheet, and also to determine the profit or loss are shown below.

This will probably include accounting policies in respect of:

Basis of accounting

The basis of accounting adopted (namely, historical cost, or modified historical cost, or current cost).

Basis of consolidation

SSAP 14
SSAP 23
para 21
4 Sch 69,
70

The basis of consolidation (for example, whether acquisition accounting or merger accounting or a combination of these methods is used, whether all subsidiaries are consolidated, whether all subsidiaries prepare their accounts to the same date as the holding company, whether uniform accounting policies are adopted by all companies in the group). The treatment of subsidiaries acquired or disposed of during the year.

SSAP 22
para 39

The treatment of goodwill arising on consolidation.

Associated companies and related companies

SSAP 1
para 18

The definition and treatment of associated companies. Whether such companies are related companies as defined in paragraph 92 of Schedule 4 and whether there are any other related companies.

Research and development

4 Sch 20(2)
SSAP 13
para 29

The fact that research expenditure is written off in the year of expenditure. The basis and the reasons for capitalising development costs, or the fact that development costs are written off in the year of expenditure, and the period over which they are being written off.

Intangible fixed assets (excluding goodwill)

4 Sch 17, 18
SSAP12
para 22

The basis for capitalising patents and trade marks and the amortisation policy adopted.

Purchased goodwill

4 Sch 21(4)
SSAP 22
paras 39, 41

The treatment of purchased goodwill. If purchased goodwill is capitalised, the period over which it is being written off, and the directors' reasons for choosing that period.

Tangible fixed assets

4 Sch 17,
18, 19
SSAP 12
para 22

The basis on which tangible fixed assets are stated (normally cost or valuation, less depreciation), the depreciation policy adopted and the rates of depreciation used. The treatment of permanent diminutions in value of fixed assets.

Investment properties

SSAP 19   *The basis on which investment properties are included in the balance sheet.*

Leased assets and obligations

SSAP 21
para 57   *For lessees, the policy adopted for accounting for operating leases and finance leases. This disclosure should include also the equivalent policies in respect of hire purchase contracts that have characteristics similar to leases. (If part of the group's business was that of a lessor, then its policy for accounting for operating leases and finance leases would need to be given. These model financial statements do not deal with the accounting disclosure required by SSAP 21 for lessors.)*

Government grants

SSAP 4
para 9   *The treatment of Government grants.*

Fixed asset investments

4 Sch 19   *The basis on which fixed asset investments are stated. The treatment of any temporary or permanent diminutions in value of fixed asset investments.*

Stocks and long-term contracts

SSAP 9
para 28   *The bases that have been used to determine the balance sheet value. In particular, the bases used to calculate cost, net realisable value, attributable profit and foreseeable losses.*

Deferred taxation

SSAP 15   *The basis and the method for providing deferred taxation.*

Contributions to pension funds

Best practice
SOI
'Accounting
for pension
costs' para
1.70   *The nature of the pension schemes. Whether they are externally funded or internally financed. The accounting policy, and the funding policy if different from the accounting policy, indicating the basis on which amounts are charged to the profit and loss account. The policy in respect of any deficiency revealed by an actuarial valuation.*

Foreign currency amounts

4 Sch 58(1)
SSAP 20
para 50   *The basis of translating amounts denominated in foreign currencies. The basis of translating the financial statements of overseas subsidiaries. The treatment of translation differences.*

Turnover

4 Sch 95
SSAP 5
para 8   *The basis on which turnover is stated.*

Departures from Accounting Standards

CO 21(a)
GU 10(a)

If any of the above accounting policies represent a significant departure from standard accounting practice, the directors' reasons for the departure must be given in the directors' report.

Consolidated Profit and Loss Account
For the year ended 31 December 1985

Based on the profit and loss account format 1 shown in Schedule 4 to the Companies Act 1985.

		Notes	1985 £	1984 £
	Turnover	2		
4 Sch Note 14	Cost of sales		——	——
	Gross profit			
4 Sch Note 14	Other operating expenses	3	——	——
	Trading profit			
SSAP 1 para 19	Share of results of associated companies			
	Investment income	5		
	Amounts written off investments	6		
	Interest payable	7	——	——
4 Sch 3(6)	Profit on ordinary activities before taxation	8		
	Taxation	9	——	——
	Profit on ordinary activities after taxation			
SSAP 14 para 35	Minority interests		——	——
	Profit before extraordinary items			
SSAP 6 para 15	Extraordinary items	10	——	——
	Profit for the financial year	11		
4 Sch 3(7) (b)	Dividends	12	——	——
4 Sch 3(7)(a)	Retained profit for year		£	£

SSAP 3 paras 14, 15	**Earnings per share**	13		
	Net basis		——p	——p
	Nil basis		——p	——p
	Fully diluted		——p	——p

SSAP 6 para 16	**Statement of retained profits for the year ended 31 December 1985**			
	Retained profits at 1 January 1985 As previously reported			
	Prior-year adjustment	14	——	——
	As restated			
	Retained profit for year			
	Transfer from revaluation reserve	25	——	——
	Retained profits at 31 December 1985	25	£	£

Balance Sheets
At 31 December 1985

Based on the balance sheet format 1 shown in Schedule 4 to the Companies Act 1985.

		Notes	Group 1985 £	Group 1984 £	Company 1985 £	Company 1984 £
Fixed Assets						
Intangible assets		15				
Tangible assets		16				
Investments		17				
Current Assets						
Stocks		19				
Debtors		20				
Investments		21				
Cash at bank and in hand						
Current Liabilities						
Creditors: amounts falling due within one year		22				
4 Sch Note 11	Net Current Assets					
Total Assets less Current Liabilities						
Creditors: amounts falling due after more than one year (including loans)		22				
Provisions for liabilities and charges						
SSAP 15 para 25	Deferred taxation	23				
Net Assets			£	£	£	£
Capital and Reserves						
Called-up share capital		24				
Share premium account		25				
Revaluation reserve		25				
Other reserves		25				
Profit and loss account		25				
Shareholders' funds						
SSAP 14 para 34	Minority interests					
			£	£	£	£

SSAP 17
para 26

The financial statements on pages   to   were approved by the board of directors on (*date*) and were signed on its behalf by:

Name ⎫
         ⎬   Directors
Name ⎭

Appendix II

Consolidated Statement of Source and Application of Funds
For the year ended 31 December 1985

	1985 £	1984 £
Source of Funds		
Profit on ordinary activities before taxation less minority interests		
Extraordinary items before taxation		
Adjustments for items not involving the movement of funds:		
Depreciation and amounts written off fixed assets		
Profit on disposals of fixed assets		
Exchange differences on consolidation		
Minority interests in retained profits		
Profits retained in associated companies		
Total funds generated from operations		
Funds from other sources		
Proceeds of disposals of tangible fixed assets		
Proceeds of disposals of fixed asset investments		
Shares issued in part consideration of the acquisition of a subsidiary*		
Total source of funds		
Application of Funds		
Development costs incurred		
Purchase of tangible fixed assets*		
Purchase of goodwill on acquisition of subsidiary*		
Purchase of fixed asset investments		
Loan repayments		
Tax paid		
Dividends paid by parent company		
Dividends paid to minority shareholders		
Total application of funds		
Net source of funds	£	£
The net source of funds is represented by the following increase in working capital:		
Stocks*		
Debtors*		
Creditors falling due within one year*		
Movements in net liquid funds:		
Current asset investments		
Cash at bank and in hand		
Bank overdraft*		
Increase in working capital	£	£

*See Note 32 for a summary of the effect of the acquisition of the subsidiary.

580

Notes to the Financial Statements
For the year ended 31 December 1985

s 228(7)   1.   As permitted by Section 228(7) of the Companies Act 1985, the holding company's profit and loss account has not been included in these financial statements.

2. **Turnover and profit on ordinary activities before taxation**

		Turnover		Profit on ordinary activities before taxation	
		1985 £	1984 £	1985 £	1984 £
4 Sch 55 (1)(4)	*Description of classes of business*				
		£	£	£	£
4 Sch 55 (2)(4) CO 21(c) GU 10(c)	*Geographical markets supplied*				
		£	£	£	£

OR

The analysis of turnover by geographical market and the analysis of turnover and profit before taxation by class of business has not been given.

SSAP 14   As a result of the acquisition of a material subsidiary, turnover
para 30   increased by £   and the profit on ordinary activities before taxation increased by £

3. **Other operating expenses**

		1985 £	1984 £
4 Sch Format 1	Distribution costs		
	Administrative expenses		
	Other operating income		
		£	£

4. **Directors and employees**

Employees

4 Sch 54(1)   The average weekly number of persons (including directors) employed by the group during the year was:

	1985 Number	1984 Number
Categories		

	1985 £	1984 £

4 Sch 56(4), 94   Staff costs (for the above persons):
Wages and salaries
Social security costs
Other pension costs

	£	£

Higher-paid employees

5 Sch 35   The number of senior employees of GAAP UK plc, other than directors, who received remuneration (excluding pension contributions) in the following ranges was:

	1985 Number	1984 Number
£30,001 — £35,000		
£35,001 — £40,000		
etc.		

Directors' remuneration

5 Sch 22   The remuneration paid to the directors of GAAP UK plc was:

	1985 £	1984 £
Fees		
Other emoluments (including pension contributions and benefits in kind)		
Pensions paid to former directors		
Compensation for loss of office		
	£	£

5 Sch 24, 25(3)   Fees and other emoluments disclosed above (excluding pension contributions) include amounts paid to:

	1985	1984
The chairman	£	£
The highest-paid director	£	£

5 Sch 25(2), 26	The number of directors (including the chairman and the highest-paid director) who received fees and other emoluments (excluding pension contributions) in the following ranges was:

	1985 Number	1984 Number
£0 — £5,000		
£5,001 — £10,000		
etc.		

5 Sch 27 CO 21(n) GU 10(k)	Emoluments amounting to £ (1984: £) have been waived by (*number*) (1984: *number*) directors.

5. Investment income

	1985 £	1984 £
Income from fixed asset investments		
Income from current asset investments		
Other interest receivable		
	£	£

4 Sch 53(4)	Income from investments includes £ (1984: £) from listed investments.

6. Amounts written off investments

		1985 £	1984 £
4 Sch 19(1) (2)	Amounts written off fixed asset investments as a result of:		
	A permanent diminution in value		
	A temporary diminution in value		
4 Sch 23(1)	Amounts written off current asset investments		
4 Sch 19(3), 23(2)	Amounts written off fixed asset or current asset investments in prior years written back as no longer necessary:		
	Fixed assets		
	Current assets		
		£	£

7. Interest payable

4 Sch 53(2)	On bank loans, overdrafts and other loans:		
	Repayable within 5 years, not by instalments		
	Repayable within 5 years, by instalments		
	Repayable wholly or partly in more than 5 years		
SSAP 21 para 53	On finance leases and hire purchase contracts		
		£	£

8. **Profit on ordinary activities before taxation**

		1985	1984
		£	£

Profit on ordinary activities before taxation is stated after crediting:

4 Sch 53(5)   Rents receivable (net of outgoings)

And after charging:

4 Sch 18, 19 (2), Note 17 SSAP 21 para 50
Depreciation of assets and amounts written off assets as a result of a permanent diminution in their value:
Depreciation charge for the year:
— intangible fixed assets
— tangible owned fixed assets
— tangible fixed assets held under finance leases and hire purchase contracts

Amounts written off fixed assets as a result of a permanent diminution in their value

4 Sch 19(3)   Amounts written off fixed assets in prior years written back as no longer necessary

4 Sch 57(3) SSAP 6 para 14
Exceptional item:
Provision made against a major contract

4 Sch 53(7)   Auditors' remuneration (including expenses)

4 Sch 53(6) SSAP 21 para 55
Hire of plant and machinery — operating leases
Hire of other assets — operating leases

4 Sch 53(6)   Amounts charged to revenue in respect of sums payable for the hire of plant and machinery under finance leases and hire purchase contracts are shown above separately under the headings of depreciation £   and finance charges £   — total £   (1984: £   ) (see note 7).

9. **Taxation**

		1985	1984
		£	£

4 Sch 54	UK corporation tax at %:
SSAP 8	Current
para 12	Deferred
SSAP 15	Tax credits on franked investment income
para 33	Irrecoverable advance corporation tax
	Double taxation relief
	Overseas taxation
	Under-provision in respect of prior years:
	Current
	Deferred
SSAP 1	Associated companies
para 20	

£   £

SSAP 15	The taxation charge for the year has been reduced by £ (1984:
para 35	£) in respect of the excess of tax allowances over depreciation, and other timing differences on which, in accordance with the group's accounting policy, no deferred taxation has been provided.

10. **Extraordinary items**

		1985	1984
		£	£

4 Sch	Extraordinary income:
format 1	Surplus on disposal of freehold land and
SSAP 6	buildings including £ transferred
para 15	from the revaluation reserve (see note 25)
	Share of associated company's extraordinary income
SSAP 1	Extraordinary charges:
para 21	Closure costs
	Extraordinary profit
4 Sch 54(3)	Taxation on the above:
	UK corporation tax at %:
	Current
	Deferred

£   £

11. **Profit for the financial year**

s 228(7)	Dealt with in the accounts of the holding
SSAP 1	company
para 22	Retained by subsidiary companies
	Retained by associated companies

£   £

12. **Dividends**

	1985 £	1984 £
Preference paid		
Ordinary:		
Interim paid of p per share		
Final proposed of p per share	___	___
	£	£

CO 21(o)
GU 10(l)

Particulars must also be given where there are any arrangements under which a shareholder has waived, or agreed to waive, any dividends.

13. **Earnings per ordinary share**

SSAP 3 paras
14, 16,
Appendix 1
para 31

The calculation of earnings per share on the net basis is based on the profit on ordinary activities after taxation but before extraordinary items and after deducting preference dividends, namely, £   (1984: £   ) and on (*number*) (1984: *number*) ordinary shares, being the weighted average number of ordinary shares in issue and ranking for dividend during the year.

The calculation of earnings per share on the nil basis is based on adjusted profits of £   (1984: £   ), after adding irrecoverable advance corporation tax, and on (*number*) (1984: *number*) ordinary shares.

The calculation of fully diluted earnings per ordinary share is based on (*number*) (1984: *number*) ordinary shares, allowing for the full exercise of outstanding share purchase options (see note 24), and adjusted profit of £   (1984: £   ), after adding interest deemed to be earned from investing the proceeds of such share options in 2½% Consolidated Stock.

14. **Prior-year adjustment**

SSAP 6
para 16
SSAP 22
para 36

During the financial year, the group changed its accounting policy regarding the treatment of goodwill in its financial statements. In accordance with SSAP 22, the group now amortises goodwill on consolidation to the profit and loss account over its estimated useful economic life. Consequently, the group wrote off goodwill of £   to reserves. £   of this balance arose in 1984, and the corresponding profit and loss results and balance sheet figures have been adjusted accordingly.

15. Intangible fixed assets

		Development costs £	Patents and trademarks £	Goodwill on consolidation £	Total £
	Group				

SSAP 13 para 17 4 Sch Note 3	Cost 1 January 1985 Exchange differences Additions Disposals At 31 December 1985				
4 Sch 42(3)	Amounts written off At 1 January 1985 Exchange differences Charge for the year Eliminated in respect of disposals				
	At 31 December 1985				
	Net book value				
	At 31 December 1985	£	£	£	£
	At 31 December 1984	£	£	£	£

If GAAP UK plc owned any intangible fixed assets, similar information would be required in respect of those assets.

s 269   *Where appropriate, the note should include a statement that capitalised development costs have not been treated as a realised loss, and the special circumstances that the directors have relied upon.*

16. Tangible fixed assets

		Investment properties £	Land and buildings £	Plant and machinery £	Fixtures fittings tools and equipment £	Total £
	Group					
4 Sch 42(1)	Cost or valuation At 1 January 1985 Exchange differences Surplus on revaluation Additions In respect of new subsidiary Disposals At 31 December 1985					

4 Sch 42(3)

Depreciation
At 1 January 1985
Exchange differences
Adjustment on
revaluation
In respect of new
subsidiary
Charge for the year
Provision for
diminution in value
Eliminated in respect
of disposals
At 31 December 1985

Net book value

At 31 December 1985 £   £   £   £   £

At 31 December 1984 £   £   £   £   £

Cost or valuation at 31 December
1985 is represented by:
Valuation in *year*
Cost

£   £   £   £   £

Where a company has made payments on account of tangible fixed assets or is in the course of constructing tangible fixed assets, it must show the amounts involved in a separate column.

SSAP 21
para 50

The net book value of tangible fixed assets includes an amount of £   (1984: £   ) in respect of assets held under finance leases and hire purchase contracts.

4 Sch 33(2),
43
SSAP 19
para 12

Investment properties were revalued at their open market value at 31 December 1985 by (*name*), a director of the subsidiary that owns the investment properties.

s 228
SSAP 19
paras 11, 13

In accordance with SSAP 19, investment properties are revalued annually and the aggregate surplus or deficit is transferred to the revaluation reserve. Depreciation is not provided in respect of freehold investment properties, and leasehold investment properties where the unexpired term of the lease is more than 20 years. The directors consider that this accounting policy results in the financial statements giving a true and fair view. Depreciation is only one of the many factors reflected in the annual valuation and the amount that might otherwise have been shown cannot be separately identified or quantified.

4 Sch 33(2),
43

Land and buildings in the UK were revalued on the basis of an open market valuation for existing use at 31 December 1985 by (*name*), Chartered Surveyors.

4 Sch 33(3), (4)	If investment properties and land and buildings had not been re-valued they would have been included at the following amounts:

		Investment properties		Land and buildings	
Group		1985	1984	1985	1984
Cost		£	£	£	£
Aggregate depreciation based on cost		£	£	£	£

4 Sch 44   Investment properties and land and buildings at net book value comprise:

	Investment properties		Land and buildings	
	1985	1984	1985	1984
	£	£	£	£
Freeholds				
Long leaseholds				
Short leaseholds				
	£	£	£	£

If GAAP UK plc had any tangible fixed assets, similar information would be required in respect of those assets.

17. Fixed asset investments

Group	Associated companies £	Loans £	Other investments £	Total £
4 Sch 42(1)				
Cost or valuation				
At 1 January 1985				
Additions				
Disposals				
At 31 December 1985				
4 Sch 42(3)				
Amounts written off				
At 1 January 1985				
Amounts written off in the year				
Amounts written off in prior years written back				
Eliminated in respect of disposals				
At 31 December 1985				
Net book value				
At 31 December 1985	£	£	£	£
At 31 December 1984	£	£	£	£

589

		Associated companies		Other investments	
		1985 £	1984 £	1985 £	1984 £

4 Sch 45(1)

Investments at net book value include:

Investments listed on a recognised stock exchange
Other listed investments

		£	£	£	£

Aggregate market value of listed investments

		£	£	£	£

SSAP 1
para 26

Interests in associated companies:
Share of associated companies' net assets (excluding goodwill)
Share of associated companies' goodwill
Premium paid on acquisition of interests in associated companies
Total interests in associated companies

		£	£	£	£

GAAP UK plc

	Subsidiaries £	Associated companies £	Other investments £	Total £

4 Sch 42(1)

Cost or valuation
At 1 January 1985
Surplus on revaluation
Additions
Disposals
At 31 December 1985

4 Sch 42(3)

Amounts written off
At 1 January 1985
Amounts written off in year
Amounts written off in prior years written back
Eliminated in respect of disposals
At 31 December 1985

Net book value

	Subsidiaries £	Associated companies £	Other investments £	Total £
At 31 December 1985	£	£	£	£
At 31 December 1984 £	£	£	£	

4 Sch 31(3), 33(2)

Investments in subsidiaries are stated at the group's share of the net assets of the subsidiaries. The directors have adopted this basis for valuing the investments in subsidiaries because they consider that it more fairly represents the investment of GAAP UK plc in subsidiary companies.

4 Sch 33(3)
(4)

If investments in subsidiaries had not been revalued they would have been included at the following amounts:

	1985 £	1984 £
Cost		
Aggregate amounts written off		
Total	£	£

Listed investments

	Associated companies		Other investments	
	1985 £	1984 £	1985 £	1984 £

4 Sch 45(1)
Investments at net book value include:
Investments listed on a recognised stock exchange
Other listed investments

	£	£	£	£

4 Sch 45(2)
(a)

Listed investments include certain investments for which the market value is considered to be higher than the stock exchange value. The market value of these investments is £   and their stock exchange value £

Group and GAAP UK plc

5 Sch 1, 7
to 9
SSAP 1
para 49
SSAP 14
para 33
CO 21(d)(e)
GU 10(d)(e)

The group holds more than 10% of the equity of the following companies:

	Country of incorporation (or re-registration)	Description of holding	Proportion held
Subsidiary companies			
Names			
Associated companies			
Names			
Other companies			
Names			

5 Sch 10,
11

Where appropriate, a statement that the information given above deals only with those companies whose results principally affect the profit or loss or amount of assets of the group.

The 25% holding in (*Company*) is not treated as an associated company because GAAP UK plc is not in a position to exercise significant influence over that company.

At 31 December 1985, the aggregate capital and reserves of that company was £   (1984: £   ). The profit of that company for the year ended 31 December 1985 was £   (1984: £   ).

18. Capital commitments

		Group		Company	
		1985	1984	1985	1984
4 Sch 50(3)	Capital expenditure that has been contracted for but has not been provided for in the financial statements	£	£	£	£
	Capital expenditure that has been authorised by the directors but has not yet been contracted for	£	£	£	£
SSAP 21 para 54	Commitments under finance leases entered into, but not yet provided for in the financial statements	£	£	£	£

19. Stocks

		Group		Company	
		1985	1984	1985	1984
		£	£	£	£
SSAP 9 paras 29, 30	Stocks comprise: Raw materials and consumables Work in progress Finished goods				
	Long-term contracts Cost plus attributable profit less provision for losses				
4 Sch Note 8	*Less:* Payments received on account				
		£	£	£	£

s 228   In accordance with the provisions of SSAP 9, attributable profit amounting to £   (1984: £   ) has been included in the value of long-term contracts. The inclusion of this attributable profit is a departure from the statutory valuation rules for current assets, but it is required to enable the financial statements to give a true and fair view.

4 Sch 26(3)
CO 21(g)
GU 10(g)   The cost of long-term contracts includes interest amounting to £   (1984: £   ) on capital borrowed to finance production. Payments received on account in excess of the value of the work done on the related contract are included in creditors.

4 Sch 27(3)
(4)

The replacement cost of raw materials and consumables is greater than the balance sheet value of raw materials and consumables by £   (1984: £   ). The replacement cost of work in progress is greater than the balance sheet value of work in progress by £   (1984: £   ).

20. Debtors

	Group 1985 £	Group 1984 £	Company 1985 £	Company 1984 £
Amounts falling due within one year:				
Trade debtors				
Amounts owed by subsidiaries				
Amounts owed by associated companies				
Other debtors				
Prepayments and accrued income				

4 Sch
Note 6

4 Sch
Note 5

Amounts falling due after more than one year:				
Amounts owed by subsidiaries				
Amounts owed by associated companies				
Other debtors				
	£	£	£	£

21. Current asset investments

	Group 1985 £	Group 1984 £	Company 1985 £	Company 1984 £
Investments listed on a recognised stock exchange				
Other listed investments				
	£	£	£	£

4 Sch 45(1)

4 Sch 45(2)
(a)

Listed investments include certain investments for which the market value is considered to be higher than the stock exchange value. The market value of these investments is £   and their stock exchange value £

22. Creditors

		Group		Company	
		1985	1984	1985	1984
		£	£	£	£
	Amounts falling due within one year:				
	Current instalments due on debenture loans				
	Bank overdrafts				
SSAP 21 para 51	Obligations under finance leases				
4 Sch Note 8	Payments received on account				
	Trade creditors				
	Bills of exchange payable				
	Amounts owed to subsidiaries				
	Amounts owed to associated companies				
4 Sch 51 (3)	Dividends payable				
SSAP 8 para 26	Corporation tax				
4 Sch Note 9	Other taxation and social security payable				
	Other creditors				
4 Sch Note 10	Accruals and deferred income				
		£	£	£	£

4 Sch 48(4) Bank overdrafts amounting to £   (1984: £   ) are secured by a floating charge on all the assets of the company.

		Group		Company	
		1985	1984	1985	1984
		£	£	£	£
	Amounts falling due after more than one year:				
	Debenture loans				
	Bank loans				
SSAP 21 para 51	Obligations under finance leases				
	Amounts owed to subsidiaries				
	Amounts owed to associated companies				
	Corporation tax				
		£	£	£	£

Debenture loans

4 Sch 48(1) (4) Repayable otherwise than by instalments in more than five years:

        % first mortgage debenture stock 1995 secured on the land and buildings, repayable at par on 1 April 1995

594

Repayable by instalments:
% debenture stock 1985/92
secured on the land and
buildings, repayable at par by
equal annual instalments
from 1 April 1985.
Instalments amounting to
£   (1984: £   ) are
repayable in more than
five years

	£	£	£	£

CO 21(f)
GU 10(f)

Debenture loans are repayable as
follows:
   In one year or less
   Between one and two years
   Between two and five years
   In five years or more

	£	£	£	£

**Bank loans and obligations under
finance leases**

4 Sch 48(1)
to (4)

Repayable otherwise than by
instalments in more than five
years:
   Bank loans at   % per
annum secured by a floating
charge on all the assets of the
company, repayable on demand
after 1 April 1992
Repayable by instalments:
   Bank loans at   % per
annum repayable in three equal
annual instalments from 1 April
1987
   Finance leases

	£	£	£	£

CO 21(f)
GU 10(f)
SSAP 21
para 52

Bank loans and obligations
under finance leases
are repayable as follows:
   In one year or less, or on demand
   Between one and two years
   Between two and five years
   In five years or more

	£	£	£	£

23. **Deferred taxation**

Deferred taxation provided in the financial statements, and the total potential liability including the amounts for which provision has been made, are as follows:

		Amount provided		Total potential liability	
		1985 £	1984 £	1985 £	1984 £
SSAP 15 paras 37 to 42	**Group** Tax effect of timing differences because of: Excess of tax allowances over depreciation Other				
SSAP 8 para 27	*Less:* Advance corporation tax				
	Tax effect of timing differences on revaluation of: Land and buildings Investment properties				
		£	£	£	£

4 Sch 46(2)   The movements on the group provision for deferred taxation are as follows:

£

Provision at 1 January 1985
Utilised in the year
Transfer from profit and loss account
Provision at 31 December 1985   £

If GAAP UK plc had any deferred taxation, similar information would be required in respect of that deferred taxation.

24. **Called-up share capital**

		1985 £	1984 £
	Authorised		
4 Sch 38(1) (a) SSAP 8 para 28	(*Number*) ordinary shares of p each (*Number*) 10% (now 7% plus tax credit) redeemable preference shares of £1 each		
		£	£

596

	1985	1984
	£	£

Allotted, called up and fully paid

4 Sch 38(1) 　(*Number*) ordinary shares of 　　p each
(b) 　　　　　　(*Number*) 10% (now 7% plus tax credit)
4 Sch 　　　　redeemable preference shares of
Note 12 　　　£1 each
SSAP 8
para 28

	£	£

4 Sch 38(2) 　The 10% (now 7% plus tax credit) redeemable preference shares must be redeemed by three equal annual instalments commencing on 1 January 1987 at a premium of 10p per £1 share.

Allotment during the year

4 Sch 39 　As part of the acquisition of (*name of new subsidiary*), GAAP UK plc made an allotment of (*number*) ordinary shares at p each.

Contingent rights to the allotment of shares

4 Sch 40 　Options have been granted to subscribe for ordinary shares of GAAP UK plc as follows:

Number and description of shares	Subscripton price per share	Period within which options exercisable

Details of directors' interests in shares and debentures of group companies are included in the directors' report.

25. **Share premium account and reserves**

	Share premium account £	Revaluation reserve £	Other reserves £	Profit and loss account £
Group				
4 Sch 46(2)				
At 1 January 1985				
Premium on allotment during the year				
Surplus arising on revaluation of investment properties and land and buildings				
Transfer from revaluation reserve to profit and loss account				
Retained profit for the year				
At 31 December 1985	£	£	£	£

SSAP 1 para 31 — GAAP UK plc and subsidiaries Associated companies

	£	£	£	£

GAAP UK plc

4 Sch 46(2)
At 1 January 1985
Premium on allotment during year
Surplus arising on revaluation of investments in subsidiaries
Retained profit for the year

At 31 December 1985	£	£	£	£

SSAP 19 para 13
The revaluation reserve includes £   (1984: £   ) in respect of surpluses on the annual revaluation of investment properties.

4 Sch 34(4)
No provision has been made for the additional United Kingdom taxation that would accrue if the investment properties, land and buildings or the investments in subsidiaries were disposed of at their revalued amounts. The potential liability to such taxation is disclosed in Note 23.

The transfer from the revaluation reserve to the profit and loss account includes £   transferred to extraordinary items (see note 10) being the realisation of a revaluation surplus on the disposal of freehold land and buildings. The balance of the transfer represents the difference between the depreciation charge for the year based on revalued amounts and the depreciation charge for the year based on cost.

SSAP1
para 31
SSAP 14
para 36
SSAP 15
para 44

Included in the group profit and loss account is an amount of £ (1984: £) in respect of profits retained in (*country*), the remittance of which is subject to approval by the (*country's*) authorities. No deferred taxation has been provided on these earnings as they are not expected to be remitted to the UK in the near future.

Not
statutory

The amount of the reserves of GAAP UK plc that may not legally be distributed under Section 264 of the Companies Act 1985 is £ (1984: £).

26. Contingent liabilities

	Group		Company	
	1985	1984	1985	1984

4 Sch 50(2)
SSAP 18
para 16

Bills discounted with recourse £ £ £ £

4 Sch 50(6)
(b)

Guarantee in respect of bank overdraft of a subsidiary £ £

27. Pension commitments

4 Sch 50(4)

The group has a number of pension funds for its employees. The actuarial valuation by (*name of actuary*) at 31 July 1985 indicated that there were insufficient assets in some of the funds to secure the benefits of existing pensioners and to provide paid-up pensions to present employees on the basis of present salaries and credited periods of service. The group intends to fund this deficiency of £ by paying contributions at an increased rate of 15% of pensionable salaries in accordance with the actuary's recommendations.

The company has annual pension commitments to past directors amounting to £ (1984: £) for which no provision has been made in these financial statements.

28. Other financial commitments

4 Sch 50(5)

GAAP UK plc has agreed to enter into a joint venture with (*name*). The initial contribution to the joint venture will amount to £   . The total contribution to the joint venture is not expected to exceed £

SSAP 21
para 56

At 31 December 1985 the company had annual commitments under non-cancellable operating leases as follows:

	1985 Land and buildings £	Other £	1984 Land and buildings £	Other £
Expiring within one year				
Expiring between two and five years inclusive				
Expiring in over five years				
	£	£	£	£

The majority of the company's leases of land and buildings are subject to rent review periods ranging between three and five years.

29. Subsequent events

SSAP 17
paras 23, 24

On (*date*), a subsidiary's factory was badly damaged by fire. The costs of repair are not expected to exceed insurance proceeds. Accordingly, no provision has been made in these financial statements.

30. Transactions with directors

6 Sch 9

During the year, the company made a loan for house purchase of £   to (*name*), a director, following his transfer to London. The loan is repayable by 24 monthly instalments. The maximum amount outstanding during the year was £   . At 31 December 1985, the amount outstanding (excluding accrued interest) was £   . The amount of interest outstanding at 31 December 1985 was £

31. Transactions with officers

6 Sch 16

Included in other debtors are loans to (*number*) officers amounting to £   and quasi-loans to (*number*) officers amounting to £

600

32. Consolidated statement of source and application of funds

SSAP 10
Appendix 1

The figures in the consolidated statement of source and application of funds include the following amounts that relate to the effect of the acquisition of a subsidiary:

	£	£
Assets acquired:		
Tangible fixed assets		
Stocks		
Debtors		___
Less: Bank overdraft		
Creditors		
Current taxation		
		___
Net assets of subsidiary		___
Less: Minority interest		___
Goodwill		___
Total consideration		£ ___

Discharged by:

	£
Allotment of ordinary shares	
Cash	___
	£ ___

The movement in creditors falling due within one year comprises the following:

	1985 £	1984 £
Current instalments due on loans		
Payments received on account		
Trade creditors		
Bills of exchange payable		
Other taxation and social security payable		
Other creditors		
Accruals and deferred income	___	___
	£ ___	£ ___

Historical Cost Five Year Summary

This statement is not required by statute, but it is customary for listed companies and companies traded on the USM to give this information.

	1985 £	1984 £	1983 £	1982 £	1981 £
Turnover					
Trading profit before interest					
Interest					
Profit on ordinary activities before taxation					
Taxation					
Profit after taxation					
Extraordinary items					
Minority interests and preference dividends					
Profit attributable to the members of the holding company	£	£	£	£	£
Earnings per share	—— p	—— p	—— p	—— p	—— p
Ordinary dividends per share	—— p	—— p	—— p	—— p	—— p
Dividend cover					
Employment of finance:					
Fixed assets					
Net current assets					
Total assets less current liabilities	£	£	£	£	£
Financed by:					
Shareholders' funds					
Minority interests					
Loans					
Provisions					
	£	£	£	£	£
Return on total assets less current liabilities	%	%	%	%	%

Summary of EC Company Law and related Directives

The UK's membership of the European Community has had a significant effect on UK company law. The Council of the European Community has a specific duty to coordinate (or 'harmonize') the company law of the Community to make it equivalent in its effects throughout the Member States (Article 54(g) of the Treaty of Rome). It also has a general duty to issue Directives harmonising the provisions directly affecting the establishing or functioning of the common market laid down in the laws, regulations or by other administrative actions of the Member States (Article 100). The Council has used these powers to introduce a number of measures, some of which have been adopted into Community and national law, whilst others are still under discussion.

The European Community law-making process is lengthy, and it takes years, rather than months, for agreement to be reached on the measures to be adopted. Each new Regulation, Directive, etc. is examined and amended by various Community bodies and by all the individual Member States before the Council finally approves it. Even then, it is unlikely that all the Member States will implement a measure into their national laws until at least two years after the Council has approved it.

The principal company law measures of the EC that the Council has already approved, and those that it is still discussing, are briefly described below.

Directives already adopted in UK law

First Company Law Directive (Publicity requirements, *ultra vires* and nullity)

This Directive deals with the disclosure and the public inspection of company documents and the protection of third parties. It was enacted in the UK in January 1973 by section 9 of the European Communities Act.

Second Company Law Directive (Formation of companies and capital and dividend requirements)

This Directive deals with the formation of public limited liability companies, the maintenance and alteration of their capital, and the payment of dividends. It was enacted in the UK in December 1980 by sections 1 to 45 and 76 to 78 of the Companies Act 1980.

Fourth Company Law Directive (Company accounts)

This Directive requires that annual accounts of certain types of companies should be presented in a standard format and to show a true and fair view. It was enacted in the UK for accounting periods beginning on or after 15 June 1982 by sections 1 to 21 of, and Schedules 1 and 2 to, the Companies Act 1981.

Directive coordinating the conditions for admission of securities to listing

This Directive coordinates the conditions for the admission of securities for listing on an official stock exchange. This was implemented in the UK with effect from 1 January 1985 by The Stock Exchange (Listing) Regulations 1984 (SI 1984/716). This regulation together with the two directives that follow were included in the revision to The Stock Exchange's 'Yellow book'. The requirements of the new Yellow book affect all announcements made by listed companies concerning accounting periods ending after 31 December 1984.

Directive on listing particulars

This Directive coordinates the requirements for drawing up, scrutinising and distributing the listing particulars that are required for securities to be admitted to an official stock exchange listing. This was implemented in the UK with effect from 1 January 1985 by The Stock Exchange (Listing) Regulations 1984 (SI 1984/716).

Directive on continuing disclosure of information

This Directive deals with the information to be published on a regular basis by companies whose shares have been admitted for listing on an official stock exchange. This was implemented in the UK with effect from 1 January 1985 by The Stock Exchange (Listing) Regulations 1984 (SI 1984/716).

Directives that have been adopted by the Council, but have not yet been implemented in the UK

Third Company Law Directive (Mergers)

This Directive deals with mergers between public limited companies within the same Member State. The Council adopted this Directive in October 1978, but deferred the deadline for the implementation of the Directive until January 1986. This date then coincides with the implementation of the Sixth Directive (described below). The UK Government issued a consultative document in August 1982 on the implementation of this Directive, but the Directive is expected to have little impact in the UK, because few mergers will fall within its scope. Regulations are expected in due course.

Sixth Company Law Directive ('Scissions')

This Directive complements the Third Directive. It deals with a public limited company that transfers all of its assets and liabilities to a number of limited companies in exchange for the issue of shares to the shareholders of the divided company.

The Directive was adopted by the Council in December 1982. Member States have until January 1986 to implement it. The UK Government issued a consultative document on the implementation of this Directive in March 1984, and regulations are expected in due course.

Seventh Company Law Directive (Group accounts)

This Directive deals with the preparation, the content and the publication of group accounts. It was adopted by the Council in June 1983. Member States have until the end of 1987 to implement it, and they need not apply its provisions until 1990. The UK Government is expected to consult interested parties about the implementation of this Directive, but no consultative document has yet been issued.

Eighth Company Law Directive (Auditors)

This Directive sets out the minimum standards for the education, the training and the qualification of auditors. The Directive was adopted by the Council in April 1984. Member States are required to implement the Directive by 1988, but they need not apply its provisions until 1990. The UK Government has not yet consulted interested parties on its implementation.

Directive to revise the amounts expressed in ECU in the Fourth Directive

This Directive provides for a revision of the thresholds for the balance sheet total and the net turnover that are relevant when determining whether a company qualifies as either a small or a medium-sized company.

The Directive was adopted by the Council in November 1984. It proposes that the thresholds for the balance sheet total should be increased by 55% and that the thresholds for the net turnover should be increased by 60%. This Directive has yet to be enacted in the UK, but the Government is expected to consult interested parties shortly.

Proposals for Directives, and other instruments still under discussion by EC institutions

Proposed Regulation for a European Economic Interest Grouping

This Regulation would introduce a new legal form of undertaking into Community law in order to encourage cooperation between those undertakings that carry on similar business across national frontiers. It would enable those undertakings to set up common, non-profit-making, support activities, and to operate with unlimited liability.

As a Regulation, this would have direct effect in the Member States. The Council is expected to approve the Regulation before the end of 1985.

Draft Directive on prospectuses to be published when securities are offered for subscription or sale to the public

This proposed Directive would require persons offering securities to the public for entities that were not listed on a stock exchange to prepare prospectuses on the lines of those called for by the Directive on listed securities. It also requires those persons to have the prospectuses vetted by a competent authority before publishing them. A Council working group is examining this draft Directive, but it has a low priority.

Draft Fifth Company Law Directive (Company structure and employee participation)

This Directive would require a public limited company to divide its board by making some directors responsible for management and other directors responsible for the supervision of the company. Companies that employ more than 1000 people would have to permit employees to participate in decision making through representation at a supervisory level. The Commission amended these proposals in July 1983 and discussions on them are expected to continue for several years.

Draft Proposal for a Ninth Company Law Directive (Conduct of groups of companies)

It is proposed that this Directive should provide for a harmonised legal structure for the 'unified management' of a public limited company that is controlled by another undertaking (for example, a company, or an individual, or a partnership), and that it should prescribe rules for the conduct of groups. It would also require those acquiring 10% or more of the shares of a company to notify the company.

This proposal is still at a very early stage, and has not yet been approved by the Commission. The DTI issued a consultative document on the proposal in February 1985.

Draft Tenth Company Law Directive (Cross-border mergers)

The proposals of this Directive would allow, on a Community-wide basis, the type of merger between public limited companies within one Member State that the Third Directive (described above) deals with. The proposals in their present form are still at an early stage.

The DTI issued a consultative document on this draft Directive in February 1985.

Draft Directive on unit trusts

This Directive proposes coordination of the laws etc. relating to undertakings for collective investment in transferable securities. These proposals would allow unit trust type funds to be marketed throughout the Community. A Council working group is currently considering this draft Directive.

Draft Directive on annual accounts of credit institutions

The Fourth Company Law Directive (referred to above) provides that Member States need not apply the provisions of that Directive to the financial statements of banks and other financial institutions. This draft Directive will provide for the harmonisation of the annual financial statements of those institutions. Negotiations are taking place in a Council working group and are likely to continue for at least a further year.

Draft proposal for a Directive on the annual accounts of insurance undertakings

The Fourth Company Law Directive also excluded insurance companies from its scope (at the option of Member States). The Commission is presently discussing a proposal for a directive on insurance company accounts, but the proposal is at a very early stage and progress is slow. The proposal has not yet been approved by the Commission for submission to the Council.

Draft Directive on procedures for informing and consulting employees ('Vredeling' Directive)

This draft Directive proposes that the head offices of large companies and other major employers (such as leading building societies and large professional partnerships) should inform and consult employees of subsidiaries or separate establishments through local management about proposed decisions likely to affect employees.

The proposal is under discussion in a Council working group, but it has proved to be highly contentious and it is unlikely that agreement will be reached on the draft Directive in its present form.

Draft bankruptcy convention

This draft convention provides for the harmonisation throughout the Community of bankruptcy proceedings, liquidation proceedings of insolvent companies and analogous proceedings. The proposal has been agreed subject to some reservations by certain Member States, but certain constitutional points have been raised which are currently being considered by the Council.

Draft convention on the mutual recognition of companies, firms and legal persons

The object of this draft convention is to ensure that companies and other business associates formed under the law of one Member State are recognised in other Member States. The proposal has run into serious difficulties, and indeed some Member States have challenged the fundamental need to have it at all. No agreement is expected on the convention in the foreseeable future.

Draft Regulation for a European company statute

This Regulation provides for the incorporation of a European company under Community law. Negotiations at Council level are expected to take many years to complete.

Draft Directive on the right of establishment for accountants

This draft Directive includes proposals for the mutual recognition of accountants' qualifications, for the right of establishment for accountants, and for the freedom for them to offer their services. The Council working party may resume its examination of this proposal now that the Eighth Directive has been approved by the Council.

Summary of maximum penalties for offences under the accounting provisions of the Companies Act 1985

This appendix refers throughout to the 'statutory maximum fine' which is currently £2,000.

Section	Who is liable	Maximum punishment
151(3)	A company that gives financial assistance for the acquisition of its own shares, and every officer of that company who is in default.	On indictment: (a) Where the company is convicted, a fine. (b) Where an officer of the company is convicted, 2 years imprisonment or a fine, or both. On summary conviction: (a) Where the company is convicted, the statutory maximum fine. (b) Where an officer of the company is convicted, 6 months imprisonment or the statutory maximum fine, or both.
156(6)	A company that fails to register a statutory declaration under Section 155, and every officer of that company who is in default.	On summary conviction, the statutory maximum fine and a daily default fine (where applicable) of one-fiftieth of the statutory maximum.
156(7)	A director who makes a statutory declaration under Section 155, without having reasonable grounds for the opinion expressed in it.	On indictment, 2 years imprisonment or a fine, or both. On summary conviction, 6 months imprisonment or the statutory maximum fine, or both.
223(1)	Every officer, who is in default, of a company that fails to keep accounting records.	On indictment, 2 years imprisonment or a fine, or both. On summary conviction, 6 months imprisonment or the statutory maximum fine, or both.
223(2)	An officer of a company who fails to secure compliance with, or intentionally causes default under, Section 222(4) (preservation of accounting records for requisite number of years).	On indictment, 2 years imprisonment or a fine, or both. On summary conviction, 6 months imprisonment or the statutory maximum fine, or both.

231(3)	A company that fails to annex to its annual return certain particulars required by Schedule 5 that are not included in its annual accounts, and every officer of that company who is in default.	On summary conviction, a fine of one-fifth of the statutory maximum, and (where applicable) a daily default fine of one-fiftieth of the statutory maximum.
231(4)	A director or an officer of a company who is in default in giving notice of matters relating to himself for purposes of Schedule 5 Part V.	On summary conviction, a fine of one-fifth of the statutory maximum.
235(7)	Directors of a company whose directors' report does not comply with the Act.	Directors are individually liable: (a) On indictment, to a fine. (b) On summary conviction, to the statutory maximum fine.
238(2)	A company that lays or delivers an unsigned balance sheet or circulates copies of the balance sheet without signatures, and every officer of that company who is in default.	On summary conviction, a fine of one-fifth of the statutory maximum.
240(5)	A company that fails to send its balance sheet, directors' report and auditors' report to those entitled to receive them, and every officer of that company who is in default.	On indictment, a fine. On summary conviction, the statutory maximum fine.
243(1)	A director who is in default regarding his duty to lay and deliver company accounts.	On summary conviction, the statutory maximum fine, and (where applicable) a daily default fine of one-tenth of the statutory maximum.
245(1)	A director of a company whose individual accounts do not conform with the requirements of this Act.	Directors are individually liable: (a) On indictment, to a fine. (b) On summary conviction, to the statutory maximum fine.
245(2)	A director of a holding company whose group accounts do not conform with Sections 229 and 230 and with other requirements of this Act.	Directors are individually liable: (a) On indictment, to a fine. (b) On summary conviction, to the statutory maximum fine.
246(2)	A company that fails to supply a copy of its accounts to a shareholder on his demand, and every officer of that company who is in default.	On summary conviction, a fine of one-fifth of the statutory maximum, and (where applicable) a daily default fine of one-fiftieth of the statutory maximum.
254(6)	A company and any officer that is in default by contravening Section 254 as regards the publication of full individual or group accounts.	On summary conviction, a fine of one-fifth of the statutory maximum.

255(5)	A company and any officer that is in default by contravening Section 255 as regards publication of abridged accounts.	On summary conviction, a fine of one-fifth of the statutory maximum.
260(3)	A director of a special category company who fails to secure compliance with the special disclosure provision regarding directors' remuneration and higher-paid employees.	On indictment, a fine. On summary conviction, the statutory maximum fine.
314(3)	A director who fails to comply with Section 314 (duty to disclose compensation payable on a takeover, etc.), or a person who fails to include required particulars in a notice he has to give of such matters.	On summary conviction, a fine of one-fifth of the statutory maximum.
317(7)	A director who fails to disclose an interest in a contract.	On indictment, a fine. On summary conviction, the statutory maximum fine.
318(8)	A company that is in default in complying with Section 318(1) or (5) (directors' service contracts to be kept at an appropriate place), or that is 14 days in default in complying with Section 318(4) (notice to Registrar as to where copies of contracts and memoranda are kept), or that refuses inspection as required under Section 318(7).	On summary conviction, a fine of one-fifth of the statutory maximum, and (where applicable) a daily default fine of one-fiftieth of the statutory maximum.
323(2)	A director who deals in options to buy or sell a listed company's shares or debentures.	On indictment, 2 years imprisonment or a fine, or both. On summary conviction, 6 months imprisonment or the statutory maximum fine, or both.
324(7)	A director who fails to notify his interest in a company's shares, or who makes a false statement in a purported notification.	On indictment, 2 years imprisonment or a fine, or both. On summary conviction, 6 months imprisonment or the statutory maximum fine, or both.
326(2), (3),(4), (5)	A company that commits various defaults in connection with a company's register of directors' interests, and any officer who is in default.	On summary conviction, a fine of one-fifth of the statutory maximum, and, except in the case of Section 326(5), a daily default fine (where applicable) of one-fiftieth of the statutory maximum.

328(6)	A director who fails to notify the company that members of his family have, or have exercised, options to buy shares or debentures, or who makes a false statement in a purported notification.	On indictment, 2 years imprisonment or a fine, or both. On summary conviction, 6 months imprisonment or the statutory maximum fine, or both.
329(3)	A company that fails to notify The Stock Exchange of an acquisition of its securities by a director, and any officer of the company who is in default.	On summary conviction, a fine of one-fifth of the statutory maximum, and (where applicable) a daily default fine of one-fiftieth of the statutory maximum.
342(1)	A director of a relevant company who authorises or permits a company to enter into a transaction or arrangement, knowing or suspecting it to contravene Section 330 (loans to directors etc.).	On indictment, 2 years imprisonment or a fine, or both. On summary conviction, 6 months imprisonment or the statutory maximum fine, or both.
342(2)	A relevant company that enters into a transaction or an arrangement for a director in contravention of Section 330.	On indictment, 2 years imprisonment or a fine, or both. On summary conviction, 6 months imprisonment or the statutory maximum fine, or both.
342(3)	A person who procures a relevant company to enter into a transaction or an arrangement knowing or suspecting it to be contrary to Section 330.	On indictment, 2 years imprisonment or a fine, or both. On summary conviction, 6 months imprisonment or the statutory maximum fine, or both.
343(8)	A director of a company that fails to maintain a register of transactions, etc. made with and for directors and not disclosed in the company's accounts or that fails to make the register available at the registered office or at the company's meeting.	On indictment, a fine. On summary conviction, a fine of the statutory maximum.
458	A person who is a party to carrying on a company's business with intent to defraud creditors, or for any fraudulent purpose.	On indictment, 7 years imprisonment or a fine, or both. On summary conviction, 6 months imprisonment or the statutory maximum fine, or both.
697(1)	An overseas company that fails to comply with any of the Sections 691 to 693 or 696 (Registration of overseas company etc.), and any officer or agent of the company who authorises or permits the default.	On summary conviction: (a) For an offence that is not a continuing offence, a fine of one-fifth of the statutory maximum. (b) For an offence that is a continuing offence, a fine of one-fifth of the statutory maximum, and (where applicable) a daily default fine of one-fiftieth of the statutory maximum.

697(2)	An overseas company that contravenes Section 694(6) (carrying on business under its corporate name after Secretary of State's direction), and any officer or agent who authorises or permits the contravention.	On indictment, a fine. On summary conviction, the statutory maximum fine, and (where applicable) a daily default fine of one-tenth of the statutory maximum.
703(1)	An overseas company that fails to comply with Section 700 as respects delivery of its annual accounts, and any officer or agent of the company who authorises or permits the default.	On indictment, a fine. On summary conviction, the statutory maximum fine, and (where applicable) a daily default fine of one-tenth of the statutory maximum.

Statements of Standard Accounting Practice and Exposure Drafts

SSAP 1	Accounting for associated companies	Revised April 1982
SSAP 2	Disclosure of accounting policies	Issued November 1971
SSAP 3	Earnings per share	Revised August 1984
SSAP 4	The accounting treatment of government grants	Issued April 1974
SSAP 5	Accounting for value added tax	Issued April 1974
SSAP 6	Extraordinary items and prior year adjustments	Revised April 1975
SSAP 8	The treatment of taxation under the imputation system in the accounts of companies	Revised December 1977
SSAP 9	Stocks and work in progress	Revised August 1980
SSAP 10	Statements of source and application of funds	Revised June 1978
SSAP 12	Accounting for depreciation	Revised November 1981
SSAP 13	Accounting for research and development	Issued December 1977
SSAP 14	Group accounts	Issued September 1978
SSAP 15	Accounting for deferred taxation	Revised May 1985
SSAP 16	Current cost accounting	Issued March 1980
SSAP 17	Accounting for post balance sheet events	Issued August 1980
SSAP 18	Accounting for contingencies	Issued August 1980

SSAP 19	Accounting for investment properties	Issued November 1981
SSAP 20	Foreign currency translation	Issued April 1983
SSAP 21	Accounting for leases and hire purchase contracts	Issued August 1984
SSAP 22	Accounting for goodwill	Issued December 1984
SSAP 23	Accounting for acquisitions and mergers	Issued April 1985
ED 32	Disclosure of pension information in company accounts	Issued October 1982
ED 34	Pension scheme accounts	Issued April 1984
ED 36	Extraordinary items and prior year adjustments	Issued January 1985
ED 37	Accounting for depreciation	Issued March 1985

Counsel's opinions on 'True and Fair'

The Accounting Standards Committee—Joint Opinion

1. The Accounting Standards Committee ("ASC") from time to time issues Statements of Standard Accounting Practice ("SSAPs"). These are declared in the Explanatory Foreword to be "methods of accounting approved. . .for application to all financial accounts intended to give a true and fair view of financial position and profit or loss." They are not intended to be "a comprehensive code of rigid rules" but departures from them should be disclosed and explained. The Committee also noted in its Explanatory Foreword that "methods of financial accounting evolve and alter in response to changing business and economic needs. From time to time new accounting standards will be drawn at progressive levels, and established standards will be reviewed with the object of improvement in the light of new needs and developments."

2. The ASC has recently undertaken a review of the standard setting process and decided that future standards will "deal only with those matters which are of major and fundamental importance and affect the generality of companies" but that, as in the past, the standards will apply "to all accounts which are intended to show a true and fair view of financial position and profit or loss". A SSAP is therefore a declaration by the ASC, on behalf of its constituent professional bodies, that save in exceptional circumstances, accounts which do not comply with the standard will not give a true and fair view.

3. But the preparation of accounts which give a true and fair view is not merely a matter of compliance with professional standards. In many important cases it is a requirement of law. Since 1947 all accounts prepared for the purpose of compliance with the Companies Acts have been required to "give a true and fair view": s 13(1) of the Companies Act 1947, re-enacted as s 149(1) of the Companies Act 1948. In 1978 the concept of a true and fair view was adopted by the EEC Council in its Fourth Directive "on the annual accounts of certain types of companies". The Directive combined the requirement of giving a true and fair view with extremely detailed provisions about the form and contents of the accounts but the obligation to give a true and fair view was declared to be overriding. Accounts must not comply with the detailed requirements if this would prevent them from giving a true and fair view. Parliament gave effect to the Directive by passing the Companies Act 1981. This substitutes a new s 149(2) in the 1948 Act [*that is now Section 228(2) of the Companies Act 1985*], reproducing

the old s 149(1) in substantially similar words. The detailed requirements of the Directive appear as a new Eighth Schedule to the 1948 Act [*now Schedule 4 to the Companies Act 1985*]. The old s 149(1) (now renumbered 149A(1)) and the old Eighth Schedule (now Sch 8A) are retained for the accounts of banking, insurance and shipping companies. [*These are now Section 258(1) of, and Schedule 9 to, the Companies Act 1985.*] So far as the requirement to give a true and fair view is concerned, a difference between 149(2) and 149A(1) is that the former has come into the law via Brussels, whereas the latter has no EEC pedigree.

4.   "True and fair view" is thus a legal concept and the question of whether company accounts comply with s 149(2) (or s 149A(1)) can be authoritatively decided only by a court. This gives rise to a number of questions about the relationship between the legal requirement and the SSAPs issued by the ASC, which also claim to be authoritative statements on what is a true and fair view. What happens if there is a conflict between the professional standards demanded by the ASC and the decisions of the courts on the requirements of the Companies Acts? Furthermore, the ASC issues new SSAPs "at progressive levels" and reviews established ones. How is this consistent with a statutory requirement of a true and fair view which has been embodied in the law in the same language sinced 1947? Can the issue of a new SSAP make it unlawful to prepare accounts in a form which would previously have been lawful? How can the ASC have power to legislate in this way?

5.   To answer these questions it is necessary first to examine the nature of the "true and fair view" concept as used in the Companies Act. It is an abstraction or philosophical concept expressed in simple English. The law uses many similar concepts, of which "reasonable care" is perhaps the most familiar example. It is a common feature of such concepts that there is seldom any difficulty in understanding what they mean but frequent controversy over their application to particular facts. One reason for this phenomenon is that because such concepts represent a very high level of abstraction which has to be applied to an infinite variety of concrete facts, there can never be a sharply defined line between, for example, what is reasonable care and what is not. There will always be a penumbral area in which views may reasonably differ.

6.   The courts have never attempted to define "true and fair" in the sense of offering a paraphrase in other languages and in our opinion have been wise not to do so. When a concept can be expressed in ordinary English words, we do not think that it illuminates their meaning to attempt to frame a definition. We doubt, for example, whether the man on the Clapham omnibus has really contributed very much to the understanding of "reasonable care" or that accountants have found it helpful to ask themselves how this imaginary passenger would have prepared a set of accounts. It is much more useful to illustrate the concept in action, for example, to explain why certain accounts do or do not give a true and fair view.

7.　　It is however important to observe that the application of the concept involves judgment in questions of degree. The information contained in accounts must be accurate and comprehensive (to mention two of the most obvious elements which contribute to a true and fair view) to within acceptable limits. What is acceptable and how is this to be achieved? Reasonable businessmen and accountants may differ over the degree of accuracy or comprehensiveness which in particular cases the accounts should attain. Equally, there may sometimes be room for differences over the method to adopt in order to give a true and fair view, cases in which there may be more than one "true and fair view" of the same financial position. Again, because "true and fair view" involves questions of degree, we think that cost-effectiveness must play a part in deciding the amount of information which is sufficient to make accounts true and fair.

8.　　In the end, as we have said, the question of whether accounts give a true and fair view in compliance with the Companies Act must be decided by a judge. But the courts look for guidance on this question to the ordinary practices of professional accountants. This is not merely because accounts are expressed in a language which judges find difficult to understand. This may sometimes be true but it is a minor reason for the importance which the courts attach to evidence of accountancy practice. The important reason is inherent in the nature of the "true and fair" concept. Accounts will not be true and fair unless the information they contain is sufficient in quantity and quality to satisfy the reasonable expectations of the readers to whom they are addressed. On this question, accountants can express an informed professional opinion on what, in current circumstances, it is thought that accounts should reasonably contain. But they can do more than that. The readership of accounts will consist of businessmen, investors, bankers and so forth, as well as professional accountants. But the expectations of the readers will have been moulded by the practices of accountants because by and large they will expect to get what they ordinarily get and that in turn will depend upon the normal practices of accountants.

9.　　For these reasons, the courts will treat compliance with accepted accounting principles as *prima facie* evidence that the accounts are true and fair. Equally, deviation from accepted principles will be *prima facie* evidence that they are not. We have not been able to find reported cases on the specific question of whether accounts are true and fair, although the question has been adverted to in the course of judgments on other matters; see for example *Willingale v. International Commercial Bank Ltd* [1978] A.C.834. There are however some cases on the analogous question arising in income tax cases of whether profit or loss has been calculated in accordance with "the correct principles of commercial accountancy" and there is a helpful statement of principle (approved in subsequent cases in the Court of Appeal) by Pennycuick V-C in *Odeon Associated Theatres Ltd v. Jones (Inspector of Taxes)* [1971] 1 W.L.R. 442 at 454:

　　　　"In order to ascertain what are the correct principles [the court] has recourse to the evidence of accountants. That evidence is conclusive on the practice of accountants in the sense of the principles on which accountants act in practice. That is a question of pure fact, but the court itself has to make a final decision as to whether that practice corresponds to the correct principles of commercial accountancy. No doubt in the vast proportion of cases the court will agree with the accountants but it will not necessarily do so. Again, there may be a divergency of views between the accountants, or there may be alternative principles, none of which can be said to be incorrect, or of course there may be no accountancy evidence at all. . . At the end of the day the court must determine what is the correct principle of commercial accountancy to be applied."

10.   This is also in our opinion the relationship between generally accepted accounting principles and the legal concept of "true and fair". The function of the ASC is to formulate what it considers should be generally accepted accounting principles. Thus the value of a SSAP to a court which has to decide whether accounts are true and fair is two-fold. First, it represents an important statement of professional opinion about the standards which readers may reasonably expect in accounts which are intended to be true and fair. The SSAP is intended to crystallise professional opinion and reduce penumbral areas in which divergent practices exist and can each have claim to being "true and fair". Secondly, because accountants are professionally obliged to comply with a SSAP, it creates in the readers an expectation that the accounts will be in conformity with the prescribed standards. This is in itself a reason why accounts which depart from the standard without adequate justification or explanation may be held not to be true and fair. The importance of expectations was emphasised by the Court of Appeal in what may be regarded as a converse case, *Re Press Caps* [1949] Ch.434. An ordinary historic cost balance sheet was said to be "true and fair" notwithstanding that it gave no information about the current value of freehold properties because, it was said, no one familiar with accounting conventions would expect it to include such information.

11.   A SSAP therefore has no direct legal effect. It is simply a rule of professional conduct for accountants. But in our opinion it is likely to have an indirect effect on the content which the courts will give to the "true and fair" concept. The effect of a SSAP may therefore be to make it likely that accounts which would previously have been considered true and fair will no longer satisfy the law. Perhaps the most dramatic example arises out of the recent statement by the ASC in connection with its review of SSAP 16 "Current Cost Accounting". The Statement puts forward for discussion the proposition that "where a company is materially affected by changing prices, pure HC accounts do not give a true and fair view". If this proposition were embodied in a new SSAP and accepted by the courts, the legal requirements of a true and fair view will have undergone a revolutionary change.

12.   There is no inconsistency between such a change brought about by changing professional opinion and the rule that words in a statute must

be construed in accordance with the meaning which they bore when the statute was passed. The *meaning* of true and fair remains what it was in 1947. It is the *content* given to the concept which has changed. This is something which constantly happens to such concepts. For example, the Bill of Rights 1688 prohibited "cruel and unusual punishments". There has been no change in the meaning of "cruel" since 1688. The definition in Dr Johnson's Dictionary of 1755 ("pleased with hurting others, inhuman, hard-hearted, without pity, barbarous") is much the same as in a modern dictionary. But changes in society mean that a judge in 1983 would unquestionably characterise punishments as "cruel" which his predecessor of 1688 would not have thought o come within this description. The meaning of the concept remains the same; the facts to which it is applied have changed.

13. The possibility of changing accounting standards has been recognised both by the courts and the legislature. In *Associated Portland Cement Manufacturers Ltd v. Price Commission* [1975] I.C.R.27, esp. at 45-6, the court recognised changes since 1945 in the permissible methods of calculating depreciation. Similarly para 90 of the new Eighth Schedule to the Companies Act 1948 refers to "principles generally accepted...at the time when those accounts are prepared."

14. We therefore see no conflict between the functions of the ASC in formulating standards which it declares to be essential to true and fair accounts and the function of the courts in deciding whether the accounts satisfy the law. The courts are of course not bound by a SSAP. A court may say that accounts which ignore them are nevertheless true and fair. But the immediate effect of a SSAP is to strengthen the likelihood that a court will hold that compliance with the prescribed standard is necessary for the accounts to give a true and fair view. In the absence of a SSAP, a court is unlikely to reject accounts drawn up in accordance with principles which command some respectable professional support. The issue of a SSAP has the effect, for the two reasons which we have given in para 10, of creating a *prima facie* presumption that accounts which do not comply are not true and fair. This presumption is then strengthened or weakened by the extent to which the SSAP is actually accepted and applied. Universal acceptance means that it is highly unlikely that a court would accept accounts drawn up according to different principles. On the other hand, if there remains a strong body of professional opinion which consistently opts out of applying the SSAP, giving reasons which the ASC may consider inadequate, the *prima facie* presumption against such accounts is weakened.

15. We therefore do not think that the ASC should be concerned by the possibility that a court may hold that compliance with one of its SSAPs is not necessary for the purposes of the Companies Acts. This possibility is inherent in the fact that the courts are not bound by professional opinion. The function of the ASC is to express their professional judgment on the standards which in their opinion are required.

16.   There are two further points to be considered. The first is the relationship between the "true and fair" requirement and the detailed provisions of the new Eighth Schedule. The Act is quite explicit on this point: the true and fair view is overriding. Nevertheless it may be said that the detailed requirements offer some guidance as to the principles which Parliament considered would give a true and fair view. In particular, the Schedule plainly regards historic cost accounting as the norm and current cost accounting as an optional alternative. In these circumstances, is a court likely to follow a SSAP which declares that for certain companies, historic cost accounts *cannot* give a true and fair view? In our opinion, whatever reasons there may be for taking one view or the other, the provisions of the Eighth Schedule are no obstacle to accepting such a SSAP. As we have already pointed out, the provisions of the Schedule are static whereas the concept of a true and fair view is dynamic. If the latter is overriding, it is not impossible that the effect in time will be to render obsolete some of the provisions of the Schedule. But we think that this is what must have been intended when overriding force was given to a concept with a changing content.

17.   Lastly, there is the effect of the adoption of "true and fair view" by the EEC. Because s 149(2) of the 1948 Act now gives effect to a Directive, it must (unlike s 149A(1)) be construed in accordance with any decision of the European Court on the meaning of Article 2.3 of the Directive. In practice we do not think that this is likely to affect the evolution of the concept in England. Just as the concept may have a different content at different times, so it may have a different content in different countries. Although the European Court may seek to achieve some uniformity by laying down minimum standards for the accounts of all EEC countries, it seems to use that they are unlikely to disapprove of higher standards being required by the professional bodies of individual states and in consequence, higher legal criteria for what is a true and fair view being adopted in the national courts of some member states.

18.   So for example Article 33 of the Directive gives member states the right to "permit or require" companies to use current cost accounting instead of historic cost principles. In the UK, as we have said, current cost accounts are permitted by the Eighth Schedule but the only circumstances in which they may be required is if a court should decide, on the basis of prevailing principles, that they were necessary to give a true and fair view. In Germany, on the other hand, the equivalent of the Eighth Schedule does not even permit current cost accounts. In Germany therefore, the only way they could be permitted would be if the German court applied "true and fair view" as an overriding requirement. For the reasons given in para 16, we do not regard it as illogical or impossible that even a German court may take this view. But having regard to the Directive, we think it is very unlikely that the European Court would decide as a matter of community law that there are circumstances in which historic cost accounts do not give a true and fair view. Developments of this kind are more likely to be left to national courts to make in the light of local professional opinion.

Leonard Hoffman
M. H. Arden

Lincoln's Inn
13 September 1983

The Joint Opinion that follows was given in relation to the Statement of Intent issued by the ASC on the proposed revision of SSAP 16. However, this Opinion has a more general application to the relationship between SSAPs and the 'true and fair' concept. In particular, it discusses the question of cost-effectiveness and whether a SSAP should apply to all companies.

The Accounting Standards Committee—Supplementary Joint Opinion

1.   This Opinion is intended to be supplementary to our Joint Opinion dated 13 September 1983. We do not propose to repeat the contents of that Opinion more than is necessary in order to make this one intelligible. The two Opinions should therefore be read together.

2.   The ASC proposed to issue a Statement of Intent concerning the future of SSAP 16 "Current Cost Accounting". In summary, the proposal is that all public limited companies ("PLCs") other than insurance companies, property companies and investment-based companies ("value-based companies") should show the effects of changing prices when these effects are material, but this should be indicated in a note and not in separate current cost accounts. The present position is that SSAP 16 applies only to large and quoted companies (as therein defined) and does not apply to value-based companies, whatever their size. The ASC is not satisfied that a method has yet been developed for producing useful information about the effects of changing prices on the businesses of private companies and value-based companies at a cost that can be justified. It is therefore commissioning further work on the application of current cost accounting to these companies. However, the ASC draws attention to the principal factors which have led them to their conclusion that significant benefits result from the disclosure of current cost information by PLCs, including the large number and wide range of users of their accounts and in many cases the sophistication of those users. These factors generally do not apply to private companies. The benefits of providing information about the effects of changing prices on the businesses of private companies are therefore likely to be significantly less than in the case of PLCs.

3.   The Statement of Intent therefore recognises that while in principle and subject to cost-effectiveness, all accounts should, in order to give a true and a fair view, show the effects of changing prices when such effects are material, there are practical difficulties about devising cost-effective methods for implementing this principle in the case of certain companies.

4. This practical approach has been criticised on the ground that if a foot-note about the effects of changing prices is regarded as necessary for accounts to give a true and fair view, this requirement should apply to all sets of accounts. Questions of cost and expediency are said to be irrelevant to whether or not the accounts give a true and fair view and it is argued that there can be no justification for the ASC distinguishing between different kinds of companies.

5. We think that this criticism is misconceived. In the first place, questions of cost-effectiveness are in our opinion relevant to whether accounts give a true and fair view or not. "True and fair view" is not an absolute and unique concept. If that was what the legislature had meant, it would no doubt have said "the true and fair view". More than one view may be true and fair and whether a particular set of accounts satisfies this test or not involves questions of degree and a consideration of many factors relating both to the affairs of the particular business and the reasonable expectations of the people likely to use the accounts. In paragraph 7 of our Joint Opinion we said:

    "Again, because 'true and fair view' involves questions of degree, we think that cost-effectiveness must play a part in deciding the amount of information which is sufficient to make accounts true and fair."

    Some elaboration of this statement may be useful. The information contained in accounts may vary in its comprehensiveness, usefulness and degree of precision. These are all factors which bear upon the question of whether the accounts are "true and fair". The accounts must satisfy criteria of acceptability in regard to each of these and other matters. But the question of whether it is necessary for particular kinds of information to be included must take into account the cost and difficulty of providing such information. There is in our opinion nothing illogical in saying: "This information would be useful to (say) investors in assessing the condition of the business. If it could be provided relatively easily, we think that fairness to investors demands that it should be included. *Prima facie* therefore, accounts which do not include such information would not be true and fair. On the other hand, if the information could be provided only with great expense and difficulty, we do not think that it would be reasonable to insist upon it. Therefore we would accept accounts without such information as still being true and fair."[1]

6. In our earlier Opinion we mentioned for another purpose the analogy of the legal concept of reasonable care. On this point too, we think that reasonable care provides a useful comparison. The question of

---

[1] In saying this we have in mind expense and difficulty applicable to any company of that kind. We are not saying that it would be right to take into account the difficulty which a particular company might have in providing certain information, e.g. because its records had been badly maintained. There is again an analogy here with "reasonable care" (see paragraph 6) in which difficulties or handicaps peculiar to an individual are usually disregarded on the ground that a person suffering from such a difficulty or handicap should not have undertaken the activity which gave rise to the risk.

whether a person has taken reasonable care to guard against some danger depends upon weighing a number of factors, including the likelihood that the risk may materialise, the seriousness of the loss or injury which may be caused if the risk does materialise, the importance of the activity giving rise to the risk, and the cost of taking various kinds of precautions. As Lord Wilberforce put it, more succinctly than we have done:

> "What is reasonable depends on the nature and degree of the danger. It also depends upon the difficulty and expense of guarding against it."[2]

This process of weighing risks against the difficulty and expense of guarding against them would apply equally to the question of whether an accountant had taken reasonable care in the preparation of a set of accounts. And although the question of whether reasonable care has been taken in the preparation of accounts is not the same as whether they are true and fair, we think that the questions of "reasonableness" and "fairness" have enough in common to make the analogy a valid one.

7.   At this point the critic may say: "Well, I can see that questions of cost-effectiveness may enter into the decision on whether accounts are true and fair and that information about the effects of price changes may have to be given in the accounts of some companies but not others. But the SSAP should still be capable of expression in general terms. How can one justify an arbitrary dividing line which requires such information in the accounts of one company which happens to be a PLC and does not require it in the accounts of a private company of the same size and carrying on a substantially similar business?"

8.   This criticism in our opinion misses the true function of SSAPs, which is to reduce the level of abstraction at which rules of good accounting practice are expressed. The more abstract the rule, the more pure and universally applicable it is, but the less useful it is to the practitioner seeking to apply it to the facts of a particular case. If universality were all that one wanted, the proposition that accounts should be true and fair would be sufficient. The point of a SSAP is to concretise that proposition, while recognising that every case must depend upon its own facts and that any rules expressed at a lower level of abstraction must to a greater or lesser extent be "rules of thumb". This point is made with great clarity in the Explanatory Foreword. We therefore see nothing illogical in a SSAP which gives guidance to the profession by taking a (necessarily) arbitrary but practical dividing line and saying that for PLCs which are not value-based companies it will ordinarily be assumed that the public benefit from the provision of information about the effects of changing prices will be sufficient to justify the cost of providing such information, whereas this will not be assumed, or will not yet be assumed, in the case of private or value-based companies.

[2] *Herrington v. British Railways Board* [1972] A.C.877, 920.

9.   We said in our earlier opinion that "true and fair" was a dynamic concept and that its detailed content could change by degrees over time. We also said that one of the functions of the ASC was to initiate and promote such changes. A SSAP in accordance with the draft Statement of Intent seems to us to give effect to that function.

Leonard Hoffman
M. H. Arden

Lincoln's Inn
20 March 1984

The two preceding opinions are reproduced with the kind permission of Accountancy, The Accounting Standards Committee, Leonard Hoffman and Mary H. Arden.

The Institute of Chartered Accountants of Scotland—Opinion

I have been asked to consider the meaning of the term 'true and fair view' from the Scottish point of view, in the light of the Joint Opinion given by English leading Counsel to the Accounting Standards Committee dated 14th September 1983.

In their Opinion English Counsel examine the nature of the 'true and fair' view concept as used in the Companies Acts in some detail. They draw attention to the fact that the Courts have never attempted to define this term, in the sense of offering a paraphrase of it, and go on to say that the application of the concept involves judgment in questions of degree. Turning to the relationship between the legal concept of 'true and fair' on the one hand and generally accepted accounting principles on the other, they say that the Courts will treat compliance with accepted accounting principles as *prima facie* evidence that the accounts are true and fair, and that equally deviation from accepted principles will be *prima facie* evidence that they are not. This leads them to consider the problem of the effect upon the 'true and fair view' concept of a new Statement of Standard Accounting Practice. ('SSAP'). Their answer to it is to say that there is no inconsistency between a change in the legal requirements for a true and fair view resulting from a new SSAP and the rule that words in a statute must be construed in accordance with the meaning which they bore when the statute was passed. As they put it, 'The *meaning* of true and fair remains what it was in 1947. It is the *content* given to the concept which has changed.' Thus the concept of the 'true and fair view' is, they say, dynamic, with a changing content as accounting practices are revised and developed with time. The importance of this conclusion is revealed when they recognise, in paragraph 16 of their Opinion, that since the 'true and fair' view requirement in section 149(2) of the Companies Act 1948 [*now Section 228(2) of the Companies Act 1985]* as amended overrides the provisions of the new Schedule 8 [*now Schedule 4*] to the Act, it may have the effect in time of rendering obsolete some of the detailed provisions of the Schedule.

Had I been approaching the matter afresh I would have reached the same conclusions as English Counsel have done, for substantially the same reasons. While the various authorities to which they refer in the course of their discussion are cases decided in the English Courts, the principles upon which their opinion is based are all familiar to a Scottish lawyer, and the statutes are of course applicable with equal force in both countries. It is equally true of Scotland to say that the Courts have not attempted to provide a definition of the term 'true and fair view', although there have been a number of recent cases where the sufficiency of a company's accounts in that regard have come under consideration. In each case the question whether or not they present a 'true and fair view' is a question of fact, which the Court will decide in the light of the evidence including evidence of current accounting practice. As in England, the Court is likely to pay close attention to the evidence of accountants without feeling bound by that evidence: cf. Lord Advocate v. Ruffle, 1979 SC 351. The statement of principle by Pennycuick V-C in Odeon Associated Theatres v. Jones (1971) 1 WLR 442 at p. 454, which English Counsel quote in paragraph 9 of their Opinion, as explained by Lord Denning MR. in Heather v. P.E. Consulting Group Limited (1973) Ch. 189, is familiar in this country, and has been referred to in the Scottish Court on a number of occasions particularly in tax cases.

The distinction which English Counsel draw between the meaning of the term 'true and fair' on the one hand and its content on the other is entirely sound in my opinion. This is because the answer to the question whether a true and fair view is given by the accounts inevitably involves questions of fact and degree, which must always be decided by reference to the state of affairs generally at the time when the accounts were prepared. An analogy can be drawn with other concepts used by the law, such as 'reasonable care' and 'reasonably practicable'. The latter expression, for instance, is used in a variety of provisions to be found in the Factories Act 1961 and its subordinate legislation. The meaning of the phrase, no doubt, must be taken to have remained the same since the date of the enactment, but it is well established in Scotland as well as in England that when it comes to considering whether in any particular case measures which might have been taken so as to avoid the accident were or were not reasonably practicable regard must be had to the state of current knowledge and invention. In my opinion an argument to the effect that the question whether a particular set of accounts gave a true and fair view had to be decided with reference to principles of accounting which, while current in 1947 or 1948, had become obsolete by the time the accounts were prepared only has to be stated to be seen to be unacceptable. I agree with English Counsel that it is reasonable to think that the reason why overriding force was given by the Companies Act 1981 to the concept of the 'true and fair view' is that it was recognised that this was a dynamic concept with a changing content, capable of rendering obsolete any particular provision in the Schedule which had become inconsistent with current practice.

For these reasons I am of opinion that the guidance which English Counsel have given to the Accounting Standards Committee can be accepted as being in accordance with the Scottish approach.

J. A. D. Hope
Edinburgh, 22 December 1983

This legal opinion is reproduced with the kind permission of The Institute of Chartered Accountants of Scotland and J. A. D. Hope.

Directors' loans decision tables

Decision table 1: Loans – relevant company

(To be read in conjunction with Chapter 11 of this book.)

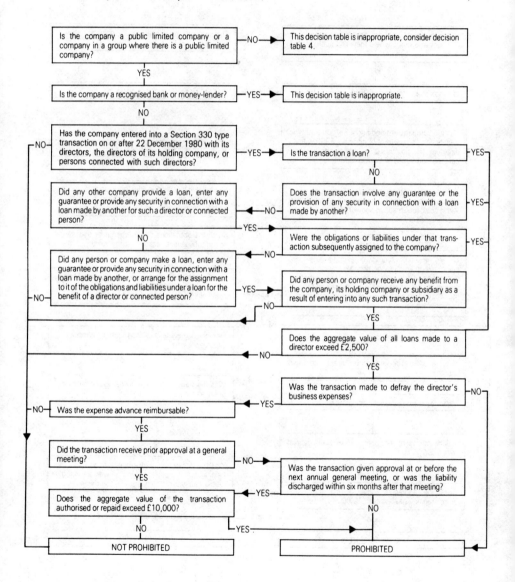

Decision table 2: Quasi-loans – relevant company

(To be read in conjunction with Chapter 11 of this book.)

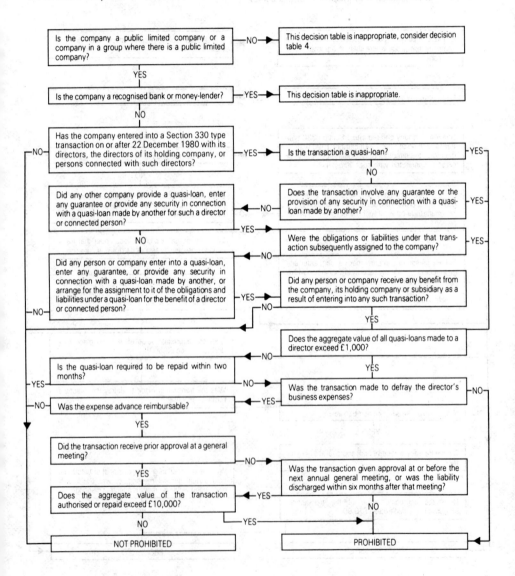

Decision table 3: Credit transactions – relevant company

(To be read in conjunction with Chapter 11 of this book.)

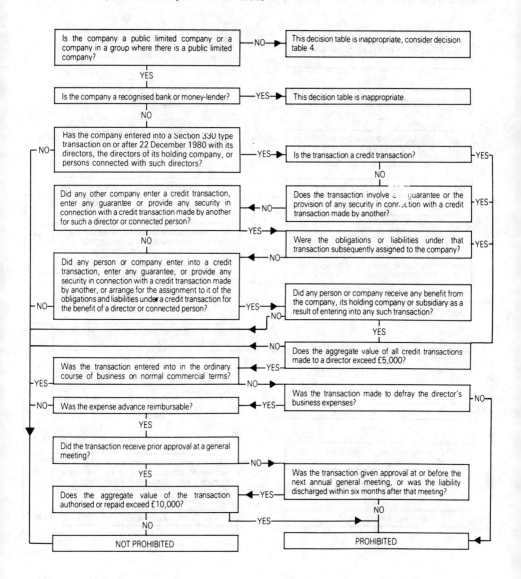

Decision table 4: Loans – non-relevant company

(To be read in conjunction with Chapter 11 of this book.)

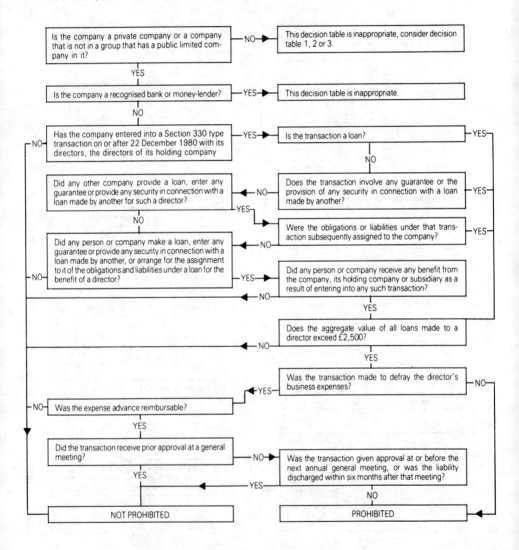

Text of TR 481 and TR 482

Technical Release 481, The Determination of Realised Profits and Disclosure of Distributable Profits in the Context of the Companies Acts 1948 to 1981, and Technical Release 482, The Determination of Distributable Profits in the Context of the Companies Acts 1948 to 1981, were issued in September 1982 by the Consultative Committee of Accountancy Bodies (CCAB), whose members are as follows: The Institute of Chartered Accountants in England and Wales; The Institute of Chartered Accountants of Scotland; The Institute of Chartered Accountants in Ireland; The Chartered Association of Certified Accountants; The Institute of Cost and Management Accountants; and The Chartered Institute of Public Finance and Accountancy.

Set out below is the complete text of Technical Release 481 and Technical Release 482. These Technical Releases refer to the Companies Acts 1948 to 1981. The appropriate references to the Companies Act 1985 that correspond to those references to the previous Acts that are included in the text are as follows:

Reference to previous Act		Reference to Companies Act 1985
Companies Act 1948,	s 56	Sec 130
	s 57	(Repealed by Companies Act 1980)
	s 58	(Repealed by Companies Act 1981)
	s 149	Sec 228
	s 152	Sec 230
	new Schedule 8	Sch 4
	para: 12	para: 12
	13	13
	15	15
	19	19
	20	20
	34	34
	61 to 66	61 to 66
	87	88
	88	89
	90	91
	Schedule 8A	Sch 9
Companies Act 1967, s 14		Sec 236
Companies Act 1976, s 1		Sec 241

Companies Act 1980, Part III	Part VIII
s 39	Sec 263 and 275
s 40	Sec 264
s 41	Sec 265 to 267
s 42	Sec 268
s 42A	Sec 269
s 43	Sec 270 to 275
s 43A	Sec 276
s 45	Sec 263 and 280
s 87	Sec 264
Companies Act 1981, s 53	Sec 170
s 60	Sec 274

Technical Release 481

Explanatory note

The Consultative Committee of Accountancy Bodies wishes to draw readers' attention to the fact that the attached (*sic*) guidance statement does not deal with the special problems arising in connection with the determination of realised profits in the context of foreign currency translation. It is intended that these problems should be dealt with in the future by the issue of an accounting standard on foreign currency translation. (*Such a standard has since been issued as SSAP 20.*)

The following statement of guidance on the determination of realised profits and disclosure of distributable profits in the context of the Companies Acts 1948 to 1981 is issued by the Councils of the member bodies of the Consultative Committee of Accountancy Bodies. The guidance given in this statement may need to be amended as the law is interpreted in particular cases, or as existing Accounting Standards are revised and new Standards are issued.

The statement and its appendix have been considered and approved by Counsel. They are, however, not definitive. Interpretation of the law rests ultimately with the courts.

References to the '1948 Act', the '1980 Act' and the '1981 Act' are to the Companies Acts 1948, 1980 and 1981 respectively.

References to the 'new Schedule 8' are to Schedule 8 to the 1948 Act as inserted by Section 1(2) of the 1981 Act, and as set out in Schedule 1 to the 1981 Act.

Realised profits: The statutory framework

1. The term 'realised profits' was introduced into UK company law statutes as a result of the implementation of the 2nd and 4th EEC directives on company law in the Companies Act 1980 (Part III) and

the Companies Act 1981 (Part I) respectively:

(1) Part III of the 1980 Act imposes statutory restrictions on the distribution of profits and assets by companies. These restrictions include a prohibition on the distribution of unrealised profits.*

(2) Paragraph 12(a) of the new Schedule 8 requires that 'Only profits realised at the balance sheet date shall be included in the profit and loss account'. Paragraph 34(4) contains a similar requirement applicable to transfers from the revaluation reserve to the profit and loss account. These requirements are extended to consolidated accounts by paragraphs 61 to 66 of the new Schedule 8. They do not apply to accounts prepared under Schedule 8A to the 1948 Act.

*There is an exception to this rule where distributions are made in kind (see Section 43A of the 1980 Act, as inserted by Section 85 of the 1981 Act).

2. The new Schedule 8 states that 'references to realised profits . . . are references to such profits . . . as fall to be treated as realised profits . . . in accordance with principles generally accepted with respect to the determination for accounting purposes of realised profits at the time when those accounts are prepared' (new Schedule 8, para. 90, extended to the 1980 Act by reason of Section 21(1) of the 1981 Act). The term 'principles generally accepted' for the determination of realised profits is not defined in the Act.

3. This statement gives guidance as to the interpretation of 'principles generally accepted' for the determination of realised profits in the context of these statutory requirements. Both the statutory requirements and the following guidance must throughout be viewed in the context of Section 149 of the 1948 Act, as amended by Section 1 of the 1981 Act, which states that the requirement for company accounts to give a true and fair view overrides all other provisions of the Companies Acts 1948 to 1981 as to the matters to be included in a company's accounts. Section 152 of the 1948 Act, as amended by Section 2 of the 1981 Act, imposes a corresponding requirement for group accounts.

'Principles generally accepted' for realised profits

4. 'Principles generally accepted' for the determination of realised profits should be considered in conjunction with, inter alia, the legal principles laid down in the new Schedule 8, statements of standard accounting practice ('SSAPs'), and in particular the fundamental accounting concepts referred to in SSAP 2 'Disclosure of accounting policies'. As stated in the Explanatory Foreword to Accounting Standards, SSAPs describe methods of accounting for all accounts intended to give a true and fair view. They must therefore, where

637

applicable, be considered to be highly persuasive in the interpretation of 'principles generally accepted' for the determination of realised profits.

5. Accounting thought and practice develop over time. This is recognised in the statutory requirement that realised profits should be determined 'in accordance with principles generally accepted . . . at the time when those accounts are prepared'. Because of this, the guidance set out in this statement is itself liable to amendment from time to time.

6. In determining whether a profit is realised, particular regard should be had to the statutory accounting principles at paragraphs 12 and 13 of the new Schedule 8, and to the parallel fundamental accounting concepts of 'prudence' and 'accruals' as set out in SSAP 2.

7. Paragraph 12 of the new Schedule 8 requires that 'The amount of any item shall be determined on a prudent basis' and, in particular, as already noted, that 'only profits realised at the balance sheet date shall be included in the profit and loss account'. SSAP 2 amplifies the prudence concept as follows:

    'revenues and profits are not anticipated, but are recognised by inclusion in the profit and loss account only when realised in the form either of cash or of other assets the ultimate cash realisation of which can be assessed with reasonable certainty'.

    In the light of the new statutory requirements, it should be borne in mind that the phrases 'ultimate cash realisation' and 'assessed with reasonable certainty' are intended to clarify the extent to which a profit can be said to be 'realised' under the prudence concept in circumstances other than where the profit has already been realised in the form of cash. 'Reasonable certainty' is the limiting factor.

8. This approach is consistent with paragraph 13 of the new Schedule 8 which requires that:

    'All income and charges relating to the financial year to which the accounts relate shall be taken into account, without regard to the date of receipt or payment'.

    The statutory requirement corresponds with the accruals concept as explained at paragraph 14(b) of SSAP 2. This states that:

    'revenue and costs are accrued (that is, recognised as they are earned or incurred, not as money is received or paid), matched with one another so far as their relationship can be established or justifiably assumed, and dealt with in the profit and loss account of the period to which they relate'.

9. In determining realised profits, it is also necessary to comply with paragraph 12(b) of the new Schedule 8, which states that:

    'all liabilities and losses which have arisen or are likely to arise in respect of the financial year to which the accounts relate or a previous financial year shall be taken into account, including those which only become apparent between the balance sheet date and the date on which it is signed on behalf of the board of directors . . . '.

This statutory requirement corresponds with the prudence concept as explained at paragraph 14(d) of SSAP 2. This states that:

'provision is made for all known liabilities (expenses and losses) whether the amount of these is known with certainty or is a best estimate in the light of the information available'.

Realised profits: Summary of guidance

10. A profit which is required by statements of standard accounting practice to be recognised in the profit and loss account should normally be treated as a realised profit, unless the SSAP specifically indicates that it should be treated as unrealised. *See Appendix.*

11. A profit may be recognised in the profit and loss account in accordance with an accounting policy which is not the subject of a SSAP, or, exceptionally, which is contrary to a SSAP. Such a profit will normally be a realised profit if the accounting policy adopted is consistent with paragraphs 12 and 13 of the new Schedule 8 and with the accruals and prudence concepts as set out in SSAP 2.

12. Where, in special circumstances, a true and fair view could not be given, even if additional information were provided, without including in the profit and loss account an unrealised profit, the effect of Section 149(3) of the 1948 Act (as amended) is to require inclusion of that unrealised profit notwithstanding paragraph 12(a) of the new Schedule 8. Moreover, paragraph 15 of the new Schedule 8 allows the directors to include an unrealised profit in the profit and loss account where there are special reasons for doing so. Where unrealised profits are thus recognised in the profit and loss account, particulars of this departure from the statutory accounting principle, the reasons for it and its effect are required to be given in a note to the accounts.

Distributable profits

13. The definition of realised profits contained in the new Schedule 8 is extended by Section 21(1) of the 1981 Act to apply to any of the Companies Acts. It therefore applies to the provisions of Part III of the 1980 Act, dealing with distributions. In that context this guidance should be read in conjunction with the statutory rules as to what constitute distributable profits and losses in particular circumstances for the purposes of that part of that Act.

14. It is essential that all companies should keep sufficient records to enable them to distinguish between those reserves which are

639

distributable and those which are not. While most realised profits will be passed through the profit and loss account, there may be some realised profits which will originally have been brought into the accounts as unrealised profits by way of direct credit to reserves. Similarly, while most unrealised profits will be credited direct to reserves, there may be some unrealised profits passed through the profit and loss account (see paragraph 12 above). Subsequently, when such profits are realised either in whole or in part, a reclassification needs to be made between unrealised and realised profits.

15. There is no legal requirement for a company to distinguish in its balance sheet between distributable and non-distributable reserves as such. However, where material non-distributable profits are included in the profit and loss account or in other reserves which might reasonably be assumed to be distributable, it may be necessary for this to be disclosed and quantified in a note to the accounts in order for them to give a true and fair view.

16. Distributions are made by companies and not by groups. It follows that the profits of a group are only distributable to members of the group's holding company to the extent of the holding company's distributable profits. The concept of distributable profit is not, therefore, strictly applicable to groups. However, it is reasonable to assume that the distributable retained profits of subsidiaries can be distributed to the holding company. Where this is not the case, the requirements of paragraph 36 of SSAP 14 'Group accounts' should be complied with. This states:

> 'If there are significant restrictions on the ability of the holding company to distribute the retained profits of the group (other than those shown as non-distributable) because of statutory, contractual or exchange control restrictions the extent of the restrictions should be indicated.'

Appendix to TR 481
Accounting standards and realised profits: Examples

1. As statements of standard accounting practice are revised and as new standards are issued, it is expected that they will deal with any matters relevant to the determination of realised profits.

2. This has already been done in the case of SSAP 1 'Accounting for Associated Companies', revised in April 1982. This provides an example of the way in which the true and fair view requirements should be satisfied by giving additional information rather than by including unrealised profits in profit and loss account (see paragraph 12 above). As far as an investing company is concerned, the profits of its associated companies are not realised until they are passed on as dividends; the true and fair view, however, requires that they should

be reflected in the investing company's financial statements. There is no problem where group accounts are prepared because specific provision is made for this situation in paragraph 65(1) of the new Schedule 8. Where, however, the investing company does not prepare group accounts, the revised SSAP 1 states that it should show the information required as to its share of the associated company's profit by preparing a separate profit and loss account or by adding the information to its own profit and loss account in supplementary form in such a way that its share of the profits of the associated company is not treated as realised.

3.   An example of the principle that profit recognised in accordance with an Accounting Standard should normally be treated as realised (see paragraph 10 above) is provided by SSAP 9 'Stocks and work in progress'. This requires that long-term contract work in progress should be stated in periodic financial statements at cost plus any attributable profit, less any foreseeable losses and progress payments received and receivable. There was initially some concern as to whether profit thus recognised on long-term contract work in progress would be construed as realised profit within the provisions of the Companies Acts. However, the relevant principles of recognising profits in SSAP 9 are based on the concept of 'reasonable certainty' as to the eventual outcome and are not in conflict with the statutory accounting principles. Such profits should be treated as realised profits. The Department of Trade does not dissent from this view.

Technical Release 482

Guidance statement issued in September 1982 on behalf of the Councils of the constituent members of the Consultative Committee of Accountancy Bodies, on the determination of distributable profits. This statement gives guidance on the interpretation of Part III of the Companies Act 1980 and on the determination of the maximum amount of profit which can be legally distributed under that Act.

It should be emphasised that it does not seek to deal with the many commercial factors which need to be taken into account before a company decides on the amount of a distribution to be recommended to its shareholders. It should also be borne in mind that its guidance relates solely to the determination of profits legally available for distribution and that it does not give guidance on the recognition of profit in the accounts.

This statement should be read in conjunction with the guidance statement issued by the Councils of the constituent members of the CCAB on 'The determination of realised profits and disclosure of distributable profits in the context of the Companies Acts 1948 to 1981', issued in September 1982.

This statement has been considered and approved by Counsel.

However, it is not definitive. Interpretation of the law rests ultimately with the courts.

References to the '1948 Act', the '1967 Act', the '1980 Act' and the '1981 Act' are to the Companies Acts 1948, 1967, 1980 and 1981 respectively. Section references without ascription refer to the 1980 Act.

References to the 'new Schedule 8' are to Schedule 8 to the 1948 Act as inserted by S 1(2) of the 1981 Act, and as set out in Schedule 1 to the 1981 Act.

Introduction

1. The 1980 Act restricts distributions of both public and private companies. Previously the determination of legally distributable reserves and profits was governed only by a company's articles of association, Sections 56 to 58 of the 1948 Act, and a significant body of case law. After the commencement of the provisions of the 1980 Act, a company must restrict its distributions to those permitted by the 1980 Act, subject to any further restrictions imposed under its memorandum or articles of association.

2. In general, companies are only able to make distributions out of realised profits less realised losses, but further restrictions are imposed on public companies (see paragraph 6 below). The 1980 Act also includes special provisions for certain investment companies and insurance companies (ss 41 and 42): these are not discussed in this guidance statement.

Provision of the Companies Act 1980 (as amended)

Distribution

3. A 'distribution' is defined (s 45(2)) as 'every description of distribution of a company's assets to members of the company, whether in cash or otherwise, except distributions made by way of –

    (*a*) an issue of shares as fully or partly paid bonus shares;

    (*b*) redemption or purchase of any of the company's own shares out of capital (including a new issue of shares) or out of unrealised profits;

    (*c*) reduction of share capital; and

    (*d*) a distribution of assets to members of the company on its winding-up.

Profits available for distribution

4.   A company may only make a distribution out of profits available for that purpose (s 39(1)). A company's profits available for distribution are stated to be its accumulated, realised profits (so far as not previously distributed or capitalised) less its accumulated, realised losses (so far as not previously written off in a reduction or reorganisation of its share capital) (s 39(2)). Realised losses may not be offset against unrealised profits. Public companies are subject to a further restriction (see paragraph 6 below).

5.   A company may only distribute an unrealised profit when the distribution is in kind and the unrealised profit arises from the writing up of the asset being distributed (s 43A, as inserted by s 85 of the 1981 Act).

Public companies

6.   A further restriction is placed on distributions by public companies (s 40). A public company may only make a distribution if, after giving effect to such distribution, the amount of its net assets (as defined in s 87(4)(c)) is not less than the aggregate of its called up share capital and undistributable reserves. This means that a public company must deduct any net unrealised losses from net realised profits before making a distribution, whereas a private company need not make such a deduction (see also paragraphs 29 to 31 below).

7.   Under Section 40(2) the following are undistributable reserves:

(*a*) share premium account (see also s 56 of the 1948 Act as amended by the 1981 Act);

(*b*) capital redemption reserve (see also s 53 of the 1981 Act);

(*c*) the excess of accumulated, unrealised profits, over the accumulated, unrealised losses so far as not previously written off in a reduction or reorganisation of its share capital;

(*d*) any other reserve which the company is prohibited from distributing by any enactment, or by its memorandum or articles of association (or equivalent).

Section 40 only applies to public companies. However, because of the effect of Section 39(2) of the 1980 Act, Section 56 of the 1948 Act, and Section 53 of the 1981 Act, none of the above mentioned reserves is distributable by private companies. (The restrictions which are placed upon public companies which have distributed or utilised unrealised profits prior to the commencement of the Act are discussed at paragraph 30 below).

Relevant accounts

8.   Whether or not a distribution may be made within the terms of the 1980 Act is determined by reference to 'relevant items' as stated in the 'relevant accounts'. A 'relevant item' is defined by s 43(8) as profits, losses, assets, liabilities, provisions, share capital and reserves. Thus, valuations or contingencies included in notes to the financial statements, but not incorporated in the accounts themselves, have no effect on the amount of distributable profit. There is no requirement that distributions can only be made out of distributable profits described as such in the accounts.

9.   The 'relevant accounts' (annual, interim or initial) are defined in Section 43(2) and, except for the initial or interim accounts of private companies, must be properly prepared in accordance with Section 43(8).

10. Annual accounts must be accompanied by an audit report complying with Section 14 of the 1967 Act, and must have been laid before the company in general meeting in accordance with Section 1 of the 1976 Act (s 43(3)). Interim and initial accounts of public companies (there is no such requirement for private companies) must have been delivered to the Registrar of Companies (s 43(5)(b) and s 43(6)(d)). Initial accounts of public companies must be accompanied by a report by the auditor stating whether in his opinion the accounts have been properly prepared (s 43(6)(b)). The interim accounts need not be accompanied by an audit report.

11. There are requirements in Section 43(3)(c) and Section 43(6)(c), where an auditor has issued a qualified report on either annual or initial accounts as appropriate, that before a distribution may be made in reliance on those accounts the auditor must issue an additional statement. In this statement he must express an opinion whether the subject of his qualification is material for the purposes of determining whether the proposed distribution complies with the requirements of the Act.

Adjustments to relevant accounts

12. Adjustments to distributable profits calculated from the relevant accounts are required where one or more distributions have already been made 'in pursuance of determinations made by reference to' those accounts (s 43(7)). Adjustments are also required where a company has, since those accounts were prepared, provided financial assistance for the purchase of its own shares which depletes its net assets or made certain payments in respect of or in connection with the purchase of its own shares (s 60(1) of the 1981 Act).

Basis for calculating profits available for distribution

13.   The starting point in determining profits available for distribution, the 'accumulated, realised profits . . . less accumulated, realised losses', will be the profit or loss recognised in the relevant accounts. That is the accumulated balance on the profit and loss account. This figure may require adjustment to take into account any items which are required to be excluded in the determination of distributable profits (e.g. see paragraph 21 below). The amount so arrived at will require further adjustment for any items taken to reserve accounts which may properly be included in the determination of distributable profits. For example, an unrealised profit on an asset revaluation will originally be credited direct to a revaluation reserve. On a subsequent disposal of the asset part or all of the profit is clearly realised notwithstanding the fact that it may not have been passed through the profit and loss account.

14.   If an item has not been recognised in the relevant accounts, it cannot be taken into account in determining the profits or net assets available for distribution.

Aspects requiring special consideration

Realised losses

15.   Section 39(4) as amended states that certain provisions are to be treated as a realised loss. These are provisions of any kind mentioned in paragraphs 87(1) and 88 of the new Schedule 8, namely:

> '. . . any amount written off by way of providing for depreciation or diminution in value of assets' and ' . . . any amount retained as reasonably necessary for the purpose of providing for any liability or loss which is likely to be incurred, or certain to be incurred but uncertain as to amount or as to the date on which it will arise.'

16.   Section 39(4) as amended makes one specific exception to the rule that any provision of any kind mentioned in these paragraphs is to be treated as a realised loss, namely a provision arising on a revaluation of a fixed asset when all the fixed assets, or all fixed assets other than goodwill, have been revalued (see paragraph 19 below).

17.   In view of the requirement of s 39(4), any loss recognised in the profit and loss account will normally be a realised loss. (An exception to this rule at s 39(5) is discussed at paragraph 21 below.)

Revaluation of assets

18.   A surplus over original cost recognised on revaluation of any asset is unrealised. There is no statutory requirement specifying whether the

645

balance, if any, of the surplus that represents the writing back of past depreciation or of provisions for diminution in value should be regarded as realised or unrealised. Moreover, there is at present no unanimity of opinion as to whether such a surplus, to the extent that it represents the writing back of a realised loss, particularly where the realised loss arises from past depreciation, constitutes a realised profit. In view of the division of opinion on this matter, and in the absence of any statutory rule or clearly decisive precedent in case law, it is considered inappropriate to offer guidance on the question in this statement. Where reliance is placed on such a profit being realised in order to make a distribution, it may be appropriate for the directors of the company to seek legal advice. To the extent that the surplus represents the writing back of an unrealised loss, it should be treated as an unrealised profit.

19.   A deficit on the revaluation of an asset (unless offsetting a previous unrealised surplus on the same asset) gives rise to a provision and is required to be treated as a realised loss. A realised loss thus created cannot be reduced by being offset wholly or partially against revaluation surpluses on other assets, whether or not of the same class. However, there is an exception to the general rule where a provision for diminution in value of a fixed asset arises on a revaluation of all the fixed assets (other than goodwill) (s 39(4) as amended). Although not explicitly stated, the Act implies that such a provision may be treated as unrealised, and therefore that it does not reduce the profits available for distribution.

20.   For the purpose of s 39(4), a 'revaluation' of all the fixed assets may comprise actual revaluations of some of the fixed assets combined with consideration by the directors of the value of the remaining fixed assets. However, if an actual revaluation of all the fixed assets has not occurred, the directors must be satisfied that the aggregate value of all fixed assets 'considered' but not actually revalued is not less than the aggregate amount at which they are for the time being stated in the company's accounts (s 39(4A): see paragraph 45(2) of Schedule 3 to the 1981 Act). If the accounts include 'revalued' fixed assets which have been 'considered', but which have not been subject to an actual revaluation, certain additional information is required to be disclosed for the 'revaluation' to be valid (s 43(7A): see paragraph 47 (c) of Schedule 3 to the 1981 Act).

Revalued fixed assets and depreciation

21.   Provisions for depreciation of revalued fixed assets require special treatment to the extent that these provisions exceed the amounts which would have been provided if an unrealised profit had not been made on revaluation (s 39(5)). For the purpose of calculating the amount of profit which is legally available for distribution, s 39(5) requires an amount equivalent to this excess depreciation to 'be treated . . . as a realised profit', thereby reducing the provision for this

purpose to that relating to the original cost of the asset. As a result, while the depreciation of a surplus on a fixed asset revaluation will affect the published profits, it will not normally affect the amount of a company's distributable profits, provided of course that this revaluation surplus has not been capitalised ('capitalisation' in this context is defined at s 45(3)).

Disposal of revalued assets

22. On the disposal of a revalued asset any surplus over cost immediately becomes realised. Any loss which has been treated as unrealised (see paragraph 20 above) should on disposal of the asset be redesignated as a realised loss.

Development costs

23. Development costs carried forward in accordance with SSAP 13 'Accounting for research and development' will not normally affect distributable profits. Although Section 42A(1) (inserted by s 84 of the 1981 Act) requires that development costs shown as an asset should be treated as a realised loss, this requirement does not apply (s 42A(3)) if the directors justify the costs carried forward not being treated as a realised loss. This they will normally be able to do if the costs are carried forward in accordance with SSAP 13. Such justification must be included in the note on capitalised development costs required by paragraph 20(2) of the new Schedule 8.

Holding company

24 It should be noted that although the whole of the distributable profits of a subsidiary are (subject to the interests of minority shareholders and tax on distributions) available to the holding company, the latter cannot distribute these profits to its own shareholders until such time as they are recognised in the accounts of the holding company.

25. It is not normal practice to take credit for dividends from investments unless the amounts are declared prior to the investing company's year-end. However, dividends receivable from subsidiaries and associates in respect of accounting periods ending on or before that of the holding company are normally accrued in the holding company's accounts even if declared after the holding company's year-end. Such dividends should be treated as realised by the holding company whether they are paid or passed through a current account, provided that, in the latter case, an appropriate reassessment of the realisable value of the current account balance is made.

26. Exchange control or other restrictions may affect the ability of overseas subsidiaries to remit dividends to the UK. In accordance with

the prudence concept such dividends receivable should be treated as realised only when their eventual receipt can be assessed with reasonable certainty.

27.   Whilst there is no legal requirement for a holding company to take into account its share of the net losses (if any) of its subsidiaries in determining its distributable profits, the holding company may need to make a provision against a permanent diminution in the value of its investment in any such subsidiary (paragraph 19(2) of the new Schedule 8).

Current cost accounts

28.   It will normally make no difference to a company's legally distributable profit whether its relevant accounts are drawn up under the historical or the current cost convention. Where net assets under the current cost convention exceed net assets under the historical cost convention, the difference consists of net unrealised profits which form part of the current cost reserve. The remainder of the current cost reserve consists of an amount equal to the cumulative current cost adjustments charged in the profit and loss account each year. According to SSAP 16 this amount is regarded as realised (in the case of the depreciation adjustment the 1980 Act specifically requires it to be so treated). This part of the current cost reserve, being realised, is legally distributable even though there would be a reduction in the operating capability of the business as a result of making such a distribution, which might, therefore, be commercially inadvisable.

Transitional provisions

Determination of distributable profits at the commencement date

29.   Where the directors of a company are, after making all reasonable enquiries, unable to determine whether a particular profit or loss made before the commencement date of the 1980 Act is realised or unrealised, they may treat such a profit as realised and such a loss as unrealised (s39(7)). Such a position will occur when there are no records of the original cost of an asset or the original amount of a liability.

30.   Where a public company has distributed or utilised (otherwise than by capitalisation) unrealised profits prior to the commencement date of the 1980 Act and such profits have not subsequently been realised, an amount equal to the unrealised profits so distributed or utilised falls to be included as part of the undistributable reserves (s 40(2) and s 45(4)). This prevents a public company which has so distributed or utilised unrealised profits in the past from making any further distribution until the shortfall has been made good.

31.　　If, prior to the commencement of the 1980 Act, a company has realised losses (insofar as they have not been previously written off in either a reduction or a reorganisation of capital), such losses must be made good before making any distribution (s 39(2)).

32.　　The part of the 1980 Act dealing with distributable profits came into operation as follows (s 45(6)):

New public companies	On their registration under Part I of the 1980 Act.
Existing public companies	On their re-registration as a public limited company under Part I of the 1980 Act, or on 22 June 1982 (18 months after the appointed day), whichever is the earlier.
Private companies	22 June 1982.

Companies Act 1985

Extracts of accounting provisions

(Reproduced by kind permission of the
Controller of Her Majesty's Stationery Office)

*Those Sections of, and Schedules to, the Act that are
reproduced in full are indicated on the Arrangement of Sections
by an asterisk.*

Companies Act 1985

CHAPTER 6

ARRANGEMENT OF SECTIONS

A 2

CHAPTER II

ISSUES BY COMPANIES INCORPORATED, OR TO BE INCORPORATED, OUTSIDE GREAT BRITAIN

PART IV

ALLOTMENT OF SHARES AND DEBENTURES

General provisions as to allotment

Pre-emption rights

Commissions and discounts

Amount to be paid for shares; the means of payment

PART V

SHARE CAPITAL, ITS INCREASE, MAINTENANCE AND
REDUCTION

CHAPTER I

GENERAL PROVISIONS ABOUT SHARE CAPITAL

CHAPTER II

CLASS RIGHTS

A 3

A 4

Debentures

Part VI

Disclosure of Interests in Shares

Individual and group acquisitions

Registration and investigation of share acquisitions and disposals

Supplementary

PART VII

ACCOUNTS AND AUDIT

CHAPTER I

PROVISIONS APPLYING TO COMPANIES GENERALLY

Modified accounts

Dormant companies

Publication of accounts

Supplementary

CHAPTER II

ACCOUNTS OF BANKING, SHIPPING AND INSURANCE COMPANIES

PART VIII

DISTRIBUTION OF PROFITS AND ASSETS

Limits of company's power of distribution

Relevant accounts

PART IX

A COMPANY'S MANAGEMENT; DIRECTORS AND SECRETARIES; THEIR QUALIFICATIONS, DUTIES AND RESPONSIBILITIES

PART XI

COMPANY ADMINISTRATION AND PROCEDURE

CHAPTER I

COMPANY IDENTIFICATION

CHAPTER II

REGISTER OF MEMBERS

Part XII

Registration of Charges

Chapter I

Registration of Charges (England and Wales)

Chapter II

Registration of Charges (Scotland)

Part XIII

Arrangements and Reconstructions

Part XV

Orders Imposing Restrictions on Shares
(Sections 210, 216, 445)

Part XVI

Fraudulent Trading by a Company

Part XVII

Protection of Company's Members against Unfair Prejudice

Part XVIII

Floating Charges and Receivers
(Scotland)

Chapter I

Floating Charges

Chapter II

Receivers

CHAPTER III

GENERAL

PART XIX

RECEIVERS AND MANAGERS
(ENGLAND AND WALES)

PART XX

WINDING UP OF COMPANIES REGISTERED
UNDER THIS ACT OR THE FORMER COMPANIES ACTS

CHAPTER I

PRELIMINARY

Modes of winding up

ELIZABETH II

Companies Act 1985

1985 CHAPTER 6

An Act to consolidate the greater part of the Companies
Acts. [11th March 1985]

B E IT ENACTED by the Queen's most Excellent Majesty, by and
with the advice and consent of the Lords Spiritual and
Temporal, and Commons, in this present Parliament
assembled, and by the authority of the same, as follows:—

CHAPTER III

SHARE PREMIUMS

Application of
share
premiums.

130.—(1) If a company issues shares at a premium, whether for cash or otherwise, a sum equal to the aggregate amount or value of the premiums on those shares shall be transferred to an account called " the share premium account ".

(2) The share premium account may be applied by the company in paying up unissued shares to be allotted to members as fully paid bonus shares, or in writing off—

    (*a*) the company's preliminary expenses ; or

    (*b*) the expenses of, or the commission paid or discount allowed on, any issue of shares or debentures of the company,

or in providing for the premium payable on redemption of debentures of the company.

(3) Subject to this, the provisions of this Act relating to the reduction of a company's share capital apply as if the share premium account were part of its paid up share capital.

(4) Sections 131 and 132 below give relief from the requirements of this section, and in those sections references to the issuing company are to the company issuing shares as above mentioned.

Merger relief.

131.—(1) With the exception made by section 132(4) (group reconstruction) this section applies where the issuing company has secured at least a 90 per cent. equity holding in another company in pursuance of an arrangement providing for the allotment of equity shares in the issuing company on terms that the consideration for the shares allotted is to be provided—

    (*a*) by the issue or transfer to the issuing company of equity shares in the other company, or

    (*b*) by the cancellation of any such shares not held by the issuing company.

(2) If the equity shares in the issuing company allotted in pursuance of the arrangement in consideration for the acquisition or cancellation of equity shares in the other company are issued at a premium, section 130 does not apply to the premiums on those shares.

(3) Where the arrangement also provides for the allotment of any shares in the issuing company on terms that the consideration for those shares is to be provided by the issue or transfer to the issuing company of non-equity shares in the other

company or by the cancellation of any such shares in that company not held by the issuing company, relief under subsection (2) extends to any shares in the issuing company allotted on those terms in pursuance of the arrangement.

(4) Subject to the next subsection, the issuing company is to be regarded for purposes of this section as having secured at least a 90 per cent. equity holding in another company in pursuance of such an arrangement as is mentioned in subsection (1) if in consequence of an acquisition or cancellation of equity shares in that company (in pursuance of that arrangement) it holds equity shares in that company (whether all or any of those shares were acquired in pursuance of that arrangement, or not) of an aggregate nominal value equal to 90 per cent. or more of the nominal value of that company's equity share capital.

(5) Where the equity share capital of the other company is divided into different classes of shares, this section does not apply unless the requirements of subsection (1) are satisfied in relation to each of those classes of shares taken separately.

(6) Shares held by a company which is the issuing company's holding company or subsidiary, or a subsidiary of the issuing company's holding company, or by its or their nominees, are to be regarded for purposes of this section as held by the issuing company.

(7) In relation to a company and its shares and capital, the following definitions apply for purposes of this section—

(a) " equity shares " means shares comprised in the company's equity share capital ; and

(b) " non-equity shares " means shares (of any class) not so comprised ;

and " arrangement " means any agreement, scheme or arrangement (including an arrangement sanctioned under section 425 (company compromise with members and creditors) or section 582 (liquidator accepting shares etc. as consideration for sale of company property)).

(8) The relief allowed by this section does not apply if the issue of shares took place before 4th February 1981.

132.—(1) This section applies where the issuing company— Relief in respect of group recon- structions.

(a) is a wholly-owned subsidiary of another company (" the holding company "), and

(b) allots shares to the holding company or to another wholly-owned subsidiary of the holding company in consideration for the transfer to the issuing company of assets other than cash, being assets of any company (" the transferor company ") which is a member of the group of companies which comprises the holding company and all its wholly-owned subsidiaries.

(2) Where the shares in the issuing company allotted in consideration for the transfer are issued at a premium, the issuing company is not required by section 130 to transfer any amount in excess of the minimum premium value to the share premium account.

(3) In subsection (2), " the minimum premium value " means the amount (if any) by which the base value of the consideration for the shares allotted exceeds the aggregate nominal value of those shares.

(4) For the purposes of subsection (3), the base value of the consideration for the shares allotted is the amount by which the base value of the assets transferred exceeds the base value of any liabilities of the transferor company assumed by the issuing company as part of the consideration for the assets transferred.

(5) For the purposes of subsection (4)—

> (a) the base value of the assets transferred is to be taken as—
>
>> (i) the cost of those assets to the transferor company, or
>>
>> (ii) the amount at which those assets are stated in the transferor company's accounting records immediately before the transfer,
>
> whichever is the less ; and
>
> (b) the base value of the liabilities assumed is to be taken as the amount at which they are stated in the transferor company's accounting records immediately before the transfer.

(6) The relief allowed by this section does not apply (subject to the next subsection) if the issue of shares took place before the date of the coming into force of the Companies (Share Premium Account) Regulations 1984 (which were made on 21st December 1984).

S.I. 1984/2007.

(7) To the extent that the relief allowed by this section would have been allowed by section 38 of the Companies Act 1981 as originally enacted (the text of which section is set out in Schedule 25 to this Act), the relief applies where the issue of shares took place before the date of the coming into force of those Regulations, but not if the issue took place before 4th February 1981.

1981 c. 62.

(8) Section 131 does not apply in a case falling within this section.

133.—(1) An amount corresponding to one representing the premiums or part of the premiums on shares issued by a company which by virtue of sections 131 or 132 of this Act, or section 12 of the Consequential Provisions Act, is not included in the company's share premium account may also be disregarded in determining the amount at which any shares or other consideration provided for the shares issued is to be included in the company's balance sheet.

(2) References in this Chapter (however expressed) to—

(*a*) the acquisition by a company of shares in another company ; and

(*b*) the issue or allotment of shares to, or the transfer of shares to or by, a company,

include (respectively) the acquisition of any of those shares by, and the issue or allotment or (as the case may be) the transfer of any of those shares to or by, nominees of that company ; and the reference in section 132 to the company transferring the shares is to be construed accordingly.

(3) References in this Chapter to the transfer of shares in a company include the transfer of a right to be included in the company's register of members in respect of those shares.

(4) In sections 131 to 133 " company ", except in references to the issuing company, includes any body corporate.

134.—(1) The Secretary of State may by regulations in a statutory instrument make such provision as appears to him to be appropriate—

Provision for extending or restricting relief from s. 130.

(*a*) for relieving companies from the requirements of section 130 in relation to premiums other than cash premiums, or

(*b*) for restricting or otherwise modifying any relief from those requirements provided by this Chapter.

(2) Regulations under this section may make different provision for different cases or classes of case and may contain such incidental and supplementary provisions as the Secretary of State thinks fit.

(3) No such regulations shall be made unless a draft of the instrument containing them has been laid before Parliament and approved by a resolution of each House.

Chapter VI

Financial Assistance by a Company for Acquisition of its Own Shares

Provisions applying to both public and private companies

Financial
assistance
generally
prohibited.

151.—(1) Subject to the following provisions of this Chapter, where a person is acquiring or is proposing to acquire shares in a company, it is not lawful for the company or any of its subsidiaries to give financial assistance directly or indirectly for the purpose of that acquisition before or at the same time as the acquisition takes place.

(2) Subject to those provisions, where a person has acquired shares in a company and any liability has been incurred (by that or any other person), for the purpose of that acquisition, it is not lawful for the company or any of its subsidiaries to give financial assistance directly or indirectly for the purpose of reducing or discharging the liability so incurred.

(3) If a company acts in contravention of this section, it is liable to a fine, and every officer of it who is in default is liable to imprisonment or a fine, or both.

Definitions for
this Chapter.

152.—(1) In this Chapter—

(*a*) " financial assistance " means—

    (i) financial assistance given by way of gift,

    (ii) financial assistance given by way of guarantee, security or indemnity, other than an indemnity in respect of the indemnifier's own neglect or default, or by way of release or waiver,

    (iii) financial assistance given by way of a loan or any other agreement under which any of the obligations of the person giving the assistance are to be fulfilled at a time when in accordance with the agreement any obligation of another party to the agreement remains unfulfilled, or by way of the novation of, or the assignment of rights arising under, a loan or such other agreement, or

    (iv) any other financial assistance given by a company the net assets of which are thereby reduced to a material extent or which has no net assets ;

(*b*) " distributable profits ", in relation to the giving of any financial assistance—

    (i) means those profits out of which the company could lawfully make a distribution equal in value to that assistance, and

    (ii) includes, in a case where the financial assistance is or includes a non-cash asset, any profit which, if the company were to make a distribution of that asset, would under section 276 (distributions in kind) be available for that purpose,

     and

(c) " distribution " has the meaning given by section 263(2).

(2) In subsection (1)(a)(iv), " net assets " means the aggregate of the company's assets, less the aggregate of its liabilities (" liabilities " to include any provision for liabilities or charges within paragraph 89 of Schedule 4).

(3) In this Chapter—

(a) a reference to a person incurring a liability includes his changing his financial position by making an agreement or arrangement (whether enforceable or unenforceable, and whether made on his own account or with any other person) or by any other means, and

(b) a reference to a company giving financial assistance for the purpose of reducing or discharging a liability incurred by a person for the purpose of the acquisition of shares includes its giving such assistance for the purpose of wholly or partly restoring his financial position to what it was before the acquisition took place.

153.—(1) Section 151(1) does not prohibit a company from giving financial assistance for the purpose of an acquisition of shares in it or its holding company if—

Transactions not prohibited by s. 151.

(a) the company's principal purpose in giving that assistance is not to give it for the purpose of any such acquisition, or the giving of the assistance for that purpose is but an incidental part of some larger purpose of the company, and

(b) the assistance is given in good faith in the interests of the company.

(2) Section 151(2) does not prohibit a company from giving financial assistance if—

(a) the company's principal purpose in giving the assistance is not to reduce or discharge any liability incurred by a person for the purpose of the acquisition of shares in the company or its holding company, or the reduction or discharge of any such liability is but an incidental part of some larger purpose of the company, and

(b) the assistance is given in good faith in the interests of the company.

(3) Section 151 does not prohibit—

(a) a distribution of a company's assets by way of dividend lawfully made or a distribution made in the course of the company's winding up, (*b*) the allotment of bonus shares ,

(*c*) a reduction of capital confirmed by order of the court under section 137,

(*d*) a redemption or purchase of shares made in accordance with Chapter VII of this Part,

(*e*) anything done in pursuance of an order of the court under section 425 (compromises and arrangements with creditors and members),

(*f*) anything done under an arrangement made in pursuance of section 582 (acceptance of shares by liquidator in winding up as consideration for sale of property), or

(*g*) anything done under an arrangement made between a company and its creditors which is binding on the creditors by virtue of section 601 (winding up imminent or in progress).

(4) Section 151 does not prohibit—

(*a*) where the lending of money is part of the ordinary business of the company, the lending of money by the company in the ordinary course of its business,

(*b*) the provision by a company in accordance with an employees' share scheme of money for the acquisition of fully paid shares in the company or its holding company,

(*c*) the making by a company of loans to persons (other than directors) employed in good faith by the company with a view to enabling those persons to acquire fully paid shares in the company or its holding company to be held by them by way of beneficial ownership.

Special restriction for public companies.

154.—(1) In the case of a public company, section 153(4) authorises the giving of financial assistance only if the company has net assets which are not thereby reduced or, to the extent that those assets are thereby reduced, if the assistance is provided out of distributable profits.

(2) For this purpose the following definitions apply—

(*a*) " net assets " means the amount by which the aggregate of the company's assets exceeds the aggregate of its liabilities (taking the amount of both assets and liabilities to be as stated in the company's accounting records immediately before the financial assistance is given) ;

(*b*) " liabilities " includes any amount retained as reasonably necessary for the purpose of providing for any liability or loss which is either likely to be incurred, or certain to be incurred but uncertain as to amount or as to the date on which it will arise.

Private companies

PART V
CHAPTER VI
Relaxation of
s. 151 for
private
companies.

155.—(1) Section 151 does not prohibit a private company from giving financial assistance in a case where the acquisition of shares in question is or was an acquisition of shares in the company or, if it is a subsidiary of another private company, in that other company if the following provisions of this section, and sections 156 to 158, are complied with as respects the giving of that assistance.

(2) The financial assistance may only be given if the company has net assets which are not thereby reduced or, to the extent that they are reduced, if the assistance is provided out of distributable profits.

Section 154(2) applies for the interpretation of this subsection.

(3) This section does not permit financial assistance to be given by a subsidiary, in a case where the acquisition of shares in question is or was an acquisition of shares in its holding company, if it is also a subsidiary of a public company which is itself a subsidiary of that holding company.

(4) Unless the company proposing to give the financial assistance is a wholly-owned subsidiary, the giving of assistance under this section must be approved by special resolution of the company in general meeting.

(5) Where the financial assistance is to be given by the company in a case where the acquisition of shares in question is or was an acquisition of shares in its holding company, that holding company and any other company which is both the company's holding company and a subsidiary of that other holding company (except, in any case, a company which is a wholly-owned subsidiary) shall also approve by special resolution in general meeting the giving of the financial assistance.

(6) The directors of the company proposing to give the financial assistance and, where the shares acquired or to be acquired are shares in its holding company, the directors of that company and of any other company which is both the company's holding company and a subsidiary of that other holding company shall before the financial assistance is given make a statutory declaration in the prescribed form complying with the section next following.

156.—(1) A statutory declaration made by a company's directors under section 155(6) shall contain such particulars of the financial assistance to be given, and of the business of the company of which they are directors, as may be prescribed, and shall identify the person to whom the assistance is to be given.

(2) The declaration shall state that the directors have formed the opinion, as regards the company's initial situation immediately following the date on which the assistance is proposed to be given, that there will be no ground on which it could then be found to be unable to pay its debts ; and either—

> (*a*) if it is intended to commence the winding up of the company within 12 months of that date, that the company will be able to pay its debts in full within 12 months of the commencement of the winding up, or

> (*b*) in any other case, that the company will be able to pay its debts as they fall due during the year immediately following that date.

(3) In forming their opinion for purposes of subsection (2), the directors shall take into account the same liabilities (including contingent and prospective liabilities) as would be relevant under section 517 (winding up by the court) to the question whether the company is unable to pay its debts.

(4) The directors' statutory declaration shall have annexed to it a report addressed to them by their company's auditors stating that—

> (*a*) they have enquired into the state of affairs of the company, and

> (*b*) they are not aware of anything to indicate that the opinion expressed by the directors in the declaration as to any of the matters mentioned in subsection (2) of this section is unreasonable in all the circumstances.

(5) The statutory declaration and auditors' report shall be delivered to the registrar of companies—

> (*a*) together with a copy of any special resolution passed by the company under section 155 and delivered to the registrar in compliance with section 380, or

> (*b*) where no such resolution is required to be passed, within 15 days after the making of the declaration.

(6) If a company fails to comply with subsection (5), the company and every officer of it who is in default is liable to a fine and, for continued contravention, to a daily default fine.

(7) A director of a company who makes a statutory declaration under section 155 without having reasonable grounds for the opinion expressed in it is liable to imprisonment or a fine, or both.

Special
resolution
under s. 155.

157.—(1) A special resolution required by section 155 to be passed by a company approving the giving of financial assistance must be passed on the date on which the directors of that company make the statutory declaration required by that section in connection with the giving of that assistance, or within the week immediately following that date.

(2) Where such a resolution has been passed, an application may be made to the court for the cancellation of the resolution—

    (*a*) by the holders of not less in the aggregate than 10 per cent. in nominal value of the company's issued share capital or any class of it, or

    (*b*) if the company is not limited by shares, by not less than 10 per cent. of the company's members ;

but the application shall not be made by a person who has consented to or voted in favour of the resolution.

(3) Subsections (3) to (10) of section 54 (litigation to cancel resolution under section 53) apply to applications under this section as to applications under section 54.

(4) A special resolution passed by a company is not effective for purposes of section 155—

    (*a*) unless the declaration made in compliance with sub-section (6) of that section by the directors of the company, together with the auditors' report annexed to it, is available for inspection by members of the company at the meeting at which the resolution is passed,

    (*b*) if it is cancelled by the court on an application under this section.

158.—(1) This section applies as to the time before and after which financial assistance may not be given by a company in pursuance of section 155.

Time for giving financial assistance under s. 155.

(2) Where a special resolution is required by that section to be passed approving the giving of the assistance, the assistance shall not be given before the expiry of the period of 4 weeks beginning with—

    (*a*) the date on which the special resolution is passed, or

    (*b*) where more than one such resolution is passed, the date on which the last of them is passed,

unless, as respects that resolution (or, if more than one, each of them), every member of the company which passed the resolution who is entitled to vote at general meetings of the company voted in favour of the resolution.

(3) If application for the cancellation of any such resolution is made under section 157, the financial assistance shall not be given before the final determination of the application unless the court otherwise orders.

(4) The assistance shall not be given after the expiry of the period of 8 weeks beginning with—

(a) the date on which the directors of the company proposing to give the assistance made their statutory declaration under section 155, or

(b) where that company is a subsidiary and both its directors and the directors of any of its holding companies made such a declaration, the date on which the earliest of the declarations is made,

unless the court, on an application under section 157, otherwise orders.

PART VII

ACCOUNTS AND AUDIT

CHAPTER I

PROVISIONS APPLYING TO COMPANIES GENERALLY

Accounting records

Companies to keep accounting records.

221.—(1) Every company shall cause accounting records to be kept in accordance with this section.

(2) The accounting records shall be sufficient to show and explain the company's transactions, and shall be such as to—

(a) disclose with reasonable accuracy, at any time, the financial position of the company at that time, and

(b) enable the directors to ensure that any balance sheet and profit and loss account prepared under this Part comply with the requirements of this Act as to the form and content of company accounts and otherwise.

(3) The accounting records shall in particular contain—

(a) entries from day to day of all sums of money received and expended by the company, and the matters in respect of which the receipt and expenditure takes place, and

(b) a record of the assets and liabilities of the company.

(4) If the company's business involves dealing in goods, the accounting records shall contain—

(a) statements of stock held by the company at the end of each financial year of the company,

(b) all statements of stocktakings from which any such statement of stock as is mentioned in paragraph (a) has been or is to be prepared, and

(c) except in the case of goods sold by way of ordinary

retail trade, statements of all goods sold and purchased, showing the goods and the buyers and sellers in sufficient detail to enable all these to be identified.

222.—(1) Subject as follows, a company's accounting records shall be kept at its registered office or such other place as the directors think fit, and shall at all times be open to inspection by the company's officers.

(2) If accounting records are kept at a place outside Great Britain, accounts and returns with respect to the business dealt with in the accounting records so kept shall be sent to, and kept at, a place in Great Britain, and shall at all times be open to such inspection.

(3) The accounts and returns to be sent to Great Britain in accordance with subsection (2) shall be such as to—

(a) disclose with reasonable accuracy the financial position of the business in question at intervals of not more than 6 months, and

(b) enable the directors to ensure that the company's balance sheet and profit and loss account comply with the requirements of this Act as to the form and content of company accounts and otherwise.

(4) Accounting records which a company is required by section 221 to keep shall be preserved by it—

(a) in the case of a private company, for 3 years from the date on which they are made, and

(b) in the case of a public company, for 6 years from that date.

This is subject to any direction with respect to the disposal of records given under winding-up rules under section 663.

223.—(1) If a company fails to comply with any provision of section 221 or 222(1) or (2), every officer of the company who is in default is guilty of an offence unless he shows that he acted honestly and that in the circumstances in which the company's business was carried on the default was excusable.

(2) An officer of a company is guilty of an offence if he fails to take all reasonable steps for securing compliance by the company with section 222(4), or has intentionally caused any default by the company under it.

(3) A person guilty of an offence under this section is liable to imprisonment or a fine, or both.

A company's accounting reference periods and financial year

224.—(1) A company's accounting reference periods are determined according to its accounting reference date.

(2) A company may give notice in the prescribed form to the registrar of companies specifying a date in the calendar year

as being the date on which in each successive calendar year an accounting reference period of the company is to be treated as coming to an end ; and the date specified in the notice is then the company's accounting reference date.

(3) However, no such notice has effect unless it is given before the end of 6 months beginning with the date of the company's incorporation ; and, failing such notice, the company's account· ing reference date is 31st March.

(4) A company's first accounting reference period is such period ending with its accounting reference date as begins on the date of its incorporation and is a period of more than 6 months and not more than 18 months ; and each successive period of 12 months beginning after the end of the first accounting reference period and ending with the accounting reference date is also an accounting reference period of the company.

(5) This section is subject to section 225, under which in certain circumstances a company may alter its accounting reference date and accounting reference periods.

Alteration of accounting reference period.

225.—(1) At any time during a period which is an accounting reference period of a company by virtue of section 224 or 226 the company may give notice in the prescribed form to the registrar of companies specifying a date in the calendar year (" the new accounting reference date ") on which that accounting reference period (" the current accounting reference period ") and each subsequent accounting reference period of the company is to be treated as coming to an end or (as the case may require) as having come to an end.

(2) At any time after the end of a period which was an accounting reference period of a company by virtue of section 224 or 226 the company may give notice in the prescribed form to the registrar of companies specifying a date in the calendar year (" the new accounting reference date ") on which that accounting reference period (" the previous accounting reference period ") and each subsequent accounting reference period of the company is to be treated as coming or (as the case may require) as having come to an end.

(3) But a notice under subsection (2)—

    (a) has no effect unless the company is a subsidiary or holding company of another company and the new accounting reference date coincides with the accounting reference date of that other company, and

    (b) has no effect if the period allowed (under section 242) for laying and delivering accounts in relation to the previous accounting reference period has already expired at the time when the notice is given.

(4) A notice under this section shall state whether the current
or previous accounting reference period of the company—

    (*a*) is to be treated as shortened, so as to come to an end
or (as the case may require) be treated as having come
to an end on the new accounting reference date on the
first occasion on which that date falls or fell after the
beginning of that accounting reference period, or

    (*b*) is to be treated as extended, so as to come to an end or
(as the case may require) be treated as having come
to an end on the new accounting reference date on the
second occasion on which that date falls or fell after
the beginning of that accounting reference period.

(5) A notice which states that the current or previous accounting reference period is to be extended has no effect if the current
or previous accounting reference period, as extended in accordance with the notice, would exceed 18 months.

(6) Subject to any direction given by the Secretary of State
under the next subsection, a notice which states that the current
or previous accounting reference period is to be extended has
no effect unless—

    (*a*) no earlier accounting reference period of the company
has been extended by virtue of a previous notice given
by the company under this section, or

    (*b*) the notice is given not less than 5 years after the date
on which any earlier accounting reference period of
the company which was so extended came to an end,
or

    (*c*) the company is a subsidiary or holding company of
another company and the new accounting reference
date coincides with the accounting reference date of
that other company.

(7) The Secretary of State may, if he thinks fit, direct that
subsection (6) shall not apply to a notice already given by a
company under this section or (as the case may be) in relation
to a notice which may be so given.

226.—(1) Where a company has given notice with effect in
accordance with section 225, and that notice has not been superseded by a subsequent notice by the company which has such
effect, the new date specified in the notice is the company's
accounting reference date, in substitution for that which, by
virtue of section 224 or this section, was its accounting reference
date at the time when the notice was given.

(2) Where by virtue of such a notice one date is substituted for another as the accounting reference date of a company—

(a) the current or previous accounting reference period, shortened or extended (as the case may be) in accordance with the notice, and

(b) each successive period of 12 months beginning after the end of that accounting reference period (as so shortened or extended) and ending with the new accounting reference date,

is or (as the case may require) is to be treated as having been an accounting reference period of the company, instead of any period which would be an accounting reference period of the company if the notice had not been given.

(3) Section 225 and this section do not affect any accounting reference period of the company which—

(a) in the case of a notice under section 225(1), is earlier than the current accounting reference period, or

(b) in the case of a notice under section 225(2), is earlier than the previous accounting reference period.

Directors'
duty to
prepare
annual
accounts.

227.—(1) In the case of every company, the directors shall in respect of each accounting reference period of the company prepare a profit and loss account for the financial year or, if it is a company not trading for profit, an income and expenditure account.

(2) Where it is the company's first accounting reference period, the financial year begins with the first day of that period and ends with—

(a) the date on which the accounting reference period ends, or

(b) such other date, not more than 7 days before or more than 7 days after the end of that period, as the directors may determine;

and after that the financial year begins with the day after the date to which the last preceding profit and loss account was made up and ends as mentioned in paragraphs (a) and (b) above.

(3) The directors shall prepare a balance sheet as at the last day of the financial year.

(4) In the case of a holding company, the directors shall secure that, except where in their opinion there are good reasons against it, the financial year of each of its subsidiaries coincides with the company's own financial year.

PART VII
CHAPTER I
Form and
content of
individual
accounts.

Form and content of company individual and group accounts

228.—(1) A company's accounts prepared under section 227 shall comply with the requirements of Schedule 4 (so far as applicable) with respect to the form and content of the balance sheet and profit and loss account and any additional information to be provided by way of notes to the accounts.

(2) The balance sheet shall give a true and fair view of the state of affairs of the company as at the end of the financial year ; and the profit and loss account shall give a true and fair view of the profit or loss of the company for the financial year.

(3) Subsection (2) overrides—

(a) the requirements of Schedule 4, and

(b) all other requirements of this Act as to the matters to be included in a company's accounts or in notes to those accounts ;

and accordingly the following two subsections have effect.

(4) If the balance sheet or profit and loss account drawn up in accordance with those requirements would not provide sufficient information to comply with subsection (2), any necessary additional information must be provided in that balance sheet or profit and loss account, or in a note to the accounts.

(5) If, owing to special circumstances in the case of any company, compliance with any such requirement in relation to the balance sheet or profit and loss account would prevent compliance with subsection (2) (even if additional information were provided in accordance with subsection (4)), the directors shall depart from that requirement in preparing the balance sheet or profit and loss account (so far as necessary in order to comply with subsection (2)).

(6) If the directors depart from any such requirement, particulars of the departure, the reasons for it and its effect shall be given in a note to the accounts.

(7) Subsections (1) to (6) do not apply to group accounts prepared under the next section ; and subsections (1) and (2) do not apply to a company's profit and loss account (or require the notes otherwise required in relation to that account) if—

(a) the company has subsidiaries, and

(b) the profit and loss account is framed as a consolidated account dealing with all or any of the company's subsidiaries as well as the company, and—

(i) complies with the requirements of this Act relating to consolidated profit and loss accounts, and

(ii) shows how much of the consolidated profit or loss for the financial year is dealt with in the company's individual accounts.

If group accounts are prepared, and advantage is taken of this subsection, that fact shall be disclosed in a note to the group accounts.

Group
accounts of
holding
company.

229.—(1) If at the end of its financial year a company has subsidiaries, the directors shall, as well as preparing individual accounts for that year, also prepare group accounts, being accounts or statements which deal with the state of affairs and profit or loss of the company and the subsidiaries.

(2) This does not apply if the company is at the end of the financial year the wholly-owned subsidiary of another body corporate incorporated in Great Britain.

(3) Group accounts need not deal with a subsidiary if the company's directors are of opinion that—

   (a) it is impracticable, or would be of no real value to the company's members, in view of the insignificant amounts involved, or

   (b) it would involve expense or delay out of proportion to the value to members, or

   (c) the result would be misleading, or harmful to the business of the company or any of its subsidiaries, or

   (d) the business of the holding company and that of the subsidiary are so different that they cannot reasonably be treated as a single undertaking;

and, if the directors are of that opinion about each of the company's subsidiaries, group accounts are not required.

(4) However, the approval of the Secretary of State is required for not dealing in group accounts with a subsidiary on the ground that the result would be harmful or on the ground of difference between the business of the holding company and that of the subsidiary.

(5) A holding company's group accounts shall be consolidated accounts comprising—

   (a) a consolidated balance sheet dealing with the state of affairs of the company and all the subsidiaries to be dealt with in group accounts, and

   (b) a consolidated profit and loss account dealing with the profit or loss of the company and those subsidiaries.

(6) However, if the directors are of opinion that it is better for the purpose of presenting the same or equivalent information about the state of affairs and profit or loss of the company and

those subsidiaries, and of so presenting it that it may be readily
appreciated by the company's members, the group accounts may
be prepared in other than consolidated form, and in particular
may consist—

  (a) of more than one set of consolidated accounts dealing
      respectively with the company and one group of sub-
      sidiaries and with other groups of subsidiaries, or

  (b) of separate accounts dealing with each of the subsidiar-
      ies, or

  (c) of statements expanding the information about the sub-
      sidiaries in the company's individual accounts,

or of any combination of those forms.

(7) The group accounts may be wholly or partly incorporated
in the holding company's individual balance sheet and profit
and loss account.

230.—(1) A holding company's group accounts shall comply Form and
with the requirements of Schedule 4 (so far as applicable to content of
group accounts in the form in which those accounts are pre- group
pared) with respect to the form and content of those accounts and accounts.
any additional information to be provided by way of notes to
those accounts.

(2) Group accounts (together with any notes to them) shall
give a true and fair view of the state of affairs and profit or
loss of the company and the subsidiaries dealt with by those
accounts as a whole, so far as concerns members of the company.

(3) Subsection (2) overrides—

  (a) the requirements of Schedule 4, and

  (b) all other requirements of this Act as to the matters to
      be included in group accounts or in notes to those
      accounts,

and accordingly the following two subsections have effect.

(4) If group accounts drawn up in accordance with those
requirements would not provide sufficient information to comply
with subsection (2), any necessary additional information must
be provided in, or in a note to, the group accounts.

(5) If, owing to special circumstances in the case of any company, compliance with any such requirement in relation to its
group accounts would prevent those accounts from complying
with subsection (2) (even if additional information were provided
in accordance with subsection (4)), the directors shall depart from
that requirement in preparing the group accounts (so far as necessary to comply with subsection (2)).

(6) If the directors depart from any such requirement, particulars of that departure, the reason for it and its effect shall be given in a note to the group accounts.

(7) If the financial year of a subsidiary does not coincide with that of the holding company, the group accounts shall (unless the Secretary of State, on the application or with the consent of the holding company's directors, otherwise directs) deal with the subsidiary's state of affairs as at the end of its relevant financial year, that is—

(a) if its financial year ends with that of the holding company, that financial year, and

(b) if not, the subsidiary's financial year ending last before the end of the financial year of the holding company dealt with in the group accounts,

and with the subsidiary's profit or loss for its relevant financial year.

(8) The Secretary of State may, on the application or with the consent of a company's directors, modify the requirements of Schedule 4 as they have effect in relation to that company by virtue of subsection (1), for the purpose of adapting them to the company's circumstances; and references above in this section to the requirements of Schedule 4 are then to be read in relation to that company as references to those requirements as modified.

Additional
disclosure
required in
notes to
accounts.

231.—(1) Schedule 5 has effect with respect to additional matters which must be disclosed in company accounts for a financial year; and in that Schedule, where a thing is required to be stated or shown, or information is required to be given, it means that the thing is to be stated or shown, or the information is to be given, in a note to those accounts.

(2) In Schedule 5—

(a) Parts I and II are concerned, respectively, with the disclosure of particulars of the company's subsidiaries and of its other shareholdings,

(b) Part III is concerned with the disclosure of financial information relating to subsidiaries,

(c) Part IV requires a company which is itself a subsidiary to disclose its ultimate holding company,

(d) Part V is concerned with the emoluments of directors (including emoluments waived), pensions of directors and past directors and compensation for loss of office to directors and past directors, and

(e) Part VI is concerned with disclosure of the number of the company's employees who are remunerated at higher rates.

(3) Whenever it is stated in Schedule 5 that this subsection applies to certain particulars or information, it means that the particulars or information shall be annexed to the annual return first made by the company after copies of its accounts have been laid before it in general meeting ; and if a company fails to satisfy an obligation thus imposed, the company and every officer of it who is in default is liable to a fine and, for continued contravention, to a daily default fine.

(4) It is the duty of any director of a company to give notice to the company of such matters relating to himself as may be necessary for purposes of Part V of Schedule 5 ; and this applies to persons who are or have at any time in the preceding 5 years been officers, as it applies to directors.

A person who makes default in complying with this subsection is liable to a fine.

232.—(1) A holding company's group accounts for a financial year shall comply with Part I of Schedule 6 (so far as applicable) as regards the disclosure of transactions, arrangements and agreements there mentioned (loans, quasi-loans and other dealings in favour of directors). *Loans in favour of directors and connected persons.*

(2) In the case of a company other than a holding company, its individual accounts shall comply with Part I of Schedule 6 (so far as applicable) as regards disclosure of those matters.

(3) Particulars which are required by Part I of Schedule 6 to be contained in any accounts shall be given by way of notes to the accounts, and are required in respect of shadow directors as well as directors.

(4) Where by virtue of section 229(2) or (3) a company does not prepare group accounts for a financial year, subsection (1) of this section requires disclosure of such matters in its individual accounts as would have been disclosed in group accounts.

(5) The requirements of this section apply with such exceptions as are mentioned in Part I of Schedule 6 (including in particular exceptions for and in respect of recognised banks).

233.—(1) A holding company's group accounts for a financial year shall comply with Part II of Schedule 6 (so far as applicable) as regards transactions, arrangements and agreements made by the company or a subsidiary of it for persons who at any time during that financial year were officers of the company (but not directors). *Loans etc. to company's officers; statement of amounts outstanding.*

(2) In the case of a company other than a holding company, its individual accounts shall comply with Part II of Schedule 6 (so far as applicable) as regards those matters.

(3) Subsections (1) and (2) do not apply in relation to any transaction, arrangement or agreement made by a recognised bank for any of its officers or for any of the officers of its holding company.

(4) Particulars required by Part II of Schedule 6 to be contained in any accounts shall be given by way of notes to the accounts.

(5) Where by virtue of section 229(2) or (3) a company does not prepare group accounts for a financial year, subsection (1) of this section requires such matters to be stated in its individual accounts as would have been stated in group accounts.

Recognised banks: disclosure of dealings with and for directors.

234.—(1) The group accounts of a company which is, or is the holding company of, a recognised bank, and the individual accounts of any other company which is a recognised bank, shall comply with Part III of Schedule 6 (so far as applicable) as regards transactions, arrangements and agreements made by the company preparing the accounts (if it is a recognised bank) and, in the case of a holding company, by any of its subsidiaries which is a recognised bank, for persons who at any time during the financial year were directors of the company or connected with a director of it.

(2) Particulars required by Part III of Schedule 6 to be contained in any accounts shall be given by way of notes to those accounts, and are required in respect of shadow directors as well as directors.

(3) Where by virtue of section 229(2) or (3) a company does not prepare group accounts for a financial year, subsection (1) of this section requires such matters to be stated in its individual accounts as would have been stated in group accounts.

Directors' and auditors' reports

Directors' report.

235.—(1) In the case of every company there shall for each financial year be prepared a report by the directors—

    (a) containing a fair review of the development of the business of the company and its subsidiaries during the financial year and of their position at the end of it, and

    (b) stating the amount (if any) which they recommend should be paid as dividend and the amount (if any) which they propose to carry to reserves.

(2) The directors' report shall state the names of the persons who, at any time during the financial year, were directors of the company, and the principal activities of the company and its subsidiaries in the course of the year and any significant change in those activities in the year.

(3) The report shall also state the matters, and give the particulars, required by Part I of Schedule 7 (changes in asset values, directors' shareholdings and other interests, contributions for political and charitable purposes, etc.).

(4) Part II of Schedule 7 applies as regards the matters to be stated in the directors' report in the circumstances there specified (company acquiring its own shares or a permitted charge on them).

(5) Parts III, IV and V of Schedule 7 apply respectively as regards the matters to be stated in the directors' report relative to the employment, training and advancement of disabled persons ; the health, safety and welfare at work of the company's employees ; and the involvement of employees in the affairs, policy and performance of the company.

(6) If the company's individual accounts are accompanied by group accounts which are special category, the directors' report shall, in addition to complying with Schedule 7, also comply with paragraphs 2 to 6 of Schedule 10 (turnover and profitability ; size of labour force and wages paid).

(7) In respect of any failure to comply with the requirements of this Act as to the matters to be stated, and the particulars to be given, in the directors' report, every person who was a director of the company immediately before the end of the relevant period (meaning whatever is under section 242 the period for laying and delivering accounts) is guilty of an offence and liable to a fine.

In proceedings for an offence under this subsection, it is a defence for the person to prove that he took all reasonable steps for securing compliance with the requirements in question.

236.—(1) A company's auditors shall make a report to its Auditors' members on the accounts examined by them, and on every report. balance sheet and profit and loss account, and on all group accounts, copies of which are to be laid before the company in general meeting during the auditors' tenure of office.

(2) The auditors' report shall state—

    (a) whether in the auditors' opinion the balance sheet and profit and loss account and (if it is a holding company submitting group accounts) the group accounts have been properly prepared in accordance with this Act ; and

    (b) without prejudice to the foregoing, whether in their opinion a true and fair view is given—

       (i) in the balance sheet, of the state of the company's affairs at the end of the financial year,

    (ii) in the profit and loss account (if not framed
as a consolidated account), of the company's profit
or loss for the financial year, and

    (iii) in the case of group accounts, of the state
of affairs and profit or loss of the company and its
subsidiaries dealt with by those accounts, so far as
concerns members of the company.

Auditors'
duties and
powers.

237.—(1) It is the duty of the company's auditors, in preparing their report, to carry out such investigations as will
enable them to form an opinion as to the following matters—

(a) whether proper accounting records have been kept by
the company and proper returns adequate for their
audit have been received from branches not visited by
them,

(b) whether the company's balance sheet and (if not consolidated) its profit and loss account are in agreement
with the accounting records and returns.

(2) If the auditors are of opinion that proper accounting
records have not been kept, or that proper returns adequate for
their audit have not been received from branches not visited
by them, or if the balance sheet and (if not consolidated) the profit and loss account are not in agreement with the accounting
records and returns, the auditors shall state that fact in their
report.

(3) Every auditor of a company has a right of access at all
times to the company's books, accounts and vouchers, and is
entitled to require from the company's officers such information
and explanations as he thinks necessary for the performance of
the auditor's duties.

(4) If the auditors fail to obtain all the information and
explanations which, to the best of their knowledge and belief,
are necessary for the purposes of their audit, they shall state
that fact in their report.

(5) If the requirements of Parts V and VI of Schedule 5 and
Parts I to III of Schedule 6 are not complied with in the
accounts, it is the auditors' duty to include in their report, so
far as they are reasonably able to do so, a statement giving
the required particulars.

(6) It is the auditors' duty to consider whether the information given in the directors' report for the financial year for
which the accounts are prepared is consistent with those
accounts; and if they are of opinion that it is not, they shall
state that fact in their report.

Procedure on completion of accounts

238.—(1) A company's balance sheet, and every copy of it which is laid before the company in general meeting or de-livered to the registrar of companies, shall be signed on behalf of the board by two of the directors of the company or, if there is only one director, by that one.

(2) If a copy of the balance sheet—

    (a) is laid before the company or delivered to the registrar without being signed as required by this section, or

    (b) not being a copy so laid or delivered, is issued, circu-lated or published in a case where the balance sheet has not been signed as so required or where (the balance sheet having been so signed) the copy does not include a copy of the signatures or signature, as the case may be,

the company and every officer of it who is in default is liable to a fine.

(3) A company's profit and loss account and, so far as not incorporated in its individual balance sheet or profit and loss account, any group accounts of a holding company shall be annexed to the balance sheet, and the auditors' report shall be attached to it.

(4) Any accounts so annexed shall be approved by the board of directors before the balance sheet is signed on their behalf.

239. For the purposes of this Part, a company's accounts for a financial year are to be taken as comprising the following docu-ments—

    (a) the company's profit and loss account and balance sheet,

    (b) the directors' report,

    (c) the auditors' report, and

    (d) where the company has subsidiaries and section 229 applies, the company's group accounts.

240.—(1) In the case of every company, a copy of the com-pany's accounts for the financial year shall, not less than 21 days before the date of the meeting at which they are to be laid in accordance with the next section, be sent to each of the following persons—

    (a) every member of the company (whether or not entitled to receive notice of general meetings),

    (b) every holder of the company's debentures (whether or not so entitled), and

    (c) all persons other than members and debenture holders, being persons so entitled.

(2) In the case of a company not having a share capital, subsection (1) does not require a copy of the accounts to be sent to a member of the company who is not entitled to receive notices of general meetings of the company, or to a holder of the company's debentures who is not so entitled.

(3) Subsection (1) does not require copies of the accounts to be sent—

(*a*) to a member of the company or a debenture holder, being in either case a person who is not entitled to receive notices of general meetings, and of whose address the company is unaware, or

(*b*) to more than one of the joint holders of any shares or debentures none of whom are entitled to receive such notices, or

(*c*) in the case of joint holders of shares or debentures some of whom are, and some not, entitled to receive such notices, to those who are not so entitled.

(4) If copies of the accounts are sent less than 21 days before the date of the meeting, they are, notwithstanding that fact, deemed to have been duly sent if it is so agreed by all the members entitled to attend and vote at the meeting.

(5) If default is made in complying with subsection (1), the company and every officer of it who is in default is liable to a fine.

Directors'
duty to lay
and deliver
accounts.

241.—(1) In respect of each financial year of a company the directors shall lay before the company in general meeting copies of the accounts of the company for that year.

(2) The auditors' report shall be read before the company in general meeting, and be open to the inspection of any member of the company.

(3) In respect of each financial year the directors—

(*a*) shall deliver to the registrar of companies a copy of the accounts for the year, and

(*b*) if any document comprised in the accounts is in a language other than English, shall annex to the copy of that document delivered a translation of it into English, certified in the prescribed manner to be a correct translation.

(4) In the case of an unlimited company, the directors are not required by subsection (3) to deliver a copy of the accounts if—

(*a*) at no time during the accounting reference period has the company been, to its knowledge, the subsidiary of a company that was then limited and at no such time, to its knowledge, have there been held or been exercisable, by or on behalf of two or more companies that were then limited, shares or powers which, if they had been held or been exercisable by one of them, would have made the company its subsidiary, and

(b) at no such time has the company been the holding company of a company which was then limited, and

(c) at no such time has the company been carrying on business as the promoter of a trading stamp scheme within the Trading Stamps Act 1964.

References here to a company that was limited at a particular time are to a body corporate (under whatever law incorporated) the liability of whose members was at that time limited.

242.—(1) The period allowed for laying and delivering a company's accounts for a financial year is as follows in this section, being determined by reference to the end of the relevant accounting reference period (that is, the accounting reference period in respect of which the financial year of the company is ascertained).

(2) Subject to the following subsections, the period allowed is—

(a) for a private company, 10 months after the end of the relevant accounting reference period, and

(b) for a public company, 7 months after the end of that period.

(3) If a company carries on business, or has interests, outside the United Kingdom, the Channel Islands and the Isle of Man and in respect of a financial year the directors (before the end of the period allowed by subsection (2)) give to the registrar of companies notice in the prescribed form—

(a) stating that the company so carries on business or has such interests, and

(b) claiming an extension of the period so allowed by a further 3 months,

the period allowed in relation to that financial year is then so extended.

(4) Where a company's first accounting reference period—

(a) begins on the date of its incorporation, and

(b) is a period of more than 12 months,

the period otherwise allowed for laying and delivering accounts is reduced by the number of days by which the relevant accounting reference period is longer than 12 months.

However, the period allowed is not by this provision reduced to less than 3 months after the end of that accounting reference period.

(5) Where a company's relevant accounting reference period has been shortened under section 226 (in consequence of notice by the company under section 225), the period allowed for laying and delivering accounts is—

(a) the period allowed in accordance with subsections (2) to (4) above, or

(b) the period of 3 months beginning with the date of the notice under section 225,

whichever of those periods last expires.

(6) If for any special reason the Secretary of State thinks fit to do so, he may by notice in writing to a company extend, by such further period as may be specified in the notice, the period otherwise allowed for laying and delivering accounts for any financial year of the company.

Penalty for
non-
compliance
with s. 241.

243.—(1) If for a financial year of a company any of the requirements of section 241(1) or (3) is not complied with before the end of the period allowed for laying and delivering accounts, every person who immediately before the end of that period was a director of the company is, in respect of each of those subsections which is not so complied with, guilty of an offence and liable to a fine and, for continued contravention, to a daily default fine.

(2) If a person is charged with that offence in respect of any of the requirements of section 241(1) or (3), it is a defence for him to prove that he took all reasonable steps for securing that those requirements would be complied with before the end of the period allowed for laying and delivering accounts.

(3) If in respect of the company's financial year any of the requirements of section 241(3) is not complied with before the end of the period allowed for laying and delivering accounts, the company is liable to a penalty, recoverable in civil proceedings by the Secretary of State.

(4) The amount of the penalty is determined by reference to the length of the period between the end of the accounting reference period and the earliest day by which all those requirements have been complied with, and is—

(a) £20 where the period is not more than one month,

(b) £50 where the period is more than 1 month but not more than 3 months,

(c) £100 where the period is more than 3 months but not more than 6 months,

(d) £200 where the period is more than 6 months but not more than 12 months, and

(e) £450 where the period is more than 12 months.

(5) In proceedings under this section with respect to a requirement to lay a copy of a document before a company in general meeting, or to deliver a copy of a document to the registrar of companies, it is not a defence to prove that the document in question was not in fact prepared as required by this Part.

(6) Subsections (3) and (4) of this section do not come into force unless and until made to do so by an order of the Secretary of State in a statutory instrument.

244.—(1) If—

(a) in respect of a company's financial year any of the requirements of section 241(3) has not been complied with before the end of the period allowed for laying and delivering accounts, and

(b) the directors of the company fail to make good the default within 14 days after the service of a notice on them requiring compliance,

the court may, on application by any member or creditor of the company, or by the registrar of companies, make an order directing the directors (or any of them) to make good the default within such time as may be specified in the order.

*Default order
in case of
non-
compliance.*

(2) The court's order may provide that all costs of and incidental to the application shall be borne by the directors.

(3) Nothing in this section prejudices section 243.

245.—(1) If any accounts of a company of which a copy is laid before the company in general meeting or delivered to the registrar of companies do not comply with the requirements of this Act as to the matters to be included in, or in a note to, those accounts, every person who at the time when the copy is so laid or delivered is a director of the company is guilty of an offence and, in respect of each offence, liable to a fine.

This subsection does not apply to a company's group accounts.

*Penalty for
laying or
delivering
defective
accounts.*

(2) If any group accounts of which a copy is laid before a company in general meeting or delivered to the registrar of companies do not comply with section 229(5) to (7) or section 230, and with the other requirements of this Act as to the

matters to be included in or in a note to those accounts, every person who at the time when the copy was so laid or delivered was a director of the company is guilty of an offence and liable to a fine.

(3) In proceedings against a person for an offence under this section, it is a defence for him to prove that he took all reasonable steps for securing compliance with the requirements in question.

Shareholders' right to obtain copies of accounts. **246.**—(1) Any member of a company, whether or not he is entitled to have sent to him copies of the company's accounts, and any holder of the company's debentures (whether or not so entitled) is entitled to be furnished (on demand and without charge) with a copy of its last accounts.

(2) If, when a person makes a demand for a document with which he is entitled by this section to be furnished, default is made in complying with the demand within 7 days after its making, the company and every officer of it who is in default is liable to a fine and, for continued contravention, to a daily default fine (unless it is proved that the person has already made a demand for, and been furnished with, a copy of the document).

Modified accounts

Entitlement to deliver accounts in modified form. **247.**—(1) In certain cases a company's directors may, in accordance with Part I of Schedule 8, deliver modified accounts in respect of a financial year ; and whether they may do so depends on the company qualifying, in particular financial years, as small or medium-sized.

(2) Modified accounts for a financial year may not be delivered in the case of a company which is, or was at any time in that year—

(a) a public company,

(b) a special category company (Chapter II of this Part), or

(c) subject to the next-but-one subsection, a member of a group which is ineligible for this purpose.

(3) " Group " here means a holding company and its subsidiaries together ; and a group is ineligible if any of its members is—

(a) a public company or a special category company, or

(b) a body corporate (other than a company) which has

power under its constitution to offer its shares or debentures to the public and may lawfully exercise that power, or

(c) a body corporate (other than a company) which is either a recognised bank or licensed institution within the Banking Act 1979 or an insurance company to which Part II of the Insurance Companies Act 1982 applies.

(4) Notwithstanding subsection (2)(c), modified accounts for a financial year may be delivered if the company is exempt under section 252 (dormant companies) from the obligation to appoint auditors and either—

(a) was so exempt throughout that year, or

(b) became so exempt by virtue of a special resolution under that section passed during that year.

(5) For purposes of sections 247 to 250 and Schedule 8, " deliver " means deliver to the registrar of companies under this Chapter; and for purposes of subsection (3)(b), " shares " and " debentures " have the same meaning as when used in relation to a company.

248.—(1) A company qualifies as small in a financial year if for that year two or more of the following conditions are satisfied—

(a) the amount of its turnover for the year is not more than £1·4 million ;

(b) its balance sheet total is not more than £700,000 ;

(c) the average number of persons employed by the company in the year (determined on a weekly basis) does not exceed 50.

(2) A company qualifies as medium-sized in a financial year if for that year two or more of the following conditions are satisfied—

(a) the amount of its turnover for the year is not more than £5·75 million ;

(b) its balance sheet total is not more than £2·8 million ;

(c) the average number of persons employed by the company in the year (determined on a weekly basis) does not exceed 250.

(3) In subsections (1) and (2), " balance sheet total " means, in relation to a company's financial year—

(a) where in the company's accounts Format 1 of the balance sheet formats set out in Part I of Schedule 4 is adopted, the aggregate of the amounts shown in the balance sheet under the headings corresponding to items A to D in that Format, and

(b) where Format 2 is adopted, the aggregate of the amounts shown under the general heading " Assets ".

(4) The average number of persons employed as mentioned in subsections (1)(c) and (2)(c) is determined by applying the method of calculation prescribed by paragraph 56(2) and (3) of Schedule 4 for determining the number required by sub-paragraph (1)(a) of that paragraph to be stated in a note to the company's accounts.

(5) In applying subsections (1) and (2) to a period which is a company's financial year but not in fact a year, the maximum figures for turnover in paragraph (a) of each subsection are to be proportionately adjusted.

Modified
individual
accounts.

249.—(1) This section specifies the cases in which a company's directors may (subject to section 250, where the company has subsidiaries) deliver individual accounts modified as for a small or a medium-sized company ; and Part I of Schedule 8 applies with respect to the delivery of accounts so modified.

(2) In respect of the company's first financial year the directors may—

    (a) deliver accounts modified as for a small company, if in that year it qualifies as small,

    (b) deliver accounts modified as for a medium-sized company, if in that year it qualifies as medium-sized.

(3) The next three subsections are concerned only with a company's financial year subsequent to the first.

(4) The directors may in respect of a financial year—

    (a) deliver accounts modified as for a small company if in that year the company qualifies as small and it also so qualified in the preceding year,

    (b) deliver accounts modified as for a medium-sized company if in that year the company qualifies as medium-sized and it also so qualified in the preceding year.

(5) The directors may in respect of a financial year—

    (a) deliver accounts modified as for a small company (although not qualifying in that year as small), if in the preceding year it so qualified and the directors were entitled to deliver accounts so modified in respect of that year, and

    (b) deliver accounts modified as for a medium-sized company (although not qualifying in that year as medium-sized), if in the preceding year it so qualified and the directors were entitled to deliver accounts so modified in respect of that year.

(6) The directors may in respect of a financial year—

(a) deliver accounts modified as for a small company, if in that year the company qualifies as small and the directors were entitled under subsection (5)(a) to deliver accounts so modified for the preceding year (although the company did not in that year qualify as small), and

(b) deliver accounts modified as for a medium-sized company if in that year the company qualifies as medium-sized and the directors were entitled under subsection (5)(b) to deliver accounts so modified for the preceding year (although the company did not in that year qualify as medium-sized).

250.—(1) This section applies to a company (" the holding company ") where in respect of a financial year section 229 requires the preparation of group accounts for the company and its subsidiaries.

Modified accounts of holding company.

(2) The directors of the holding company may not under section 249—

(a) deliver accounts modified as for a small company, unless the group (meaning the holding company and its subsidiaries together) is in that year a small group,

(b) deliver accounts modified as for a medium-sized company, unless in that year the group is medium-sized ;

and the group is small or medium-sized if it would so qualify under section 248 (applying that section as directed by subsections (3) and (4) below), if it were all one company.

(3) The figures to be taken into account in determining whether the group is small or medium-sized (or neither) are the group account figures, that is—

(a) where the group accounts are prepared as consolidated accounts, the figures for turnover, balance sheet total and numbers employed which are shown in those accounts, and

(b) where not, the corresponding figures given in the group accounts, with such adjustment as would have been made if the accounts had been prepared in consolidated form,

aggregated in either case with the relevant figures for the subsidiaries (if any) omitted from the group accounts (excepting those for any subsidiary omitted under section 229(3)(a) on the ground of impracticability).

(4) In the case of each subsidiary omitted from the group accounts, the figures relevant as regards turnover, balance sheet total and numbers employed are those which are included in the accounts of that subsidiary prepared in respect of its relevant financial year (with such adjustment as would have been made if those figures had been included in group accounts prepared in consolidated form).

(5) For the purposes of subsection (4), the relevant financial year of the subsidiary is—

(a) if its financial year ends with that of the holding company to which the group accounts relate, that financial year, and

(b) if not, the subsidiary's financial year ending last before the end of the financial year of the holding company.

(6) If the directors are entitled to deliver modified accounts (whether as for a small or a medium-sized company), they may also deliver modified group accounts; and this means that the group accounts—

(a) if consolidated, may be in accordance with Part II of Schedule 8 (while otherwise comprising or corresponding with group accounts prepared under section 229), and

(b) if not consolidated, may be such as (together with any notes) give the same or equivalent information as required by paragraph (a) above;

and Part III of the Schedule applies to modified group accounts, whether consolidated or not.

Power of
Secretary of
State to
modify
ss. 247–250
and Sch. 8.

251.—(1) The Secretary of State may by regulations in a statutory instrument modify the provisions of sections 247(1) to (3), 248 to 250 and Schedule 8; and those provisions then apply as modified by regulations for the time being in force.

(2) Regulations under this section reducing the classes of companies which have the benefit of those provisions, or rendering the requirements of those provisions more onerous, shall not be made unless a draft of the instrument containing the regulations has been laid before Parliament and approved by a resolution of each House.

(3) Otherwise, a statutory instrument containing such regulations is subject to annulment in pursuance of a resolution of either House.

Dormant companies

Company
resolution
not to
appoint
auditors.

252.—(1) In certain circumstances a company may, with a view to the subsequent laying and delivery of unaudited accounts, pass a special resolution making itself exempt from the obligation to appoint auditors as otherwise required by section 384.

(2) Such a resolution may be passed at a general meeting of the company at which its accounts for a financial year are laid as required by section 241 (if it is not a year for which the directors are required to lay group accounts) ; but the following conditions must be satisfied—

   (a) the directors must be entitled under section 249 to deliver, in respect of that financial year, accounts modified as for a small company (or would be so entitled but for the company being, or having at any time in the financial year been, a member of an ineligible group within section 247 (3)), and

   (b) the company must have been dormant since the end of the financial year.

(3) A company may by such a resolution make itself exempt from the obligation to appoint auditors if the resolution is passed at some time before the first general meeting of the company at which accounts are laid as required by section 241, provided that the company has been dormant from the time of its formation until the resolution is passed.

(4) A company may not under subsection (3) pass such a resolution if it is a public company or a special category company.

(5) For purposes of this and the next section, a company is " dormant " during any period in which no transaction occurs which is for the company a significant accounting transaction ; and—

   (a) this means a transaction which is required by section 221 to be entered in the company's accounting records (disregarding any which arises from the taking of shares in the company by a subscriber to the memorandum in pursuance of an undertaking of his in the memorandum), and

   (b) a company which has been dormant for any period ceases to be so on the occurrence of any such transaction.

(6) A company which has under this section made itself exempt from the obligation to appoint auditors loses that exemption if—

   (a) it ceases to be dormant, or

   (b) it would no longer qualify (for any other reason) to exclude that obligation by passing a resolution under this section.

(7) Where the exemption is lost, the directors may, at any time before the next meeting of the company at which accounts are to be laid, appoint an auditor or auditors, to hold office until the conclusion of that meeting ; and if they fail to exercise that

Part VII
Chapter I
Laying and
delivery of
unaudited
accounts.
power, the company in general meeting may exercise it.

253.—(1) The following applies in respect of a company's accounts for a financial year if the company is exempt under section 252 from the obligation to appoint auditors and either—

(a) was so exempt throughout that year, or

(b) became so exempt by virtue of a special resolution passed during that year, and retained the exemption until the end of that year.

(2) A report by the company's auditors need not be included (as otherwise required by preceding provisions of this Chapter) with the accounts laid before the company in general meeting and delivered to the registrar of companies.

(3) If the auditors' report is omitted from the accounts so delivered, then—

(a) the balance sheet shall contain a statement by the directors (in a position immediately above their signatures to the balance sheet) that the company was dormant throughout the financial year, and

(b) if the accounts delivered to the registrar are modified as permitted by sections 247 to 249—

(i) the modified balance sheet need not contain the statement otherwise required by paragraph 9 of Schedule 8, and

(ii) the modified accounts need not include the special report of the auditors otherwise required by paragraph 10 of that Schedule.

Publication of accounts

254.—(1) This section applies to the publication by a company of full individual or group accounts, that is to say the accounts required by section 241 to be laid before the company in general meeting and delivered to the registrar of companies (including the directors' report, unless dispensed with under paragraph 3 of Schedule 8).

(2) If a company publishes individual accounts (modified or other) for a financial year, it shall publish with them the relevant auditors' report.

(3) If a company required by section 229 to prepare group accounts for a financial year publishes individual accounts for that year, it shall also publish with them its group accounts (which may be modified accounts, but only if the individual accounts are modified).

(4) If a company publishes group accounts (modified or other), otherwise than together with its individual accounts, it shall publish with them the relevant auditors' report.

(5) References above to the relevant auditors' report are to
the auditors' report under section 236 or, in the case of modified
accounts (individual or group), the auditors' special report
under paragraph 10 of Schedule 8.

(6) A company which contravenes any provision of this section, and any officer of it who is in default, is liable to a fine.

255.—(1) This section applies to the publication by a company of abridged accounts, that is to say any balance sheet or
profit and loss account relating to a financial year of the
company or purporting to deal with any such financial year,
otherwise than as part of full accounts (individual or group) to
which section 254 applies.

(2) The reference above to a balance sheet or profit and loss
account, in relation to accounts published by a holding company,
includes an account in any form purporting to be a balance
sheet or profit and loss account for the group consisting of
the holding company and its subsidiaries.

(3) If the company publishes abridged accounts, it shall
publish with those accounts a statement indicating—

(a) that the accounts are not full accounts,

(b) whether full individual or full group accounts (according as the abridged accounts deal solely with the company's own affairs or with the affairs of the company
and any subsidiaries) have been delivered to the registrar of companies or, in the case of an unlimited
company exempt under section 241(4) from the requirement to deliver accounts, that the company is so
exempt,

(c) whether the company's auditors have made a report
under section 236 on the company's accounts for any
financial year with which the abridged accounts purport to deal, and

(d) whether any report so made was unqualified (meaning
that it was a report, without qualification, to the effect
that in the opinion of the person making it the company's accounts had been properly prepared).

(4) Where a company publishes abridged accounts, it shall not
publish with those accounts any such report of the auditors as is
mentioned in subsection (3)(c).

(5) A company which contravenes any provision of this section,
and any officer of it who is in default, is liable to a fine.

PART VII
CHAPTER I
Power of
Secretary of
State to alter
accounting
requirements.

Supplementary

256.—(1) The Secretary of State may by regulations in a statutory instrument—

    (a) add to the classes of documents—

        (i) to be comprised in a company's accounts for a financial year to be laid before the company in general meeting as required by section 241, or

        (ii) to be delivered to the registrar of companies under that section,

    and make provision as to the matters to be included in any document to be added to either class ;

    (b) modify the requirements of this Act as to the matters to be stated in a document of any such class ;

    (c) reduce the classes of documents to be delivered to the registrar of companies under section 241.

(2) In particular, the Secretary of State may by such regulations alter or add to the requirements of Schedule 4 and Schedule 9 (special category companies) ; and any reference in this Act to a provision of it then refers to that provision as it has effect subject to regulations in force under this section.

(3) Where regulations made under subsection (1)(a) add to either class of documents there mentioned documents dealing with the state of affairs and profit or loss of a company and other bodies, the regulations may also—

    (a) extend the provisions of this Act relating to group accounts (or such of those provisions as may be specified) to such documents,

    (b) exempt that company from the requirement to prepare group accounts in respect of any period for which it has prepared such a document.

(4) Regulations under this section may make different provision for different cases or classes of case, and may contain such incidental and supplementary provisions as the Secretary of State thinks fit.

(5) Regulations under subsection (1)(a), or extending the classes of company to which any requirement mentioned in subsection (1)(b) applies or rendering those requirements more onerous, shall not be made unless a draft of the instrument containing them has been laid before Parliament and approved by a resolution of each House.

(6) Otherwise, a statutory instrument containing such regulations is subject to annulment in pursuance of a resolution of either House.

ACCOUNTS OF BANKING, SHIPPING AND INSURANCE COMPANIES

257.—(1) For purposes of this Act, " special category com-panies " are banking companies, shipping companies and insurance companies ; and—

Special category companies and their accounts.

> (a) " banking company " means a company which is a recognised bank for the purposes of the Banking Act 1979 or is a licensed institution within that Act ;

1979 c. 37.

> (b) " insurance company " means an insurance company to which Part II of the Insurance Companies Act 1982 applies ; and

1982 c. 50.

> (c) " shipping company " means a company which, or a subsidiary of which, owns ships or includes among its activities the management or operation of ships and which satisfies the Secretary of State that it ought in the national interest to be treated under this Part of this Act as a shipping company.

(2) Except as otherwise provided below, Chapter I of this Part applies to a special category company and its accounts as it applies to, and to the accounts of, any other company.

(3) The individual accounts of a special category company, and the group accounts of a holding company which is, or has as its subsidiary, a special category company, may be prepared under this Chapter and not under Chapter I, and contain a statement that they are so prepared ; and a reference in this Act to a company's accounts (individual or group) being " special category " is to their being so prepared and containing that statement.

(4) Subject as follows, a reference in any enactment or other document to section 228 or 230 of this Act or to Schedule 4 is, in relation to special category accounts, to be read as a reference to section 258 or 259 or Schedule 9 (as the case may require) ; but this is subject to any contrary context.

258.—(1) Where a company's individual accounts are special category, section 228 and Schedule 4 do not apply, but—

Special category individual accounts.

> (a) the balance sheet shall give a true and fair view of the state of affairs of the company as at the end of the financial year, and

> (b) the profit and loss account shall give a true and fair view of the company's profit or loss for the financial year.

(2) The balance sheet and profit and loss account shall comply with the requirements of Schedule 9, so far as applicable.

(3) Except as expressly provided by this section or Part III of Schedule 9, the requirements of subsection (2) and that

Schedule are without prejudice to the general requirements of subsection (1) or to any other requirements of this Act.

(4) The Secretary of State may, on the application or with the consent of the company's directors, modify in relation to that company any of the requirements of this Chapter as to the matters to be stated in a company's balance sheet or profit and loss account (except the requirements of subsection (1) above), for the purpose of adapting them to the circumstances of the company.

(5) So much of subsections (1) and (2) as relates to the profit and loss account does not apply if—

    (a) the company has subsidiaries, and

    (b) the profit and loss account is framed as a consolidated account dealing with all or any of the company's subsidiaries as well as the company and—

        (i) complies with the requirements of this Act relating to consolidated profit and loss accounts (as those requirements apply in the case of special category companies), and

        (ii) shows how much of the consolidated profit or loss for the financial year is dealt with in the company's accounts.

Special
category
group
accounts.
    259.—(1) Where a holding company's group accounts are special category, those accounts shall give a true and fair view of the state of affairs and profit or loss of the company and the subsidiaries dealt with by those accounts as a whole, so far as concerns members of the company.

(2) Where the financial year of a subsidiary does not coincide with that of the holding company, the group accounts shall (unless the Secretary of State on the application or with the consent of the holding company's directors otherwise directs) deal with the subsidiary's state of affairs as at the end of its relevant financial year, that is—

    (a) if its financial year ends with that of the holding company, that financial year, and

    (b) if not, the subsidiary's financial year ending last before the end of the financial year of the holding company dealt with in the group accounts,

and with the subsidiary's profit or loss for its relevant financial year.

(3) Without prejudice to subsection (1), the group accounts, if prepared as consolidated accounts, shall comply with the requirements of Schedule 9 (so far as applicable), and if not so prepared shall give the same or equivalent information.

(4) However, the Secretary of State may, on the application or with the consent of the holding company's directors, modify

the requirements of Schedule 9 in relation to that company for the purpose of adapting them to the company's circumstances.

260.—(1) In Schedule 5 (matters to be dealt with in notes to accounts)—

  (*a*) paragraph 8 in Part II (disclosure of shareholdings in other bodies corporate, not being subsidiaries), and

  (*b*) Part III (financial information about subsidiaries),

do not apply in the case of special category accounts.

(2) Where an item is given in a note to special category accounts, to comply with Part V or VI of Schedule 5 (directors' emoluments, pensions etc. ; emoluments of higher-paid employees), the corresponding amount for the immediately preceding financial year shall be included in the note.

(3) If a person, being a director of a company preparing special category accounts, fails to take all reasonable steps to secure compliance with subsection (2), he is in respect of each offence liable to a fine ; but in proceedings against a person for that offence it is a defence to prove that he had reasonable ground to believe, and did believe, that a competent and reliable person was charged with the duty of seeing that subsection (2) was complied with and was in a position to discharge that duty.

261.—(1) Where a company's individual accounts are special category, the following applies with respect to the directors' report accompanying the accounts.

(2) Paragraphs (*a*) and (*b*) of section 235(1) do not apply as regards the contents of the report ; but the report shall deal with the company's state of affairs, the amount (if any) which the directors recommend should be paid as dividend, and the amount (if any) which they propose to carry to reserves (within the meaning of Schedule 9).

(3) Information which is otherwise required to be given in the accounts, and allowed to be given in a statement annexed, may be given in the directors' report instead of in the accounts.

If any information is so given, the report is treated as forming part of the accounts for the purposes of audit, except that the auditors shall report on it only so far as it gives that information.

(4) Where advantage is taken of subsection (3) to show an item in the directors' report instead of in the accounts, the report shall also show the corresponding amount for (or, as the case may require, as at the end of) the immediately preceding financial year of that item, except where the amount would not have had to be shown had the item been shown in the accounts.

(5) Schedule 7 applies to the directors' report only in respect of the matters to be stated, and the information to be given, under paragraphs 1 to 5 (but excluding paragraph 2(3)) and 9, 10 and 11 ; and paragraph 1 of the Schedule does not apply if the company has the benefit of any provision of Part III of Schedule 9.

(6) The report shall, in addition to complying with those paragraphs of Schedule 7, also comply with Schedule 10, where and so far as applicable (disclosure of recent share and debenture issues ; turnover and profitability ; size of labour force and wages paid ; and other general matters) ; but in that Schedule, paragraphs 2 to 4 and 6 do not apply to a directors' report attached to any accounts unless the documents required to be comprised in those accounts include group accounts which are special category.

(7) Section 237(6) does not apply.

Auditors' report.

262.—(1) The following applies where a company is entitled to avail itself, and has availed itself, of the benefit of any of the provisions of Part III of Schedule 9.

(2) In that case section 236(2) does not apply ; and the auditors' report shall state whether in their opinion the company's balance sheet and profit and loss account and (if it is a holding company submitting group accounts) the group accounts have been properly prepared in accordance with this Act.

PART VIII

DISTRIBUTION OF PROFITS AND ASSETS

Limits of company's power of distribution

Certain distributions prohibited.

263.—(1) A company shall not make a distribution except out of profits available for the purpose.

(2) In this Part, " distribution " means every description of distribution of a company's assets to its members, whether in cash or otherwise, except distribution by way of—

(a) an issue of shares as fully or partly paid bonus shares,

(b) the redemption or purchase of any of the company's own shares out of capital (including the proceeds of any fresh issue of shares) or out of unrealised profits in accordance with Chapter VII of Part V,

(c) the reduction of share capital by extinguishing or reducing the liability of any of the members on any of the company's shares in respect of share capital not paid up, or by paying off paid up share capital, and

(d) a distribution of assets to members of the company on its winding up.

(3) For purposes of this Part, a company's profits available for distribution are its accumulated, realised profits, so far as

not previously utilised by distribution or capitalisation, less its accumulated, realised losses, so far as not previously written off in a reduction or reorganisation of capital duly made.

This is subject to the provision made by sections 265 and 266 for investment and other companies.

(4) A company shall not apply an unrealised profit in paying up debentures, or any amounts unpaid on its issued shares.

(5) Where the directors of a company are, after making all reasonable enquiries, unable to determine whether a particular profit made before 22nd December 1980 is realised or unrealised, they may treat the profit as realised ; and where after making such enquiries they are unable to determine whether a particular loss so made is realised or unrealised, they may treat the loss as unrealised.

264.—(1) A public company may only make a distribution at any time—

(a) if at that time the amount of its net assets is not less than the aggregate of its called-up share capital and undistributable reserves, and

(b) if, and to the extent that, the distribution does not reduce the amount of those assets to less than that aggregate.

This is subject to the provision made by sections 265 and 266 for investment and other companies.

(2) In subsection (1), " net assets " means the aggregate of the company's assets less the aggregate of its liabilities (" liabilities " to include any provision for liabilities or charges within paragraph 89 of Schedule 4).

(3) A company's undistributable reserves are—

(a) the share premium account,

(b) the capital redemption reserve,

(c) the amount by which the company's accumulated, unrealised profits, so far as not previously utilised by capitalisation of a description to which this paragraph applies, exceed its accumulated, unrealised losses (so far as not previously written off in a reduction or reorganisation of capital duly made), and

(d) any other reserve which the company is prohibited from distributing by any enactment (other than one contained in this Part) or by its memorandum or articles ;

and paragraph (c) applies to every description of capitalisation except a transfer of profits of the company to its capital redemption reserve on or after 22nd December 1980.

(4) A public company shall not include any uncalled share capital as an asset in any accounts relevant for purposes of this section.

Restriction on distribution of assets.

265.—(1) Subject to the following provisions of this section, an investment company (defined in section 266) may also make a distribution at any time out of its accumulated, realised revenue profits, so far as not previously utilised by distribution or capitalisation, less its accumulated revenue losses (whether realised or unrealised), so far as not previously written off in a reduction or reorganisation of capital duly made—

(a) if at that time the amount of its assets is at least equal to one and a half times the aggregate of its liabilities, and

(b) if, and to the extent that, the distribution does not reduce that amount to less than one and a half times that aggregate.

(2) In subsection (1)(a), " liabilities " includes any provision for liabilities or charges (within the meaning of paragraph 89 of Schedule 4).

(3) The company shall not include any uncalled share capital as an asset in any accounts relevant for purposes of this section.

(4) An investment company may not make a distribution by virtue of subsection (1) unless—

(a) its shares are listed on a recognised stock exchange, and

(b) during the relevant period it has not—

(i) distributed any of its capital profits, or

(ii) applied any unrealised profits or any capital profits (realised or unrealised) in paying up debentures or amounts unpaid on its issued shares.

(5) The " relevant period " under subsection (4) is the period beginning with—

(a) the first day of the accounting reference period immediately preceding that in which the proposed distribution is to be made, or

(b) where the distribution is to be made in the company's first accounting reference period, the first day of that period,

and ending with the date of the distribution.

(6) An investment company may not make a distribution by virtue of subsection (1) unless the company gave to the registrar of companies the requisite notice (that is, notice under section 266(1)) of the company's intention to carry on business as an investment company—

(a) before the beginning of the relevant period under subsection (4), or (*b*) in the case of a company incorporated on or after 22nd December 1980, as soon as may have been reasonably practicable after the date of its incorporation.

266.—(1) In section 265 "investment company" means a public company which has given notice in the prescribed form (which has not been revoked) to the registrar of companies of its intention to carry on business as an investment company, and has since the date of that notice complied with the requirements specified below.

Meaning of "investment company".

Part VIII

(2) Those requirements are—

(*a*) that the business of the company consists of investing its funds mainly in securities, with the aim of spreading investment risk and giving members of the company the benefit of the results of the management of its funds,

(*b*) that none of the company's holdings in companies (other than those which are for the time being in investment companies) represents more than 15 per cent. by value of the investing company's investments,

(*c*) that distribution of the company's capital profits is prohibited by its memorandum or articles of association,

(*d*) that the company has not retained, otherwise than in compliance with this Part, in respect of any accounting reference period more than 15 per cent. of the income it derives from securities.

(3) Notice to the registrar of companies under subsection (1) may be revoked at any time by the company on giving notice in the prescribed form to the registrar that it no longer wishes to be an investment company within the meaning of this section; and, on giving such notice, the company ceases to be such a company.

(4) Section 359(2) and (3) of the Income and Corporation Taxes Act 1970 and section 93(6)(*b*) of the Finance Act 1972 apply for purposes of subsection (2)(*b*) as for those of section 359(1)(*b*) of the Act first mentioned.

1970 c. 10.
1972 c. 41.

267.—(1) The Secretary of State may by regulations in a statutory instrument extend the provisions of sections 265 and 266 (with or without modifications) to companies whose principal business consists of investing their funds in securities, land or other assets with the aim of spreading investment risk and giving their members the benefit of the results of the management of the assets.

Extension of ss. 265, 266 to other companies.

(2) Regulations under this section—

(*a*) may make different provision for different classes of companies and may contain such transitional and supplemental provisions as the Secretary of State considers necessary, and

(*b*) shall not be made unless a draft of the statutory instrument containing them has been laid before Parliament and approved by a resolution of each House.

Realised profits of insurance company with long term business.
1982 c. 50.

268.—(1) Where an insurance company to which Part II of the Insurance Companies Act 1982 applies carries on long term business—

(*a*) any amount properly transferred to the profit and loss account of the company from a surplus in the fund or funds maintained by it in respect of that business, and

(*b*) any deficit in that fund or those funds,

are to be (respectively) treated, for purposes of this Part, as a realised profit and a realised loss ; and, subject to this, any profit or loss arising in that business is to be left out of account for those purposes.

(2) In subsection (1)—

(*a*) the reference to a surplus in any fund or funds of an insurance company is to an excess of the assets representing that fund or those funds over the liabilities of the company attributable to its long term business, as shown by an actuarial investigation, and

(*b*) the reference to a deficit in any such fund or funds is to the excess of those liabilities over those assets, as so shown.

(3) In this section—

(*a*) " actuarial investigation " means an investigation to which section 18 of the Insurance Companies Act 1982 (periodic actuarial investigation of company with long term business) applies or which is made in pursuance of a requirement imposed by section 42 of that Act (actuarial investigation required by Secretary of State) ; and

(*b*) " long term business " has the same meaning as in that Act.

Treatment of development costs.

269.—(1) Subject as follows, where development costs are shown as an asset in a company's accounts, any amount shown in respect of those costs is to be treated—

(*a*) under section 263, as a realised loss, and

(*b*) under section 265, as a realised revenue loss.

(2) This does not apply to any part of that amount representing an unrealised profit made on revaluation of those costs ; nor
does it apply if—

  (a) there are special circumstances in the company's case
      justifying the directors in deciding that the amount
      there mentioned is not to be treated as required by
      subsection (1), and

  (b) the note to the accounts required by paragraph 20 of
      Schedule 4 (reasons for showing development costs as
      an asset) states that the amount is not to be so treated
      and explains the circumstances relied upon to justify
      the decision of the directors to that effect.

Relevant accounts

270.—(1) This section and sections 271 to 276 below are for Distribution to
determining the question whether a distribution may be made be justified by
by a company without contravening sections 263, 264 or 265. reference to
company's
(2) The amount of a distribution which may be made is accounts.
determined by reference to the following items as stated in the
company's accounts—

  (a) profits, losses, assets and liabilities,

  (b) provisions of any of the kinds mentioned in paragraphs
      88 and 89 of Schedule 4 (depreciation, diminution in
      value of assets, retentions to meet liabilities, etc.), and

  (c) share capital and reserves (including undistributable re-
      serves).

(3) Except in a case falling within the next subsection, the
company's accounts which are relevant for this purpose are its
last annual accounts, that is to say those prepared under Part
VII which were laid in respect of the last preceding accounting
reference period in respect of which accounts so prepared were
laid ;·and for this purpose accounts are laid if section 241 (1)
has been complied with in relation to them.

(4) In the following two cases—

  (a) where the distribution would be found to contravene
      the relevant section if reference were made only to
      the company's last annual accounts, or

  (b) where the distribution is proposed to be declared during
      the company's first accounting reference period, or
      before any accounts are laid in respect of that period,

the accounts relevant under this section (called "interim
accounts" in the first case, and "initial accounts" in the
second) are those necessary to enable a reasonable judgment to
be made as to the amounts of the items mentioned in subsection
(2) above.

PART VIII

(5) The relevant section is treated as contravened in the case of a distribution unless the statutory requirements about the relevant accounts (that is, the requirements of this and the following three sections, as and where applicable) are complied with in relation to that distribution.

Requirements for last annual accounts.

271.—(1) If the company's last annual accounts constitute the only accounts relevant under section 270, the statutory requirements in respect of them are as follows.

(2) The accounts must have been properly prepared in accordance with this Act, or have been so prepared subject only to matters which are not material for determining, by reference to items mentioned in section 270(2), whether the distribution would contravene the relevant section ; and, without prejudice to the foregoing—

(a) so much of the accounts as consists of a balance sheet must give a true and fair view of the state of the company's affairs as at the balance sheet date, and

(b) so much of the accounts as consists of a profit and loss account must give a true and fair view of the company's profit or loss for the period in respect of which the accounts were prepared.

(3) The auditors must have made their report on the accounts under section 236 ; and the following subsection applies if the report is a qualified report, that is to say, it is not a report without qualification to the effect that in the auditors' opinion the accounts have been properly prepared in accordance with this Act.

(4) The auditors must in that case also have stated in writing (either at the time of their report or subsequently) whether, in their opinion, the matter in respect of which their report is qualified is material for determining, by reference to items mentioned in section 270(2), whether the distribution would contravene the relevant section ; and a copy of the statement must have been laid before the company in general meeting.

(5) A statement under subsection (4) suffices for purposes of a particular distribution not only if it relates to a distribution which has been proposed but also if it relates to distributions of any description which includes that particular distribution, notwithstanding that at the time of the statement it has not been proposed.

Requirements for interim accounts.

272.—(1) The following are the statutory requirements in respect of interim accounts prepared for a proposed distribution by a public company.

(2) The accounts must have been properly prepared, or have been so prepared subject only to matters which are not material

for determining, by reference to items mentioned in section
270(2), whether the proposed distribution would contravene the
relevant section.

(3) " Properly prepared " means that the accounts must comply with section 228 (applying that section and Schedule 4 with
such modifications as are necessary because the accounts are
prepared otherwise than in respect of an accounting reference
period) and any balance sheet comprised in the accounts must
have been signed in accordance with section 238 ; and, without
prejudice to the foregoing—

> (a) so much of the accounts as consists of a balance sheet
> must give a true and fair view of the state of the com-
> pany's affairs as at the balance sheet date, and

> (b) so much of the accounts as consists of a profit and loss
> account must give a true and fair view of the com-
> pany's profit or loss for the period in respect of which
> the accounts were prepared.

(4) A copy of the accounts must have been delivered to the
registrar of companies.

(5) If the accounts are in a language other than English and
section 241(3)(b) (translation) does not apply, a translation into
English of the accounts, certified in the prescribed manner to
be a correct translation, must also have been delivered to the
registrar.

273.—(1) The following are the statutory requirements in Requirements
respect of initial accounts prepared for a proposed distribution for initial
by a public company. accounts.

(2) The accounts must have been properly prepared, or they
must have been so prepared subject only to matters which are
not material for determining, by reference to items mentioned
in section 270(2), whether the proposed distribution would
contravene the relevant section.

(3) Section 272(3) applies as respects the meaning of " properly prepared ".

(4) The company's auditors must have made a report stating
whether, in their opinion, the accounts have been properly
prepared ; and the following subsection applies if their report is
a qualified report, that is to say it is not a report without qualification to the effect that in the auditors' opinion the accounts
have been so prepared.

(5) The auditors must in that case also have stated in writing
whether, in their opinion, the matter in respect of which their
report is qualified is material for determining, by reference to

PART VIII items mentioned in section 270(2), whether the distribution would contravene the relevant section.

(6) A copy of the accounts, of the auditors' report under subsection (4) and of the auditors' statement (if any) under subsection (5) must have been delivered to the registrar of companies.

(7) If the accounts are, or the auditors' report under subsection (4) or their statement (if any) under subsection (5) is, in a language other than English and section 241(3)(*b*) (translation) does not apply, a translation into English of the accounts, the report or the statement (as the case may be), certified in the prescribed manner to be a correct translation, must also have been delivered to the registrar.

Method of applying s. 270 to successive distributions.

274.—(1) For the purpose of determining by reference to particular accounts whether a proposed distribution may be made by a company, section 270 has effect, in a case where one or more distributions have already been made in pursuance of determinations made by reference to those same accounts, as if the amount of the proposed distribution was increased by the amount of the distributions so made.

(2) Subsection (1) of this section applies (if it would not otherwise do so) to—

(*a*) financial assistance lawfully given by a public company out of its distributable profits in a case where the assistance is required to be so given by section 154,

(*b*) financial assistance lawfully given by a private company out of its distributable profits in a case where the assistance is required to be so given by section 155(2),

(*c*) financial assistance given by a company in contravention of section 151, in a case where the giving of that assistance reduces the company's net assets or increases its net liabilities,

(*d*) a payment made by a company in respect of the purchase by it of shares in the company (except a payment lawfully made otherwise than out of distributable profits), and

(*e*) a payment of any description specified in section 168 (company's purchase of right to acquire its own shares, etc.),

being financial assistance given or payment made since the relevant accounts were prepared, as if any such financial assistance or payment were a distribution already made in pursuance of a determination made by reference to those accounts.

(3) In this section the following definitions apply—

" financial assistance " means the same as in Chapter VI of Part V ;

"net assets" has the meaning given by section 154(2)(*a*);   **PART VIII**
and

"net liabilities", in relation to the giving of financial assistance by a company, means the amount by which the
aggregate amount of the company's liabilities (within
the meaning of section 154(2)(*b*)) exceeds the aggregate amount of its assets, taking the amount of the
assets and liabilities to be as stated in the company's
accounting records immediately before the financial
assistance is given.

(4) Subsections (2) and (3) of this section are deemed to be
included in Chapter VII of Part V for purposes of the Secretary
of State's power to make regulations under section 179.

275.—(1) For purposes of sections 263 and 264, a provision Treatment of
of any kind mentioned in paragraphs 88 and 89 of Schedule 4, assets in the
other than one in respect of a diminution in value of a fixed relevant
asset appearing on a revaluation of all the fixed assets of the accounts.
company, or of all of its fixed assets other than goodwill, is
treated as a realised loss.

(2) If, on the revaluation of a fixed asset, an unrealised profit
is shown to have been made and, on or after the revaluation, a
sum is written off or retained for depreciation of that asset over
a period, then an amount equal to the amount by which that
sum exceeds the sum which would have been so written off or
retained for the depreciation of that asset over that period, if
that profit had not been made, is treated for purposes of sections
263 and 264 as a realised profit made over that period.

(3) Where there is no record of the original cost of an asset,
or a record cannot be obtained without unreasonable expense
or delay, then for the purpose of determining whether the company has made a profit or loss in respect of that asset, its cost
is taken to be the value ascribed to it in the earliest available
record of its value made on or after its acquisition by the company.

(4) Subject to subsection (6), any consideration by the directors
of the value at a particular time of a fixed asset is treated as a
revaluation of the asset for the purposes of determining whether
any such revaluation of the company's fixed assets as is required
for purposes of the exception from subsection (1) has taken place
at that time.

(5) But where any such assets which have not actually been
revalued are treated as revalued for those purposes under subsection (4), that exception applies only if the directors are
satisfied that their aggregate value at the time in question is

PART VIII   not less than the aggregate amount at which they are for the time being stated in the company's accounts.

(6) Where section 271(2), 272(2) or 273(2) applies to the relevant accounts, subsections (4) and (5) above do not apply for the purpose of determining whether a revaluation of the company's fixed assets affecting the amount of the relevant items (that is, the items mentioned in section 270(2)) as stated in those accounts has taken place, unless it is stated in a note to the accounts—

(a) that the directors have considered the value at any time of any fixed assets of the company, without actually revaluing those assets,

(b) that they are satisfied that the aggregate value of those assets at the time in question is or was not less than the aggregate amount at which they are or were for the time being stated in the company's accounts, and

(c) that the relevant items in question are accordingly stated in the relevant accounts on the basis that a revaluation of the company's fixed assets which by virtue of subsections (4) and (5) included the assets in question took place at that time.

Distributions
in kind.
276. Where a company makes a distribution of or including a non-cash asset, and any part of the amount at which that asset is stated in the accounts relevant for the purposes of the distribution in accordance with sections 270 to 275 represents an unrealised profit, that profit is to be treated as a realised profit—

(a) for the purpose of determining the lawfulness of the distribution in accordance with this Part (whether before or after the distribution takes place), and

(b) for the purpose of the application of paragraphs 12(a) and 34(4)(b) of Schedule 4 (only realised profits to be included in or transferred to the profit and loss account) in relation to anything done with a view to or in connection with the making of that distribution.

Supplementary

Consequences
of unlawful
distribution.
277.—(1) Where a distribution, or part of one, made by a company to one of its members is made in contravention of this Part and, at the time of the distribution, he knows or has reasonable grounds for believing that it is so made, he is liable to repay it (or that part of it, as the case may be) to the company or (in the case of a distribution made otherwise than in cash) to pay the company a sum equal to the value of the distribution (or part) at that time.

(2) The above is without prejudice to any obligation imposed apart from this section on a member of a company to repay a

distribution unlawfully made to him ; but this section does not apply in relation to—

  (a) financial assistance given by a company in contravention of section 151, or

  (b) any payment made by a company in respect of the redemption or purchase by the company of shares in itself.

(3) Subsection (2) of this section is deemed included in Chapter VII of Part V for purposes of the Secretary of State's power to make regulations under section 179.

278. Where immediately before 22nd December 1980 a company was authorised by a provision of its articles to apply its unrealised profits in paying up in full or in part unissued shares to be allotted to members of the company as fully or partly paid bonus shares, that provision continues (subject to any alteration of the articles) as authority for those profits to be so applied after that date. Saving for provision in articles operative before Act of 1980.

279. Where a company's accounts relevant for the purposes of this Part are special category, sections 265 to 275 apply with the modifications shown in Schedule 11. Distributions by special category companies.

280.—(1) The following has effect for the interpretation of this Part. Definitions for Part VIII.

(2) " Capitalisation ", in relation to a company's profits, means any of the following operations (whenever carried out)—

  (a) applying the profits in wholly or partly paying up unissued shares in the company to be allotted to members of the company as fully or partly paid bonus shares, or

  (b) transferring the profits to capital redemption reserve.

(3) References to profits and losses of any description are (respectively) to profits and losses of that description made at any time and, except where the context otherwise requires, are (respectively) to revenue and capital profits and revenue and capital losses.

281. The provisions of this Part are without prejudice to any enactment or rule of law, or any provision of a company's memorandum or articles, restricting the sums out of which, or the cases in which, a distribution may be made. Saving for other restraints on distribution.

PART X

ENFORCEMENT OF FAIR DEALING BY DIRECTORS

Restrictions on directors taking financial advantage

Prohibition
on tax-free
payments to
directors.

311.—(1) It is not lawful for a company to pay a director remuneration (whether as director or otherwise) free of income tax, or otherwise calculated by reference to or varying with the amount of his income tax, or to or with any rate of income tax.

(2) Any provision contained in a company's articles, or in any contract, or in any resolution of a company or a company's directors, for payment to a director of remuneration as above mentioned has effect as if it provided for payment, as a gross sum subject to income tax, of the net sum for which it actually provides.

Payment to
director for
loss of office
etc.

312. It is not lawful for a company to make to a director of the company any payment by way of compensation for loss of office, or as consideration for or in connection with his retirement from office, without particulars of the proposed payment (including its amount) being disclosed to members of the company and the proposal being approved by the company.

PART X
Company
approval for
property
transfer.

313.—(1) It is not lawful, in connection with the transfer of the whole or any part of the undertaking or property of a company, for any payment to be made to a director of the company by way of compensation for loss of office, or as consideration for or in connection with his retirement from office, unless particulars of the proposed payment (including its amount) have been disclosed to members of the company and the proposal approved by the company.

(2) Where a payment unlawful under this section is made to a director, the amount received is deemed to be received by him in trust for the company.

Director's
duty of
disclosure on
takeover, etc.

314.—(1) This section applies where, in connection with the transfer to any persons of all or any of the shares in a company, being a transfer resulting from—

    (*a*) an offer made to the general body of shareholders ; or

    (*b*) an offer made by or on behalf of some other body corporate with a view to the company becoming its subsidiary or a subsidiary of its holding company ; or

    (*c*) an offer made by or on behalf of an individual with a view to his obtaining the right to exercise or control the exercise of not less than one-third of the voting power at any general meeting of the company ; or (*d*) any other offer which is conditional on acceptance to a given extent,

a payment is to be made to a director of the company by way of compensation for loss of office, or as consideration for or in connection with his retirement from office.

(2) It is in those circumstances the director's duty to take all reasonable steps to secure that particulars of the proposed payment (including its amount) are included in or sent with any notice of the offer made for their shares which is given to any shareholders.

(3) If—

(*a*) the director fails to take those steps, or

(*b*) any person who has been properly required by the director to include those particulars in or send them with the notice required by subsection (2) fails to do so,

he is liable to a fine.

315.—(1) If in the case of any such payment to a director as is mentioned in section 314(1)—

(*a*) his duty under that section is not complied with, or

(*b*) the making of the proposed payment is not, before the transfer of any shares in pursuance of the offer, approved by a meeting (summoned for the purpose) of the holders of the shares to which the offer relates and of other holders of shares of the same class as any of those shares,

any sum received by the director on account of the payment is deemed to have been received by him in trust for persons who have sold their shares as a result of the offer made ; and the expenses incurred by him in distributing that sum amongst those persons shall be borne by him and not retained out of that sum.

(2) Where—

(*a*) the shareholders referred to in subsection (1)(*b*) are not all the members of the company, and

(*b*) no provision is made by the articles for summoning or regulating the meeting referred to in that paragraph,

the provisions of this Act and of the company's articles relating to general meetings of the company apply (for that purpose) to the meeting either without modification or with such modifications as the Secretary of State on the application of any person concerned may direct for the purpose of adapting them to the circumstances of the meeting.

(3) If at a meeting summoned for the purpose of approving any payment as required by subsection (1)(b) a quorum is not present and, after the meeting has been adjourned to a later date, a quorum is again not present, the payment is deemed for the purposes of that subsection to have been approved.

Provisions supplementing ss. 312 to 315.

316.—(1) Where in proceedings for the recovery of any payment as having, by virtue of section 313(2) or 315(1), been received by any person in trust, it is shown that—

    (a) the payment was made in pursuance of any arrangement entered into as part of the agreement for the transfer in question, or within one year before or two years after that agreement or the offer leading to it ; and

    (b) the company or any person to whom the transfer was made was privy to that arrangement,

the payment is deemed, except in so far as the contrary is shown, to be one to which the provisions mentioned above in this subsection apply.

(2) If in connection with any such transfer as is mentioned in any of sections 313 to 315—

    (a) the price to be paid to a director of the company whose office is to be abolished or who is to retire from office for any shares in the company held by him is in excess of the price which could at the time have been obtained by other holders of the like shares ; or

    (b) any valuable consideration is given to any such director,

the excess or the money value of the consideration (as the case may be) is deemed for the purposes of that section to have been a payment made to him by way of compensation for loss of office or as consideration for or in connection with his retirement from office.

(3) References in sections 312 to 315 to payments made to a director by way of compensation for loss of office or as consideration for or in connection with his retirement from office, do not include any bona fide payment by way of damages for breach of contract or by way of pension in respect of past services.

" Pension " here includes any superannuation allowance, superannuation gratuity or similar payment.

(4) Nothing in sections 313 to 315 prejudices the operation of any rule of law requiring disclosure to be made with respect to such payments as are there mentioned, or with respect to any other like payments made or to be made to a company's directors.

317.—(1) It is the duty of a director of a company who is in any way, whether directly or indirectly, interested in a contract or proposed contract with the company to declare the nature of his interest at a meeting of the directors of the company.

(2) In the case of a proposed contract, the declaration shall be made—

(a) at the meeting of the directors at which the question of entering into the contract is first taken into consideration ; or

(b) if the director was not at the date of that meeting interested in the proposed contract, at the next meeting of the directors held after he became so interested ;

and, in a case where the director becomes interested in a contract after it is made, the declaration shall be made at the first meeting of the directors held after he becomes so interested.

(3) For purposes of this section, a general notice given to the directors of a company by a director to the effect that—

(a) he is a member of a specified company or firm and is to be regarded as interested in any contract which may, after the date of the notice, be made with that company or firm ; or

(b) he is to be regarded as interested in any contract which may after the date of the notice be made with a specified person who is connected with him (within the meaning of section 346 below),

is deemed a sufficient declaration of interest in relation to any such contract.

(4) However, no such notice is of effect unless either it is given at a meeting of the directors or the director takes reasonable steps to secure that it is brought up and read at the next meeting of the directors after it is given.

(5) A reference in this section to a contract includes any transaction or arrangement (whether or not constituting a contract) made or entered into on or after 22nd December 1980.

(6) For purposes of this section, a transaction or arrangement of a kind described in section 330 (prohibition of loans, quasi-loans etc. to directors) made by a company for a director of the company or a person connected with such a director is treated (if it would not otherwise be so treated, and whether or not it is prohibited by that section) as a transaction or arrangement in which that director is interested.

(7) A director who fails to comply with this section is liable to a fine.

(8) This section applies to a shadow director as it applies to a director, except that a shadow director shall declare his interest, not at a meeting of the directors, but by a notice in writing to the directors which is either—

> (a) a specific notice given before the date of the meeting at which, if he had been a director, the declaration would be required by subsection (2) to be made ; or
>
> (b) a notice which under subsection (3) falls to be treated as a sufficient declaration of that interest (or would fall to be so treated apart from subsection (4)).

(9) Nothing in this section prejudices the operation of any rule of law restricting directors of a company from having an interest in contracts with the company.

318.—(1) Subject to the following provisions, every company shall keep at an appropriate place—

> (a) in the case of each director whose contract of service with the company is in writing, a copy of that contract ;
>
> (b) in the case of each director whose contract of service with the company is not in writing, a written memorandum setting out its terms ; and
>
> (c) in the case of each director who is employed under a contract of service with a subsidiary of the company, a copy of that contract or, if it is not in writing, a written memorandum setting out its terms.

(2) All copies and memoranda kept by a company in pursuance of subsection (1) shall be kept at the same place.

(3) The following are appropriate places for the purposes of subsection (1)—

> (a) the company's registered office ;
>
> (b) the place where its register of members is kept (if other than its registered office) ;
>
> (c) its principal place of business, provided that is situated in that part of Great Britain in which the company is registered.

(4) Every company shall send notice in the prescribed form to the registrar of companies of the place where copies and memoranda are kept in compliance with subsection (1), and of any change in that place, save in a case in which they have at all times been kept at the company's registered office.

(5) Subsection (1) does not apply to a director's contract of service with the company or with a subsidiary of it if that contract required him to work wholly or mainly outside the United

Kingdom ; but the company shall keep a memorandum—
- (*a*) in the case of a contract of service with the company, giving the director's name and setting out the provisions of the contract relating to its duration ;
- (*b*) in the case of a contract of service with a subsidiary, giving the director's name and the name and place of incorporation of the subsidiary, and setting out the provisions of the contract relating to its duration,

at the same place as copies and memoranda are kept by the company in pursuance of subsection (1).

(6) A shadow director is treated for purposes of this section as a director.

(7) Every copy and memorandum required by subsection (1) or (5) to be kept shall, during business hours (subject to such reasonable restrictions as the company may in general meeting impose, so that not less than 2 hours in each day be allowed for inspection), be open to inspection of any member of the company without charge.

(8) If—
- (*a*) default is made in complying with subsection (1) or (5), or
- (*b*) an inspection required under subsection (7) is refused, or
- (*c*) default is made for 14 days in complying with subsection (4),

the company and every officer of it who is in default is liable to a fine and, for continued contravention, to a daily default fine.

(9) In the case of a refusal of an inspection required under subsection (7) of a copy or memorandum, the court may by order compel an immediate inspection of it.

(10) Subsections (1) and (5) apply to a variation of a director's contract of service as they apply to the contract.

(11) This section does not require that there be kept a copy of, or memorandum setting out the terms of, a contract (or its variation) at a time when the unexpired portion of the term for which the contract is to be in force is less than 12 months, or at a time at which the contract can, within the next ensuing 12 months, be terminated by the company without payment of compensation.

319.—(1) This section applies in respect of any term of an agreement whereby a director's employment with the company   Director's contract of employment for more than 5 years.

PART X   of which he is a director or, where he is the director of a holding company, his employment within the group is to continue, or may be continued, otherwise than at the instance of the company (whether under the original agreement or under a new agreement entered into in pursuance of it), for a period of more than 5 years during which the employment—

    (a) cannot be terminated by the company by notice ; or

    (b) can be so terminated only in specified circumstances.

(2) In any case where—

    (a) a person is or is to be employed with a company under an agreement which cannot be terminated by the company by notice or can be so terminated only in specified circumstances ; and

    (b) more than 6 months before the expiration of the period for which he is or is to be so employed, the company enters into a further agreement (otherwise than in pursuance of a right conferred by or under the original agreement on the other party to it) under which he is to be employed with the company or, where he is a director of a holding company, within the group,

this section applies as if to the period for which he is to be employed under that further agreement there were added a further period equal to the unexpired period of the original agreement.

(3) A company shall not incorporate in an agreement such a term as is mentioned in subsection (1), unless the term is first approved by a resolution of the company in general meeting and, in the case of a director of a holding company, by a resolution of that company in general meeting.

(4) No approval is required to be given under this section by any body corporate unless it is a company within the meaning of this Act, or is registered under section 680, or if it is a wholly-owned subsidiary of any body corporate, wherever incorporated.

(5) A resolution of a company approving such a term as is mentioned in subsection (1) shall not be passed at a general meeting of the company unless a written memorandum setting out the proposed agreement incorporating the term is available for inspection by members of the company both—

    (a) at the company's registered office for not less than 15 days ending with the date of the meeting ; and

    (b) at the meeting itself.

(6) A term incorporated in an agreement in contravention

of this section is, to the extent that it contravenes the section, void; and that agreement and, in a case where subsection (2) applies, the original agreement are deemed to contain a term entitling the company to terminate it at any time by the giving of reasonable notice.

(7) In this section—

(a) " employment " includes employment under a contract for services ; and

(b) " group ", in relation to a director of a holding company, means the group which consists of that company and its subsidiaries ;

and for purposes of this section a shadow director is treated as a director.

320.—(1) With the exceptions provided by the section next following, a company shall not enter into an arrangement—

(a) whereby a director of the company or its holding company, or a person connected with such a director, acquires or is to acquire one or more non-cash assets of the requisite value from the company ; or

(b) whereby the company acquires or is to acquire one or more non-cash assets of the requisite value from such a director or a person so connected,

unless the arrangement is first approved by a resolution of the company in general meeting and, if the director or connected person is a director of its holding company or a person connected with such a director, by a resolution in general meeting of the holding company.

(2) For this purpose a non-cash asset is of the requisite value if at the time the arrangement in question is entered into its value is not less than £1,000 but (subject to that) exceeds £50,000 or 10 per cent. of the company's asset value, that is—

(a) except in a case falling within paragraph (b) below, the value of the company's net assets determined by reference to the accounts prepared and laid under Part VII in respect of the last preceding financial year in respect of which such accounts were so laid ; and

(b) where no accounts have been so prepared and laid before that time, the amount of the company's called-up share capital.

(3) For purposes of this section and sections 321 and 322, a shadow director is treated as a director.

321.—(1) No approval is required to be given under section 320 by any body corporate unless it is a company within the meaning of this Act or registered under section 680 or, if it is a wholly-owned subsidiary of any body corporate, wherever incorporated.

(2) Section 320(1) does not apply to an arrangement for the acquisition of a non-cash asset—

    (*a*) if the asset is to be acquired by a holding company from any of its wholly-owned subsidiaries or from a holding company by any of its wholly-owned subsidiaries, or by one wholly-owned subsidiary of a holding company from another wholly-owned subsidiary of that same holding company, or

    (*b*) if the arrangement is entered into by a company which is being wound up, unless the winding up is a members' voluntary winding up.

(3) Section 320(1)(*a*) does not apply to an arrangement whereby a person is to acquire an asset from a company of which he is a member, if the arrangement is made with that person in his character as a member.

322.—(1) An arrangement entered into by a company in contravention of section 320, and any transaction entered into in pursuance of the arrangement (whether by the company or any other person) is voidable at the instance of the company unless one or more of the conditions specified in the next subsection is satisfied.

(2) Those conditions are that—

    (*a*) restitution of any money or other asset which is the subject-matter of the arrangement or transaction is no longer possible or the company has been indemnified in pursuance of this section by any other person for the loss or damage suffered by it; or

    (*b*) any rights acquired bona fide for value and without actual notice of the contravention by any person who is not a party to the arrangement or transaction would be affected by its avoidance ; or

    (*c*) the arrangement is, within a reasonable period, affirmed by the company in general meeting and, if it is an arrangement for the transfer of an asset to or by a director of its holding company or a person who is connected with such a director, is so affirmed with the approval of the holding company given by a resolution in general meeting.

(3) If an arrangement is entered into with a company by a director of the company or its holding company or a person connected with him in contravention of section 320, that director and the person so connected, and any other director of the company who authorised the arrangement or any transaction entered into in pursuance of such an arrangement, is liable—

(a) to account to the company for any gain which he has made directly or indirectly by the arrangement or transaction, and

(b) (jointly and severally with any other person liable under this subsection) to indemnify the company for any loss or damage resulting from the arrangement or transaction.

(4) Subsection (3) is without prejudice to any liability imposed otherwise than by that subsection, and is subject to the following two subsections; and the liability under subsection (3) arises whether or not the arrangement or transaction entered into has been avoided in pursuance of subsection (1).

(5) If an arrangement is entered into by a company and a person connected with a director of the company or its holding company in contravention of section 320, that director is not liable under subsection (3) if he shows that he took all reasonable steps to secure the company's compliance with that section.

(6) In any case, a person so connected and any such other director as is mentioned in subsection (3) is not so liable if he shows that, at the time the arrangement was entered into, he did not know the relevant circumstances constituting the contravention.

Share dealings by directors and their families

323.—(1) It is an offence for a director of a company to buy—

(a) a right to call for delivery at a specified price and within a specified time of a specified number of relevant shares or a specified amount of relevant debentures; or

(b) a right to make delivery at a specified price and within a specified time of a specified number of relevant shares or a specified amount of relevant debentures; or

(c) a right (as he may elect) to call for delivery at a specified price and within a specified time or to make delivery at a specified price and within a specified time of a specified number of relevant shares or a specified amount of relevant debentures.

Part X   (2) A person guilty of an offence under subsection (1) is liable to imprisonment or a fine, or both.

(3) In subsection (1)—

(a) " relevant shares ", in relation to a director of a company, means shares in the company or in any other body corporate, being the company's subsidiary or holding company, or a subsidiary of the company's holding company, being shares as respects which there has been granted a listing on a stock exchange (whether in Great Britain or elsewhere) ;

(b) " relevant debentures ", in relation to a director of a company, means debentures of the company or of any other body corporate, being the company's subsidiary or holding company or a subsidiary of the company's holding company, being debentures as respects which there has been granted such a listing ; and

(c) " price " includes any consideration other than money.

(4) This section applies to a shadow director as to a director.

(5) This section is not to be taken as penalising a person who buys a right to subscribe for shares in, or debentures of, a body corporate or buys debentures of a body corporate that confer upon the holder of them a right to subscribe for, or to convert the debentures (in whole or in part) into, shares of that body.

Duty of director to disclose shareholdings in own company.

324.—(1) A person who becomes a director of a company and at the time when he does so is interested in shares in, or debentures of, the company or any other body corporate, being the company's subsidiary or holding company or a subsidiary of the company's holding company, is under obligation to notify the company in writing—

(a) of the subsistence of his interests at that time ; and

(b) of the number of shares of each class in, and the amount of debentures of each class of, the company or other such body corporate in which each interest of his subsists at that time.

(2) A director of a company is under obligation to notify the company in writing of the occurrence, while he is a director, of any of the following events—

(a) any event in consequence of whose occurrence he becomes, or ceases to be, interested in shares in, or debentures of, the company or any other body corporate, being the company's subsidiary or holding company or a subsidiary of the company's holding company ;

(*b*) the entering into by him of a contract to sell any such
shares or debentures ;

(*c*) the assignment by him of a right granted to him by the
company to subscribe for shares in, or debentures of,
the company ; and

(*d*) the grant to him by another body corporate, being the
company's subsidiary or holding company or a subsidiary of the company's holding company, of a right
to subscribe for shares in, or debentures of, that other
body corporate, the exercise of such a right granted to
him and the assignment by him of such a right so
granted ;

and notification to the company must state the number or
amount, and class, of shares or debentures involved.

(3) Schedule 13 has effect in connection with subsections (1)
and (2) above ; and of that Schedule—

(*a*) Part I contains rules for the interpretation of, and
otherwise in relation to, those subsections and applies
in determining, for purposes of those subsections,
whether a person has an interest in shares or debentures ;

(*b*) Part II applies with respect to the periods within which
obligations imposed by the subsections must be fulfilled ; and

(*c*) Part III specifies certain circumstances in which obligations arising from subsection (2) are to be treated as not
discharged ;

and subsections (1) and (2) are subject to any exceptions for
which provision may be made by regulations made by the
Secretary of State by statutory instrument.

(4) Subsection (2) does not require the notification by a person
of the occurrence of an event whose occurrence comes to his
knowledge after he has ceased to be a director.

(5) An obligation imposed by this section is treated as not discharged unless the notice by means of which it purports to be discharged is expressed to be given in fulfilment of that obligation.

(6) This section applies to shadow directors as to directors ; but
nothing in it operates so as to impose an obligation with respect
to shares in a body corporate which is the wholly-owned subsidiary of another body corporate.

(7) A person who—

(*a*) fails to discharge, within the proper period, an obligation
to which he is subject under subsection (1) or (2), or

(*b*) in purported discharge of an obligation to which he is so subject, makes to the company a statement which he knows to be false, or recklessly makes to it a statement which is false,

is guilty of an offence and liable to imprisonment or a fine, or both.

(8) Section 732 (restriction on prosecutions) applies to an offence under this section.

Register of directors' interests notified under s. 324.

325.—(1) Every company shall keep a register for the purposes of section 324.

(2) Whenever a company receives information from a director given in fulfilment of an obligation imposed on him by that section, it is under obligation to enter in the register, against the director's name, the information received and the date of the entry.

(3) The company is also under obligation, whenever it grants to a director a right to subscribe for shares in, or debentures of, the company to enter in the register against his name—

(a) the date on which the right is granted,

(b) the period during which, or time at which, it is exercisable,

(c) the consideration for the grant (or, if there is no consideration, that fact), and

(d) the description of shares or debentures involved and the number or amount of them, and the price to be paid for them (or the consideration, if otherwise than in money).

(4) Whenever such a right as is mentioned above is exercised by a director, the company is under obligation to enter in the register against his name that fact (identifying the right), the number or amount of shares or debentures in respect of which it is exercised and, if they were registered in his name, that fact and, if not, the name or names of the person or persons in whose name or names they were registered, together (if they were registered in the names of two persons or more) with the number or amount of the shares or debentures registered in the name of each of them.

(5) Part IV of Schedule 13 has effect with respect to the register to be kept under this section, to the way in which entries in it are to be made, to the right of inspection, and generally.

(6) For purposes of this section, a shadow director is deemed a director.

326.—(1) The following applies with respect to defaults in
complying with, and to contraventions of, section 325 and Part
IV of Schedule 13.

(2) If default is made in complying with any of the following
provisions—

    (a) section 325(1), (2), (3) or (4), or

    (b) Schedule 13, paragraph 21, 22 or 28,

the company and every officer of it who is in default is liable
to a fine and, for continued contravention, to a daily default
fine.

(3) If an inspection of the register required under paragraph
25 of the Schedule is refused, or a copy required under paragraph 26 is not sent within the proper period, the company
and every officer of it who is in default is liable to a fine and,
for continued contravention, to a daily default fine.

(4) If default is made for 14 days in complying with paragraph
27 of the Schedule (notice to registrar of where register is kept),
the company and every officer of it who is in default is liable
to a fine and, for continued contravention, to a daily default fine.

(5) If default is made in complying with paragraph 29 of the
Schedule (register to be produced at annual general meeting),
the company and every officer of it who is in default is liable
to a fine.

(6) In the case of a refusal of an inspection of the register
required under paragraph 25 of the Schedule, the court may by
order compel an immediate inspection of it; and in the case
of failure to send within the proper period a copy required
under paragraph 26, the court may by order direct that the
copy be sent to the person requiring it.

327.—(1) Section 323 applies to—

    (a) the wife or husband of a director of a company (not
        being herself or himself a director of it), and

    (b) an infant son or infant daughter of a director (not
        being himself or herself a director of the company),

as it applies to the director; but it is a defence for a person
charged by virtue of this section with an offence under section
323 to prove that he (she) had no reason to believe that his (her)
spouse or, as the case may be, parent was a director of the
company in question.

(2) For purposes of this section—

    (a) "son" includes step-son, and "daughter" includes
        step-daughter ("parent" being construed accordingly),

    (b) " infant " means, in relation to Scotland, pupil or minor, and

    (c) a shadow director of a company is deemed a director of it.

328.—(1) For the purposes of section 324—

    (a) an interest of the wife or husband of a director of a company (not being herself or himself a director of it) in shares or debentures is to be treated as the director's interest ; and

    (b) the same applies to an interest of an infant son or infant daughter of a director of a company (not being himself or herself a director of it) in shares or debentures.

(2) For those purposes—

    (a) a contract, assignment or right of subscription entered into, exercised or made by, or a grant made to, the wife or husband of a director of a company (not being herself or himself a director of it) is to be treated as having been entered into, exercised or made by, or (as the case may be) as having been made to, the director ; and

    (b) the same applies to a contract, assignment or right of subscription entered into, exercised or made by, or grant made to, an infant son or infant daughter of a director of a company (not being himself or herself a director of it).

(3) A director of a company is under obligation to notify the company in writing of the occurrence while he or she is a director, of either of the following events, namely—

    (a) the grant by the company to his (her) spouse, or to his or her infant son or infant daughter, of a right to subscribe for shares in, or debentures of, the company ; and

    (b) the exercise by his (her) spouse or by his or her infant son or infant daughter of such a right granted by the company to the wife, husband, son or daughter.

(4) In a notice given to the company under subsection (3) there shall be stated—

    (a) in the case of the grant of a right, the like information as is required by section 324 to be stated by the director on the grant to him by another body corporate of a right to subscribe for shares in, or debentures of, that other body corporate ; and

    (b) in the case of the exercise of a right, the like information as is required by that section to be stated by the director on the exercise of a right granted to him by another body corporate to subscribe for shares in, or debentures of, that other body corporate.

(5) An obligation imposed by subsection (3) on a director must be fulfilled by him before the end of 5 days beginning with the day following that on which the occurrence of the event giving rise to it comes to his knowledge ; but in reckoning that period of days there is disregarded any Saturday or Sunday, and any day which is a bank holiday in any part of Great Britain.

(6) A person who—

(a) fails to fulfil, within the proper period, an obligation to which he is subject under subsection (3), or

(b) in purported fulfilment of such an obligation, makes to a company a statement which he knows to be false, or recklessly makes to a company a statement which is false,

is guilty of an offence and liable to imprisonment or a fine, or both.

(7) The rules set out in Part I of Schedule 13 have effect for the interpretation of, and otherwise in relation to, subsections (1) and (2) ; and subsections (5), (6) and (8) of section 324 apply with any requisite modification.

(8) In this section, " son " includes step-son, " daughter " includes step-daughter, and " infant " means, in relation to Scotland, pupil or minor.

(9) For purposes of section 325, an obligation imposed on a director by this section is to be treated as if imposed by section 324.

329.—(1) Whenever a company whose shares or debentures are listed on a recognised stock exchange is notified of any matter by a director in consequence of the fulfilment of an obligation imposed by section 324 or 328, and that matter relates to shares or debentures so listed, the company is under obligation to notify that stock exchange of that matter ; and the stock exchange may publish, in such manner as it may determine, any information received by it under this subsection.

(2) An obligation imposed by subsection (1) must be fulfilled before the end of the day next following that on which it arises ; but there is disregarded for this purpose a day which is a Saturday or a Sunday or a bank holiday in any part of Great Britain.

(3) If default is made in complying with this section, the company and every officer of it who is in default is guilty of an offence and liable to a fine and, for continued contravention, to a daily default fine.

PART X

Section 732 (restriction on prosecutions) applies to an offence under this section.

Restrictions on a company's power to make loans, etc., to directors and persons connected with them

General restriction on loans etc. to directors and persons connected with them.

330.—(1) The prohibitions listed below in this section are subject to the exceptions in sections 332 to 338.

(2) A company shall not—

    (a) make a loan to a director of the company or of its holding company ;

    (b) enter into any guarantee or provide any security in connection with a loan made by any person to such a director.

(3) A relevant company shall not—

    (a) make a quasi-loan to a director of the company or of its holding company ;

    (b) make a loan or a quasi-loan to a person connected with such a director ;

    (c) enter into a guarantee or provide any security in connection with a loan or quasi-loan made by any other person for such a director or a person so connected.

(4) A relevant company shall not—

    (a) enter into a credit transaction as creditor for such a director or a person so connected ;

    (b) enter into any guarantee or provide any security in connection with a credit transaction made by any other person for such a director or a person so connected.

(5) For purposes of sections 330 to 346, a shadow director is treated as a director.

(6) A company shall not arrange for the assignment to it, or the assumption by it, of any rights, obligations or liabilities under a transaction which, if it had been entered into by the company, would have contravened subsection (2), (3) or (4) ; but for the purposes of sections 330 to 347 the transaction is to be treated as having been entered into on the date of the arrangement.

(7) A company shall not take part in any arrangement whereby—

    (a) another person enters into a transaction which, if it had been entered into by the company, would have contravened any of subsections (2), (3), (4) or (6) ; and (*b*) that other person, in pursuance of the arrangement, has obtained or is to obtain any benefit from the company or its holding company or a subsidiary of the company or its holding company.

331.—(1) The following subsections apply for the interpretation of sections 330 to 346.

(2) " Guarantee " includes indemnity, and cognate expressions are to be construed accordingly.

(3) A quasi-loan is a transaction under which one party (" the creditor ") agrees to pay, or pays otherwise than in pursuance of an agreement, a sum for another (" the borrower ") or agrees to reimburse, or reimburses otherwise than in pursuance of an agreement, expenditure incurred by another party for another (" the borrower ")—

(*a*) on terms that the borrower (or a person on his behalf) will reimburse the creditor ; or

(*b*) in circumstances giving rise to a liability on the borrower to reimburse the creditor.

(4) Any reference to the person to whom a quasi-loan is made is a reference to the borrower ; and the liabilities of a borrower under a quasi-loan include the liabilities of any person who has agreed to reimburse the creditor on behalf of the borrower.

(5) " Recognised bank " means a company which is recognised as a bank for the purposes of the Banking Act 1979.

(6) " Relevant company " means a company which—

(*a*) is a public company, or

(*b*) is a subsidiary of a public company, or

(*c*) is a subsidiary of a company which has as another subsidiary a public company, or

(*d*) has a subsidiary which is a public company.

(7) A credit transaction is a transaction under which one party (" the creditor ")—

(*a*) supplies any goods or sells any land under a hire-purchase agreement or a conditional sale agreement ;

(*b*) leases or hires any land or goods in return for periodical payments ;

(*c*) otherwise disposes of land or supplies goods or services on the understanding that payment (whether in a lump sum or instalments or by way of periodical payments or otherwise) is to be deferred.

(8) " Services " means anything other than goods or land.

(9) A transaction or arrangement is made " for " a person if—

    (a) in the case of a loan or quasi-loan, it is made to him ;

    (b) in the case of a credit transaction, he is the person to whom goods or services are supplied, or land is sold or otherwise disposed of, under the transaction ;

    (c) in the case of a guarantee or security, it is entered into or provided in connection with a loan or quasi-loan made to him or a credit transaction made for him ;

    (d) in the case of an arrangement within subsection (6) or (7) of section 330, the transaction to which the arrangement relates was made for him ; and

    (e) in the case of any other transaction or arrangement for the supply or transfer of, or of any interest in, goods, land or services, he is the person to whom the goods, land or services (or the interest) are supplied or transferred.

(10) " Conditional sale agreement " means the same as in the Consumer Credit Act 1974.

332.—(1) Subsection (3) of section 300 does not prohibit a company (" the creditor ") from making a quasi-loan to one of its directors or to a director of its holding company if—

    (a) the quasi-loan contains a term requiring the director or a person on his behalf to reimburse the creditor his expenditure within 2 months of its being incurred ; and

    (b) the aggregate of the amount of that quasi-loan and of the amount outstanding under each relevant quasi-loan does not exceed £1,000.

(2) A quasi-loan is relevant for this purpose if it was made to the director by virtue of this section by the creditor or its subsidiary or, where the director is a director of the creditor's holding company, any other subsidiary of that company ; and " the amount outstanding " is the amount of the outstanding liabilities of the person to whom the quasi-loan was made.

333. In the case of a relevant company which is a member of a group of companies (meaning a holding company and its subsidiaries), paragraphs (b) and (c) of section 330(3) do not prohibit the company from—

    (a) making a loan or quasi-loan to another member of that group ; or

    (b) entering into a guarantee or providing any security in connection with a loan or quasi-loan made by any person to another member of the group, by reason only that a director of one member of the group is associated with another.

PART X

334. Without prejudice to any other provision of sections 332 to 338, paragraph (*a*) of section 330(2) does not prohibit a company from making a loan to a director of the company or of its holding company if the aggregate of the relevant amounts does not exceed £2,500.

Loans of small amounts.

335.—(1) Section 330(4) does not prohibit a company from entering into a transaction for a person if the aggregate of the relevant amounts does not exceed £5,000.

Minor and business transactions.

(2) Section 330(4) does not prohibit a company from entering into a transaction for a person if—

(*a*) the transaction is entered into by the company in the ordinary course of its business ; and

(*b*) the value of the transaction is not greater, and the terms on which it is entered into are no more favourable, in respect of the person for whom the transaction is made, than that or those which it is reasonable to expect the company to have offered to or in respect of a person of the same financial standing but unconnected with the company.

336. The following transactions are excepted from the prohibitions of section 330—

Transactions at behest of holding company.

(*a*) a loan or quasi-loan by a company to its holding company, or a company entering into a guarantee or providing any security in connection with a loan or quasi-loan made by any person to its holding company ;

(*b*) a company entering into a credit transaction as creditor for its holding company, or entering into a guarantee or providing any security in connection with a credit transaction made by any other person for its holding company.

337.—(1) A company is not prohibited by section 330 from doing anything to provide a director with funds to meet expenditure incurred or to be incurred by him for the purposes of the company or for the purpose of enabling him properly to perform his duties as an officer of the company.

Funding of director's expenditure on duty to company.

(2) Nor does the section prohibit a company from doing anything to enable a director to avoid incurring such expenditure.

(3) Subsections (1) and (2) apply only if one of the following conditions is satisfied—

(a) the thing in question is done with prior approval of the company given at a general meeting at which there are disclosed all the matters mentioned in the next subsection ;

(b) that thing is done on condition that, if the approval of the company is not so given at or before the next annual general meeting, the loan is to be repaid, or any other liability arising under any such transaction discharged, within 6 months from the conclusion of that meeting ;

but those subsections do not authorise a relevant company to enter into any transaction if the aggregate of the relevant amounts exceeds £10,000.

(4) The matters to be disclosed under subsection (3)(a) are—

(a) the purpose of the expenditure incurred or to be incurred, or which would otherwise be incurred, by the director,

(b) the amount of the funds to be provided by the company, and

(c) the extent of the company's liability under any transaction which is or is connected with the thing in question.

Loan or quasi-loan by money-lending company. **338.**—(1) There is excepted from the prohibitions in section 330—

(a) a loan or quasi-loan made by a money-lending company to any person ; or

(b) a money-lending company entering into a guarantee in connection with any other loan or quasi-loan.

(2) " Money-lending company " means a company whose ordinary business includes the making of loans or quasi-loans, or the giving of guarantees in connection with loans or quasi-loans.

(3) Subsection (1) applies only if both the following conditions are satisfied—

(a) the loan or quasi-loan in question is made by the company, or it enters into the guarantee, in the ordinary course of the company's business ; and

(b) the amount of the loan or quasi-loan, or the amount guaranteed, is not greater, and the terms of the loan, quasi-loan or guarantee are not more favourable, in

the case of the person to whom the loan or quasi-loan
is made or in respect of whom the guarantee is entered
into, than that or those which it is reasonable to expect
that company to have offered to or in respect of a
person of the same financial standing but unconnected
with the company.

(4) But subsection (1) does not authorise a relevant company
(unless it is a recognised bank) to enter into any transaction if
the aggregate of the relevant amounts exceeds £50,000.

(5) In determining that aggregate, a company which a
director does not control is deemed not to be connected with
him.

(6) The condition specified in subsection (3)(b) does not of
itself prevent a company from making a loan to one of its
directors or a director of its holding company—

(a) for the purpose of facilitating the purchase, for use as
that director's only or main residence, of the whole or
part of any dwelling-house together with any land to be
occupied and enjoyed with it ;

(b) for the purpose of improving a dwelling-house or part
of a dwelling-house so used or any land occupied and
enjoyed with it ;

(c) in substitution for any loan made by any person and
falling within paragraph (a) or (b) of this subsection,

if loans of that description are ordinarily made by the company
to its employees and on terms no less favourable than those on
which the transaction in question is made, and the aggregate of
the relevant amounts does not exceed £50,000.

339.—(1) This section has effect for defining the " relevant " Relevant
amounts " to be aggregated under sections 334, 335(1), 337(3) amounts " for
and 338(4) ; and in relation to any proposed transaction or ar- purposes of
rangement and the question whether it falls within one or other ss. 334 ff.
of the exceptions provided by those sections, " the relevant
exception " is that exception ; but where the relevant exception
is the one provided by section 334 (loan of small amount), references in this section to a person connected with a director are to
be disregarded.

(2) Subject as follows, the relevant amounts in relation to a
proposed transaction or arrangement are—

(a) the value of the proposed transaction or arrangement,

  (*b*) the value of any existing arrangement which—

   (i) **falls within subsection (6) or (7) of section 330, and**

   (ii) **also falls within subsection (3) of this section, and**

   (iii) was entered into by virtue of the relevant exception by the company or by a subsidiary of the company or, where the proposed transaction or arrangement is to be made for a director of its holding company or a person connected with such a director, by that holding company or any of its subsidiaries ;

  (*c*) the amount outstanding under any other transaction—

   (i) **falling within subsection (3) below, and**

   (ii) made by virtue of the relevant exception, and

   (iii) **made by the company or by a subsidiary of the company or, where the proposed transaction or arrangement is to be made for a director of its holding company or a person connected with such a director, by that holding company or any of its subsidiaries.**

(3) A transaction falls within this subsection if it was made—

  (*a*) for the director for whom the proposed transaction or arrangement is to be made, or for any person connected with that director ; or

  (*b*) where the proposed transaction or arrangement is to be made for a person connected with a director of a company, for that director or any person connected with him ;

and an arrangement also falls within this subsection if it relates to a transaction which does so.

(4) But where the proposed transaction falls within section 338 and is one which a recognised bank proposes to enter into under subsection (6) of that section (housing loans, etc.), any other transaction or arrangement which apart from this subsection would fall within subsection (3) of this section does not do so unless it was entered into in pursuance of section 338(6).

(5) A transaction entered into by a company which is (at the time of that transaction being entered into) a subsidiary of the company which is to make the proposed transaction, or is a subsidiary of that company's holding company, does not fall within subsection (3) if at the time when the question arises (that is to say, the question whether the proposed transaction or arrangement falls within any relevant exception), it no longer is such a subsidiary.

(6) Values for purposes of subsection (2) of this section are to be determined in accordance with the section next following; and " the amount outstanding " for purposes of subsection (2)(c) above is the value of the transaction less any amount by which that value has been reduced. PART X

340.—(1) This section has effect for determining the value of a transaction or arrangement for purposes of sections 330 to 339. " Value " of transactions and arrangements.

(2) The value of a loan is the amount of its principal.

(3) The value of a quasi-loan is the amount, or maximum amount, which the person to whom the quasi-loan is made is liable to reimburse the creditor.

(4) The value of a guarantee or security is the amount guaranteed or secured.

(5) The value of an arrangement to which section 330(6) or (7) applies is the value of the transaction to which the arrangement relates less any amount by which the liabilities under the arrangement or transaction of the person for whom the transaction was made have been reduced.

(6) The value of a transaction or arrangement not falling within subsections (2) to (5) above is the price which it is reasonable to expect could be obtained for the goods, land or services to which the transaction or arrangement relates if they had been supplied (at the time the transaction or arrangement is entered into) in the ordinary course of business and on the same terms (apart from price) as they have been supplied, or are to be supplied, under the transaction or arrangement in question.

(7) For purposes of this section, the value of a transaction or arrangement which is not capable of being expressed as a specific sum of money (because the amount of any liability arising under the transaction or arrangement is unascertainable, or for any other reason), whether or not any liability under the transaction or arrangement has been reduced, is deemed to exceed £50,000.

341.—(1) If a company enters into a transaction or arrangement in contravention of section 330, the transaction or arrangement is voidable at the instance of the company unless— Civil remedies for breach of s. 330.

(a) restitution of any money or any other asset which is the subject matter of the arrangement or transaction is no longer possible, or the company has been indemnified in pursuance of subsection (2)(b) below for the loss or damage suffered by it, or

(b) any rights acquired bona fide for value and without actual notice of the contravention by a person other than the person for whom the transaction or arrangement was made would be affected by its avoidance.

(2) Where an arrangement or transaction is made by a company for a director of the company or its holding company or a person connected with such a director in contravention of section 330, that director and the person so connected and any other director of the company who authorised the transaction or arrangement (whether or not it has been avoided in pursuance of subsection (1)) is liable—

(a) to account to the company for any gain which he has made directly or indirectly by the arrangement or transaction ; and

(b) (jointly and severally with any other person liable under this subsection) to indemnify the company for any loss or damage resulting from the arrangement or transaction.

(3) Subsection (2) is without prejudice to any liability imposed otherwise than by that subsection, but is subject to the next two subsections.

(4) Where an arrangement or transaction is entered into by a company and a person connected with a director of the company or its holding company in contravention of section 330, that director is not liable under subsection (2) of this section if he shows that he took all reasonable steps to secure the company's compliance with that section.

(5) In any case, a person so connected and any such other director as is mentioned in subsection (2) is not so liable if he shows that, at the time the arrangement or transaction was entered into, he did not know the relevant circumstances constituting the contravention.

Criminal penalties for breach of s. 330.

342.—(1) A director of a relevant company who authorises or permits the company to enter into a transaction or arrangement knowing or having reasonable cause to believe that the company was thereby contravening section 330 is guilty of an offence.

(2) A relevant company which enters into a transaction or arrangement for one of its directors or for a director of its holding company in contravention of section 330 is guilty of an offence.

(3) A person who procures a relevant company to enter into a transaction or arrangement knowing or having reasonable cause to believe that the company was thereby contravening section 330 is guilty of an offence.

(4) A person guilty of an offence under this section is liable to imprisonment or a fine, or both.

(5) A relevant company is not guilty of an offence under subsection (2) if it shows that, at the time the transaction or arrangement was entered into, it did not know the relevant circumstances.

343.—(1) The following provisions of this section—

   (a) apply in the case of a company which is, or is the holding company of, a recognised bank, and

   (b) are subject to the exceptions provided by section 344.

Record of transactions not disclosed in company accounts.

(2) Such a company shall maintain a register containing a copy of every transaction, arrangement or agreement of which particulars would, but for paragraph 4 of Schedule 6, be required by section 232 to be disclosed in the company's accounts or group accounts for the current financial year and for each of the preceding 10 financial years.

(3) In the case of a transaction, arrangement or agreement which is not in writing, there shall be contained in the register a written memorandum setting out its terms.

(4) Such a company shall before its annual general meeting make available at its registered office for not less than 15 days ending with the date of the meeting a statement containing the particulars of transactions, arrangements and agreements which the company would, but for paragraph 4 of Schedule 6, be required by section 232 to disclose in its accounts or group accounts for the last complete financial year preceding that meeting.

(5) The statement shall be so made available for inspection by members of the company ; and such a statement shall also be made available for their inspection at the annual general meeting.

(6) It is the duty of the company's auditors to examine the statement before it is made available to members of the company and to make a report to the members on it ; and the report shall be annexed to the statement before it is made so available.

(7) The auditors' report shall state whether in their opinion the statement contains the particulars required by subsection (4) ; and, where their opinion is that it does not, they shall include in the report, so far as they are reasonably able to do so, a statement giving the required particulars.

(8) If a company fails to comply with any provision of subsections (2) to (5), every person who at the time of the failure is a director of it is guilty of an offence and liable to a fine ; but—

(a) it is a defence in proceedings against a person for this offence to prove that he took all reasonable steps for securing compliance with the subsection concerned, and

(b) a person is not guilty of the offence by virtue only of being a shadow director of the company.

(9) For purposes of the application of this section to loans and quasi-loans made by a company to persons connected with a person who at any time is a director of the company or of its holding company, a company which a person does not control is not connected with him.

344.—(1) Section 343 does not apply in relation to—

(a) transactions or arrangements made or subsisting during a financial year by a company or by a subsidiary of a company for a person who was at any time during that year a director of the company or of its holding company or was connected with such a director, or

(b) an agreement made or subsisting during that year to enter into such a transaction or arrangement,

if the aggregate of the values of each transaction or arrangement made for that person, and of each agreement for such a transaction or arrangement, less the amount (if any) by which the value of those transactions, arrangements and agreements has been reduced, did not exceed £1,000 at any time during the financial year.

For purposes of this subsection, values are to be determined as under section 340.

(2) Section 343(4) and (5) do not apply to a recognised bank which is the wholly-owned subsidiary of a company incorporated in the United Kingdom.

Supplementary

345.—(1) The Secretary of State may by order in a statutory instrument substitute for any sum of money specified in this Part a larger sum specified in the order.

(2) An order under this section is subject to annulment in pursuance of a resolution of either House of Parliament.

(3) Such an order does not have effect in relation to anything done or not done before its coming into force ; and accordingly, proceedings in respect of any liability (whether civil or criminal) incurred before that time may be continued or instituted as if the order had not been made.

346.—(1) This section has effect with respect to references in this Part to a person being " connected " with a director of a company, and to a director being " associated with " or " controlling " a body corporate.

(2) A person is connected with a director of a company if, but only if, he (not being himself a director of it) is—

(a) that director's spouse, child or step-child ; or

(b) except where the context otherwise requires, a body corporate with which the director is associated ; or

(c) a person acting in his capacity as trustee of any trust the beneficiaries of which include—

(i) the director, his spouse or any children or step-children of his, or

(ii) a body corporate with which he is associated, or of a trust whose terms confer a power on the trustees that may be exercised for the benefit of the director, his spouse, or any children or step-children of his, or any such body corporate ; or

(d) a person acting in his capacity as partner of that director or of any person who, by virtue of paragraph (a), (b) or (c) of this subsection, is connected with that director ; or

(e) a Scottish firm in which—

(i) that director is a partner,

(ii) a partner is a person who, by virtue of paragraph (a), (b) or (c) above, is connected with that director, or

(iii) a partner is a Scottish firm in which that director is a partner or in which there is a partner who, by virtue of paragraph (a), (b) or (c) above, is connected with that director.

(3) In subsection (2)—

(a) a reference to the child or step-child of any person includes an illegitimate child of his, but does not include any person who has attained the age of 18 ; and

(b) paragraph (c) does not apply to a person acting in his capacity as trustee under an employees' share scheme or a pension scheme.

(4) A director of a company is associated with a body corporate if, but only if, he and the persons connected with him, together—

(a) are interested in shares comprised in the equity share capital of that body corporate of a nominal value equal to at least one-fifth of that share capital ; or (*b*) are entitled to exercise or control the exercise of more than one-fifth of the voting power at any general meeting of that body.

(5) A director of a company is deemed to control a body corporate if, but only if—

(*a*) he or any person connected with him is interested in any part of the equity share capital of that body or is entitled to exercise or control the exercise of any part of the voting power at any general meeting of that body ; and

(*b*) that director, the persons connected with him and the other directors of that company, together, are interested in more than one-half of that share capital or are entitled to exercise or control the exercise of more than one-half of that voting power.

(6) For purposes of subsections (4) and (5)—

(*a*) a body corporate with which a director is associated is not to be treated as connected with that director unless it is also connected with him by virtue of subsection (2)(*c*) or (*d*) ; and

(*b*) a trustee of a trust the beneficiaries of which include (or may include) a body corporate with which a director is associated is not to be treated as connected with a director by reason only of that fact.

(7) The rules set out in Part I of Schedule 13 apply for the purposes of subsections (4) and (5).

(8) References in those subsections to voting power the exercise of which is controlled by a director include voting power whose exercise is controlled by a body corporate controlled by him ; but this is without prejudice to other provisions of subsections (4) and (5).

Transactions under foreign law.

347. For purposes of sections 319 to 322 and 330 to 343, it is immaterial whether the law which (apart from this Act) governs any arrangement or transaction is the law of the United Kingdom, or of a part of it, or not.

Chapter V

Auditors

384.—(1) Every company shall, at each general meeting of the company at which accounts are laid in accordance with section 241, appoint an auditor or auditors to hold office from the conclusion of that meeting until the conclusion of the next general meeting at which the requirements of section 241 are complied with. *Annual appointment of auditors.*

This is subject to section 252 (exemption for dormant companies).

(2) The first auditors of a company may be appointed by the directors at any time before the first general meeting of the company at which accounts are laid ; and auditors so appointed shall hold office until the conclusion of that meeting.

(3) If the directors fail to exercise their powers under subsection (2), those powers may be exercised by the company in general meeting.

(4) The directors, or the company in general meeting, may fill any casual vacancy in the office of auditor ; but while any such vacancy continues, the surviving or continuing auditor or auditors (if any) may act.

(5) If at any general meeting of a company at which accounts are laid as required by section 241 no auditors are appointed or reappointed, the Secretary of State may appoint a person to fill the vacancy ; and the company shall, within one week of that power of the Secretary of State becoming exercisable, give to him notice of that fact.

If a company fails to give the notice required by this subsection, the company and every officer of it who is in default is guilty of an offence and liable to a fine and, for continued contravention, to a daily default fine.

385.—(1) The remuneration of a company's auditors shall be fixed by the company in general meeting, or in such manner as the company in general meeting may determine. *Remuneration of auditors.*

(2) This does not apply in the case of auditors appointed by the directors or by the Secretary of State ; and in that case their remuneration may be fixed by the directors or by the Secretary of State (as the case may be).

(3) For the purpose of this section, " remuneration " includes any sums paid by the company in respect of the auditor's expenses.

PART XI
CHAPTER V
Removal of auditors.

386.—(1) A company may by ordinary resolution remove an auditor before the expiration of his term of office, notwithstanding anything in any agreement between it and him.

(2) Where a resolution removing an auditor is passed at a general meeting of a company, the company shall within 14 days give notice of that fact in the prescribed form to the registrar of companies.

If a company fails to give the notice required by this subsection, the company and every officer of it who is in default is guilty of an offence and liable to a fine and, for continued contravention, to a daily default fine.

(3) Nothing in this section is to be taken as depriving a person removed under it of compensation or damages payable to him in respect of the termination of his appointment as auditor or of any appointment terminating with that as auditor.

Auditors' right to attend company meetings.

387.—(1) A company's auditors are entitled to attend any general meeting of the company and to receive all notices of, and other communications relating to, any general meeting which a member of the company is entitled to receive, and to be heard at any general meeting which they attend on any part of the business of the meeting which concerns them as auditors.

(2) An auditor of a company who has been removed is entitled to attend—

(a) the general meeting at which his term of office would otherwise have expired, and

(b) any general meeting at which it is proposed to fill the vacancy caused by his removal,

and to receive all notices of, and other communications relating to, any such meeting which any member of the company is entitled to receive, and to be heard at any such meeting which he attends on any part of the business of the meeting which concerns him as former auditor of the company.

Supplementary provisions as to auditors.

388.—(1) Special notice is required for a resolution at a general meeting of a company—

(a) appointing as auditor a person other than a retiring auditor ; or

(b) filling a casual vacancy in the office of auditor ; or

(c) reappointing as auditor a retiring auditor who was appointed by the directors to fill a casual vacancy ; or

(d) removing an auditor before the expiration of his term of office.

(2) On receipt of notice of such an intended resolution as is mentioned above the company shall forthwith send a copy of it—

 (a) to the person proposed to be appointed or removed, as the case may be;

 (b) in a case within subsection (1)(a), to the retiring auditor; and

 (c) where, in a case within subsection (1)(b) or (c), the casual vacancy was caused by the resignation of an auditor, to the auditor who resigned.

(3) Where notice is given of such a resolution as is mentioned in subsection (1) (a) or (d), and the retiring auditor or (as the case may be) the auditor proposed to be removed makes with respect to the intended resolution representations in writing to the company (not exceeding a reasonable length) and requests their notification to members of the company, the company shall (unless the representations are received by it too late for it to do so)—

 (a) in any notice of the resolution given to members of the company state the fact of the representations having been made, and

 (b) send a copy of the representations to every member of the company to whom notice of the meeting is or has been sent.

(4) If a copy of any such representations is not sent out as required by subsection (3) because received too late or because of the company's default, the auditor may (without prejudice to his right to be heard orally) require that the representations shall be read out at the meeting.

(5) Copies of the representations need not be sent out and the representations need not be read out at the meeting if, on the application either of the company or of any other person claiming to be aggrieved, the court is satisfied that the rights conferred by this section are being abused to secure needless publicity for defamatory matter; and the court may order the company's costs on the application to be paid in whole or in part by the auditor, notwithstanding that he is not a party to the application.

389.—(1) Subject to the next subsection, a person is not qualified for appointment as auditor of a company unless either—

 (a) he is a member of a body of accountants established in the United Kingdom and for the time being recognised for the purposes of this provision by the Secretary of State; or

(b) he is for the time being authorised by the Secretary of State to be so appointed, as having similar qualifications obtained outside the United Kingdom or else he retains an authorisation formerly granted by the Board of Trade or the Secretary of State under section 161(1) (b) of the Companies Act 1948 (adequate knowledge and experience, or pre-1947 practice).

1948 c. 38.

(2) Subject to subsections (6) to (8) below, a person is qualified for appointment as auditor of an unquoted company if he retains an authorisation granted by the Board of Trade or the Secretary of State under section 13(1) of the Companies Act 1967.

1967 c. 81.

In this subsection—

(a) " unquoted company " means a company in the case of which, at the time of the person's appointment, the following condition is satisfied, namely, that no shares or debentures of the company, or of a body corporate of which it is the subsidiary, have been quoted on a stock exchange (whether in Great Britain or elsewhere) to the public for subscription or purchase, and

(b) " company " does not include a company that carries on business as the promoter of a trading stamp scheme within the meaning of the Trading Stamps Act 1964.

1964 c. 71.

(3) Subject to the next subsection, the bodies of accountants recognised for the purposes of subsection (1)(a) are—

(a) the Institute of Chartered Accountants in England and Wales,

(b) the Institute of Chartered Accountants of Scotland,

(c) the Chartered Association of Certified Accountants, and

(d) the Institute of Chartered Accountants in Ireland.

(4) The Secretary of State may by regulations in a statutory instrument amend subsection (3) by adding or deleting any body, but shall not make regulations—

(a) adding any body, or

(b) deleting any body which has not considered in writing to its deletion,

unless he has published notice of his intention to do so in the London and Edinburgh Gazettes at least 4 months before making the regulations.

(5) The Secretary of State may refuse an authorisation under subsection (1)(b) to a person as having qualifications obtained outside the United Kingdom if it appears to him that the country in which the qualifications were obtained does not confer

on persons qualified in the United Kingdom privileges corresponding to those conferred by that subsection.

(6) None of the following persons is qualified for appointment
as auditor of a company—

(a) an officer or servant of the company ;

(b) a person who is a partner of or in the employment of an
officer or servant of the company ;

(c) a body corporate ;

and for this purpose an auditor of a company is not to be regarded as either officer or servant of it.

(7) A person is also not qualified for appointment as auditor
of a company if he is, under subsection (6), disqualified
for appointment as auditor of any other body corporate which
is that company's subsidiary or holding company or a subsidiary
of that company's holding company, or would be so disqualified
if the body corporate were a company.

(8) Notwithstanding subsections (1), (6) and (7), a Scottish firm
is qualified for appointment as auditor of a company if, but only
if, all the partners are qualified for appointment as auditors of it.

(9) No person shall act as auditor of a company at a time
when he knows that he is disqualified for appointment to that
office ; and if an auditor of a company to his knowledge becomes so disqualified during his term of office he shall thereupon
vacate his office and give notice in writing to the company that
he has vacated it by reason of that disqualification.

(10) A person who acts as auditor in contravention of subsection (9), or fails without reasonable excuse to give notice of
vacating his office as required by that subsection, is guilty of an
offence and liable to a fine and, for continued contravention, to
a daily default fine.

390.—(1) An auditor of a company may resign his office by
depositing a notice in writing to that effect at the company's
registered office ; and any such notice operates to bring his term
of office to an end on the date on which the notice is deposited,
or on such later date as may be specified in it.

Resignation of
auditors.

(2) An auditor's notice of resignation is not effective unless
it contains either—

(a) a statement to the effect that there are no circumstances
connected with his resignation which he considers
should be brought to the notice of the members or
creditors of the company ; or

(b) a statement of any such circumstances as are mentioned above.

(3) Where a notice under this section is deposited at a company's registered office, the company shall within 14 days send a copy of the notice—

  (a) to the registrar of companies ; and

  (b) if the notice contained a statement under subsection (2)(b), to every person who under section 240 is entitled to be sent copies of the accounts.

(4) The company or any person claiming to be aggrieved may, within 14 days of the receipt by the company of a notice containing a statement under subsection (2)(b), apply to the court for an order under the next subsection.

(5) If on such an application the court is satisfied that the auditor is using the notice to secure needless publicity for defamatory matter, it may by order direct that copies of the notice need not be sent out; and the court may further order the company's costs on the application to be paid in whole or in part by the auditor, notwithstanding that he is not a party to the application.

(6) The company shall, within 14 days of the court's decision, send to the persons mentioned in subsection (3)—

  (a) if the court makes an order under subsection (5), a statement setting out the effect of the order ;

  (b) if not, a copy of the notice containing the statement under subsection (2)(b).

(7) If default is made in complying with subsection (3) or (6), the company and every officer of it who is in default is liable to a fine and, for continued contravention, to a daily default fine.

Right of resigning auditor to requisition company meeting.

391.—(1) Where an auditor's notice of resignation contains a statement under section 390(2)(b) there may be deposited with the notice a requisition signed by the auditor calling on the directors of the company forthwith duly to convene an extraordinary general meeting of the company for the purpose of receiving and considering such explanation of the circumstances connected with his resignation as he may wish to place before the meeting.

(2) Where an auditor's notice of resignation contains such a statement, the auditor may request the company to circulate to its members—

  (a) before the general meeting at which his term of office would otherwise have expired ; or

(*b*) before any general meeting at which it is proposed to
fill the vacancy caused by his resignation or convened
on his requisition,

a statement in writing (not exceeding a reasonable length) of
the circumstances connected with his resignation.

(3) The company shall in that case (unless the statement is
received by it too late for it to comply)—

(*a*) in any notice of the meeting given to members of the
company state the fact of the statement having been
made, and

(*b*) send a copy of the statement to every member of the
company to whom notice of the meeting is or has been
sent.

(4) If the directors do not within 21 days from the date of
the deposit of a requisition under this section proceed duly
to convene a meeting for a day not more than 28 days after the
date on which the notice convening the meeting is given, every
director who failed to take all reasonable steps to secure that a
meeting was convened as mentioned above is guilty of an
offence and liable to a fine.

(5) If a copy of the statement mentioned in subsection (2)
is not sent out as required by subsection (3) because received
too late or because of the company's default, the auditor may
(without prejudice to his right to be heard orally) require that
the statement shall be read out at the meeting.

(6) Copies of a statement need not be sent out and the statement need not be read out at the meeting if, on the application
either of the company or of any other person who claims to be
aggrieved, the court is satisfied that the rights conferred by
this section are being abused to secure needless publicity for
defamatory matter ; and the court may order the company's
costs on such an application to be paid in whole or in part by
the auditor, notwithstanding that he is not a party to the
application.

(7) An auditor who has resigned his office is entitled to attend
any such meeting as is mentioned in subsection (2)(*a*) or (*b*)
and to receive all notices of, and other communications relating
to, any such meeting which any member of the company is entitled to receive, and to be heard at any such meeting which he
attends on any part of the business of the meeting which concerns him as former auditor of the company.

Part XI
Chapter V
Powers of
auditors in
relation to
subsidiaries.

392.—(1) Where a company (" the holding company ") has a subsidiary, then—

> (a) if the subsidiary is a body corporate incorporated in Great Britain, it is the duty of the subsidiary and its auditors to give to the auditors of the holding company such information and explanation as those auditors may reasonably require for the purposes of their duties as auditors of the holding company ;

> (b) in any other case, it is the duty of the holding company, if required by its auditors to do so, to take all such steps as are reasonably open to it to obtain from the subsidiary such information and explanation as are mentioned above.

(2) If a subsidiary or holding company fails to comply with subsection (1), the subsidiary or holding company and every officer of it who is in default is guilty of an offence and liable to a fine; and if an auditor fails without reasonable excuse to comply with paragraph (a) of the subsection, he is guilty of an offence and so liable.

393. An officer of a company commits an offence if he knowingly or recklessly makes to a company's auditors a statement (whether written or oral) which—

> (a) conveys or purports to convey any information or explanation which the auditors require, or are entitled to require, as auditors of the company, and

> (b) is misleading, false or deceptive in a material particular.

A person guilty of an offence under this section is liable to imprisonment or a fine, or both.

394.—(1) Subject as follows, this section applies to every body which is both a company and a trade union or an employers' association to which section 11 of the Trade Union and Labour Relations Act 1974 applies.

(2) Section 11(3) of the Act of 1974 and paragraphs 6 to 15 of Schedule 2 to that Act (qualifications, appointment and removal of auditors) do not have effect in relation to bodies to which this section applies.

(3) The rights and powers conferred, and the duties imposed, by paragraphs 16 to 21 of that Schedule on the auditors of a body to which this section applies belong to the auditors from time to time appointed by or on behalf of that body under section 384 of this Act.

Part XVI

Fraudulent Trading by a Company

458. If any business of a company is carried on with intent to defraud creditors of the company or creditors of any other person, or for any fraudulent purpose, every person who was knowingly a party to the carrying on of the business in that manner is liable to imprisonment or a fine, or both. *Punishment for fraudulent trading.*

This applies whether or not the company has been, or is in the course of being, wound up.

Part XXIII

Oversea Companies

Chapter I

Registration, Etc.

691.—(1) When a company incorporated outside Great Britain establishes a place of business in Great Britain, it shall within one month of doing so deliver to the registrar of companies for registration— *Documents to be delivered to registrar.*

(a) a certified copy of the charter, statutes or memorandum and articles of the company or other instrument constituting or defining the company's constitution, and, if the instrument is not written in the English language, a certified translation of it ; and

(b) a return in the prescribed form containing—

(i) a list of the company's directors and secretary, containing the particulars specified in the next subsection,

(ii) a list of the names and addresses of some one or more persons resident in Great Britain authorised to accept on the company's behalf service of process and any notices required to be served on it,

(iii) a list of the documents delivered in compliance with paragraph (a) of this subsection, and

(iv) a statutory declaration (made by a director or secretary of the company or by any person whose name and address are given in the list required by sub-paragraph (ii)), stating the date on which the company's place of business in Great Britain was established.

(2) The list referred to in subsection (1)(*b*)(i) shall contain the following particulars—

(*a*) with respect to each director—

(i) in the case of an individual, his present Christian name and surname and any former Christian name or surname, his usual residential address, his nationality and his business occupation (if any), or, if he has no business occupation but holds other directorships, particulars of any of them,

(ii) in the case of a corporation, its corporate name and registered or principal office ;

(*b*) with respect to the secretary (or, where there are joint secretaries, with respect to each of them)—

(i) in the case of an individual, his present Christian name and surname, any former Christian name and surname and his usual residential address,

(ii) in the case of a corporation or a Scottish firm, its corporate or firm name and registered or principal office.

Where all the partners in a firm are joint secretaries of the company, the name and principal office of the firm may be stated instead of the particulars mentioned in paragraph (*b*).

Section 289(2) applies for the purposes of the construction of references above to present and former Christian names and surnames.

Registration of altered particulars.

692.—(1) If any alteration is made in—

(*a*) the charter, statutes, or memorandum and articles of an oversea company or any such instrument as is mentioned above, or

(*b*) the directors or secretary of an oversea company or the particulars contained in the list of the directors and secretary, or

(*c*) the names or addresses of the persons authorised to accept service on behalf of an oversea company,

the company shall, within the time specified below, deliver to the registrar of companies for registration a return containing the prescribed particulars of the alteration.

(2) If any change is made in the corporate name of an oversea company, the company shall, within the time specified below, deliver to the registrar of companies for registration a return containing the prescribed particulars of the change.

(3) The time for delivery of the returns required by subsections (1) and (2) is—

(*a*) in the case of an alteration to which subsection (1)(*c*) applies, 21 days after the making of the alteration, and (*b*) otherwise, 21 days after the date on which notice of the alteration or change in question could have been re- ceived in Great Britain in due course of post (if despatched with due diligence).

693. Every oversea company shall—
(*a*) in every prospectus inviting subscriptions for its shares or debentures in Great Britain, state the country in which the company is incorporated,
(*b*) conspicuously exhibit on every place where it carries on business in Great Britain the company's name and the country in which it is incorporated,
(*c*) cause the company's name and the country in which it is incorporated to be stated in legible characters in all bill-heads and letter paper, and in all notices and other official publications of the company, and
(*d*) if the liability of the members of the company is limited, cause notice of that fact to be stated in legible characters in every such prospectus as above mentioned and in all bill-heads, letter paper, notices and other official publications of the company in Great Britain, and to be affixed on every place where it carries on its business.

694.—(1) If it appears to the Secretary of State that the corporate name of an oversea company is a name by which the company, had it been formed under this Act, would on the rele- vant date (defined below in subsection (3)) have been precluded from being registered by section 26 either—
(*a*) because it falls within subsection (1) of that section, or
(*b*) if it falls within subsection (2) of that section, because the Secretary of State would not approve the company's being registered with that name,
the Secretary of State may serve a notice on the company, stating why the name would not have been registered.

(2) If the corporate name of an oversea company is in the Secretary of State's opinion too like a name appearing on the relevant date in the index of names kept by the registrar of companies under section 714 or which should have appeared in that index on that date, or is the same as a name which should have so appeared, the Secretary of State may serve a notice on the company specifying the name in the index which the company's name is too like or which is the same as the company's name.

(3) No notice shall be served on a company under subsection

(1) or (2) later than 12 months after the relevant date, being the date on which the company has complied with—

    (*a*) section 691 in this Part, or

    (*b*) if there has been a change in the company's corporate name, section 692(2).

(4) An oversea company on which a notice is served under subsection (1) or (2)—

    (*a*) may deliver to the registrar of companies for registration a statement in the prescribed form specifying a name approved by the Secretary of State other than its corporate name under which it proposes to carry on business in Great Britain, and

    (*b*) may, after that name has been registered, at any time deliver to the registrar for registration a statement in the prescribed form specifying a name approved by the Secretary of State (other than its corporate name) in substitution for the name previously registered.

(5) The name by which an oversea company is for the time being registered under subsection (4) is, for all purposes of the law applying in Great Britain (including this Act and the Business Names Act 1985), deemed to be the company's corporate name ; but—

    (*a*) this does not affect references to the corporate name in this section, or any rights or obligations of the company, or render defective any legal proceedings by or against the company, and

    (*b*) any legal proceedings that might have been continued or commenced against the company by its corporate name or its name previously registered under this section may be continued or commenced against it by its name for the time being so registered.

(6) An oversea company on which a notice is served under subsection (1) or (2) shall not at any time after the expiration of 2 months from the service of that notice (or such longer period as may be specified in that notice carry on business in Great Britain under its corporate name.

Nothing in this subsection, or in section 697(2) (which imposes penalties for its contravention) invalidates any transaction entered into by the company.

(7) The Secretary of State may withdraw a notice served under subsection (1) or (2) at any time before the end of the period mentioned in subsection (6) ; and that subsection does not apply to a company served with a notice which has been withdrawn.

695.—(1) Any process or notice required to be served on an oversea company is sufficiently served if addressed to any person whose name has been delivered to the registrar under preceding sections in this Part and left at or sent by post to the address which has been so delivered.

(2) However—

(a) where such a company makes default in delivering to the registrar the name and address of a person resident in Great Britain who is authorised to accept on behalf of the company service of process or notices, or

(b) if at any time all the persons whose names and addresses have been so delivered are dead or have ceased so to reside, or refuse to accept service on the company's behalf, or for any reason cannot be served,

a document may be served on the company by leaving it at, or sending it by post to, any place of business established by the company in Great Britain.

696.—(1) Any document which an oversea company is required to deliver to the registrar of companies shall be delivered to the registrar at the registration office in England and Wales or Scotland, according to where the company has established a place of business.

(2) If the company has established a place of business both in England and Wales and in Scotland, the document shall be delivered at the registration office both in England and Wales and in Scotland.

(3) References in this Part to the registrar of companies are to be construed in accordance with the above subsections.

(4) If an oversea company ceases to have a place of business in either part of Great Britain, it shall forthwith give notice of that fact to the registrar of companies for that part ; and as from the date on which notice is so given the obligation of the company to deliver any document to the registrar ceases.

697.—(1) If an oversea company fails to comply with any of sections 691 to 693 and 696, the company, and every officer or agent of the company who knowingly and wilfully authorises or permits the default, is liable to a fine and, in the case of a continuing offence, to a daily default fine for continued contravention.

(2) If an oversea company contravenes section 694(6), the company and every officer or agent of it who knowingly and wilfully authorises or permits the contravention is guilty of an offence and liable to a fine and, for continued contravention, to a daily default fine.

PART XXIII
CHAPTER I
Definitions for
this Chapter.

698. For purposes of this Chapter—

" certified " means certified in the prescribed manner to be a true copy or a correct translation ;

" director ", in relation to an oversea company, includes shadow director ; and

" secretary " includes any person occupying the position of secretary by whatever name called.

Channel
Islands and
Isle of Man
companies.

699.—(1) With the exceptions specified in subsection (3) below, the provisions of this Act requiring documents to be forwarded or delivered to or filed with the registrar of companies and applying to companies formed and registered under Part I apply also (if they would not otherwise) to an oversea company incorporated in the Channel Islands or the Isle of Man.

(2) Those provisions apply to such a company—

(a) if it has established a place of business in England and Wales, as if it were registered in England and Wales,

(b) if it has established a place of business in Scotland, as if it were registered in Scotland, and

(c) if it has established a place of business both in England and Wales and in Scotland, as if it were registered in both England and Wales and Scotland,

with such modifications as may be necessary and, in particular, apply in a similar way to documents relating to things done outside Great Britain as if they had been done in Great Britain.

(3) The exceptions are—

section 6(1) (resolution altering company's objects),

section 18 (alteration of memorandum or articles by statute or statutory instrument),

section 241(3) (directors' duty to file accounts),

section 288(2) (notice to registrar of change of directors or secretary), and

section 380 (copies of certain resolutions and agreements to be sent to registrar within 15 days), so far as applicable to a resolution altering a company's memorandum or articles.

CHAPTER II

DELIVERY OF ACCOUNTS

Preparation
and delivery
of accounts
by oversea
companies.

700.—(1) Every oversea company shall in respect of each accounting reference period of the company prepare such accounts, made up by reference to such date or dates, and in such form, containing such particulars and having annexed to

them such documents, as would have been required if it were
a company formed and registered under this Act.

(2) An oversea company shall, in respect of each accounting reference period of the company, deliver to the registrar of companies copies of the accounts and other documents required by subsection (1) ; and, if such an account or other document is in a language other than English, there shall be annexed to the copy so delivered a translation of it into English certified in the prescribed manner to be a correct translation.

(3) If in relation to an accounting reference period the company's directors would be exempt under section 241(4) from compliance with subsection (3) of that section (independent company with unlimited liability), if the company were otherwise subject to that section, compliance with this section is not required in respect of that accounting reference period.

(4) The Secretary of State may by order in a statutory instrument—

    (a) modify the requirements referred to in subsection (1) for the purpose of their application to oversea companies,

    (b) exempt an oversea company from those requirements or from such of them as may be specified in the order.

(5) An order under subsection (4) may make different provision in relation to different cases or classes of case and may contain such incidental and supplementary provisions as the Secretary of State thinks fit ; and a statutory instrument containing an order so made is subject to annulment in pursuance of a resolution of either House of Parliament.

701.—(1) An oversea company's accounting reference periods are determined according to its accounting reference date.

Oversea company's accounting reference period and date.

(2) The company may give notice in the prescribed form to the registrar of companies specifying a date in the calendar year as being the date on which in each successive calendar year an accounting reference period of the company is to be treated as coming to an end ; and the date specified in the notice is then the company's accounting reference date.

(3) No such notice has effect unless it is given before the end of 6 months beginning with the date on which a place of business in Great Britain is or was established by the company ; and, failing such a notice, the company's accounting reference date is 31st March.

(4) The company's first accounting reference period is such period ending with its accounting reference date as—

(a) begins or began on a date determined by the company, but not later than that on which a place of business is or was established in Great Britain, and

(b) is a period exceeding 6 months and not exceeding 18 months.

(5) Each successive period of 12 months beginning after the end of the first accounting reference period and ending with the company's accounting reference date is also an accounting reference period of the company.

(6) Subsections (2) to (5) are subject to section 225 of this Act, under which in certain circumstances a company's accounting reference period may be altered, and which applies to oversea companies as well as to companies subject to Part VII, but omitting subsections (6) and (7).

Period
allowed for
delivering
accounts.

702.—(1) In the case of an oversea company, the period allowed for delivering accounts in relation to an accounting reference period is 13 months after the end of the period.

(2) Where the company's first accounting reference period—

(a) begins or began on the date determined by the company for the purposes of section 701(4)(a) and

(b) is or was a period of more than 12 months,

the period which would otherwise be allowed for delivering accounts in relation to that accounting reference period is treated as reduced by the number of days by which the accounting reference period is or was longer than 12 months.

(3) But the period allowed in relation to a company's first accounting reference period is not by subsection (2) reduced to less than 3 months after the end of that accounting reference period.

(4) In relation to an accounting reference period of an oversea company as respects which notice is given by the company under section 225 (as applied) and which by virtue of that section is treated as shortened in accordance with the notice, the period allowed for delivering accounts is—

(a) the period allowed in relation to that accounting reference period in accordance with the preceding subsections, or

(b) the period of 3 months beginning with the date of the notice,

whichever of those periods last expires.

(5) If for any special reason the Secretary of State thinks fit to do so, he may by notice in writing to an oversea company extend,

by such further period as may be specified in the notice, the
period which in accordance with the preceding subsections is the
period allowed for delivering accounts in relation to any accounting reference period of the company.

703.—(1) If in respect of an accounting reference period of Penalty for
an oversea company any of the requirements of section 700(2) non-
is not complied with before the end of the period allowed for compliance.
delivering accounts, the company and every officer or agent of
it who knowingly and wilfully authorises or permits the default
is, in respect of the company's failure to comply with the requirements in question, guilty of an offence and liable to a fine
and, for continued contravention, to a daily default fine.

(2) For purposes of any proceedings under this section with
respect to a requirement to deliver a copy of a document to the
registrar of companies, it is not a defence to prove that the document in question was not in fact prepared as required by section
700.

PART XXVI

INTERPRETATION

"Company",
etc.

25 & 26 Vict. c. 89.

8 Edw. 7 c. 69.

1929 c. 23.

735.—(1) In this Act—

(a) " company " means a company formed and registered under this Act, or an existing company ;

(b) " existing company " means a company formed and registered under the former Companies Acts, but does not include a company registered under the Joint Stock Companies Acts, the Companies Act 1862 or the Companies (Consolidation) Act 1908 in what was then Ireland ;

(c) " the former Companies Acts " means the Joint Stock Companies Acts, the Companies Act 1862, the Companies (Consolidation) Act 1908, the Companies Act 1929 and the Companies Acts 1948 to 1983.

(2) " Public company " and " private company " have the meanings given by section 1(3).

20 & 21 Vict. c. 14.

20 & 21 Vict. c. 49.

21 & 22 Vict. c. 91.

7 & 8 Vict. c. 110.

(3) " The Joint Stock Companies Acts " means the Joint Stock Companies Act 1856, the Joint Stock Companies Acts 1856, 1857, the Joint Stock Banking Companies Act 1857 and the Act to enable Joint Stock Banking Companies to be formed on the principle of limited liability, or any one or more of those Acts (as the case may require), but does not include the Joint Stock Companies Act 1844.

(4) The definitions in this section apply unless the contrary intention appears.

"Holding
company ",
" subsidiary "
and " wholly-
owned
subsidiary".

736.—(1) For the purposes of this Act, a company is deemed to be a subsidiary of another if (but only if)—

(a) that other either—

(i) is a member of it and controls the composition of its board of directors, or

(ii) holds more than half in nominal value of its equity share capital, or

(b) the first-mentioned company is a subsidiary of any company which is that other's subsidiary.

The above is subject to subsection (4) below in this section.

(2) For purposes of subsection (1), the composition of a company's board of directors is deemed to be controlled by another company if (but only if) that other company by the exercise of some power exercisable by it without the consent or concurrence of any other person can appoint or remove the holders of all or a majority of the directorships.

(3) For purposes of this last provision, the other company is deemed to have power to appoint to a directorship with respect

to which any of the following conditions is satisfied—

(a) that a person cannot be appointed to it without the exercise in his favour by the other company of such a power as is mentioned above, or

(b) that a person's appointment to the directorship follows necessarily from his appointment as director of the other company, or

(c) that the directorship is held by the other company itself or by a subsidiary of it.

(4) In determining whether one company is a subsidiary of another—

(a) any shares held or power exercisable by the other in a fiduciary capacity are to be treated as not held or exercisable by it,

(b) subject to the two following paragraphs, any shares held or power exercisable—

(i) by any person as nominee for the other (except where the other is concerned only in a fiduciary capacity), or

(ii) by, or by a nominee for, a subsidiary of the other (not being a subsidiary which is concerned only in a fiduciary capacity),

are to be treated as held or exercisable by the other,

(c) any shares held or power exercisable by any person by virtue of the provisions of any debentures of the first-mentioned company or of a trust deed for securing any issue of such debentures are to be disregarded,

(d) any shares held or power exercisable by, or by a nominee for, the other or its subsidiary (not being held or exercisable as mentioned in paragraph (c)) are to be treated as not held or exercisable by the other if the ordinary business of the other or its subsidiary (as the case may be) includes the lending of money and the shares are held or the power is exercisable as above mentioned by way of security only for the purposes of a transaction entered into in the ordinary course of that business.

(5) For purposes of this Act—

(a) a company is deemed to be another's holding company if (but only if) the other is its subsidiary, and

(b) a body corporate is deemed the wholly-owned subsidiary of another if it has no members except that other and that other's wholly-owned subsidiaries and its or their nominees.

(6) In this section " company " includes any body corporate.

PART XXVI
" Called-up
share
capital ".

737.—(1) In this Act, " called-up share capital ", in relation to a company, means so much of its share capital as equals the aggregate amount of the calls made on its shares (whether or not those calls have been paid), together with any share capital paid up without being called and any share capital to be paid on a specified future date under the articles, the terms of allotment of the relevant shares or any other arrangements for payment of those shares.

(2) " Uncalled share capital " is to be construed accordingly.

(3) The definitions in this section apply unless the contrary intention appears.

"Allotment"
and " paid
up ".

738.—(1) In relation to an allotment of shares in a company, the shares are to be taken for the purposes of this Act to be allotted when a person acquires the unconditional right to be included in the company's register of members in respect of those shares.

(2) For purposes of this Act, a share in a company is deemed paid up (as to its nominal value or any premium on it) in cash, or allotted for cash, if the consideration for the allotment or payment up is cash received by the company, or is a cheque received by it in good faith which the directors have no reason for suspecting will not be paid, or is a release of a liability of the company for a liquidated sum, or is an undertaking to pay cash to the company at a future date.

(3) In relation to the allotment or payment up of any shares in a company, references in this Act (except sections 89 to 94) to consideration other than cash and to the payment up of shares and premiums on shares otherwise than in cash include the payment of, or any undertaking to pay, cash to any person other than the company.

(4) For the purpose of determining whether a share is or is to be allotted for cash, or paid up in cash, " cash " includes foreign currency.

" Non-cash
asset ".

739.—(1) In this Act " non-cash asset " means any property or interest in property other than cash ; and for this purpose " cash " includes foreign currency.

(2) A reference to the transfer or acquisition of a non-cash asset includes the creation or extinction of an estate or interest in, or a right over, any property and also the discharge of any person's liability, other than a liability for a liquidated sum.

" Body
corporate "
and
" corpora-
tion ".

740. References in this Act to a body corporate or to a corporation do not include a corporation sole, but include a company incorporated elsewhere than in Great Britain.

Such references to a body corporate do not include a Scottish firm.

741.—(1) In this Act, " director " includes any person occupying the position of director, by whatever name called.

(2) In relation to a company, " shadow director " means a person in accordance with whose directions or instructions the directors of the company are accustomed to act.

However, a person is not deemed a shadow director by reason only that the directors act on advice given by him in a professional capacity.

(3) For the purposes of the following provisions of this Act, namely—

> section 309 (directors' duty to have regard to interests of employees),
>
> section 319 (directors' long-term contracts of employment),
>
> sections 320 to 322 (substantial property transactions involving directors), and
>
> sections 330 to 346 (general restrictions on power of companies to make loans, etc., to directors and others connected with them),

(being provisions under which shadow directors are treated as directors), a body corporate is not to be treated as a shadow director of any of its subsidiary companies by reason only that the directors of the subsidiary are accustomed to act in accordance with its directions or instructions.

742.—(1) In this Act, unless the contrary intention appears—

> (a) " accounting reference period " has the meaning given by sections 224 to 226 ;
>
> (b) " accounts " includes a company's group accounts (within the meaning of section 229), whether prepared in the form of accounts or not ;
>
> (c) " balance sheet date ", in relation to a balance sheet, means the date as at which the balance sheet was prepared ;
>
> (d) " financial year "—
>
>> (i) in relation to a body corporate to which Part VII applies, means a period in respect of which a profit and loss account under section 227 in that Part is made up, and
>>
>> (ii) in relation to any other body corporate, means a period in respect of which a profit and loss account of the body laid before it in general meeting is made up,
>
> (whether, in either case, that period is a year or not) ;

(e) any reference to a profit and loss account, in the case of a company not trading for profit, is to its income and expenditure account, and references to profit or loss and, if the company has subsidiaries, references to a consolidated profit and loss account are to be construed accordingly.

(2) Except in relation to special category accounts, any reference to a balance sheet or profit and loss account includes any notes to the account in question giving information which is required by any provision of this Act, and required or allowed by any such provision to be given in a note to company accounts.

(3) In relation to special category accounts, any reference to a balance sheet or profit and loss account includes any notes thereon or document annexed thereto giving information which is required by this Act and is thereby allowed to be so given.

(4) References to special category companies and special category accounts are to be construed in accordance with Chapter II of Part VII.

(5) For the purposes of Part VII, a body corporate is to be regarded as publishing any balance sheet or other account if it publishes, issues or circulates it or otherwise makes it available for public inspection in a manner calculated to invite members of the public generally, or any class of members of the public, to read it.

(6) Expressions which, when used in Schedule 4, fall to be construed in accordance with any provision of Part VII of that Schedule have the same meaning (unless the contrary intention appears) when used in any provision of this Act.

" Employees' share scheme ".

743. For purposes of this Act, an employees' share scheme is a scheme for encouraging or facilitating the holding of shares or debentures in a company by or for the benefit of—

(a) the bona fide employees or former employees of the company, the company's subsidiary or holding company or a subsidiary of the company's holding company, or

(b) the wives, husbands, widows, widowers or children or step-children under the age of 18 of such employees or former employees.

Expressions used generally in this Act.

744. In this Act, unless the contrary intention appears, the following definitions apply—

" agent " does not include a person's counsel acting as such ;

" annual return " means the return to be made by a company under section 363 or 364 (as the case may be) ;

" articles " means, in relation to a company, its articles   PART XXVI
of association, as originally framed or as altered by
resolution, including (so far as applicable to the company) regulations contained in or annexed to any enactment relating to companies passed before this Act, as
altered by or under any such enactment ;

" authorised minimum " has the meaning given by section
118 ;

" bank holiday " means a holiday under the Banking and
Financial Dealings Act 1971 ;   1971 c. 80.

" books and papers " and " books or papers " include accounts, deeds, writings and documents ;

" the Companies Acts " means this Act, the Insider Dealing
Act and the Consequential Provisions Act ;

" the Consequential Provisions Act " means the Companies   1985 c. 9.
Consolidation (Consequential Provisions) Act 1985 ;

" the court ", in relation to a company, means the court
having jurisdiction to wind up the company ;

" debenture " includes debenture stock, bonds and any other
securities of a company, whether constituting a charge
on the assets of the company or not ;

" document " includes summons, notice, order, and other
legal process, and registers ;

" equity share capital " means, in relation to a company, its
issued share capital excluding any part of that capital
which, neither as respects dividends nor as respects
capital, carries any right to participate beyond a specified amount in a distribution ;

" expert " has the meaning given by section 62 ;

" floating charge " includes a floating charge within the
meaning given by section 462 ;

" the Gazette " means, as respects companies registered in
England and Wales, the London Gazette and, as res-
pects companies registered in Scotland, the Edinburgh
Gazette ;

" general rules " means general rules made under section
663, and includes forms ;

" hire-purchase agreement " has the same meaning as in
the Consumer Credit Act 1974 ;   1974 c. 39.

" the Insider Dealing Act " means the Company Securities   1985 c. 8.
(Insider Dealing) Act 1985 ;

" insurance company " means the same as in the Insurance   1982 c. 50.
Companies Act 1982 ;

" joint stock company " has the meaning given by section
683 ;

" memorandum ", in relation to a company, means its memorandum of association, as originally framed or as altered in pursuance of any enactment ;

" number ", in relation to shares, includes amount, where the context admits of the reference to shares being construed to include stock ;

" officer ", in relation to a body corporate, includes a director, manager or secretary ;

" official seal ", in relation to the registrar of companies, means a seal prepared under section 704(4) for the authentication of documents required for or in connection with the registration of companies ;

" oversea company " means—

(a) a company incorporated elsewhere than in Great Britain which, after the commencement of this Act, establishes a place of business in Great Britain, and

(b) a company so incorporated which has, before that commencement, established a place of business and continues to have an established place of business in Great Britain at that commencement ;

" place of business " includes a share transfer or share registration office ;

" prescribed " means—

(a) as respects provisions of this Act relating to winding up, prescribed by general rules under section 663, and

(b) otherwise, prescribed by statutory instrument made by the Secretary of State ;

" prospectus " means any prospectus, notice, circular, advertisement, or other invitation, offering to the public for subscription or purchase any shares in or debentures of a company ;

" prospectus issued generally " means a prospectus issued to persons who are not existing members of the company or holders of its debentures ;

" recognised bank " means a company which is recognised as a bank for the purposes of the Banking Act 1979 ;

1979 c. 37.

" recognised stock exchange " means any body of persons which is for the time being a recognised stock exchange for the purposes of the Prevention of Fraud (Investments) Act 1958 ;

1958 c. 45.

" the registrar of companies " and " the registrar " mean the registrar or other officer performing under this Act the duty of registration of companies in England and Wales or in Scotland, as the case may require ;

" share " means share in the share capital of a company, and includes stock (except where a distinction between shares and stock is express or implied) ; and

" undistributable reserves " has the meaning given by section 264(3).

Part XXVII

Final Provisions

745.—(1) Except where otherwise expressly provided, nothing Northern in this Act (except provisions relating expressly to companies Ireland. registered or incorporated in Northern Ireland or outside Great Britain) applies to or in relation to companies so registered or incorporated.

(2) Subject to any such provision, and to any express provision as to extent, this Act does not extend to Northern Ireland.

746. Except as provided by section 243(6), this Act comes into Commence- force on 1st July 1985. ment.

747. This Act may be cited as the Companies Act 1985. Citation.

SCHEDULE 4

FORM AND CONTENT OF COMPANY ACCOUNTS

PART I

GENERAL RULES AND FORMATS

SECTION A

GENERAL RULES

1.—(1) Subject to the following provisions of this Schedule—

   (*a*) every balance sheet of a company shall show the items listed in either of the balance sheet formats set out below in section B of this Part ; and

   (*b*) every profit and loss account of a company shall show the items listed in any one of the profit and loss account formats so set out ;

in either case in the order and under the headings and sub-headings given in the format adopted.

(2) Sub-paragraph (1) above is not to be read as requiring the heading or sub-heading for any item to be distinguished by any letter or number assigned to that item in the format adopted.

2.—(1) Where in accordance with paragraph 1 a company's balance sheet or profit and loss account for any financial year has been prepared by reference to one of the formats set out in section B below, the directors of the company shall adopt the same format in preparing the accounts for subsequent financial years of the company unless in their opinion there are special reasons for a change.

(2) Particulars of any change in the format adopted in preparing a company's balance sheet or profit and loss account in accordance with paragraph 1 shall be disclosed, and the reasons for the change shall be explained, in a note to the accounts in which the new format is first adopted.

3.—(1) Any item required in accordance with paragraph 1 to be shown in a company's balance sheet or profit and loss account may be shown in greater detail than required by the format adopted.

(2) A company's balance sheet or profit and loss account may include an item representing or covering the amount of any asset or liability, income or expenditure not otherwise covered by any of the items listed in the format adopted, but the following shall not be treated as assets in any company's balance sheet—

   (*a*) preliminary expenses ;

   (*b*) expenses of and commission on any issue of shares or debentures ; and

   (*c*) costs of research.

(3) In preparing a company's balance sheet or profit and loss account the directors of the company shall adapt the arrangement and headings and sub-headings otherwise required by paragraph 1 in respect of items to which an Arabic number is assigned in the format adopted, in any case where the special nature of the company's business requires such adaptation.

(4) Items to which Arabic numbers are assigned in any of the formats set out in section B below may be combined in a company's accounts for any financial year if either—

(a) their individual amounts are not material to assessing the state of affairs or profit or loss of the company for that year ; or

(b) the combination facilitates that assessment ;

but in a case within paragraph (b) the individual amounts of any items so combined shall be disclosed in a note to the accounts.

(5) Subject to paragraph 4(3) below, a heading or sub-heading corresponding to an item listed in the format adopted in preparing a company's balance sheet or profit and loss account shall not be included if there is no amount to be shown for that item in respect of the financial year to which the balance sheet or profit and loss account relates.

(6) Every profit and loss account of a company shall show the amount of the company's profit or loss on ordinary activities before taxation.

(7) Every profit and loss account of a company shall show separately as additional items—

(a) any amount set aside or proposed to be set aside to, or withdrawn or proposed to be withdrawn from, reserves ; and

(b) the aggregate amount of any dividends paid and proposed.

4.—(1) In respect of every time shown in a company's balance sheet or profit and loss account the corresponding amount for the financial year immediately preceding that to which the balance sheet or profit and loss account relates shall also be shown.

(2) Where that corresponding amount is not comparable with the amount to be shown for the item in question in respect of the financial year to which the balance sheet or profit and loss account relates, the former amount shall be adjusted and particulars of the adjustment and the reasons for it shall be disclosed in a note to the accounts.

(3) Paragraph 3(5) does not apply in any case where an amount can be shown for the item in question in respect of the financial year immediately preceding that to which the balance sheet or profit and loss account relates, and that amount shall be shown under the heading or sub-heading required by paragraph 1 for that item.

5. Amounts in respect of items representing assets or income may not be set off against amounts in respect of items representing liabilities or expenditure (as the case may be), or vice versa.

SECTION B

THE REQUIRED FORMATS FOR ACCOUNTS

Preliminary

6. References in this Part of this Schedule to the items listed in any of the formats set out below are to those items read together with any of the notes following the formats which apply to any of those items, and the requirement imposed by paragraph 1 to show the items listed in any such format in the order adopted in the format is subject to any provision in those notes for alternative positions for any particular items.

7. A number in brackets following any item in any of the formats set out below is a reference to the note of that number in the notes following the formats.

8. In the notes following the formats—

   (a) the heading of each note gives the required heading or sub-heading for the item to which it applies and a reference to any letters and numbers assigned to that item in the formats set out below (taking a reference in the case of Format 2 of the balance sheet formats to the item listed under " Assets " or under " Liabilities " as the case may require) ; and

   (b) references to a numbered format are to the balance sheet format or (as the case may require) to the profit and loss account format of that number set out below.

Balance Sheet Formats

Format 1

A.   Called up share capital not paid (*1*)

B.   Fixed assets
   I   Intangible assets
     1. Development costs
     2. Concessions, patents, licences, trade marks and similar rights and assets (*2*)
     3. Goodwill (*3*)
     4. Payments on account

   II   Tangible assets
     1. Land and buildings
     2. Plant and machinery
     3. Fixtures, fittings, tools and equipment
     4. Payments on account and assets in course of construction

   III   Investments
     1. Shares in group companies
     2. Loans to group companies
     3. Shares in related companies
     4. Loans to related companies
     5. Other investments other than loans
     6. Other loans
     7. Own shares (*4*)

C.   Current assets

   I   Stocks
     1. Raw materials and consumables
     2. Work in progress
     3. Finished goods and goods for resale
     4. Payments on account

   II   Debtors (*5*)
     1. Trade debtors
     2. Amounts owed by group companies
     3. Amounts owed by related companies
     4. Other debtors
     5. Called up share capital not paid (*1*)
     6. Prepayments and accrued income (*6*)

   III   Investments
     1. Shares in group companies
     2. Own shares (*4*)
     3. Other investments

   IV   Cash at bank and in hand

D.   Prepayments and accrued income (*6*).

E.   Creditors: amounts falling due within one year
     1. Debenture loans (*7*)
     2. Bank loans and overdrafts
     3. Payments received on account (*8*)

4. Trade creditors
5. Bills of exchange payable
6. Amounts owed to group companies
7. Amounts owed to related companies
8. Other creditors including taxation and social security (*9*)
9. Accruals and deferred income (*10*)

F. Net current assets (liabilities) (*11*)

G. Total assets less current liabilities

H.   Creditors: amounts falling due after more than one year
1. Debenture loans (*7*)
2. Bank loans and overdrafts
3. Payments received on account (*8*)
4. Trade creditors
5. Bills of exchange payable
6. Amounts owed to group companies
7. Amounts owed to related companies
8. Other creditors including taxation and social security (*9*)
9. Accruals and deferred income (*10*)

I. Provisions for liabilities and charges
1. Pensions and similar obligations
2. Taxation, including deferred taxation
3. Other provisions

J. Accruals and deferred income (*10*)

K. Capital and reserves

   I   Called up share capital (*12*)

  II   Share premium account

 III   Revaluation reserve

 IV   Other reserves
1. Capital redemption reserve
2. Reserve for own shares
3. Reserves provided for by the articles of association
4. Other reserves

   V   Profit and loss account

Balance Sheet Formats

Format 2

ASSETS

A. Called up share capital not paid (*1*)

B. Fixed assets

I Intangible assets
   1. Development costs
   2. Concessions, patents, licences, trade marks and similar
      rights and assets (*2*)
   3. Goodwill (*3*)
   4. Payments on account

II Tangible assets
   1. Land and buildings
   2. Plant and machinery
   3. Fixtures, fittings, tools and equipment
   4. Payments on account and assets in course of construction

III Investments
   1. Shares in group companies
   2. Loans to group companies
   3. Shares in related companies
   4. Loans to related companies
   5. Other investments other than loans
   6. Other loans
   7. Own shares (*4*)

C. Current assets

I Stocks
   1. Raw materials and consumables
   2. Work in progress
   3. Finished goods and goods for resale
   4. Payments on account

II Debtors (*5*)
   1. Trade debtors
   2. Amounts owed by group companies
   3. Amounts owed by related companies
   4. Other debtors
   5. Called up share capital not paid (*1*)
   6. Prepayments and accrued income (*6*)

III Investments
   1. Shares in group companies
   2. Own shares (*4*)
   3. Other investments

IV Cash at bank and in hand

D. Prepayments and accrued income (*6*)

LIABILITIES

A. Capital and reserves

    I   Called up share capital (*12*)

    II Share premium account

    III Revaluation reserve

    IV Other reserves
        1. Capital redemption reserve
        2. Reserve for own shares
        3. Reserves provided for by the articles of association
        4. Other reserves

    V Profit and loss account

B. Provisions for liabilities and charges
    1. Pensions and similar obligations
    2. Taxation including deferred taxation
    3. Other provisions

C. Creditors (*13*)
    1. Debenture loans (*7*)
    2. Bank loans and overdrafts
    3. Payments received on account (*8*)
    4. Trade creditors
    5. Bills of exchange payable
    6. Amounts owed to group companies
    7. Amounts owed to related companies
    8. Other creditors including taxation and social security (*9*)
    9. Accruals and deferred income (*10*)

D. Accruals and deferred income (*10*)

Notes on the balance sheet formats

(1) Called up share capital not paid

(Formats 1 and 2, items A and C.II.5.)

This item may be shown in either of the two positions given in Formats 1 and 2.

(2) Concessions, patents, licences, trade marks and similar rights and assets

(Formats 1 and 2, item B.I.2.)

Amounts in respect of assets shall only be included in a company's balance sheet under this item if either—

(*a*) the assets were acquired for valuable consideration and are not required to be shown under goodwill ; or

(*b*) the assets in question were created by the company itself.

(3) Goodwill

(Formats 1 and 2, item B.I.3.)

Amounts representing goodwill shall only be included to the extent that the goodwill was acquired for valuable consideration.

(4) Own shares

(Formats 1 and 2, items B.III.7 and C.III.2.)

The nominal value of the shares held shall be shown separately.

(5) Debtors

(Formats 1 and 2, items C.II.1 to 6.)

The amount falling due after more than one year shall be shown separately for each item included under debtors.

(6) Prepayments and accrued income

(Formats 1 and 2, items C.II.6 and D.)

This item may be shown in either of the two positions given in Formats 1 and 2.

(7) Debenture loans

(Format 1, items E.1 and H.1 and Format 2, item C.1.)

The amount of any convertible loans shall be shown separately.

(8) Payments received on account

(Format 1, items E.3 and H.3 and Format 2, item C.3.)

Payments received on account of orders shall be shown for each of these items in so far as they are not shown as deductions from stocks.

(9) Other creditors including taxation and social security

(Format 1, items E.8 and H.8 and Format 2, item C.8.)

The amount for creditors in respect of taxation and social security shall be shown separately from the amount for other creditors.

(10) Accruals and deferred income

(Format 1, items E.9, H.9 and J and Format 2, items C.9 and D.)

The two positions given for this item in Format 1 at E.9 and H.9 are an alternative to the position at J, but if the item is not shown in a position corresponding to that at J it may be shown in either or both of the other two positions (as the case may require).

The two positions given for this item in Format 2 are alternatives.

(11) Net current assets (liabilities)

(Format 1, item F.)

In determining the amount to be shown for this item any amounts shown under " prepayments and accrued income " shall be taken into account wherever shown.

(12) Called up share capital

(Format 1, item K.I and Format 2, item A.I.)

The amount of allotted share capital and the amount of called up share capital which has been paid up shall be shown separately.

(13) Creditors

(Format 2, items C.1 to 9.)

Amounts falling due within one year and after one year shall be shown separately for each of these items and their aggregate shall be shown separately for all of these items.

Profit and loss account formats

Format 1

(see note (*17*) below)

1. Turnover
2. Cost of sales (*14*)
3. Gross profit or loss
4. Distribution costs (*14*)
5. Administrative expenses (*14*)
6. Other operating income
7. Income from shares in group companies
8. Income from shares in related companies
9. Income from other fixed asset investments (*15*)
10. Other interest receivable and similar income (*15*)
11. Amounts written off investments
12. Interest payable and similar charges (*16*)
13. Tax on profit or loss on ordinary activities
14. Profit or loss on ordinary activities after taxation
15. Extraordinary income
16. Extraordinary charges
17. Extraordinary profit or loss
18. Tax on extraordinary profit or loss
19. Other taxes not shown under the above items
20. Profit or loss for the financial year

Profit and loss account formats

Format 2

1. Turnover
2. Change in stocks of finished goods and in work in progress
3. Own work capitalised
4. Other operating income
5. (a) Raw materials and consumables
   (b) Other external charges
6. Staff costs:
   (a) wages and salaries
   (b) social security costs
   (c) other pension costs
7. (a) Depreciation and other amounts written off tangible and intangible fixed assets
   (b) Exceptional amounts written off current assets
8. Other operating charges
9. Income from shares in group companies
10. Income from shares in related companies
11. Income from other fixed asset investments (*15*)
12. Other interest receivable and similar income (*15*)
13. Amounts written off investments
14. Interest payable and similar charges (*16*)
15. Tax on profit or loss on ordinary activities
16. Profit or loss on ordinary activities after taxation
17. Extraordinary income
18. Extraordinary charges
19. Extraordinary profit or loss
20. Tax on extraordinary profit or loss
21. Other taxes not shown under the above items
22. Profit or loss for the financial year

Profit and loss account formats

Format 3

(see note (*17*) below)

A. Charges
  1. Cost of sales (*14*)
  2. Distribution costs (*14*)
  3. Administrative expenses (*14*)
  4. Amounts written off investments
  5. Interest payable and similar charges (*16*)
  6. Tax on profit or loss on ordinary activities
  7. Profit or loss on ordinary activities after taxation
  8. Extraordinary charges
  9. Tax on extraordinary profit or loss
  10. Other taxes not shown under the above items
  11. Profit or loss for the financial year

B. Income
  1. Turnover
  2. Other operating income
  3. Income from shares in group companies
  4. Income from shares in related companies
  5. Income from other fixed asset investments (*15*)
  6. Other interest receivable and similar income (*15*)
  7. Profit or loss on ordinary activities after taxation
  8. Extraordinary income
  9. Profit or loss for the financial year

Profit and loss account formats

Format 4

A. Charges
1. Reduction in stocks of finished goods and in work in progress
2. (*a*) Raw materials and consumables
   (*b*) Other external charges
3. Staff costs:
   (*a*) wages and salaries
   (*b*) social security costs
   (*c*) other pension costs
4. (*a*) Depreciation and other amounts written off tangible and intangible fixed assets
   (*b*) Exceptional amounts written off current assets
5. Other operating charges
6. Amounts written off investments
7. Interest payable and similar charges (*16*)
8. Tax on profit or loss on ordinary activities
9. Profit or loss on ordinary activities after taxation
10. Extraordinary charges
11. Tax on extraordinary profit or loss
12. Other taxes not shown under the above items
13. Profit or loss for the financial year

B. Income
1. Turnover
2. Increase in stocks of finished goods and in work in progress
3. Own work capitalised
4. Other operating income
5. Income from shares in group companies
6. Income from shares in related companies
7. Income from other fixed asset investments (*15*)
8. Other interest receivable and similar income (*15*)
9. Profit or loss on ordinary activities after taxation
10. Extraordinary income
11. Profit or loss for the financial year

Notes on the profit and loss account formats

(14) Cost of sales: distribution costs: administrative expenses

(Format 1, items 2, 4 and 5 and Format 3, items A.1, 2 and 3.)

These items shall be stated after taking into account any necessary provisions for depreciation or diminution in value of assets.

(15) Income from other fixed asset investments: other interest receivable and similar income

(Format 1, items 9 and 10: Format 2, items 11 and 12: Format 3, items B.5 and 6: Format 4, items B.7 and 8.)

Income and interest derived from group companies shall be shown separately from income and interest derived from other sources.

(16) Interest payable and similar charges

(Format 1, item 12: Format 2, item 14: Format 3, item A.5: Format 4, item A.7.)

The amount payable to group companies shall be shown separately.

(17) Formats 1 and 3

The amount of any provisions for depreciation and diminution in value of tangible and intangible fixed assets falling to be shown under items 7(*a*) and A.4(*a*) respectively in Formats 2 and 4 shall be disclosed in a note to the accounts in any case where the profit and loss account is prepared by reference to Format 1 or Format 3.

PART II

ACCOUNTING PRINCIPLES AND RULES

SECTION A

ACCOUNTING PRINCIPLES

Preliminary

9. Subject to paragraph 15 below, the amounts to be included in respect of all items shown in a company's accounts shall be determined in accordance with the principles set out in paragraphs 10 to 14.

Accounting principles

10. The company shall be presumed to be carrying on business as a going concern.

11. Accounting policies shall be applied consistently from one financial year to the next.

12. The amount of any item shall be determined on a prudent basis, and in particular—

(*a*) only profits realised at the balance sheet date shall be included in the profit and loss account ; and

(*b*) all liabilities and losses which have arisen or are likely to arise in respect of the financial year to which the accounts relate or a previous financial year shall be taken into account, including those which only become apparent between the balance sheet date and the date on which it is signed on behalf of the board of directors in pursuance of section 238 of this Act.

13. All income and charges relating to the financial year to which the accounts relate shall be taken into account, without regard to the date of receipt or payment.

14. In determining the aggregate amount of any item the amount of each individual asset or liability that falls to be taken into account shall be determined separately.

Departure from the accounting principles

15. If it appears to the directors of a company that there are special reasons for departing from any of the principles stated above in preparing the company's accounts in respect of any financial year they may do so, but particulars of the departure, the reasons for it and its effect shall be given in a note to the accounts.

SECTION B

HISTORICAL COST ACCOUNTING RULES

Preliminary

16. Subject to section C of this Part of this Schedule, the amounts to be included in respect of all items shown in a company's accounts shall be determined in accordance with the rules set out in paragraphs 17 to 28.

Fixed assets

General rules

17. Subject to any provision for depreciation or diminution in value made in accordance with paragraph 18 or 19 the amount to be included in respect of any fixed asset shall be its purchase price or production cost.

18. In the case of any fixed asset which has a limited useful economic life, the amount of—

(a) its purchase price or production cost ; or

(b) where it is estimated that any such asset will have a residual value at the end of the period of its useful economic life, its purchase price or production cost less that estimated residual value ;

shall be reduced by provisions for depreciation calculated to write off that amount systematically over the period of the asset's useful economic life.

19.—(1) Where a fixed asset investment of a description falling to be included under item B.III of either of the balance sheet formats set out in Part I of this Schedule has diminished in value provisions for diminution in value may be made in respect of it and the amount to be included in respect of it may be reduced accordingly ; and any such provisions which are not shown in the profit and loss account shall be disclosed (either separately or in aggregate) in a note to the accounts.

(2) Provisions for diminution in value shall be made in respect of any fixed asset which has diminished in value if the reduction in its value is expected to be permanent (whether its useful economic life is limited or not), and the amount to be included in respect of it shall be reduced accordingly ; and any such provisions which are not shown in the profit and loss account shall be disclosed (either separately or in aggregate) in a note to the accounts.

(3) Where the reasons for which any provision was made in accordance with sub-paragraph (1) or (2) have ceased to apply to any extent, that provision shall be written back to the extent that it is no longer necessary ; and any amounts written back in accordance with this sub-paragraph which are not shown in the profit and loss account shall be disclosed (either separately or in aggregate) in a note to the accounts.

Rules for determining particular fixed asset items

20.—(1) Notwithstanding that an item in respect of " development costs " is included under " fixed assets " in the balance sheet formats set out in Part I of this Schedule, an amount may only be included in a company's balance sheet in respect of development costs in special circumstances.

(2) If any amount is included in a company's balance sheet in respect of development costs the following information shall be given in a note to the accounts—

> (a) the period over which the amount of those costs originally capitalised is being or is to be written off ; and

> (b) the reasons for capitalising the development costs in question.

21.—(1) The application of paragraphs 17 to 19 in relation to goodwill (in any case where goodwill is treated as an asset) is subject to the following provisions of this paragraph.

(2) Subject to sub-paragraph (3) below, the amount of the consideration for any goodwill acquired by a company shall be reduced by provisions for depreciation calculated to write off that amount systematically over a period chosen by the directors of the company.

(3) The period chosen shall not exceed the useful economic life of the goodwill in question.

(4) In any case where any goodwill acquired by a company is shown or included as an asset in the company's balance sheet the period chosen for writing off the consideration for that goodwill and the reasons for choosing that period shall be disclosed in a note to the accounts.

Current assets

22. Subject to paragraph 23, the amount to be included in respect of any current asset shall be its purchase price or production cost.

23.—(1) If the net realisable value of any current asset is lower than its purchase price or production cost the amount to be included in respect of that asset shall be the net realisable value.

(2) Where the reasons for which any provision for diminution in value was made in accordance with sub-paragraph (1) have ceased to apply to any extent, that provision shall be written back to the extent that it is no longer necessary.

Miscellaneous and supplementary provisions

Excess of money owed over value received as an asset item

24.—(1) Where the amount repayable on any debt owed by a company is greater than the value of the consideration received in the transaction giving rise to the debt, the amount of the difference may be treated as an asset.

(2) Where any such amount is so treated—

> (a) it shall be written off by reasonable amounts each year and must be completely written off before repayment of the debt ; and

> (b) if the current amount is not shown as a separate item in the company's balance sheet it must be disclosed in a note to the accounts.

Assets included at a fixed amount

25.—(1) Subject to the following sub-paragraph, assets which fall
to be included—

(a) amongst the fixed assets of a company under the item
" tangible assets " ; or

(b) amongst the current assets of a company under the item
" raw materials and consumables " ;

may be included at a fixed quantity and value.

(2) Sub-paragraph (1) applies to assets of a kind which are
constantly being replaced, where—

(a) their overall value is not material to assessing the company's
state of affairs ; and

(b) their quantity, value and composition are not subject to
material variation.

Determination of purchase price or production cost

26.—(1) The purchase price of an asset shall be determined by
adding to the actual price paid any expenses incidental to its
acquisition.

(2) The production cost of an asset shall be determined by adding
to the purchase price of the raw materials and consumables used
the amount of the costs incurred by the company which are directly
attributable to the production of that asset.

(3) In addition, there may be included in the production cost of
an asset—

(a) a reasonable proportion of the costs incurred by the company
which are only indirectly attributable to the production of
that asset, but only to the extent that they relate to the
period of production ; and

(b) interest on capital borrowed to finance the production of that
asset, to the extent that it accrues in respect of the period
of production ;

provided, however, in a case within paragraph (b) above, that the
inclusion of the interest in determining the cost of that asset and the
amount of the interest so included is disclosed in a note to the
accounts.

(4) In the case of current assets distribution costs may not be
included in production costs.

27.—(1) Subject to the qualification mentioned below, the purchase
price or production cost of—

(a) any assets which fall to be included under any item shown
in a company's balance sheet under the general item
" stocks " ; and

(b) any assets which are fungible assets (including investments) ;

may be determined by the application of any of the methods
mentioned in sub-paragraph (2) below in relation to any such assets
of the same class.

The method chosen must be one which appears to the directors to
be appropriate in the circumstances of the company.

(2) Those methods are—

   (*a*) the method known as " first in, first out " (FIFO) ;

   (*b*) the method known as " last in, first out " (LIFO) ;

   (*c*) a weighted average price ; and

   (*d*) any other method similar to any of the methods mentioned above.

(3) Where in the case of any company—

   (*a*) the purchase price or production cost of assets falling to be included under any item shown in the company's balance sheet has been determined by the application of any method permitted by this paragraph ; and

   (*b*) the amount shown in respect of that item differs materially from the relevant alternative amount given below in this paragraph ;

the amount of that difference shall be disclosed in a note to the accounts.

(4) Subject to sub-paragraph (5) below, for the purposes of sub-paragraph (3)(*b*) above, the relevant alternative amount, in relation to any item shown in a company's balance sheet, is the amount which would have been shown in respect of that item if assets of any class included under that item at an amount determined by any method permitted by this paragraph had instead been included at their replacement cost as at the balance sheet date.

(5) The relevant alternative amount may be determined by reference to the most recent actual purchase price or production cost before the balance sheet date of assets of any class included under the item in question instead of by reference to their replacement cost as at that date, but only if the former appears to the directors of the company to constitute the more appropriate standard of comparison in the case of assets of that class.

(6) For the purposes of this paragraph, assets of any description shall be regarded as fungible if assets of that description are substantially indistinguishable one from another.

Substitution of original stated amount where price or cost unknown

28. Where there is no record of the purchase price or production cost of any asset of a company or of any price, expenses or costs relevant for determining its purchase price or production cost in accordance with paragraph 26, or any such record cannot be obtained without unreasonable expense or delay, its purchase price or production cost shall be taken for the purposes of paragraphs 17 to 23 to be the value ascribed to it in the earliest available record of its value made on or after its acquisition or production by the company.

SECTION C
ALTERNATIVE ACCOUNTING RULES

Preliminary

29.—(1) The rules set out in section B are referred to below in this Schedule as the historical cost accounting rules.

(2) Those rules, with the omission of paragraphs 16, 21 and 25 to 28, are referred to below in this Part of this Schedule as the depreciation rules ; and references below in this Schedule to the historical cost accounting rules do not include the depreciation rules as they apply by virtue of paragraph 32.

30. Subject to paragraphs 32 to 34, the amounts to be included in respect of assets of any description mentioned in paragraph 31 may be determined on any basis so mentioned.

Alternative accounting rules

31.—(1) Intangible fixed assets, other than goodwill, may be included at their current cost.

(2) Tangible fixed assets may be included at a market value determined as at the date of their last valuation or at their current cost.

(3) Investments of any description falling to be included under item B.III of either of the balance sheet formats set out in Part I of this Schedule may be included either—

   (a) at a market value determined as at the date of their last valuation ; or

   (b) at a value determined on any basis which appears to the directors to be appropriate in the circumstances of the company ;

but in the latter case particulars of the method of valuation adopted and of the reasons for adopting it shall be disclosed in a note to the accounts.

(4) Investments of any description falling to be included under item C.III of either of the balance sheet formats set out in Part 1 of this Schedule may be included at their current cost.

(5) Stocks may be included at their current cost.

Application of the depreciation rules

32.—(1) Where the value of any asset of a company is determined on any basis mentioned in paragraph 31, that value shall be, or (as the case may require) be the starting point for determining, the amount to be included in respect of that asset in the company's accounts, instead of its purchase price or production cost or any value previously so determined for that asset ; and the depreciation rules shall apply accordingly in relation to any such asset with the substitution for any reference to its purchase price or production cost of a reference to the value most recently determined for that asset on any basis mentioned in paragraph 31.

(2) The amount of any provision for depreciation required in the case of any fixed asset by paragraph 18 or 19 as it applies by virtue of sub-paragraph (1) is referred to below in this paragraph as the adjusted amount, and the amount of any provision which would be required by that paragraph in the case of that asset according to the historical cost accounting rules is referred to as the historical cost amount.

(3) Where sub-paragraph (1) applies in the case of any fixed asset the amount of any provision for depreciation in respect of that asset—

(a) included in any item shown in the profit and loss account in respect of amounts written off assets of the description in question ; or

(b) taken into account in stating any item so shown which is required by note (*14*) of the notes on the profit and loss account formats set out in Part I of this Schedule to be stated after taking into account any necessary provisions for depreciation or diminution in value of assets included under it ;

may be the historical cost amount instead of the adjusted amount, provided that the amount of any difference between the two is shown separately in the profit and loss account or in a note to the accounts.

Additional information to be provided in case of departure from historical cost accounting rules

33.—(1) This paragraph applies where the amounts to be included in respect of assets covered by any items shown in a company's accounts have been determined on any basis mentioned in paragraph 31.

(2) The items affected and the basis of valuation adopted in determining the amounts of the assets in question in the case of each such item shall be disclosed in a note to the accounts.

(3) In the case of each balance sheet item affected (except stocks) either—

(a) the comparable amounts determined according to the historical cost accounting rules ; or

(b) the differences between those amounts and the corresponding amounts actually shown in the balance sheet in respect of that item ;

shall be shown separately in the balance sheet or in a note to the accounts.

(4) In sub-paragraph (3) above, references in relation to any item to the comparable amounts determined as there mentioned are references to—

(a) the aggregate amount which would be required to be shown in respect of that item if the amounts to be included in respect of all the assets covered by that item were determined according to the historical cost accounting rules ; and

(b) the aggregate amount of the cumulative provisions for depreciation or diminution in value which would be permitted or required in determining those amounts according to those rules.

Revaluation reserve

34.—(1) With respect to any determination of the value of an asset of a company on any basis mentioned in paragraph 31, the amount of any profit or loss arising from that determination (after allowing, where appropriate, for any provisions for depreciation or diminution in value made otherwise than by reference to the value so determined and any adjustments of any such provisions made in the light of that determination) shall be credited or (as the case may be) debited to a separate reserve (" the revaluation reserve ").

(2) The amount of the revaluation reserve shall be shown in the company's balance sheet under a separate sub-heading in the position given for the item "revaluation reserve" in Format 1 or 2 of the balance sheet formats set out in Part I of this Schedule, but need not be shown under that name.

(3) The revaluation reserve shall be reduced to the extent that the amounts standing to the credit of the reserve are in the opinion of the directors of the company no longer necessary for the purpose of the accounting policies adopted by the company ; but an amount may only be transferred from the reserve to the profit and loss account if either—

    (*a*) the amount in question was previously charged to that account ; or

    (*b*) it represents realised profit.

(4) The treatment for taxation purposes of amounts credited or debited to the revaluation reserve shall be disclosed in a note to the accounts.

Part III

Notes to the Accounts

Preliminary

35. Any information required in the case of any company by the following provisions of this Part of this Schedule shall (if not given in the company's accounts) be given by way of a note to those accounts.

Disclosure of accounting policies

36. The accounting policies adopted by the company in determining the amounts to be included in respect of items shown in the balance sheet and in determining the profit or loss of the company shall be stated (including such policies with respect to the depreciation and diminution in value of assets).

Information supplementing the balance sheet

37. Paragraphs 38 to 51 require information which either supplements the information given with respect to any particular items shown in the balance sheet or is otherwise relevant to assessing the company's state of affairs in the light of the information so given.

Share capital and debentures

38.—(1) The following information shall be given with respect to the company's share capital—

(a) the authorised share capital ; and

(b) where shares of more than one class have been allotted, the number and aggregate nominal value of shares of each class allotted.

(2) In the case of any part of the allotted share capital that consists of redeemable shares, the following information shall be given—

(a) the earliest and latest dates on which the company has power to redeem those shares ;

(b) whether those shares must be redeemed in any event or are liable to be redeemed at the option of the company or of the shareholder ; and

(c) whether any (and, if so, what) premium is payable on redemption.

39. If the company has allotted any shares during the financial year, the following information shall be given—

(a) the reason for making the allotment ;

(b) the classes of shares allotted ; and

(c) as respects each class of shares, the number allotted, their aggregate nominal value, and the consideration received by the company for the allotment.

40.—(1) With respect to any contingent right to the allotment of shares in the company the following particulars shall be given—

(a) the number, description and amount of the shares in relation to which the right is exercisable ;

(b) the period during which it is exercisable ; and

(c) the price to be paid for the shares allotted.

(2) In sub-paragraph (1) above "contingent right to the allotment of shares" means any option to subscribe for shares and any other right to require the allotment of shares to any person whether arising on the conversion into shares of securities of any other description or otherwise.

41.—(1) If the company has issued any debentures during the financial year to which the accounts relate, the following information shall be given—

(a) the reason for making the issue ;

(b) the classes of debentures issued ; and

(c) as respects each class of debentures, the amount issued and the consideration received by the company for the issue.

(2) Particulars of any redeemed debentures which the company has power to reissue shall also be given.

(3) Where any of the company's debentures are held by a nominee of or trustee for the company, the nominal amount of the debentures and the amount at which they are stated in the accounting records kept by the company in accordance with section 221 of this Act shall be stated.

Fixed assets

42.—(1) In respect of each item which is or would but for paragraph 3(4)(*b*) be shown under the general item " fixed assets " in the company's balance sheet the following information shall be given—

(*a*) the appropriate amounts in respect of that item as at the date of the beginning of the financial year and as at the balance sheet date respectively ;

(*b*) the effect on any amount shown in the balance sheet in respect of that item of—

(i) any revision of the amount in respect of any assets included under that item made during that year on any basis mentioned in paragraph 31 ;

(ii) acquisitions during that year of any assets ;

(iii) disposals during that year of any assets ; and

(iv) any transfers of assets of the company to and from that item during that year.

(2) The reference in sub-paragraph (1)(*a*) to the appropriate amounts in respect of any item as at any date there mentioned is a reference to amounts representing the aggregate amounts determined, as at that date, in respect of assets falling to be included under that item on either of the following bases, that is to say—

(*a*) on the basis of purchase price or production cost (determined in accordance with paragraphs 26 and 27) ; or

(*b*) on any basis mentioned in paragraph 31,

(leaving out of account in either case any provisions for depreciation or diminution in value).

(3) In respect of each item within sub-paragraph (1)—

(*a*) the cumulative amount of provisions for depreciation or diminution in value of assets included under that item as at each date mentioned in sub-paragraph (1)(*a*) ;

(*b*) the amount of any such provisions made in respect of the financial year ;

(*c*) the amount of any adjustments made in respect of any such provisions during that year in consequence of the disposal of any assets ; and

(*d*) the amount of any other adjustments made in respect of any such provisions during that year ;

shall also be stated.

43. Where any fixed assets of the company (other than listed investments) are included under any item shown in the company's balance sheet at an amount determined on any basis mentioned in paragraph 31, the following information shall be given—

    (a) the years (so far as they are known to the directors) in which the assets were severally valued and the several values ; and

    (b) in the case of assets that have been valued during the financial year, the names of the persons who valued them or particulars of their qualifications for doing so and (whichever is stated) the bases of valuation used by them.

44. In relation to any amount which is or would but for paragraph 3(4)(b) be shown in respect of the item " land and buildings " in the company's balance sheet there shall be stated—

    (a) how much of that amount is ascribable to land of freehold tenure and how much to land of leasehold tenure ; and

    (b) how much of the amount ascribable to land of leasehold tenure is ascribable to land held on long lease and how much to land held on short lease.

Investments

45.—(1) In respect of the amount of each item which is or would but for paragraph 3(4)(b) be shown in the company's balance sheet under the general item " investments " (whether as fixed assets or as current assets) there shall be stated—

    (a) how much of that amount is ascribable to listed investments ; and

    (b) how much of any amount so ascribable is ascribable to investments as respects which there has been granted a listing on a recognised stock exchange and how much to other listed investments.

(2) Where the amount of any listed investments is stated for any item in accordance with sub-paragraph (1)(a), the following amounts shall also be stated—

    (a) the aggregate market value of those investments where it differs from the amount so stated ; and

    (b) both the market value and the stock exchange value of any investments of which the former value is, for the purposes of the accounts, taken as being higher than the latter.

Reserves and provisions

46.—(1) Where any amount is transferred—

    (a) to or from any reserves ; or

    (b) to any provisions for liabilities and charges ; or

    (c) from any provision for liabilities and charges otherwise than for the purpose for which the provision was established ;

and the reserves or provisions are or would but for paragraph 3(4)(b) be shown as separate items in the company's balance sheet, the information mentioned in the following sub-paragraph shall be given in respect of the aggregate of reserves or provisions included in the same item.

(2) That information is—

(a) the amount of the reserves or provisions as at the date of the beginning of the financial year and as at the balance sheet date respectively ;

(b) any amounts transferred to or from the reserves or provisions during that year ; and

(c) the source and application respectively of any amounts so transferred.

(3) Particulars shall be given of each provision included in the item " other provisions " in the company's balance sheet in any case where the amount of that provision is material.

Provision for taxation

47. The amount of any provisions for taxation other than deferred taxation shall be stated.

Details of indebtedness

48.—(1) In respect of each item shown under " creditors " in the company's balance sheet there shall be stated—

(a) the aggregate amount of any debts included under that item which are payable or repayable otherwise than by instalments and fall due for payment or repayment after the end of the period of five years beginning with the day next following the end of the financial year ; and

(b) the aggregate amount of any debts so included which are payable or repayable by instalments any of which fall due for payment after the end of that period ;

and in the case of debts within paragraph (b) above the aggregate amount of instalments falling due after the end of that period shall also be disclosed for each such item.

(2) Subject to sub-paragraph (3), in relation to each debt falling to be taken into account under sub-paragraph (1), the terms of payment or repayment and the rate of any interest payable on the debt shall be stated.

(3) If the number of debts is such that, in the opinion of the directors, compliance with sub-paragraph (2) would result in a statement of excessive length, it shall be sufficient to give a general indication of the terms of payment or repayment and the rates of any interest payable on the debts.

(4) In respect of each item shown under " creditors " in the company's balance sheet there shall be stated—

(a) the aggregate amount of any debts included under that item in respect of which any security has been given by the company ; and

(b) an indication of the nature of the securities so given.

(5) References above in this paragraph to an item shown under " creditors " in the company's balance sheet include references,

where amounts falling due to creditors within one year and after more than one year are distinguished in the balance sheet—

    (*a*) in a case within sub-paragraph (1), to an item shown under the latter of those categories ; and

    (*b*) in a case within sub-paragraph (4), to an item shown under either of those categories ;

and references to items shown under " creditors " include references to items which would but for paragraph 3(4)(*b*) be shown under that heading.

49. If any fixed cumulative dividends on the company's shares are in arrear, there shall be stated—

    (*a*) the amount of the arrears ; and

    (*b*) the period for which the dividends or, if there is more than one class, each class of them are in arrear.

Guarantees and other financial commitments

50.—(1) Particulars shall be given of any charge on the assets of the company to secure the liabilities of any other person, including, where practicable, the amount secured.

(2) The following information shall be given with respect to any other contingent liability not provided for—

    (*a*) the amount or estimated amount of that liability ;

    (*b*) its legal nature ; and

    (*c*) whether any valuable security has been provided by the company in connection with that liability and if so, what.

(3) There shall be stated, where practicable—

    (*a*) the aggregate amount or estimated amount of contracts for capital expenditure, so far as not provided for ; and

    (*b*) the aggregate amount or estimated amount of capital expenditure authorised by the directors which has not been contracted for.

(4) Particulars shall be given of—

    (*a*) any pension commitments included under any provision shown in the company's balance sheet ; and

    (*b*) any such commitments for which no provision has been made ;

and where any such commitment relates wholly or partly to pensions payable to past directors of the company separate particulars shall be given of that commitment so far as it relates to such pensions.

(5) Particulars shall also be given of any other financial commitments which—

    (*a*) have not been provided for ; and

    (*b*) are relevant to assessing the company's state of affairs.

(6) Commitments within any of the preceding sub-paragraphs undertaken on behalf of or for the benefit of—

(a) any holding company or fellow subsidiary of the company ; or

(b) any subsidiary of the company ;

shall be stated separately from the other commitments within that sub-paragraph (and commitments within paragraph (a) shall also be stated separately from those within paragraph (b)).

Miscellaneous matters

51.—(1) Particulars shall be given of any case where the purchase price or production cost of any asset is for the first time determined under paragraph 28.

(2) Where any outstanding loans made under the authority of section 153(4)(b) or (c) or section 155 of this Act (various cases of financial assistance by a company for purchase of its own shares) are included under any item shown in the company's balance sheet, the aggregate amount of those loans shall be disclosed for each item in question.

(3) The aggregate amount which is recommended for distribution by way of dividend shall be stated.

Information supplementing the profit and loss account

52. Paragraphs 53 to 57 require information which either supplements the information given with respect to any particular items shown in the profit and loss account or otherwise provides particulars of income or expenditure of the company or of circumstances affecting the items shown in the profit and loss account.

Separate statement of certain items of income and expenditure

53.—(1) Subject to the following provisions of this paragraph, each of the amounts mentioned below shall be stated.

(2) The amount of the interest on or any similar charges in respect of—

(a) bank loans and overdrafts, and loans made to the company (other than bank loans and overdrafts) which—

(i) are repayable otherwise than by instalments and fall due for repayment before the end of the period of five years beginning with the day next following the end of the financial year ; or

(ii) are repayable by instalments the last of which falls due for payment before the end of that period ; and

(b) loans of any other kind made to the company.

This sub-paragraph does not apply to interest or charges on loans to the company from group companies, but, with that exception, it applies to interest or charges on all loans, whether made on the security of debentures or not.

(3) The amounts respectively set aside for redemption of share capital and for redemption of loans.

(4) The amount of income from listed investments.

(5) The amount of rents from land (after deduction of ground rents, rates and other outgoings).

This amount need only be stated if a substantial part of the company's revenue for the financial year consists of rents from land.

(6) The amount charged to revenue in respect of sums payable in respect of the hire of plant and machinery.

(7) The amount of the remuneration of the auditors (taking " remuneration ", for the purposes of this sub-paragraph, as including any sums paid by the company in respect of the auditors' expenses).

Particulars of tax

54.—(1) The basis on which the charge for United Kingdom corporation tax and United Kingdom income tax is computed shall be stated.

(2) Particulars shall be given of any special circumstances which affect liability in respect of taxation of profits, income or capital gains for the financial year or liability in respect of taxation of profits, income or capital gains for succeeding financial years.

(3) The following amounts shall be stated—

(*a*) the amount of the charge for United Kingdom corporation tax ;

(*b*) if that amount would have been greater but for relief from double taxation, the amount which it would have been but for such relief ;

(*c*) the amount of the charge for United Kingdom income tax ; and

(*d*) the amount of the charge for taxation imposed outside the United Kingdom of profits, income and (so far as charged to revenue) capital gains.

These amounts shall be stated separately in respect of each of the amounts which is or would but for paragraph 3(4)(*b*) be shown under the following items in the profit and loss account, that is to say " tax on profit or loss on ordinary activities " and " tax on extraordinary profit or loss ".

Particulars of turnover

55.—(1) If in the course of the financial year the company has carried on business of two or more classes that, in the opinion of the directors, differ substantially from each other, there shall be stated in respect of each class (describing it)—

(*a*) the amount of the turnover attributable to that class ; and

(*b*) the amount of the profit or loss of the company before taxation which is in the opinion of the directors attributable to that class.

(2) If in the course of the financial year the company has supplied markets that, in the opinion of the directors, differ substantially from each other, the amount of the turnover attributable to each such market shall also be stated.

In this paragraph "market" means a market delimited by geographical bounds.

(3) In analysing for the purposes of this paragraph the source (in terms of business or in terms of market) of turnover or (as the case may be) of profit or loss, the directors of the company shall have regard to the manner in which the company's activities are organised.

(4) For the purposes of this paragraph—

(a) classes of business which, in the opinion of the directors, do not differ substantially from each other shall be treated as one class ; and

(b) markets which, in the opinion of the directors, do not differ substantially from each other shall be treated as one market ;

and any amounts properly attributable to one class of business or (as the case may be) to one market which are not material may be included in the amount stated in respect of another.

(5) Where in the opinion of the directors the disclosure of any information required by this paragraph would be seriously prejudicial to the interests of the company, that information need not be disclosed, but the fact that any such information has not been disclosed must be stated.

Particulars of staff

56.—(1) The following information shall be given with respect to the employees of the company—

(a) the average number of persons employed by the company in the financial year ; and

(b) the average number of persons so employed within each category of persons employed by the company.

(2) The average number required by sub-paragraph (1)(a) or (b) shall be determined by dividing the relevant annual number by the number of weeks in the financial year.

(3) The relevant annual number shall be determined by ascertaining for each week in the financial year—

(a) for the purposes of sub-paragraph (1)(a), the number of persons employed under contracts of service by the company in that week (whether throughout the week or not) ;

(b) for the purposes of sub-paragraph (1)(b), the number of persons in the category in question of persons so employed ;

and, in either case, adding together all the weekly numbers.

(4) In respect of all persons employed by the company during the financial year who are taken into account in determining the relevant annual number for the purposes of sub-paragraph (1)(*a*) there shall also be stated the aggregate amounts respectively of—

(*a*) wages and salaries paid or payable in respect of that year to those persons ;

(*b*) social security costs incurred by the company on their behalf ; and

(*c*) other pension costs so incurred ;

save in so far as those amounts or any of them are stated in the profit and loss account.

(5) The categories of persons employed by the company by reference to which the number required to be disclosed by sub-paragraph (1)(*b*) is to be determined shall be such as the directors may select, having regard to the manner in which the company's activities are organised.

Miscellaneous matters

57.—(1) Where any amount relating to any preceding financial year is included in any item in the profit and loss account, the effect shall be stated.

(2) Particulars shall be given of any extraordinary income or charges arising in the financial year.

(3) The effect shall be stated of any transactions that are exceptional by virtue of size or incidence though they fall within the ordinary activities of the company.

General

58.—(1) Where sums originally denominated in foreign currencies have been brought into account under any items shown in the balance sheet or profit and loss account, the basis on which those sums have been translated into sterling shall be stated.

(2) Subject to the following sub-paragraph, in respect of every item stated in a note to the accounts the corresponding amount for the financial year immediately preceding that to which the accounts relate shall also be stated and where the corresponding amount is not comparable, it shall be adjusted and particulars of the adjustment and the reasons for it shall be given.

(3) Sub-paragraph (2) does not apply in relation to any amounts stated by virtue of any of the following provisions of this Act—

(*a*) section 231 as applying Parts I and II of Schedule 5 (proportion of share capital of subsidiaries and other bodies corporate held by the company, etc.),

(*b*) sections 232 to 234 and Schedule 6 (particulars of loans to directors, etc.), and

(*c*) paragraphs 42 and 46 above.

PART IV

SPECIAL PROVISIONS WHERE THE COMPANY IS A HOLDING OR SUBSIDIARY COMPANY

Company's own accounts

59. Where a company is a holding company or a subsidiary of another body corporate and any item required by Part I of this Schedule to be shown in the company's balance sheet in relation to group companies includes—

(a) amounts attributable to dealings with or interests in any holding company or fellow subsidiary of the company ; or

(b) amounts attributable to dealings with or interests in any subsidiary of the company ;

the aggregate amounts within paragraphs (a) and (b) respectively shall be shown as separate items, either by way of subdivision of the relevant item in the balance sheet or in a note to the company's accounts.

60.—(1) Subject to the following sub-paragraph, where the company is a holding company, the number, description and amount of the shares in and debentures of the company held by its subsidiaries or their nominees shall be disclosed in a note to the company's accounts.

(2) Sub-paragraph (1) does not apply in relation to any shares or debentures—

(a) in the case of which the subsidiary is concerned as personal representative ; or

(b) in the case of which it is concerned as trustee ;

provided that in the latter case neither the company nor any subsidiary of the company is beneficially interested under the trust, otherwise than by way of security only for the purposes of a transaction entered into by it in the ordinary course of a business which includes the lending of money.

Schedule 2 to this Act has effect for the interpretation of the reference in this sub-paragraph to a beneficial interest under a trust.

Consolidated accounts of holding company and subsidiaries

61. Subject to paragraphs 63 and 66, the consolidated balance sheet and profit and loss account shall combine the information contained in the separate balance sheets and profit and loss accounts of the holding company and of the subsidiaries dealt with by the consolidated accounts, but with such adjustments (if any) as the directors of the holding company think necessary.

62. Subject to paragraphs 63 to 66, and to Part V of this Schedule, the consolidated accounts shall, in giving the information required by paragraph 61, comply so far as practicable with the requirements of this Schedule and with the other requirements of this Act as if they were the accounts of an actual company.

63. The following provisions of this Act, namely—

  (a) section 231 as applying Schedule 5, but only Parts II, III, V and VI of that Schedule, and

  (b) sections 232 to 234 and Schedule 6, so far as relating to accounts other than group accounts,

do not, by virtue of paragraphs 61 and 62, apply for the purposes of the consolidated accounts.

64. Paragraph 62 is without prejudice to any requirement of this Act which applies (otherwise than by virtue of paragraph 61 or 62) to group accounts.

65.—(1) Notwithstanding paragraph 62, the consolidated accounts prepared by a holding company may deal with an investment of any member of the group in the shares of any other body corporate by way of the equity method of accounting in any case where it appears to the directors of the holding company that that body corporate is so closely associated with any member of the group as to justify the use of that method in dealing with investments by that or any other member of the group in the shares of that body corporate.

(2) In this paragraph, references to the group, in relation to consolidated accounts prepared by a holding company, are references to the holding company and the subsidiaries dealt with by the accounts.

66. Notwithstanding paragraphs 61 and 62, paragraphs 17 to 19 and 21 do not apply to any amount shown in the consolidated balance sheet in respect of goodwill arising on consolidation.

67. In relation to any subsidiaries of the holding company not dealt with by the consolidated accounts paragraphs 59 and 60 apply for the purpose of those accounts as if those accounts were the accounts of an actual company of which they were subsidiaries.

Group accounts not prepared as consolidated accounts

68. Group accounts which are not prepared as consolidated accounts, together with any notes to those accounts, shall give the same or equivalent information as that required to be given by consolidated accounts by virtue of paragraphs 61 to 67.

Provisions of general application

69.—(1) This paragraph applies where the company is a holding company and either—

  (a) does not prepare group accounts ; or

  (b) prepares group accounts which do not deal with one or more of its subsidiaries ;

and references below in this paragraph to the company's subsidiaries shall be read in a case within paragraph (b) as references to such of the company's subsidiaries as are excluded from the group accounts.

(2) Subject to the following provisions of this paragraph—

(a) the reasons why the subsidiaries are not dealt with in group accounts ; and

(b) a statement showing any qualifications contained in the reports of the auditors of the subsidiaries on their accounts for their respective financial years ending with or during the financial year of the company, and any note or saving contained in those accounts to call attention to a matter which, apart from the note or saving, would properly have been referred to in such a qualification, in so far as the matter which is the subject of the qualification or note is not covered by the company's own accounts and is material from the point of view of its members,

shall be given in a note to the company's accounts.

(3) Subject to the following provisions of this paragraph, the aggregate amount of the total investment of the holding company in the shares of the subsidiaries shall be stated in a note to the company's accounts by way of the equity method of valuation.

(4) Sub-paragraph (3) does not apply where the company is a wholly-owned subsidiary of another body corporate incorporated in Great Britain if there is included in a note to the company's accounts a statement that in the opinion of the directors of the company the aggregate value of the assets of the company consisting of shares in, or amounts owing (whether on account of a loan or otherwise) from, the company's subsidiaries is not less than the aggregate of the amounts at which those assets are stated or included in the company's balance sheet.

(5) In so far as information required by any of the preceding provisions of this paragraph to be stated in a note to the company's accounts is not obtainable, a statement to that effect shall be given instead in a note to those accounts.

(6) The Secretary of State may, on the application or with the consent of the company's directors, direct that in relation to any subsidiary sub-paragraphs (2) and (3) shall not apply, or shall apply only to such extent as may be provided by the direction.

(7) Where in any case within sub-paragraph (1)(b) the group accounts are consolidated accounts, references above in this paragraph to the company's accounts and the company's balance sheet respectively shall be read as references to the consolidated accounts and the consolidated balance sheet.

70. Where a company has subsidiaries whose financial years did not end with that of the company, the following information shall be given in relation to each such subsidiary (whether or not dealt with in any group accounts prepared by the company) by way of

a note to the company's accounts or (where group accounts are prepared) to the group accounts, that is to say—

- (a) the reasons why the company's directors consider that the subsidiaries' financial years should not end with that of the company ; and
- (b) the dates on which the subsidiaries' financial years ending last before that of the company respectively ended or the earliest and latest of those dates.

PART V

SPECIAL PROVISIONS WHERE THE COMPANY IS AN INVESTMENT COMPANY

71.—(1) Paragraph 34 does not apply to the amount of any profit or loss arising from a determination of the value of any investments of an investment company on any basis mentioned in paragraph 31(3).

(2) Any provisions made by virtue of paragraph 19(1) or (2) in the case of an investment company in respect of any fixed asset investments need not be charged to the company's profit and loss account provided they are either—

- (a) charged against any reserve account to which any amount excluded by sub-paragraph (1) from the requirements of paragraph 34 has been credited ; or
- (b) shown as a separate item in the company's balance sheet under the sub-heading " other reserves ".

(3) For the purposes of this paragraph, as it applies in relation to any company, " fixed asset investment " means any asset falling to be included under any item shown in the company's balance sheet under the subdivision " investments " under the general item " fixed assets ".

72.—(1) Any distribution made by an investment company which reduces the amount of its net assets to less than the aggregate of its called-up share capital and undistributable reserves shall be disclosed in a note to the company's accounts.

(2) For purposes of this paragraph, a company's net assets are the aggregate of its assets less the aggregate of its liabilities (including any provision for liabilities or charges within paragraph 89) ; and " undistributable reserves " has the meaning given by section 264 (3) of this Act.

73. A company shall be treated as an investment company for the purposes of this Part of this Schedule in relation to any financial year of the company if—

- (a) during the whole of that year it was an investment company as defined by section 266 of this Act, and
- (b) it was not at any time during that year prohibited under section 265(4) of this Act (no distribution where capital profits have been distributed, etc.) from making a distribution by virtue of that section.

74. Where a company entitled to the benefit of any provision contained in this Part of this Schedule is a holding company, the reference in paragraph 62 to consolidated accounts complying with the requirements of this Act shall, in relation to consolidated accounts of that company, be construed as referring to those requirements in so far only—

(a) as they apply to the individual accounts of that company ; and

(b) as they apply otherwise than by virtue of paragraphs 61 and 62 to any group accounts prepared by that company.

PART VI

SPECIAL PROVISIONS WHERE THE COMPANY HAS ENTERED INTO ARRANGEMENTS SUBJECT TO MERGER RELIEF

75.—(1) Where during the financial year the company has allotted shares in consideration for the issue, transfer or cancellation of shares in another body corporate (" the other company ") in circumstances where by virtue of section 131(2) of this Act (merger relief) section 130 did not apply to the premiums on those shares, the following information shall be given by way of a note to the company's accounts—

(a) the name of the other company ;

(b) the number, nominal value and class of shares so allotted ;

(c) the number, nominal value and class of shares in the other company so issued, transferred or cancelled ;

(d) particulars of the accounting treatment adopted in the company's accounts (including any group accounts) in respect of such issue, transfer or cancellation ; and

(e) where the company prepares group accounts, particulars of the extent to which and manner in which the profit or loss for the year of the group which appears in those accounts is affected by any profit or loss of the other company or any of its subsidiaries which arose at any time before the allotment.

(2) Where the company has during the financial year or during either of the two financial years immediately preceding it made such an allotment of shares as is mentioned in sub-paragraph (1) above and there is included in the company's consolidated profit and loss account or, if it has no such account, in its individual profit and loss account, any profit or loss (or part thereof) to which this sub-paragraph applies then the net amount of any such profit or loss (or part thereof) shall be shown in a note to the accounts together with an explanation of the transactions to which that information relates.

(3) Sub-paragraph (2) applies—

(a) to any profit or loss realised during the financial year by the company, or any of its subsidiaries, on the disposal of any shares in the other company or of any assets which were

fixed assets of the other company, or of any of its subsidiaries, at the time of the allotment ; and

(b) to any part of any profit or loss realised during the financial
year by the company, or any of its subsidiaries, on the
disposal of any shares (not being shares in the other company), which was attributable to the fact that at the time of
the disposal there were amongst the assets of the company
which issued those shares, or any of its subsidiaries, such
shares or assets as are described in sub-paragraph (a) above.

(4) Where in pursuance of the arrangement in question shares
are allotted on different dates, the time of allotment for the purposes of sub-paragraphs (1)(e) and (3)(a) above is taken to be—

(a) if the other company becomes a subsidiary of the company
as a result of the arrangement—

(i) if the arrangement becomes binding only upon
the fulfilment of a condition, the date on which that
condition is fulfilled, and

(ii) in any other case, the date on which the other
company becomes a subsidiary of the company ;

(b) if the other company is a subsidiary of the company when
the arrangement is proposed, the date of the first allotment
pursuant to that arrangement.

PART VII

INTERPRETATION OF SCHEDULE

76. The following paragraphs apply for the purposes of this Schedule and its interpretation.

Assets : fixed or current

77. Assets of a company are taken to be fixed assets if they are
intended for use on a continuing basis in the company's activities,
and any assets not intended for such use shall be taken to be current
assets.

Balance sheet date

78. " Balance sheet date ", in relation to a balance sheet, means the
date as at which the balance sheet was prepared.

Capitalisation

79. References to capitalising any work or costs are to treating
that work or those costs as a fixed asset.

Fellow subsidiary

80. A body corporate is treated as a fellow subsidiary of another
body corporate if both are subsidiaries of the same body corporate
but neither is the other's.

Group companies

81. " Group company ", in relation to any company, means any
body corporate which is that company's subsidiary or holding company, or a subsidiary of that company's holding company.

Historical cost accounting rules

82. References to the historical cost accounting rules shall be read in accordance with paragraph 29.

Leases

83.—(1) " Long lease " means a lease in the case of which the portion of the term for which it was granted remaining unexpired at the end of the financial year is not less than 50 years.

(2) " Short lease " means a lease which is not a long lease.

(3) " Lease " includes an agreement for a lease.

Listed investments

84. " Listed investment " means an investment as respects which there has been granted a listing on a recognised stock exchange, or on any stock exchange of repute (other than a recognised stock exchange) outside Great Britain.

Loans

85. A loan is treated as falling due for repayment, and an instalment of a loan is treated as falling due for payment, on the earliest date on which the lender could require repayment or (as the case may be) payment, if he exercised all options and rights available to him.

Materiality

86. Amounts which in the particular context of any provision of this Schedule are not material may be disregarded for the purposes of that provision.

Notes to the accounts

87. Notes to a company's accounts may be contained in the accounts or in a separate document annexed to the accounts.

Provisions

88.—(1) References to provisions for depreciation or diminution in value of assets are to any amount written off by way of providing for depreciation or diminution in value of assets.

(2) Any reference in the profit and loss account formats set out in Part I of this Schedule to the depreciation of, or amounts written off, assets of any description is to any provision for depreciation or diminution in value of assets of that description.

89. References to provisions for liabilities or charges are to any amount retained as reasonably necessary for the purpose of providing for any liability or loss which is either likely to be incurred, or certain to be incurred but uncertain as to amount or as to the date on which it will arise.

Purchase price

90. References (however expressed) to the purchase price of any asset of a company or of any raw materials or consumables used in the production of any such asset include any consideration (whether in cash or otherwise) given by the company in respect of that asset or in respect of those materials or consumables (as the case may require).

Realised profits

91. Without prejudice to—

(a) the construction of any other expression (where appropriate) by reference to accepted accounting principles or practice, or

(b) any specific provision for the treatment of profits of any description as realised,

it is hereby declared for the avoidance of doubt that references in this Schedule to realised profits, in relation to a company's accounts, are to such profits of the company as fall to be treated as realised profits for the purposes of those accounts in accordance with principles generally accepted with respect to the determination for accounting purposes of realised profits at the time when those accounts are prepared.

Related companies

92.—(1) " Related company ", in relation to any company, means any body corporate (other than one which is a group company in relation to that company) in which that company holds on a long-term basis a qualifying capital interest for the purpose of securing a contribution to that company's own activities by the exercise of any control or influence arising from that interest.

(2) In this paragraph " qualifying capital interest " means, in relation to any body corporate, an interest in shares comprised in the equity share capital of that body corporate of a class carrying rights to vote in all circumstances at general meetings of that body corporate.

(3) Where—

(a) a company holds a qualifying capital interest in a body corporate ; and

(b) the nominal value of any relevant shares in that body corporate held by that company is equal to twenty per cent. or more of the nominal value of all relevant shares in that body corporate ;

it shall be presumed to hold that interest on the basis and for the purpose mentioned in sub-paragraph (1), unless the contrary is shown.

In this sub-paragraph " relevant shares " means, in relation to any body corporate, any such shares in that body corporate as are mentioned in sub-paragraph (2).

Scots land tenure

93. In the application of this Schedule to Scotland, " land of free-hold tenure " means land in respect of which the company is the proprietor of the *dominium utile* or, in the case of land not held on feudal tenure, is the owner ; " land of leasehold tenure " means land of which the company is the tenant under a lease ; and the reference to ground-rents, rates and other outgoings includes feu-duty and ground annual.

Staff costs

94.—(1) " Social security costs " means any contributions by the company to any state social security or pension scheme, fund or arrangement.

(2) " Pension costs " includes any other contributions by the company for the purposes of any pension scheme established for the purpose of providing pensions for persons employed by the company, any sums set aside for that purpose and any amounts paid by the company in respect of pensions without first being so set aside.

(3) Any amount stated in respect of either of the above items or in respect of the item " wages and salaries " in the company's profit and loss account shall be determined by reference to payments made or costs incurred in respect of all persons employed by the company during the financial year who are taken into account in determining the relevant annual number for the purposes of paragraph 56(1)(*a*).

Turnover

95. " Turnover ", in relation to a company, means the amounts derived from the provision of goods and services falling within the company's ordinary activities, after deduction of—

    (*a*) trade discounts,

    (*b*) value added tax, and

    (*c*) any other taxes based on the amounts so derived.

SCHEDULE 5

MISCELLANEOUS MATTERS TO BE DISCLOSED IN NOTES TO COMPANY ACCOUNTS

PART I

PARTICULARS OF SUBSIDIARIES

1. If at the end of the financial year the company has subsidiaries, there shall in the case of each subsidiary be stated—

    (*a*) the name of the subsidiary and—

        (i) if it is incorporated in Great Britain and if it is registered in England and Wales and the company is registered in Scotland (or vice versa), the part of Great Britain in which it is registered, and

        (ii) if it is incorporated outside Great Britain, the country in which it is incorporated ; and

T

(*b*) in relation to shares of each class of the subsidiary held by the company, the identity of the class and the proportion of the nominal value of the allotted shares of that class represented by the shares held.

2. The particulars required by paragraph 1 include, with reference to the proportion of the nominal value of the allotted shares of a class represented by shares held by the company, a statement of the extent (if any) to which it consists in shares held by, or by a nominee for, a subsidiary of the company and the extent (if any) to which it consists in shares held by, or by a nominee for, the company itself.

3. Paragraph 1 does not require the disclosure of information with respect to a body corporate which is the subsidiary of another and is incorporated outside the United Kingdom or, being incorporated in the United Kingdom, carries on business outside it if the disclosure would, in the opinion of the directors of that other, be harmful to the business of that other or of any of its subsidiaries and the Secretary of State agrees that the information need not be disclosed.

4. If at the end of its financial year the company has subsidiaries and the directors are of the opinion that the number of them is such that compliance with paragraph 1 would result in particulars of excessive length being given, compliance with that paragraph is required only in the case of the subsidiaries carrying on the businesses the results of the carrying on of which (in the opinion of the directors) principally affected the amount of the profit or loss of the company and its subsidiaries or the amount of the assets of the company and its subsidiaries.

5. If advantage is taken of paragraph 4, there must be included in the statement required by this Part the information that it deals only with the subsidiaries carrying on such businesses as are referred to in that paragraph; and in that case section 231(3) (subsequent disclosure with annual return) applies to the particulars given in compliance with paragraph 1, together with those which (but for the fact that advantage is so taken) would have to be so given.

6. For purposes of this Part, shares of a body corporate are treated as held, or not held, by another such body if they would, by virtue of section 736(4) of this Act, be treated as being held or (as the case may be) not held by that other body for the purpose of determining whether the first-mentioned body is its subsidiary.

PART II

SHAREHOLDINGS IN COMPANIES ETC. OTHER THAN SUBSIDIARIES

7. If at the end of its financial year the company holds shares of any class comprised in the equity share capital of another body corporate (not being its subsidiary) exceeding in nominal value one-tenth of the nominal value of the allotted shares of that class, there shall be stated—

(*a*) the name of that other body corporate and—

(i) if it is incorporated in Great Britain and if it is

registered in England and Wales and the company is registered in Scotland (or vice versa), the part of Great Britain in which it is registered, and

    (ii) if it is incorporated outside Great Britain, the country in which it is incorporated ;

(b) the identity of the class and the proportion of the nominal value of the allotted shares of that class represented by the shares held ; and

(c) if the company also holds shares in that other body corporate of another class (whether or not comprised in its equity share capital), or of other classes (whether or not so comprised), the like particulars as respects that other class or (as the case may be) those other classes.

8. If at the end of its financial year the company holds shares comprised in the share capital of another body corporate (not being its subsidiary) exceeding in nominal value one-tenth of the allotted share capital of that other body, there shall be stated—

(a) with respect to that other body corporate, the same information as is required by paragraph 7(a), and

(b) the identity of each class of such shares held and the proportion of the nominal value of the allotted shares of that class represented by the shares of that class held by the company.

9. If at the end of its financial year the company holds shares in another body corporate (not being its subsidiary) and the amount of all shares in it which the company holds (as stated or included in the company's accounts) exceeds one-tenth of the amount of the company's assets (as so stated), there shall be stated—

(a) with respect to the other body corporate, the same information as is required by paragraph 7(a), and

(b) in relation to shares in that other body corporate of each class held, the identity of the class and the proportion of the nominal value of the allotted shares of that class represented by the shares held.

10. None of the foregoing provisions of this Part requires the disclosure by a company of information with respect to another body corporate if that other is incorporated outside the United Kingdom or, being incorporated in the United Kingdom, carries on business outside it if the disclosure would, in the opinion of the company's directors, be harmful to the business of the company or of that other body and the Secretary of State agrees that the information need not be disclosed.

11. If at the end of its financial year the company falls within paragraph 7 or 8 in relation to more bodies corporate than one, and the number of them is such that, in the directors' opinion, compliance with either or both of those paragraphs would result in particulars of excessive length being given, compliance with paragraph 7 or (as the case may be) paragraph 8 is not required except in the case of the bodies carrying on the businesses the results of the

carrying on of which (in the directors' opinion) principally affected the amount of the profit or loss of the company or the amount of its assets.

12. If advantage is taken of paragraph 11, there must be included in the statement dealing with the bodies last mentioned in that paragraph the information that it deals only with them ; and section 231(3) of this Act (subsequent disclosure in annual return) applies to the particulars given in compliance with paragraph 7 or 8 (as the case may be), together with those which, but for the fact that advantage is so taken, would have to be so given.

13. For purposes of this Part, shares of a body corporate are treated as held, or not held, by another such body if they would, by virtue of section 736(4) of this Act (but on the assumption that paragraph (b)(ii) were omitted from that subsection) be treated as being held or (as the case may be), not held by that other body for the purpose of determining whether the first-mentioned body is its subsidiary.

PART III

FINANCIAL INFORMATION ABOUT SUBSIDIARIES

14. If—
   (a) at the end of its financial year the company has subsidiaries, and
   (b) it is required by paragraph 1 in Part I above to disclose particulars with respect to any of those subsidiaries,

the additional information specified below shall be given with respect to each subsidiary to which the requirement under paragraph 1 applies.

15. If—
   (a) at the end of the financial year the company holds shares in another body corporate, and
   (b) it is required by paragraph 8 in Part II above to disclose particulars with respect to that body corporate, and
   (c) the shares held by the company in that body corporate exceed in nominal value one-fifth of the allotted share capital of that body,

the additional information specified below shall be given with respect to that body corporate.

16. The information required by paragraphs 14 and 15 is, in relation to any body corporate (whether a subsidiary of the company or not) the aggregate amount of the capital and reserves of that body corporate as at the end of its relevant financial year, and its profit or loss for that year ; and for this purpose the relevant financial year is—
   (a) if the financial year of the body corporate ends with that of the company giving the information in a note to its accounts, that financial year, and

(b) if not, the body corporate's financial year ending last before the end of the financial year of the company giving that information.

This is subject to the exceptions and other provisions in the next paragraph.

17.—(1) The information otherwise required by paragraph 16 need not be given in respect of a subsidiary of a company if either—

(a) the company is exempt under this Act from the requirement to prepare group accounts, as being at the end of its financial year the wholly-owned subsidiary of another body corporate incorporated in Great Britain, or

(b) the company prepares group accounts and—

(i) the accounts of the subsidiary are included in the group accounts, or

(ii) the investment of the company in the shares of the subsidiary is included in, or in a note to, the company's accounts by way of the equity method of valuation.

(2) That information need not be given in respect of another body corporate in which the company holds shares if the company's investment in those shares is included in, or in a note to, the accounts by way of the equity method of valuation.

(3) That information need not be given in respect of any body corporate if—

(a) that body is not required by any provision of this Act to deliver a copy of its balance sheet for its relevant financial year mentioned in paragraph 16, and does not otherwise publish that balance sheet in Great Britain or elsewhere, and

(b) the shares held by the company in that body do not amount to at least one half in nominal value of the body's allotted share capital.

(4) Information otherwise required by paragraph 16 need not be given if it is not material.

18. Where, with respect to any subsidiary of the company or any other body corporate, particulars which would otherwise be required by paragraph 1 in Part I or paragraph 8 in Part II of this Schedule to be stated in a note to the company's accounts are omitted by virtue of paragraph 4 or (as the case may be) paragraph 11, section 231(3) of this Act (subsequent disclosure in next annual return) applies—

(a) to any information with respect to any other subsidiary or body corporate which is given in or in a note to the company's accounts in accordance with this Part, and

(b) to any information which would have been required by this Part to be given in relation to a subsidiary or other body corporate but for the exemption under paragraph 4 or 11.

19. For purposes of this Part, shares of a body corporate are treated as held, or not held, by the company if they would, by

T 3

virtue of section 736(4) of this Act (but on the assumption that paragraph (b)(ii) were omitted from that subsection), be treated as being held or (as the case may be) not held by the company for the purpose of determining whether that body corporate is the company's subsidiary.

PART IV
IDENTIFICATION OF ULTIMATE HOLDING COMPANY

20. If at the end of its financial year the company is the subsidiary of another body corporate, there shall be stated the name of the body corporate regarded by the directors as being the company's ultimate holding company and, if known to them, the country in which it is incorporated.

21. Paragraph 20 does not require the disclosure by a company which carries on business outside the United Kingdom of information with respect to the body corporate regarded by the directors as being its ultimate holding company if the disclosure would, in their opinion, be harmful to the business of that holding company or of the first-mentioned company, or any other of that holding company's subsidiaries, and the Secretary of State agrees that the information need not be disclosed.

PART V
CHAIRMAN'S AND DIRECTORS' EMOLUMENTS, PENSIONS AND COMPENSATION FOR LOSS OF OFFICE
Emoluments

22.—(1) There shall be shown the aggregate amount of the directors' emoluments.

(2) This amount—

    (a) includes any emoluments paid to or receivable by a person in respect of his services as director of the company or in respect of his services, while director of the company, as director of any subsidiary of it or otherwise in connection with the management of the affairs of the company or any subsidiary of it ; and

    (b) shall distinguish between emoluments in respect of services as director, whether of the company or its subsidiary, and other emoluments.

(3) For purposes of this paragraph " emoluments ", in relation to a director, includes fees and percentages, any sums paid by way of expenses allowance (insofar as those sums are charged to United Kingdom income tax), any contributions paid in respect of him under any pension scheme and the estimated money value of any other benefits received by him otherwise than in cash.

23. A company which is neither a holding company nor a subsidiary of another body corporate need not comply with paragraphs 24 to 27 below as respects a financial year in the case of which the amount shown in compliance with paragraph 22 above does not exceed £60,000.

24.—(1) The following applies as respects the emoluments of the company's chairman; and for this purpose "chairman" means the person elected by the directors to be chairman of their meetings and includes a person who, though not so elected, holds any office (however designated) which in accordance with the company's constitution carries with it functions substantially similar to those discharged by a person so elected.

(2) If one person has been chairman throughout the financial year, there shall be shown his emoluments, unless his duties as chairman were wholly or mainly discharged outside the United Kingdom.

(3) Otherwise, there shall be shown with respect to each person who has been chairman during the year his emoluments so far as attributable to the period during which he was chairman, unless his duties as chairman were wholly or mainly discharged outside the United Kingdom.

25.—(1) The following applies as respects the emoluments of directors.

(2) With respect to all the directors (other than any who discharged their duties as such wholly or mainly outside the United Kingdom), there shall be shown—

> (a) the number (if any) who had no emoluments or whose several emoluments amounted to not more than £5,000; and

> (b) by reference to each pair of adjacent points on a scale whereon the lowest point is £5,000 and the succeeding ones are successive integral multiples of £5,000, the number (if any) whose several emoluments exceeded the lower point but did not exceed the higher.

(3) If, of the directors (other than any who discharged their duties as such wholly or mainly outside the United Kingdom), the emoluments of one only exceed the relevant amount, his emoluments (so far as so ascertainable) shall also be shown.

(4) If, of the directors (other than any who discharged their duties as such wholly or mainly outside the United Kingdom), the emoluments of each of two or more exceed the relevant amount, the emoluments of him (or them, in the case of equality) who had the greater or, as the case may be, the greatest shall also be shown.

(5) "The relevant amount"—

> (a) if one person has been chairman throughout the year, means the amount of his emoluments; and

> (b) otherwise, means an amount equal to the aggregate of the emoluments, so far as attributable to the period during which he was chairman, of each person who has been chairman during the year.

26. There shall under paragraphs 24 and 25 be brought into account as emoluments of a person all such amounts (other than

contributions paid in respect of him under a pension scheme) as in his case are to be included in the amount shown under paragraph 22.

Emoluments waived

27.—(1) There shall be shown—

(a) the number of directors who have waived rights to receive emoluments which, but for the waiver, would have fallen to be included in the amount shown under paragraph 22, and

(b) the aggregate amount of those emoluments.

(2) For these purposes—

(a) it is assumed that a sum not receivable in respect of a period would have been paid at the time at which it was due to be paid,

(b) a sum not so receivable that was payable only on demand, being a sum the right to receive which has been waived, is deemed to have been due to be paid at the time of the waiver.

Pensions of directors and past directors

28.—(1) There shall be shown the aggregate amount of directors' or past directors' pensions.

(2) This amount does not include any pension paid or receivable under a pension scheme if the scheme is such that the contributions under it are substantially adequate for the maintenance of the scheme; but, subject to this, it includes any pension paid or receivable in respect of any such services of a director or past director as are mentioned in paragraph 22(2), whether to or by him or, on his nomination or by virtue of dependence on or other connection with him, to or by any other person.

(3) The amount shown shall distinguish between pensions in respect of services as director, whether of the company or its subsidiary, and other pensions.

Compensation to directors for loss of office

29.—(1) There shall be shown the aggregate amount of any compensation to directors or past directors in respect of loss of office.

(2) This amount—

(a) includes any sums paid to or receivable by a director or past director by way of compensation for the loss of office as director of the company or for the loss, while director of the company or on or in connection with his ceasing to be a director of it, of any other office in connection with the management of the company's affairs or of any office as director or otherwise in connection with the management of the affairs of any subsidiary of the company; and

(b) shall distinguish between compensation in respect of the office of director, whether of the company or its subsidiary, and compensation in respect of other offices.

(3) References to compensation for loss of office include sums paid as consideration for or in connection with a person's retirement from office.

Supplementary

30.—(1) The following applies with respect to the amounts to be shown under paragraphs 22, 28 and 29.

(2) The amount in each case includes all relevant sums paid by or receivable from—

(a) the company ; and

(b) the company's subsidiaries ; and

(c) any other person,

except sums to be accounted for to the company or any of its subsidiaries or, by virtue of sections 314 and 315 of this Act (duty of directors to make disclosure on company takeover ; consequence of non-compliance), to past or present members of the company or any of its subsidiaries or any class of those members.

(3) The amount to be shown under paragraph 29 shall distinguish between the sums respectively paid by or receivable from the company, the company's subsidiaries and persons other than the company and its subsidiaries.

31.—(1) The amounts to be shown for any financial year under paragraphs 22, 28 and 29 are the sums receivable in respect of that year (whenever paid) or, in the case of sums not receivable in respect of a period, the sums paid during that year.

(2) But where—

(a) any sums are not shown in a note to the accounts for the relevant financial year on the ground that the person receiving them is liable to account for them as mentioned in paragraph 30(2), but the liability is thereafter wholly or partly released or is not enforced within a period of 2 years ; or

(b) any sums paid by way of expenses allowance are charged to United Kingdom income tax after the end of the relevant financial year,

those sums shall, to the extent to which the liability is released or not enforced or they are charged as mentioned above (as the case may be), be shown in a note to the first accounts in which it is practicable to show them and shall be distinguished from the amounts to be shown apart from this provision.

32. Where it is necessary to do so for the purpose of making any distinction required by the preceding paragraphs in an amount to be shown in compliance with this Part, the directors may apportion any payments between the matters in respect of which these have been paid or are receivable in such manner as they think appropriate.

Interpretation

33.—(1) The following applies for the interpretation of paragraphs 22 to 32.

(2) A reference to the company's subsidiary—

(a) in relation to a person who is or was, while a director of the company, a director also, by virtue of the company's nomination (direct or indirect) of any other body corporate, includes (subject to the following sub-paragraph) that body corporate, whether or not it is or was in fact the company's subsidiary, and

(b) for purposes of paragraphs 22 to 28 (including any provision of this Part referring to paragraph 22) is to a subsidiary at the time the services were rendered, and for purposes of paragraph 29 to a subsidiary immediately before the loss of office as director.

(3) The following definitions apply—

(a) " pension " includes any superannuation allowance, superannuation gratuity or similar payment,

(b) " pension scheme " means a scheme for the provision of pensions in respect of services as director or otherwise which is maintained in whole or in part by means of contributions, and

(c) " contribution ", in relation to a pension scheme, means any payment (including an insurance premium) paid for the purposes of the scheme by or in respect of persons rendering services in respect of which pensions will or may become payable under the scheme, except that it does not include any payment in respect of two or more persons if the amount paid in respect of each of them is not ascertainable.

Supplementary

34. This Part of this Schedule requires information to be given only so far as it is contained in the company's books and papers or the company has the right to obtain it from the persons concerned.

PART VI

PARTICULARS RELATING TO NUMBER OF EMPLOYEES REMUNERATED AT HIGHER RATES

35.—(1) There shall be shown by reference to each pair of adjacent points on a scale whereon the lowest point is £30,000 and the succeeding ones are successive integral multiples of £5,000 beginning with that in the case of which the multiplier is 7, the number (if any) of persons in the company's employment whose several emoluments exceeded the lower point but did not exceed the higher.

(2) The persons whose emoluments are to be taken into account for this purpose do not include—

(a) directors of the company ; or

(b) persons (other than directors of the company) who—

(i) if employed by the company throughout the financial year, worked wholly or mainly during that year outside the United Kingdom, or

(ii) if employed by the company for part only of that year, worked wholly or mainly during that part outside the United Kingdom.

36.—(1) For these purposes, a person's emoluments include any paid to or receivable by him from the company, the company's subsidiaries and any other person in respect of his services as a person in the employment of the company or a subsidiary of it or as a director of a subsidiary of the company (except sums to be accounted for to the company or any of its subsidiaries).

(2) " Emoluments " here includes fees and percentages, any sums paid by way of expenses allowance in so far as those sums are charged to United Kingdom income tax, and the estimated money value of any other benefits received by a person otherwise than in cash.

(3) The amounts to be brought into account for the purpose of complying with paragraph 35 are the sums receivable in respect of the financial year (whenever paid) or, in the case of sums not receivable in respect of a period, the sums paid during that year.

(4) But where—

(a) any sums are not brought into account for the financial year on the ground that the person receiving them is liable to account for them as mentioned in sub-paragraph (1), but the liability is wholly or partly released or is not enforced within a period of 2 years ; or

(b) any sums paid to a person by way of expenses allowance are charged to United Kingdom income tax after the end of the financial year,

those sums shall, to the extent to which the liability is released or not enforced or they are charged as above mentioned (as the case may be), be brought into account for the purpose of complying with paragraph 35 on the first occasion on which it is practicable to do so.

37. References in paragraph 36 to a company's subsidiary—

(a) in relation to a person who is or was, while employed by the company a director, by virtue of the company's nomination (direct or indirect), of any other body corporate, include that body corporate (but subject to the following sub-paragraph), whether or not it is or was in fact the company's subsidiary ; and

(b) are to be taken as referring to a subsidiary at the time the services were rendered.

SCHEDULE 6

PARTICULARS IN COMPANY ACCOUNTS OF LOAN AND OTHER TRANSACTIONS FAVOURING DIRECTORS AND OFFICERS

PART I

MATTERS TO BE DISCLOSED UNDER SECTION 232

1. Group accounts shall contain the particulars required by this Schedule of—

(a) any transaction or arrangement of a kind described in

section 330 entered into by the company or by a subsidiary of the company for a person who at any time during the financial year was a director of the company or its holding company, or was connected with such a director ;

(b) an agreement by the company or by a subsidiary of the company to enter into any such transaction or arrangement for a person who was at any time during the financial year a director of the company or its holding company, or was connected with such a director ; and

(c) any other transaction or arrangement with the company or a subsidiary of it in which a person who at any time during the financial year was a director of the company or its holding company had, directly or indirectly, a material interest.

2. The accounts prepared by a company other than a holding company shall contain the particulars required by this Schedule of—

(a) any transaction or arrangement of a kind described in section 330 entered into by the company for a person who at any time during the financial year was a director of it or of its holding company or was connected with such a director ;

(b) an agreement by the company to enter into any such transaction or arrangement for a person who at any time during the financial year was a director of the company or its holding company or was connected with such a director ; and

(c) any other transaction or arrangement with the company in which a person who at any time during the financial year was a director of the company or of its holding company had, directly or indirectly, a material interest.

3.—(1) For purposes of paragraphs 1(c) and 2(c), a transaction or arrangement between a company and a director of it or of its holding company, or a person connected with such a director, is to be treated (if it would not otherwise be so) as a transaction, arrangement or agreement in which that director is interested.

(2) An interest in such a transaction or arrangement is not " material " for purposes of those sub-paragraphs if in the board's opinion it is not so ; but this is without prejudice to the question whether or not such an interest is material in a case where the board have not considered the matter.

" The board " here means the directors of the company preparing the accounts, or a majority of those directors, but excluding in either case the director whose interest it is.

4. Paragraphs 1 and 2 do not apply, for the purposes of accounts prepared by a company which is, or is the holding company of, a recognised bank, in relation to a transaction or arrangement of a kind described in section 330 or an agreement to enter into such a transaction or arrangement, to which that recognised bank is a party.

5. Paragraphs 1 and 2 do not apply in relation to the following
transactions, arrangements and agreements—

   (*a*) a transaction, arrangement or agreement between one company and another in which a director of the former or of its subsidiary or holding company is interested only by virtue of his being a director of the latter ;

   (*b*) a contract of service between a company and one of its directors or a director of its holding company, or between a director of a company and any of that company's subsidiaries ;

   (*c*) a transaction, arrangement or agreement which was not entered into during the financial year and which did not subsist at any time during that year.

6. Paragraphs 1 and 2 apply whether or not—

   (*a*) the transaction or arrangement was prohibited by section 330 ;

   (*b*) the person for whom it was made was a director of the company or was connected with a director of it at the time it was made ;

   (*c*) in the case of a transaction or arrangement made by a company which at any time during a financial year is a subsidiary of another company, it was a subsidiary of that other company at the time the transaction or arrangement was made.

7. Neither paragraph 1(*c*) nor paragraph 2 (*c*) applies in relation to any transaction or arrangement if—

   (*a*) each party to the transaction or arrangement which is a member of the same group of companies (meaning a holding company and its subsidiaries) as the company entered into the transaction or arrangement in the ordinary course of business, and

   (*b*) the terms of the transaction or arrangement are not less favourable to any such party than it would be reasonable to expect if the interest mentioned in that sub-paragraph had not been an interest of a person who was a director of the company or of its holding company.

8. Neither paragraph 1(*c*) nor paragraph 2(*c*) applies in relation to any transaction or arrangement if—

   (*a*) the company is a member of a group of companies (meaning a holding company and its subsidiaries), and

   (*b*) either the company is a wholly-owned subsidiary or no body corporate (other than the company or a subsidiary of the company) which is a member of the group of companies which includes the company's ultimate holding company was a party to the transaction or arrangement, and

   (*c*) the director in question was at some time during the relevant period associated with the company, and

(*d*) the material interest of the director in question in the transaction or arrangement would not have arisen if he had
not been associated with the company at any time during
the relevant period.

The particulars required by this Part

9.—(1) Subject to the next paragraph, the particulars required by
this Part are those of the principal terms of the transaction, arrangement or agreement.

(2) Without prejudice to the generality of sub-paragraph (1), the
following particulars are required—

(*a*) a statement of the fact either that the transaction, arrangement or agreement was made or subsisted (as the case
may be) during the financial year ;

(*b*) the name of the person for whom it was made and, where
that person is or was connected with a director of the
company or of its holding company, the name of that
director ;

(*c*) in a case where paragraph 1(*c*) or 2(*c*) applies, the name of
the director with the material interest and the nature of
that interest ;

(*d*) in the case of a loan or an agreement for a loan or an
arrangement within section 330(6) or (7) of this Act relating
to a loan—

(i) the amount of the liability of the person to whom
the loan was or was agreed to be made, in respect of
principal and interest, at the beginning and at the end
of the financial year ;

(ii) the maximum amount of that liability during that
year ;

(iii) the amount of any interest which, having fallen
due, has not been paid ; and

(iv) the amount of any provision (within the meaning
of Schedule 4 to this Act) made in respect of any failure
or anticipated failure by the borrower to repay the whole
or part of the loan or to pay the whole or part of any
interest on it ;

(*e*) in the case of a guarantee or security or an arrangement
within section 330(6) relating to a guarantee or security—

(i) the amount for which the company (or its subsidiary) was liable under the guarantee or in respect of
the security both at the beginning and at the end of the
financial year ;

(ii) the maximum amount for which the company (or
its subsidiary) may become so liable ; and

(iii) any amount paid and any liability incurred by the
company (or its subsidiary) for the purpose of fulfilling
the guarantee or discharging the security (including any
loss incurred by reason of the enforcement of the
guarantee or security) ; and

(*f*) in the case of any transaction, arrangement or agreement other than those mentioned in sub-paragraphs (*d*) and (*e*), the value of the transaction or arrangement or (as the case may be) the value of the transaction or arrangement to which the agreement relates.

10. In paragraph 9(2) above, sub-paragraphs (*c*) to (*f*) do not apply in the case of a loan or quasi-loan made or agreed to be made by a company to or for a body corporate which is either—

(*a*) a body corporate of which that company is a wholly-owned subsidiary, or

(*b*) a wholly-owned subsidiary of a body corporate of which that company is a wholly-owned subsidiary, or

(*c*) a wholly-owned subsidiary of that company,

if particulars of that loan, quasi-loan or agreement for it would not have been required to be included in that company's annual accounts if the first-mentioned body corporate had not been associated with a director of that company at any time during the relevant period.

Transactions excluded from section 232

11.—(1) In relation to a company's accounts for a financial year, compliance with this Part is not required in the case of transactions of a kind mentioned in the following sub-paragraph which are made by the company or a subsidiary of it for a person who at any time during that financial year was a director of the company or of its holding company, or was connected with such a director, if the aggregate of the values of each transaction, arrangement or agreement so made for that director or any person connected with him, less the amount (if any) by which the liabilities of the person for whom the transaction or arrangement was made has been reduced, did not at any time during the financial year exceed £5,000.

(2) The transactions in question are—

(*a*) credit transactions,

(*b*) guarantees provided or securities entered into in connection with credit transactions,

(*c*) arrangements within subsection (6) or (7) of section 330 relating to credit transactions,

(*d*) agreements to enter into credit transactions.

12. In relation to a company's accounts for a financial year, compliance with this Part is not required by virtue of paragraph 1(*c*) or 2(*c*) in the case of any transaction or arrangement with a company or any of its subsidiaries in which a director of the company or its holding company had, directly or indirectly, a material interest if—

(*a*) the value of each transaction or arrangement within paragraph 1(*c*) or 2(*c*) (as the case may be) in which that director had (directly or indirectly) a material interest and which was made after the commencement of the financial year with the company or any of its subsidiaries, and

(*b*) the value of each such transaction or arrangement which was made before the commencement of the financial year less the amount (if any) by which the liabilities of the person for whom the transaction or arrangement was made have been reduced,

did not at any time during the financial year exceed in the aggregate £1,000 or, if more, did not exceed £5,000 or 1 per cent. of the value of the net assets of the company preparing the accounts in question as at the end of the financial year, whichever is the less.

For this purpose a company's net assets are the aggregate of its assets, less the aggregate of its liabilities ("liabilities" to include any provision for liabilities or charges within paragraph 89 of Schedule 4).

13. Section 345 of this Act (power of Secretary of State to alter sums by statutory instrument subject to negative resolution in Parliament) applies as if the money sums specified in paragraph 11 or 12 above were specified in Part X.

Interpretation

14. The following provisions of this Act apply for purposes of this Part of this Schedule—

    (a) section 331(2), (5) and (7), as regards the meaning of "guarantee", "recognised bank" and "credit transaction";

    (b) section 331(9), as to the interpretation of references to a transaction or arrangement being made "for" a person;

    (c) section 340, in assigning values to transactions and arrangements, and

    (d) section 346, as to the interpretation of references to a person being "connected with" a director of a company.

PART II

MATTERS TO BE DISCLOSED UNDER SECTION 233

15. This Part of this Schedule applies in relation to the following classes of transactions, arrangements and agreements—

    (a) loans, guarantees and securities relating to loans, arrangements of a kind described in subsection (6) or (7) of section 330 of this Act relating to loans and agreements to enter into any of the foregoing transactions and arrangements;

    (b) quasi-loans, guarantees and securities relating to quasi-loans arrangements of a kind described in either of those subsections relating to quasi-loans and agreements to enter into any of the foregoing transactions and arrangements;

    (c) credit transactions, guarantees and securities relating to credit transactions, arrangements of a kind described in either of those subsections relating to credit transactions and agreements to enter into any of the foregoing transactions and arrangements.

16.—(1) To comply with this Part of this Schedule, the accounts must contain a statement, in relation to transactions, arrangements and agreements made as mentioned in section 233(1), of—

    (a) the aggregate amounts outstanding at the end of the financial year under transactions, arrangements and agreements within sub-paragraphs (*a*), (*b*) and (*c*) respectively of paragraph 15 above, and

(*b*) the numbers of officers for whom the transactions, arrangements and agreements falling within each of those sub-paragraphs were made.

(2) This paragraph does not apply to transactions, arrangements and agreements made by the company or any of its subsidiaries for an officer of the company if the aggregate amount outstanding at the end of the financial year under the transactions, arrangements and agreements so made for that officer does not exceed £2,500.

(3) Section 345 of this Act (power of Secretary of State to alter money sums by statutory instrument subject to negative resolution in Parliament) applies as if the money sum specified above in this paragraph were specified in Part X.

17. The following provisions of this Act apply for purposes of this Part—

(*a*) section 331(2), (3), (5) and (7), as regards the meaning of "guarantee", "quasi-loan", "recognised bank" and "credit transaction", and

(*b*) section 331(9), as to the interpretation of references to a transaction or arrangement being made "for" a person ;

and "amount outstanding" means the amount of the outstanding liabilities of the person for whom the transaction, arrangement or agreement was made or, in the case of a guarantee or security, the amount guaranteed or secured.

PART III

MATTERS TO BE DISCLOSED UNDER SECTION 234 (RECOGNISED BANKS)

18. This Part of this Schedule applies in relation to the same classes of transactions, arrangements and agreements as does Part II.

19. To comply with this Part, the accounts must contain a statement, in relation to such transactions, arrangements and agreements made as mentioned in section 234(1), of—

(*a*) the aggregate amounts outstanding at the end of the financial year under transactions, arrangements and agreements within sub-paragraphs (*a*), (*b*) and (*c*) respectively of paragraph 15 of this Schedule, and

(*b*) the numbers of persons for whom the transactions, arrangements and agreements falling within each of those sub-paragraphs were made.

20. For the purposes of the application of paragraph 19 in relation to loans and quasi-loans made by a company to persons connected with a person who at any time is a director of the company or of its holding company, a company which a person does not control is not connected with him.

c. 6 — Companies Act 1985

SCH. 6
PART III

21. The following provisions of this Act apply for purposes of this Part—

(a) section 331(3), as regards the meaning of "quasi-loan";

(b) section 331(9), as to the interpretation of references to a transaction or arrangement being made "for" a person; and

(c) section 346, as to the interpretation of references to a person being connected with a director, or to a director controlling a company;

and "amount outstanding" means the amount of the outstanding liabilities of the person for whom the transaction, arrangement or agreement was made or, in the case of a guarantee or security, the amount guaranteed or secured.

Section 235.

SCHEDULE 7

MATTERS TO BE DEALT WITH IN DIRECTORS' REPORT

PART I

MATTERS OF A GENERAL NATURE

Asset values

1.—(1) If significant changes in the fixed assets of the company or of any of its subsidiaries have occurred in the financial year, the report shall contain particulars of the changes.

(2) If, in the case of such of those assets as consist in interests in land, their market value (as at the end of the financial year) differs substantially from the amount at which they are included in the balance sheet, and the difference is, in the directors' opinion, of such significance as to require that the attention of members of the company or of holders of its debentures should be drawn to it, the report shall indicate the difference with such degree of precision as is practicable.

Directors' interests

2.—(1) The report shall state the following, with respect to each person who, at the end of the financial year, was a director of the company—

(a) whether or not, according to the register kept by the company for the purposes of sections 324 to 328 of this Act (director's obligation to notify his interests in the company and companies in the same group), he was at the end of that year interested in shares in, or debentures of, the company or any other body corporate, being the company's subsidiary or holding company or a subsidiary of the company's holding company;

(b) if he was so interested—

(i) the number and amount of shares in, and debentures of, each body (specifying it) in which, according to that register, he was then interested,

846

(ii) whether or not (according to that register) he was, at the beginning of that year (or, if he was not then a director, when he became one), interested in shares in, or debentures of, the company or any other such body corporate, and

(iii) if he was, the number and amount of shares in, and debentures of, each body (specifying it) in which, according to that register, he was interested at the beginning of the financial year or (as the case may be) when he became a director.

(2) An interest in shares or debentures which, under sections 324 to 328, falls to be treated as being the interest of a director is so treated for the purposes of this paragraph ; and the references above to the time when a person became a director, in the case of a person who became a director on more than one occasion, is to the time when he first became a director.

(3) The particulars required by this paragraph may be given by way of notes to the company's accounts in respect of the financial year, instead of being stated in the directors' report.

Political and charitable gifts

3.—(1) The following applies if the company (not being the wholly-owned subsidiary of a company incorporated in Great Britain) has in the financial year given money for political purposes or charitable purposes or both.

(2) If the money given exceeded £200 in amount, there shall be contained in the directors' report for the year—

    (*a*) in the case of each of the purposes for which money has been given, a statement of the amount of money given for that purpose, and

    (*b*) in the case of political purposes for which money has been given, the following particulars (so far as applicable)—

        (i) the name of each person to whom money has been given for those purposes exceeding £200 in amount and the amount of money given,

        (ii) if money exceeding £200 in amount has been given by way of donation or subscription to a political party, the identity of the party and the amount of money given.

4.—(1) Paragraph 3 does not apply to a company which, at the end of the financial year, has subsidiaries which have, in that year. given money as mentioned above, but is not itself the wholly-owned subsidiary of a company incorporated in Great Britain.

(2) But in such a case there shall (if the amount of money so given in that year by the company and the subsidiaries between them exceeds £200) be contained in the directors' report for the year—

    (*a*) in the case of each of the purposes for which money has been given by the company and the subsidiaries between them, a statement of the amount of money given for that purpose, and

    (b) in the case of political purposes for which money has been given, the like particulars (so far as applicable) as are required by paragraph 3.

5.—(1) The following applies for the interpretation of paragraphs 3 and 4.

(2) A company is to be treated as giving money for political purposes if, directly or indirectly—

    (a) it gives a donation or subscription to a political party of the United Kingdom or any part of it ; or

    (b) it gives a donation or subscription to a person who, to the company's knowledge, is carrying on, or proposing to carry on, any activities which can, at the time at which the donation or subscription was given, reasonably be regarded as likely to affect public support for such a political party as is mentioned above.

(3) Money given for charitable purposes to a person who, when it was given, was ordinarily resident outside the United Kingdom is to be left out of account.

(4) " Charitable purposes " means purposes which are exclusively charitable ; and, as respects Scotland, " charitable " is to be construed as if it were contained in the Income Tax Acts.

Miscellaneous

6. The directors' report shall contain—

    (a) particulars of any important events affecting the company or any of its subsidiaries which have occurred since the end of the financial year,

    (b) an indication of likely future developments in the business of the company and of its subsidiaries, and

    (c) an indication of the activities (if any) of the company and its subsidiaries in the field of research and development.

PART II

DISCLOSURE REQUIRED BY COMPANY ACQUIRING ITS OWN SHARES, ETC.

7. This Part of this Schedule applies where shares in a company—

    (a) are purchased by the company or are acquired by it by forfeiture or surrender in lieu of forfeiture, or in pursuance of section 143(3) of this Act (acquisition of own shares by company limited by shares), or

    (b) are acquired by another person in circumstances where paragraph (c) or (d) of section 146(1) applies (acquisition by company's nominee, or by another with company financial assistance, the company having a beneficial interest), or

(c) are made subject to a lien or other charge taken (whether
    expressly or otherwise) by the company and permitted by
    section 150(2) or (4), or section 6(3) of the Consequential
    Provisions Act (exceptions from general rule against a
    company having a lien or charge on its own shares).

8. The directors' report with respect to a financial year shall
state—

  (a) the number and nominal value of the shares so purchased,
      the aggregate amount of the consideration paid by the
      company for such shares and the reasons for their purchase ;

  (b) the number and nominal value of the shares so acquired
      by the company, acquired by another person in such cir-
      cumstances and so charged respectively during the financial
      year ;

  (c) the maximum number and nominal value of shares which,
      having been so acquired by the company, acquired by
      another person in such circumstances or so charged (whether
      or not during that year) are held at any time by the com-
      pany or that other person during that year ;

  (d) the number and nominal value of the shares so acquired by
      the company, acquired by another person in such circum-
      stances or so charged (whether or not during that year)
      which are disposed of by the company or that other person
      or cancelled by the company during that year ;

  (e) where the number and nominal value of the shares of any
      particular description are stated in pursuance of any of
      the preceding sub-paragraphs, the percentage of the called-
      up share capital which shares of that description repre-
      sent ;

  (f) where any of the shares have been so charged the amount
      of the charge in each case ; and

  (g) where any of the shares have been disposed of by the
      company or the person who acquired them in such circum-
      stances for money or money's worth the amount or value
      of the consideration in each case.

PART III

DISCLOSURE CONCERNING EMPLOYMENT, ETC,
OF DISABLED PERSONS

9.—(1) This Part of this Schedule applies to the directors' report
where the average number of persons employed by the company in
each week during the financial year exceeded 250.

(2) That average number is the quotient derived by dividing,
by the number of weeks in the financial year, the number derived
by ascertaining, in relation to each of those weeks, the number of
persons who, under contracts of service, were employed in the week
(whether throughout it or not) by the company, and adding up the
numbers ascertained.

(3) The directors' report shall in that case contain a statement describing such policy as the company has applied during the financial year—

(*a*) for giving full and fair consideration to applications for employment by the company made by disabled persons, having regard to their particular aptitudes and abilities,

(*b*) for continuing the employment of, and for arranging appropriate training for, employees of the company who have become disabled persons during the period when they were employed by the company, and

(*c*) otherwise for the training, career development and promotion of disabled persons employed by the company.

(4) In this Part—

(*a*) " employment " means employment other than employment to work wholly or mainly outside the United Kingdom, and " employed " and " employee " shall be construed accordingly ; and

1944 c. 10.
(*b*) " disabled person " means the same as in the Disabled Persons (Employment) Act 1944.

PART IV

HEALTH, SAFETY AND WELFARE AT WORK OF COMPANY'S EMPLOYEES

10.—(1) In the case of companies of such classes as may be prescribed by regulations made by the Secretary of State, the directors' report shall contain such information as may be so prescribed about the arrangements in force in the financial year for securing the health, safety and welfare at work of employees of the company and its subsidiaries, and for protecting other persons against risks to health or safety arising out of or in connection with the activities at work of those employees.

(2) Regulations under this Part may—

(*a*) make different provision in relation to companies of different classes,

(*b*) enable any requirements of the regulations to be dispensed with or modified in particular cases by any specified person or by any person authorised in that behalf by a specified authority,

(*c*) contain such transitional provisions as the Secretary of State thinks necessary or expedient in connection with any provision made by the regulations.

(3) The power to make regulations under this paragraph is exercisable by statutory instrument subject to annulment in pursuance of a resolution of either House of Parliament.

1974 c. 37.
(4) Any expression used in sub-paragraph (1) above and in Part I of the Health and Safety at Work etc. Act 1974 has the same meaning

here as it has in that Part of that Act ; section 1(3) of that Act
applies for interpreting that sub-paragraph ; and in sub-paragraph (2)
" specified " means specified in regulations made under that sub-
paragraph.

Part V
Employee Involvement

11.—(1) This Part of this Schedule applies to the directors' report
where the average number of persons employed by the company in
each week during the financial year exceeded 250.

(2) That average number is the quotient derived by dividing by the
number of weeks in the financial year the number derived by ascertaining, in relation to each of those weeks, the number of persons who,
under contracts of service, were employed in the week (whether
throughout it or not) by the company, and adding up the numbers
ascertained.

(3) The directors' report shall in that case contain a statement describing the action that has been taken during the financial year to
introduce, maintain or develop arrangements aimed at—

(a) providing employees systematically with information on
matters of concern to them as employees,

(b) consulting employees or their representatives on a regular
basis so that the views of employees can be taken into
account in making decisions which are likely to affect their
interests,

(c) encouraging the involvement of employees in the company's
performance through an employees' share scheme or by
some other means,

(d) achieving a common awareness on the part of all employees
of the financial and economic factors affecting the performance of the company.

(4) In sub-paragraph (3) " employee " does not include a person
employed to work wholly or mainly outside the United Kingdom ;
and for the purposes of sub-paragraph (2) no regard is to be had to
such a person.

SCHEDULE 8
Modified Accounts of Companies Qualifying as Small or Medium Sized

Part I
Modified Individual Accounts

Introductory

1. In this Part of this Schedule—

(a) paragraphs 2 to 6 relate to a company's individual accounts
modified as for a small company,

(*b*) paragraphs 7 and 8 relate to a company's individual accounts modified as for a medium-sized company, and

(*c*) paragraphs 9 to 11 relate to both cases.

Accounts modified as for a small company

2.—(1) In respect of the relevant financial year, there may be delivered a copy of a modified balance sheet, instead of the full balance sheet.

(2) The modified balance sheet shall be an abbreviated version of the full balance sheet, showing only those items to which a letter or Roman number is assigned in the balance sheet format adopted under Schedule 4, Part I, but in other respects corresponding to the full balance sheet.

(3) The copy of the modified balance sheet shall be signed as required by section 238.

3. A copy of the company's profit and loss account need not be delivered, nor a copy of the directors' report otherwise required by section 241.

4. The information required by Parts V and VI of Schedule 5 need not be given.

5. The information required by Schedule 4 to be given in notes to the accounts need not be given, with the exception of any information required by the following provisions of that Schedule—

paragraph 36 (accounting policies),

paragraph 38 (share capital),

paragraph 39 (particulars of allotments),

paragraph 48(1) and (4) (particulars of debts),

paragraph 58(1) (basis of translation of foreign currency amounts into sterling), and

paragraph 58(2) (corresponding amounts for preceding financial year) ;

and the reference here to paragraph 58(2) includes that sub-paragraph as applied to any item stated in a note to the company's accounts, whether by virtue of a requirement of Schedule 4 or under any other provision of this Act.

6. If a modified balance sheet is delivered, there shall be disclosed in it (or in a note to the company's accounts delivered)—

(*a*) the aggregate of the amounts required by note (5) of the notes on the balance sheet formats set out in Schedule 4 Part I to be shown separately for each item included under debtors (amounts falling due after one year), and

(*b*) the aggregate of the amounts required by note (*13*) of those notes to be shown separately for each item included under creditors in Format 2 (amounts falling due within one year or after more than one year).

Accounts modified as for a medium-sized company

7.—(1) There may be delivered a copy of a modified profit and loss account, instead of the company's full profit and loss account (that is, the profit and loss account prepared as under section 227).

(2) The modified profit and loss account shall, save for one exception, correspond to the full profit and loss account; and that exception is the combination as one item, under the heading "gross profit or loss", of the following items listed in the profit and loss account formats set out in Schedule 4 Part I—

Items 1, 2, 3 and 6 in Format 1;

Items 1 to 5 in Format 2;

Items A.1, B.1 and B.2 in Format 3; and

Items A.1, A.2 and B.1 to B.4 in Format 4.

8. The information required by paragraph 55 of Schedule 4 (particulars of turnover) need not be given.

Both cases

9. The company's balance sheet shall contain a statement by the directors that—

(a) they rely on sections 247 to 249 of this Act as entitling them to deliver modified accounts, and

(b) they do so on the ground that the company is entitled to the benefit of those sections as a small or (as the case may be) a medium-sized company;

and the statement shall appear in the balance sheet immediately above the signatures of the directors.

10.—(1) The accounts delivered shall be accompanied by a special report of the auditors stating that in their opinion—

(a) the directors are entitled to deliver modified accounts in respect of the financial year, as claimed in the directors' statement, and

(b) any accounts comprised in the documents delivered as modified accounts are properly prepared as such in accordance with this Schedule.

(2) A copy of the auditors' report under section 236 need not be delivered; but the full text of it shall be reproduced in the special report under this paragraph.

(3) If the directors propose to rely on sections 247 to 249 as entitling them to deliver modified accounts, it is the auditors' duty to provide them with a report stating whether in their opinion the directors are so entitled, and whether the documents to be delivered as modified accounts are properly prepared in accordance with this Act.

11. Subject as above, where the directors rely on sections 247 to 249 in delivering any documents, and—

(a) the company is entitled to the benefit of those sections on the ground claimed by the directors in their statement under paragraph 9, and

(*b*) the accounts comprised in the documents delivered as modified accounts are properly prepared in accordance with
this Schedule,

then section 241(3) has effect as if any document which by virtue
of this Part of this Schedule is included in or omitted from
the documents delivered as modified accounts were (or, as the case
may be, were not) required by this Act to be comprised in the company's accounts in respect of the financial year.

PART II

MODIFIED GROUP ACCOUNTS (IN CONSOLIDATED FORM)

Introductory

12. In this Part of this Schedule—

(*a*) paragraphs 13 to 17 relate to modified accounts for a small
group, and

(*b*) paragraphs 18 and 19 relate to modified accounts for a
medium-sized group.

Small groups

13.—(1) In respect of the relevant financial year, there may be
delivered a copy of a modified balance sheet, instead of the full
consolidated balance sheet.

(2) The modified balance sheet shall be an abbreviated version of
the full consolidated balance sheet, showing only those items to which
a letter or Roman numeral is assigned in the balance sheet format
adopted under Schedule 4 Part I, but in other respects corresponding to the full consolidated balance sheet.

14. A copy of the profit and loss account need not be delivered,
nor a copy of the directors' report otherwise required by section 241.

15. The information required by Schedule 4 to be given in
notes to group accounts need not be given, with the exception
of any information required by provisions of that Schedule listed in
paragraph 5 above.

16. There shall be disclosed in the modified balance sheet, or in
a note to the group accounts delivered, aggregate amounts corresponding to those specified in paragraph 6 above.

17. The information required by Parts V and VI of Schedule 5
need not be given.

Medium-sized groups

18.—(1) There may be delivered a copy of a modified profit and
loss account, instead of a full consolidated profit and loss account
prepared as under section 229.

(2) The modified profit and loss account shall, save for one
exception, correspond to the full consolidated profit and loss

account ; and that exception is the combination as one item, under the heading " gross profit or loss ", of the items listed in the profit and loss account formats set out in Schedule 4 Part I which are specified in paragraph 7(2) above.

19. The information required by paragraph 55 of Schedule 4 (particulars of turnover) need not be given.

PART III

MODIFIED GROUP ACCOUNTS (CONSOLIDATED OR OTHER)

20. If modified group accounts are delivered, the following paragraphs apply.

21. The directors' statement required by paragraph 9 to be contained in the balance sheet shall include a statement that the documents delivered include modified group accounts, in reliance on section 250.

22.—(1) The auditors' special report under paragraph 10 shall include a statement that in their opinion—

    (*a*) the directors are entitled to deliver modified group accounts, as claimed in their statement in the balance sheet, and

    (*b*) any accounts comprised in the documents delivered as modified group accounts are properly prepared as such in accordance with this Schedule.

(2) A copy of the auditors' report under section 236 need not be delivered ; but the full text of it shall be reproduced in the special report under paragraph 10.

(3) If the directors propose to rely on section 250 as entitling them to deliver modified group accounts, it is the auditors' duty to provide them with a report stating whether in their opinion the directors are so entitled, and whether the documents to be delivered as modified group accounts are properly prepared in accordance with this Schedule.

23. Subject as above, where the directors rely on section 250 in delivering any documents, and

    (*a*) the company is entitled to the benefit of that section on the ground claimed by the directors in their statement in the balance sheet, and

    (*b*) the accounts comprised in the documents delivered as modified accounts are properly prepared in accordance with this Schedule,

then section 241(3) has effect as if any document which by virtue of this Schedule is included in or omitted from the documents delivered as modified group accounts were (or, as the case may be, were not) required by this Act to be comprised in the company's accounts in respect of the financial year.

SCHEDULE 9

FORM AND CONTENT OF SPECIAL CATEGORY ACCOUNTS

Preliminary

1. Paragraphs 2 to 13 of this Schedule apply to the balance sheet and 14 to 18 to the profit and loss account, and are subject to the exceptions and modifications provided for by Part II of this Schedule in the case of a holding or subsidiary company and by Part III thereof in the case of companies of the classes there mentioned.

PART I

GENERAL PROVISIONS AS TO BALANCE SHEET AND PROFIT AND LOSS ACCOUNT

Balance sheet

2. The authorised share capital, issued share capital, liabilities and assets shall be summarised, with such particulars as are necessary to disclose the general nature of the assets and liabilities, and there shall be specified—

   (a) any part of the issued capital that consists of redeemable shares, the earliest and latest dates on which the company has power to redeem those shares, whether those shares must be redeemed in any event or are liable to be redeemed at the option of the company or of the shareholder and whether any (and, if so, what) premium is payable on redemption ;

   (b) so far as the information is not given in the profit and loss account, any share capital on which interest has been paid out of capital during the financial year, and the rate at which interest has been so paid ;

   (c) the amount of the share premium account ;

   (d) particulars of any redeemed debentures which the company has power to re-issue.

3. There shall be stated under separate headings, so far as they are not written off,—

   (a) the preliminary expenses ;

   (b) any expenses incurred in connection with any issue of share capital or debentures ;

   (e) the amount of the discount allowed on any issue of shares or debentures ;

   (d) any sums allowed by way of discount in respect of any debentures ; and

   (e) the amount of the discount allowed on any issue of shares at a discount.

4.—(1) The reserves, provisions, liabilities and assets shall be classified under headings appropriate to the company's business:

Provided that—

(a) where the amount of any class is not material, it may be included under the same heading as some other class ; and

(b) where any assets of one class are not separable from assets of another class, those assets may be included under the same heading.

(2) Fixed assets, current assets and assets that are neither fixed nor current shall be separately identified.

(3) The method or methods used to arrive at the amount of the fixed assets under each heading shall be stated.

5.—(1) The method of arriving at the amount of any fixed asset shall, subject to the next following sub-paragraph, be to take the difference between—

(a) its cost or, if it stands in the company's books at a valuation, the amount of the valuation ; and

(b) the aggregate amount provided or written off since the date of acquisition or valuation, as the case may be, for depreciation or diminution in value ;

and for the purposes of this paragraph the net amount at which any assets stood in the company's books on 1st July 1948 (after deduction of the amounts previously provided or written off for depreciation or diminution in value) shall, if the figures relating to the period before that date cannot be obtained without unreasonable expense or delay, be treated as if it were the amount of a valuation of those assets made at that date and, where any of those assets are sold, the said net amount less the amount of the sales shall be treated as if it were the amount of a valuation so made of the remaining assets.

(2) The foregoing sub-paragraph shall not apply—

(a) to assets for which the figures relating to the period beginning with 1st July 1948 cannot be obtained without unreasonable expense or delay ; or

(b) to assets the replacement of which is provided for wholly or partly—

(i) by making provision for renewals and charging the cost of replacement against the provision so made ; or

(ii) by charging the cost of replacement direct to revenue ; or

(c) to any listed investments or to any unlisted investments of which the value as estimated by the directors is shown either as the amount of the investments or by way of note ; or

(d) to goodwill, patents or trade marks.

(3) For the assets under each heading whose amount is arrived at in accordance with sub-paragraph (1) of this paragraph, there shall be shown—

(a) the aggregate of the amounts referred to in paragraph (a) of that sub-paragraph ; and

(b) the aggregate of the amounts referred to in paragraph (b) thereof.

(4) As respects the assets under each heading whose amount is not arrived at in accordance with the said sub-paragraph (1) because their replacement is provided for as mentioned in sub-paragraph (2)(b) of this paragraph, there shall be stated—

(a) the means by which their replacement is provided for ; and

(b) the aggregate amount of the provision (if any) made for renewals and not used.

6. In the case of unlisted investments consisting in equity share capital of other bodies corporate (other than any whose values as estimated by the directors are separately shown, either individually or collectively or as to some individually and as to the rest collectively, and are so shown either as the amount thereof, or by way of note), the matters referred to in the following heads shall, if not otherwise shown, be stated by way of note or in a statement or report annexed : —

(a) the aggregate amount of the company's income for the financial year that is ascribable to the investments ;

(b) the amount of the company's share before taxation, and the amount of that share after taxation, of the net aggregate amount of the profits of the bodies in which the investments are held, being profits for the several periods to which accounts sent by them during the financial year to the company related, after deducting those bodies' losses for those periods (or vice versa) ;

(c) the amount of the company's share of the net aggregate amount of the undistributed profits accumulated by the bodies in which the investments are held since the time when the investments were acquired after deducting the losses accumulated by them since that time (or vice versa) ;

(d) the manner in which any losses incurred by the said bodies have been dealt with in the company's accounts.

7. The aggregate amounts respectively of reserves and provisions (other than provisions for depreciation, renewals or diminution in value of assets) shall be stated under separate headings ;

Provided that—

(a) this paragraph shall not require a separate statement of either of the said amounts which is not material ; and

(b) the Secretary of State may direct that a separate statement shall not be required of the amount of provisions where he is satisfied that that is not required in the public interest and would prejudice the company, but subject to the condition that any heading stating an amount arrived at after taking into account a provision (other than as aforesaid) shall be so framed or marked as to indicate that fact.

8.—(1) There shall also be shown (unless it is shown in the profit and loss account or a statement or report annexed thereto, or the amount involved is not material)—

(*a*) where the amount of the reserves or of the provisions (other than provisions for depreciation, renewals or diminution in value of assets) shows an increase as compared with the amount at the end of the immediately preceding financial year, the source from which the amount of the increase has been derived ; and

(*b*) where—

(i) the amount of the reserves shows a decrease as compared with the amount at the end of the immediately preceding financial year ; or

(ii) the amount at the end of the immediately preceding financial year of the provisions (other than provisions for depreciation, renewals or diminution in value of assets) exceeded the aggregate of the sums since applied and amounts still retained for the purposes thereof ;

the application of the amounts derived from the difference.

(2) Where the heading showing the reserves or any of the provisions aforesaid is divided into sub-headings, this paragraph shall apply to each of the separate amounts shown in the sub-headings instead of applying to the aggregate amount thereof.

9. If an amount is set aside for the purpose of its being used to prevent undue fluctuations in charges for taxation, it shall be stated.

10.—(1) There shall be shown under separate headings—

(*a*) the aggregate amounts respectively of the company's listed investments and unlisted investments ;

(*b*) if the amount of the goodwill and of any patents and trade marks or part of that amount is shown as a separate item in or is otherwise ascertainable from the books of the company, or from any contract for the sale or purchase of any property to be acquired by the company, or from any documents in the possession of the company relating to the stamp duty payable in respect of any such contract or the conveyance of any such property, the said amount so shown or ascertained as far as not written off or, as the case may be, the said amount so far as it is so shown or ascertainable and as so shown or ascertained, as the case may be ;

(*c*) the aggregate amount of any outstanding loans made under the authority of section 153(4)(*b*) or (*c*) or 155 of this Act ;

(d) the aggregate amount of bank loans and overdrafts and the aggregate amount of loans made to the company which—

(i) are repayable otherwise than by instalments and fall due for repayment after the expiration of the period of five years beginning with the day next following the expiration of the financial year ; or

(ii) are repayable by instalments any of which fall due for payment after the expiration of that period ;

not being, in either case, bank loans or overdrafts ;

(e) the aggregate amount which is recommended for distribution by way of dividend.

(2) Nothing in head (b) of the foregoing sub-paragraph shall be taken as requiring the amount of the goodwill, patents and trade marks to be stated otherwise than as a single item.

(3) The heading showing the amount of the listed investments shall be subdivided, where necessary, to distinguish the investments as respects which there has, and those as respects which there has not, been granted a listing on a recognised stock exchange.

(4) In relation to each loan falling within head (d) of sub-paragraph (1) of this paragraph (other than a bank loan or overdraft), there shall be stated by way of note (if not otherwise stated) the terms on which it is repayable and the rate at which interest is payable thereon:

Provided that if the number of loans is such that, in the opinion of the directors, compliance with the foregoing requirement would result in a statement of excessive length, it shall be sufficient to give a general indication of the terms on which the loans are repayable and the rates at which interest is payable thereon.

11. Where any liability of the company is secured otherwise than by operation of law on any assets of the company, the fact that that liability is so secured shall be stated, but it shall not be necessary to specify the assets on which the liability is secured.

12. Where any of the company's debentures are held by a nominee of or trustee for the company, the nominal amount of the debentures and the amount at which they are stated in the books of the company shall be stated.

13.—(1) The matters referred to in the following sub-paragraphs shall be stated by way of note, or in a statement or report annexed, if not otherwise shown.

(2) The number, description and amount of any shares in the company which any person has an option to subscribe for, together with the following particulars of the option, that is to say—

(a) the period during which it is exercisable ;

(b) the price to be paid for shares subscribed for under it.

(3) Where shares in a public company (other than an old public company within the meaning of section 1 of the Consequential

Provisions Act) are purchased or are acquired by the company by forfeiture or surrender in lieu of forfeiture, or as expressly permitted by section 143(3) of this Act, or are acquired by another person in circumstances where paragraph (c) or (d) of section 146(1) applies or are made subject to a lien or charge taken (whether expressly or otherwise) by the company and permitted by section 150(2) or (4), or section 6(3) of the Consequential Provisions Act—

(a) the number and nominal value of the shares so purchased, the aggregate amount of the consideration paid by the company for such shares and the reasons for their purchase ;

(b) the number and nominal value of the shares so acquired by the company, acquired by another person in such circumstances and so charged respectively during the financial year ;

(c) the maximum number and nominal value of shares which, having been so acquired by the company, acquired by another person in such circumstances or so charged (whether or not during the financial year) are held at any time by the company or that other person during that year ;

(d) the number and nominal value of shares so acquired by the company, acquired by another person in such circumstances or so charged (whether or not during that year) which are disposed of by the company or that other person or cancelled by the company during that year ;

(e) where the number and nominal value of the shares of any particular description are stated in pursuance of any of the preceding paragraphs, the percentage of the called-up share capital which shares of that description represent ;

(f) where any of the shares have been so charged, the amount of the charge in each case ;

(g) where any of the shares have been disposed of by the company or the person who acquired them in such circumstances for money or money's worth, the amount or value of the consideration in each case.

(4) Any distribution made by an investment company within the meaning of Part VIII of this Act which reduces the amount of its net assets to less than the aggregate of its called-up share capital and undistributable reserves.

For purposes of this sub-paragraph, a company's net assets are the aggregate of its assets less the aggregate of its liabilities ; and " undistributable reserves " has the meaning given by section 264(3).

(5) The amount of any arrears of fixed cumulative dividends on the company's shares and the period for which the dividends or, if there is more than one class, each class of them are in arrear.

(6) Particulars of any charge on the assets of the company to secure the liabilities of any other person, including, where practicable, the amount secured.

(7) The general nature of any other contingent liabilities not provided for and, where practicable, the aggregate amount or estimated amount of those liabilities, if it is material.

(8) Where practicable the aggregate amount or estimated amount, if it is material, of contracts for capital expenditure, so far as not provided for and, where practicable, the aggregate amount or estimated amount, if it is material, of capital expenditure authorised by the directors which has not been contracted for.

(9) In the case of fixed assets under any heading whose amount is required to be arrived at in accordance with paragraph 5(1) of this Schedule (other than unlisted investments) and is so arrived at by reference to a valuation, the years (so far as they are known to the directors) in which the assets were severally valued and the several values, and, in the case of assets that have been valued during the financial year, the names of the persons who valued them or particulars of their qualifications for doing so and (whichever is stated) the bases of valuation used by them.

(10) If there are included amongst fixed assets under any heading (other than investments) assets that have been acquired during the financial year, the aggregate amount of the assets acquired as determined for the purpose of making up the balance sheet, and if during that year any fixed assets included under a heading in the balance sheet made up with respect to the immediately preceding financial year (other than investments) have been disposed of or destroyed, the aggregate amount thereof as determined for the purpose of making up that balance sheet.

(11) Of the amount of fixed assets consisting of land, how much is ascribable to land of freehold tenure and how much to land of leasehold tenure, and, of the latter, how much is ascribable to land held on long lease and how much to land held on short lease.

(12) If in the opinion of the directors any of the current assets have not a value, on realisation in the ordinary course of the company's business, at least equal to the amount at which they are stated, the fact that the directors are of that opinion.

(13) The aggregate market value of the company's listed investments where it differs from the amount of the investments as stated and the stock exchange value of any investments of which the market value is shown (whether separately or not) and is taken as being higher than their stock exchange value.

(14) If a sum set aside for the purpose of its being used to prevent undue fluctuations in charges for taxation has been used during the financial year for another purpose, the amount thereof and the fact that it has been so used.

(15) If the amount carried forward for stock in trade or work in progress is material for the appreciation by its members of the company's state of affairs or of its profit or loss for the financial year, the manner in which that amount has been computed.

(16) The basis on which foreign currencies have been converted into sterling, where the amount of the assets or liabilities affected is material.

(17) The basis on which the amount, if any, set aside for United Kingdom corporation tax is computed.

(18) The corresponding amounts at the end of the immediately preceding financial year for all items shown in the balance sheet other than any item the amount for which is shown—

(a) in pursuance of sub-paragraph (10) of this paragraph, or

(b) as an amount the source or application of which is required by paragraph 8 to be shown.

Profit and loss account

14.—(1) There shall be shown—

(a) the amount charged to revenue by way of provision for depreciation, renewals or diminution in value of fixed assets ;

(b) the amount of the interest on loans of the following kinds made to the company (whether on the security of debentures or not), namely, bank loans, overdrafts and loans which, not being bank loans or overdrafts,—

(i) are repayable otherwise than by instalments and fall due for repayment before the expiration of the period of five years beginning with the day next following the expiration of the financial year ; or

(ii) are repayable by instalments the last of which falls due for payment before the expiration of that period ;

and the amount of the interest on loans of other kinds so made (whether on the security of debentures or not) ;

(c) the amount of the charge to revenue for United Kingdom corporation tax and, if that amount would have been greater but for relief from double taxation, the amount which it would have been but for such relief, the amount of the charge for United Kingdom income tax, and the amount of the charge for taxation imposed outside the United Kingdom of profits, income and (so far as charged to revenue) capital gains ;

(d) the amounts respectively set aside for redemption of share capital and for redemption of loans ;

(e) the amount, if material, set aside or proposed to be set aside to, or withdrawn from, reserves ;

(f) subject to sub-paragraph (2) of this paragraph, the amount, if material, set aside to provisions other than provisions for depreciation, renewals, or diminution in value of assets or, as the case may be, the amount, if material, withdrawn from such provisions and not applied for the purposes thereof ;

(g) the amounts respectively of income from listed investments and income from unlisted investments ;

(h) if a substantial part of the company's revenue for the financial year consists in rents from land, the amount thereof (after deduction of ground-rents, rates and other outgoings);

(j) the amount, if material, charged to revenue in respect of sums payable in respect of the hire of plant and machinery;

(k) the aggregate amount of the dividends paid and proposed.

(2) The Secretary of State may direct that a company shall not be obliged to show an amount set aside to provisions in accordance with sub-paragraph (1)(f) of this paragraph, if he is satisfied that that is not required in the public interest and would prejudice the company, but subject to the condition that any heading stating an amount arrived at after taking into account the amount set aside as aforesaid shall be so framed or marked as to indicate that fact.

(3) If, in the case of any assets in whose case an amount is charged to revenue by way of provision for depreciation or diminution in value, an amount is also so charged by way of provision for renewal thereof, the last-mentioned amount shall be shown separately.

(4) If the amount charged to revenue by way of provision for depreciation or diminution in value of any fixed assets (other than investments) has been determined otherwise than by reference to the amount of those assets as determined for the purpose of making up the balance sheet, that fact shall be stated.

15. The amount of any charge arising in consequence of the occurrence of an event in a preceding financial year and of any credit so arising shall, if not included in a heading relating to other matters, be stated under a separate heading.

16. The amount of the remuneration of the auditors shall be shown under a separate heading, and for the purposes of this paragraph, any sums paid by the company in respect of the auditors' expenses shall be deemed to be included in the expression "remuneration".

17.—(1) The following matters shall be stated by way of note, if not otherwise shown.

(2) The turnover for the financial year, except in so far as it is attributable to the business of banking or discounting or to business of such other class as may be prescribed for the purposes of this sub-paragraph.

(3) If some or all of the turnover is omitted by reason of its being attributable as aforesaid, the fact that it is so omitted.

(4) The method by which turnover stated is arrived at.

(5) A company shall not be subject to the requirements of this paragraph if it is neither a holding company nor a subsidiary of another body corporate and the turnover which, apart from this sub-paragraph, would be required to be stated does not exceed £1 million.

18.—(1) The following matters shall be stated by way of note, if not otherwise shown.

(2) If depreciation or replacement of fixed assets is provided for by some method other than a depreciation charge or provision for renewals, or is not provided for, the method by which it is provided for or the fact that it is not provided for, as the case may be.

(3) The basis on which the charge for United Kingdom corporation tax and United Kingdom income tax is computed.

(4) Any special circumstances which affect liability in respect of taxation of profits, income or capital gains for the financial year or liability in respect of taxation of profits, income or capital gains for succeeding financial years.

(5) The corresponding amounts for the immediately preceding financial year for all items shown in the profit and loss account.

(6) Any material respects in which items shown in the profit and loss account are affected—

(a) by transactions of a sort not usually undertaken by the company or otherwise by circumstances of an exceptional or non-recurrent nature ; or

(b) by any change in the basis of accounting.

PART II

SPECIAL PROVISIONS WHERE THE COMPANY IS A HOLDING OR SUBSIDIARY COMPANY

Modifications of and additions to requirements as to company's own accounts

19.—(1) This paragraph applies where the company is a holding company, whether or not it is itself a subsidiary of another body corporate.

(2) The aggregate amount of assets consisting of shares in, or amounts owing (whether on account of a loan or otherwise) from, the company's subsidiaries, distinguishing shares from indebtedness, shall be set out in the balance sheet separately from all the other assets of the company, and the aggregate amount of indebtedness (whether on account of a loan or otherwise) to the company's subsidiaries shall be so set out separately from all its other liabilities and—

(a) the references in Part I of this Schedule to the company's investments (except those in paragraphs 13(10) and 14(4)) shall not include investments in its subsidiaries required by this paragraph to be separately set out ; and

(b) paragraph 5, sub-paragraph (1)(a) of paragraph 14, and sub-paragraph (2) of paragraph 18 of this Schedule shall not apply in relation to fixed assets consisting of interests in the company's subsidiaries.

(3) There shall be shown by way of note on the balance sheet or in a statement or report annexed thereto the number, description and amount of the shares in and debentures of the company held

by its subsidiaries or their nominees, but excluding any of those shares or debentures in the case of which the subsidiary is concerned as personal representative or in the case of which it is concerned as trustee and neither the company nor any subsidiary thereof is beneficially interested under the trust, otherwise than by way of security only for the purposes of a transaction entered into by it in the ordinary course of a business which includes the lending of money.

Schedule 2 has effect for the interpretation of the reference in this sub-paragraph to a beneficial interest under a trust.

(4) Where group accounts are not submitted, there shall be annexed to the balance sheet a statement showing—

> (a) the reasons why subsidiaries are not dealt with in group accounts ;
>
> (b) the net aggregate amount, so far as it concerns members of the holding company and is not dealt with in the company's accounts, of the subsidiaries' profits after deducting the subsidiaries' losses (or vice versa)—
>
>> (i) for the respective financial years of the subsidiaries ending with or during the financial year of the company ; and
>>
>> (ii) for their previous financial years since they respectively became the holding company's subsidiary ;
>
> (c) the net aggregate amount of the subsidiaries' profits after deducting the subsidiaries' losses (or vice versa)—
>
>> (i) for the respective financial years of the subsidiaries ending with or during the financial year of the company ; and
>>
>> (ii) for their other financial years since they respectively became the holding company's subsidiary ;
>
> so far as those profits are dealt with, or provision is made for those losses, in the company's accounts ;
>
> (d) any qualifications contained in the report of the auditors of the subsidiaries on their accounts for their respective financial years ending as aforesaid, and any note or saving contained in those accounts to call attention to a matter which, apart from the note or saving, would properly have been referred to in such a qualification, in so far as the matter which is the subject of the qualification or note is not covered by the company's own accounts and is material from the point of view of its members ;

or, in so far as the information required by this sub-paragraph is not obtainable, a statement that it is not obtainable:

Provided that the Secretary of State may, on the application or with the consent of the company's directors, direct that in relation to any subsidiary this sub-paragraph shall not apply or shall apply only to such extent as may be provided by the direction.

(5) Paragraphs (b) and (c) of the last foregoing sub-paragraph shall apply only to profits and losses of a subsidiary which may properly be treated in the holding company's accounts as revenue profits or

losses, and the profits or losses attributable to any shares in a subsidiary for the time being held by the holding company or any other of its subsidiaries shall not (for the purposes of those paragraphs) be treated as aforesaid so far as they are profits or losses for the period before the date on or as from which the shares were acquired by the company or any of its subsidiaries, except that they may in a proper case be so treated where—

(a) the company is itself the subsidiary of another body corporate ; and

(b) the shares were acquired from that body corporate or a subsidiary of it ;

and for the purpose of determining whether any profits or losses are to be treated as profits or losses for the said period the profit or loss for any financial year of the subsidiary may, if it is not practicable to apportion it with reasonable accuracy by reference to the facts, be treated as accruing from day to day during that year and be apportioned accordingly.

The amendment of the previous corresponding provision by section 40(3) of the Companies Act 1981 (substituting " (for the purposes of those paragraphs) " for " (for that or any other purpose) ") is without prejudice to any other restriction with respect to the manner in which a holding company may treat pre-acquisition profits or losses of a subsidiary in its accounts. 1981 c. 62.

(6) Paragraphs (b) and (c) of sub-paragraph (4) above shall not apply where the company is a wholly-owned subsidiary of another body corporate incorporated in Great Britain if there is annexed to the balance sheet a statement that in the opinion of the directors of the company the aggregate value of the assets of the company consisting of shares in, or amounts owing (whether on account of a loan or otherwise) from, the company's subsidiaries is not less than the aggregate of the amounts at which those assets are stated or included in the balance sheet.

(7) Where group accounts are not submitted, there shall be annexed to the balance sheet a statement showing, in relation to the subsidiaries (if any) whose financial years did not end with that of the company—

(a) the reasons why the company's directors consider that the subsidiaries' financial years should not end with that of the company ; and

(b) the dates on which the subsidiaries' financial years ending last before that of the company respectively ended or the earliest and latest of those dates.

20.—(1) The balance sheet of a company which is a subsidiary of another body corporate, whether or not it is itself a holding company, shall show the aggregate amount of its indebtedness to all bodies corporate of which it is a subsidiary or a fellow subsidiary and the aggregate amount of indebtedness of all such bodies corporate to it, distinguishing in each case between indebtedness in respect of debentures and otherwise, and the aggregate amount of assets consisting of shares in fellow subsidiaries.

(2) For the purposes of this paragraph a company shall be deemed to be a fellow subsidiary of another body corporate if both are subsidiaries of the same body corporate but neither is the other's.

Consolidated accounts of holding company and subsidiaries

21. Subject to the following paragraphs of this Part of this Schedule the consolidated balance sheet and profit and loss account shall combine the information contained in the separate balance sheets and profit and loss accounts of the holding company and of the subsidiaries dealt with by the consolidated accounts, but with such adjustments (if any) as the directors of the holding company think necessary.

22. Subject as aforesaid and to Part III of this Schedule, the consolidated accounts shall, in giving the said information, comply so far as practicable, with the requirements of this Act as if they were the accounts of an actual company.

23. The following provisions of this Act, namely—

(a) section 231 as applying Schedule 5, but only Parts II, V and VI of that Schedule, and

(b) sections 232 to 234 and Schedule 6, so far as relating to accounts other than group accounts,

do not by virtue of the two last foregoing paragraphs apply for the purpose of the consolidated accounts.

24. Paragraph 22 above is without prejudice to any requirement of this Act which applies (otherwise than by virtue of paragraph 21 or 22) to group accounts.

25. In relation to any subsidiaries of the holding company not dealt with by the consolidated accounts—

(a) sub-paragraphs (2) and (3) of paragraph 19 of this Schedule shall apply for the purpose of those accounts as if those accounts were the accounts of an actual company of which they were subsidiaries ; and

(b) there shall be annexed the like statement as is required by sub-paragraph (4) of that paragraph where there are no group accounts, but as if references therein to the holding company's accounts were references to the consolidated accounts.

26. In relation to any subsidiary (whether or not dealt with by the consolidated accounts), whose financial year did not end with that of the company, there shall be annexed the like statement as is required by sub-paragraph (7) of paragraph 19 of this Schedule where there are no group accounts.

PART III

EXCEPTIONS FOR CERTAIN SPECIAL CATEGORY COMPANIES

27.—(1) The following applies to a banking company (if not subject to the Banking Companies (Accounts) Regulations 1970) which satisfies the Secretary of State that it ought to have the benefit of this paragraph.

(2) The company shall not be subject to the requirements of Part I of this Schedule other than—

    (*a*) as respects its balance sheet, those of paragraphs 2 and 3, paragraph 4 (so far as it relates to assets), paragraph 10 (except sub-paragraphs (1)(*d*) and (4)), paragraphs 11 and 12 and paragraph 13 (except sub-paragraphs (9), (10), (11), (13) and (14)) ; and

    (*b*) as respects its profit and loss account, those of sub-paragraph (1)(*h*) and (*k*) of paragraph 14, paragraphs 15 and 16 and sub-paragraphs (1) and (5) of paragraph 18.

(3) But, where in the company's balance sheet reserves or provisions (other than provisions for depreciation, renewals or diminution in value of assets) are not stated separately, any heading stating an amount arrived at after taking into account a reserve or such a provision shall be so framed or marked as to indicate that fact, and its profit and loss account shall indicate by appropriate words the manner in which the amount stated for the company's profit or loss has been arrived at.

(4) The company's accounts shall not be deemed, by reason only of the fact that they do not comply with any requirements of the said Part I from which the company is exempt by virtue of this paragraph, not to give the true and fair view required by this Act.

28.—(1) An insurance company to which Part II of the Insurance Companies Act 1982 applies shall not be subject to the following requirements of Part I of this Schedule, that is to say— 1982 c. 50.

    (*a*) as respects its balance sheet, those of paragraphs 4 to 8 (both inclusive), sub-paragraphs (1)(*a*) and (3) of paragraph 10 and sub-paragraphs (6), (7) and (9) to (13) (both inclusive) of paragraph 13 ;

    (*b*) as respects its profit and loss account, those of paragraph 14 (except sub-paragraph (1)(*b*), (*c*), (*d*) and (*k*)) and paragraph 18(2) ;

but, where in its balance sheet reserves or provisions (other than provisions for depreciation, renewals or diminution in value of assets) are not stated separately, any heading stating an amount arrived at after taking into account a reserve or such a provision shall be so framed or marked as to indicate that fact, and its profit and loss account shall indicate by appropriate words the manner in which the amount stated for the company's profit or loss has been arrived at:

Provided that the Secretary of State may direct that any such insurance company whose business includes to a substantial extent business other than insurance business shall comply with all the requirements of the said Part I or such of them as may be specified in the direction and shall comply therewith as respects either the whole of its business or such part thereof as may be so specified.

(2) The accounts of a company shall not be deemed, by reason only of the fact that they do not comply with any requirement of Part I of this Schedule from which the company is exempt by virtue

of this paragraph, not to give the true and fair view required by this Act.

29.—(1) A shipping company shall not be subject to the following requirements of Part I of this Schedule, that is to say—

(a) as respects its balance sheet, those of paragraph 4 (except so far as it relates to assets), paragraphs 5, 7 and 8 and sub-paragraphs (9) and (10) of paragraph 13 ;

(b) as respects its profit and loss account, those of sub-paragraph (1)(a), (e) and (f) and sub-paragraphs (3) and (4) of paragraph 14 and paragraph 17.

(2) The accounts of a company shall not be deemed, by reason only of the fact that they do not comply with any requirements of Part I of this Schedule from which the company is exempt by virtue of this paragraph, not to give the true and fair view required by this Act.

30. Where a company entitled to the benefit of any provision contained in this Part of this Schedule is a holding company, the reference in Part II of this Schedule to consolidated accounts complying with the requirements of this Act shall, in relation to consolidated accounts of that company, be construed as referring to those requirements in so far only—

(a) as they apply to the individual accounts of that company, and

(b) as they apply (otherwise than by virtue of paragraphs 21 and 22) to the group accounts prepared by that company.

Part IV

Special Provisions Where the Company Has Entered into Arrangements Subject to Merger Relief

31.—(1) Where during the financial year the company has allotted shares in consideration for the issue, transfer or cancellation of shares in another body corporate (" the other company ") in circumstances where by virtue of section 131(2) (merger relief) section 130 did not apply to the premiums on those shares, the following information shall be given by way of a note to the company's accounts—

(a) the name of the other company ;

(b) the number, nominal value and class of shares so allotted ;

(c) the number, nominal value and class of shares in the other company so issued, transferred or cancelled ;

(d) particulars of the accounting treatment adopted in the company's accounts (including any group accounts) in respect of such issue, transfer or cancellation ; and

(e) where the company prepares group accounts, particulars of the extent to which and manner in which the profit or loss for the year of the group which appears in those accounts is affected by any profit or loss of the other company or any of its subsidiaries which arose at any time before the allotment.

(2) Where the company has during the financial year or during
either of the two financial years immediately preceding it made such
an allotment of shares as is mentioned in sub-paragraph (1) above
and there is included in the company's consolidated profit and loss
account, or if it has no such account, in its individual profit and loss
account, any profit or loss (or part thereof) to which this sub-paragraph applies then the net amount of any such profit or loss (or
part thereof) shall be shown in a note to the accounts together with
an explanation of the transactions to which that information relates.

(3) Sub-paragraph (2) applies—

(a) to any profit or loss realised during the financial year by the
company, or any of its subsidiaries, on the disposal of any
shares in the other company or of any assets which were
fixed assets of the other company, or of any of its subsidiaries, at the time of the allotment; and

(b) to any part of any profit or loss realised during the financial
year by the company, or any of its subsidiaries, on the
disposal of any shares (not being shares in the other
company), which was attributable to the fact that at the
time of the disposal there were amongst the assets of the
company which issued those shares, or any of its subsidiaries,
such shares or assets as are described in paragraph (a)
above.

(4) Where in pursuance of the arrangement in question shares are
allotted on different dates, the time of allotment for the purposes of
sub-paragraphs (1)(e) and (3)(a) above is taken to be—

(a) if the other company becomes a subsidiary of the company
as a result of the arrangement—

(i) if the arrangement becomes binding only upon the
fulfilment of a condition, the date on which that condition is fulfilled, and

(ii) in any other case, the date on which the other company becomes a subsidiary of the company;

(b) if the other company is a subsidiary of the company when
the arrangement is proposed, the date of the first allotment
pursuant to that arrangement.

PART V

INTERPRETATION OF SCHEDULE

32.—(1) For the purposes of this Schedule, unless the context
otherwise requires,—

(a) the expression " provision " shall, subject to sub-paragraph
(2) of this paragraph, mean any amount written off or
retained by way of providing for depreciation, renewals
or diminution in value of assets or retained by way of providing for any known liability of which the amount cannot
be determined with substantial accuracy;

(b) the expression "reserve" shall not, subject as aforesaid,
include any amount written off or retained by way of
providing for depreciation, renewals or diminution in value

of assets or retained by way of providing for any known liability or any sum set aside for the purpose of its being used to prevent undue fluctuations in charges for taxation ;

and in this paragraph the expression " liability " shall include all liabilities in respect of expenditure contracted for and all disputed or contingent liabilities.

(2) Where—

(a) any amount written off or retained by way of providing for depreciation, renewals or diminution in value of assets ; or

(b) any amount retained by way of providing for any known liability ;

is in excess of that which in the opinion of the directors is reasonably necessary for the purpose, the excess shall be treated for the purposes of this Schedule as a reserve and not as a provision.

33. For the purposes aforesaid, the expression " listed investment " means an investment as respects which there has been granted a listing on a recognised stock exchange, or on any stock exchange of repute outside Great Britain and the expression " unlisted investment " shall be construed accordingly.

34. For the purposes aforesaid, the expression " long lease " means a lease in the case of which the portion of the term for which it was granted remaining unexpired at the end of the financial year is not less than fifty years, the expression " short lease " means a lease which is not a long lease and the expression " lease " includes an agreement for a lease.

35. For the purposes aforesaid, a loan shall be deemed to fall due for repayment, and an instalment of a loan shall be deemed to fall due for payment, on the earliest date on which the lender could require repayment or, as the case may be, payment if he exercised all options and rights available to him.

36. In the application of this Schedule to Scotland, " land of freehold tenure " means land in respect of which the company is the proprietor of the *dominium utile* or, in the case of land not held on feudal tenure, is the owner ; " land of leasehold tenure " means land of which the company is the tenant under a lease ; and the reference to ground-rents, rates and other outgoings includes a reference to feu-duty and ground annual.

SCHEDULE 10

ADDITIONAL MATTERS TO BE DEALT WITH IN DIRECTORS' REPORT ATTACHED TO SPECIAL CATEGORY ACCOUNTS

Recent issues

1.—(1) If in the financial year to which the accounts relate the company has issued any shares, the directors' report shall state the reason for making the issue, the classes of shares issued and, as respects each class of shares, the number issued and the consideration received by the company for the issue.

(2) If in that year the company has issued any debentures, the report shall state the reason for making the issue, the classes of debentures issued, and, as respects each class of debentures, the amount issued and the consideration received by the company for the issue.

Turnover and profitability

2. If in the course of the financial year the company (being one subject to the requirements of paragraph 17 of Schedule 9, but not one that has subsidiaries at the end of the year and submits in respect of that year group accounts prepared as consolidated accounts) has carried on business of two or more classes (other than banking or discounting or a class prescribed for the purpose of paragraph 17(2) of that Schedule) that, in the opinion of the directors, differ substantially from each other, there shall be contained in the directors' report a statement of—

(a) the proportions in which the turnover for the year (so far as stated in the accounts in respect of the year in pursuance of that Schedule) is divided amongst those classes (describing them), and

(b) as regards business of each class, the extent or approximate extent (expressed, in either case, in monetary terms) to which, in the opinion of the directors, the carrying on of business of that class contributed to, or restricted, the profit or loss of the company for that year before taxation.

3.—(1) This paragraph applies if—

(a) the company has subsidiaries at the end of the financial year and submits in respect of that year group accounts prepared as consolidated accounts, and

(b) the company and the subsidiaries dealt with by the accounts carried on between them in the course of the year business of two or more classes (other than banking or discounting or a class prescribed for the purposes of paragraph 17(2) of Schedule 9) that, in the opinion of the directors, differ substantially from each other.

(2) There shall be contained in the directors' report a statement of—

(a) the proportions in which the turnover for the financial year (so far as stated in the accounts for that year in pursuance of Schedule 9) is divided amongst those classes (describing them), and

(b) as regards business of each class, the extent or approximate extent (expressed, in either case, in monetary terms) to which, in the opinion of the directors of the company, the carrying on of business of that class contributed to, or restricted, the profit or loss for that year (before taxation) of the company and the subsidiaries dealt with by the accounts.

4. For the purposes of the preceding two paragraphs, classes of business which, in the opinion of the directors, do not differ substantially from each other, are to be treated as one class.

Labour force and wages paid

5.—(1) If at the end of the financial year the company does not have subsidiaries, there shall be contained in the directors' report a statement of—

> (a) the average number of persons employed by the company in each week in the year, and

> (b) the aggregate remuneration paid or payable in respect of the year to the persons by reference to whom the number stated under sub-paragraph (a) is ascertained.

(2) The number to be stated under that sub-paragraph is the quotient derived by dividing, by the number of weeks in the financial year, the number derived by ascertaining, in relation to each of those weeks, the number of persons who, under contracts of service, were employed in the week (whether throughout it or not) by the company and adding up the numbers ascertained.

6.—(1) If at the end of the financial year the company has subsidiaries, there shall be contained in the directors' report a statement of—

> (a) the average number of persons employed between them in each week in that year by the company and the subsidiaries, and

> (b) the aggregate remuneration paid or payable in respect of that year to the persons by reference to whom the number stated under sub-paragraph (a) is ascertained.

(2) The number to be stated under that sub-paragraph is the quotient derived by dividing, by the number of weeks in the financial year, the number derived by ascertaining, in relation to each of those weeks, the number of persons who, under contracts of service, were employed between them in the week (whether throughout it or not) by the company and its subsidiaries and adding up the numbers ascertained.

7. The remuneration to be taken into account under paragraphs 5(1)(b) and 6(1)(b) is the gross remuneration paid or payable in respect of the financial year ; and for this purpose " remuneration " includes bonuses (whether payable under contract or not).

8.—(1) Paragraphs 5 and 6 are qualified as follows.

(2) Neither paragraph applies if the number that, apart from this sub-paragraph, would fall to be stated under paragraph 5(1)(a) or 6(1)(a) is less than 100.

(3) Neither paragraph applies to a company which is a wholly-   SCH. 10
owned subsidiary of a company incorporated in Great Britain.

(4) For purposes of both paragraphs, no regard is to be had to any
person who worked wholly or mainly outside the United Kingdom.

General matters

9. The directors' report shall contain particulars of any matters
(other than those required to be dealt with in it by section 261(5) and
the preceding provisions of this Schedule) so far as they are material
for the appreciation of the state of the company's affairs by its
members, being matters the disclosure of which will not, in the
opinion of the directors, be harmful to the business of the company
or of any of its subsidiaries.

SCHEDULE 11   Section 279.

MODIFICATIONS OF PART VIII WHERE COMPANY'S RELEVANT ACCOUNTS ARE SPECIAL CATEGORY

1. Section 264 applies as if in subsection (2) for the words following "the aggregate of its liabilities" there were substituted
"("liabilities" to include any provision within the meaning of
Schedule 9, except to the extent that that provision is taken into
account in calculating the value of any asset of the company)".

2. Section 265 applies as if—

(a) for subsection (2) there were substituted—

> "(2) In subsection (1)(a), "liabilities" includes any
> provision (within the meaning of Schedule 9) except
> to the extent that that provision is taken into account for
> the purposes of that subsection in calculating the value
> of any asset of the company", and

(b) there were added at the end of the section—

> "(7) In determining capital and revenue profits and
> losses, an asset which is not a fixed asset or a current
> asset is treated as a fixed asset".

3. Section 269 does not apply.

4. Section 270 applies as if—

(a) in subsection (2) the following were substituted for paragraph
(b)—

> "(b) provisions (within the meaning of Schedule 9)";

(b) in subsection (3), for the words from "which were laid"
onwards there were substituted—

> "which were laid or filed in respect of the last pre-
> ceding accounting reference period in respect of which

accounts so prepared were laid or filed ; and for this purpose accounts are laid or filed if section 241(1) or (as the case may be) (3) has been complied with in relation to them " ; and

(c) in subsection (4)(b) the words " or filed " were inserted after " laid ".

5. Section 271 applies as if—

    (a) in subsection (2), immediately before paragraph (a) there were inserted " except where the company is entitled to avail itself, and has availed itself, of any of the provisions of Part III of Schedule 9 ", and

    (b) at the end of subsection (4) there were added the words " or delivered to the registrar of companies according as those accounts have been laid or filed ".

6. Sections 272 and 273 apply as if in section 272(3)—

    (a) for the references to section 228 and Schedule 4 there were substituted references to section 258 and Schedule 9, and

    (b) immediately before paragraph (a) there were inserted " except where the company is entitled to avail itself, and has availed itself, of any of the provisions of Part III of Schedule 9 ".

7. Section 275 applies as if—

    (a) for subsection (1) there were substituted—

        " (1) For purposes of section 263, any provision (within the meaning of Schedule 9), other than one in respect of any diminution of value of a fixed asset appearing on a revaluation of all the fixed assets of the company, or of all its fixed assets other than goodwill, is to be treated as a realised loss " ; and

    (b) " fixed assets " were defined to include any other asset which is not a current asset.

SCHEDULE 13

PROVISIONS SUPPLEMENTING AND INTERPRETING SECTIONS 324 TO 328

PART I

RULES FOR INTERPRETATION OF THE SECTIONS
AND ALSO SECTION 346(4) AND (5)

1.—(1) A reference to an interest in shares or debentures is to be read as including any interest of any kind whatsoever in shares or debentures.

(2) Accordingly, there are to be disregarded any restraints or restrictions to which the exercise of any right attached to the interest is or may be subject.

2. Where property is held on trust and any interest in shares or debentures is comprised in the property, any beneficiary of the trust who (apart from this paragraph) does not have an interest in the shares or debentures is to be taken as having such an interest ; but this paragraph is without prejudice to the following provisions of this Part of this Schedule.

3.—(1) A person is taken to have an interest in shares or debentures if—

    (a) he enters into a contract for their purchase by him (whether for cash or other consideration), or

    (b) not being the registered holder, he is entitled to exercise any right conferred by the holding of the shares or debentures, or is entitled to control the exercise of any such right.

(2) For purposes of sub-paragraph (1)(b), a person is taken to be entitled to exercise or control the exercise of a right conferred by the holding of shares or debentures if he—

    (a) has a right (whether subject to conditions or not) the exercise of which would make him so entitled, or

    (b) is under an obligation (whether or not so subject) the fulfilment of which would make him so entitled.

(3) A person is not by virtue of sub-paragraph (1)(b) taken to be interested in shares or debentures by reason only that he—

    (a) has been appointed a proxy to vote at a specified meeting of a company or of any class of its members and at any adjournment of that meeting, or

    (b) has been appointed by a corporation to act as its representative at any meeting of a company or of any class of its members.

4. A person is taken to be interested in shares or debentures if a body corporate is interested in them and—

    (a) that body corporate or its directors are accustomed to act in accordance with his directions or instructions, or

    (b) he is entitled to exercise or control the exercise of one-third or more of the voting power at general meetings of that body corporate.

As this paragraph applies for the purposes of section 346(4) and (5), " more than one-half " is substituted for " one-third or more ".

5. Where a person is entitled to exercise or control the exercise of one-third or more of the voting power at general meetings of a body corporate, and that body corporate is entitled to exercise or control the exercise of any of the voting power at general meetings of another body corporate (" the effective voting power "), then, for purposes of paragraph 4(*b*), the effective voting power is taken to be exercisable by that person.

As this paragraph applies for the purposes of section 346(4) and (5), " more than one-half " is substituted for " one-third or more ".

6.—(1) A person is taken to have an interest in shares or debentures if, otherwise than by virtue of having an interest under a trust—

(*a*) he has a right to call for delivery of the shares or debentures to himself or to his order, or

(*b*) he has a right to acquire an interest in shares or debentures or is under an obligation to take an interest in shares or debentures ;

whether in any case the right or obligation is conditional or absolute.

(2) Rights or obligations to subscribe for shares or debentures are not to be taken, for purposes of sub-paragraph (1), to be rights to acquire, or obligations to take, an interest in shares or debentures.

This is without prejudice to paragraph 1.

7. Persons having a joint interest are deemed each of them to have that interest.

8. It is immaterial that shares or debentures in which a person has an interest are unidentifiable.

9. So long as a person is entitled to receive, during the lifetime of himself or another, income from trust property comprising shares or debentures, an interest in the shares or debentures in reversion or remainder or (as regards Scotland) in fee, are to be disregarded.

10. A person is to be treated as uninterested in shares or debentures if, and so long as, he holds them under the law in force in England and Wales as a bare trustee or as a custodian trustee, or under the law in force in Scotland, as a simple trustee.

11. There is to be disregarded an interest of a person subsisting by virtue of—

(*a*) any unit trust scheme declared by an order of the Secretary of State (or any predecessor of his) for the time being in force under the Prevention of Fraud (Investments) Act 1958 to be an authorised unit trust scheme for the purposes of that Act ;

(b) a scheme made under section 22 of the Charities Act 1960, section 11 of the Trustee Investments Act 1961 or section 1 of the Administration of Justice Act 1965 ; or

(c) the scheme set out in the Schedule to the Church Funds Investment Measure 1958.

12. There is to be disregarded any interest—

(a) of the Church of Scotland General Trustees or of the Church of Scotland Trust in shares or debentures held by them ;

(b) of any other person in shares or debentures held by those Trustees or that Trust otherwise than as simple trustees.

"The Church of Scotland General Trustees" are the body incorporated by the order confirmed by the Church of Scotland (General Trustees) Order Confirmation Act 1921 ; and "the Church of Scotland Trust" is the body incorporated by the order confirmed by the Church of Scotland Trust Order Confirmation Act 1932.

13. Delivery to a person's order of shares or debentures in fulfilment of a contract for the purchase of them by him or in satisfaction of a right of his to call for their delivery, or failure to deliver shares or debentures in accordance with the terms of such a contract or on which such a right falls to be satisfied, is deemed to constitute an event in consequence of the occurrence of which he ceases to be interested in them, and so is the lapse of a person's right to call for delivery of shares or debentures.

PART II

PERIODS WITHIN WHICH OBLIGATIONS IMPOSED BY SECTION 324 MUST BE FULFILLED

14.—(1) An obligation imposed on a person by section 324(1) to notify an interest must, if he knows of the existence of the interest on the day on which he becomes a director, be fulfilled before the expiration of the period of 5 days beginning with the day following that day.

(2) Otherwise, the obligation must be fulfilled before the expiration of the period of 5 days beginning with the day following that on which the existence of the interest comes to his knowledge.

15.—(1) An obligation imposed on a person by section 324(2) to notify the occurrence of an event must, if at the time at which the event occurs he knows of its occurrence and of the fact that its occurrence gives rise to the obligation, be fulfilled before the expiration of the period of 5 days beginning with the day following that on which the event occurs.

SCH. 13
PART I
1958 c. 45.

1960 c. 58.
1961 c. 62.
1965 c. 2.

1958 No. 1.

1921 c. xxv.

1932 c. xxi.

(2) Otherwise, the obligation must be fulfilled before the expiration of a period of 5 days beginning with the day following that on which the fact that the occurrence of the event gives rise to the obligation comes to his knowledge.

16. In reckoning, for purposes of paragraphs 14 and 15, any period of days, a day that is a Saturday or Sunday, or a bank holiday in any part of Great Britain, is to be disregarded.

PART III

CIRCUMSTANCES IN WHICH OBLIGATION IMPOSED BY SECTION 324 IS NOT DISCHARGED

17.—(1) Where an event of whose occurrence a director is, by virtue of section 324(2)(*a*), under obligation to notify a company consists of his entering into a contract for the purchase by him of shares or debentures, the obligation is not discharged in the absence of inclusion in the notice of a statement of the price to be paid by him under the contract.

(2) An obligation imposed on a director by section 324(2)(*b*) is not discharged in the absence of inclusion in the notice of the price to be received by him under the contract.

18.—(1) An obligation imposed on a director by virtue of section 324(2)(*c*) to notify a company is not discharged in the absence of inclusion in the notice of a statement of the consideration for the assignment (or, if it be the case that there is no consideration, that fact).

(2) Where an event of whose occurrence a director is, by virtue of section 324(2)(*d*), under obligation to notify a company consists in his assigning a right, the obligation is not discharged in the absence of inclusion in the notice of a similar statement.

19.—(1) Where an event of whose occurrence a director is, by virtue of section 324(2)(*d*), under obligation to notify a company consists in the grant to him of a right to subscribe for shares or debentures, the obligation is not discharged in the absence of inclusion in the notice of a statement of—

    (*a*) the date on which the right was granted,

    (*b*) the period during which or the time at which the right is exercisable.

    (*c*) the consideration for the grant (or, if it be the case that there is no consideration, that fact), and

    (*d*) the price to be paid for the shares or debentures.

(2) Where an event of whose occurrence a director is, by section 324(2)(*d*), under obligation to notify a company consists in the exercise of a right granted to him to subscribe for shares or debentures, the obligation is not discharged in the absence of inclusion in the notice of a statement of—

    (*a*) the number of shares or amount of debentures in respect of which the right was exercised, and (*b*) if it be the case that they were registered in his name, that fact, and, if not, the name or names of the person or persons in whose name or names they were registered, together (if they were registered in the names of 2 persons or more) with the number or amount registered in the name of each of them.

20. In this Part, a reference to price paid or received includes any consideration other than money.

Part IV

Provisions with Respect to Register of Directors' Interests to be Kept Under Section 325

21. The register must be so made up that the entries in it against the several names appear in chronological order.

22. An obligation imposed by section 325(2) to (4) must be fulfilled before the expiration of the period of 3 days beginning with the day after that on which the obligation arises; but in reckoning that period, a day which is a Saturday or Sunday or a bank holiday in any part of Great Britain is to be disregarded.

23. The nature and extent of an interest recorded in the register of a director in any shares or debentures shall, if he so requires, be recorded in the register.

24. The company is not, by virtue of anything done for the purposes of section 325 or this Part of this Schedule, affected with notice of, or put upon enquiry as to, the rights of any person in relation to any shares or debentures.

25. The register shall—

(*a*) if the company's register of members is kept at its registered office, be kept there;

(*b*) if the company's register of members is not so kept, be kept at the company's registered office or at the place where its register of members is kept;

and shall during business hours (subject to such reasonable restrictions as the company in general meeting may impose, so that not less than 2 hours in each day be allowed for inspection) be open to the inspection of any member of the company without charge and of any other person on payment of 5 pence, or such less sum as the company may prescribe, for each inspection.

26.—(1) Any member of the company or other person may require a copy of the register, or of any part of it, on payment of 10 pence, or such less sum as the company may prescribe, for every 100 words or fractional part of 100 words required to be copied.

(2) The company shall cause any copy so required by a person to be sent to him within the period of 10 days beginning with the day after that on which the requirement is received by the company.

27. The company shall send notice in the prescribed form to the registrar of companies of the place where the register is kept and of any change in that place, save in a case in which it has at all times been kept at its registered office.

28. Unless the register is in such a form as to constitute in itself an index, the company shall keep an index of the names inscribed in it, which shall—

   (a) in respect of each name, contain a sufficient indication to enable the information entered against it to be readily found ; and

   (b) be kept at the same place as the register ;

and the company shall, within 14 days after the date on which a name is entered in the register, make any necessary alteration in the index.

29. The register shall be produced at the commencement of the company's annual general meeting and remain open and accessible during the continuance of the meeting to any person attending the meeting.

SCHEDULE 25

COMPANIES ACT 1981, SECTION 38, AS ORIGINALLY ENACTED

38.—(1) This section applies where the issuing company—

(a) is a wholly-owned subsidiary of another company (" the holding company ") ; and

(b) allots shares to the holding company or to another wholly-owned subsidiary of the holding company in consideration for the transfer to it of shares in another subsidiary (whether wholly-owned or not) of the holding company.

Relief from section 56 in respect of group reconstructions.

(2) Where the shares in the issuing company allotted in consideration for the transfer are issued at a premium, the issuing company shall not be required by section 56 of the 1948 Act to transfer any amount in excess of the minimum premium value to the share premium account.

(3) In subsection (2) above " the minimum premium value " means the amount (if any) by which the base value of the shares transferred exceeds the aggregate nominal value of the shares allotted in consideration for the transfer.

(4) For the purposes of subsection (3) above, the base value of the shares transferred shall be taken as—

(a) the cost of those shares to the company transferring them ; or

(b) the amount at which those shares are stated in that company's accounting records immediately before the transfer ;

whichever is the less.

(5) Section 37 of this Act shall not apply in a case to which this section applies.

Table of Legislation and of other regulations

Exposure Drafts

The Stock Exchange's Continuing Obligations for listed companies

CO	1.13, 2.01, 3.07, 6.59, 9.06, 10.12, 11.80, 11.99, 11.102, 13.34, 13.41, 13.95, 14.01, 19.17, 20.16, 21.13, 21.41	
para 14		11.100
para 20		17.19, 20.16, 21.21
para 21 (a)		3.05
(b)		12.12
(c)		10.10
(d)		8.42
(e)		8.18
(f)		9.05, 17.14
(g)		4.31
(h)		12.35, 12.38
(i)		12.42
(j)		12.42
(k)		11.102, 11.103
(l)(m)		12.42
(n)		10.68
(o)		10.129
(p)		12.14, 12.17
(q)		14.14
(r)		14.10
para 25		6.60
para 43 (b)(c)		12.42
para 44		14.09

The Stock Exchange's General Undertaking for companies traded on the USM

GU	1.13, 2.01, 3.07, 6.59, 6.61, 6.62, 9.06, 10.12, 11.99, 11.101, 13.34, 13.41, 13.95, 19.17, 21.13, 21.41	
para 1 (d)		11.101
para 8		21.21
para 10 (a)		3.05
(b)		12.12
(c)		10.10
(d)		8.42
(e)		8.20
(f)		9.05, 17.14
(g)		4.31
(h)		12.38
(i)(j)		12.42
(k)		10.68
(l)		10.129
para 11		12.42

Table of Cases

References are to paragraph numbers of this book.

Table of Companies

References are to page numbers of this book where extracts from the financial statements of these companies are reproduced.

Index

References are to paragraph numbers of this book.